THE REPUBLIC OF IRELAND

INTERNATIONAL FOOTBALL FACTS

DEAN HAYES

THE REPUBLIC OF IRELAND
INTERNATIONAL FOOTBALL FACTS

DEAN HAYES

The Collins Press

Published in 2008 by
The Collins Press
West Link Park
Doughcloyne
Wilton
Cork

Photographs © *Irish Examiner* pages 50, 76, 100, 162, 165, 166, 184, 187, 190, 281,
291, 295, 301, 311, 317, 320, 328, 335, 338, 345, 348, 353, 356, 359, 380.
© **Inpho**photography page 260.
© PA Photo page 286.
© *Lancashire Evening Post* pages 65, 68, 83, 84, 85, 87, 90, 91, 92, 95, 99, 105, 111,
113, 115, 127, 228, 229, 240, 242, 305, 309, 313, 318, 323, 325, 326, 329, 332, 334,
337, 340, 342, 344, 352, 358, 361, 363, 369, 372, 373, 375, 377, 382, 384.
Memorabilia images supplied by the Woods family pages 20, 43,
154, 159, 170, 265, 284, 404, 405.

British Library Cataloguing in Publication Data
Hayes, Dean, 1949-

The Republic of Ireland international football facts
1. Soccer teams - Ireland - Miscellanea 2. Soccer players -
Ireland - Miscellanea
I. Title
796.3'34'09417

ISBN-13: 9781905172832

Cover and text design by Anú Design
Typesetting by Carole Lynch
Printed in Spain by Edelvives

Cover photos
Clockwise from top left: Roy Keane; Jim McDonagh; Mick McCarthy; Noel Cantwell; the Irish
team that defeated England 2–0 at Goodison Park in 1949; Kevin Kilbane; Jack Charlton.

Contents

THE STORY

PLAYERS

MANAGERS

MATCHES

TOP 50 PLAYERS

STATISTICS

1

The Republic of Ireland Story

The Republic of Ireland Story

Although the game of football has been played in Ireland since the 1860s, it was mainly based in Ulster and it was some twenty years later that the game spread to other parts of the country. The first club outside Ulster was the Dublin Association Football Club which was formed in 1883. At that time the Irish Football Association (IFA) was the game's governing body. However, being based in Belfast, it found it very difficult to promote the game throughout the entire country. As the game grew in popularity, this led to the formation of the Leinster FA in 1892.

Even so, there was always a feeling from the clubs outside the Belfast area that the IFA favoured Ulster-based, Protestant clubs – especially when it came to the selection of sides for international duty.

Despite this, it wasn't until after the 1916 Rising and the upsurge of nationalism that southern affiliates such as the Leinster FA took a more aggressive approach with the IFA. Clubs had often threatened to break away and in 1921, Bohemians, St James's Gate and Shelbourne all withdrew from the Irish League, though the three clubs opted to remain in the various Cup competitions.

Towards the end of 1921, the matter reached a crisis point when the IFA failed to keep their word, having promised to hold the IFA Cup Final replay between Glenavon and Shelbourne in Dublin and re-scheduled the game for Belfast. Shelbourne refused to comply with this decision and in doing so, forfeited the Cup. This led to a meeting of the southern associations and on 1 June 1921, the Football Association of the Irish Free State (FAIFS) was formed in Molesworth Hall in the centre of Dublin.

A Free State Football League was quickly formed with eight teams involved. At the outset, the eight teams were all from Dublin but the following season, Athlone became the first provincial club to join the competition. St James's Gate won the first-ever Championship and they also won the first Football Association of Ireland (FAI) Cup

– then called the Free State Cup in 1922. However, the FAIFS had much more difficulty in arranging international fixtures.

Though all the home countries associations had decided to blacklist the FAIFS, the Association had more luck in their dealings with Fédération Internationale de Football Association (FIFA). France defied the home nation's wishes and in 1923, sent Athletic Club of Gallia to play a series of challenge matches against Bohemians and Pioneers. In the summer of that year, FIFA decided to accept Ireland's application for membership and the FAIFS joined the international scene.

However, a further three years passed before Ireland fulfilled its very first international fixture. Though a Free State side participated in the 1924 Olympic Games in Paris, it was under the auspices of the Olympic Council of Ireland.

The first fixture organised by the FAIFS was in March 1926 against Italy in Turin and though the game ended in a 3–0 defeat for the Irish, the first steps had been taken. At this time, both the FAIFS and the IFA selected their teams from all over Ireland, meaning that a number of players won caps for both Associations. In April 1927, the Italian Football Federation sent their 'B' team to Dublin for Ireland's first-ever home international. A crowd of 20,000 fans gathered at Lansdowne Road to see Bob Fullam open the scoring after six minutes – according to the game's folklore, the visitors were so frightened of Fullam's powerful shooting that they begged the Irish team not to let him take any free-kicks! Even so, Italy ran out 2–1 winners with two goals from Munerati.

The following year, Ireland won their first international match, against Belgium in Liege. The Irish were trailing 2–0 at half-time but fought back to win 4–2 with Jimmy White (2), Billy Lacey and Jack Sullivan from the penalty spot, the scorers. It was another fourteen months before the return match took place with Ireland winning 4–0 at Dalymount Park – their first victory on home soil – with Shamrock Rovers' Joe Flood netting a hat-trick.

Ireland's first World Cup campaign in 1934 was a short-lived affair as a 4–4 draw against Belgium in which Paddy Moore scored all his side's goals, was followed by a 5–2 defeat by the Dutch in Amsterdam. The qualifying campaign for the next World Cup tournament in 1938 lasted only two matches. Despite a 3–2 defeat against Norway in Oslo, the Irish team were confident of overturning the deficit in the return match at Dalymount Park and of booking a place in the finals. A crowd of 25,000 saw Manchester United's Johnny Carey put the ball into the net with his first touch but the referee disallowed the 'goal' for offside. This did not deflate the home side and Jimmy Dunne put them ahead with a legitimate strike. However, Norway replied with three well taken goals and though Kevin O'Flanagan and Harry Duggan netted to level the game, it was the Norwegians who won through to the finals.

Ireland's last match before the outbreak of the Second World War was against Germany in Bremen in May 1939. To the resentment of Britain and Northern Ireland, the Republic stayed neutral during the hostilities. Germany's sporting punishment for her wartime aggression was to be barred from FIFA and therefore from competing in the next World Cup. Hostilities prevented competition in Brazil in 1942 and the tournament's earmarked successor four years later was a non-starter.

Did you know?

There is an urban myth in Ireland that says Germany's common use of a green-coloured away shirt is in recognition of Ireland being the first team to play Germany after the Second World War, in spite of the fact that the Swiss were actually the Germans' first opponents!

At the end of the fighting came news from across the Irish Sea that the British Home Associations had mended their fences with FIFA and had condescended to rejoin, taking part in the World Cup for the first time. This spelled trouble for the Emerald Isle, because the two Irelands were now embarked on a quest for the same prize. They would now have to stop their habit of selecting players from both north and south of the border.

Politically, the split from Britain was finalised in 1949 when the Republic of Ireland declared its intention to leave the Commonwealth. In footballing terms, the friction with Northern Ireland continued a while due to both Dublin and Belfast seeking exclusive rights to the use of the word 'Ireland'.

The Republic of Ireland were placed in a World Cup pool with Finland and Sweden, the only European section – other than the British one of the four home countries – to comprise more than two nations.

Ireland might have been celebrating the birth of the Republic but they had little to celebrate on the football pitch. Since the war ended, they had played ten matches – seven of them against Portugal and Spain, who had likewise stayed neutral during the hostilities – even so, the Republic must have been sick of the sight of them!

The breakthrough came on 30 September 1946 when the Republic entertained England, who had thrashed Northern Ireland 7–2 in Belfast a couple of days earlier. The Irish were just eight minutes away from a draw when Preston's Tom Finney pounced to score the game's only goal. The new era brought down the curtain on Republic of Ireland sides dominated by Irish-based players. With the exception of the

Johnny Careys, Tommy Eglingtons and Peter Farrells – of whom there were not that many – the selectors had to scour the lower divisions of the English Football League in search of eligible players to represent the Republic.

Towards the end of the nation's failed World Cup bid, the Republic of Ireland became the first side to defeat England on English soil when they won the Goodison Park encounter 2–0 with goals from Con Martin and Peter Farrell. The result entered the nation's folklore, though in England little significance was attached because nine of the Republic's side played in the Football League.

The Republic learned a painful lesson when Sweden beat them 3–1 in both home and away games prior to the 1950 World Cup Finals and their form in the following years showed more low spots than high. The Irish looked particularly fragile away from home, where they found themselves beaten 5–1 by Belgium, 3–0 by Germany, and 6–0 by both Austria and Spain. Two of these defeats were reversed in Dublin – with soon-to-be World Champions Germany beaten 3–2 and Austria defeated 4–0.

When FIFA convened to announce the draw for the 1954 World Cup, the Republic found themselves in the same group as favourites France and Luxembourg. The French were developing into one of Europe's more enterprising sides, having held England to a 2–2 draw at Wembley and beaten World Champions West Germany 3–1. They also got off to a great start in the group matches by beating Luxembourg 6–1.

The 1954 World Cup campaign saw a new Republic of Ireland team, one without the services of that magnificent captain Johnny Carey. He was by now the Republic of Ireland's team coach, some might even have said manager except that the selection committee continued to pull the strings. The Republic's new skipper was Everton wing-half Peter Farrell. He was one of seven players – the others being club teammates Tommy Eglington, Arthur Fitzsimons, Con Martin, Tommy Moroney, Reg Ryan and Davy Walsh – who were embarking on their second World Cup quest.

The Republic's first match in the World Cup against France brought a feast of football. The then largest crowd to cram into Dalymount Park – 45,000 – saw Ireland go down 5–3 to a side that they were accustomed to beating. The plain fact of the matter was that their opponents rose to the big occasions when the Republic could not. Despite beating Luxembourg home and away, the Irish lost 1–0 in the return game against the French at Parc des Princes, Paris and failed to reach the finals.

It was only in this World Cup year that FIFA finally bowed to the reality of the Republic's existence – five years after Dublin's proclamation of a republic, the world's governing body of the sport agreed to refer to its footballers as representing the Republic of Ireland. The new designation was employed for the first time in the home match against Norway in November 1954, a match the Republic won 2–1.

Between the 1954 and 1958 World Cup qualifying matches, the Republic of Ireland played just seven games, yet they strung together a series of results to suggest that they could possibly win through to the finals. They defeated Norway twice, Holland twice and in a heroic display in Hamburg, went down narrowly (2–1) to Germany, the World Cup holders. The Republic's other defeat prior to the 1958 qualifiers was a 4–1 home reversal against Yugoslavia – the first occasion that Ireland had entertained a team from a communist country. This was such a controversial occasion that both church and state objected and their interventions almost caused the game to be cancelled. The draw for the qualifiers saw the Republic grouped with England and Denmark – the whole of the Republic looked forward to two tussles with their mighty neighbours – after all, the Republic had beaten England at Goodison the last time the two countries met.

Having beaten the Danes 2–1, the Republic travelled to Wembley for their first game on the hallowed turf – this followed one of the country's greatest wins when they beat World Champions Germany 3–0. Sadly, there was to be no repeat performance as the boys in green, who were 4–0 down at the interval, were beaten 5–1. Manchester United centre-forward Tommy Taylor netted a hat-trick to add to his treble in his side's previous group match against Denmark. Just eleven days later, the Republic faced England at Dalymount Park – if the Republic could win at home, then beat the Danes away, they would force England into a play-off.

Dalymount Park's previous record attendance had been established against France in the 1954 World Cup qualifiers, but for the return game against England, the ground was bursting at the seams with 47,600 crammed inside. The Irish got the start they dreamed of when Sheffield United's Alf Ringstead netted after only three minutes and though England had plenty of chances to draw level, the Republic still led 1–0 as the game entered its final minute. Tom Finney's cross was met by John Atyeo, who buried the ball in the net. The whole of Dalymount Park fell silent – in fact, one Irish newspaper went as far as to insist that the silence could be heard in O'Connell Street.

The Republic of Ireland also entered the newly created European Championships. They had the honour of lining up in the first-ever match in the competition. However, it was a short-lived experience as they went out in the first qualifying round, over two legs to Czechoslovakia.

In the games played between the 1958 and 1962 World Cups, the Irish recorded some memorable victories – notably over Sweden (3–2), who arrived fresh from beating England at Wembley, and West Germany (1–0) in Dusseldorf.

The countries in Ireland's group for the 1962 World Cup were Scotland and Czechoslovakia. Just weeks before the Irish travelled to Hampden Park, the Scots had been crushed 9–3 by the English at Wembley but they bounced back, beating the

Republic 4–1. In the return game at Dalymount Park, the Scots completed the double by winning 3–0. It was obvious that the referee was no Irishman as he clearly demonstrated towards the end of the game when Fitzgerald was upended well inside the penalty area and the official gave the Republic a free-kick a good five yards outside. After losing 3–1 at home to the Czechs, the Irish suffered their heaviest World Cup defeat to that day or since, when they were beaten 7–1 in Prague. Four matches, four defeats and seventeen goals conceded – these were the Republic's worst-ever figures in the World Cup.

By the time the 1964 European Championships came around, numbers entering the competition had swelled with the inclusion of the majority of Europe's major footballing powers. Having defeated Iceland and Austria, the Republic faced Spain for a place in the semi-finals. Sadly, they proved far too strong for Ireland, winning 5–1 in Seville and 2–0 in Dublin. Not surprisingly, they went on to win the tournament.

With the 1966 World Cup Finals being held in England, it was certain that Republic of Ireland fans would flood across the Irish Sea should the boys in green qualify. Their opponents were Spain and Syria but the latter nation decided to pull out of the competition, leaving the Republic of Ireland and Spain to fight out a double header. A win for the Irish in their first meeting at Dalymount Park would guarantee them a money-spinning play-off. Spain were the better side and it was against the run of play that Ireland scored. Johnny Giles was fouled out wide and O'Neill flighted in the free-kick for which Noel Cantwell, playing at centre-forward, defender Zoco and goalkeeper Iribar rose as one. The Spanish keeper won the race but the ball spilled from his grasp and dropped behind him and into the net. The Spanish pressed hard but Ireland held on for a memorable victory.

All the Republic needed in Seville was a draw. Despite taking the lead through Blackburn's Andy McEvoy, the home side dominated the rest of the proceedings and ran out 4–1 winners. As aggregate scores were not used at the time, a play-off match was needed. There was some controversy that Paris was chosen as the venue – it had a large Spanish population – and a seventy-ninth-minute goal by Ufarte meant that Ireland missed out on a World Cup Finals place.

After finishing third in their 1968 European Championships group, in matches against Czechoslovakia, Turkey and again Spain, the Republic suffered defeat after defeat with great regularity, though they shocked the whole of Europe by beating the Czechs 2–1 in their final qualification match in Prague.

To take part in the next World Cup in Mexico, the Irish found themselves for the first time in a four-team group with Czechoslovakia (again), Denmark and Hungary. Few gave the boys in green much of a chance and so it transpired with the side's only point coming in a 1–1 home draw with Denmark.

The Republic of Ireland's poor results in the 1970 World Cup qualifiers were followed by a similar outcome in the qualifying matches for the 1972 European Championships. Their last games in the group stages of this tournament saw them take on Austria, who scored four times at Dalymount Park. It was time for a change of manager. The Republic's first manager, Mick Meagan had been in charge for two years – he had overseen twelve internationals but the Republic had not won any.

Meagan's replacement was Liam Tuohy, who knew that one of the national side's greatest problems was the lack of preparation before international matches. His first game in charge was the return with Austria in Linz. The new manager played six debutants and sent on a seventh from the bench. With the exception of Paddy Mulligan, the Irish side had been selected entirely from players from the League of Ireland. The Republic were beaten 6–0. Tuohy made a number of changes for the Brazilian Independence Cup, a tournament in which the Irish had not previously participated. When the Republic beat Iran 2–1 in their opening match, it was their first victory in almost five years – a run of 21 games without any success. They then followed it up with a 3–2 defeat of Ecuador before losing to both Chile and Portugal.

Did you know?

Both Tony Grealish and Kevin Sheedy have scored goals at three different home grounds – Dalymount Park, Lansdowne Road and Tolka Park.

It was around this time that the Republic began to play some of the international games at Lansdowne Road and their first game there in modern times was the European Championship qualifier against Italy which the visitors won 2–1. Despite coming to Dublin as World Cup runners-up, they attracted a crowd of just 25,000. There were many Irish fans who mourned the loss of the Bohemians' grand old stadium at Dalymount Park and especially the famed 'Dalymount Roar' which some viewed was worth a goal start – but it was not lost completely as the Republic alternated between Dalymount and Lansdowne for a number of years.

With the 1974 World Cup Finals being held in West Germany, the Republic of Ireland had to get past France and the Soviet Union. Whilst this seemed most unlikely, they were not sure of a place even if they succeeded, because the winners of this group were scheduled to play against a South American group which included Chile and Peru.

Having been beaten 2–1 at home by the Soviet Union, the situation was desperate. The Republic now needed to collect five or six points from their three remaining games and many Irish fans had given up hope. For the home game against the French, Liam Tuohy made Giles captain and brought back the experienced Givens and Mulligan. Jimmy Holmes – just four days past his nineteenth birthday, became the youngest Republic of Ireland player to appear in a World Cup game. Terry Conroy gave the Irish the lead when his shot smashed into the net via the underside of the bar. The French – up until then the better team – drew level midway through the second-half before Treacy inadvertently scored what proved to be the winning goal. The Irish had won but sadly, Dalymount Park never again hosted another World Cup match. Even though the Republic lost the return against the Soviet Union 1–0, they could still head the group if they beat France in Paris and France in turn won in Moscow. It all proved immaterial for despite a spirited showing by the Irish, they drew 1–1, with Mick Martin netting the Republic's goal.

Did you know?

The Republic of Ireland's youngest full cap is Jimmy Holmes who was just 17 years 200 days when he made his debut against Austria in May 1971.

At underage level, the Republic of Ireland had its first success with the youths qualifying for the 1972 UEFA Youth Championship in 1972, after the Welsh team refused to travel over to Ireland for a qualifying match. In 1973, Sean Thomas, then Bohemians manager, managed Ireland for one match, a friendly away game against Norway which resulted in a 1–1 draw.

Johnny Giles, the Republic's fourth manager in as many years, was appointed player-manager in October 1973. It was his view that the League of Ireland players had neither the fitness nor the know-how to cope with international football: the only League of Ireland player he ever selected in World Cup games was himself, when seeing out his career with Shamrock Rovers.

For the 1976 European Championships, the Irish were in the same group as Switzerland, Turkey and the Soviet Union. They started off brilliantly with a 3–0 defeat of the Soviet Union before a creditable 1–1 draw against Turkey in Izmir and a 2–1 home win over Switzerland. After completing their six group games, the Republic of Ireland were top of the table, leaving the Soviet Union needing two points from their remaining two games to pip Ireland at the post – unfortunately they got them.

With a string of solid performances behind them, including a 1–1 draw against England at Wembley, the Republic of Ireland embarked on the qualifying games for the 1978 World Cup Finals. Their opponents were France and Bulgaria. Though the Irish lost 2–0 in Paris, a goal by Liam Brady brought them victory in the return at Lansdowne Road in March 1977. The attendance for this game was put at 48,000 – a record for a football game in Ireland. The Republic needed at least one point from their visit to Bulgaria but they lost 2–1 in a bad-tempered game which saw two players from each side being sent off. With their hopes hanging by a thread, the Irish had to beat Bulgaria by four goals in Dublin and hope that France and Bulgaria played out a draw. As it transpired, the Republic were held to a goalless draw by the Bulgarians and the Irish slid anticlimactically out of the World Cup.

For the qualification campaign of the 1980 European Championships, the Republic of Ireland were drawn in the same group as England and Northern Ireland, along with Bulgaria and Denmark. During the qualifiers, the Republic of Ireland took on Northern Ireland in an historic meeting between the two sides. A goalless draw was marred by rioting in Dublin on the day of the match. Unfortunately for the boys in green, England ran away with the group, dropping just one point – a 1–1 draw against the Republic in front of a vast crowd of 50,000.

For the 1982 World Cup tournament, held in Spain, the Republic were grouped with Belgium, Cyprus, France and Holland. It was certainly a tough group and one in which they would have to finish in the top two to qualify. Although they had never played Cyprus before, the Irish won 3–2 in Nicosia to record their first away victory in the World Cup since beating Denmark in 1957.

A few weeks after this success, Johnny Giles resigned as Republic of Ireland manager and Alan Kelly took over for just one friendly – a 2–0 win over Switzerland – before new boss Eoin Hand took over the reins. Ireland's next opponents in this World Cup group were Holland, who in the past had lost two World Cup Finals, both to the tournament hosts. Though the Dutch side were in a transitional state, they took the lead and held it until the seventy-ninth minute when Daly levelled the scores. Shortly afterwards, Mark Lawrenson netted the winner – the defender had scored in both qualifying matches. The Republic then drew 1–1 at home to Belgium before losing 2–0 in France. This match is best remembered for its pre-match controversy. Determined that the Republic would be permitted to field its strongest side, the FAI compelled FIFA to intervene. English clubs who refused to release players because of League Cup ties found their games postponed – the FAI had won a famous victory.

The boys in green then thrashed Cyprus 6–0 with Gerry Daly netting a hat-trick. A late goal by Ceulmans gave Belgium a 1–0 win over the Irish before the Republic drew 2–2 against Holland in Rotterdam. Normally that would be hailed as an outstanding result but it was just what France and Belgium were hoping for. For their final group game at home to France, the Irish got off to a flying start when Mahut, under pressure from Stapleton, put through his own goal. The lead was short-lived and three minutes later the French were level but goals by Stapleton and Robinson gave the Republic a 3–1 lead and though Platini reduced the arrears, the Republic held on to win 3–2. Sadly, other results did not go Ireland's way and though they finished level on points with France, they lost out on goal difference.

After a badly-arranged tour of South America, where the Republic lost all three games, the national team embarked on the series of qualification games for Euro '84. Two defeats by Holland and three points dropped against the Spanish left Ireland adrift of the pace from the outset. Even though in November 1983, the team had ended on a high note with an 8–0 demolition of Malta, Irish supporters were beginning to turn against the manager. But, despite an increasing lack of support, Eoin Hand remained in charge.

Denmark, Switzerland, Norway and the Soviet Union were in Ireland's qualifying group for the 1986 World Cup due to be held in Mexico. The Republic's first match was at Lansdowne Road against the highly-tipped Soviet Union. Micky Walsh gave the Irish the lead and though in the dying moments Rodinov smashed a shot against the crossbar and Litovchenko rattled the post from the rebound, the Irish held on to record the win.

Unfortunately, there followed a lacklustre display against Norway in Oslo – the home side recording only their second success in twelve attempts against the Irish. Worse was to come when Ireland were beaten 3–0 by Denmark, who could, if they had so desired, have won by a much bigger margin. Then the Republic gave one of their worst-ever displays in a goalless home draw against Norway.

The Irish returned to winning ways with a 3–0 defeat of Switzerland but the return in Berne failed to produce any goals. The Republic then faced the challenge of playing the Soviet Union in Moscow. Unbeaten in nineteen World Cup matches, they had not conceded a goal in thirteen of those games and duly beat the Irish 2–0. Denmark, who had already qualified for the finals, were the Republic's final opponents. Though Frank Stapleton gave Ireland an early lead, the Danes came back to win 4–1.

Following the departure of Eoin Hand, Jack Charlton was named as the Republic of Ireland's new manager in February 1986. However, the former England international centre-half who had managed at Middlesbrough, Sheffield Wednesday and Newcastle United, could not realistically hope to qualify for Euro 1988, certainly not after Ireland's first five games had yielded just five points. But following Gary Mackay's late winner for Scotland in Bulgaria, the Republic found themselves playing in the European Championship finals.

In their opening game against England at Stuttgart, Ray Houghton's fifth-minute header, after blunders by full-backs Gary Stevens and Kenny Sansom had allowed John

Aldridge to fire in a cross, knocked England back on their heels. England's forwards missed numerous chances whilst Packie Bonner pulled off a string of spectacular saves to seal England's fate. The boys in green then played out a goalless draw with the Soviet Union and lost only 1–0 to tournament favourites Holland, narrowly missing out on a place in the semi-finals. Not surprisingly they returned home as national heroes.

Following this success, the Republic of Ireland were drawn in a World Cup qualifying group alongside Hungary, Spain, Malta and Northern Ireland. With second place being good enough, there was all to play for.

Jack Charlton arranged to start the qualifying games by visiting the three toughest sides first. Opening up against Northern Ireland in Belfast was especially tricky, more so as the Republic's supporters would not be able to lend their massive support for security reasons, but the game had 'goalless draw' written all over it. A decimated Ireland squad then travelled to Spain where they lost 2–0, before playing out another goalless draw in Hungary. The Irish side entertained Spain at Lansdowne Road, having yet to score a goal in the competition. An own goal by Michel gave the team a 1–0 win. Ireland now faced back-to-back visits from Malta and Hungary and after a 2–0 win over Malta, the Republic played Hungary in what was tantamount to a cup final for both countries. McGrath and Cascarino scored the goals in another 2–0 win. A 3–0 defeat of Northern Ireland was followed by a 2–0 triumph in Malta and at the thirteenth attempt, the Republic of Ireland were set for the World Cup Finals.

Did you know?

Packie Bonner made his international debut on his twenty-first birthday in 1981 but conceded three goals to Poland.

In the months leading up to the World Cup Final, the Irish stretched their unbeaten run to thirteen games. Having conceded just two goals, they arrived in Italy looking to cause an upset or two.

The Republic's opponents in the group games were England, Egypt and Holland. Their first game against England at Cagliari was played at a tremendous pace and could not in any way be described as a classic. Gary Lineker gave England the lead but the Republic refused to give up and twenty minutes from the end, Kevin Sheedy netted a deserved equaliser. The Irish players celebrated deep into the night but with their next opponents Egypt rarely venturing across the halfway line, Jack Charlton's side had to be content with a goalless draw. Ireland's last opponents Holland had also drawn 0–0 with England, leaving all four sides with identical records. The Irish boss made just one change bringing in Niall Quinn for the out-of-form Cascarino. Ruud Gullit gave the Dutch the lead but Quinn equalised to ensure that both teams qualified for the second round.

Lots were drawn to see which teams would be placed second and third – the Republic took the higher place and their opponents in the second round were Romania. Ireland dominated the game and created the better chances but the game remained goalless, even after extra-time and became the first one of the tournament to be decided on penalties. The shoot-out had reached 4–4 when Bonner saved Timofte's spot-kick. Now it was all down to David O'Leary and as he sent the Romanian keeper the wrong way, the Irish players and fans went wild. Jack Charlton's side were now in the quarter-finals where they would face hosts Italy. It was a thrilling encounter but the Irish couldn't penetrate the Italian defence – this was the Italian side's tenth successive game without conceding a goal – and Schillaci scored the game's only goal. The boys in green returned home with dignity from a World Cup competition that had certainly exceeded all expectations.

After these heroics, the boys in green knew they were capable of qualifying for Euro '92 and started off well with a 5–0 defeat of Turkey that included a hat-trick by John Aldridge. The other teams in the group were Poland and England – the third consecutive major competition in which Ireland and England had been drawn together. The first game against England proved to be as unwatchable as the one in the World Cup but a 1–1 draw was by no means a disaster. It was a similar scoreline in the return at Wembley and with both games against Poland also being drawn, a 3–1 win in the second game against Turkey, meant that the Republic were unbeaten in the group. However, a late strike by Gary Lineker against Poland took England into the Euro finals.

Though Ireland managed to avoid England in the World Cup qualifiers for USA '94, they were grouped with European Championship winners Denmark, Spain, Northern Ireland and three of the lesser footballing powers in Albania, Latvia and Lithuania. It was the only one of the qualifying groups to comprise seven teams – meaning that Ireland would play twelve qualifying games.

The Irish made a convincing start with good home victories over Albania (2–0) and Latvia (4–0) followed by a couple of goalless draws in Denmark and Spain. In the latter match, the main talking point was the linesman's flag that denied the Republic of Ireland a precious goal. The following day, the Spanish press agreed it should have been allowed to stand. Yet to concede a goal, the Republic defeated Northern Ireland 3–0 before being held to a 1–1 draw at Lansdowne Road by Denmark. Ireland beat Albania, Latvia and Lithuania on their travels before beating the Lithuanians at home, in what Jack Charlton described as the side's worst performance since he took over the reins. The Irish knew that if they defeated Spain, they would be through to the World Cup Finals but they were well beaten 3–1 and to make matters worse, Denmark scored a late goal in their match with Northern Ireland. With two teams to qualify, there was just a point separating the top three teams prior to Ireland's final group game in Belfast.

An Irish victory would secure second place whilst a draw might be good enough if the match between the two teams ahead of the Republic – Denmark v Spain – didn't finish all-square. The Republic's supporters could not flock to Belfast for security reasons, just as the Ulster fans couldn't descend on Dublin. Despite a number of injuries hampering Jack Charlton's selection, the Republic played out a goalless first-half – not a shot on goal by either side. News filtered through that the Danes were trailing 1–0 to Spain but that mattered little when Jimmy Quinn gave Northern Ireland the lead. However, three minutes later, substitute Alan McLoughlin levelled the scores and with ten-man Spain holding onto their narrow advantage, the boys in green had reached their second World Cup Finals.

The Republic's first game of USA '94 was against Italy, the team that had beaten them in the quarter-finals four years previously. Supported by a large part of the 74,826 who were packed into the Giants Stadium, Ireland didn't take long to show the Italians that they meant business. Only eleven minutes had been played when Ray Houghton ran the ball along the edge of the Italian penalty area. Seeing Pagliuca off his line, he dipped a shot just under the bar. The Italians were stunned and failed to respond with anything approaching a cohesive attack. In fact, they were lucky not to concede a second goal when John Sheridan rifled a powerful shot against the bar. The Irish retained their edge and composure and held on for a shock win.

The Republic's next game against Mexico was played in the steaming heat of Orlando and is probably best remembered for the antics of Jack Charlton, who again found himself in confrontation with FIFA officials. Mexico were 2–0 up when the Irish boss had his infamous altercation with FIFA officials who seemed intent on pre-venting substitute John Aldridge from taking to the field even though Coyne had already been withdrawn. The Irish fought back well and Aldridge reduced the arrears – a goal which was to prove vital in deciding their final position in the group. The Republic then played out a goalless draw with Norway to finish in second place, level on points with leaders Mexico but with an inferior goal difference. Ireland's oppo-nents in the last sixteen were Holland but two slip-ups by full-back Terry Phelan and another by goalkeeper Packie Bonner put an end to the Republic's hopes of progress-ing to the quarter-finals.

There were many people who thought Jack Charlton would stand down but they were wrong. His final qualifying campaign was to end in disappointment when the Republic missed out on a place at Euro '96 after a play-off match against Holland at

Anfield, which they lost 2–0. Eight days later, Jack Charlton announced his resignation – he had taken the Republic of Ireland to the finals of three major tournaments and to the dizzy heights of sixth place in the FIFA world rankings.

Charlton's successor was Mick McCarthy. Though he started the campaign for the 1998 World Cup Finals with victories over Liechtenstein away and Macedonia in Dublin, he led the team to a goalless home draw with Iceland and a disastrous 3–2 defeat in Macedonia. Following a 1–0 reversal in Romania, the best the Republic could hope for was to finish in second place, thereby securing a play-off match against another second-placed country. The Irish recovered their form and were unbeaten in their last six games to earn a two-legged head-to-head with Belgium. The first leg in Dublin ended all-square at 1–1 but a defeat in Brussels meant there would be no trip to France for the boys in green in 1998.

At the same time that McCarthy was building a senior team, Brian Kerr was establishing Ireland as one of the best in the world at the underage level. In 1997, Ireland finished third in the World Under-20 Championships in Malaysia and the following year, Brian Kerr led both Under-16 and Under-18 teams to victory in their respective European Championships, making Ireland the only country to win both Championships in the same year.

The Irish fans were also getting some long overdue credit as FIFA honoured them with a FIFA Fair Play Award in 1997

The Republic of Ireland started the Euro 2000 qualifiers with a fine 2–0 win over Croatia, whilst in their next game at home to Malta, eighteen-year-old Robbie Keane went into the record books as Ireland's youngest-ever scorer, hitting two goals in three minutes in a 5–0 win. Although they lost 1–0 to group favourites, Yugoslavia, the Republic put up a fine display and won the return 2–1. Despite losing to a last-gasp goal against Croatia, there was more heartache for the Irish in their final group game against Macedonia. Ireland, who were leading 1–0 with a little over ten seconds remaining, were heading for automatic qualification but on conceding an added-time equaliser, they had to try and make it through the play-offs.

Their opponents were Turkey. In the first leg in Dublin, the Irish were yet again undone in the closing minutes, allowing the Turks to grab an all-important equaliser from the penalty-spot after Robbie Keane had put Ireland ahead. Sadly, Ireland's campaign came to a bitter end after a scoreless draw in Turkey. They failed on the away-goal rule whilst Tony Cascarino, who was involved in some unsavoury scenes with opposition players at the finish, announced his retirement from the international game.

The attack-minded Republic of Ireland team made a good start to their 2002 World Cup campaign. They shocked the Dutch by taking a 2–0 lead in Amsterdam through Robbie Keane and Jason McAteer but wobbled late on, allowing the home side to snatch a draw. After another draw, this time in Portugal, the boys in green won four games on the trot to go to the top of their group. In the return game at home to Portugal, the Irish survived an early mauling to draw 1–1. Then on a rutted surface well below international standard, the Republic overcame Estonia to remain undefeated at the top of their group. Down to ten men after Gary Kelly was sent off for picking up two yellow cards, the Republic pulled off a shock 1–0 home win over favourites Holland which effectively left the Dutch requiring miracles to make the World Cup Finals.

In Ireland's final group game, 35–year-old Niall Quinn headed his way into the record books with his twenty-first goal for the Republic. They got the required win over Cyprus and finished joint-top with Portugal. They then had to beat Iran (runners-up from the Asian qualifiers) in a play-off match to make the finals. Following a 2–0 win in Dublin, the Irish clinched their World Cup Finals place, despite conceding a goal 30 seconds from the final whistle in Iran.

The 2002 World Cup tournament started controversially with captain Roy Keane being sent home after an argument with manager Mick McCarthy.

In their opening game of the World Cup Finals, a Matt Holland goal earned the Republic a draw with Cameroon. Four days later, Steve Staunton became the first Republic of Ireland player to earn 100 caps as Robbie Keane snatched a last-gasp equaliser against the mighty Germany. The Republic then progressed to the second round by scoring three goals without reply against Saudi Arabia. Their opponents in the next stage of the tournament were the much-fancied Spain. Ian Harte had a sixty-second-minute penalty saved and Kevin Kilbane hit the rebound wide but Robbie Keane sent the game into extra-time at 1–1 with a last minute spot-kick.

There were no further goals but Ireland lost the ensuing penalty shoot-out. However, the squad still returned home as heroes with Robbie Keane and Damien Duff proving they will be superstars for many years to come.

In the Euro 2004 qualifiers, the Republic of Ireland didn't get off to the best of starts, losing 4–2 in Russia and then going down 2–1 at home to Switzerland. This defeat put more pressure on beleaguered boss Mick McCarthy and the following month he resigned his post as Europe's longest-serving national manager. His departure came just four months after leading the side into the last sixteen of the World Cup.

Two months later, Brian Kerr was named as McCarthy's successor. His first competitive match in charge saw the Irish win 2–1 in Georgia, a match in which winger Kevin Kilbane was hit by an open penknife, thrown by opposition fans. After a disappointing goalless draw in Albania, the Republic snatched a last-gasp vital win over the same opponents in Dublin followed by another home victory four days later over Georgia. In the home game against Russia, the Irish lost the plot in a match which was strewn with goalkeeping errors and had to be satisfied with a 1–1 draw. The team's final game in Switzerland saw them miss out on the chance of reaching the finals when they lost 2–0 to the eventual group winners. The game ended Brian Kerr's nine-game unbeaten run since starting as manager.

Did you know?

The comedy musical *I, Keano* opened in the Olympia Theatre, Dublin in February 2005.

With no European Championships to look forward to, Kerr began planning for the 2006 World Cup qualifiers and Ireland recorded some great results against some of the top teams in the world including wins over the Czech Republic and Holland and a draw with World Champions, Brazil.

In the first of the 2006 World Cup qualifiers, Robbie Keane equalled the country's goalscoring record by netting from the penalty-spot in a 3–0 win over Cyprus. The Irish missed a host of chances before coming away from Switzerland with a 1–1 draw. A goalless home draw against favourites France was followed by a 2–0 victory over the Faroes with Robbie Keane netting both goals to overtake Niall Quinn's overall scoring record. Ireland drew both games with Israel – matches they should have won. Another victory over the Faroes took Ireland to the top of the group before Thierry Henry's goal was enough to defeat the Irish in the second meeting between the two countries. A 1–0 win over Cyprus meant that the Irish needed to beat Switzerland in their final group game to qualify for the World Cup Finals in Germany. The game ended goalless and they missed out.

Following the Republic of Ireland's failure to reach the 2006 World Cup, the tenure of Brian Kerr came to an end, though the FAI were accused by many of acting too hastily due to the lack of viable successors for the post of Ireland team manager. The FAI did not waste too much in time in making what was seen as a crucial appointment, unveiling Steve Staunton and Sir Bobby Robson as the new Irish managerial team.

Staunton's international management career got off to a dream start when he led Ireland to an impressive 3–0 victory over Sweden. His honeymoon period didn't last too long though as the victory was followed by two friendly defeats against Chile and Holland – the Dutch winning 4–0 at Lansdowne Road, Ireland's worst home reversal in 40 years.

His first competitive match in charge of the national team saw Ireland lose 1–0 to Germany in Stuttgart despite a battling performance. Staunton himself was sent-off by the referee for kicking a water bottle onto the pitch in frustration in the second-half. Worse was to follow when, in their second Euro 2008 qualifier, the Irish were beaten 5–2 by Cyprus in Nicosia. An improved performance against the Czech Republic brought a 1–1 draw before Ireland beat San Marino 5–0 on what was to be the last match to be played on the old Lansdowne Road pitch. After an injury-time goal was needed to beat lowly San Marino in the return, there were calls for the manager's resignation.

Thankfully, the Irish returned to form with successive 1–0 home victories over Wales and Slovakia and a 4–0 friendly win against Denmark in Copenhagen. However, these victories proved to be something of a false dawn as in the space of five days an injury-hit side dropped five points from games against Slovakia and the Czech Republic to see their qualifying campaign come to an end. A goalless draw with Germany at Croke Park was followed by a 1–1 draw with Cyprus at the same venue – a chorus of boos greeting the final whistle.

Amid the fans' dissatisfaction, Staunton was now on borrowed time and it came as no surprise when the FAI brought his turbulent 21-month reign to an end. He was replaced by Don Givens for the final Euro 2008 group game against Wales which ended all-square at 2–2. In February 2008, the FAI confirmed that Giovanni Trapatoni as the Republic of Ireland's new manager, ending a 112-day wait for an appointment since Steve Staunton's sacking. The former Italy coach agreed a contract worth around €1.8 million a year until the 2010 World Cup.

**The Republic of Ireland
Soccer Supporters Club
(London Branch)**
In association with
Allied Dunbar PLC
PRESENTS THE

CHRIS HUGHTON

ST. PATRICKS DAY
TESTIMONIAL DINNER DANCE

SUNDAY 15TH MARCH 1992
ROYAL LANCASTER HOTEL, LANCASTER TERRACE, LONDON W2
SOUVENIR BROCHURE & MENU CARD

Chris Hughton who appeared in almost 300 League games for Spurs was honoured by the London Branch of the Republic of Ireland Supporters Club on 15 March 1992.

The Players

The Players

1. FRANK BRADY

Position	Full-back
Born	Glasgow
Club	Fordsons; Aldershot
Caps	2

Date	Team	Result	Goals
21 Mar 1926	Italy	0–3	
27 Apr 1927	Italy 'B'	1–2	

2. HARRY CANNON

Position	Goalkeeper
Club	Bohemians
Caps	2

Date	Team	Result	Goals
21 Mar 1926	Italy	0–3	
12 Feb 1928	Belgium	4–2	

3. JAMES 'Sally' CONNOLLY

Position	Wing-half
Club	Fordsons
Caps	1

Date	Team	Result	Goals
21 Mar 1926	Italy	0–3	

4. DENIS 'Dinny' DOYLE

Position	Centre-half
Club	Shamrock Rovers
Caps	1

Date	Team	Result	Goals
21 Mar 1926	Italy	0–3	

5. JACK 'Kruger' FAGAN

Position	Outside-left
Club	Shamrock Rovers
Caps	1

Date	Team	Result	Goals
21 Mar 1926	Italy	0–3	

6. JOHN JOE FLOOD

Position	Outside-right
Born	Dublin
Club	Shamrock Rovers; Leeds United; Crystal Palace; Reds United
Caps	5

Date	Team	Result	Goals
21 Mar 1926	Italy	0–3	
20 Apr 1929	Belgium	4–0	3
11 May 1930	Belgium	3–1	1
26 Apr 1931	Spain	1–1	
13 Dec 1931	Spain	0–5	

7. MICK 'Boxer' FOLEY

Position	Wing-half
Born	Dublin
Club	Shelbourne; Leeds City
Caps	1

Date	Team	Result	Goals
21 Mar 1926	Italy	0–3	

8. BOB FULLAM

Position	Inside-forward
Born	Ringstead 1897
Club	St Brendan's North End; Olympic; Shelbourne; Shamrock Rovers; Leeds United; Philadelphia Celtic; Holly Carburetors (Detroit)
Caps	2

Date	Team	Result	Goals
21 Mar 1926	Italy	0–3	
27 Apr 1927	Italy 'B'	1–2	1

9. JOE GRACE

Position	Inside-forward
Club	Drumcondra
Caps	1

Date	Team	Result	Goals
21 Mar 1926	Italy	0–3	

10. JACK McCARTHY

Position	Left-back
Club	Bohemians
Caps	3

Date	Team	Result	Goals
21 Mar 1926	Italy	0–3	
12 Feb 1928	Belgium	4–2	
11 May 1930	Belgium	3–1	

11. FRAN WATTERS

Position	Centre-forward
Club	Shelbourne
Caps	1

Date	Team	Result	Goals
21 Mar 1926	Italy	0–3	

12. FRANK COLLINS

Position	Goalkeeper
Club	Jacobs
Caps	1

Date	Team	Result	Goals
27 Apr 1927	Italy	1–2	

13. HARRY DUGGAN

Position	Forward
Born	Dublin, 8 June 1903
Died	1968
Club	Richmond United; Leeds United; Newport County
Caps	5

Date	Team	Result	Goals
27 Apr 1927	Italy 'B'	1–2	
11 May 1930	Belgium	3–1	
3 May 1936	Hungary	3–3	
9 May 1936	Luxembourg	5–1	
7 Nov 1937	Norway	3–3	1

14. WILLIAM 'Sacky' GLEN

Position	Right-half
Club	Shamrock Rovers
Caps	8

Date	Team	Result	Goals
27 Apr 1927	Italy 'B'	1–2	
20 Apr 1929	Belgium	4–0	
11 May 1930	Belgium	3–1	
13 Dec 1931	Spain	0–5	
8 Dec 1935	Holland	3–5	
17 Mar 1936	Switzerland	1–0	
3 May 1936	Hungary	3–3	
9 May 1936	Luxembourg	5–1	

15. JOE KENDRICK

Position	Outside-left; Left-half
Club	Everton; Dolphin
Caps	4

Date	Team	Result	Goals
27 Apr 1927	Italy 'B'	1–2	
25 Feb 1934	Belgium	4–4	
8 Apr 1934	Holland	2–5	
8 Dec 1935	Holland	3–5	

16. ALEC KIRKLAND

Position	Right-Back
Born	Dublin, 26 August 1900
Club	Pontypridd; Bradford Park Avenue; Shamrock Rovers
Caps	1

Date	Team	Result	Goals
27 Apr 1927	Italy 'B'	1–2	

17. BILLY LACEY

Position	Winger; Right-half
Born	Wexford, 24 December 1889
Died	1969
Club	Shelbourne; Everton; Liverpool; New Brighton; Cork Bohemians
Caps	3

Date	Team	Result	Goals
27 Apr 1927	Italy 'B'	1–2	
12 Feb 1928	Belgium	4–2	1
11 May 1930	Belgium	3–1	

18. C MARTIN

Position	Centre-forward
Club	Bo'ness
Caps	1

Date	Team	Result	Goals
27 Apr 1927	Italy 'B'	1–2	

19. TOMMY MULDOON

Position	Wing-half
Born	Athlone, 14 February 1901
Club	Athlone Town; Aston Villa; Tottenham Hotspur; Walsall
Caps	1

Date	Team	Result	Goals
27 Apr 1927	Italy 'B'	1–2	

20. MICK O'BRIEN

Position	Centre-half; Left-half
Born	Kilcock, 10 August 1893
Died	1940
Club	Walker Celtic; Wallsend; Blyth Spartans; Newcastle East End; Celtic; Brentford; Norwich City; South Shields; Queen's Park Rangers; Leicester City; Hull City; Brooklyn Wanderers (US); Derby County; Walsall; Watford
Caps	4

Date	Team	Result	Goals
27 Apr 1927	Italy 'B'	1–2	
20 Apr 1929	Belgium	4–0	
11 May 1930	Belgium	3–1	
8 May 1932	Holland	2–0	

Did you know?

Bill Lacey was the oldest player to make his debut for the Republic of Ireland when he lined up against Italy in March 1926 aged 37 years 87 days. He also became the oldest international for the Irish when he played against Belgium in May 1930, aged 41 years 138 days.

21. PADDY BARRY

Position	Left-half
Club	Fordsons
Caps	2

Date	Team	Result	Goals
12 Feb 1928	Belgium	4–2	
20 Apr 1929	Belgium	4–0	

22. JACK 'Squib' BYRNE

Position	Centre-half
Club	Bray Unknowns
Caps	1

Date	Team	Result	Goals
12 Feb 1928	Belgium	4–2	

23. CHARLIE DOWDALL

Position	Inside-right
Born	Dublin
Club	St James's Gate; Fordsons; Barnsley; Swindon Town; Cork
Caps	3

Date	Team	Result	Goals
12 Feb 1928	Belgium	4–2	
20 Apr 1929	Belgium	4–0	
26 Apr 1931	Spain	1–1	

24. JOSEPH 'Lye' GOLDING

Position	Outside-left
Club	Shamrock Rovers
Caps	2

Date	Team	Result	Goals
12 Feb 1928	Belgium	4–2	
11 May 1930	Belgium	3–1	

25. JOE KINSELLA

Position	Right-half
Club	Shelbourne
Caps	1

Date	Team	Result	Goals
12 Feb 1928	Belgium	4–2	

26. JEREMIAH 'Sam' ROBINSON

Position	Right-back; Right-half
Club	Bohemians; Dolphin
Caps	2

Date	Team	Result	Goals
12 Feb 1928	Belgium	4–2	
26 Apr 1931	Spain	1–1	

27. JACK SULLIVAN

Position	Outside-right
Club	Fordsons
Caps	1

Date	Team	Result	Goals
12 Feb 1928	Belgium	4–2	1

28. JIMMY WHITE

Position	Centre-forward
Club	Bohemians
Caps	1

Date	Team	Result	Goals
12 Feb 1928	Belgium	4–2	2

29. JIMMY BERMINGHAM

Position	Outside-right
Club	Bohemians
Caps	1

Date	Team	Result	Goals
20 Apr 1929	Belgium	4–0	

30. JOHN BURKE

Position	Left-back
Club	Shamrock Rovers
Caps	1

Date	Team	Result	Goals
20 Apr 1929	Belgium	4–0	

31. DAVID 'Babby' BYRNE

Position	Centre-forward
Born	Dublin, 28 April 1905
Club	St Brendan's; Shamrock Rovers; Bradford City; Shelbourne; Manchester United; Coleraine
Caps	3

Date	Team	Result	Goals
20 Apr 1929	Belgium	4–0	1
13 Dec 1931	Spain	0–5	
25 Feb 1934	Belgium	4–4	

32. ROBERT EGAN

Position	Outside-left
Club	Dundalk
Caps	1

Date	Team	Result	Goals
20 Apr 1929	Belgium	4–0	

33. TOM FARQUHARSON

Position	Goalkeeper
Born	Dublin, 4 December 1900
Died	1970
Club	Abertillery; Cardiff City
Caps	4

Date	Team	Result	Goals
20 Apr 1929	Belgium	4–0	
11 May 1930	Belgium	3–1	
26 Apr 1931	Spain	1–1	
13 Dec 1931	Spain	0–5	

34. JIM MAGUIRE

Position	Right-back
Club	Shamrock Rovers
Caps	1

Date	Team	Result	Goals
20 Apr 1929	Belgium	4–0	

35. JIMMY 'Snowy' DUNNE

Position	Centre-forward
Born	Ringstead, 3 September 1905
Died	1949
Club	Shamrock Rovers; New Brighton; Sheffield United; Arsenal; Southampton
Caps	15

Date	Team	Result	Goals
11 May 1930	Belgium	3–1	2
17 Mar 1936	Switzerland	1–0	1
3 May 1936	Hungary	3–3	2
9 May 1936	Luxembourg	5–1	2
17 May 1937	Switzerland	1–0	1
23 May 1937	France	2–0	
10 Oct 1937	Norway	2–3	1
7 Nov 1937	Norway	3–3	1
18 May 1938	Czechoslovakia	2–2	1
22 May 1938	Poland	0–6	
18 Sep 1938	Switzerland	4–0	1
13 Nov 1938	Poland	3–2	1
19 Mar 1939	Hungary	2–2	
18 May 1939	Hungary	2–2	
23 May 1939	Germany	1–1	

36. FRED HORLACHER

Position	Inside-left
Club	Bohemians
Caps	7

Date	Team	Result	Goals
11 May 1930	Belgium	3–1	
13 Dec 1931	Spain	0–5	
8 May 1932	Holland	2–0	
8 Apr 1934	Holland	2–5	
16 Dec 1934	Hungary	2–4	
8 Dec 1935	Holland	3–5	2
17 Mar 1936	Switzerland	1–0	

37. FRAN McLOUGHLIN

Position	Left-half
Club	Fordsons; Cork
Caps	2

Date	Team	Result	Goals
11 May 1930	Belgium	3–1	
13 Dec 1931	Spain	0–5	

38. PADDY 'Babs' BYRNE

Position	Left-back
Club	Dolphin; Shelbourne; Drumcondra
Caps	3

Date	Team	Result	Goals
26 Apr 1931	Spain	1–1	
8 May 1932	Holland	2–0	
8 Apr 1934	Holland	2–5	

39. SEAN BYRNE

Position	Wing-half
Club	Bohemians
Caps	1

Date	Team	Result	Goals
26 Apr 1931	Spain	1–1	

40. HARRY CHATTON

Position	Centre-half
Club	Shelbourne; Dumbarton; Cork
Caps	3

Date	Team	Result	Goals
26 Apr 1931	Spain	1–1	
13 Dec 1931	Spain	0–5	
8 Apr 1934	Holland	2–5	

41. PETER KAVANAGH

Position	Outside-left
Born	Dublin, 1910
Died	Glasgow, 15 February 1993
Club	Drumcondra; Bohemians; Glasgow Celtic; Northampton Town; Guildford City; Hibernian; Stranraer; Waterford
Caps	2

Date	Team	Result	Goals
26 Apr 1931	Spain	1–1	
13 Dec 1931	Spain	0–5	

42. GEORGE LENNOX

Position	Right-back
Club	Dolphin; Shelbourne
Caps	2

Date	Team	Result	Goals
26 Apr 1931	Spain	1–1	
13 Dec 1931	Spain	0–5	

43. PADDY MOORE

Position	Centre-forward
Born	Ballybough, 1909
Died	1951
Club	Richmond Rovers; Shamrock Rovers; Cardiff City; Merthyr Town; Tranmere Rovers; Aberdeen; Shelbourne; Brideville
Caps	9

Date	Team	Result	Goals
26 Apr 1931	Spain	1–1	1
8 May 1932	Holland	2–0	1
25 Feb 1934	Belgium	4–4	4
8 Apr 1934	Holland	2–5	1
16 Dec 1934	Hungary	2–4	
8 May 1935	Germany	1–3	
8 Dec 1935	Holland	3–5	
17 Oct 1936	Germany	5–2	
6 Dec 1936	Hungary	2–3	

Did you know?

Paddy Moore became the first player to score four goals in a World Cup game when he netted for the Republic of Ireland in their 4–4 draw with Belgium in 1934.

44. CHARLIE REID

Position Inside-left
Club Brideville
Caps 1

Date	Team	Result	Goals
26 Apr 1931	Spain	1–1	

45. LARRY DOYLE

Position Left-back
Club Dolphins
Caps 1

Date	Team	Result	Goals
13 Dec 1931	Spain	0–5	

46. PATSY GALLAGHER

Position Inside-forward
Club Falkirk
Caps 1

Date	Team	Result	Goals
13 Dec 1931	Spain	0–5	

47. JIMMY DALY

Position Right-back; Outside-right
Club Shamrock Rovers
Caps 2

Date	Team	Result	Goals
8 May 1932	Holland	2–0	
5 May 1935	Switzerland	0–1	

48. JIMMY KELLY

Position Outside-left
Club Derry City
Caps 4

Date	Team	Result	Goals
8 May 1932	Holland	2–0	
25 Feb 1934	Belgium	4–4	
17 Mar 1936	Switzerland	1–0	
9 May 1936	Luxembourg	5–1	2

49. BILLY KENNEDY

Position Outside-right
Club St James's Gate
Caps 3

Date	Team	Result	Goals
8 May 1932	Holland	2–0	
25 Feb 1934	Belgium	4–4	
8 Apr 1934	Holland	2–5	

50. OWEN KINSELLA

Position Left-half
Club Shamrock Rovers
Caps 2

Date	Team	Result	Goals
8 May 1932	Holland	2–0	
10 Oct 1937	Norway	2–3	

51. MICK McCARTHY

Position Goalkeeper
Born Cork, 22 December 1911
Died 1973
Club Shamrock Rovers; Sheffield United; Brideville
Caps 1

Date	Team	Result	Goals
8 May 1932	Holland	2–0	

52. JOE O'REILLY

Position Wing-half; Centre-half
Club Brideville; Aberdeen; St James's Gate
Caps 20

Date	Team	Result	Goals
8 May 1932	Holland	2–0	1
25 Feb 1934	Belgium	4–4	
8 Apr 1934	Holland	2–5	
8 Dec 1935	Holland	3–5	
17 Mar 1936	Switzerland	1–0	
3 May 1936	Hungary	3–3	
9 May 1936	Luxembourg	5–1	

17 Oct 1936	Germany	5–2
6 Dec 1936	Hungary	2–3
17 May 1937	Switzerland	1–0
23 May 1937	France	2–0
10 Oct 1937	Norway	2–3
7 Nov 1937	Norway	3–3
18 May 1938	Czechoslovakia	2–2
22 May 1938	Poland	0–6
18 Sep 1938	Switzerland	4–0
13 Nov 1938	Poland	3–2
19 Mar 1939	Hungary	2–2
18 May 1939	Hungary	2–2
23 May 1939	Germany	1–1

53. ALEX STEVENSON

Position	Inside-forward
Born	Dublin, 9 August 1912
Died	1985
Club	Dolphin; Glasgow Rangers; Everton; Bootle
Caps	7

Date	Team	Result	Goals
8 May 1932	Holland	2–0	
30 Sep 1946	England	0–1	
2 Mar 1947	Spain	3–2	
4 May 1947	Portugal	0–2	
23 May 1948	Portugal	0–2	
30 May 1948	Spain	1–2	
5 Dec 1948	Switzerland	0–1	

54. TOM BURKE

Position	Left-back
Club	Cork
Caps	1

Date	Team	Result	Goals
25 Feb 1934	Belgium	4–4	

55. JIM 'Fox' FOLEY

Position	Goalkeeper
Born	Cork, 1914
Club	Cork; Glasgow Celtic; Plymouth Argyle; Cork City; Cork United
Caps	7

Date	Team	Result	Goals
25 Feb 1934	Belgium	4–4	
8 Apr 1934	Holland	2–5	
16 Dec 1934	Hungary	2–4	
5 May 1935	Switzerland	0–1	
8 May 1935	Germany	1–3	
17 Oct 1936	Germany	5–2	
6 Dec 1936	Hungary	2–3	

56. PADDY GASKINS

Position	Right-back; Right-half
Club	Shamrock Rovers; St James's Gate
Caps	7

Date	Team	Result	Goals
25 Feb 1934	Belgium	4–4	
8 Apr 1934	Holland	2–5	
16 Dec 1934	Hungary	2–4	

Did you know?

Alex Stevenson holds the record for having the longest gap between his first and second caps. He made his debut for the Republic of Ireland in their 2–0 win against Holland on 8 May 1932 and his second match was the 1–0 home defeat by England in September 1946 – a break of fourteen years!

Date	Team	Result	Goals
5 May 1935	Switzerland	0–1	
8 May 1935	Germany	1–3	
18 May 1938	Czechoslovakia	2–2	
22 May 1938	Poland	0–6	

57. MIAH LYNCH

Position Right-back
Club Cork Bohemians
Caps 1

Date	Team	Result	Goals
25 Feb 1934	Belgium	4–4	

58. TIM O'KEEFFE

Position Inside-left
Club Cork; Waterford
Caps 3

Date	Team	Result	Goals
25 Feb 1934	Belgium	4–4	
18 May 1938	Czechoslovakia	2–2	
22 May 1938	Poland	0–6	

59. BILLY JORDAN

Position Inside-forward
Club Bohemians
Caps 2

Date	Team	Result	Goals
8 Apr 1934	Holland	2–5	
10 Oct 1937	Norway	2–3	

60. PADDY 'Woodere' MEEHAN

Position Outside-left
Club Drumcondra
Caps 1

Date	Team	Result	Goals
8 Apr 1934	Holland	2–5	

61. JOHNNY SQUIRES

Position Inside-right
Club Shelbourne
Caps 1

Date	Team	Result	Goals
8 Apr 1934	Holland	2–5	1

62. PADDY BERMINGHAM

Position Left-back
Club St James's Gate
Caps 1

Date	Team	Result	Goals
16 Dec 1934	Hungary	2–4	1

63. JOEY DONNELLY

Position Inside-forward
Club Dundalk
Caps 10

Date	Team	Result	Goals
16 Dec 1934	Hungary	2–4	1
5 May 1935	Switzerland	0–1	
8 May 1935	Germany	1–3	
8 Dec 1935	Holland	3–5	
17 Mar 1936	Switzerland	1–0	
3 May 1936	Hungary	3–3	
9 May 1936	Luxembourg	5–1	1
17 Oct 1936	Germany	5–2	2
6 Dec 1936	Hungary	2–3	
10 Oct 1937	Norway	2–3	

64. BILL FALLON

Position Outside-left
Born Larne, 14 January 1912
Died 1989
Club Brideville, Dolphin, Notts County; Sheffield Wednesday; Shamrock Rovers; Shelbourne; Dundalk; Exeter City; Peterborough United
Caps 9

Date	Team	Result	Goals
16 Dec 1934	Hungary	2–4	
3 May 1936	Hungary	3–3	
6 Dec 1936	Hungary	2–3	1
17 May 1937	Switzerland	1–0	
23 May 1937	France	2–0	
18 Sep 1938	Switzerland	4–0	
13 Nov 1938	Poland	3–2	1
18 May 1939	Hungary	2–2	
23 May 1939	Germany	1–1	

65. BOB GRIFFITH

Position   Outside-right
Born   Dublin, 28 September 1907
Died   1976
Club   Hillview; Great Southern Railway;
            Tottenham Hotspur; Drumcondra;
            Shelbourne; Southport; Walsall
Caps   1

Date	Team	Result	Goals
16 Dec 1934	Hungary	2–4	

66. CHARLIE LENNON

Position   Centre-half
Club   St James's Gate
Caps   3

Date	Team	Result	Goals
16 Dec 1934	Hungary	2–4	
5 May 1935	Switzerland	0–1	
8 May 1935	Germany	1–3	

67. PADDY O'KANE

Position   Wing-half
Club   Bohemians
Caps   3

Date	Team	Result	Goals
16 Dec 1934	Hungary	2–4	
5 May 1935	Switzerland	0–1	
8 May 1935	Germany	1–3	

68. ALF RIGBY

Position   Centre-forward
Club   St James's Gate
Caps   3

Date	Team	Result	Goals
16 Dec 1934	Hungary	2–4	
5 May 1935	Switzerland	0–1	
8 May 1935	Germany	1–3	

69. LEO DUNNE

Position   Full-back
Born   Dublin
Club   Drumcondra; Manchester City; Hull
            City
Caps   2

Date	Team	Result	Goals
5 May 1935	Switzerland	0–1	
8 May 1935	Germany	1–3	

70. PLEV ELLIS

Position   Inside-right; Outside-right
Club   Bohemians
Caps   7

Date	Team	Result	Goals
5 May 1935	Switzerland	0–1	
8 May 1935	Germany	1–3	1
8 Dec 1935	Holland	3–5	1
17 Mar 1936	Switzerland	1–0	
9 May 1936	Luxembourg	5–1	
17 Oct 1936	Germany	5–2	
6 Dec 1936	Hungary	2–3	

71. FREDDIE HUTCHINSON

Position   Left-half
Club   Drumcondra
Caps   2

Date	Team	Result	Goals
5 May 1935	Switzerland	0–1	
8 May 1935	Germany	1–3	

72. PADDY MONAHAN

Position	Outside-left
Club	Sligo Rovers
Caps	2

Date	Team	Result	Goals
5 May 1935	Switzerland	0–1	
8 May 1935	Germany	1–3	

73. PADDY ANDREWS

Position	Centre-half
Club	Bohemians
Caps	1

Date	Team	Result	Goals
8 Dec 1935	Holland	3–5	

74. WILLIAM HARRINGTON

Position	Goalkeeper
Club	Cork
Caps	5

Date	Team	Result	Goals
8 Dec 1935	Holland	3–5	
17 Mar 1936	Switzerland	1–0	
3 May 1936	Hungary	3–3	
9 May 1936	Luxembourg	5–1	
22 May 1938	Poland	0–6	

75. BILL McGUIRE

Position	Left-back
Club	Bohemians
Caps	1

Date	Team	Result	Goals
8 Dec 1935	Holland	3–5	

76. WILLIAM O'NEILL

Position	Right-back
Club	Dundalk
Caps	11

Date	Team	Result	Goals
8 Dec 1935	Holland	3–5	

Date	Team	Result	Goals
17 Mar 1936	Switzerland	1–0	
3 May 1936	Hungary	3–3	
9 May 1936	Luxembourg	5–1	
17 Oct 1936	Germany	5–2	
6 Dec 1936	Hungary	2–3	
17 May 1937	Switzerland	1–0	
23 May 1937	France	2–0	
7 Nov 1937	Norway	3–3	
18 May 1939	Hungary	2–2	
23 May 1939	Germany	1–1	

77. BILL GORMAN

Position	Full-back
Born	Sligo, 13 July 1911
Died	1978
Club	Shettleston Juniors; Bury; Brentford
Caps	13

Date	Team	Result	Goals
17 Mar 1936	Switzerland	1–0	
3 May 1936	Hungary	3–3	
9 May 1936	Luxembourg	5–1	
17 Oct 1936	Germany	5–2	
6 Dec 1936	Hungary	2–3	
7 Nov 1937	Norway	3–3	
18 May 1938	Czechoslovakia	2–2	
22 May 1938	Poland	0–6	
18 Sep 1938	Switzerland	4–0	
13 Nov 1938	Poland	3–2	
19 Mar 1939	Hungary	2–2	
30 Sep 1946	England	0–1	
4 May 1947	Portugal	0–2	

78. CHARLIE TURNER

Position	Centre-half
Born	Athlone 1911
Club	Manchester Central; Stalybridge Celtic; Leeds United; Southend United; West Ham United; Hartlepool United
Caps	10

Date	Team	Result	Goals
17 Mar 1936	Switzerland	1–0	
17 Oct 1936	Germany	5–2	
6 Dec 1936	Hungary	2–3	
17 May 1937	Switzerland	1–0	
23 May 1937	France	2–0	
10 Oct 1937	Norway	2–3	
7 Nov 1937	Norway	3–3	
18 May 1938	Czechoslovakia	2–2	
22 May 1938	Poland	0–6	
19 Mar 1939	Hungary	2–2	

79. OWEN MADDEN

Position	Inside-left; Outside-left
Born	Cork, 5 December 1916
Died	1981
Club	Cork Southern Rovers; Cork; Norwich City; Birmingham; Sligo Rovers; Cork City; Cork United; Cork Athletic
Caps	1

Date	Team	Result	Goals
3 May 1936	Hungary	3–2	1

80. CON MOULSON

Position	Centre-half; Left-back
Born	Clogheen, 3 September 1906
Died	1989
Club	Cleethorpes Town; Grimsby Town; Bristol City; Lincoln City; Notts County
Caps	5

Date	Team	Result	Goals
3 May 1936	Hungary	3–3	
9 May 1936	Luxembourg	5–1	
6 Dec 1936	Hungary	2–3	
17 May 1937	Switzerland	1–0	
23 May 1937	France	2–0	

81. HUGH CONNOLLY

Position	Left-half
Club	Cork
Caps	1

Date	Team	Result	Goals
17 Oct 1936	Germany	5–2	

82. TOM DAVIS

Position	Centre-forward, Inside-right
Born	Dublin 1911
Club	Midland Athletic; Cork; Shelbourne; Boston Town; Torquay United; New Brighton; FC de Metz; Oldham Athletic; Tranmere Rovers; York City; Workington; Belfast Distillery
Caps	4

Date	Team	Result	Goals
17 Oct 1936	Germany	5–2	2
6 Dec 1936	Hungary	2–3	1
18 May 1938	Czechoslovakia	2–2	1
22 May 1938	Poland	0–6	

83. MATT GEOGHEGAN

Position	Outside-left
Club	St James's Gate
Caps	2

Date	Team	Result	Goals
17 Oct 1936	Germany	5–2	1
10 Oct 1937	Norway	2–3	1

84. TOMMY BREEN

Position	Goalkeeper
Born	Drogheda, 27 April 1917
Died	1988
Club	Newry Town; Belfast Celtic; Manchester United; Linfield; Shamrock Rovers; Glentoran
Caps	5

Date	Team	Result	Goals
17 May 1937	Switzerland	1–0	
23 May 1937	France	2–0	
30 Sep 1946	England	0–1	
2 Mar 1947	Spain	3–2	
4 May 1947	Portugal	0–2	

85. JOHNNY BROWN

Position	Outside-right
Born	Belfast, 8 November 1914
Club	Belfast Celtic; Wolverhampton Wanderers; Coventry City; Birmingham; Barry Town; Ipswich Town
Caps	2

Date	Team	Result	Goals
17 May 1937	Switzerland	1–0	
23 May 1937	France	2–0	1

86. PADDY FARRELL

Position	Inside-left
Club	Hibernian
Caps	2

Date	Team	Result	Goals
17 May 1937	Switzerland	1–0	
23 May 1937	France	2–0	

87. JOHNNY FEENAN

Position	Full-back
Born	Newry, 1 July 1914
Died	1994
Club	Newry Town; Belfast Celtic; Sunderland
Caps	2

Date	Team	Result	Goals
17 May 1937	Switzerland	1–0	
23 May 1937	France	2–0	

88. DAVY JORDAN

Position	Centre-forward; Right-half; Right-back
Born	Belfast
Club	Ards; Hull City; Wolverhampton Wanderers; Crystal Palace
Caps	2

Date	Team	Result	Goals
17 May 1937	Switzerland	1–0	
23 May 1937	France	2–0	1

89. TOM DONNELLY

Position	Outside-right
Club	Drumcondra; Shamrock Rovers
Caps	2

Date	Team	Result	Goals
10 Oct 1937	Norway	2–3	
18 Sep 1938	Switzerland	4–0	1

90. MICK HOY

Position	Left-back
Club	Dundalk
Caps	6

Date	Team	Result	Goals
10 Oct 1937	Norway	2–3	
18 Sep 1938	Switzerland	4–0	
13 Nov 1938	Poland	3–2	
19 Mar 1939	Hungary	2–2	
18 May 1939	Hungary	2–2	
23 May 1939	Germany	1–1	

91. GEORGE McKENZIE

Position	Goalkeeper
Born	Dublin
Club	Arthurlie; Plymouth Argyle; Southend United; Hereford United
Caps	9

Date	Team	Result	Goals
10 Oct 1937	Norway	2–3	
7 Nov 1937	Norway	3–3	
18 May 1938	Czechoslovakia	2–2	
22 May 1938	Poland	0–6	
18 Sep 1938	Switzerland	4–0	
13 Nov 1938	Poland	3–2	
19 Mar 1939	Hungary	2–2	
18 May 1939	Hungary	2–2	
23 May 1939	Germany	1–1	

92. JOE WILLIAMS

Position	Right-back
Club	Shamrock Rovers
Caps	1

Date	Team	Result	Goals
10 Oct 1937	Norway	2–3	

93. TOM ARRIGAN

Position	Left-half
Club	Waterford
Caps	1

Date	Team	Result	Goals
7 Nov 1937	Norway	3–3	

94. JOHNNY CAREY

Position	Defender
Born	Dublin, 23 February 1919
Died	August 1995
Club	St James's Gate; Manchester United
Caps	29

Date	Team	Result	Goals
7 Nov 1937	Norway	3–3	
18 May 1937	Czechoslovakia	2–2	
22 May 1938	Poland	0–6	
18 Sep 1938	Switzerland	4–0	
13 Nov 1938	Poland	3–2	1
19 Mar 1939	Hungary	2–2	1
18 May 1939	Hungary	2–2	
23 May 1939	Germany	1–1	
16 Jun 1946	Portugal	1–3	
23 Jun 1946	Spain	1–0	
30 Sep 1946	England	0–1	
2 Mar 1947	Spain	3–2	
4 May 1947	Portugal	0–2	
23 May 1948	Portugal	0–2	
30 May 1948	Spain	1–2	
5 Dec 1948	Switzerland	0–1	
24 Apr 1949	Belgium	0–2	
22 May 1949	Portugal	1–0	
2 Jun 1949	Sweden	1–3	
12 Jun 1949	Spain	1–4	
8 Sep 1949	Finland	3–0	
21 Sep 1949	England	2–0	
9 Oct 1949	Finland	1–1	
13 Nov 1949	Sweden	1–3	
26 Nov 1950	Norway	2–2	1
13 May 1951	Argentina	0–1	
30 May 1951	Norway	3–2	
16 Nov 1952	France	1–1	
25 Mar 1953	Austria	4–0	

95. TOMMY FOY

Position	Outside-left
Born	Croydon, 1911
Club	Bohemians; St James's Gate; Bradford City; Scarborough; Bristol City; Barrow; Shamrock Rovers
Caps	2

Date	Team	Result	Goals
7 Nov 1937	Norway	3–3	
19 Mar 1939	Hungary	2–2	

96. KEVIN O'FLANAGAN

Position	Winger
Born	Dublin, 10 June 1919
Club	Bohemians; Arsenal; Barnet; Brentford
Caps	10

Date	Team	Result	Goals
7 Nov 1937	Norway	3–3	1
18 May 1938	Czechoslovakia	2–2	
22 May 1938	Poland	0–6	
13 Nov 1938	Poland	3–2	
19 Mar 1939	Hungary	2–2	
18 May 1939	Hungary	2–2	2
23 May 1939	Germany	1–1	
30 Sep 1946	England	0–1	
2 Mar 1947	Spain	3–2	
4 May 1947	Portugal	0–2	

97. MATT O'MAHONEY

Position	Centre-half
Born	Mullinavat, County Kilkenny, 9 January 1913
Died	1992
Club	Liverpool; New Brighton; Hoylake; Southport; Wolverhampton Wanderers; Newport County; Bristol Rovers; Ipswich Town; Yarmouth Town
Caps	6

Date	Team	Result	Goals
18 May 1938	Czechoslovakia	2–2	
22 May 1938	Poland	0–6	
18 Sep 1938	Switzerland	4–0	
13 Nov 1938	Poland	3–2	
18 May 1939	Hungary	2–2	
23 May 1939	Germany	1–1	

98. PADDY BRADSHAW

Position	Centre-forward
Club	St James's Gate
Caps	5

Date	Team	Result	Goals
18 Sep 1938	Switzerland	4–0	2
13 Nov 1938	Poland	3–2	
19 Mar 1939	Hungary	2–2	1
18 May 1939	Hungary	2–2	
23 May 1939	Germany	1–1	1

99. DICK LUNN

Position	Left-half
Club	Dundalk
Caps	2

Date	Team	Result	Goals
18 Sep 1938	Switzerland	4–0	
13 Nov 1938	Poland	3–2	

100. ERIC WEIR

Position	Left-half
Club	Clyde
Caps	3

Date	Team	Result	Goals
19 Mar 1939	Hungary	2–2	
18 May 1939	Hungary	2–2	
23 May 1939	Germany	1–1	

101. BUD AHERNE

Position	Full-back
Born	Limerick, 26 January 1919
Died	January 2000
Club	Limerick; Belfast Celtic; Luton Town
Caps	16

Did you know?

The fastest goal scored by an Irish player came from the boot of Paddy Bradshaw after just 20 seconds of play during the Republic's 4–0 win over Switzerland in 1938.

Date	Team	Result	Goals
16 Jun 1946	Portugal	1–3	
23 Jun 1946	Spain	1–0	
8 Sep 1949	Finland	3–0	
21 Sep 1949	England	2–0	
9 Oct 1949	Finland	1–1	
13 Nov 1949	Sweden	1–3	
10 May 1950	Belgium	1–5	
26 Nov 1950	Norway	2–2	
13 May 1951	Argentina	0–1	
30 May 1951	Norway	3–2	
17 Oct 1951	West Germany	3–2	
4 May 1952	West Germany	0–3	
7 May 1952	Austria	0–6	
1 Jun 1952	Spain	0–6	
16 Nov 1952	France	1–1	
4 Oct 1953	France	3–5	

Date	Team	Result	Goals
5 Dec 1948	Switzerland	0–1	
22 May 1949	Portugal	1–0	
2 Jun 1949	Sweden	1–3	
26 Nov 1950	Norway	2–2	
13 May 1951	Argentina	0–1	
17 Oct 1951	West Germany	3–2	
4 May 1952	West Germany	0–3	
7 May 1952	Austria	0–6	
1 Jun 1952	Spain	0–6	
16 Nov 1952	France	1–1	
25 Mar 1953	Austria	4–0	1
4 Oct 1953	France	3–5	
28 Oct 1953	Luxembourg	4–0	1
25 Nov 1953	France	0–1	
7 Nov 1954	Norway	2–1	
1 May 1955	Holland	1–0	
28 May 1955	West Germany	1–2	
27 Nov 1955	Spain	2–2	

102. NED COURTNEY

Position	Goalkeeper
Born	Dublin
Club	Cork United; Cork Athletic
Caps	1

Date	Team	Result	Goals
16 Jun 1946	Portugal	1–3	

103. TOMMY EGLINGTON

Position	Outside-left
Born	Dublin, 15 January 1923
Died	18 February 2004
Club	Shamrock Rovers; Everton; Tranmere Rovers
Caps	24

Date	Team	Result	Goals
16 Jun 1946	Portugal	1–3	
23 Jun 1946	Spain	1–0	
30 Sep 1946	England	0–1	
2 Mar 1947	Spain	3–2	
4 May 1947	Portugal	0–2	
23 May 1947	Portugal	0–2	

Did you know?

When a player has played 25 times for Ireland he is awarded a 25-cap statuette although Tommy Eglington was awarded one in special circumstances – he had 24 caps with the Republic of Ireland but had played for Northern Ireland a number of times, bringing his total up to the required total.

104. PETER FARRELL

Position	Wing-half
Born	Dublin, 16 August 1922
Died	16 March 1999
Club	Shamrock Rovers; Everton; Tranmere Rovers
Caps	28

Date	Team	Result	Goals
16 Jun 1946	Portugal	1–3	
23 Jun 1946	Spain	1–0	
2 Mar 1947	Spain	3–2	
4 May 1947	Portugal	0–2	
23 May 1948	Portugal	0–2	
30 May 1948	Spain	1–2	
5 Dec 1948	Switzerland	0–1	
22 May 1949	Portugal	1–0	
12 Jun 1949	Spain	1–4	
21 Sep 1949	England	2–0	1
9 Oct 1949	Finland	1–1	1
13 Nov 1949	Sweden	1–3	
13 May 1951	Argentina	0–1	
30 May 1951	Norway	3–2	1
17 Oct 1951	West Germany	3–2	
4 May 1952	West Germany	0–3	
7 May 1952	Austria	0–6	
1 Jun 1952	Spain	0–6	
16 Nov 1952	France	1–1	
25 Mar 1953	Austria	4–0	
4 Oct 1953	France	3–5	
25 Nov 1953	France	0–1	
7 Nov 1954	Norway	2–1	
1 May 1955	Holland	1–0	
28 May 1955	West Germany	1–2	
19 Oct 1955	Yugoslavia	1–4	
27 Nov 1955	Spain	2–2	
8 May 1957	England	1–5	

Did you know?

When Everton-player Peter Farrell scored for the Republic of Ireland against England at Goodison Park on 21 September 1949, he became the only international to score an away goal on his home ground.

105. JIMMY McALINDEN

Position	Centre-forward
Born	Belfast, 31 December 1917
Died	15 November 1993
Club	Belfast Celtic; Portsmouth; Stoke City; Southend United; Glenavon
Caps	2

Date	Team	Result	Goals
16 Jun 1946	Portugal	1–3	
23 Jun 1946	Spain	1–0	

106. BILLY McMILLAN

Position	Right-back
Born	Carrickfergus
Died	1991
Club	Belfast Celtic; Ballymena United
Caps	2

Date	Team	Result	Goals
16 Jun 1946	Portugal	1–3	
23 Jun 1946	Spain	1–0	

107. CON MARTIN

Position	Defender; Goalkeeper
Born	Dublin, 20 March 1923
Club	Drumcondra; Glentoran; Leeds United; Aston Villa
Caps	30

Date	Team	Result	Goals
16 Jun 1946	Portugal	1–3	
23 Jun 1946	Spain	1–0	
30 Sep 1946	England	0–1	
2 Mar 1947	Spain	3–2	
23 May 1948	Portugal	0–2	
30 May 1948	Spain	1–2	
5 Dec 1948	Switzerland	0–1	
24 Apr 1949	Belgium	0–2	
22 May 1949	Portugal	1–0	
2 Jun 1949	Sweden	1–3	
12 Jun 1949	Spain	1–4	1
8 Sep 1949	Finland	3–0	2
21 Sep 1949	England	2–0	1

Date	Team	Result	Goals
9 Oct 1949	Finland	1–1	
13 Nov 1949	Sweden	1–3	1
10 May 1950	Belgium	1–5	
13 May 1951	Argentina	0–1	
4 May 1952	West Germany	0–3	
7 May 1952	Austria	0–6	
1 Jun 1952	Spain	0–6	
4 Oct 1953	France	3–5	
25 Nov 1953	France	0–1	
7 Mar 1954	Luxembourg	1–0	
7 Nov 1954	Norway	2–1	1
1 May 1955	Holland	1–0	
25 May 1955	Norway	3–1	
28 May 1955	West Germany	1–2	
19 Oct 1955	Yugoslavia	1–4	
27 Nov 1955	Spain	2–2	
10 May 1956	Holland	4–1	

108. JACKIE O'REILLY

Position	Winger
Born	Cobh, County Cork, 7 May 1914
Club	Cork Bohemians; Cobh Wanderers; Cobh Ramblers; Cork United; Norwich City; Cork United
Caps	2

Date	Team	Result	Goals
16 Jun 1946	Portugal	1–3	1
23 Jun 1946	Spain	1–0	

109. PADDY SLOAN

Position	Inside-forward; Wing-half
Born	Lurgan, 30 April 1920
Died	19 January 1993
Club	Glenavon; Manchester United; Arsenal; Sheffield United; Milan; Torino; Udinese; Brescia; Norwich City; Peterborough United; Rabat FC (Malta); Hastings United; Leamington Lockheed; Bath City
Caps	2

Date	Team	Result	Goals
16 Jun 1946	Portugal	1–3	
23 Jun 1946	Spain	1–0	1

110. JACKIE VERNON

Position	Centre-half
Born	Belfast, 26 September 1918
Died	June 1981
Club	Dundela; Belfast Celtic; West Bromwich Albion; Crusaders
Caps	2

Date	Team	Result	Goals
16 Jun 1946	Portugal	1–3	
23 Jun 1946	Spain	1–0	

111. DAVY WALSH

Position	Centre-forward
Born	Waterford, 28 April 1923
Club	Shelbourne; Limerick; Linfield; West Bromwich Albion; Aston Villa; Walsall; Worcester City
Caps	20

Date	Team	Result	Goals
16 Jun 1946	Portugal	1–3	
23 Jun 1946	Spain	1–0	
2 Mar 1947	Spain	3–2	2
4 May 1947	Portugal	0–2	
23 May 1948	Portugal	0–2	
30 May 1948	Spain	1–2	
5 Dec 1948	Switzerland	0–1	

Date	Team	Result	Goals
22 May 1949	Portugal	1–0	
2 Jun 1949	Sweden	1–3	1
12 Jun 1949	Spain	1–4	
21 Sep 1949	England	2–0	
9 Oct 1949	Finland	1–1	
13 Nov 1949	Sweden	1–3	
26 Nov 1950	Norway	2–2	1
13 May 1951	Argentina	0–1	
30 May 1951	Norway	3–2	
1 Jun 1952	Spain	0–6	
25 Mar 1953	Austria	4–0	
4 Oct 1953	France	3–5	1
25 Nov 1953	France	0–1	

Did you know?

Davy Walsh is the only player to have represented both the Republic of Ireland and Northern Ireland in World Cup matches.

112. PADDY COAD

Position Wing-half; Forward
Born Waterford, 1920
Club Corinthians; Waterford; Glenavon; Shamrock Rovers; Waterford
Caps 11

Date	Team	Result	Goals
30 Sep 1946	England	0–1	
2 Mar 1947	Spain	3–2	1
4 May 1947	Portugal	0–2	
23 May 1948	Portugal	0–2	
30 May 1948	Spain	1–2	
5 Dec 1948	Switzerland	0–1	
24 Apr 1949	Belgium	0–2	
22 May 1949	Portugal	1–0	1
2 Jun 1949	Sweden	1–3	
30 May 1951	Norway	3–2	1
1 Jun 1952	Spain	0–6	

113. BILLY HAYES

Position Full-back
Born Cork, 7 November 1915
Died 22 April 1987
Club Sheffield St Vincents; Huddersfield Town; Burnley
Caps 2

Date	Team	Result	Goals
30 Sep 1946	England	0–1	
4 May 1947	Portugal	0–2	

114. MICHAEL O'FLANAGAN

Position Winger
Born Dublin, 29 September 1922
Club Bohemians; Belfast Celtic
Caps 1

Date	Team	Result	Goals
30 Sep 1946	England	0–1	

115. BILLY WALSH

Position Wing-half
Born Dublin, 31 May 1921
Club Manchester United; Manchester City; Chelmsford City; Canterbury
Caps 9

Date	Team	Result	Goals
30 Sep 1946	England	0–1	
2 Mar 1947	Spain	3–2	
4 May 1947	Portugal	0–2	
23 May 1948	Portugal	0–2	
30 May 1948	Spain	1–2	
24 Apr 1949	Belgium	0–2	
21 Sep 1949	England	2–0	
13 Nov 1949	Sweden	1–3	
10 May 1950	Belgium	1–5	

116. JOHN McGOWAN

Position Defender
Born Cork, 8 June 1920
Club Cobh Wanderers; Cork United; West Ham United
Caps 1

Date	Team	Result	Goals
2 Mar 1947	Spain	3–2	

117. KEVIN CLARKE

Position	Half-back
Born	Dublin, 3 December 1921
Club	Drumcondra; Swansea City; Gravesend and Northfleet
Caps	2

Date	Team	Result	Goals
23 May 1948	Portugal	0–2	
30 May 1948	Spain	1–2	

118. BENNY HENDERSON

Position	Outside-right
Born	Dublin
Club	Bohemians; Transport and Ierne; Drumcondra; Dundalk
Caps	2

Date	Team	Result	Goals
23 May 1948	Portugal	0–2	
30 May 1948	Spain	1–2	

119. GEORGE MOULSON

Position	Goalkeeper
Born	Clogheen, County Tipperary, 6 August 1914
Died	May 1994
Club	Grimsby Town; Lincoln City; Peterborough United
Caps	3

Date	Team	Result	Goals
23 May 1948	Portugal	0–2	
30 May 1948	Spain	1–2	
5 Dec 1948	Switzerland	0–1	

120. TOMMY MORONEY

Position	Wing-half
Born	Cork, 10 November 1923
Died	16 May 1981
Club	Cork United; West Ham United; Evergreen United
Caps	12

Date	Team	Result	Goals
30 May 1948	Spain	1–2	1
22 May 1949	Portugal	1–0	
2 Jun 1949	Sweden	1–3	
12 Jun 1949	Spain	1–4	
8 Sep 1949	Finland	3–0	
21 Sep 1949	England	2–0	
9 Oct 1949	Finland	1–1	
10 May 1950	Belgium	1–5	
26 Nov 1950	Norway	2–2	
30 May 1951	Norway	3–2	
17 Oct 1951	West Germany	3–2	
4 Oct 1953	France	3–5	

121. EDDIE GANNON

Position	Wing-half
Born	Dublin, 3 January 1921
Died	31 July 1989
Club	Shelbourne; Distillery; Shelbourne; Notts County; Sheffield Wednesday; Shelbourne
Caps	14

Date	Team	Result	Goals
5 Dec 1948	Switzerland	0–1	
24 Apr 1949	Belgium	0–2	
22 May 1949	Portugal	1–0	
2 Jun 1949	Sweden	1–3	
12 Jun 1949	Spain	1–4	
8 Sep 1949	Finland	3–0	
26 Nov 1950	Norway	2–2	
4 May 1952	West Germany	0–3	
7 May 1952	Austria	0–6	
28 Oct 1953	Luxembourg	4–0	
25 Nov 1953	France	0–1	
7 Nov 1954	Norway	2–1	
25 May 1955	Norway	3–1	
28 May 1955	West Germany	1–2	

SOUVENIR BROCHURE £5

The cover for Matt Busby's testimonial match on 11 August 1991 shows two Manchester United greats – Paul McGrath in the green of the Republic of Ireland and Norman Whiteside (Northern Ireland) in the red of Manchester United.

122. RORY KEANE

Position	Full-back
Born	Limerick, 31 August 1922
Club	Limerick; Swansea Town
Caps	4

Date	Team	Result	Goals
5 Dec 1948	Switzerland	0–1	
22 May 1949	Portugal	1–0	
2 Jun 1949	Sweden	1–3	
12 Jun 1949	Spain	1–4	

123. JACKIE O'DRISCOLL

Position	Winger
Born	Cork, 20 September 1921
Died	November 1988
Club	Cork City; Waterford; Shelbourne; Cork United; Swansea Town; Llanelli
Caps	3

Date	Team	Result	Goals
5 Dec 1948	Switzerland	0–1	
24 Apr 1949	Belgium	0–2	
2 Jun 1949	Sweden	1–3	

124. BRENDAN O'CARROLL

Position	Centre-forward
Born	Bray, County Wicklow
Club	Bray Wanderers; Shelbourne; Transport
Caps	2

Date	Team	Result	Goals
24 Apr 1949	Belgium	0–2	
8 Sep 1949	Finland	3–0	

125. BILL HAYES

Position	Goalkeeper
Born	Limerick, 30 March 1928
Club	Limerick; Wrexham; Ellesmere Port; Torquay United
Caps	1

Date	Team	Result	Goals
24 Apr 1949	Belgium	0–2	

126. KIT LAWLOR

Position	Forward
Born	Dublin, 3 December 1922
Club	Shamrock Rovers; Drumcondra; Doncaster Rovers; Drumcondra; Dundalk
Caps	3

Date	Team	Result	Goals
24 Apr 1949	Belgium	0–2	
26 Nov 1950	Norway	2–2	
13 May 1951	Argentina	0–1	

127. GERRY MALONE

Position	Outside-left
Born	Dublin
Club	Shelbourne
Caps	1

Date	Team	Result	Goals
24 Apr 1949	Belgium	0–2	

128. LAR O'BYRNE

Position	Left-back
Born	Dublin
Club	Shamrock Rovers; St Patrick's Athletic; Transport
Caps	1

Date	Team	Result	Goals
24 Apr 1949	Belgium	0–2	

129. PETER CORR

Position	Outside-right
Born	Dundalk, 26 June 1923
Club	Dundalk; Preston North End; Everton; Bangor
Caps	4

Date	Team	Result	Goals
22 May 1949	Portugal	1–0	
12 Jun 1949	Spain	1–4	
21 Sep 1949	England	2–0	
13 Nov 1949	Sweden	1–3	

130. TOMMY GODWIN

Position	Goalkeeper
Born	Dublin, 20 August 1927
Died	8 August 1996
Club	Home Farm; Shamrock Rovers; Leicester City; Bournemouth
Caps	13

Date	Team	Result	Goals
22 May 1949	Portugal	1–0	
2 Jun 1949	Sweden	1–3	
12 Jun 1949	Spain	1–4	
8 Sep 1949	Finland	3–0	
21 Sep 1949	England	2–0	
9 Oct 1949	Finland	1–1	
13 Nov 1949	Sweden	1–3	
10 May 1950	Belgium	1–5	
26 Nov 1950	Norway	2–2	
10 May 1956	Holland	4–1	
19 May 1957	England	1–1	
2 Oct 1957	Denmark	2–0	
11 May 1958	Poland	2–2	

131. DANNY McGOWAN

Position	Wing-half
Born	Dublin, 8 November 1924
Died	25 April 1994
Club	Shelbourne; West Ham United; Chelmsford City
Caps	3

Date	Team	Result	Goals
22 May 1949	Portugal	1–0	
2 Jun 1949	Sweden	1–3	
12 Jun 1949	Spain	1–4	

132. JIM HARTNETT

Position	Outside-left
Born	Dublin, 17 February 1927
Died	June 1988
Club	Dundalk; Middlesbrough; Barry Town; Hartlepool United; York City
Caps	2

Date	Team	Result	Goals
12 Jun 1949	Spain	1–4	
7 Mar 1954	Luxembourg	1–0	

133. PADDY DALY

Position	Centre-half
Born	Dublin, 4 December 1927
Club	Jacobs; Shamrock Rovers; Aston Villa
Caps	1

Date	Team	Result	Goals
8 Sep 1949	Finland	3–0	

134. PETER DESMOND

Position	Inside-forward
Born	Cork, 23 November 1926
Died	July 1990
Club	Waterford; Shelbourne; Middlesbrough; Southport; York City; Fleetwood; Hartlepool United;
Caps	4

Date	Team	Result	Goals
8 Sep 1949	Finland	3–0	
21 Sep 1949	England	2–0	
9 Oct 1949	Finland	1–1	
13 Nov 1949	Sweden	1–3	

135. ARTHUR FITZSIMONS

Position	Inside-forward
Born	Dublin, 16 December 1929
Club	Shelbourne; Middlesbrough; Lincoln City; Mansfield Town
Caps	26

Date	Team	Result	Goals
8 Sep 1949	Finland	3–0	
10 May 1950	Belgium	1–5	
17 Oct 1951	West Germany	3–2	1
4 May 1952	West Germany	0–3	
7 May 1952	Austria	0–6	
1 Jun 1952	Spain	0–6	
16 Nov 1952	France	1–1	

Date	Team	Result	Goals
25 Mar 1953	Austria	4–0	
4 Oct 1953	France	3–5	
28 Oct 1953	Luxembourg	4–0	2
25 Nov 1953	France	0–1	
1 May 1955	Holland	1–0	
25 May 1955	Norway	3–1	1
28 May 1955	West Germany	1–2	
19 Oct 1955	Yugoslavia	1–4	1
27 Nov 1955	Spain	2–2	1
10 May 1956	Holland	4–1	2
3 Oct 1956	Denmark	2–1	
25 Nov 1956	West Germany	2–1	
8 May 1957	England	1–5	
19 May 1957	England	1–1	
2 Oct 1957	Denmark	2–0	
11 May 1958	Poland	2–2	
14 May 1958	Austria	1–3	
5 Oct 1958	Poland	2–2	
10 May 1959	Czechoslovakia	0–4	

136. JOHNNY GAVIN

Position Outside-right
Born Limerick, 20 April 1928
Club Limerick; Norwich City; Tottenham Hotspur; Norwich City; Watford; Crystal Palace; Cambridge City; Newmarket Town
Caps 7

Date	Team	Result	Goals
8 Sep 1949	Finland	3–0	1
9 Oct 1949	Finland	1–1	
16 Nov 1952	France	1–1	
7 Mar 1954	Luxembourg	1–0	
1 May 1955	Holland	1–0	
28 May 1955	West Germany	1–2	
3 Oct 1956	Denmark	2–1	1

137. TOMMY O'CONNOR

Position Winger
Born Dublin
Club Shamrock Rovers
Caps 4

Date	Team	Result	Goals
8 Sep 1949	Finland	3–0	
21 Sep 1949	England	2–0	
9 Oct 1949	Finland	1–1	
13 Nov 1949	Sweden	1–3	

138. TIMMY COFFREY

Position Left-half
Born Dublin
Club Drumcondra
Caps 1

Date	Team	Result	Goals
9 Oct 1949	Finland	1–1	

139. REG RYAN

Position Inside-forward
Born Dublin, 30 October 1925
Died 13 February 1997
Club Nuneaton Borough; Coventry City; West Bromwich Albion; Derby County; Coventry City
Caps 16

Date	Team	Result	Goals
13 Nov 1949	Sweden	1–3	
10 May 1950	Belgium	1–5	
26 Nov 1950	Norway	2–2	
13 May 1951	Argentina	0–1	
30 May 1951	Norway	3–2	
17 Oct 1951	West Germany	3–2	
4 May 1952	West Germany	0–3	
7 May 1952	Austria	0–6	
1 Jun 1952	Spain	0–6	
16 Nov 1952	France	1–1	
25 Mar 1953	Austria	4–0	
4 Oct 1953	France	3–5	1
28 Oct 1953	Luxembourg	4–0	1
25 Nov 1953	France	0–1	
7 Nov 1954	Norway	2–1	1
27 Nov 1955	Spain	2–2	

140. MATTIE CLARKE

Position	Full-back
Born	Dublin
Club	Shamrock Rovers; Dundalk
Caps	1

Date	Team	Result	Goals
10 May 1950	Belgium	1–5	

141. MARTIN COLFER

Position	Centre-forward
Born	Dublin
Club	St James's Gate; Shelbourne
Caps	2

Date	Team	Result	Goals
10 May 1950	Belgium	1–5	
30 May 1951	Norway	3–2	

142. BOBBY DUFFY

Position	Centre-forward
Born	Dublin
Club	St James's Gate; Shamrock Rovers; Drumcondra
Caps	1

Date	Team	Result	Goals
10 May 1950	Belgium	1–5	1

143. TERRY MURRAY

Position	Inside-forward
Born	Dublin, 22 May 1928
Club	Dundalk; Hull City; Bournemouth
Caps	1

Date	Team	Result	Goals
10 May 1950	Belgium	1–5	

144. SEAN FALLON

Position	Defender; Centre-forward
Born	Sligo, 31 July 1922
Club	Sligo Rovers; Glenavon; Glasgow Celtic
Caps	8

Date	Team	Result	Goals
26 Nov 1950	Norway	2–2	
17 Oct 1951	West Germany	3–2	
4 May 1952	West Germany	0–3	
7 May 1952	Austria	0–6	
1 Jun 1952	Spain	0–6	
16 Nov 1952	France	1–1	1
25 May 1955	Norway	3–1	
28 May 1955	West Germany	1–2	1

145. CHRISTY GILES

Position	Outside-right
Born	Dublin, 17 July 1928
Club	Drumcondra; Doncaster Rovers; Aldershot; Portadown; Distillery
Caps	1

Date	Team	Result	Goal
26 Nov 1950	Norway	2–2	

146. JIM HIGGINS

Position	Centre-forward
Born	Dublin, 3 February 1926
Club	Home Farm; Dundalk; Birmingham City; Hereford United; Dundalk
Caps	1

Date	Team	Result	Goals
13 May 1951	Argentina	0–1	

147. FRED KIERNAN

Position	Goalkeeper
Born	Dublin, 7 July 1919
Died	May 1981
Club	Shelbourne; Dundalk; Shamrock Rovers; Southampton; Yeovil Town
Caps	5

Date	Team	Result	Goals
13 May 1951	Argentina	0–1	
30 May 1951	Norway	3–2	
17 Oct 1951	West Germany	3–2	
4 May 1952	West Germany	0–3	
7 May 1952	Austria	0–6	

148. ALF RINGSTEAD

Position	Outside-left
Born	Dublin, 14 October 1927
Club	Northwich Victoria; Sheffield United; Mansfield Town
Caps	20

Date	Team	Result	Goals
13 May 1951	Argentina	0–1	
30 May 1951	Norway	3–2	1
17 Oct 1951	West Germany	3–2	
4 May 1952	West Germany	0–3	
7 May 1952	Austria	0–6	
1 Jun 1952	Spain	0–6	
25 Mar 1953	Austria	4–0	2
25 Nov 1953	France	0–1	
25 May 1955	Norway	3–1	
19 Oct 1955	Yugoslavia	1–4	
27 Nov 1955	Spain	2–2	1
10 May 1956	Holland	4–1	1
8 May 1957	England	1–5	
19 May 1957	England	1–1	1
2 Oct 1957	Denmark	2–0	
11 May 1958	Poland	2–2	
14 May 1958	Austria	1–3	
5 Oct 1958	Poland	2–2	
5 Apr 1959	Czechoslovakia	2–0	
10 May 1959	Czechoslovakia	0–4	

149. TOMMY CLINTON

Position	Full-back
Born	Dublin, 13 April 1926
Club	Dundalk; Everton; Blackburn Rovers; Tranmere Rovers; Runcorn
Caps	3

Date	Team	Result	Goals
30 May 1951	Norway	3–2	
25 Nov 1953	France	0–1	
7 Mar 1954	Luxembourg	1–0	

150. TIM CUNEEN

Position	Inside-right
Born	Limerick, 1924
Club	Pike Rovers; Limerick; Coleraine; Limerick
Caps	1

Date	Team	Result	Goals
30 May 1951	Norway	3–2	

151. FLORRIE BURKE

Position	Centre-half
Born	Ballintemple, County Cork 1921
Died	July 1995
Club	Cork Athletic; Evergreen United
Caps	1

Date	Team	Result	Goals
17 Oct 1951	West Germany	3–2	

152. DESSIE GLYNN

Position	Centre-forward
Born	Dublin, 7 June 1928
Club	Clifton United; Drumcondra; Shelbourne
Caps	2

Date	Team	Result	Goals
17 Oct 1951	West Germany	3–2	1
25 May 1955	Norway	3–1	

Did you know?

In November 1951, Drumcondra's Irish international forward Dessie Glynn scored five goals against Transport. His fifth came from the penalty-spot: it not only beat the goalkeeper but burst the net and knocked out a seventeen–year-old fan in the stands!

153. SHAY GIBBONS

Position	Centre-forward
Born	Dublin, 19 May 1929
Club	Home Farm; Bohemians; St Patrick's Athletic; Holyhead Town; Cork Hibernians; Dundalk
Caps	4

Date	Team	Result	Goals
4 May 1952	West Germany	0–3	
28 Oct 1953	Luxembourg	4–0	
19 Oct 1955	Yugoslavia	1–4	
27 Nov 1955	Spain	2–2	

154. FRANK O'FARRELL

Position	Wing-half
Born	Cork, 9 October 1927
Club	Cork United; West Ham United; Preston North End; Weymouth
Caps	9

Date	Team	Result	Goals
7 May 1952	Austria	0–6	
25 Mar 1953	Austria	4–0	1
4 Oct 1953	France	3–5	1
1 May 1955	Holland	1–0	
25 May 1955	Norway	3–1	
19 Oct 1955	Yugoslavia	1–4	
10 May 1956	Holland	4–1	
2 Oct 1957	Denmark	2–0	
10 May 1959	Czechoslovakia	0–4	

155. JIMMY O'NEILL

Position	Goalkeeper
Born	Dublin, 13 October 1931
Club	Buffin United; Everton; Stoke City; Darlington; Port Vale
Caps	17

Date	Team	Result	Goals
1 Jun 1952	Spain	0–6	
16 Nov 1952	France	1–1	
25 Mar 1953	Austria	4–0	
4 Oct 1953	France	3–5	
28 Oct 1953	Luxembourg	4–0	
25 Nov 1953	France	0–1	
7 Nov 1954	Norway	2–1	
1 May 1955	Holland	1–0	
25 May 1955	Norway	3–1	
28 May 1955	West Germany	1–2	
19 Oct 1955	Yugoslavia	1–4	
27 Nov 1955	Spain	2–2	
3 Oct 1956	Denmark	2–1	
14 May 1958	Austria	1–3	
5 Oct 1958	Poland	2–2	
5 Apr 1959	Czechoslovakia	2–0	
10 May 1959	Czechoslovakia	0–4	

156. SEAN CUSACK

Position	Defender
Born	Limerick
Club	Limerick
Caps	1

Date	Team	Result	Goals
16 Nov 1952	France	1–1	

157. SHAY DUNNE

Position	Full-back
Born	Wicklow, 13 April 1930
Club	Drogheda United; Wicklow Town; Shelbourne; Luton Town; Yiewsley; Dunstable Town
Caps	15

Date	Team	Result	Goals
16 Nov 1952	France	1–1	
25 Mar 1953	Austria	4–0	
4 Oct 1953	France	3–5	
28 Oct 1953	Luxembourg	4–0	
27 Nov 1955	Spain	2–2	
10 May 1956	Holland	4–1	
3 Oct 1956	Denmark	2–1	
25 Nov 1956	West Germany	3–0	
19 May 1957	England	1–1	
2 Oct 1957	Denmark	2–0	
11 May 1958	Poland	2–2	

14 May 1958	Austria	1–3
5 Oct 1958	Poland	2–2
11 May 1960	West Germany	1–0
18 May 1960	Sweden	1–4

158. ROBIN LAWLER

Position	Defender
Born	Dublin, 28 August 1925
Died	17 April 1998
Club	Home Farm; Distillery; Transport; Drumcondra; Belfast Celtic; Fulham; Yiewsley
Caps	8

Date	Team	Result	Goals
25 Mar 1953	Austria	4–0	
28 Oct 1953	Luxembourg	4–0	
25 Nov 1953	France	0–1	
7 Nov 1954	Norway	2–1	
1 May 1955	Holland	1–0	
25 May 1955	Norway	3–1	
28 May 1955	West Germany	1–2	
19 Oct 1955	Yugoslavia	1–4	

159. NOEL CANTWELL

Position	Left-back
Born	Cork, 28 December 1932
Died	September 2005
Club	Cork Athletic; West Ham United; Manchester United
Caps	36

Date	Team	Result	Goals
28 Oct 1953	Luxembourg	4–0	
27 Nov 1955	Spain	2–2	
10 May 1956	Holland	4–1	
3 Oct 1956	Denmark	2–1	
25 Nov 1956	West Germany	3–0	1
8 May 1957	England	1–5	
19 May 1957	England	1–1	
2 Oct 1957	Denmark	2–0	
11 May 1958	Poland	2–2	
14 May 1958	Austria	1–3	
5 Oct 1958	Poland	2–2	2
5 Apr 1959	Czechoslovakia	2–0	1
10 May 1959	Czechoslovakia	0–4	
1 Nov 1959	Sweden	3–2	

The 1953 Limerick team that won the League of Ireland Trophy for the first time. Back row (left to right): G. Lynam, P. Bradley, B. Neilan, S. O'Dwyer, W. Ahearne, W. O'Grady. Front row (left to right): J. Neilan, S. Cusack, G. O'Grady (Capt.), P. Cronin, M. Hayes. Republic of Ireland international Sean Cusack won his only cap against France in November 1952.

30 Mar 1960	Chile	2–0	1
18 May 1960	Sweden	1–4	
6 Nov 1960	Norway	3–1	
3 May 1961	Scotland	1–4	
7 May 1961	Scotland	0–3	
8 Oct 1961	Czechoslovakia	1–3	
29 Oct 1961	Czechoslovakia	1–7	
8 Apr 1962	Austria	2–3	1
12 Aug 1962	Iceland	4–2	2
2 Sep 1962	Iceland	1–1	
9 Jun 1963	Scotland	1–0	1
13 Oct 1963	Austria	3–2	2
8 Apr 1964	Spain	0–2	
24 May 1964	England	1–3	
25 Oct 1964	Poland	3–2	
5 May 1965	Spain	1–0	
27 Oct 1965	Spain	1–4	
10 Nov 1965	Spain	0–1	
22 May 1966	Austria	0–1	
25 May 1966	Belgium	3–2	2
23 Oct 1966	Spain	0–0	
22 Feb 1967	Turkey	1–2	1

160. GEORGE CUMMINS

Position Inside-forward
Born Dublin, 12 March 1931
Club St Patrick's Athletic; Everton; Luton Town; Cambridge City; Hull City
Caps 19

Date	Team	Result	Goals
28 Oct 1953	Luxembourg	4–0	
7 Mar 1954	Luxembourg	1–0	1
7 Nov 1954	Norway	2–1	
25 May 1955	Norway	3–1	2
28 May 1955	West Germany	1–2	
19 Oct 1955	Yugoslavia	1–4	
27 Nov 1955	Spain	2–2	
2 Oct 1957	Denmark	2–0	1
11 May 1958	Poland	2–2	1
14 May 1958	Austria	1–3	
5 Oct 1958	Poland	2–2	

5 Apr 1959	Czechoslovakia	2–0	
10 May 1959	Czechoslovakia	0–4	
1 Nov 1959	Sweden	3–2	
30 Mar 1960	Chile	2–0	
11 May 1960	West Germany	1–0	
18 May 1960	Sweden	1–4	
3 May 1961	Scotland	1–4	
7 May 1961	Scotland	0–3	

161. LIAM MOORE

Position Forward
Born Dublin
Club Shamrock Rovers
Caps 1

Date	Team	Result	Goals
28 Oct 1953	Luxembourg	4–0	

162. MICK GALLAGHER

Position Half-back
Born Donegal
Club Alloa Athletic; Hibernian
Caps 1

Date	Team	Result	Goals
7 Mar 1954	Luxembourg	1–0	

163. FRED KEARNS

Position Centre-forward
Born Dublin, 8 January 1927
Died 1987
Club Shamrock Rovers; West Ham United; Norwich City
Caps 1

Date	Team	Result	Goals
7 Mar 1954	Luxembourg	1–0	

164. NOEL KELLY

Position Inside-forward
Born Dublin, 28 December 1921
Died 1991
Club Bohemians; Shamrock Rovers; Glentoran; Arsenal; Crystal Palace; Nottingham Forest; Tranmere Rovers; Ellesmere Port
Caps 1

Date	Team	Result	Goals
7 Mar 1954	Luxembourg	1–0	

165. PAT SAWARD

Position	Wing-half
Born	Cork, 17 August 1928
Died	20 September 2002
Club	Crystal Palace; Buckingham Town; Millwall Aston Villa; Huddersfield Town
Caps	18

Date	Team	Result	Goals
7 Mar 1954	Luxembourg	1–0	
8 May 1957	England	1–5	
19 May 1957	England	1–1	
2 Oct 1957	Denmark	2–0	
11 May 1958	Poland	2–2	
14 May 1958	Austria	1–3	
5 Oct 1958	Poland	2–2	
5 Apr 1959	Czechoslovakia	2–o	
1 Nov 1959	Sweden	3–2	
30 Mar 1960	Chile	2–0	
11 May 1960	West Germany	1–0	
18 May 1960	Sweden	1–4	
28 Sep 1960	Wales	2–3	
6 Nov 1960	Norway	3–1	
3 May 1961	Scotland	1–4	
8 Apr 1962	Austria	2–3	
12 Aug 1962	Iceland	4–2	
2 Sep 1962	Iceland	1–1	

166. TOMMY SCANNELL

Position	Goalkeeper
Born	Youghal, 3 June 1925
Died	1992
Club	Grays Athletic; Tilbury; Southend United
Caps	1

Date	Team	Result	Goals
7 Mar 1954	Luxembourg	1–0	

167. TOMMY TRAYNOR

Position	Left-back
Born	Dundalk, 22 July 1933
Died 20 September 2006	
Club	Dundalk; Southampton
Caps	8

Date	Team	Result	Goals
7 Mar 1954	Luxembourg	1–0	
8 Apr 1962	Austria	2–3	
12 Aug 1962	Iceland	4–2	
2 Sep 1962	Iceland	1–1	
9 Jun 1963	Scotland	1–0	
23 Sep 1963	Austria	0–0	
13 Oct 1963	Austria	3–2	
11 Mar 1964	Spain	1–5	

168. PADDY AMBROSE

Position	Inside-forward; Centre-forward
Born	Dublin, 17 October 1929
Club	Clontarf; Shamrock Rovers
Caps	5

Date	Team	Result	Goals
7 Nov 1954	Norway	2–1	
1 May 1955	Holland	1–0	
10 May 1964	Poland	1–3	1
13 May 1964	Norway	4–1	
24 May 1964	England	1–3	

169. DON DONOVAN

Position	Full-back
Born	Cork, 23 December 1929
Club	Maymount Rovers; Dalymount Rovers; Everton; Grimsby Town; Boston United
Caps	5

Date	Team	Result	Goals
7 Nov 1954	Norway	2–1	
1 May 1955	Holland	1–0	
25 May 1955	Norway	3–1	
28 May 1955	West Germany	1–2	
8 May 1957	England	1–5	

170. PADDY FAGAN

Position	Winger
Born	Dublin, 7 June 1930
Club	Transport; Hull City; Manchester City; Derby County; Altrincham; Northwich Victoria; Ashton United
Caps	8

Date	Team	Result	Goals
7 Nov 1954	Norway	2–1	
1 Nov 1959	Sweden	3–2	
30 Mar 1960	Chile	2–0	
11 May 1960	West Germany	1–0	1
18 May 1960	Sweden	1–4	1
28 Sep 1960	Wales	2–3	2
6 Nov 1960	Norway	3–1	1
7 May 1961	Scotland	0–3	

171. JACK FITZGERALD

Position	Centre-forward
Born	Waterford, 3 April 1930
Club	Bohemians; Waterford; Cork Hibernians
Caps	2

Date	Team	Result	Goals
1 May 1955	Holland	1–0	1
10 May 1956	Holland	4–1	

172. ALBIE MURPHY

Position	Right-half
Born	Dublin, 15 November 1930
Club	Transport; Clyde; Shamrock Rovers; Clyde
Caps	1

Date	Team	Result	Goals
19 Oct 1955	Yugoslavia	1–4	

173. LIAM TUOHY

Position	Outside-left
Born	Dublin, 27 April 1933
Club	Shamrock Rovers; Newcastle United; Shamrock Rovers
Caps	8

Date	Team	Result	Goals
19 Oct 1955	Yugoslavia	1–4	
5 Apr 1959	Czechoslovakia	2–0	1
10 May 1959	Czechoslovakia	0–4	
8 Apr 1962	Austria	2–3	1
12 Aug 1962	Iceland	4–2	1
2 Sep 1962	Iceland	1–1	1
23 Sep 1963	Austria	0–0	
24 Mar 1965	Belgium	0–2	

174. TOMMY DUNNE

Position	Right-half
Born	Dublin, 1932
Club	Shamrock Rovers; St Patrick's Athletic; Sligo Rovers; Dundalk
Caps	3

Date	Team	Result	Goals
10 May 1956	Holland	4–1	
3 Oct 1956	Denmark	2–1	
25 Nov 1956	West Germany	3–0	

175. JOE HAVERTY

Position	Outside-left
Born	Dublin, 17 February 1936
Club	Home Farm; St Patrick's Athletic; Arsenal; Blackburn Rovers; Millwall; Bristol Rovers; Glasgow Celtic; Shelbourne; Chicago Spurs (United States)
Caps	32

Date	Team	Result	Goals
10 May 1956	Holland	4–1	1
3 Oct 1956	Denmark	2–1	
25 Nov 1956	West Germany	3–0	1
8 May 1957	England	1–5	
19 May 1957	England	1–1	
2 Oct 1957	Denmark	2–0	
11 May 1958	Poland	2–2	
14 May 1958	Austria	1–3	
5 Oct 1958	Poland	2–2	
1 Nov 1959	Sweden	3–2	

Date	Team	Record	Goals
30 Mar 1960	Chile	2–0	
28 Sep 1960	Wales	2–3	
6 Nov 1960	Norway	3–1	
3 May 1961	Scotland	1–4	1
7 May 1961	Scotland	0–3	
8 Oct 1961	Czechoslovakia	1–3	
29 Oct 1961	Czechoslovakia	1–7	
9 Jun 1963	Scotland	1–0	
13 Oct 1963	Austria	3–2	
11 Mar 1964	Spain	1–5	
10 May 1964	Poland	1–3	
13 May 1964	Norway	4–1	
24 May 1964	England	1–3	
25 Oct 1964	Poland	3–2	
5 May 1965	Spain	1–0	
27 Oct 1965	Spain	1–4	
10 Nov 1965	Spain	0–1	
4 May 1966	West Germany	0–4	
22 May 1966	Austria	0–1	
25 May 1966	Belgium	3–2	
16 Nov 1966	Turkey	2–1	
7 Dec 1966	Spain	0–2	

176. BILLY WHELAN

Position Inside-forward
Born Dublin, 1 April 1935
Died 6 February 1958
Club Home Farm; Manchester United
Caps 4

Date	Team	Record	Goals
10 May 1956	Holland	4–1	
3 Oct 1956	Denmark	2–1	
8 May 1957	England	1–5	
19 May 1957	England	1–1	

177. DERMOT CURTIS

Position Centre-forward
Born Dublin, 26 August 1932
Club Shelbourne; Bristol City; Ipswich Town; Exeter City; Torquay United; Exeter City; Bideford; Elmore
Caps 17

Date	Team	Record	Goals
3 Oct 1956	Denmark	2–1	1
25 Nov 1956	West Germany	3–0	
8 May 1957	England	1–5	1
19 May 1957	England	1–1	
2 Oct 1957	Denmark	2–0	1
11 May 1958	Poland	2–2	1
14 May 1958	Austria	1–3	1
5 Oct 1958	Poland	2–2	
1 Nov 1959	Sweden	3–2	2
30 Mar 1960	Chile	2–0	1
11 May 1960	West Germany	1–0	
18 May 1960	Sweden	1–4	
6 Nov 1960	Norway	3–1	
3 May 1961	Scotland	1–4	
8 Apr 1962	Austria	2–3	
2 Sep 1962	Iceland	1–1	
23 Sep 1962	Austria	0–0	

178. GERRY MACKEY

Position Defender
Born Dublin, 10 June 1933
Club Shamrock Rovers; King's Lynn
Caps 3

Date	Team	Result	Goals
3 Oct 1956	Denmark	2–1	
25 Nov 1956	West Germany	3–0	
8 May 1957	England	1–5	

179. RONNIE NOLAN

Position Right-half
Born Dublin, 1935
Club Shamrock Rovers; Bohemians
Caps 10

Date	Team	Result	Goals
3 Oct 1956	Denmark	2–1	
25 Nov 1956	West Germany	3–0	
19 May 1957	England	1–1	
11 May 1958	Poland	2–2	
30 Mar 1960	Chile	2–0	

11 May 1960	West Germany	1–0
18 May 1960	Sweden	1–4
8 Oct 1961	Czechoslovakia	1–3
29 Oct 1961	Czechoslovakia	1–7
2 Sep 1962	Iceland	1–1

180. ALAN KELLY SNR

Position	Goalkeeper
Born	Dublin, 5 July 1936
Club	Drumcondra; Preston North End;
Caps	47

Date	Team	Result	Goals
25 Nov 1956	West Germany	3–0	
8 May 1957	England	1–5	
8 Apr 1962	Austria	2–3	
12 Aug 1962	Iceland	4–2	
2 Sep 1962	Iceland	1–1	
9 Jun 1963	Scotland	1–0	
23 Sep 1963	Austria	0–0	
13 Oct 1963	Austria	3–2	
11 Mar 1964	Spain	1–5	
8 Apr 1964	Spain	0–2	
10 May 1964	Poland	1–3	
24 Mar 1965	Belgium	0–2	
22 May 1966	Austria	0–1	
25 May 1966	Belgium	3–2	
23 Oct 1966	Spain	0–0	
7 Dec 1966	Spain	0–2	
22 Feb 1967	Turkey	1–2	
21 May 1967	Czechoslovakia	0–2	
22 Nov 1967	Czechoslovakia	2–1	
15 May 1968	Poland	2–2	
30 Oct 1968	Poland	0–1	
10 Nov 1968	Austria	2–2	
4 Dec 1968	Denmark	1–1	
4 May 1969	Czechoslovakia	1–2	
27 May 1969	Denmark	0–2	
8 Jun 1969	Hungary	1–2	
21 Sep 1969	Scotland	1–1	
15 Oct 1969	Denmark	1–1	

5 Nov 1969	Hungary	0–4
6 May 1970	Poland	1–2
9 May 1970	West Germany	1–2
23 Sep 1970	Poland	0–2
14 Oct 1970	Sweden	1–1
28 Oct 1970	Sweden	0–1
8 Dec 1970	Italy	0–3
10 May 1971	Italy	1–2
30 May 1971	Austria	1–4
11 Jun 1972	Iran	2–1
18 Jun 1972	Ecuador	3–2
21 Jun 1972	Chile	1–2
25 Jun 1972	Portugal	1–2
18 Oct 1972	USSR	1–2
15 Nov 1972	France	2–1
13 May 1973	USSR	0–1
16 May 1973	Poland	0–2
19 May 1973	France	1–1
6 Jun 1973	Norway	1–1

> ## Did you know?
> Alan Kelly Snr is the only goalkeeper to have captained the Republic of Ireland.

181. JIMMY McCANN

Position	Outside-right
Born	Dublin
Club	Clontarf; Shamrock Rovers; Drumcondra; Dundalk
Caps	1

Date	Team	Result	Goals
25 Nov 1956	West Germany	3–0	1

182. NOEL PEYTON

Position	Inside-forward
Born	Dublin, 4 December 1935
Club	East Wall; Shamrock Rovers; Leeds United; York City; Barnstaple Town; St Patrick's Athletic
Caps	6

Date	Team	Result	Goals
25 Nov 1956	West Germany	3–0	
11 May 1960	West Germany	1–0	
18 May 1960	Sweden	1–4	
28 Sep 1960	Wales	2–3	
2 Sep 1962	Iceland	1–1	
9 Jun 1963	Scotland	1–0	

183. CHARLIE HURLEY

Position	Centre-half
Born	Cork, 4 October 1936
Club	Millwall; Sunderland; Bolton Wanderers
Caps	40

Date	Team	Result	Goals
19 May 1957	England	1–1	
2 Oct 1957	Denmark	2–0	
11 May 1958	Poland	2–2	
14 May 1958	Austria	1–3	
5 Apr 1959	Czechoslovakia	2–0	
10 May 1959	Czechoslovakia	0–4	
1 Nov 1959	Sweden	3–2	
30 Mar 1960	Chile	2–0	
11 May 1960	West Germany	1–0	
18 May 1960	Sweden	1–4	
28 Sep 1960	Wales	2–3	
6 Nov 1960	Norway	3–1	
3 May 1961	Scotland	1–4	
7 May 1961	Scotland	0–3	
8 Oct 1961	Czechoslovakia	1–3	
29 Oct 1961	Czechoslovakia	1–7	
8 Apr 1962	Austria	2–3	
12 Aug 1962	Iceland	4–2	
2 Sep 1962	Iceland	1–1	
9 Jun 1963	Scotland	1–0	
23 Sep 1963	Austria	0–0	
13 Oct 1963	Austria	3–2	
11 Mar 1964	Spain	1–5	
8 Apr 1964	Spain	0–2	
10 May 1964	Poland	1–3	
13 May 1964	Norway	4–1	2
5 May 1965	Spain	1–0	
4 May 1966	West Germany	0–4	
22 May 1966	Austria	0–1	
25 May 1966	Belgium	3–2	
16 Nov 1966	Turkey	2–1	
7 Dec 1966	Spain	0–2	
22 Feb 1967	Turkey	1–2	
21 May 1967	Czechoslovakia	0–2	
22 Nov 1967	Czechoslovakia	2–1	
15 May 1968	Poland	2–2	
30 Oct 1968	Poland	0–1	
4 Dec 1968	Denmark	1–1	
4 May 1969	Czechoslovakia	1–2	
8 Jun 1969	Hungary	1–2	

184. MICK McGRATH

Position	Wing-half
Born	Dublin, 7 April 1936
Club	Home Farm; Blackburn Rovers; Bradford Park Avenue; Bangor City
Caps	22

Date	Team	Result	Goals
14 May 1958	Austria	1–3	
5 Oct 1958	Poland	2–2	
5 Apr 1969	Czechoslovakia	2–0	
10 May 1959	Czechoslovakia	0–4	
1 Nov 1959	Sweden	3–2	
11 May 1960	West Germany	1–0	
18 May 1960	Sweden	1–4	
28 Sep 1960	Wales	2–3	
8 Oct 1961	Czechoslovakia	1–3	
29 Oct 1961	Czechoslovakia	1–7	
9 Jun 1963	Scotland	1–0	

Date	Team	Result
23 Sep 1963	Austria	0–0
13 Oct 1963	Austria	3–2
24 May 1964	England	1–3
25 Oct 1964	Poland	3–2
24 Mar 1965	Belgium	0–2
5 May 1965	Spain	1–0
27 Oct 1965	Spain	1–4
4 May 1966	West Germany	0–4
22 May 1966	Austria	0–1
25 May 1966	Belgium	3–2
22 Feb 1967	Turkey	1–2

185. SHAY KEOGH

Position	Defender
Born	Dublin
Club	Shamrock Rovers; St Patrick's Athletic
Caps	1

Date	Team	Result	Goals
5 Oct 1958	Poland	2–2	

186. TOMMY TAYLOR

Position	Goalkeeper
Born	Dublin
Club	Home Farm; Waterford United
Caps	1

Date	Team	Result	Goals
5 Oct 1958	Poland	2–2	

187. CHRISTY DOYLE

Position	Forward
Born	Dublin
Club	Shelbourne
Caps	1

Date	Team	Result	Goals
5 Apr 1959	Czechoslovakia	2–0	

188. TOMMY HAMILTON

Position	Midfield
Born	Dublin
Club	Shamrock Rovers; Cork Hibernians; Limerick
Caps	2

Date	Team	Result	Goals
5 Apr 1959	Czechoslovakia	2–0	
10 May 1959	Czechoslovakia	0–4	

189. BRENDAN McNALLY

Position	Full-back
Born	Dublin, 22 January 1935
Club	Shelbourne; Luton Town
Caps	3

Date	Team	Result	Goals
5 Apr 1959	Czechoslovakia	2–0	
3 May 1961	Scotland	1–4	
2 Sep 1962	Iceland	1–1	

190. DICK WHITTAKER

Position	Full-back
Born	Dublin, 10 October 1934
Club	St Mary's Boy's Club; Chelsea; Peterborough United; Queen's Park Rangers
Caps	1

Date	Team	Result	Goals
10 May 1959	Czechoslovakia	0–4	

191. JOE CAROLAN

Position	Full-back
Born	Dublin, 8 September 1937
Club	Home Farm; Manchester United; Brighton and Hove Albion
Caps	2

Date	Team	Result	Goals
1 Nov 1959	Sweden	3–2	
30 Mar 1960	Chile	2–0	

192. NOEL DWYER

Position	Goalkeeper
Born	Dublin, 30 October 1934
Died	January 1993
Club	Ormeau; Wolverhampton Wanderers; West Ham United; Swansea City; Plymouth Argyle; Charlton Athletic
Caps	14

Date	Team	Result	Goals
1 Nov 1959	Sweden	3–2	
30 Mar 1960	Chile	2–0	
11 May 1960	West Germany	1–0	
18 May 1960	Sweden	1–4	
28 Sep 1960	Wales	2–3	
6 Nov 1960	Norway	3–1	
3 May 1961	Scotland	1–4	
7 May 1961	Scotland	0–3	
8 Oct 1961	Czechoslovakia	1–3	
29 Oct 1961	Czechoslovakia	1–7	
10 May 1964	Poland	1–3	
13 May 1964	Norway	4–1	
24 May 1964	England	1–3	
25 Oct 1964	Poland	3–2	

193. JOHNNY GILES

Position	Midfield
Born	Dublin, 6 November 1940
Club	Home Farm; Manchester United; Leeds United; West Bromwich Albion; Shamrock Rovers
Caps	59

Date	Team	Result	Goals
1 Nov 1959	Sweden	3–2	1
30 Mar 1960	Chile	2–0	
28 Sep 1960	Wales	2–3	
6 Nov 1960	Norway	3–1	
3 May 1961	Scotland	1–4	
7 May 1961	Scotland	0–3	
8 Oct 1961	Czechoslovakia	1–3	1
29 Oct 1961	Czechoslovakia	1–7	
8 Apr 1962	Austria	2–3	
12 Aug 1962	Iceland	4–2	
9 Jun 1963	Scotland	1–0	
23 Sep 1963	Austria	0–0	
13 Oct 1963	Austria	3–2	
11 Mar 1964	Spain	1–5	
8 Apr 1964	Spain	0–2	
10 May 1964	Poland	1–3	
13 May 1964	Norway	4–1	1
24 May 1964	England	1–3	
5 May 1965	Spain	1–0	
27 Oct 1965	Spain	1–4	
10 Nov 1965	Spain	0–1	
22 May 1966	Austria	0–1	
25 May 1966	Belgium	3–2	
23 Oct 1966	Spain	0–0	
16 Nov 1966	Turkey	2–1	
22 Feb 1967	Turkey	1–2	
10 Nov 1968	Austria	2–2	
4 Dec 1968	Denmark	1–1	1
4 May 1969	Czechoslovakia	1–2	
21 Sep 1969	Scotland	1–1	
6 May 1970	Poland	1–2	
9 May 1970	West Germany	1–2	
10 May 1971	Italy	1–2	
15 Nov 1972	France	2–1	
13 May 1973	USSR	0–1	
5 May 1974	Brazil	1–2	
8 May 1974	Uruguay	0–2	
12 May 1974	Chile	2–1	
30 Oct 1974	USSR	3–0	
20 Nov 1974	Turkey	1–1	
10 May 1975	Switzerland	2–1	
18 May 1975	USSR	1–2	
21 May 1975	Switzerland	0–1	
29 Oct 1975	Turkey	4–0	
8 Sep 1976	England	1–1	
13 Oct 1976	Turkey	3–3	
17 Nov 1976	France	0–2	
30 Mar 1977	France	1–0	

Date	Team	Result	Goals
24 Apr 1977	Poland	0–0	
1 Jun 1977	Bulgaria	1–2	
12 Oct 1977	Bulgaria	0–0	
5 Apr 1978	Turkey	4–2	1
12 Apr 1978	Poland	0–3	
21 May 1978	Norway	0–0	
24 May 1978	Denmark	3–3	
20 Sep 1978	Northern Ireland	0–0	
2 May 1979	Denmark	2–0	
19 May 1979	Bulgaria	0–1	
22 May 1979	West Germany	1–3	

194. AMBROSE FOGARTY

Position Inside-forward
Born Dublin, 11 September 1933
Club Bohemians; Glentoran; Sunderland; Hartlepool United; Cork Hibernians; Cork Celtic; Drumcondra
Caps 11

Date	Team	Result	Goals
11 May 1960	West Germany	1–0	
18 May 1960	Sweden	1–4	
3 May 1961	Scotland	1–4	
8 Oct 1961	Czechoslovakia	1–3	
29 Oct 1961	Czechoslovakia	1–7	1
12 Aug 1962	Iceland	4–2	1
2 Sep 1962	Iceland	1–1	
9 Jun 1963	Scotland	1–0	
23 Sep 1963	Austria	0–0	
13 Oct 1963	Austria	3–2	1
11 Mar 1964	Spain	1–5	

195. MAURICE SWAN

Position Goalkeeper
Born Dublin, 27 September 1938
Club Drumcondra; Cardiff City; Hull City; Dundalk; Drumcondra
Caps 1

Date	Team	Result	Goals
18 May 1960	Sweden	1–4	

196. PETER FITZGERALD

Position Forward
Born Waterford, 17 June 1937
Club Waterford United; Sparta Club Rotterdam (Holland); Leeds United; Chester City; Waterford
Caps 5

Date	Team	Result	Goals
28 Sep 1960	Wales	2–3	
6 Nov 1960	Norway	3–1	2
7 May 1961	Scotland	0–3	
8 Oct 1961	Czechoslovakia	1–3	
29 Oct 1961	Czechoslovakia	1–7	

197. PHIL KELLY

Position Full-back
Born Dublin, 10 July 1939
Club Sheldon Town; Wolverhampton Wanderers; Norwich City
Caps 5

Date	Team	Result	Goals
28 Sep 1960	Wales	2–3	
6 Nov 1960	Norway	3–1	
7 May 1961	Scotland	0–3	
8 Oct 1961	Czechoslovakia	1–3	
29 Oct 1961	Czechoslovakia	1–7	

198. JOHN O'NEILL

Position Defender
Born Dublin, 9 September 1935
Club Drumcondra; Preston North End; Barrow; Druimcondra; Waterford
Caps 1

Date	Team	Result	Goals
28 Sep 1960	Wales	2–3	

199. JOHNNY FULLAM

Position Wing-half
Born Dublin, 22 March 1940
Club Home Farm; Preston North End; Shamrock Rovers; Bohemians; Shamrock Rovers; Athlone Town
Caps 11

Date	Team	Result	Goals
6 Nov 1960	Norway	3–1	
8 Apr 1964	Spain	0–2	
10 May 1964	Poland	1–3	
13 May 1964	Norway	4–1	
22 May 1966	Austria	0–1	
25 May 1966	Belgium	3–2	1
15 May 1968	Poland	2–2	
30 Oct 1968	Poland	0–1	
10 Nov 1968	Austria	2–2	
4 Dec 1968	Denmark	1–1	
7 Oct 1969	Czechoslovakia	0–3	

200. ANDY McEVOY

Position	Inside-forward
Born	Dublin, 15 July 1938
Club	Bray Wanderers; Blackburn Rovers; Limerick
Caps	17

Date	Team	Result	Goals
3 May 1961	Scotland	1–4	
7 May 1961	Scotland	0–3	
9 Jun 1963	Scotland	1–0	
13 Oct 1963	Austria	3–2	
11 Mar 1964	Spain	1–5	1
8 Apr 1964	Spain	0–2	
10 May 1964	Poland	1–3	
13 May 1964	Norway	4–1	1
24 May 1964	England	1–3	
25 Oct 1964	Poland	3–2	2
24 Mar 1965	Belgium	0–2	
5 May 1965	Spain	1–0	
27 Oct 1965	Spain	1–4	1
10 Nov 1965	Spain	0–1	
23 Oct 1966	Spain	0–0	
16 Nov 1966	Turkey	2–1	1
21 May 1967	Czechoslovakia	0–2	

201. MICK MEAGAN

Position	Full-back
Born	Dublin, 29 May 1934
Club	Johnville; Everton; Huddersfield Town; Halifax Town; Drogheda United
Caps	17

Date	Team	Result	Goals
7 May 1961	Scotland	0–3	
8 Apr 1962	Austria	2–3	
12 Aug 1962	Iceland	4–2	
11 Mar 1964	Spain	1–5	
24 Mar 1965	Belgium	0–2	
27 Oct 1965	Spain	1–4	
10 Nov 1965	Spain	0–1	
22 May 1966	Austria	0–1	
25 May 1966	Belgium	3–2	
23 Oct 1966	Spain	0–0	
16 Nov 1966	Turkey	2–1	
7 Dec 1966	Spain	0–2	
22 Feb 1967	Turkey	1–2	
21 May 1967	Czechoslovakia	0–2	
22 Nov 1967	Czechoslovakia	2–1	
15 May 1968	Poland	2–2	
21 Sep 1969	Scotland	1–1	

202. FRANK O'NEILL

Position	Outside-right
Born	Dublin, 13 April 1940
Club	Home Farm; Arsenal; Shamrock Rovers; Waterford
Caps	20

Date	Team	Result	Goals
8 Oct 1961	Czechoslovakia	1–3	
29 Oct 1961	Czechoslovakia	1–7	
25 Oct 1964	Poland	3–2	
24 Mar 1965	Belgium	0–2	
5 May 1965	Spain	1–0	
27 Oct 1965	Spain	1–4	
10 Nov 1965	Spain	0–1	
4 May 1966	West Germany	0–4	

Date	Team	Result	Goals
22 May 1966	Austria	0–1	
23 Oct 1966	Spain	0–0	
16 Nov 1966	Turkey	2–1	1
7 Dec 1966	Spain	0–2	
22 Feb 1967	Turkey	1–2	
30 Oct 1968	Poland	0–1	
10 Nov 1968	Austria	2–2	
4 Dec 1968	Denmark	1–1	
4 May 1969	Czechoslovakia	1–2	
27 May 1969	Denmark	0–2	
8 Jun 1969	Hungary	1–2	
10 Oct 1971	Austria	0–6	

8 Jun 1969	Hungary	1–2
5 Nov 1969	Hungary	0–4
14 Oct 1970	Sweden	1–1
10 May 1971	Italy	1–2
30 May 1971	Austria	1–4
5 May 1974	Brazil	1–2
8 May 1974	Uruguay	0–2
12 May 1974	Chile	2–1
20 Nov 1974	Turkey	1–1
11 Mar 1975	West Germany 'B'	1–0
10 May 1975	Switzerland	2–1
18 May 1975	USSR	1–2
21 May 1975	Switzerland	0–1
29 Oct 1975	Turkey	4–0

203. TONY DUNNE

Position Left-back
Born Dublin, 24 July 1941
Club St Finbar's; Tara United; Shelbourne; Manchester United; Bolton Wanderers; Detroit Express (United States)
Caps 33

Date	Team	Result	Goals
8 Apr 1962	Austria	2–3	
12 Aug 1962	Iceland	4–2	
9 Jun 1963	Scotland	1–0	
13 Oct 1963	Austria	3–2	
8 Apr 1964	Spain	0–2	
10 May 1964	Poland	1–3	
13 May 1964	Norway	4–1	
24 May 1964	England	1–3	
25 Oct 1964	Poland	3–2	
5 May 1965	Spain	1–0	
27 Oct 1965	Spain	1–4	
10 Nov 1965	Spain	0–1	
22 May 1966	Austria	0–1	
25 May 1966	Belgium	3–2	
23 Oct 1966	Spain	0–0	
16 Nov 1966	Turkey	2–1	
7 Dec 1966	Spain	0–2	
30 Oct 1968	Poland	0–1	
4 Dec 1968	Denmark	1–1	

204. ALFIE HALE

Position Inside-forward
Born Waterford, 28 August 1939
Club Waterford; Cork Hibernians; Waterford; Aston Villa; Doncaster Rovers; Newport County; Waterford; St Patrick's Athletic; Limerick; Thurles Town
Caps 14

Date	Team	Result	Goals
8 Apr 1962	Austria	2–3	
12 Aug 1962	Iceland	4–2	
11 Mar 1964	Spain	1–5	
8 Apr 1964	Spain	0–2	
7 Dec 1966	Spain	0–2	
15 May 1968	Poland	2–2	1
30 Oct 1968	Poland	0–1	
10 Nov 1968	Austria	2–2	1
4 Dec 1968	Denmark	1–1	
21 Sep 1969	Scotland	1–1	
7 Oct 1969	Czechoslovakia	0–3	
23 Sep 1970	Poland	0–2	
10 Oct 1971	Austria	0–6	
21 Oct 1973	Poland	1–0	

205. DINNY LOWRY

Position	Goalkeeper
Born	Dublin 1936
Club	Bulfin United; St Patrick's Athletic; Bohemians
Caps	1

Date	Team	Result	Goals
8 Apr 1962	Austria	2–3	

206. PADDY TURNER

Position	Inside-right
Born	Dublin, 1940
Club	Shamrock Rovers; Shelbourne; Morton; Glasgow Celtic; Glentoran; Dundalk; Bohemians
Caps	2

Date	Team	Result	Goals
9 Jun 1963	Scotland	1–0	
8 Apr 1964	Spain	0–2	

207. RAY BRADY

Position	Centre-half
Born	Dublin, 3 June 1937
Club	Transport; Home Farm; Millwall; Queen's Park Rangers; Hastings United
Caps	6

Date	Team	Result	Goals
23 Sep 1963	Austria	0–0	
13 Oct 1963	Austria	3–2	
11 Mar 1964	Spain	1–5	
8 Apr 1964	Spain	0–2	
10 May 1964	Poland	1–3	
13 May 1964	Norway	4–1	

208. WILLIE BROWNE

Position	Right-back
Born	Longford, 1936
Died	14 October 2004
Club	University College Dublin; Bohemians
Caps	3

Date	Team	Result	Goals
23 Sep 1963	Austria	0–0	
8 Apr 1964	Spain	0–2	
24 May 1964	England	1–3	

209. RONNIE WHELAN SNR

Position	Inside-forward
Born	Dublin, 17 November 1936
Died	1993
Club	Home Farm; St Patrick's Athletic; Drogheda; Aer Lingus
Caps	2

Date	Team	Result	Goals
23 Sep 1963	Austria	0–0	
24 May 1964	England	1–3	

210. THEO FOLEY

Position	Full-back
Born	Dublin, 2 April 1937
Club	Home Farm; Exeter City; Northampton Town; Charlton Athletic
Caps	9

Date	Team	Result	Goals
11 Mar 1964	Spain	1–5	
10 May 1964	Poland	1–3	
13 May 1964	Norway	4–1	
25 Oct 1964	Poland	3–2	
24 Mar 1965	Belgium	0–2	
27 Oct 1965	Spain	1–4	
10 Nov 1965	Spain	0–1	
4 May 1965	West Germany	0–4	
21 May 1967	Czechoslovakia	0–2	

211. FREDDIE STRAHAN

Position	Centre-half
Born	Dublin
Club	Shelbourne; Rialto
Caps	5

Date	Team	Result	Goals
10 May 1964	Poland	1–3	

13 May 1964	Norway	4–1	
24 May 1964	England	1–3	1
25 Oct 1964	Poland	3–2	
4 May 1966	West Germany	0–4	

212. EDDIE BAILHAM

Position Centre-forward
Born Dublin, 1941
Club Home Farm; Cork Hibernians;
Shamrock Rovers
Caps 1

Date	Team	Result	Goals
24 May 1964	England	1–3	

213. JACKIE HENNESSEY

Position Wing-half; Inside-forward
Born Dublin
Club Shelbourne; Derry City; St Patrick's
Athletic
Caps 5

Date	Team	Result	Goals
25 Oct 1964	Poland	3–2	
24 Mar 1965	Belgium	0–2	
5 May 1965	Spain	1–0	
4 May 1966	West Germany	0–4	
10 Nov 1968	Austria	2–2	

214. JACKIE MOONEY

Position Centre-forward
Born Dublin, 1938
Club Home Farm; Manchester United;
Bangor City; Cork Hibernians;
Shamrock Rovers; Athlone Town;
Bohemians
Caps 2

Date	Team	Result	Goals
25 Oct 1964	Poland	3–2	1
24 Mar 1965	Belgium	0–2	

215. FRAN BRENNAN

Position Defender
Born Dublin
Club Drumcondra; Dundalk
Caps 1

Date	Team	Result	Goals
24 Mar 1965	Belgium	0–2	

216. OLLIE CONMY

Position Winger
Born Mulrany, 13 November 1939
Club St Paulinus YC; Huddersfield Town;
Peterborough United; Cambridge
City; Ely City; March Town
Caps 5

Date	Team	Result	Goals
24 Mar 1965	Belgium	0–2	
21 May 1967	Czechoslovakia	0–2	
22 Nov 1967	Czechoslovakia	2–1	
15 May 1968	Poland	2–2	
7 Oct 1969	Czechoslovakia	0–3	

217. SHAY BRENNAN

Position Full-back
Born Manchester, 6 May 1937
Died 9 June 2000
Club Manchester United; Waterford
United
Caps 19

Date	Team	Result	Goals
5 May 1965	Spain	1–0	
10 Nov 1965	Spain	0–1	
22 May 1966	Austria	0–1	
25 May 1966	Belgium	3–2	
23 Oct 1966	Spain	0–0	
16 Nov 1966	Turkey	2–1	
7 Dec 1966	Spain	0–2	
4 May 1969	Czechoslovakia	1–2	
27 May 1969	Denmark	0–2	
8 Jun 1969	Hungary	1–2	
21 Sep 1969	Scotland	1–1	

Date	Team	Result	Goals
7 Oct 1969	Czechoslovakia	0–3	
15 Oct 1969	Denmark	1–1	
5 Nov 1969	Hungary	0–4	
6 May 1970	Poland	1–2	
9 May 1970	West Germany	1–2	
23 Sep 1970	Poland	0–2	
28 Oct 1970	Sweden	0–1	
8 Dec 1970	Italy	0–3	

218. PAT DUNNE

Position Goalkeeper
Born Dublin, 9 February 1943
Club Everton; Shamrock Rovers; Manchester United; Plymouth Argyle
Caps 5

Date	Team	Result	Goals
5 May 1965	Spain	1–0	
27 Oct 1965	Spain	1–4	
10 Nov 1965	Spain	0–1	
4 May 1966	West Germany	0–4	
16 Nov 1966	Turkey	2–1	

219. ERIC BARBER

Position Forward
Born Dublin, 18 January 1942
Club St Finbar's; Shelbourne; Birmingham City; Chicago Spurs (United States); Shamrock Rovers; Wiener Sportclub (Austria); Shelbourne
Caps 2

Date	Team	Result	Goals
27 Oct 1965	Spain	1–4	
25 May 1966	Belgium	3–2	

220. EAMONN DUNPHY

Position Midfield
Born Dublin, 3 August 1945
Club Manchester United; York City; Millwall; Charlton Athletic; Reading
Caps 23

Date	Team	Result	Goals
10 Nov 1965	Spain	0–1	
4 May 1966	West Germany	0–4	
16 Nov 1966	Turkey	2–1	
7 Dec 1966	Spain	0–2	
22 Feb 1967	Turkey	1–2	
21 May 1967	Czechoslovakia	0–2	
22 Nov 1967	Czechoslovakia	2–1	
15 May 1968	Poland	2–2	
30 Oct 1968	Poland	0–1	
10 Nov 1968	Austria	2–2	
4 Dec 1968	Denmark	1–1	
27 May 1969	Denmark	0–2	
8 Jun 1969	Hungary	1–2	
15 Oct 1969	Denmark	1–1	
5 Nov 1969	Hungary	0–4	
6 May 1970	Poland	1–2	
9 May 1970	West Germany	1–2	
23 Sep 1970	Poland	0–2	
14 Oct 1970	Sweden	1–1	
28 Oct 1970	Sweden	0–1	
8 Dec 1970	Italy	0–3	
10 May 1971	Italy	1–2	
30 May 1971	Austria	1–4	

221. BOBBY GILBERT

Position Centre-forward
Born Dublin
Club Derry City; Shamrock Rovers; Drumcondra; Dundalk
Caps 1

Date	Team	Result	Goals
4 May 1966	West Germany	0–4	

222. JOHN KEOGH

Position Right-back
Born Dublin, 1942
Club Stella Maris; Shamrock Rovers; Cork Celtic
Caps 1

Date	Team	Result	Goals
4 May 1966	West Germany	0–4	

Ray Treacy

223. RAY TREACY

Position	Forward
Born	Dublin, 18 June 1946
Club	West Bromwich Albion; Charlton Athletic; Swindon Town; Preston North End; Oldham Athletic; West Bromwich Albion; Shamrock Rovers; Toronto Mets (Canada)
Caps	42

Date	Team	Result	Goals
4 May 1966	West Germany	0–4	
23 Oct 1966	Spain	0–0	
21 May 1967	Czechoslovakia	0–2	
22 Nov 1967	Czechoslovakia	2–1	1
15 May 1968	Poland	2–2	
30 Oct 1968	Poland	0–1	
4 May 1969	Czechoslovakia	1–2	
27 May 1969	Denmark	0–2	
21 Sep 1969	Scotland	1–1	
15 Oct 1969	Denmark	1–1	
5 Nov 1969	Hungary	0–4	
6 May 1970	Poland	1–2	
9 May 1970	West Germany	1–2	
23 Sep 1970	Poland	0–2	
14 Oct 1970	Sweden	1–1	
28 Oct 1970	Sweden	0–1	
8 Dec 1970	Italy	0–3	
30 May 1971	Austria	1–4	
11 Jun 1972	Iran	2–1	
18 Jun 1972	Ecuador	3–2	
21 Jun 1972	Chile	1–2	
25 Jun 1972	Portugal	1–2	
18 Oct 1972	USSR	1–2	
15 Nov 1972	France	2–1	1
13 May 1973	USSR	0–1	
16 May 1973	Poland	0–2	
19 May 1973	France	1–1	
6 Jun 1973	Norway	1–1	
21 Oct 1973	Poland	1–0	
5 May 1974	Brazil	1–2	
30 Oct 1974	USSR	3–0	
11 Mar 1975	West Germany 'B'	1–0	
10 May 1975	Switzerland	2–1	1
21 May 1975	Switzerland	0–1	
29 Oct 1975	Turkey	4–0	
24 Mar 1976	Norway	3–0	
26 May 1976	Poland	2–0	
30 Mar 1977	France	1–0	
24 Apr 1977	Poland	0–0	
5 Apr 1978	Turkey	4–2	2
12 Apr 1978	Poland	0–3	
26 Sep 1979	Czechoslovakia	1–4	

224. JIMMY CONWAY

Position	Outside-right
Born	Dublin, 10 August 1946
Club	Bohemians; Fulham; Manchester City
Caps	20

Date	Team	Result	Goals
23 Oct 1966	Spain	0–0	
16 Nov 1966	Turkey	2–1	
7 Dec 1966	Spain	0–2	
22 Nov 1967	Czechoslovakia	2–1	
10 Nov 1968	Austria	2–2	
8 Jun 1969	Hungary	1–2	
21 Sep 1969	Scotland	1–1	
7 Oct 1969	Czechoslovakia	0–3	
15 Oct 1969	Denmark	1–1	
5 Nov 1969	Hungary	0–4	
6 May 1970	Poland	1–2	
9 May 1970	West Germany	1–2	
10 May 1971	Italy	1–2	1
30 May 1971	Austria	1–4	
8 May 1974	Uruguay	0–2	
12 May 1974	Chile	2–1	1
11 Mar 1975	West Germany 'B'	1–0	1
24 Mar 1976	Norway	3–0	
26 May 1976	Poland	2–0	
24 Apr 1977	Poland	0–0	

225. TONY O'CONNELL

Position	Outside-left
Born	Dublin, 1941
Club	Stella Maris; Shamrock Rovers; Dundalk; Bohemians
Caps	2

Date	Team	Result	Goals
23 Oct 1966	Spain	0–0	
23 Sep 1970	Poland	0–2	

226. JOHN DEMPSEY

Position	Central defender
Born	Hampstead, 15 March 1946
Club	Fulham; Chelsea; Philadelphia Furies (United States)
Caps	19

Date	Team	Result	Goals
7 Dec 1966	Spain	0–2	
21 May 1967	Czechoslovakia	0–2	
22 Nov 1967	Czechoslovakia	2–1	
15 May 1968	Poland	2–2	1
30 Oct 1968	Poland	0–1	
10 Nov 1968	Austria	2–2	
4 Dec 1968	Denmark	1–1	
4 May 1969	Czechoslovakia	1–2	
27 May 1969	Denmark	0–2	
5 Nov 1969	Hungary	0–4	
9 May 1970	West Germany	1–2	
23 Sep 1970	Poland	0–2	
14 Oct 1970	Sweden	1–1	
28 Oct 1970	Sweden	0–1	
8 Dec 1970	Italy	0–3	
11 Jun 1972	Iran	2–1	
18 Jun 1972	Ecuador	3–2	
21 Jun 1972	Chile	1–2	
25 Jun 1972	Portugal	1–2	

227. AL FINUCANE

Position	Centre-half
Born	Limerick, 1943
Club	Limerick; Waterford
Caps	11

Date	Team	Result	Goals
22 Feb 1967	Turkey	1–2	
21 May 1967	Czechoslovakia	0–2	
4 May 1969	Czechoslovakia	1–2	

Did you know?

John Dempsey holds the unenviable record of being the first Republic of Ireland player to be sent off when he received his marching orders in the game against Hungary in 1969.

27 May 1969	Denmark	0–2
8 Jun 1969	Hungary	1–2
21 Sep 1969	Scotland	1–1
7 Oct 1969	Czechoslovakia	0–3
28 Oct 1970	Sweden	0–1
8 Dec 1970	Italy	0–3
10 May 1971	Italy	1–2
10 Oct 1971	Austria	0–6

228. CHARLIE GALLAGHER

Position	Inside-forward
Born	Glasgow, 3 November 1940
Club	Glasgow Celtic; Dumbarton
Caps	2

Date	Team	Result	Goals
22 Feb 1967	Turkey	1–2	
21 May 1967	Czechoslovakia	0–2	

229. JOE KINNEAR

Position	Right-back
Born	Dublin, 27 December 1946
Club	St Alban's City; Tottenham Hotspur; Brighton & Hove Albion
Caps	26

Date	Team	Result	Goals
22 Feb 1967	Turkey	1–2	
22 Nov 1967	Czechoslovakia	2–1	
15 May 1968	Poland	2–2	
10 Nov 1968	Austria	2–2	
7 Oct 1969	Czechoslovakia	0–3	
15 Oct 1969	Denmark	1–1	
5 Nov 1969	Hungary	0–4	
6 May 1970	Poland	1–2	
14 Oct 1970	Sweden	1–1	
10 May 1971	Italy	1–2	
11 Jun 1972	Iran	2–1	
18 Jun 1972	Ecuador	3–2	
21 Jun 1972	Chile	1–2	
25 Jun 1972	Portugal	1–2	
18 Oct 1972	USSR	1–2	

15 Nov 1972	France	2–1
21 Oct 1973	Poland	1–0
5 May 1974	Brazil	1–2
8 May 1974	Uruguay	0–2
12 May 1974	Chile	2–1
30 Oct 1974	USSR	3–0
20 Nov 1974	Turkey	1–1
11 Mar 1975	West Germany 'B'	1–0
10 May 1975	Switzerland	2–1
18 May 1975	USSR	1–2
29 Oct 1975	Turkey	4–0

230. TURLOUGH O'CONNOR

Position	Centre-forward
Born	Athlone County Westmeath, 22 July 1946
Club	Limerick; Athlone Town; Bohemians; Fulham; Dundalk; Bohemians; Athlone Town
Caps	7

Date	Team	Result	Goals
22 Nov 1967	Czechoslovakia	2–1	1
10 Oct 1971	Austria	0–6	
11 Jun 1972	Iran	2–1	
18 Jun 1972	Ecuador	3–2	1
21 Jun 1972	Chile	1–2	
25 Jun 1972	Portugal	1–2	
15 Nov 1972	France	2–1	

231. EAMONN ROGERS

Position	Winger
Born	Dublin, 16 April 1947
Club	Blackburn Rovers; Charlton Athletic; Northampton Town
Caps	19

Date	Team	Result	Goals
22 Nov 1967	Czechoslovakia	2–1	
15 May 1968	Poland	2–2	
30 Oct 1968	Poland	0–1	
10 Nov 1968	Austria	2–2	1
4 Dec 1968	Denmark	1–1	

Date	Team	Result	Goals
4 May 1969	Czechoslovakia	1–2	1
27 May 1969	Denmark	0–2	
8 Jun 1969	Hungary	1–2	
21 Sep 1969	Scotland	1–1	
15 Oct 1969	Denmark	1–1	
5 Nov 1969	Hungary	0–4	
8 Dec 1970	Italy	0–3	
10 May 1971	Italy	1–2	
30 May 1971	Austria	1–4	1
11 Jun 1972	Iran	2–1	
18 Jun 1972	Ecuador	3–2	1
21 Jun 1972	Chile	1–2	1
25 Jun 1972	Portugal	1–2	
18 Oct 1972	USSR	1–2	

Date	Team	Result	Goals
15 May 1968	Poland	2–2	
30 Oct 1968	Poland	0–1	
10 Nov 1968	Austria	2–2	
4 Dec 1968	Denmark	1–1	
7 Oct 1969	Czechoslovakia	0–3	
6 May 1970	Poland	1–2	
9 May 1970	West Germany	1–2	
14 Oct 1970	Sweden	1–1	1
11 Jun 1972	Iran	2–1	
18 Jun 1972	Ecuador	3–2	
21 Jun 1972	Chile	1–2	
25 Jun 1972	Portugal	1–2	
18 Oct 1972	USSR	1–2	
13 May 1973	USSR	0–1	
16 May 1973	Poland	0–2	
19 May 1973	France	1–1	
6 Jun 1973	Norway	1–1	

Eamonn Rogers

232. TOMMY CARROLL

Position Right-back
Born Dublin, 18 August 1942
Club St Finbar's; Shelbourne; Cambridge City; Ipswich Town; Birmingham City
Caps 17

233. MICK SMYTH

Position Goalkeeper
Born Dublin, 13 May 1940
Club St Patrick's CYMS; Drumcondra; Barrow; Altrincham; Shamrock Rovers; Bohemians; Athlone Town
Caps 1

Date	Team	Result	Goals
30 Oct 1968	Poland	0–1	

234. MICK LEECH

Position Centre-forward
Born Dublin, 6 August 1948
Club Ormeau; Shamrock Rovers; Waterford; Shamrock Rovers; Bohemians; Drogheda; St Patrick's Athletic
Caps 8

Date	Team	Result	Goals
4 May 1969	Czechoslovakia	1–2	
27 May 1969	Denmark	0–2	
8 Jun 1969	Hungary	1–2	

10 Oct 1971	Austria	0–6	
11 Jun 1972	Iran	2–1	1
18 Jun 1972	Ecuador	3–2	
25 Jun 1972	Portugal	1–2	1
18 Oct 1972	USSR	1–2	

235. PADDY MULLIGAN

Position	Right-back
Born	Dublin, 17 March 1945
Club	Home Farm; Bohemians; Shamrock Rovers; Chelsea; Crystal Palace; West Bromwich Albion; Shamrock Rovers; Galway
Caps	50

Date	Team	Result	Goals
4 May 1969	Czechoslovakia	1–2	
27 May 1969	Denmark	0–2	
8 Jun 1969	Hungary	1–2	
21 Sep 1969	Scotland	1–1	
7 Oct 1969	Czechoslovakia	0–3	
15 Oct 1969	Denmark	1–1	
5 Nov 1969	Hungary	0–4	
6 May 1970	Poland	1–2	
9 May 1970	West Germany	1–2	1
23 Sep 1970	Poland	0–2	
14 Oct 1970	Sweden	1–1	
10 May 1971	Italy	1–2	
10 Oct 1971	Austria	0–6	
11 Jun 1972	Iran	2–1	
18 Jun 1972	Ecuador	3–2	
21 Jun 1972	Chile	1–2	
25 Jun 1972	Portugal	1–2	
15 Nov 1972	France	2–1	
13 May 1973	USSR	0–1	
16 May 1973	Poland	0–2	
19 May 1973	France	1–1	
6 Jun 1973	Norway	1–1	
21 Oct 1973	Poland	1–0	
5 May 1974	Brazil	1–2	
8 May 1974	Uruguay	0–2	
12 May 1974	Chile	2–1	

30 Oct 1974	USSR	3–0	
20 Nov 1974	Turkey	1–1	
10 May 1975	Switzerland	2–1	
18 May 1975	USSR	1–2	
21 May 1975	Switzerland	0–1	
20 Oct 1975	Turkey	4–0	
26 May 1976	Poland	2–0	
8 Sep 1976	England	1–1	
13 Oct 1976	Turkey	3–3	
17 Nov 1976	France	0–2	
30 Mar 1977	France	1–0	
24 Apr 1977	Poland	0–0	
1 Jun 1977	Bulgaria	1–2	
12 Oct 1977	Bulgaria	0–0	
21 May 1978	Norway	0–0	
24 May 1978	Denmark	3–3	
25 Oct 1978	England	1–1	
2 May 1979	Denmark	2–0	
19 May 1979	Bulgaria	0–1	
22 May 1979	West Germany	1–3	
11 Sep 1979	Wales	1–2	
26 Sep 1979	Czechoslovakia	1–4	
17 Oct 1979	Bulgaria	3–0	
29 Oct 1979	United States	3–2	

236. EOIN HAND

Position	Central defender
Born	Dublin, 30 March 1946
Club	Stella Maris; Swindon Town; Dundalk; Drumcondra; Portsmouth; Shamrock Rovers; Limerick
Caps	20

Date	Team	Result	Goals
4 May 1969	Czechoslovakia	1–2	
6 May 1970	Poland	1–2	
9 May 1970	West Germany	1–2	
23 Sep 1970	Poland	0–2	
30 May 1971	Austria	1–4	
18 Oct 1972	USSR	1–2	
15 Nov 1972	France	2–1	

Date	Team	Result	Goals
13 May 1973	USSR	0–1	
16 May 1973	Poland	0–2	
19 May 1973	France	1–1	
21 Oct 1973	Poland	1–0	
5 May 1974	Brazil	1–2	
8 May 1974	Uruguay	0–2	
12 May 1974	Chile	2–1	1
20 Nov 1974	Turkey	1–1	
11 Mar 1975	West Germany 'B'	1–0	
10 May 1975	Switzerland	2–1	
18 May 1975	USSR	1–2	1
21 May 1975	Switzerland	0–1	
29 Oct 1975	Turkey	4–0	

237. DON GIVENS

Position	Forward
Born	Limerick, 9 August 1949
Club	Manchester United; Luton Town; Queen's Park Rangers; Birmingham City; Bournemouth (loan); Sheffield United; Xamax Neuchatel (Switzerland)
Caps	56

Date	Team	Result	Goals
27 May 1969	Denmark	0–2	
8 Jun 1969	Hungary	1–2	1
21 Sep 1969	Scotland	1–1	1
7 Oct 1969	Czechoslovakia	0–3	
15 Oct 1969	Denmark	1–1	1
5 Nov 1969	Hungary	0–4	
6 May 1970	Poland	1–2	1
9 May 1970	West Germany	1–2	
14 Oct 1970	Sweden	1–1	
8 Dec 1970	Italy	0–3	
10 May 1971	Italy	1–2	
30 May 1971	Austria	1–4	
11 Jun 1972	Iran	2–1	1
18 Jun 1972	Ecuador	3–2	
25 Jun 1972	Portugal	1–2	
15 Nov 1972	France	2–1	
13 May 1973	USSR	0–1	
16 May 1973	Poland	0–2	
19 May 1973	France	1–1	
6 Jun 1973	Norway	1–1	
21 Oct 1973	Poland	1–0	
5 May 1974	Brazil	1–2	
8 May 1974	Uruguay	0–2	
12 May 1974	Chile	2–1	
30 Oct 1974	USSR	3–0	3
20 Nov 1974	Turkey	1–1	1
11 Mar 1975	West Germany 'B'	1–0	
10 May 1975	Switzerland	2–1	
18 May 1975	USSR	1–2	
21 May 1975	Switzerland	0–1	
29 Oct 1975	Turkey	4–0	4
24 Mar 1976	Norway	3–0	
26 May 1976	Poland	2–0	2
8 Sep 1976	England	1–1	
13 Oct 1976	Turkey	3–3	
17 Nov 1976	France	0–2	
9 Feb 1977	Spain	0–1	
30 Mar 1977	France	1–0	
1 Jun 1977	Bulgaria	1–2	1
12 Oct 1977	Bulgaria	0–0	
21 May 1978	Norway	0–0	
24 May 1978	Denmark	3–3	
20 Sep 1978	Northern Ireland	0–0	
25 Oct 1978	England	1–1	
2 May 1979	Denmark	2–0	1
19 May 1979	Bulgaria	0–1	
22 May 1979	West Germany	1–3	
29 Oct 1979	United States	3–2	1
21 Nov 1979	Northern Ireland	0–1	
30 Apr 1980	Switzerland	2–0	1
16 May 1980	Argentina	0–1	
10 Sep 1980	Holland	2–1	
15 Oct 1980	Belgium	1–1	
19 Nov 1980	Cyprus	6–0	
24 Feb 1981	Wales	1–3	
14 Oct 1981	France	3–2	

238. BILLY NEWMAN

Position	Midfield
Born	Dublin, 1947
Club	Bohemians; Shelbourne
Caps	1

Date	Team	Result	Goals
27 May 1969	Denmark	0–2	

239. TERRY CONROY

Position	Forward
Born	Dublin, 2 October 1946
Club	Home Farm; Glentoran; Stoke City; Bulova (Hong Kong); Crewe Alexandra
Caps	27

Date	Team	Result	Goals
7 Oct 1969	Czechoslovakia	0–3	
15 Oct 1969	Denmark	1–1	
5 Nov 1969	Hungary	0–4	
6 May 1970	Poland	1–2	
9 May 1970	West Germany	1–2	
23 Sep 1970	Poland	0–2	
14 Oct 1970	Sweden	1–1	
28 Oct 1970	Sweden	0–1	
8 Dec 1970	Italy	0–3	
18 Oct 1972	USSR	1–2	1
15 Nov 1972	France	2–1	1
13 May 1973	USSR	0–1	
6 Jun 1973	Norway	1–1	
21 Oct 1973	Poland	1–0	
5 May 1974	Brazil	1–2	
8 May 1974	Uruguay	0–2	
12 May 1974	Chile	2–1	
20 Nov 1974	Turkey	1–1	

11 Mar 1975	West Germany 'B'	1–0	
10 May 1975	Switzerland	2–1	
18 May 1975	USSR	1–2	
21 May 1975	Switzerland	0–1	
29 Oct 1975	Turkey	4–0	
26 May 1976	Poland	2–0	
8 Sep 1976	England	1–1	
13 Oct 1976	Turkey	3–3	
24 Apr 1977	Poland	0–0	

240. KEVIN FITZPATRICK

Position	Goalkeeper
Born	Limerick, 1943
Club	Limerick
Caps	1

Date	Team	Result	Goals
7 Oct 1969	Czechoslovakia	0–3	

241. TONY BYRNE

Position	Defender
Born	Rathdowney, 2 February 1946
Club	Millwall; Southampton; Hereford United; Newport County
Caps	14

Date	Team	Result	Goals
15 Oct 1969	Denmark	1–1	
6 May 1970	Poland	1–2	
9 May 1970	West Germany	1–2	
23 Sep 1970	Poland	0–2	
14 Oct 1970	Sweden	1–1	
28 Oct 1970	Sweden	0–1	
8 Dec 1970	Italy	0–3	
10 May 1971	Italy	1–2	

30 May 1971	Austria	1–4
15 Nov 1972	France	2–1
13 May 1973	USSR	0–1
19 May 1973	France	1–1
6 Jun 1973	Norway	1–1
21 Oct 1973	Poland	1–0

242. STEVE HEIGHWAY

Position	Winger
Born	Dublin, 25 November 1947
Club	Skelmersdale United; Liverpool; Minnesota Kicks (United States)
Caps	34

Date	Team	Result	Goals
23 Sep 1970	Poland	0–2	
14 Oct 1970	Sweden	1–1	
28 Oct 1970	Sweden	0–1	
10 May 1971	Italy	1–2	
30 May 1971	Austria	1–4	
18 Oct 1972	USSR	1–2	
30 Oct 1974	USSR	3–0	
20 Nov 1974	Turkey	1–1	
11 Mar 1975	West Germany 'B'	1–0	
18 May 1975	USSR	1–2	
29 Oct 1975	Turkey	4–0	
24 Mar 1976	Norway	3–0	
8 Sep 1976	England	1–1	
17 Nov 1976	France	0–2	
9 Feb 1977	Spain	0–1	
30 Mar 1977	France	1–0	
1 Jun 1977	Bulgaria	1–2	
12 Oct 1977	Bulgaria	0–0	
21 May 1978	Norway	0–0	
24 May 1978	Denmark	3–3	
20 Sep 1978	Northern Ireland	0–0	
19 May 1979	Bulgaria	0–1	
17 Oct 1979	Bulgaria	3–0	
29 Oct 1979	United States	3–2	
21 Nov 1979	Northern Ireland	0–1	
6 Feb 1980	England	0–2	

26 Mar 1980	Cyprus	3–2
16 May 1980	Argentina	0–1
15 Oct 1980	Belgium	1–1
28 Oct 1980	France	0–2
19 Nov 1980	Cyprus	6–0
24 Feb 1981	Wales	1–3
25 Mar 1981	Belgium	0–1
9 Sep 1981	Holland	2–2

243. MICK KEARNS

Position	Goalkeeper
Born	Banbury, 26 November 1950
Club	Oxford United; Plymouth Argyle (loan); Charlton Athletic (loan); Walsall; Wolverhampton Wanderers; Walsall
Caps	18

Date	Team	Result	Goals
23 Sep 1970	Poland	0–2	
21 Oct 1973	Poland	1–0	
8 May 1974	Uruguay	0–2	
12 May 1974	Chile	2–1	
24 Mar 1976	Norway	3–0	
26 May 1976	Poland	2–0	
8 Sep 1976	England	1–1	
13 Oct 1976	Turkey	3–3	
17 Nov 1976	France	0–2	
9 Feb 1977	Spain	0–1	
30 Mar 1977	France	1–0	
1 Jun 1977	Bulgaria	1–2	
21 May 1978	Norway	0–0	
24 May 1978	Denmark	3–3	
20 Sep 1978	Northern Ireland	0–0	
25 Oct 1978	England	1–1	
29 Oct 1979	United States	3–2	
21 Nov 1979	Northern Ireland	0–1	

244. MICK LAWLOR

Position	Midfield; Forward
Born	Dublin, 1948
Club	Shamrock Rovers; Shelbourne; Dundalk; Shelbourne; Home Farm
Caps	5

Date	Team	Result	Goals
23 Sep 1970	Poland	0–2	
14 Oct 1970	Sweden	1–1	
28 Oct 1970	Sweden	0–1	
8 Dec 1970	Italy	0–3	
16 May 1973	Poland	0–2	

245. PADDY DUNNING

Position	Centre-half
Born	Dublin, 1951
Club	Shelbourne; Dundalk; Los Angeles Skyhawks (United States); University College Dublin
Caps	2

Date	Team	Result	Goals
28 Oct 1970	Sweden	0–1	
8 Dec 1970	Italy	0–3	

246. NOEL CAMPBELL

Position	Inside-forward
Born	Dublin, 11 December 1949
Club	St Patrick's Athletic; Fortuna Cologne (Germany)
Caps	11

Date	Team	Result	Goals
30 May 1971	Austria	1–4	
11 Jun 1972	Iran	2–1	
18 Jun 1972	Ecuador	3–2	
21 Jun 1972	Chile	1–2	
25 Jun 1972	Portugal	1–2	
18 Oct 1972	USSR	1–2	
15 Nov 1972	France	2–1	
11 Mar 1975	West Germany 'B'	1–0	
24 Mar 1976	Norway	3–0	
9 Feb 1977	Spain	0–1	
1 Jun 1977	Bulgaria	1–2	

247. JIMMY DUNNE

Position	Central defender
Born	Dublin, 1 December 1947
Club	Shelbourne; Millwall; Torquay United; Fulham; Torquay United
Caps	1

Date	Team	Result	Goals
30 May 1971	Austria	1–4	

248. JIMMY HOLMES

Position	Left-back
Born	Dublin, 11 November 1953
Club	Coventry City; Tottenham Hotspur; Vancouver Whitecaps (Canada); Leicester City; Brentford; Torquay United; Peterborough United; Nuneaton Borough
Caps	30

Date	Team	Result	Goals
30 May 1971	Austria	1–4	
15 Nov 1972	France	2–1	
13 May 1973	USSR	0–1	
16 May 1971	Poland	0–2	
19 May 1973	France	1–1	
6 Jun 1973	Norway	1–1	
21 Oct 1973	Poland	1–0	
5 May 1974	Brazil	1–2	
30 Oct 1974	USSR	3–0	
21 May 1975	Switzerland	0–1	
29 Oct 1975	Turkey	4–0	
24 Mar 1976	Norway	3–0	1
26 May 1976	Poland	2–0	
8 Sep 1976	England	1–1	
13 Oct 1976	Turkey	3–3	
17 Nov 1976	France	0–2	
9 Feb 1977	Spain	0–1	
30 Mar 1977	France	1–0	
24 Apr 1977	Poland	0–0	
1 Jun 1977	Bulgaria	1–2	
12 Oct 1977	Bulgaria	0–0	
5 Apr 1978	Turkey	4–2	

PLAYERS

12 Apr 1978	Poland	0–3
21 May 1978	Norway	0–0
24 May 1978	Denmark	3–3
20 Sep 1978	Northern Ireland	0–0
25 Oct 1978	England	1–1
2 May 1979	Denmark	2–0
19 May 1979	Bulgaria	0–1
24 Feb 1981	Wales	1–3

249. MICK GANNON

Position	Right-back
Born	Dublin, 2 February 1947
Club	Shelbourne; Shamrock Rovers; Shelbourne; Aer Lingus
Caps	1

Date	Team	Result	Goals
10 Oct 1971	Austria	0–6	

250. JOHN HERRICK

Position	Defender
Born	Cork, 1947
Club	Cork Hibernians; Limerick
Caps	3

Date	Team	Result	Goals
10 Oct 1971	Austria	0–6	
21 Jun 1972	Chile	1–2	
19 May 1973	France	1–1	

251. MICK KEARIN

Position	Left-half
Born	Dublin, 1948
Club	Bohemians; Shamrock Rovers; Bohemians; Athlone Town
Caps	1

Date	Team	Result	Goals
10 Oct 1971	Austria	0–6	

252. TOMMY McCONVILLE

Position	Centre-half
Born	Dundalk, County Louth, 1947
Club	Dundalk; Waterford; Shamrock Rovers; Dundalk
Caps	6

Date	Team	Result	Goals
10 Oct 1971	Austria	0–6	
18 Oct 1972	USSR	1–2	
15 Nov 1972	France	2–1	
13 May 1973	USSR	0–1	
16 May 1973	Poland	0–2	
19 May 1973	France	1–1	

253. MICK MARTIN

Position	Midfield
Born	Dublin, 9 July 1951
Club	Home Farm; Bohemians; Manchester United; West Bromwich Albion; Newcastle United; Vancouver Whitecaps (Canada); Cardiff City; Peterborough United; Rotherham United; Preston North End
Caps	52

Date	Team	Result	Goals
10 Oct 1971	Austria	0–6	
11 Jun 1972	Iran	2–1	
18 Jun 1972	Ecuador	3–2	1
21 Jun 1972	Chile	1–2	
25 Jun 1972	Portugal	1–2	
18 Oct 1972	USSR	1–2	
13 May 1973	USSR	0–1	
16 May 1973	Poland	0–2	
19 May 1973	France	1–1	1
6 Jun 1973	Norway	1–1	
21 Oct 1973	Poland	1–0	
5 May 1974	Brazil	1–2	
8 May 1974	Uruguay	0–2	
12 May 1974	Chile	2–1	
30 Oct 1974	USSR	3–0	

Date	Team	Result	Goals
20 Nov 1974	Turkey	1–1	
11 Mar 1975	West Germany 'B'	1–0	
10 May 1975	Switzerland	2–1	1
18 May 1975	USSR	1–2	
21 May 1975	Switzerland	0–1	
29 Oct 1975	Turkey	4–0	
24 Mar 1976	Norway	3–0	
26 May 1976	Poland	2–0	
8 Sep 1976	England	1–1	
13 Oct 1976	Turkey	3–3	
17 Nov 1976	France	0–2	
9 Feb 1977	Spain	0–1	
30 Mar 1977	France	1–0	
24 Apr 1977	Poland	0–0	
1 Jun 1977	Bulgaria	1–2	
2 May 1979	Denmark	2–0	
19 May 1979	Bulgaria	0–1	
22 May 1979	West Germany	1–3	
11 Sep 1979	Wales	1–2	
26 Sep 1979	Czechoslovakia	1–4	
17 Oct 1979	Bulgaria	3–0	1
29 Oct 1979	United States	3–2	
21 Nov 1979	Northern Ireland	0–1	
28 Oct 1980	France	0–2	
25 Mar 1981	Belgium	0–1	
29 Apr 1981	Czechoslovakia	3–1	
21 May 1981	West Germany 'B'	0–3	
9 Sep 1981	Holland	2–2	
14 Oct 1981	France	3–2	
28 Apr 1982	Algeria	0–2	
21 May 1982	Chile	0–1	
27 May 1982	Brazil	0–7	
30 May 1982	Trinidad & Tobago	1–2	
22 Sep 1982	Holland	1–2	
17 Nov 1982	Spain	3–3	
30 Mar 1983	Malta	1–0	
27 Apr 1983	Spain	0–2	

254. DAMIEN RICHARDSON

Position Forward
Born Dublin, 2 August 1947
Club Shamrock Rovers; Gillingham; Gravesend; Folkestone; Faversham; Chatham
Caps 3

Date	Team	Result	Goals
10 Oct 1971	Austria	0–6	
6 Jun 1973	Norway	1–1	
26 Sep 1979	Czechoslovakia	1–4	

255. PADDY ROCHE

Position Goalkeeper
Born Dublin, 4 January 1951
Club Shelbourne; Manchester United; Brentford; Halifax Town
Caps 8

Date	Team	Result	Goals
10 Oct 1971	Austria	0–6	
30 Oct 1974	USSR	3–0	
20 Nov 1974	Turkey	1–1	
11 Mar 1975	West Germany 'B'	1–0	
10 May 1975	Switzerland	2–1	
18 May 1975	USSR	1–2	
21 May 1975	Switzerland	0–1	
29 Oct 1975	Turkey	4–0	

256. MIAH DENNEHY

Position Winger
Born Cork, 29 March 1950
Club Cork Hibernians; Nottingham Forest; Walsall; Bristol Rovers; Cardiff City
Caps 11

Date	Team	Result	Goals
18 Jun 1972	Ecuador	3–2	
21 Jun 1972	Chile	1–2	
13 May 1973	USSR	0–1	
16 May 1973	Poland	0–2	
19 May 1973	France	1–1	

Miah Dennehy scoring against Waterford during the 1972 FAI Cup Final at Dalymount Park

6 Jun 1973	Norway	1–1	1
21 Oct 1973	Poland	1–0	1
20 Nov 1974	Turkey	1–1	
11 Mar 1975	West Germany 'B' 1–0		
26 May 1976	Poland	2–0	
24 Apr 1977	Poland	0–0	

257. GERRY DALY

Position	Midfield
Born	Dublin, 30 April 1954
Club	Bohemians; Manchester United; Derby County; Coventry City; Leicester City (loan); Birmingham City; Shrewsbury Town; Stoke City; Doncaster Rovers
Caps	48

Date	Team	Result	Goals
16 May 1973	Poland	0–2	
6 Jun 1973	Norway	1–1	
5 May 1974	Brazil	1–2	
8 May 1974	Uruguay	0–2	

11 Mar 1975	West Germany 'B' 1–0		
21 May 1975	Switzerland	0–1	
8 Sep 1976	England	1–1	1
13 Oct 1976	Turkey	3–3	1
17 Nov 1976	France	0–2	
30 Mar 1977	France	1–0	
1 Jun 1977	Bulgaria	1–2	
12 Oct 1977	Bulgaria	0–0	
5 Apr 1978	Turkey	4–2	
24 May 1978	Denmark	3–3	1
20 Sep 1978	Northern Ireland	0–0	
25 Oct 1978	England	1–1	1
2 May 1979	Denmark	2–0	1
19 May 1979	Bulgaria	0–1	
21 Nov 1979	Northern Ireland	0–1	
6 Feb 1980	England	0–2	
26 Mar 1980	Cyprus	3–2	
30 Apr 1980	Switzerland	2–0	1
16 May 1980	Argentina	0–1	
10 Sep 1980	Holland	2–1	1

Date	Team	Result	Goals
15 Oct 1980	Belgium	1–1	
19 Nov 1980	Cyprus	6–0	2
24 Feb 1981	Wales	1–3	
25 Mar 1981	Belgium	0–1	
29 Apr 1981	Czechoslovakia	3–1	
21 May 1981	West Germany 'B'	0–3	
24 May 1981	Poland	0–3	
28 Apr 1982	Algeria	0–2	
21 May 1982	Chile	0–1	
27 May 1982	Brazil	0–7	
30 May 1982	Trinidad & Tobago	1–2	
22 Sep 1982	Holland	1–2	1
27 Apr 1983	Spain	0–2	
16 Nov 1983	Malta	8–0	1
4 Apr 1984	Israel	0–3	
8 Aug 1984	Mexico	0–0	
1 May 1985	Norway	0–0	
26 May 1985	Spain	0–0	
2 Jun 1985	Switzerland	3–0	
11 Sep 1985	Switzerland	0–0	
23 Apr 1986	Uruguay	1–1	1
25 May 1986	Iceland	2–1	1
27 May 1986	Czechoslovakia	1–0	
15 Oct 1986	Scotland	0–0	

258. EAMONN FAGAN

Position Defender
Born Dublin, 1950
Club Shamrock Rovers; Athlone Town
Caps 1

Date	Team	Result	Goals
6 Jun 1973	Norway	1–1	

259. TERRY MANCINI

Position Central defender
Born Camden Town, 4 October 1942
Club Watford; Port Elizabeth (South Africa); Leyton Orient; Queen's Park Rangers; Arsenal; Aldershot
Caps 5

Date	Team	Result	Goals
21 Oct 1973	Poland	1–0	
5 May 1974	Brazil	1–2	1
8 May 1974	Uruguay	0–2	
12 May 1974	Chile	2–1	
30 Oct 1974	USSR	3–0	

260. PETER THOMAS

Position Goalkeeper
Born Coventry, 20 November 1944
Club Coventry City; Waterford
Caps 2

Date	Team	Result	Goals
21 Oct 1973	Poland	1–0	
5 May 1974	Brazil	1–2	

261. LIAM BRADY

Position Midfield
Born Dublin, 13 February 1956
Club Arsenal; Juventus (Italy); Sampdoria (Italy); Inter Milan (Italy); Ascoli (Italy); West Ham United
Caps 72

Date	Team	Result	Goals
30 Oct 1974	USSR	3–0	
20 Nov 1974	Turkey	1–1	
11 Mar 1975	West Germany 'B'	1–0	
10 May 1975	Switzerland	2–1	
18 May 1975	USSR	1–2	
21 May 1975	Switzerland	0–1	
29 Oct 1975	Turkey	4–0	
24 Mar 1976	Norway	3–0	1
26 May 1976	Poland	2–0	
8 Sep 1976	England	1–1	
13 Oct 1976	Turkey	3–3	
17 Nov 1976	France	0–2	
9 Feb 1977	Spain	0–1	
30 Mar 1977	France	1–0	1
1 Jun 1977	Bulgaria	1–2	
12 Oct 1977	Bulgaria	0–0	

Date	Team	Result	Goals
21 May 1978	Norway	0–0	
20 Sep 1978	Northern Ireland	0–0	
25 Oct 1978	England	1–1	
2 May 1979	Denmark	2–0	
19 May 1979	Bulgaria	0–1	
22 May 1979	West Germany	1–3	
11 Sep 1979	Wales	1–2	
17 Oct 1979	Bulgaria	3–0	
6 Feb 1980	England	0–2	
26 Mar 1980	Cyprus	3–2	
16 May 1980	Argentina	0–1	
10 Sep 1980	Holland	2–1	
15 Oct 1980	Belgium	1–1	
28 Oct 1980	France	0–2	
19 Nov 1980	Cyprus	6–0	
25 Mar 1981	Belgium	0–1	
9 Sep 1981	Holland	2–2	
14 Oct 1981	France	3–2	
21 May 1982	Chile	0–1	
27 May 1982	Brazil	0–7	
30 May 1982	Trinidad & Tobago	1–2	1
22 Sep 1982	Holland	1–2	
13 Oct 1982	Iceland	2–0	
17 Nov 1982	Spain	3–3	
30 Mar 1983	Malta	1–0	
21 Sep 1983	Iceland	3–0	
12 Oct 1983	Holland	2–3	1
16 Nov 1983	Malta	8–0	2
4 Apr 1984	Israel	0–3	
23 May 1984	Poland	0–0	
12 Sep 1984	USSR	1–0	
17 Oct 1984	Norway	0–1	
14 Nov 1984	Denmark	0–3	
5 Feb 1985	Italy	1–2	
26 Mar 1985	England	1–2	1
1 May 1985	Norway	0–0	
26 May 1985	Spain	0–0	
2 Jun 1985	Switzerland	3–0	
11 Sep 1985	Switzerland	0–0	
16 Oct 1985	USSR	0–2	
13 Nov 1985	Denmark	1–4	
26 Mar 1986	Wales	0–1	
10 Sep 1986	Belgium	2–2	1
15 Oct 1986	Scotland	0–0	
12 Nov 1986	Poland	0–1	
18 Feb 1987	Scotland	1–0	
1 Apr 1987	Bulgaria	1–2	
29 Apr 1987	Belgium	0–0	
23 May 1987	Brazil	1–0	1
28 May 1987	Luxembourg	2–0	
9 Sep 1987	Luxembourg	2–1	
14 Oct 1987	Bulgaria	2–0	
8 Mar 1989	Hungary	0–0	
4 Jul 1989	Hungary	2–0	
6 Sep 1989	West Germany	1–1	
16 May 1990	Finland	1–1	

262. TONY GREALISH

Position	Midfield
Born	Paddington, 21 September 1956
Club	Leyton Orient; Luton Town; Brighton & Hove Albion; West Bromwich Albion; Manchester City; Rotherham United; Walsall; Bromsgrove Rovers; Halesowen Harriers;
Caps	45

Date	Team	Result	Goals
24 Mar 1976	Norway	3–0	
26 May 1976	Poland	2–0	
21 May 1978	Norway	0–0	
24 May 1978	Denmark	3–3	1
20 Sep 1978	Northern Ireland	0–0	
25 Oct 1978	England	1–1	
22 May 1979	West Germany	1–3	
11 Sep 1979	Wales	1–2	
26 Sep 1979	Czechoslovakia	1–4	
17 Oct 1979	Bulgaria	3–0	1
29 Oct 1979	United States	3–2	1
21 Nov 1979	Northern Ireland	0–1	
6 Feb 1980	England	0–2	

Date	Team	Result	Goals
26 Mar 1980	Cyprus	3–2	
30 Apr 1980	Switzerland	2–0	
16 May 1980	Argentina	0–1	
10 Sep 1980	Holland	2–1	
15 Oct 1980	Belgium	1–1	1
28 Oct 1980	France	0–2	
19 Nov 1980	Cyprus	6–0	1
24 Feb 1981	Wales	1–3	1
25 Mar 1981	Belgium	0–1	
21 May 1981	West Germany 'B'	0–3	
24 May 1981	Poland	0–3	
9 Sep 1981	Holland	2–2	
28 Apr 1982	Algeria	0–2	
21 May 1982	Chile	0–1	
27 May 1982	Brazil	0–7	
30 May 1982	Trinidad & Tobago	1–2	
22 Sep 1982	Holland	1–2	
13 Oct 1982	Iceland	2–0	1
17 Nov 1982	Spain	3–3	
27 Apr 1983	Spain	0–2	
21 Sep 1983	Iceland	3–0	
12 Oct 1983	Holland	2–3	
23 May 1984	Poland	0–0	
3 Jun 1984	China	1–0	
8 Aug 1984	Mexico	0–0	
12 Sep 1984	USSR	1–0	
17 Oct 1984	Norway	0–1	
14 Nov 1984	Denmark	0–3	
26 May 1985	Spain	0–0	
2 Jun 1985	Switzerland	3–0	1
16 Oct 1985	USSR	0–2	
13 Nov 1985	Denmark	1–4	

263. RAY O'BRIEN

Position	Full-back
Born	Dublin, 21 May 1951
Club	Shelbourne; Manchester United; Notts County; Derby County (loan); Boston United
Caps	5

Date	Team	Result	Goals
24 Mar 1976	Norway	3–0	
26 May 1976	Poland	2–0	
9 Feb 1977	Spain	0–1	
24 Apr 1977	Poland	0–0	
16 May 1980	Argentina	0–1	

264. MICKY WALSH

Position	Forward
Born	Chorley, 13 August 1954
Club	Chorley; Blackpool; Everton; Queen's Park Rangers; FC Porto (Portugal); Sal Gueiros (Portugal); Espinho (Portugal); Rio Avenue (Portugal)
Caps	21

Date	Team	Result	Goals
24 Mar 1976	Norway	3–0	1
26 May 1976	Poland	2–0	
17 Nov 1976	France	0–2	
24 Apr 1977	Poland	0–0	
20 Sep 1978	Northern Ireland	0–0	
2 May 1979	Denmark	2–0	
19 May 1979	Bulgaria	0–1	
22 May 1979	West Germany	1–3	
25 Mar 1981	Belgium	0–1	
29 Apr 1981	Czechoslovakia	3–1	
28 Apr 1982	Algeria	0–2	
22 Sep 1982	Holland	1–2	
17 Nov 1982	Spain	3–3	
27 Apr 1983	Spain	0–2	
21 Sep 1983	Iceland	3–0	1
16 Nov 1983	Malta	8–0	
23 May 1984	Poland	0–0	
3 Jun 1984	China	1–0	
12 Sep 1984	USSR	1–0	1
17 Oct 1984	Norway	0–1	
14 Nov 1984	Denmark	0–3	

265. DAVID O'LEARY

Position	Central defender
Born	Stoke Newington, 2 May 1958
Club	Arsenal; Leeds United
Caps	68

Date	Team	Result	Goals
8 Sep 1976	England	1–1	
17 Nov 1976	France	0–2	
9 Feb 1977	Spain	0–1	
30 Mar 1977	France	1–0	
1 Jun 1977	Bulgaria	1–2	
12 Oct 1977	Bulgaria	0–0	
21 May 1978	Norway	0–0	
24 May 1978	Denmark	3–3	
25 Oct 1978	England	1–1	
19 May 1979	Bulgaria	0–1	
22 May 1979	West Germany	1–3	
11 Sep 1979	Wales	1–2	
17 Oct 1979	Bulgaria	3–0	
21 Nov 1979	Northern Ireland	0–1	
6 Feb 1980	England	0–2	
26 Mar 1980	Cyprus	3–2	
10 Sep 1980	Holland	2–1	
29 Apr 1981	Czechoslovakia	3–1	
21 May 1981	West Germany 'B'	0–3	
24 May 1981	Poland	0–3	
9 Sep 1981	Holland	2–2	
14 Oct 1981	France	3–2	
22 Sep 1982	Holland	1–2	
13 Oct 1982	Iceland	2–0	
27 Apr 1983	Spain	0–2	
4 Apr 1984	Israel	0–3	
23 May 1984	Poland	0–0	
3 Jun 1984	China	1–0	
12 Sep 1984	USSR	1–0	
17 Oct 1984	Norway	0–1	
14 Nov 1984	Denmark	0–3	
27 Feb 1985	Israel	0–0	
26 Mar 1985	England	1–2	
1 May 1985	Norway	0–0	
26 May 1985	Spain	0–0	
2 Jun 1985	Switzerland	3–0	
11 Sep 1985	Switzerland	0–0	
16 Oct 1985	USSR	0–2	
13 Nov 1985	Denmark	1–4	
26 Mar 1986	Wales	0–1	
16 Nov 1988	Spain	0–2	
28 May 1989	Malta	2–0	
4 Jul 1989	Hungary	2–0	
6 Sep 1989	West Germany	1–1	
11 Oct 1989	Northern Ireland	3–0	
15 Nov 1989	Malta	2–0	
28 Mar 1990	Wales	1–0	
25 Apr 1990	USSR	1–0	
16 May 1990	Finland	1–1	
27 May 1990	Turkey	0–0	
2 Jun 1990	Malta	3–0	
25 Jun 1990	Romania	0–0 won 5–4 on penalties	
12 Sep 1990	Morocco	1–0	
17 Oct 1990	Turkey	5–0	1
14 Nov 1990	England	1–1	
27 Mar 1991	England	1–1	
1 May 1991	Poland	0–0	
22 May 1991	Chile	1–1	
11 Sep 1991	Hungary	2–1	
16 Oct 1991	Poland	3–3	
13 Nov 1991	Turkey	3–1	
19 Feb 1992	Wales	0–1	
25 Mar 1992	Switzerland	2–1	
29 Apr 1992	United States	4–1	
26 May 1992	Albania	2–0	
4 Jun 1992	Italy	0–2	
7 Jun 1992	Portugal	2–0	
17 Feb 1993	Wales	2–1	

266. FRANK STAPLETON

Position	Forward
Born	Dublin, 10 July 1956
Club	Arsenal; Manchester United; Ajax (Holland); Derby County; Le Havre (France); Blackburn Rovers; Aldershot; Huddersfield Town; Bradford City; Brighton & Hove Albion
Caps	71

Date	Team	Result	Goals
13 Oct 1976	Turkey	3–3	1
17 Nov 1976	France	0–2	
9 Feb 1977	Spain	0–1	
1 Jun 1977	Bulgaria	1–2	
12 Oct 1977	Bulgaria	0–0	
21 May 1978	Norway	0–0	
24 May 1978	Denmark	3–3	1
20 Sep 1978	Northern Ireland	0–0	
25 Oct 1978	England	1–1	
2 May 1979	Denmark	2–0	
22 May 1979	West Germany	1–3	
11 Sep 1979	Wales	1–2	
17 Oct 1979	Bulgaria	3–0	1
21 Nov 1979	Northern Ireland	0–1	
6 Feb 1980	England	0–2	
26 Mar 1980	Cyprus	3–2	
10 Sep 1980	Holland	2–1	
15 Oct 1980	Belgium	1–1	
28 Oct 1980	France	0–2	
19 Nov 1980	Cyprus	6–0	1
25 Mar 1981	Belgium	0–1	
29 Apr 1981	Czechoslovakia	3–1	1
21 May 1981	West Germany 'B'	0–3	
24 May 1981	Poland	0–3	
9 Sep 1981	Holland	2–2	1
14 Oct 1981	France	3–2	1
28 Apr 1982	Algeria	0–2	
22 Sep 1982	Holland	1–2	
13 Oct 1982	Iceland	2–0	1
17 Nov 1982	Spain	3–3	2
30 Mar 1983	Malta	1–0	1
27 Apr 1983	Spain	0–2	
21 Sep 1983	Iceland	3–0	
12 Oct 1983	Holland	2–3	
16 Nov 1983	Malta	8–0	1
4 Apr 1984	Israel	0–3	
23 May 1984	Poland	0–0	
3 Jun 1984	China	1–0	
17 Oct 1984	Norway	0–1	
14 Nov 1984	Denmark	0–3	
5 Feb 1985	Italy	1–2	
27 Feb 1985	Israel	0–0	
26 Mar 1985	England	1–2	
1 May 1985	Norway	0–0	
2 Jun 1985	Switzerland	3–0	1
11 Sep 1985	Switzerland	0–0	
16 Oct 1985	USSR	0–2	
13 Nov 1985	Denmark	1–4	1
23 Apr 1986	Uruguay	1–1	
25 May 1986	Iceland	2–1	
27 May 1986	Czechoslovakia	1–0	1
10 Sep 1986	Belgium	2–2	1
15 Oct 1986	Scotland	0–0	
12 Nov 1986	Poland	0–1	
18 Feb 1987	Scotland	1–0	
1 Apr 1987	Bulgaria	1–2	1
29 Apr 1987	Belgium	0–0	
28 May 1987	Luxembourg	2–0	
9 Sep 1987	Luxembourg	2–1	1
14 Oct 1987	Bulgaria	2–0	
23 Mar 1988	Romania	2–0	
27 Apr 1988	Yugoslavia	2–0	
1 Jun 1988	Norway	0–0	
12 Jun 1988	England	1–0	
15 Jun 1988	USSR	1–1	
18 Jun 1988	Holland	0–1	
7 Feb 1989	France	0–0	
26 Apr 1989	Spain	1–0	
28 May 1989	Malta	2–0	
6 Sep 1989	West Germany	1–1	
2 Jun 1990	Malta	3–0	1

267. JOE WATERS

Position Midfield
Born Limerick, 20 September 1953
Club Leicester City; Grimsby Town
Caps 2

Date	Team	Result	Goals
13 Oct 1976	Turkey	3–3	1
21 Nov 1979	Northern Ireland	0–1	

268. TONY MACKEN

Position Right-back
Born Dublin, 30 July 1950
Club Home Farm; Glentoran; Waterford; Derby County; Portsmouth (loan); Washington Diplomats (United States); Dallas Tornado (United States); Walsall; Drogheda; Waterford United; Home Farm
Caps 1

Date	Team	Result	Goals
9 Feb 1977	Spain	0–1	

269. GERRY PEYTON

Position Goalkeeper
Born Birmingham, 20 May 1956
Club Atherstone Town; Burnley; Fulham; Southend United (loan); Bournemouth; Everton; Bolton Wanderers (loan); Brentford (loan); Chelsea (loan); Brentford; West Ham United
Caps 33

Date	Team	Result	Goals
9 Feb 1977	Spain	0–1	
12 Oct 1977	Bulgaria	0–0	
5 Apr 1978	Turkey	4–2	
12 Apr 1978	Poland	0–3	
2 May 1979	Denmark	2–0	
19 May 1979	Bulgaria	0–1	
22 May 1979	West Germany	1–3	
11 Sep 1979	Wales	1–2	
26 Sep 1979	Czechoslovakia	1–4	
17 Oct 1979	Bulgaria	3–0	
6 Feb 1980	England	0–2	
26 Mar 1980	Cyprus	3–2	
30 Apr 1980	Switzerland	2–0	
16 May 1980	Argentina	0–1	
10 Sep 1980	Holland	2–1	
15 Oct 1980	Belgium	1–1	
28 Oct 1980	France	0–2	
19 Nov 1980	Cyprus	6–0	
30 May 1982	Trinidad & Tobago	1–2	
8 Aug 1984	Mexico	0–0	
26 Mar 1986	Wales	0–1	
27 May 1986	Czechoslovakia	1–0	
9 Sep 1987	Luxembourg	2–0	
22 May 1988	Poland	3–1	
14 Sep 1988	Northern Ireland	0–0	
19 Oct 1988	Tunisia	4–0	
25 Apr 1990	USSR	1–0	
2 Jun 1990	Malta	3–0	
22 May 1991	Chile	1–1	
29 Apr 1992	United States	4–1	
30 May 1992	United States	1–3	
4 Jun 1992	Italy	0–2	
7 Jun 1992	Portugal	2–0	

270. RON HEALEY

Position Goalkeeper
Born Manchester, 30 August 1952
Club Manchester City; Altrincham (loan); Coventry City (loan); Preston North End (loan); Cardiff City
Caps 2

Date	Team	Result	Goals
24 Apr 1977	Poland	0–0	
6 Feb 1980	England	0–2	

271. MARK LAWRENSON

Position Defender
Born Preston, 2 June 1957
Club Preston North End; Brighton & Hove Albion; Liverpool; Tampa Bay Rowdies (United States)
Caps 39

Date	Team	Result	Goals
24 Apr 1977	Poland	0–0	
12 Oct 1977	Bulgaria	0–0	
12 Apr 1978	Poland	0–3	
21 May 1978	Norway	0–0	
24 May 1978	Denmark	3–3	
20 Sep 1978	Northern Ireland	0–0	
25 Oct 1978	England	1–1	
6 Feb 1980	England	0–2	
26 Mar 1980	Cyprus	3–2	1
30 Apr 1980	Switzerland	2–0	
10 Sep 1980	Holland	2–1	1
15 Oct 1980	Belgium	1–1	
28 Oct 1980	France	0–2	
19 Nov 1980	Cyprus	6–0	
24 May 1981	Poland	0–3	
9 Sep 1981	Holland	2–2	
14 Oct 1981	France	3–2	
22 Sep 1982	Holland	1–2	
13 Oct 1982	Iceland	2–0	
17 Nov 1982	Spain	3–3	
30 Mar 1983	Malta	1–0	
27 Apr 1983	Spain	0–2	
21 Sep 1983	Iceland	3–0	
12 Oct 1983	Holland	2–3	
16 Nov 1983	Malta	8–0	2
4 Apr 1984	Israel	0–3	
12 Sep 1984	USSR	1–0	
17 Oct 1984	Norway	0–1	
14 Nov 1984	Denmark	0–3	
5 Feb 1985	Italy	1–2	
26 Mar 1985	England	1–2	
1 May 1985	Norway	0–0	
11 Sep 1985	Switzerland	0–0	
16 Oct 1985	USSR	0–2	
13 Nov 1985	Denmark	1–4	
10 Sep 1986	Belgium	2–2	
18 Feb 1987	Scotland	1–0	1
14 Oct 1987	Bulgaria	2–0	
10 Nov 1987	Israel	5–0	

Ron Healey

272. SYNAN BRADDISH

Position	Midfield
Born	Dublin, 27 January 1958
Club	Dundalk; Liverpool; Dundalk; St Patrick's Athletic; Athlone Town; Kilkenny City; Longford Town
Caps	2

Date	Team	Result	Goals
5 Apr 1978	Turkey	4–2	
12 Apr 1978	Poland	0–3	

273. MAURICE DALY

Position	Left-back
Born	Dublin, 28 November 1955
Club	Home Farm; Wolverhampton Wanderers
Caps	2

Date	Team	Result	Goals
5 Apr 1978	Turkey	4–2	
12 Apr 1978	Poland	0–3	

274. ASHLEY GRIMES

Position	Midfield
Born	Dublin, 2 August 1957
Club	Stella Maris; Bohemians; Manchester United; Coventry City; Luton Town; Osasuna (Spain); Stoke City
Caps	18

Date	Team	Result	Goals
5 Apr 1978	Turkey	4–2	
12 Apr 1978	Poland	0–3	
21 May 1978	Norway	0–0	
17 Oct 1979	Bulgaria	3–0	
29 Oct 1979	United States	3–2	
21 Nov 1979	Northern Ireland	0–1	
6 Feb 1980	England	0–2	
26 Mar 1980	Cyprus	3–2	
29 Apr 1981	Czechoslovakia	3–1	
21 May 1981	West Germany 'B'	0–3	
24 May 1981	Poland	0–3	
28 Apr 1982	Algeria	0–2	
17 Nov 1982	Spain	3–3	1
27 Apr 1983	Spain	0–2	
4 Apr 1984	Israel	0–3	
23 May 1984	Poland	0–0	
9 Sep 1987	Luxembourg	2–1	
23 Mar 1988	Romania	2–0	

275. DAVE LANGAN

Position	Right-back
Born	Dublin, 15 February 1957
Club	Derby County; Birmingham City; Oxford United; Leicester City (loan); Bournemouth; Peterborough United
Caps	26

Date	Team	Result	Goals
5 Apr 1978	Turkey	4–2	
21 May 1978	Norway	0–0	
30 Apr 1980	Switzerland	2–0	
16 May 1980	Argentina	0–1	

Dave Langan

Date	Team	Result	Goals
10 Sep 1980	Holland	2–1	
15 Oct 1980	Belgium	1–1	
28 Oct 1980	France	0–2	
19 Nov 1980	Cyprus	6–0	
24 Feb 1981	Wales	1–3	
25 Mar 1981	Belgium	0–1	
29 Apr 1981	Czechoslovakia	3–1	
21 May 1981	West Germany 'B'	0–3	
24 May 1981	Poland	0–3	
9 Sep 1981	Holland	2–2	
14 Oct 1981	France	3–2	
1 May 1985	Norway	0–0	
26 May 1985	Spain	0–0	
2 Jun 1985	Switzerland	3–0	
26 Mar 1986	Wales	0–1	
23 Apr 1986	Uruguay	1–1	
10 Sep 1986	Belgium	2–2	
15 Oct 1986	Scotland	0–0	
12 Nov 1986	Poland	0–1	
23 May 1987	Brazil	1–0	
28 May 1987	Luxembourg	2–0	
9 Sep 1987	Luxembourg	2–1	

276. PAUL McGEE

Position	Forward
Born	Sligo, 19 June 1954
Club	Sligo Rovers; Hereford United; Finn Harps; Sligo Rovers; Queen's Park Rangers; Preston North End; Burnley; Dundalk; Shamrock Rovers; Waterford; Sligo Rovers; Galway; Haarlem (Holland); Derry City; Athlone Town
Caps	15

Date	Team	Result	Goals
5 Apr 1978	Turkey	4–2	1
21 May 1978	Norway	0–0	
24 May 1978	Denmark	3–3	
20 Sep 1978	Northern Ireland	0–0	
25 Oct 1978	England	1–1	
2 May 1979	Denmark	2–0	
19 May 1979	Bulgaria	0–1	
26 Sep 1979	Czechoslovakia	1–4	1
17 Oct 1979	Bulgaria	3–0	
29 Oct 1979	United States	3–2	
21 Nov 1979	Northern Ireland	0–1	
26 Mar 1980	Cyprus	3–2	2
30 Apr 1980	Switzerland	2–0	
16 May 1980	Argentina	0–1	
15 Oct 1980	Belgium	1–1	

277. GERRY RYAN

Position	Winger
Born	Dublin, 4 October 1955
Club	Bohemians; Derby County; Brighton & Hove Albion
Caps	18

Date	Team	Result	Goals
5 Apr 1978	Turkey	4–2	
25 Oct 1978	England	1–1	
22 May 1979	West Germany	1–3	1
11 Sep 1979	Wales	1–2	
26 Mar 1980	Cyprus	3–2	
30 Apr 1980	Switzerland	2–0	

Date	Team	Result
16 May 1980	Argentina	0–1
28 Oct 1980	France	0–2
21 May 1981	West Germany 'B'	0–3
24 May 1981	Poland	0–3
9 Sep 1981	Holland	2–2
28 Apr 1982	Algeria	0–2
21 May 1982	Chile	0–1
27 May 1982	Brazil	0–7
30 May 1982	Trinidad & Tobago	1–2
23 May 1984	Poland	0–0
3 Jun 1984	China	1–0
8 Aug 1984	Mexico	0–0

Paul McGee

278. NOEL SYNNOTT

Position	Centre-half
Born	Dublin, 1952
Club	Ealing; Guildford City; Sligo Rovers; Shamrock Rovers; Waterford
Caps	3

Date	Team	Result	Goals
5 Apr 1978	Turkey	4–2	
12 Apr 1978	Poland	0–3	
20 Sep 1978	Northern Ireland	0–0	

279. JEROME CLARKE

Position	Forward
Born	Drogheda, County Louth, 15 July 1951
Club	Drogheda United; Dundalk
Caps	1

Date	Team	Result	Goals
12 Apr 1978	Poland	0–3	

280. EAMONN GREGG

Position	Right-back
Born	Dublin, 1953
Club	Shamrock Rovers; Bohemians; Dundalk; St Patrick's Athletic; Shamrock Rovers; Kilkenny City
Caps	8

Date	Team	Result	Goals
12 Apr 1978	Poland	0–3	
24 May 1978	Denmark	3–3	
25 Oct 1978	England	1–1	
2 May 1979	Denmark	2–0	
19 May 1979	Bulgaria	0–1	
22 May 1979	West Germany	1–3	
11 Sep 1979	Wales	1–2	
26 Sep 1979	Czechoslovakia	1–4	

281. CATHAL MUCKIAN

Position	Forward
Born	Dundalk, County Louth, 1952
Club	Drogheda United; Dundalk; Shamrock Rovers; Shelbourne
Caps	1

Date	Team	Result	Goals
12 Apr 1978	Poland	0–3	

282. AUSTIN HAYES

Position	Winger
Born	Hammersmith, 15 July 1958
Died	December 1986
Club	Southampton; Millwall; Northampton Town; Barnet
Caps	1

Date	Team	Result	Goals
2 May 1979	Denmark	2–0	

283. BRENDAN O'CALLAGHAN

Position	Forward; Central defender
Born	Bradford, 23 July 1955
Club	Doncaster Rovers; Stoke City; Oldham Athletic
Caps	6

Date	Team	Result	Goals
22 May 1979	West Germany	1–3	
11 Sep 1979	Wales	1–2	
29 Oct 1979	United States	3–2	
24 Feb 1981	Wales	1–3	
27 May 1982	Brazil	0–7	
30 May 1982	Trinidad & Tobago	1–2	

284. JERRY MURPHY

Position	Midfield
Born	Stepney, 23 September 1959
Club	Crystal Palace; Chelsea
Caps	3

Date	Team	Result	Goals
11 Sep 1979	Wales	1–2	
29 Oct 1979	United States	3–2	
26 Mar 1980	Cyprus	3–2	

285. JOHN ANDERSON

Position	Defender
Born	Dublin, 7 November 1959
Club	West Bromwich Albion; Preston North End; Newcastle United
Caps	16

Date	Team	Result	Goals
26 Sep 1979	Czechoslovakia	1–4	
29 Oct 1979	United States	3–2	1
21 May 1982	Chile	0–1	
27 May 1982	Brazil	0–7	
30 May 1982	Trinidad & Tobago	1–2	
3 Jun 1984	China	1–0	

26 Mar 1986	Wales	0–1
25 May 1986	Iceland	2–1
27 May 1986	Czechoslovakia	1–0
1 Apr 1987	Bulgaria	1–2
29 Apr 1987	Belgium	0–0
23 May 1987	Brazil	1–0
28 May 1987	Luxembourg	2–0
23 Mar 1988	Romania	2–0
27 Apr 1988	Yugoslavia	2–0
19 Oct 1988	Tunisia	4–0

Jeff Chandler

286. JEFF CHANDLER

Position Winger
Born Hammersmith, 19 June 1959
Club Blackpool; Leeds United; Bolton
Wanderers; Derby County;
Mansfield Town (loan); Bolton
Wanderers; Cardiff City
Caps 2

Date	Team	Result	Goals
26 Sep 1979	Czechoslovakia	1–4	
29 Oct 1979	United States	3–2	

287. JOHN DEVINE

Position Midfield
Born Dublin, 11 November 1958
Club Arsenal; Norwich City; Stoke City; IK
Start (Norway); Shamrock Rovers
Caps 13

Date	Team	Result	Goals
26 Sep 1979	Czechoslovakia	1–4	
21 Nov 1979	Northern Ireland	0–1	
29 Apr 1981	Czechoslovakia	3–1	
21 May 1981	West Germany 'B'	0–3	
9 Sep 1981	Holland	2–2	
28 Apr 1982	Algeria	0–2	
17 Nov 1982	Spain	3–3	
30 Mar 1983	Malta	1–0	
21 Sep 1983	Iceland	3–0	
12 Oct 1983	Holland	2–3	
4 Apr 1984	Israel	0–3	
12 Sep 1984	USSR	1–0	
17 Oct 1984	Norway	0–1	

288. TERRY DONOVAN

Position Forward
Born Liverpool, 27 February 1958
Club Louth United; Grimsby Town; Aston
Villa; Oxford United (loan); Burnley;
Rotherham United; Blackpool (loan)
Caps 2

Date	Team	Result	Goals
26 Sep 1979	Czechoslovakia	1–4	
21 May 1981	West Germany 'B'	0–3	

289. FRAN O'BRIEN

Position Full-back
Born Dublin, 1955
Club Bohemians; Philadelphia Fury
(United States)
Caps 3

Date	Team	Result	Goals
26 Sep 1979	Czechoslovakia	1–4	
6 Feb 1980	England	0–2	
26 Mar 1980	Cyprus	3–2	

290. PIERCE O'LEARY

Position	Centre-half
Born	Dublin, 5 November 1959
Club	Shamrock Rovers; Philadelphia Fury (United States); Vancouver Whitecaps (Canada); Glasgow Celtic
Caps	7

Date	Team	Result	Goals
26 Sep 1979	Czechoslovakia	1–4	
17 Oct 1979	Bulgaria	3–0	
29 Oct 1979	United States	3–2	
21 Nov 1979	Northern Ireland	0–1	
6 Feb 1980	England	0–2	
16 May 1980	Argentina	0–1	
10 Sep 1980	Holland	2–1	

291. CHRIS HUGHTON

Position	Full-back
Born	Stratford, 1 December 1958
Club	Tottenham Hotspur; West Ham United; Brentford
Caps	53

Date	Team	Result	Goals
29 Oct 1979	United States	3–2	
6 Feb 1980	England	0–2	
30 Apr 1980	Switzerland	2–0	
16 May 1980	Argentina	0–1	
10 Sep 1980	Holland	2–1	
15 Oct 1980	Belgium	1–1	
28 Oct 1980	France	0–2	
19 Nov 1980	Cyprus	6–0	1
24 Feb 1981	Wales	1–3	
25 Mar 1981	Belgium	0–1	
24 May 1981	Poland	0–3	
14 Oct 1981	France	3–2	
22 Sep 1982	Holland	1–2	
17 Nov 1982	Spain	3–3	
30 Mar 1983	Malta	1–0	
27 Apr 1983	Spain	0–2	
21 Sep 1983	Iceland	3–0	
12 Oct 1983	Holland	2–3	
16 Nov 1983	Malta	8–0	
8 Aug 1984	Mexico	0–0	
12 Sep 1984	USSR	1–0	
17 Oct 1984	Norway	0–1	
5 Feb 1985	Italy	1–2	
27 Feb 1985	Israel	0–0	
26 Mar 1985	England	1–2	
26 May 1985	Spain	0–0	
11 Sep 1985	Switzerland	0–0	
16 Oct 1985	USSR	0–2	
23 Apr 1986	Uruguay	1–1	
25 May 1986	Iceland	2–1	
10 Sep 1986	Belgium	2–2	
1 Apr 1987	Bulgaria	1–2	
10 Nov 1987	Israel	5–0	
27 Apr 1988	Yugoslavia	2–0	
22 May 1988	Poland	3–1	
1 Jun 1988	Norway	0–0	
12 Jun 1988	England	1–0	
15 Jun 1988	USSR	1–1	
18 Jun 1988	Holland	0–1	
14 Sep 1988	Northern Ireland	0–0	
7 Feb 1989	France	0–0	
8 Mar 1989	Hungary	0–0	
26 Apr 1989	Spain	1–0	
28 May 1989	Malta	2–0	
4 Jul 1989	Hungary	2–0	
28 Mar 1990	Wales	1–0	
25 Apr 1990	USSR	1–0	
16 May 1990	Finland	1–1	
27 May 1990	Turkey	0–0	
2 Jun 1990	Malta	3–0	
17 Oct 1990	Turkey	5–0	
22 May 1991	Chile	1–1	
13 Nov 1991	Turkey	3–1	

Did you know?

The Republic of Ireland's longest competitive winning streak is five games. This was achieved in 1989 during the 1990 World Cup qualification campaign.

292. KEVIN MORAN

Position	Central defender
Born	Dublin, 29 April 1956
Club	Manchester United; Sporting Gijon (Spain); Blackburn Rovers
Caps	71

Date	Team	Result	Goals
30 Apr 1980	Switzerland	2–0	
16 May 1980	Argentina	0–1	
15 Oct 1980	Belgium	1–1	
28 Oct 1980	France	0–2	
19 Nov 1980	Cyprus	6–0	
24 Feb 1981	Wales	1–3	
25 Mar 1981	Belgium	0–1	
29 Apr 1981	Czechoslovakia	3–1	2
21 May 1981	West Germany 'B'	0–3	
24 May 1981	Poland	0–3	
14 Oct 1981	France	3–2	
28 Apr 1982	Algeria	0–2	
13 Oct 1982	Iceland	2–0	
21 Sep 1983	Iceland	3–0	
12 Oct 1983	Holland	2–3	
16 Nov 1983	Malta	8–0	
4 Apr 1984	Israel	0–3	
8 Aug 1984	Mexico	0–0	
13 Nov 1985	Denmark	1–4	
25 May 1986	Iceland	2–1	
27 May 1986	Czechoslovakia	1–0	
10 Sep 1986	Belgium	2–2	
15 Oct 1986	Scotland	0–0	
12 Nov 1986	Poland	0–1	
18 Feb 1987	Scotland	1–0	

Date	Team	Result	Goals
1 Apr 1987	Bulgaria	1–2	
29 Apr 1987	Belgium	0–0	
23 May 1987	Brazil	1–0	
28 May 1987	Luxembourg	2–0	
9 Sep 1987	Luxembourg	2–1	
14 Oct 1987	Bulgaria	2–0	1
10 Nov 1987	Israel	5–0	
23 Mar 1988	Romania	2–0	1
27 Apr 1988	Yugoslavia	2–0	1
22 May 1988	Poland	3–1	
1 Jun 1988	Norway	0–0	
12 Jun 1988	England	1–0	
15 Jun 1988	USSR	1–1	
18 Jun 1988	Holland	0–1	
14 Sep 1988	Northern Ireland	0–0	
16 Nov 1988	Spain	0–2	
8 Mar 1989	Hungary	0–0	
26 Apr 1989	Spain	1–0	
28 May 1989	Malta	2–0	1
4 Jul 1989	Hungary	2–0	
11 Oct 1989	Northern Ireland	3–0	
15 Nov 1989	Malta	2–0	
28 Mar 1990	Wales	1–0	
25 Apr 1990	USSR	1–0	
2 Jun 1990	Malta	3–0	
11 Jun 1990	England	1–1	
17 Jun 1990	Egypt	0–0	
21 Jun 1990	Holland	1–1	
25 Jun 1990	Romania	0–0 won 5–4 on penalties	
30 Jun 1990	Italy	0–1	

Date	Team	Result
17 Oct 1990	Turkey	5–0
6 Feb 1991	Wales	3–0
27 Mar 1991	England	1–1
1 May 1991	Poland	0–0
22 May 1991	Chile	1–1
1 Jun 1991	United States	1–1
16 Oct 1991	Poland	3–3
30 May 1992	United States	1–3
14 Oct 1992	Denmark	0–0
18 Nov 1992	Spain	0–0
31 Mar 1993	Northern Ireland	3–0
26 May 1993	Albania	2–1
16 Jun 1993	Lithuania	1–0
13 Oct 1993	Spain	1–3
20 Apr 1994	Holland	1–0
24 May 1994	Bolivia	1–0

Gary Waddock

293. GARY WADDOCK

Position	Midfield
Born	Kingsbury, 17 March 1962
Club	Queen's Park Rangers; Charleroi (Belgium); Millwall; Queen's Park Rangers; Swindon Town (loan); Bristol Rovers; Luton Town
Caps	21

Date	Team	Result	Goals
30 Apr 1980	Switzerland	2–0	
16 May 1980	Argentina	0–1	
24 Feb 1981	Wales	1–3	
24 May 1981	Poland	0–3	
28 Apr 1982	Algeria	0–2	
22 Sep 1982	Holland	1–2	
13 Oct 1982	Iceland	2–0	
30 Mar 1983	Malta	1–0	
27 Apr 1983	Spain	0–2	
21 Sep 1983	Iceland	3–0	1
12 Oct 1983	Holland	2–3	1
16 Nov 1983	Malta	8–0	
4 Apr 1984	Israel	0–3	
5 Feb 1985	Italy	1–2	1
27 Feb 1985	Israel	0–0	
26 Mar 1985	England	1–2	
1 May 1985	Norway	0–0	
26 May 1985	Spain	0–0	
16 Oct 1985	USSR	0–2	
25 Apr 1990	USSR	1–0	
27 May 1990	Turkey	0–0	

294. MICHAEL ROBINSON

Position	Forward
Born	Leicester, 12 July 1958
Club	Preston North End; Manchester City; Brighton & Hove Albion; Liverpool; Queen's Park Rangers; Osasuna (Spain)
Caps	24

Date	Team	Result	Goals
28 Oct 1980	France	0–2	

Michael Robinson

Date	Team	Result	Goals
19 Nov 1980	Cyprus	6–0	1
25 Mar 1981	Belgium	0–1	
21 May 1981	West Germany 'B'	0–3	
24 May 1981	Poland	0–3	
9 Sep 1981	Holland	2–2	1
14 Oct 1981	France	3–2	1
28 Apr 1982	Algeria	0–2	
21 May 1982	Chile	0–1	
22 Sep 1982	Holland	1–2	
13 Oct 1982	Iceland	2–0	
17 Nov 1982	Spain	3–3	
30 Mar 1983	Malta	1–0	
21 Sep 1983	Iceland	3–0	1
12 Oct 1983	Holland	2–3	
4 Apr 1984	Israel	0–3	
8 Aug 1984	Mexico	0–0	
17 Oct 1984	Norway	0–1	
1 May 1985	Norway	0–0	
26 May 1985	Spain	0–0	
2 Jun 1985	Switzerland	3–0	
13 Nov 1985	Denmark	1–4	
26 Mar 1986	Wales	0–1	
27 May 1986	Czechoslovakia	1–0	

295. JIM McDONAGH

Position	Goalkeeper
Born	Rotherham, 6 October 1952
Club	Rotherham United; Bolton Wanderers; Everton; Bolton Wanderers; Notts County; Birmingham City (loan); Gillingham (loan); Sunderland (loan); Wichita Wings (United States); Scarborough; Huddersfield Town (loan); Charlton Athletic
Caps	25

Date	Team	Result	Goals
24 Feb 1981	Wales	1–3	
25 Mar 1981	Belgium	0–1	
29 Apr 1981	Czechoslovakia	3–1	
21 May 1981	West Germany 'B'	0–3	
9 Sep 1981	Holland	2–2	
14 Oct 1981	France	3–2	
21 May 1982	Chile	0–1	
27 May 1982	Brazil	0–7	
22 Sep 1982	Holland	1–2	
13 Oct 1982	Iceland	2–0	
17 Nov 1982	Spain	3–3	
30 Mar 1983	Malta	1–0	
27 Apr 1983	Spain	0–2	
21 Sep 1983	Iceland	3–0	
12 Oct 1983	Holland	2–3	
23 May 1984	Poland	0–0	
8 Aug 1984	Mexico	0–0	
12 Sep 1984	USSR	1–0	

Jim McDonagh

17 Oct 1984	Norway	0–1
14 Nov 1984	Denmark	0–3
26 May 1985	Spain	0–0
2 Jun 1985	Switzerland	3–0
11 Sep 1985	Switzerland	0–0
16 Oct 1985	USSR	0–2
13 Nov 1985	Denmark	1–4

296. EAMONN O'KEEFE

Position Forward
Born Manchester, 13 October 1953
Club Stalybridge Celtic; Plymouth Argyle;
Hyde United; Mossley; Everton;
Wigan Athletic; Port Vale;
Blackpool; St Patrick's Athletic;
Chester City
Caps 5

Date	Team	Result	Goal
24 Feb 1981	Wales	1–3	
3 Jun 1984	China	1–0	1
8 Aug 1984	Mexico	0–0	
12 Sep 1984	USSR	1–0	
26 Mar 1985	England	1–2	

Eamonn O'Keefe

297. KEVIN O'CALLAGHAN

Position Left-winger
Born Dagenham, 19 October 1961
Club Millwall; Ipswich Town;
Portsmouth; Millwall; Southend
United
Caps 21

Date	Team	Result	Goals
29 Apr 1981	Czechoslovakia	3–1	
21 May 1981	West Germany 'B'	0–3	
24 May 1981	Poland	0–3	
28 Apr 1982	Algeria	0–2	
21 May 1982	Chile	0–1	
27 May 1982	Brazil	0–7	
30 May 1982	Trinidad & Tobago	1–2	
13 Oct 1982	Iceland	2–0	
17 Nov 1982	Spain	3–3	
30 Mar 1983	Malta	1–0	
27 Apr 1983	Spain	0–2	
21 Sep 1983	Iceland	3–0	
12 Oct 1983	Holland	2–3	
16 Nov 1983	Malta	8–0	1
8 Aug 1984	Mexico	0–0	
17 Oct 1984	Norway	0–1	
14 Nov 1984	Denmark	0–3	
26 Mar 1985	England	1–2	
11 Sep 1985	Switzerland	0–0	
16 Oct 1985	USSR	0–2	
23 May 1987	Brazil	1–0	

298. RONNIE WHELAN JNR

Position Midfield
Born Dublin, 25 September 1961
Club Home Farm; Liverpool; Southend
United
Caps 53

Date	Team	Result	Goals
29 Apr 1981	Czechoslovakia	3–1	
9 Sep 1981	Holland	2–2	
14 Oct 1981	France	3–2	
13 Oct 1982	Iceland	2–0	

30 Mar 1983	Malta	1–0	
27 Apr 1983	Spain	0–2	
4 Apr 1984	Israel	0–3	
12 Sep 1984	USSR	1–0	
17 Oct 1984	Norway	0–1	
5 Feb 1985	Italy	1–2	
27 Feb 1985	Israel	0–0	
26 Mar 1985	England	1–2	
1 May 1985	Norway	0–0	
2 Jun 1985	Switzerland	3–0	
16 Oct 1985	USSR	0–2	
26 Mar 1986	Wales	0–1	
10 Sep 1986	Belgium	2–2	
18 Feb 1987	Scotland	1–0	
1 Apr 1987	Bulgaria	1–2	
29 Apr 1987	Belgium	0–0	
23 May 1987	Brazil	1–0	
28 May 1987	Luxembourg	2–0	1
9 Sep 1987	Luxembourg	2–1	
14 Oct 1987	Bulgaria	2–0	
22 May 1988	Poland	3–1	
1 Jun 1988	Norway	0–0	
12 Jun 1988	England	1–0	
15 Jun 1988	USSR	1–1	1
18 Jun 1988	Holland	0–1	
14 Sep 1988	Northern Ireland	0–0	
7 Feb 1989	France	0–0	
8 Mar 1989	Hungary	0–0	
26 Apr 1989	Spain	1–0	
28 May 1989	Malta	2–0	
6 Sep 1989	West Germany	1–1	
11 Oct 1989	Northern Ireland	3–0	1
15 Nov 1989	Malta	2–0	
28 Mar 1990	Wales	1–0	
21 Jun 1990	Holland	1–1	
12 Sep 1990	Morocco	1–0	
14 Nov 1990	England	1–1	
25 Mar 1992	Switzerland	2–1	
9 Sep 1992	Latvia	4–0	
17 Feb 1993	Wales	2–1	

16 Jun 1993	Lithuania	1–0
8 Sep 1993	Lithuania	2–0
13 Oct 1993	Spain	1–3
23 Mar 1994	Russia	0–0
20 Apr 1994	Holland	1–0
29 May 1994	Germany	2–0
28 Jun 1994	Norway	0–0
3 Jun 1995	Liechtenstein	0–0
11 Jun 1995	Austria	1–3

299. PACKIE BONNER

Position	Goalkeeper
Born	Clochglas, County Donegal, 24 May 1960
Club	Keadue Rovers; Glasgow Celtic; Kilmarnock; Glasgow Celtic
Caps	80

Date	Team	Result	Goals
24 May 1981	Poland	0–3	
28 Apr 1982	Algeria	0–2	
16 Nov 1983	Malta	8–0	
4 Apr 1984	Israel	0–3	
3 Jun 1984	China	1–0	
5 Feb 1985	Italy	1–2	
27 Feb 1985	Israel	0–0	
26 Mar 1985	England	1–2	
1 May 1985	Norway	0–0	
23 Apr 1986	Uruguay	1–1	
25 May 1986	Iceland	2–1	
10 Sep 1986	Belgium	2–2	
15 Oct 1986	Scotland	0–0	
12 Nov 1986	Poland	0–1	
18 Feb 1987	Scotland	1–0	
1 Apr 1987	Bulgaria	1–2	
29 Apr 1987	Belgium	0–0	
23 May 1987	Brazil	1–0	
28 May 1987	Luxembourg	2–0	
14 Oct 1987	Bulgaria	2–0	
23 Mar 1988	Romania	2–0	
27 Apr 1988	Yugoslavia	2–0	

Date	Team	Result		Date	Team	Result
1 Jun 1988	Norway	0–0		17 Feb 1993	Wales	2–1
12 Jun 1988	England	1–0		31 Mar 1993	Northern Ireland	3–0
15 Jun 1988	USSR	1–1		28 Apr 1993	Denmark	1–1
18 Jun 1988	Holland	0–1		26 May 1993	Albania	2–1
16 Nov 1988	Spain	0–2		9 Jun 1993	Latvia	2–0
7 Feb 1989	France	0–0		16 Jun 1993	Lithuania	1–0
8 Mar 1989	Hungary	0–0		8 Sep 1993	Lithuania	2–0
26 Apr 1989	Spain	1–0		13 Oct 1993	Spain	1–3
28 May 1989	Malta	2–0		17 Nov 1993	Northern Ireland	1–1
4 Jul 1989	Hungary	2–0		23 Mar 1994	USSR	0–0
6 Sep 1989	West Germany	1–1		20 Apr 1994	Holland	1–0
11 Oct 1989	Northern Ireland	3–0		24 May 1994	Bolivia	1–0
15 Nov 1989	Malta	2–0		5 Jun 1994	Czech Republic	1–3
28 Mar 1990	Wales	1–0		18 Jun 1994	Italy	1–0
16 May 1990	Finland	1–1		24 Jun 1994	Mexico	1–2
27 May 1990	Turkey	0–0		28 Jun 1994	Norway	0–0
11 Jun 1990	England	1–1		4 Jul 1994	Holland	0–2
17 Jun 1990	Egypt	0–0		12 Oct 1994	Liechtenstein	4–0
21 Jun 1990	Holland	1–1		12 Jun 1996	Mexico	2–2
25 Jun 1990	Romania	0–0 won 5–4 on penalties		15 Jun 1996	Bolivia	3–0
30 Jun 1990	Italy	0–1				
12 Sep 1990	Morocco	1–0				
17 Oct 1990	Turkey	5–0				
14 Nov 1990	England	1–1				
6 Feb 1991	Wales	3–0				
27 Mar 1991	England	1–1				
1 May 1991	Poland	0–0				
1 Jun 1991	United States	1–1				
11 Sep 1991	Hungary	2–1				
16 Oct 1991	Poland	3–3				
13 Nov 1991	Turkey	3–1				
19 Feb 1992	Wales	0–1				
25 Mar 1992	Switzerland	2–1				
26 May 1992	Albania	2–0				
4 Jun 1992	Italy	0–2				
9 Sep 1992	Latvia	4–0				
14 Oct 1992	Denmark	0–0				
18 Nov 1992	Spain	0–0				

Did you know?

Packie Bonner, Celtic's Republic of Ireland goalkeeper in the 1990 World Cup, played for Leicester City in the 1975–76 FA Youth Cup.

300. EAMONN DEACY

Position	Full-back
Born	Galway, 1 October 1958
Club	Galway Rovers; Aston Villa; Derby County (loan); Galway United
Caps	4

Date	Team	Result	Goals
28 Apr 1982	Algeria	0–2	
21 May 1982	Chile	0–1	
27 May 1982	Brazil	0–7	
30 May 1982	Trinidad & Tobago	1–2	

301. MICK FAIRCLOUGH

Position	Midfield; Forward
Born	Drogheda, 22 October 1952
Club	Drogheda; Huddersfield Town; Dundalk; Sligo Rovers; Newry Town
Caps	2

Date	Team	Result	Goals
21 May 1982	Chile	0–1	
30 May 1982	Trinidad & Tobago	1–2	

302. SEAN O'DRISCOLL

Position	Midfield
Born	Wolverhampton, 1 July 1957
Club	Alvechurch; Fulham; Bournemouth
Caps	3

Date	Team	Result	Goals
21 May 1982	Chile	0–1	
27 May 1982	Brazil	0–7	
30 May 1982	Trinidad & Tobago	1–2	

303. MIKE WALSH

Position	Central defender
Born	Manchester, 20 June 1956
Club	Bolton Wanderers; Everton; Norwich City (loan); Burnley (loan); Fort Lauderdale Strikers (United States); Manchester City; Blackpool; Bury
Caps	4

Date	Team	Result	Goals
21 May 1982	Chile	0–1	
27 May 1982	Brazil	0–7	
30 May 1982	Trinidad & Tobago	1–2	
13 Oct 1982	Iceland	2–0	

304. JOHNNY WALSH

Position	Forward
Born	Limerick, 8 November 1957
Club	Wembley Rovers; Limerick
Caps	1

Date	Team	Result	Goals
30 May 1982	Trinidad & Tobago	1–2	

305. TONY GALVIN

Position	Left-winger
Born	Huddersfield, 12 July 1956
Club	Goole Town; Tottenham Hotspur; Sheffield Wednesday; Swindon Town
Caps	29

Date	Team	Result	Goals
22 Sep 1982	Holland	1–2	
30 Mar 1983	Malta	1–0	
12 Oct 1983	Holland	2–3	
4 Apr 1984	Israel	0–3	
8 Aug 1984	Mexico	0–0	
12 Sep 1984	USSR	1–0	
17 Oct 1984	Norway	0–1	
14 Nov 1984	Denmark	0–3	
5 Feb 1985	Italy	1–2	
1 May 1985	Norway	0–0	

Mike Walsh

Date	Team	Result	Goals
26 May 1985	Spain	0–0	
23 Apr 1986	Uruguay	1–1	
25 May 1986	Iceland	2–1	
27 May 1986	Czechoslovakia	1–0	
10 Sep 1986	Belgium	2–2	
18 Feb 1987	Scotland	1–0	
1 Apr 1987	Bulgaria	1–2	
29 Apr 1987	Belgium	0–0	
28 May 1987	Luxembourg	2–0	1
9 Sep 1987	Luxembourg	2–1	
14 Oct 1987	Bulgaria	2–0	
23 Mar 1988	Romania	2–0	
22 May 1988	Poland	3–1	
1 Jun 1988	Norway	0–0	
12 Jun 1988	England	1–0	
15 Jun 1988	USSR	1–1	
18 Jun 1988	Holland	0–1	
16 Nov 1988	Spain	0–2	
6 Sep 1989	West Germany	1–1	

306. KEVIN SHEEDY

Position	Midfield
Born	Builth Wells, 21 October 1959
Club	Hereford United; Liverpool; Everton; Newcastle United; Blackpool
Caps	45

Date	Team	Result	Goals
12 Oct 1983	Holland	2–3	
16 Nov 1983	Malta	8–0	1
14 Nov 1984	Denmark	0–3	
5 Feb 1985	Italy	1–2	
27 Feb 1985	Israel	0–0	
2 Jun 1985	Switzerland	3–0	1
11 Sep 1985	Switzerland	0–0	
13 Nov 1985	Denmark	1–4	
15 Oct 1986	Scotland	0–0	
12 Nov 1986	Poland	0–1	
10 Nov 1987	Israel	5–0	
23 Mar 1988	Romania	2–0	
22 May 1988	Poland	3–1	1

Date	Team	Result	Goals
12 Jun 1988	England	1–0	
15 Jun 1988	USSR	1–1	
14 Sep 1988	Northern Ireland	0–0	
19 Oct 1988	Tunisia	4–0	1
8 Mar 1989	Hungary	0–0	
26 Apr 1989	Spain	1–0	
28 May 1989	Malta	2–0	
4 July 1989	Hungary	2–0	
11 Oct 1989	Northern Ireland	3–0	
15 Nov 1989	Malta	2–0	
28 Mar 1990	Wales	1–0	
25 Apr 1990	USSR	1–0	
16 May 1990	Finland	1–1	1
27 May 1990	Turkey	0–0	
11 Jun 1990	England	1–1	1
17 Jun 1990	Egypt	0–0	
21 Jun 1990	Holland	1–1	
25 Jun 1990	Romania	0–0 won 5–4 on penalties	
30 Jun 1990	Italy	0–1	
6 Feb 1991	Wales	3–0	
27 Mar 1991	England	1–1	
1 May 1991	Poland	0–0	
22 May 1991	Chile	1–1	
1 Jun 1991	United States	1–1	
11 Sep 1991	Hungary	2–1	1
16 Oct 1991	Poland	3–3	
13 Nov 1991	Turkey	3–1	
19 Feb 1992	Wales	0–1	
25 Mar 1992	Switzerland	2–1	
26 May 1992	Albania	2–0	
9 Sep 1992	Latvia	4–0	1
17 Feb 1993	Wales	2–1	1

307. JACKO McDONAGH

Position	Centre-half
Born	Dublin, 1960
Club	Bohemians; Shamrock Rovers; Nimes Olympic (France)
Caps	3

Date	Team	Result	Goals
16 Nov 1983	Malta	8–0	
23 May 1984	Poland	0–0	
8 Aug 1984	Mexico	0–0	

308. KIERAN O'REGAN

Position	Defender; Midfield
Born	Cork, 9 November 1963
Club	Tramore Athletic; Brighton & Hove Albion; Swindon Town; Huddersfield Town; West Bromwich Albion
Caps	4

Date	Team	Result	Goals
16 Nov 1983	Malta	8–0	
23 May 1984	Poland	0–0	
8 Aug 1984	Mexico	0–0	
26 May 1985	Spain	0–0	

309. LIAM BUCKLEY

Position	Forward
Born	Dublin, 14 April 1960
Club	Shelbourne; Shamrock Rovers; KSV Waregem (Belgium); Shamrock Rovers; St Patrick's Athletic
Caps	2

Date	Team	Result	Goals
23 May 1984	Poland	0–0	
8 Aug 1984	Mexico	0–0	

310. PAT BYRNE

Position	Midfield
Born	Dublin, 15 May 1956
Club	Bohemians; Philadelphia Fury (United States); Shelbourne; Leicester City; Heart of Midlothian; Shamrock Rovers; Shelbourne; Cobh Ramblers
Caps	8

Date	Team	Result	Goals
23 May 1984	Poland	0–0	
3 Jun 1984	China	1–0	

Date	Team	Result	Goals
8 Aug 1984	Mexico	0–0	
26 May 1985	Spain	0–0	
13 Nov 1985	Denmark	1–4	
26 Mar 1986	Wales	0–1	
25 May 1986	Iceland	2–1	
27 May 1986	Czechoslovakia	1–0	

311. MICK McCARTHY

Position	Central defender
Born	Barnsley, 7 February 1959
Club	Barnsley; Manchester City; Glasgow Celtic; Olympique Lyon (France); Millwall
Caps	57

Date	Team	Result	Goals
23 May 1984	Poland	0–0	
3 Jun 1984	China	1–0	
8 Aug 1984	Mexico	0–0	
14 Nov 1984	Denmark	0–3	
5 Feb 1985	Italy	1–2	
27 Feb 1985	Israel	0–0	
26 Mar 1985	England	1–2	
26 May 1985	Spain	0–0	
2 Jun 1985	Switzerland	3–0	
11 Sep 1985	Switzerland	0–0	
16 Oct 1985	USSR	0–2	
26 Mar 1986	Wales	0–1	
23 Apr 1986	Uruguay	1–1	
25 May 1986	Iceland	2–1	
27 May 1986	Czechoslovakia	1–0	
15 Oct 1986	Scotland	0–0	
12 Nov 1986	Poland	0–1	
18 Feb 1987	Scotland	1–0	
1 Apr 1987	Bulgaria	1–2	
29 Apr 1987	Belgium	0–0	
23 May 1987	Brazil	1–0	
28 May 1987	Luxembourg	2–0	
14 Oct 1987	Bulgaria	2–0	
10 Nov 1987	Israel	5–0	
23 Mar 1988	Romania	2–0	
27 Apr 1988	Yugoslavia	2–0	1

Date	Team	Result	Goals
1 Jun 1988	Norway	0–0	
12 Jun 1988	England	1–0	
15 Jun 1988	USSR	1–1	
18 Jun 1988	Holland	0–1	
14 Sep 1988	Northern Ireland	0–0	
19 Oct 1988	Tunisia	4–0	
16 Nov 1988	Spain	0–2	
7 Feb 1989	France	0–0	
8 Mar 1989	Hungary	0–0	
26 Apr 1989	Spain	1–0	
6 Sep 1989	West Germany	1–1	
11 Oct 1989	Northern Ireland	3–0	
28 Mar 1990	Wales	1–0	
25 Apr 1990	USSR	1–0	
16 May 1990	Finland	1–1	
27 May 1990	Turkey	0–0	
11 Jun 1990	England	1–1	
17 Jun 1990	Egypt	0–0	
21 Jun 1990	Holland	1–1	
25 Jun 1990	Romania	0–0 won 5–4 on penalties	
30 Jun 1990	Italy	0–1	
12 Sep 1990	Morocco	1–0	
17 Oct 1990	Turkey	5–0	
14 Nov 1990	England	1–1	
1 Jun 1991	United States	1–1	
11 Sep 1991	Hungary	2–1	
13 Nov 1991	Turkey	3–1	
26 May 1992	Albania	2–0	
30 May 1992	United States	1–3	1
4 Jun 1992	Italy	0–2	
7 Jun 1992	Portugal	2–0	

312. JIM BEGLIN

Position	Left-back
Born	Waterford, 29 July 1963
Club	Shamrock Rovers; Liverpool; Leeds United; Plymouth Argyle (loan); Blackburn Rovers (loan)
Caps	15

Date	Team	Result	Goals
3 Jun 1984	China	1–0	
8 Aug 1984	Mexico	0–0	
14 Nov 1984	Denmark	0–3	
5 Feb 1985	Italy	1–2	
27 Feb 1985	Israel	0–0	
26 Mar 1985	England	1–2	
1 May 1985	Norway	0–0	
2 Jun 1985	Switzerland	3–0	
11 Sep 1985	Switzerland	0–0	
16 Oct 1985	USSR	0–2	
13 Nov 1985	Denmark	1–4	
26 Mar 1986	Wales	0–1	
10 Sep 1986	Belgium	2–2	
15 Oct 1986	Scotland	0–0	
12 Nov 1986	Poland	0–1	

313. GARY HOWLETT

Position	Midfield
Born	Dublin, 2 April 1963
Club	Home Farm; Coventry City; Brighton & Hove Albion; Bournemouth; Aldershot (loan); Chester City (loan); York City; Shelbourne
Caps	1

Date	Team	Result	Goals
3 Jun 1984	China	1–0	

314. JOHN BYRNE

Position	Forward
Born	Manchester, 1 February 1961
Club	York City; Queen's Park Rangers; Le Havre (France); Brighton & Hove Albion; Sunderland; Millwall; Brighton & Hove Albion (loan); Oxford United; Brighton & Hove Albion; Crawley Town;
Caps	23

Date	Team	Result	Goals
5 Feb 1985	Italy	1–2	
27 Feb 1985	Israel	0–0	

26 Mar 1985	England	1–2	
23 Apr 1986	Uruguay	1–1	
18 Feb 1987	Scotland	1–0	
29 Apr 1987	Belgium	0–0	
23 May 1987	Brazil	1–0	
28 May 1987	Luxembourg	2–0	
9 Sep 1987	Luxembourg	2–1	
14 Oct 1987	Bulgaria	2–0	
10 Nov 1987	Israel	5–0	1
23 Mar 1988	Romania	2–0	
27 Apr 1988	Yugoslavia	2–0	
22 May 1988	Poland	3–1	
6 Sep 1989	West Germany	1–1	
28 Mar 1990	Wales	1–0	
16 May 1990	Finland	1–1	
27 May 1990	Turkey	0–0	
2 Jun 1990	Malta	3–0	
6 Feb 1991	Wales	3–0	1
13 Nov 1991	Turkey	3–1	2
19 Feb 1992	Wales	0–1	
17 Feb 1993	Wales	2–1	

John Byrne

315. ALAN CAMPBELL

Position	Centre-forward
Born	Dublin, 1958
Club	Shamrock Rovers; Racing Santander (Spain)
Caps	3

Date	Team	Result	Goals
5 Feb 1985	Italy	1–2	
27 Feb 1985	Israel	0–0	
26 May 1985	Spain	0–0	

316. PAUL McGRATH

Position	Central defender; Midfield
Born	Ealing, 4 December 1959
Club	St Patrick's Athletic; Manchester United; Aston Villa; Derby County; Sheffield United
Caps	83

Date	Team	Result	Goals
5 Feb 1985	Italy	1–2	
27 Feb 1985	Israel	0–0	
26 Mar 1985	England	1–2	
1 May 1985	Norway	0–0	
2 Jun 1985	Switzerland	3–0	
11 Sep 1985	Switzerland	0–0	
13 Nov 1985	Denmark	1–4	
26 Mar 1986	Wales	0–1	
25 May 1986	Iceland	2–1	1
27 May 1986	Czechoslovakia	1–0	
10 Sep 1986	Belgium	2–2	
15 Oct 1986	Scotland	0–0	
12 Nov 1986	Poland	0–1	
18 Feb 1987	Scotland	1–0	
1 Apr 1987	Bulgaria	1–2	
29 Apr 1987	Belgium	0–0	
23 May 1987	Brazil	1–0	
28 May 1987	Luxembourg	2–0	
9 Sep 1987	Luxembourg	2–1	1
14 Oct 1987	Bulgaria	2–0	1
27 Apr 1988	Yugoslavia	2–0	
22 May 1988	Poland	3–1	

1 Jun 1988	Norway	0–0	
12 Jun 1988	England	1–0	
18 Jun 1988	Holland	0–1	
14 Sep 1988	Northern Ireland	0–0	
7 Feb 1989	France	0–0	
8 Mar 1989	Hungary	0–0	
26 Apr 1989	Spain	1–0	
28 May 1989	Malta	2–0	
4 Jul 1989	Hungary	2–0	1
6 Sep 1989	West Germany	1–1	
15 Nov 1989	Malta	2–0	
25 Apr 1990	USSR	1–0	
16 May 1990	Finland	1–1	
27 May 1990	Turkey	0–0	
11 Jun 1990	England	1–1	
17 Jun 1990	Egypt	0–0	
21 Jun 1990	Holland	1–1	
25 Jun 1990	Romania	0–0 won 5–4 on penalties	
30 Jun 1990	Italy	0–1	
14 Nov 1990	England	1–1	
6 Feb 1991	Wales	3–0	
27 Mar 1991	England	1–1	
1 May 1991	Poland	0–0	
22 May 1991	Chile	1–1	
1 Jun 1991	United States	1–1	
16 Oct 1991	Poland	3–3	1
13 Nov 1991	Turkey	3–1	
25 Mar 1992	Switzerland	2–1	
29 Apr 1992	United States	4–1	
26 May 1992	Albania	2–0	1
30 May 1992	United States	1–3	
4 Jun 1992	Italy	0–2	
7 Jun 1992	Portugal	2–0	
9 Sep 1992	Latvia	4–0	
18 Nov 1992	Spain	0–0	
31 Mar 1993	Northern Ireland	3–0	
28 Apr 1993	Denmark	1–1	
9 Jun 1993	Latvia	2–0	1

Paul McGrath

16 Jun 1993	Lithuania	1–0	
8 Sep 1993	Lithuania	2–0	
17 Nov 1993	Northern Ireland	1–1	
29 May 1994	Germany	2–0	
5 Jun 1994	Czech Republic	1–3	
18 Jun 1994	Italy	1–0	
24 Jun 1994	Mexico	1–2	
28 Jun 1994	Norway	0–0	
4 Jul 1994	Holland	0–2	
7 Sep 1994	Latvia	3–0	
16 Nov 1994	Northern Ireland	4–0	
15 Feb 1995	England	1–0	
29 Mar 1995	Northern Ireland	1–1	
26 Apr 1995	Portugal	1–0	
3 Jun 1995	Liechtenstein	0–0	
11 Jun 1995	Austria	1–3	
6 Sep 1995	Austria	1–3	1
11 Oct 1995	Latvia	2–1	
15 Nov 1995	Portugal	0–3	
13 Dec 1995	Holland	0–2	

Date	Team	Result	Goals
27 Mar 1996	Russia	0–2	
24 Apr 1996	Czech Republic	0–2	
11 Feb 1997	Wales	0–0	

317. TONY CASCARINO

Position	Forward
Born	Orpington, 1 September 1962
Club	Crockenhill; Gillingham; Millwall; Aston Villa; Glasgow Celtic; Chelsea; Olympique Marseille (France); AS Nancy-Lorraine (France)
Caps	88

Date	Team	Result	Goals
11 Sep 1985	Switzerland	0–0	
16 Oct 1985	USSR	0–2	
13 Nov 1985	Denmark	1–4	
22 May 1988	Poland	3–1	1
1 Jun 1988	Norway	0–0	
15 Jun 1988	USSR	1–1	
18 Jun 1988	Holland	0–1	
14 Sep 1988	Northern Ireland	0–0	
19 Oct 1988	Tunisia	4–0	2
16 Nov 1988	Spain	0–2	
7 Feb 1989	France	0–0	
8 Mar 1989	Hungary	0–0	
26 Apr 1989	Spain	1–0	
28 May 1989	Malta	2–0	
4 Jul 1989	Hungary	2–0	1
6 Sep 1989	West Germany	1–1	
11 Oct 1989	Northern Ireland	3–0	1
15 Nov 1989	Malta	2–0	
28 Mar 1990	Wales	1–0	
16 May 1990	Finland	1–1	
27 May 1990	Turkey	0–0	
11 Jun 1990	England	1–1	
17 Jun 1990	Egypt	0–0	
21 Jun 1990	Holland	1–1	
25 Jun 1990	Romania	0–0 won 5–4 on penalties	
30 Jun 1990	Italy	0–1	
12 Sep 1990	Morocco	1–0	
17 Oct 1990	Turkey	5–0	
14 Nov 1990	England	1–1	1
27 Mar 1991	England	1–1	
1 May 1991	Poland	0–0	
22 May 1991	Chile	1–1	
1 Jun 1991	United States	1–1	1
16 Oct 1991	Poland	3–3	1
13 Nov 1991	Turkey	3–1	1
19 Feb 1992	Wales	0–1	
25 Mar 1992	Switzerland	2–1	
29 Apr 1992	United States	4–1	1
17 Feb 1993	Wales	2–1	
31 Mar 1993	Northern Ireland	3–0	
28 Apr 1993	Denmark	1–1	
26 May 1993	Albania	2–1	1
9 Jun 1993	Latvia	2–0	
8 Sep 1993	Lithuania	2–0	
13 Oct 1993	Spain	1–3	
17 Nov 1993	Northern Ireland	1–1	
23 Mar 1994	Russia	0–0	
24 May 1994	Bolivia	1–0	
29 May 1994	Germany	2–0	1
5 Jun 1994	Czech Republic	1–3	
4 Jul 1994	Holland	0–2	
7 Sep 1994	Latvia	3–0	
29 Mar 1995	Northern Ireland	1–1	
26 Apr 1995	Portugal	1–0	
3 Jun 1995	Liechtenstein	0–0	
11 Jun 1995	Austria	1–3	
6 Sep 1995	Austria	1–3	
15 Nov 1995	Portugal	0–3	
13 Dec 1995	Holland	0–2	
27 Mar 1996	Russia	0–2	
29 May 1996	Portugal	0–1	
2 Jun 1996	Croatia	2–2	
4 Jun 1996	Holland	1–3	
31 Aug 1996	Liechtenstein	5–0	
9 Oct 1996	Macedonia	3–0	2

Date	Team	Result	Goals
10 Nov 1996	Iceland	0–0	
11 Feb 1997	Wales	0–0	
2 Apr 1997	Macedonia	2–3	
30 Apr 1997	Romania	0–1	
21 May 1997	Liechtenstein	5–0	2
20 Aug 1997	Lithuania	0–0	
6 Sep 1997	Iceland	4–2	
10 Sep 1997	Lithuania	2–1	2
11 Oct 1997	Romania	1–1	1
29 Oct 1997	Belgium	1–1	
16 Nov 1997	Belgium	1–2	
5 Sep 1998	Croatia	2–0	
14 Oct 1998	Malta	5–0	
18 Nov 1998	Yugoslavia	0–1	
10 Feb 1999	Paraguay	2–0	
28 Apr 1999	Sweden	2–0	
29 May 1999	Northern Ireland	0–1	
9 Jun 1999	Macedonia	1–0	
1 Sep 1999	Yugoslavia	2–1	
4 Sep 1999	Croatia	0–1	
9 Oct 1999	Macedonia	1–1	
13 Nov 1999	Turkey	1–1	
17 Nov 1999	Turkey	0–0	

318. JOHN ALDRIDGE

Position	Forward
Born	Liverpool, 18 September 1958
Club	South Liverpool; Newport County; Oxford United; Liverpool; Real Sociedad (Spain); Tranmere Rovers
Caps	69

Date	Team	Result	Goals
26 Mar 1986	Wales	0–1	
23 Apr 1986	Uruguay	1–1	
25 May 1986	Iceland	2–1	
27 May 1986	Czechoslovakia	1–0	
10 Sep 1986	Belgium	2–2	
15 Oct 1986	Scotland	0–0	
12 Nov 1986	Poland	0–1	
18 Feb 1987	Scotland	1–0	
1 Apr 1987	Bulgaria	1–2	
29 Apr 1987	Belgium	0–0	
23 May 1987	Brazil	1–0	
28 May 1987	Luxembourg	2–0	
14 Oct 1987	Bulgaria	2–0	
22 May 1988	Poland	3–0	
1 Jun 1988	Norway	0–0	
12 Jun 1988	England	1–0	
15 Jun 1988	USSR	1–1	
18 Jun 1988	Holland	0–1	
14 Sep 1988	Northern Ireland	0–0	
19 Oct 1988	Tunisia	4–0	1
16 Nov 1988	Spain	0–2	
7 Feb 1989	France	0–0	
8 Mar 1989	Hungary	0–0	
28 May 1989	Malta	2–0	
4 Jul 1989	Hungary	2–0	
6 Sep 1989	West Germany	1–1	
11 Oct 1989	Northern Ireland	3–0	
15 Nov 1989	Malta	2–0	2
16 May 1990	Finland	1–1	
27 May 1990	Turkey	0–0	

Did you know?

John Anderson scored after just three minutes on the field in a match against the United States in 1979, the quickest goal by a substitute. This achievement was later equalled by Tony Cascarino against Albania in 1993.

Date	Team	Result	Goals
11 Jun 1990	England	1–1	
17 Jun 1990	Egypt	0–0	
21 Jun 1990	Holland	1–1	
25 Jun 1990	Romania	0–0 won 5–4 on penalties	
30 Jun 1990	Italy	0–1	
17 Oct 1990	Turkey	5–0	3
14 Nov 1990	England	1–1	
27 Mar 1991	England	1–1	
1 May 1991	Poland	0–0	
11 Sep 1991	Hungary	2–1	
13 Nov 1991	Turkey	3–1	
19 Feb 1992	Wales	0–1	
25 Mar 1992	Switzerland	2–1	1
29 Apr 1992	United States	4–1	
26 May 1992	Albania	2–0	1
4 Jun 1992	Italy	0–2	
7 Jun 1992	Portugal	2–0	
9 Sep 1992	Latvia	4–0	3
14 Oct 1992	Denmark	0–0	
18 Nov 1992	Spain	0–0	
28 Apr 1993	Denmark	1–1	
26 May 1993	Albania	2–1	
9 Jun 1993	Latvia	2–0	1
16 Jun 1993	Lithuania	1–0	
8 Sep 1993	Lithuania	2–0	1
17 Nov 1993	Northern Ireland	1–1	
5 Jun 1994	Czech Republic	1–3	
18 Jun 1994	Italy	1–0	
24 Jun 1994	Mexico	1–2	1
28 Jun 1994	Norway	0–0	
7 Sep 1994	Latvia	3–0	2
16 Nov 1994	Northern Ireland	4–0	1
26 Apr 1995	Portugal	1–0	
3 Jun 1995	Liechtenstein	0–0	
11 Oct 1995	Latvia	2–1	2
15 Nov 1995	Portugal	0–3	
13 Dec 1995	Holland	0–2	
27 Mar 1996	Russia	0–2	
9 Oct 1996	Macedonia	3–0	

319. RAY HOUGHTON

Position	Midfield
Born	Glasgow, 9 January 1962
Club	West Ham United; Fulham; Oxford United; Liverpool; Aston Villa; Crystal Palace; Reading
Caps	73

Date	Team	Result	Goals
26 Mar 1986	Wales	0–1	
23 Apr 1986	Uruguay	1–1	
25 May 1986	Iceland	2–1	
27 May 1986	Czechoslovakia	1–0	
10 Sep 1986	Belgium	2–2	
15 Oct 1986	Scotland	0–0	
12 Nov 1986	Poland	0–1	
18 Feb 1987	Scotland	1–0	
29 Apr 1987	Belgium	0–0	
28 May 1987	Luxembourg	2–0	
9 Sep 1987	Luxembourg	2–1	
14 Oct 1987	Bulgaria	2–0	
10 Nov 1987	Israel	5–0	
27 Apr 1988	Yugoslavia	2–0	
1 Jun 1988	Norway	0–0	
12 Jun 1988	England	1–0	1
15 Jun 1988	USSR	1–1	
18 Jun 1988	Holland	0–1	
14 Sep 1988	Northern Ireland	0–0	
19 Oct 1988	Tunisia	4–0	
16 Nov 1988	Spain	0–2	
7 Feb 1989	France	0–0	
8 Mar 1989	Hungary	0–0	
26 Apr 1989	Spain	1–0	
28 May 1989	Malta	2–0	1
4 Jul 1989	Hungary	2–0	
11 Oct 1989	Northern Ireland	3–0	1
15 Nov 1989	Malta	2–0	
16 May 1990	Finland	1–1	
11 Jun 1990	England	1–1	
17 Jun 1990	Egypt	0–0	
21 Jun 1990	Holland	1–1	

25 Jun 1990	Romania	0–0 won 5–4 on penalties	
30 Jun 1990	Italy	0–1	
12 Sep 1990	Morocco	1–0	
17 Oct 1990	Turkey	5–0	
14 Nov 1990	England	1–1	
27 Mar 1991	England	1–1	
1 May 1991	Poland	0–0	
22 May 1991	Chile	1–1	
1 Jun 1991	United States	1–1	
11 Sep 1991	Hungary	2–1	
26 May 1992	Albania	2–0	
30 May 1992	United States	1–3	
4 Jun 1992	Italy	0–2	
7 Jun 1992	Portugal	2–0	
14 Oct 1992	Denmark	0–0	
18 Nov 1992	Spain	0–0	
31 Mar 1993	Northern Ireland	3–0	
28 Apr 1993	Denmark	1–1	
26 May 1993	Albania	2–1	
9 Jun 1993	Latvia	2–0	
16 Jun 1993	Lithuania	1–0	
8 Sep 1993	Lithuania	2–0	
13 Oct 1993	Spain	1–3	
17 Nov 1993	Northern Ireland	1–1	
24 May 1994	Bolivia	1–0	
29 May 1994	Germany	2–0	
18 Jun 1994	Italy	1–0	1
24 Jun 1994	Mexico	1–2	
28 Jun 1994	Norway	0–0	
4 Jul 1994	Holland	0–2	
26 Apr 1995	Portugal	1–0	
11 Jun 1995	Austria	1–3	1
6 Sep 1995	Austria	1–3	
24 Apr 1996	Czech Republic	0–2	
31 Aug 1996	Liechtenstein	5–0	
30 Apr 1997	Romania	0–1	
21 May 1997	Liechtenstein	5–0	
20 Aug 1997	Lithuania	0–0	

11 Oct 1997	Romania	1–1	
29 Oct 1997	Belgium	1–1	
16 Nov 1997	Belgium	1–2	1

Did you know?

When journalists were asked to pick their Scottish Man-of-the-Match in Scotland's 1–0 home defeat by the Republic of Ireland in a European Championship qualifier in 1987, they chose Glasgow-born Ray Houghton in the Irish midfield.

320. PETER ECCLES

Position	Central defender
Born	Dublin, 24 August 1962
Club	Shamrock Rovers; Kingston Olympic (Australia); Dundalk; Leicester City; Stafford Rangers (loan); Dundalk; Shamrock Rovers; Crusaders
Caps	1

Date	Team	Result	Goals
23 Apr 1986	Uruguay	1–1	

321. BARRY MURPHY

Position	Centre-half
Born	Dublin, 1 April 1959
Club	St Patrick's Athletic; Bohemians; Shamrock Rovers; Kilkenny City; Athlone Town
Caps	1

Date	Team	Result	Goals
23 Apr 1986	Uruguay	1–1	

322. LIAM O'BRIEN

Position	Midfield
Born	Dublin, 5 September 1964
Club	Stella Maris; Bohemians; Cleveland (United States); Shamrock Rovers; Manchester United; Newcastle United; Tranmere Rovers
Caps	16

Date	Team	Result	Goals
23 Apr 1986	Uruguay	1–1	
23 May 1987	Brazil	1–0	
10 Nov 1987	Israel	5–0	
23 Mar 1988	Romania	2–0	
27 Apr 1988	Yugoslavia	2–0	
22 May 1988	Poland	3–1	
19 Oct 1988	Tunisia	4–0	
16 Nov 1988	Spain	0–2	
25 Mar 1992	Switzerland	2–1	
17 Feb 1993	Wales	2–1	
23 Mar 1994	Russia	0–0	
2 Jun 1996	Croatia	2–2	
4 Jun 1996	Holland	1–3	

Liam O'Brien

9 Jun 1996	United States	1–2
15 Jun 1996	Bolivia	3–0
9 Oct 1996	Macedonia	3–0

323. MICK KENNEDY

Position	Midfield
Born	Salford, 9 April 1961
Club	Halifax Town; Huddersfield Town; Middlesbrough; Portsmouth; Bradford City; Leicester City; Luton Town; Stoke City; Chesterfield; Wigan Athletic
Caps	2

Date	Team	Result	Goals
25 May 1986	Iceland	2–1	
27 May 1986	Czechoslovakia	1–0	

324. NIALL QUINN

Position	Forward
Born	Dublin, 6 October 1966
Club	Arsenal; Manchester City; Sunderland
Caps	91

Date	Team	Result	Goals
25 May 1986	Iceland	2–1	
27 May 1986	Czechoslovakia	1–0	
1 Apr 1987	Bulgaria	1–2	
23 May 1987	Brazil	1–0	
9 Sep 1987	Luxembourg	2–1	
14 Oct 1987	Bulgaria	2–0	
10 Nov 1987	Israel	5–0	1
23 Mar 1988	Romania	2–0	
22 May 1988	Poland	3–1	
12 Jun 1988	England	1–0	
19 Oct 1988	Tunisia	4–0	
16 Nov 1988	Spain	0–2	
8 Mar 1989	Hungary	0–0	
25 Apr 1990	USSR	1–0	
2 Jun 1990	Malta	3–0	1
17 Jun 1990	Egypt	0–0	
21 Jun 1990	Holland	1–1	1

Date	Opponent	Score	
25 Jun 1990	Romania	0–0 won 5–4 on penalties	
30 Jun 1990	Italy	0–1	
12 Sep 1990	Morocco	1–0	
17 Oct 1990	Turkey	5–0	1
14 Nov 1990	England	1–1	
6 Feb 1991	Wales	3–1	2
27 Mar 1991	England	1–1	1
1 May 1991	Poland	0–0	
11 Sep 1991	Hungary	2–1	
19 Feb 1992	Wales	0–1	
29 Apr 1992	United States	4–1	1
26 May 1992	Albania	2–0	
30 May 1992	United States	1–3	
4 Jun 1992	Italy	0–2	
7 Jun 1992	Portugal	2–0	
9 Sep 1992	Latvia	4–0	
14 Oct 1992	Denmark	0–0	
18 Nov 1992	Spain	0–0	
31 Mar 1993	Northern Ireland	3–0	1
28 Apr 1993	Denmark	1–1	1
26 May 1993	Albania	2–1	
9 Jun 1993	Latvia	2–0	
16 Jun 1993	Lithuania	1–0	
8 Sep 1993	Lithuania	2–0	
13 Oct 1993	Spain	1–3	
17 Nov 1993	Northern Ireland	1–1	
7 Sep 1994	Latvia	3–0	
12 Oct 1994	Liechtenstein	4–0	2
16 Nov 1994	Northern Ireland	4–0	
15 Feb 1995	England	1–0	
29 Mar 1995	Northern Ireland	1–1	1
26 Apr 1995	Portugal	1–0	
3 Jun 1995	Liechtenstein	0–0	
11 Jun 1995	Austria	1–3	
6 Sep 1995	Austria	1–3	
11 Oct 1995	Latvia	2–1	
15 Nov 1995	Portugal	0–3	
27 Mar 1996	Russia	0–2	
24 Apr 1996	Czech Republic	0–2	
29 May 1996	Portugal	0–1	
2 Jun 1996	Croatia	2–2	1
4 Jun 1996	Holland	1–3	
9 Jun 1996	United States	1–2	
31 Aug 1996	Liechtenstein	5–0	2
20 Aug 1997	Lithuania	0–0	
22 Apr 1998	Argentina	0–2	
14 Oct 1998	Malta	5–0	1
18 Nov 1998	Yugoslavia	0–1	
10 Feb 1999	Paraguay	2–0	
28 Apr 1999	Sweden	2–0	
29 May 1999	Northern Ireland	0–1	
9 Jun 1999	Macedonia	1–0	1
1 Sep 1999	Yugoslavia	2–1	
4 Sep 1999	Croatia	0–1	
8 Sep 1999	Malta	3–2	
9 Oct 1999	Macedonia	1–1	1
17 Nov 1999	Turkey	0–0	
23 Feb 2000	Czech Republic	3–2	
30 May 2000	Scotland	1–2	
4 Jun 2000	Mexico	2–2	
6 Jun 2000	United States	1–1	
11 Jun 2000	South Africa	2–1	1
2 Sep 2000	Holland	2–2	
7 Oct 2000	Portugal	1–1	
11 Oct 2000	Estonia	2–0	
2 Jun 2001	Portugal	1–1	
6 Jun 2001	Estonia	2–0	
1 Sep 2001	Holland	1–0	
6 Oct 2001	Cyprus	4–0	1
10 Nov 2001	Iran	2–0	
13 Feb 2002	Russia	2–0	
5 Jun 2002	Germany	1–1	
11 Jun 2002	Saudi Arabia	3–0	
16 Jun 2002	Spain	1–1 lost 3–2 on penalties	

325. KEN DE MANGE

Position	Midfield
Born	Dublin, 3 September 1964
Club	Home Farm; Liverpool; Scunthorpe United (loan); Leeds United; Hull City; Cardiff City (loan); Limerick; Ards; Bohemians; Dundalk
Caps	2

Date	Team	Result	Goals
23 May 1987	Brazil	1–0	
19 Oct 1988	Tunisia	4–0	

326. DAVID KELLY

Position	Forward
Born	Birmingham, 25 November 1965
Club	Alvechurch; Walsall; West Ham United; Leicester City; Newcastle United; Wolverhampton Wanderers; Sunderland; Tranmere Rovers; Sheffield United; Motherwell; Mansfield Town; Derry City
Caps	26

Date	Team	Result	Goals#
10 Nov 1987	Israel	5–0	3
23 Mar 1987	Romania	2–0	1
27 Apr 1987	Yugoslavia	2–0	
19 Oct 1988	Tunisia	4–0	
25 Apr 1990	USSR	1–0	
2 Jun 1990	Malta	3–0	
12 Sep 1990	Morocco	1–0	1
6 Feb 1991	Wales	3–0	
22 May 1991	Chile	1–1	1
1 Jun 1991	United States	1–1	
11 Sep 1991	Hungary	2–1	1
4 Jun 1992	Italy	0–2	
7 Jun 1992	Portugal	2–0	
14 Oct 1992	Denmark	0–0	
17 Feb 1993	Wales	2–1	
23 Mar 1994	Russia	0–0	
28 Jun 1994	Norway	0–0	
15 Feb 1995	England	1–0	1

Date	Team	Result	Goals
29 Mar 1995	Northern Ireland	1–1	
11 Oct 1995	Latvia	2–1	
10 Nov 1996	Iceland	0–0	
11 Feb 1997	Wales	0–0	
2 Apr 1997	Macedonia	2–3	1
20 Aug 1997	Lithuania	0–0	
11 Oct 1997	Romania	1–1	
16 Nov 1997	Belgium	1–2	

327. CHRIS MORRIS

Position	Full-back
Born	Newquay, 24 December 1963
Club	Sheffield Wednesday; Glasgow Celtic; Middlesbrough
Caps	35

Date	Team	Result	Goals
10 Nov 1987	Israel	5–0	
23 Mar 1988	Romania	2–0	
27 Apr 1988	Yugoslavia	2–0	
22 May 1988	Poland	3–1	
1 Jun 1988	Norway	0–0	
12 Jun 1988	England	1–0	
15 Jun 1988	USSR	1–1	
18 Jun 1988	Holland	0–1	
14 Sep 1988	Northern Ireland	0–0	
19 Oct 1988	Tunisia	4–0	
16 Nov 1988	Spain	0–2	
7 Feb 1989	France	0–0	
8 Mar 1989	Hungary	0–0	
4 Jul 1989	Hungary	2–0	
6 Sep 1989	West Germany	1–1	
11 Oct 1989	Northern Ireland	3–0	
15 Nov 1989	Malta	2–0	
28 Mar 1990	Wales	1–0	
25 Apr 1990	USSR	1–0	
18 May 1990	Finland	1–1	
27 May 1990	Turkey	0–0	
11 Jun 1990	England	1–1	
17 Jun 1990	Egypt	0–0	
21 Jun 1990	Holland	1–1	

Date	Team	Result	
25 Jun 1990	Romania	0–0 won 5–4 on penalties	
30 Jun 1990	Italy	0–1	
14 Nov 1990	England	1–1	
11 Sep 1991	Hungary	2–1	
16 Oct 1991	Poland	3–3	
19 Feb 1992	Wales	0–1	
25 Mar 1992	Switzerland	2–1	
29 Apr 1992	United States	4–1	
30 May 1992	United States	1–3	
7 Jun 1992	Portugal	2–0	
17 Feb 1993	Wales	2–1	

328. KELHAM O'HANLON

Position	Goalkeeper
Born	Saltburn, 16 May 1962
Club	Middlesbrough; Rotherham United; Carlisle United; Preston North End; Dundee United; Preston North End
Caps	1

Date	Team	Result	Goals
10 Nov 1987	Israel	5–0	

329. JOHN SHERIDAN

Position	Midfield
Born	Manchester, 1 October 1964
Club	Manchester City; Leeds United; Nottingham Forest; Sheffield Wednesday; Birmingham City (loan); Bolton Wanderers; Doncaster Rovers; Oldham Athletic
Caps	34

Date	Team	Result	Goals
23 Mar 1988	Romania	2–0	
27 Apr 1988	Yugoslavia	2–0	
22 May 1988	Poland	3–1	1
1 Jun 1988	Norway	0–0	
16 Nov 1988	Spain	0–2	
28 Mar 1990	Wales	1–0	
27 May 1990	Turkey	0–0	

Date	Team	Result	Goals
2 Jun 1990	Malta	3–0	
30 Jun 1990	Italy	0–1	
12 Sep 1990	Morocco	1–0	
17 Oct 1990	Turkey	5–0	
22 May 1991	Chile	1–1	
1 Jun 1991	United States	1–1	
11 Sep 1991	Hungary	2–1	
9 Jun 1993	Latvia	2–0	
13 Oct 1993	Spain	1–3	1
20 Apr 1994	Holland	1–0	
24 May 1994	Bolivia	1–0	1
29 May 1994	Germany	2–0	
5 Jun 1994	Czech Republic	1–3	
18 Jun 1994	Italy	1–0	
24 Jun 1994	Mexico	1–2	
28 Jun 1994	Norway	0–0	
4 Jul 1994	Holland	0–2	
7 Sep 1994	Latvia	3–0	1
12 Oct 1994	Liechtenstein	4–0	
16 Nov 1994	Northern Ireland	4–0	1
15 Feb 1995	England	1–0	
29 Mar 1995	Northern Ireland	1–1	
26 Apr 1995	Portugal	1–0	
3 Jun 1995	Liechtenstein	0–0	
11 Jun 1995	Austria	1–3	
6 Sep 1995	Austria	1–3	
13 Dec 1995	Holland	0–2	

330. MARK KELLY

Position	Winger
Born	Sutton, 27 November 1969
Club	Portsmouth
Caps	4

Date	Team	Result	Goals
27 Apr 1988	Yugoslavia	2–0	
22 May 1988	Poland	3–1	
19 Oct 1988	Tunisia	4–0	
12 Sep 1990	Morocco	1–0	

331. PAT SCULLY

Position	Central defender
Born	Dublin, 23 June 1970
Club	Arsenal; Preston North End (loan); Northampton Town (loan); Southend United; Huddersfield Town
Caps	1

Date	Team	Result	Goals
19 Oct 1988	Tunisia	4–0	

332. STEVE STAUNTON

Position	Left-back; Midfield
Born	Dundalk, 19 January 1969
Club	Dundalk; Liverpool; Bradford City (loan); Aston Villa; Liverpool; Crystal Palace (loan); Aston Villa; Coventry City
Caps	102

Date	Team	Result	Goals
19 Oct 1988	Tunisia	4–0	
16 Nov 1988	Spain	0–2	
26 Apr 1989	Spain	1–0	
28 May 1989	Malta	2–0	
4 Jul 1989	Hungary	2–0	
6 Sep 1989	West Germany	1–1	
11 Oct 1989	Northern Ireland	3–0	
15 Nov 1989	Malta	2–0	
28 Mar 1990	Wales	1–0	
25 Apr 1990	USSR	1–0	1
16 May 1990	Finland	1–1	
27 May 1990	Turkey	0–0	
2 Jun 1990	Malta	3–0	
11 Jun 1990	England	1–1	
17 Jun 1990	Egypt	0–0	
21 Jun 1990	Holland	1–1	
25 Jun 1990	Romania	0–0 won 5–4 on penalties	
30 Jun 1990	Italy	0–1	
12 Sep 1990	Morocco	1–0	
17 Oct 1990	Turkey	5–0	
14 Nov 1990	England	1–1	
6 Feb 1991	Wales	3–0	
27 Mar 1991	England	1–1	
1 May 1991	Poland	0–0	
22 May 1991	Chile	1–1	
1 Jun 1991	United States	1–1	
16 Oct 1991	Poland	3–3	
13 Nov 1991	Turkey	3–1	
25 Mar 1992	Switzerland	2–1	
29 Apr 1992	United States	4–1	
26 May 1992	Albania	2–0	
30 May 1992	United States	1–3	
4 Jun 1992	Italy	0–2	
7 Jun 1992	Portugal	2–0	1
9 Sep 1992	Latvia	4–0	
18 Nov 1992	Spain	0–0	
31 Mar 1993	Northern Ireland	3–0	1
28 Apr 1993	Denmark	1–1	
26 May 1993	Albania	2–1	1
9 Jun 1993	Latvia	2–0	
16 Jun 1993	Lithuania	1–0	1
8 Sep 1993	Lithuania	2–0	
13 Oct 1993	Spain	1–3	
20 Apr 1994	Holland	1–0	
24 May 1994	Bolivia	1–0	
29 May 1994	Germany	2–0	
5 Jun 1994	Czech Republic	1–3	
18 Jun 1994	Italy	1–0	
24 Jun 1994	Mexico	1–2	
28 Jun 1994	Norway	0–0	
4 Jul 1994	Holland	0–2	
7 Sep 1994	Latvia	3–0	
12 Oct 1994	Liechtenstein	4–0	
16 Nov 1994	Northern Ireland	4–0	
15 Feb 1995	England	1–0	
29 Mar 1995	Northern Ireland	1–1	
26 Apr 1995	Portugal	1–0	1
3 Jun 1995	Liechtenstein	0–0	
11 Jun 1995	Austria	1–3	
11 Oct 1995	Latvia	2–1	

15 Nov 1995	Portugal	0–3	
27 Mar 1996	Russia	0–2	
31 Aug 1996	Liechtenstein	5–0	
9 Oct 1996	Macedonia	3–0	
11 Feb 1997	Wales	0–0	
2 Apr 1997	Macedonia	2–3	
30 Apr 1997	Romania	0–1	
21 May 1997	Liechtenstein	5–0	
20 Aug 1997	Lithuania	0–0	
6 Sep 1997	Iceland	4–2	
10 Sep 1997	Lithuania	2–1	
29 Oct 1997	Belgium	1–1	
16 Nov 1997	Belgium	1–2	
22 Apr 1998	Argentina	0–2	
5 Sep 1998	Croatia	2–0	
14 Oct 1998	Malta	5–0	
18 Nov 1998	Yugoslavia	0–1	
28 Apr 1999	Sweden	2–0	
1 Sep 1999	Yugoslavia	2–1	
4 Sep 1999	Croatia	0–1	
8 Sep 1999	Malta	3–2	1
9 Oct 1999	Macedonia	1–1	
23 Feb 2000	Czech Republic	3–2	
26 Apr 2000	Greece	0–1	
2 Sep 2000	Holland	2–2	
15 Nov 2000	Finland	3–0	1
25 Apr 2001	Andorra	3–1	
2 Jun 2001	Portugal	1–1	
6 Jun 2001	Estonia	2–0	
15 Aug 2001	Croatia	2–2	
1 Sep 2001	Holland	1–0	
6 Oct 2001	Cyprus	4–0	
10 Nov 2001	Iran	2–0	
15 Nov 2001	Iran	0–1	
13 Feb 2002	Russia	2–0	
27 Mar 2002	Denmark	3–0	
17 Apr 2002	United States	2–1	
16 May 2002	Nigeria	1–2	
1 Jun 2002	Cameroon	1–1	
5 Jun 2002	Germany	1–1	
11 Jun 2002	Saudi Arabia	3–0	
16 Jun 2002	Spain	1–1 lost 3–2 on penalties	

> ## Did you know?
> Steve Staunton twice scored goals direct from a corner-kick, against Portugal in 1992 and against Northern Ireland in 1993.

333. ANDY TOWNSEND

Position Midfield
Born Maidstone, 23 July 1963
Club Welling United; Weymouth; Southampton; Norwich City; Chelsea; Aston Villa; Middlesbrough; West Bromwich Albion
Caps 70

Date	Team	Result	Goals
7 Feb 1989	France	0–0	
26 Apr 1989	Spain	1–0	
28 May 1989	Malta	2–0	
4 Jul 1989	Hungary	2–0	
6 Sep 1989	West Germany	1–1	
11 Oct 1989	Northern Ireland	3–0	
15 Nov 1989	Malta	2–0	
28 Mar 1990	Wales	1–0	
25 Apr 1990	USSR	1–0	
16 May 1990	Finland	1–1	
27 May 1990	Turkey	0–0	
2 Jun 1990	Malta	3–0	1
11 Jun 1990	England	1–1	
17 Jun 1990	Egypt	0–0	
21 Jun 1990	Holland	1–1	
25 Jun 1990	Romania	0–0 won 5–4 on penalties	
30 Jun 1990	Italy	0–1	

12 Sep 1990	Morocco	1–0	
17 Oct 1990	Turkey	5–0	
14 Nov 1990	England	1–1	
6 Feb 1991	Wales	3–0	
27 Mar 1991	England	1–1	
1 May 1991	Poland	0–0	
22 May 1991	Chile	1–1	
1 Jun 1991	United States	1–1	
16 Oct 1991	Poland	3–3	1
19 Feb 1992	Wales	0–1	
29 Apr 1992	United States	4–1	1
26 May 1992	Albania	2–0	
30 May 1992	United States	1–3	
4 Jun 1992	Italy	0–2	
9 Sep 1992	Latvia	4–0	
14 Oct 1992	Denmark	0–0	
18 Nov 1992	Spain	0–0	
31 Mar 1993	Northern Ireland	3–0	1
28 Apr 1993	Denmark	1–1	
26 May 1993	Albania	2–1	
9 Jun 1993	Latvia	2–0	
16 Jun 1993	Lithuania	1–0	
8 Sep 1993	Lithuania	2–0	
17 Nov 1993	Northern Ireland	1–1	
20 Apr 1994	Holland	1–0	
24 May 1994	Bolivia	1–0	
29 May 1994	Germany	2–0	
5 Jun 1994	Czech Republic	1–3	1
18 Jun 1994	Italy	1–0	
24 Jun 1994	Mexico	1–2	
28 Jun 1994	Norway	0–0	
4 Jul 1994	Holland	0–2	
7 Sep 1994	Latvia	3–0	
16 Nov 1994	Northern Ireland	4–0	1
15 Feb 1995	England	1–0	
29 Mar 1995	Northern Ireland	1–1	
26 Apr 1995	Portugal	1–0	
6 Sep 1995	Austria	1–3	
11 Oct 1995	Latvia	2–1	
13 Dec 1995	Holland	0–2	

27 Mar 1996	Russia	0–2	
24 Apr 1996	Czech Republic	0–2	
29 May 1996	Portugal	0–1	
31 Aug 1996	Liechtenstein	5–0	1
9 Oct 1996	Macedonia	3–0	
10 Nov 1996	Iceland	0–0	
2 Apr 1997	Macedonia	2–3	
30 Apr 1997	Romania	0–1	
21 May 1997	Liechtenstein	5–0	
20 Aug 1997	Lithuania	0–0	
6 Sep 1997	Iceland	4–2	
29 Oct 1997	Belgium	1–1	
16 Nov 1997	Belgium	1–2	

Bernie Slaven

334. BERNIE SLAVEN

Position	Forward
Born	Paisley, 13 November 1960
Club	Morton; Airdrieonians; Queen of the South; Albion Rovers; Middlesbrough; Port Vale; Darlington
Caps	7

Date	Team	Result	Goals
28 Mar 1990	Wales	1–0	1
16 May 1990	Finland	1–1	
27 May 1990	Turkey	0–0	
2 Jun 1990	Malta	3–0	
6 Feb 1991	Wales	3–0	
1 May 1991	Poland	0–0	
17 Feb 1993	Wales	2–1	

335. ALAN McLOUGHLIN

Position	Midfield
Born	Manchester, 20 April 1967
Club	Manchester United; Swindon Town; Torquay United (loan); Southampton; Portsmouth; Wigan Athletic; Rochdale; Forest Green Rovers
Caps	42

Date	Team	Result	Goals
2 Jun 1990	Malta	3–0	
11 Jun 1990	England	1–1	
17 Jun 1990	Egypt	0–0	
12 Sep 1990	Morocco	1–0	
14 Nov 1990	England	1–1	
6 Feb 1991	Wales	3–0	
22 May 1991	Chile	1–1	
11 Sep 1991	Hungary	2–1	
19 Feb 1992	Wales	0–1	
29 Apr 1992	United States	4–1	
30 May 1992	United States	1–3	
4 Jun 1992	Italy	0–2	
7 Jun 1992	Portugal	2–0	
17 Feb 1993	Wales	2–1	
17 Nov 1993	Northern Ireland	1–1	1
23 Mar 1994	Russia	0–0	
20 Apr 1994	Holland	1–0	
12 Oct 1994	Liechtenstein	4–0	
29 May 1996	Portugal	0–1	
2 Jun 1996	Croatia	2–2	
4 Jun 1996	Holland	1–3	
9 Jun 1996	United States	1–2	
12 Jun 1996	Mexico	2–2	
15 Jun 1996	Bolivia	3–0	
31 Aug 1996	Liechtenstein	5–0	
9 Oct 1996	Macedonia	3–0	
10 Nov 1996	Iceland	0–0	
11 Feb 1997	Wales	0–0	
2 Apr 1997	Macedonia	2–3	1
20 Aug 1997	Lithuania	0–0	
6 Sep 1997	Iceland	4–2	
10 Sep 1997	Lithuania	2–1	
11 Oct 1997	Romania	1–1	
16 Nov 1997	Belgium	1–2	
25 Mar 1998	Czech Republic	1–2	
18 Nov 1998	Yugoslavia	0–1	
10 Feb 1999	Paraguay	2–0	
28 Apr 1999	Sweden	2–0	
29 May 1999	Northern Ireland	0–1	
4 Sep 1999	Croatia	0–1	
8 Sep 1999	Malta	3–2	
9 Oct 1999	Macedonia	1–1	

336. DENIS IRWIN

Position	Full-back
Born	Cork, 31 October 1965
Club	Leeds United; Oldham Athletic; Manchester United; Wolverhampton Wanderers
Caps	56

Date	Team	Result	Goals
12 Sep 1990	Morocco	1–0	
17 Oct 1990	Turkey	5–0	
6 Feb 1991	Wales	3–0	
27 Mar 1991	England	1–1	
1 May 1991	Poland	0–0	
1 Jun 1991	United States	1–1	
11 Sep 1991	Hungary	2–1	
16 Oct 1991	Poland	3–3	
19 Feb 1992	Wales	0–1	
29 Apr 1992	United States	4–1	1
26 May 1992	Albania	2–0	

30 May 1992	United States	1–3	
4 Jun 1992	Italy	0–2	
9 Sep 1992	Latvia	4–0	
14 Oct 1992	Denmark	0–0	
18 Nov 1992	Spain	0–0	
31 Mar 1993	Northern Ireland	3–0	
28 Apr 1993	Denmark	1–1	
26 May 1993	Albania	2–1	
9 Jun 1993	Latvia	2–0	
16 Jun 1993	Lithuania	1–0	
8 Sep 1993	Lithuania	2–0	
13 Oct 1993	Spain	1–3	
17 Nov 1993	Northern Ireland	1–1	
24 May 1994	Bolivia	1–0	
29 May 1994	Germany	2–0	
18 Jun 1994	Italy	1–0	
24 Jun 1994	Mexico	1–2	
7 Sep 1994	Latvia	3–0	
12 Oct 1994	Liechtenstein	4–0	
16 Nov 1994	Northern Ireland	4–0	
15 Feb 1995	England	1–0	
29 Mar 1995	Northern Ireland	1–1	
26 Apr 1995	Portugal	1–0	
3 Jun 1995	Liechtenstein	0–0	
11 Jun 1995	Austria	1–3	
6 Sep 1995	Austria	1–3	
15 Nov 1995	Portugal	0–3	
13 Dec 1995	Holland	0–2	
24 Apr 1996	Czech Republic	0–2	
31 Aug 1996	Liechtenstein	5–0	
9 Oct 1996	Macedonia	3–0	
10 Nov 1996	Iceland	0–0	
2 Apr 1997	Macedonia	2–3	
30 Apr 1997	Romania	0–1	
10 Sep 1997	Lithuania	2–1	
29 Oct 1997	Belgium	1–1	1
22 Apr 1998	Argentina	0–2	
5 Sep 1998	Croatia	2–0	1
18 Nov 1998	Yugoslavia	0–1	
10 Feb 1999	Paraguay	2–0	1

9 Jun 1999	Macedonia	1–0
1 Sep 1999	Yugoslavia	2–1
9 Oct 1999	Macedonia	1–1
13 Nov 1999	Turkey	1–1
17 Nov 1999	Turkey	0–0

Roy Keane

337. ROY KEANE

Position	Midfield
Born	Cork, 10 August 1971
Club	Cobh Ramblers; Nottingham Forest; Manchester United; Glasgow Celtic
Caps	67

Date	Team	Result	Goals
22 May 1991	Chile	1–1	
11 Sep 1991	Hungary	2–1	
16 Oct 1991	Poland	3–3	
19 Feb 1992	Wales	0–1	

Date	Team	Result	Goals
25 Mar 1992	Switzerland	2–1	
26 May 1992	Albania	2–0	
30 May 1992	United States	1–3	
9 Sep 1992	Latvia	4–0	
14 Oct 1992	Denmark	0–0	
18 Nov 1992	Spain	0–0	
17 Feb 1993	Wales	2–1	
31 Mar 1993	Northern Ireland	3–0	
28 Apr 1993	Denmark	1–1	
26 May 1993	Albania	2–1	
9 Jun 1993	Latvia	2–0	
16 Jun 1993	Lithuania	1–0	
8 Sep 1993	Lithuania	2–0	
13 Oct 1993	Spain	1–3	
17 Nov 1993	Northern Ireland	1–1	
24 May 1994	Bolivia	1–0	
29 May 1994	Germany	2–0	
5 Jun 1994	Czech Republic	1–3	
18 Jun 1994	Italy	1–0	
24 Jun 1994	Mexico	1–2	
28 Jun 1994	Norway	0–0	
4 Jul 1994	Holland	0–2	
16 Nov 1994	Northern Ireland	4–0	1
29 Mar 1995	Northern Ireland	1–1	
6 Sep 1995	Austria	1–3	
27 Mar 1996	Russia	0–2	
10 Nov 1996	Iceland	0–0	
11 Feb 1997	Wales	0–0	
2 Apr 1997	Macedonia	2–3	
30 Apr 1997	Romania	0–1	
21 May 1997	Liechtenstein	5–0	
20 Aug 1997	Lithuania	0–0	
6 Sep 1997	Iceland	4–2	2
10 Sep 1997	Lithuania	2–1	
5 Sep 1998	Croatia	2–0	1
14 Oct 1998	Malta	5–0	1
18 Nov 1998	Yugoslavia	0–1	
10 Feb 1999	Paraguay	2–0	
1 Sep 1999	Yugoslavia	2–1	
13 Nov 1999	Turkey	1–1	
17 Nov 1999	Turkey	0–0	
23 Feb 2000	Czech Republic	3–2	
2 Sep 2000	Holland	2–2	
7 Oct 2000	Portugal	1–1	
11 Oct 2000	Estonia	2–0	
24 Mar 2001	Cyprus	4–0	2
28 Mar 2001	Andorra	3–0	
2 Jun 2001	Portugal	1–1	1
15 Aug 2001	Croatia	2–2	
1 Sep 2001	Holland	1–0	
6 Oct 2001	Cyprus	4–0	1
10 Nov 2001	Iran	2–0	
13 Feb 2002	Russia	2–0	
16 May 2002	Nigeria	1–2	
27 May 2004	Romania	1–0	
18 Aug 2004	Bulgaria	1–1	
8 Sep 2004	Switzerland	1–1	
9 Oct 2004	France	0–0	
13 Oct 2004	Faroe Islands	2–0	
26 Mar 2005	Israel	1–1	
29 Mar 2005	China	1–0	
8 Jun 2005	Faroe Islands	2–0	
7 Sep 2005	France	0–1	

338. TERRY PHELAN

Position	Left-back
Born	Manchester, 16 March 1967
Club	Leeds United; Swansea City; Wimbledon; Manchester City; Chelsea; Everton; Crystal Palace (loan); Fulham; Sheffield United; Charleston Battery (United States)
Caps	42

Date	Team	Result	Goals
11 Sep 1991	Hungary	2–1	
16 Oct 1991	Poland	3–3	
13 Nov 1991	Turkey	3–1	
19 Feb 1992	Wales	0–1	
25 Mar 1992	Switzerland	2–1	
30 May 1992	United States	1–3	
4 Jun 1992	Italy	0–2	

29 May 1996	Portugal	0–1
2 Jun 1996	Croatia	2–2
4 Jun 1996	Holland	1–3
9 Jun 1996	United States	1–2
12 Jun 1996	Mexico	2–2
15 Jun 1996	Bolivia	3–0
11 Feb 1997	Wales	0–0
2 Apr 1997	Macedonia	2–3
11 Oct 1997	Romania	1–1
30 May 2000	Scotland	1–2
4 Jun 2000	Mexico	2–2
6 Jun 2000	United States	1–1
11 Jun 2000	South Africa	2–1

Terry Phelan

7 Jun 1992	Portugal	2–0
9 Sep 1992	Latvia	4–0
14 Oct 1992	Denmark	0–0
18 Nov 1992	Spain	0–0
31 Mar 1993	Northern Ireland	3–0
26 May 1993	Albania	2–1
9 Jun 1993	Latvia	3–0
16 Jun 1993	Lithuania	1–0
8 Sep 1993	Lithuania	2–0
13 Oct 1993	Spain	1–3
17 Nov 1993	Northern Ireland	1–1
20 Apr 1994	Holland	1–0
24 May 1994	Bolivia	1–0
29 May 1994	Germany	2–0
5 Jun 1994	Czech Republic	1–3
18 Jun 1994	Italy	1–0
24 Jun 1994	Mexico	1–2
4 Jul 1994	Holland	0–2
15 Feb 1995	England	1–0
11 Oct 1995	Latvia	2–1
13 Dec 1995	Holland	0–2
27 Mar 1996	Russia	0–2

339. LIAM DAISH

Position	Central defender
Born	Portsmouth, 23 September 1968
Club	Portsmouth; Cambridge United; Birmingham City; Coventry City
Caps	5

Date	Team	Result	Goals
19 Feb 1992	Wales	0–1	
25 Mar 1992	Switzerland	2–1	
24 Apr 1996	Czech Republic	0–2	
2 Jun 1996	Croatia	2–2	
12 Jun 1996	Mexico	2–2	

340. TOMMY COYNE

Position	Forward
Born	Glasgow, 14 November 1962
Club	Clydebank; Dundee United; Dundee; Glasgow Celtic; Tranmere Rovers; Motherwell; Dundee; Falkirk (loan); Clydebank; Albion Rovers
Caps	22

Date	Team	Result	Goals
25 Mar 1992	Switzerland	2–1	1
29 Apr 1992	United States	4–1	
26 May 1992	Albania	2–0	
30 May 1992	United States	1–3	

Date	Team	Result	Goals
4 Jun 1992	Italy	0–2	
7 Jun 1992	Portugal	2–0	1
9 Sep 1992	Latvia	4–0	
17 Feb 1993	Wales	2–1	1
31 Mar 1993	Northern Ireland	3–0	
23 Mar 1994	Russia	0–0	
20 Apr 1994	Holland	1–0	1
24 May 1994	Bolivia	1–0	
29 May 1994	Germany	2–0	
5 Jun 1994	Czech Republic	1–3	
18 Jun 1994	Italy	1–0	
24 Jun 1994	Mexico	1–2	
4 Jul 1994	Holland	0–2	
12 Oct 1994	Liechtenstein	4–0	2
16 Nov 1994	Northern Ireland	4–0	
11 Jun 1995	Austria	1–3	
27 Mar 1996	Russia	0–2	
29 Oct 1997	Belgium	1–1	

341. EDDIE McGOLDRICK

Position	Midfield
Born	Islington, 30 April 1965
Club	Kettering Town; Nuneaton Borough; Northampton Town; Crystal Palace; Arsenal; Manchester City; Stockport County
Caps	15

Date	Team	Result	Goals
25 Mar 1992	Switzerland	2–1	
29 Apr 1992	United States	4–1	
4 Jun 1992	Italy	0–2	
7 Jun 1992	Portugal	2–0	
14 Oct 1992	Denmark	0–0	
17 Feb 1993	Wales	2–1	
31 Mar 1993	Northern Ireland	3–0	
28 Apr 1993	Denmark	1–1	
17 Nov 1993	Northern Ireland	1–1	
23 Mar 1994	Russia	0–0	
20 Apr 1994	Holland	1–0	
5 Jun 1994	Czech Republic	1–3	
7 Sep 1994	Latvia	3–0	

Date	Team	Result	Goals
12 Oct 1994	Liechtenstein	4–0	
15 Feb 1995	England	1–0	

342. BRIAN CAREY

Position	Central defender
Born	Cork, 31 May 1968
Club	Cork City; Manchester United; Wrexham (loan); Leicester City; Wrexham
Caps	3

Date	Team	Result	Goals
29 Apr 1992	United States	4–1	
17 Feb 1993	Wales	2–1	
23 Mar 1994	Russia	0–0	

343. MIKE MILLIGAN

Position	Midfield
Born	Manchester, 20 February 1967
Club	Oldham Athletic; Everton; Oldham Athletic; Norwich City; Blackpool
Caps	1

Date	Team	Result	Goals
29 Apr 1992	United States	4–1	

344. ALAN KERNAGHAN

Position	Central defender
Born	Otley, 25 April 1967
Club	Middlesbrough; Charlton Athletic (loan); Manchester City; Bolton Wanderers (loan); Bradford City (loan); St Johnstone
Caps	22

Date	Team	Result	Goals
9 Sep 1992	Latvia	4–0	
14 Oct 1992	Denmark	0–0	
28 Apr 1993	Denmark	1–1	
26 May 1993	Albania	2–1	
9 Jun 1993	Latvia	2–0	
16 Jun 1993	Lithuania	1–0	
8 Sep 1993	Lithuania	2–0	1
13 Oct 1993	Spain	1–3	

Date	Team	Result	Goals
17 Nov 1993	Northern Ireland	1–1	
24 May 1994	Bolivia	1–0	
5 Jun 1994	Czech Republic	1–3	
12 Oct 1994	Liechtenstein	4–0	
15 Feb 1995	England	1–0	
6 Sep 1995	Austria	1–3	
15 Nov 1995	Portugal	0–3	
13 Dec 1995	Holland	0–2	
27 Mar 1996	Russia	0–2	
29 May 1996	Portugal	0–1	
2 Jun 1996	Croatia	2–2	
4 Jun 1996	Holland	1–3	
9 Jun 1996	United States	1–2	
15 Jun 1996	Bolivia	3–0	

345. ALAN KELLY JNR

Position	Goalkeeper
Born	Preston, 11 August 1968
Club	Preston North End; Sheffield United; Blackburn Rovers; Stockport County (loan); Birmingham City (loan)
Caps	34

Date	Team	Result	Goals
17 Feb 1993	Wales	2–1	
23 Mar 1994	Russia	0–0	
29 May 1994	Germany	2–0	
7 Sep 1994	Latvia	3–0	
16 Nov 1994	Northern Ireland	4–0	
15 Feb 1995	England	1–0	
29 Mar 1995	Northern Ireland	1–1	
26 Apr 1995	Portugal	1–0	
3 Jun 1995	Liechtenstein	0–0	
11 Jun 1995	Austria	1–3	
6 Sep 1995	Austria	1–3	
11 Oct 1995	Latvia	2–1	
15 Nov 1995	Portugal	0–3	
13 Dec 1995	Holland	0–2	
9 Oct 1996	Macedonia	3–0	
10 Nov 1996	Iceland	0–0	
2 Apr 1997	Macedonia	2–3	

Date	Team	Result	Goals
30 Apr 1997	Romania	0–1	
11 Oct 1997	Romania	1–1	
22 Apr 1998	Argentina	0–2	
10 Feb 1999	Paraguay	2–0	
9 Jun 1999	Macedonia	1–0	
1 Sep 1999	Yugoslavia	2–1	
4 Sep 1999	Croatia	0–1	
8 Sep 1999	Malta	3–2	
9 Oct 1999	Macedonia	1–1	
13 Nov 1999	Turkey	1–1	
23 Feb 2000	Czech Republic	3–2	
30 May 2000	Scotland	1–2	
6 Jun 2000	United States	1–1	
2 Sep 2000	Holland	2–2	
7 Oct 2000	Portugal	1–1	
11 Oct 2000	Estonia	2–0	
15 Aug 2001	Croatia	2–2	

346. PHIL BABB

Position	Central defender
Born	Lambeth, 30 November 1970
Club	Millwall; Bradford City; Coventry City; Liverpool; Tranmere Rovers (loan); Sporting Lisbon (Portugal); Sunderland
Caps	35

Date	Team	Result	Goals
23 Mar 1994	Russia	0–0	
20 Apr 1994	Holland	1–0	
24 May 1994	Bolivia	1–0	
29 May 1994	Germany	2–0	
5 Jun 1994	Czech Republic	1–3	
18 Jun 1994	Italy	1–0	
24 Jun 1994	Mexico	1–2	
28 Jun 1994	Norway	0–0	
4 Jul 1994	Holland	0–2	
7 Sep 1994	Latvia	3–0	
12 Oct 1994	Liechtenstein	4–0	
16 Nov 1994	Northern Ireland	4–0	
29 Mar 1995	Northern Ireland	1–1	
26 Apr 1995	Portugal	1–0	

3 Jun 1995	Liechtenstein	0–0
11 Jun 1995	Austria	1–3
11 Oct 1995	Latvia	2–1
15 Nov 1995	Portugal	0–3
13 Dec 1995	Holland	0–2
24 Apr 1996	Czech Republic	0–2
10 Nov 1996	Iceland	0–0
10 Sep 1997	Lithuania	2–1
11 Oct 1997	Romania	1–1
22 Apr 1998	Argentina	0–2
23 May 1998	Mexico	0–0
5 Sep 1998	Croatia	2–0
10 Feb 1999	Paraguay	2–0
28 Apr 1999	Sweden	2–0
29 May 1999	Northern Ireland	0–1
23 Feb 2000	Czech Republic	3–2
30 May 2000	Scotland	1–2
4 Jun 2000	Mexico	2–2
6 Jun 2000	United States	1–1
11 Jun 2000	South Africa	2–1
7 Sep 2002	Russia	2–4

347. GARY KELLY

Position Right-back
Born Drogheda, 9 July 1974
Club Home Farm; Leeds United
Caps 52

Date	Team	Result	Goals
23 Mar 1994	Russia	0–0	
20 Apr 1994	Holland	1–0	
24 May 1994	Bolivia	1–0	
29 May 1994	Germany	2–0	1
5 Jun 1994	Czech Republic	1–3	
28 Jun 1994	Norway	0–0	
4 Jul 1994	Holland	0–2	
7 Sep 1994	Latvia	3–0	
12 Oct 1994	Liechtenstein	4–0	
16 Nov 1994	Northern Ireland	4–0	
29 Mar 1995	Northern Ireland	1–1	
26 Apr 1995	Portugal	1–0	
3 Jun 1995	Liechtenstein	0–0	
11 Jun 1995	Austria	1–3	
6 Sep 1995	Austria	1–3	
11 Oct 1995	Latvia	2–1	
15 Nov 1995	Portugal	0–3	
13 Dec 1995	Holland	0–2	
11 Feb 1997	Wales	0–0	
30 Apr 1997	Romania	0–1	
21 May 1997	Liechtenstein	5–0	
6 Sep 1997	Iceland	4–2	
10 Sep 1997	Lithuania	2–1	
29 Oct 1997	Belgium	1–1	
16 Nov 1997	Belgium	1–2	
25 Mar 1998	Czech Republic	1–2	
22 Apr 1998	Argentina	0–2	
23 May 1998	Mexico	0–0	
4 Sep 1999	Croatia	0–1	
9 Oct 1999	Macedonia	1–1	
23 Feb 2000	Czech Republic	3–2	
2 Sep 2000	Holland	2–2	
15 Nov 2000	Finland	3–0	
24 Mar 2001	Cyprus	4–0	1
28 Mar 2001	Andorra	3–0	
25 Apr 2001	Andorra	3–1	
2 Jun 2001	Portugal	1–1	
6 Jun 2001	Estonia	2–0	
15 Aug 2001	Croatia	2–2	
1 Sep 2001	Holland	1–0	
10 Nov 2001	Iran	2–0	
15 Nov 2001	Iran	0–1	
13 Feb 2002	Russia	2–0	
27 Mar 2002	Denmark	3–0	
17 Apr 2002	United States	2–1	
16 May 2002	Nigeria	1–2	
1 Jun 2002	Cameroon	2–2	
5 Jun 2002	Germany	1–1	
11 Jun 2002	Saudi Arabia	3–0	
16 Jun 2002	Spain	1–1 lost 3–2 on penalties	

| 21 Aug 2002 | Finland | 3–0 |
| 16 Oct 2002 | Switzerland | 1–2 |

348. JASON McATEER

Position	Midfield
Born	Birkenhead, 18 June 1971
Club	Marine; Bolton Wanderers; Liverpool; Blackburn Rovers; Sunderland; Tranmere Rovers
Caps	52

Date	Team	Result	Goals
23 Mar 1994	Russia	0–0	
20 Apr 1994	Holland	1–0	
24 May 1994	Bolivia	1–0	
29 May 1994	Germany	2–0	
5 Jun 1994	Czech Republic	1–3	
18 Jun 1994	Italy	1–0	
24 Jun 1994	Mexico	1–2	
28 Jun 1994	Norway	0–0	
4 Jul 1994	Holland	0–2	
7 Sep 1994	Latvia	3–0	
12 Oct 1994	Liechtenstein	4–0	
16 Nov 1994	Northern Ireland	4–0	
29 Mar 1995	Northern Ireland	1–1	
3 Jun 1995	Liechtenstein	0–0	
11 Oct 1995	Latvia	2–1	
15 Nov 1995	Portugal	0–3	
13 Dec 1995	Holland	0–2	
27 Mar 1996	Russia	0–2	
9 Oct 1996	Macedonia	3–0	1
10 Nov 1996	Iceland	0–0	
11 Feb 1997	Wales	0–0	
2 Apr 1997	Macedonia	2–3	
6 Sep 1997	Iceland	4–2	
10 Sep 1997	Lithuania	2–1	
11 Oct 1997	Romania	1–1	
5 Sep 1998	Croatia	2–0	
14 Oct 1998	Malta	5–0	
18 Nov 1998	Yugoslavia	0–1	
10 Feb 1999	Paraguay	2–0	

28 Apr 1999	Sweden	2–0	
23 Feb 2000	Czech Republic	3–2	
30 May 2000	Scotland	1–2	
4 Jun 2000	Mexico	2–2	
6 Jun 2000	United States	1–1	
11 Jun 2000	South Africa	2–1	
2 Sep 2000	Holland	2–2	1
7 Oct 2000	Portugal	1–1	
11 Oct 2000	Estonia	2–0	
15 Nov 2000	Finland	3–0	
24 Mar 2001	Cyprus	4–0	
15 Aug 2001	Croatia	2–2	
1 Sep 2001	Holland	1–0	1
10 Nov 2001	Iran	2–0	
15 Nov 2001	Iran	0–1	
13 Feb 2002	Russia	2–0	
27 Mar 2002	Denmark	3–0	
16 May 2002	Nigeria	1–2	
1 Jun 2002	Cameroon	1–1	
11 Jun 2002	Saudi Arabia	3–0	
21 Aug 2002	Finland	3–0	
7 Sep 2002	Russia	2–4	
18 Feb 2004	Brazil	0–0	

349. OWEN COYLE

Position	Forward
Born	Glasgow, 14 July 1966
Club	Dumbarton; Clydebank; Airdrieonians; Bolton Wanderers; Dundee United; Motherwell; Dunfermline Athletic; Ross County (loan); Airdrieonians; Falkirk; Dundee United; Airdrie United; St Johnstone
Caps	1

Date	Team	Result	Goals
20 Apr 1994	Holland	1–0	

350. JEFF KENNA

Position	Full-back
Born	Dublin, 27 August 1970
Club	Southampton; Blackburn Rovers; Tranmere Rovers (loan); Wigan Athletic; Birmingham City; Derby County; Kidderminster Harriers
Caps	27

Date	Team	Result	Goals
26 Apr 1995	Portugal	1–0	
3 Jun 1995	Liechtenstein	0–0	
11 Jun 1995	Austria	1–3	
11 Oct 1995	Latvia	2–1	
15 Nov 1995	Portugal	0–3	
13 Dec 1995	Holland	0–2	
27 Mar 1996	Russia	0–2	
24 Apr 1996	Czech Republic	0–2	
29 May 1996	Portugal	0–1	
2 Jun 1996	Croatia	2–2	
4 Jun 1996	Holland	1–3	
9 Jun 1996	United States	1–2	
31 Aug 1996	Liechtenstein	5–0	
9 Oct 1996	Macedonia	3–0	
10 Nov 1996	Iceland	0–0	
30 Apr 1997	Romania	0–1	
21 May 1997	Liechtenstein	5–0	
20 Aug 1997	Lithuania	0–0	
6 Sep 1997	Iceland	4–2	
11 Oct 1997	Romania	1–1	
29 Oct 1997	Belgium	1–1	
16 Nov 1997	Belgium	1–2	
25 Mar 1998	Czech Republic	1–2	
22 Apr 1998	Argentina	0–2	
5 Sep 1998	Croatia	2–0	
14 Oct 1998	Malta	5–0	
17 Nov 1999	Turkey	0–0	

351. MARK KENNEDY

Position	Left-winger
Born	Dublin, 15 May 1976
Club	Millwall; Liverpool; Queen's Park Rangers (loan); Wimbledon; Manchester City; Wolverhampton Wanderers
Caps	34

Date	Team	Result	Goals
6 Sep 1995	Austria	1–3	
11 Oct 1995	Latvia	2–1	
15 Nov 1995	Portugal	0–3	
27 Mar 1996	Russia	0–2	
24 Apr 1996	Czech Republic	0–2	
2 Jun 1996	Croatia	2–2	
4 Jun 1996	Holland	1–3	
9 Jun 1996	United States	1–2	
12 Jun 1996	Mexico	2–2	
15 Jun 1996	Bolivia	3–0	
30 Apr 1997	Romania	0–1	
21 May 1997	Liechtenstein	5–0	
20 Aug 1997	Lithuania	0–0	
6 Sep 1997	Iceland	4–2	
11 Oct 1997	Romania	1–1	
29 Oct 1997	Belgium	1–1	
16 Nov 1997	Belgium	1–2	
23 May 1998	Mexico	0–0	
14 Oct 1998	Malta	5–0	
28 Apr 1999	Sweden	2–0	1
29 May 1999	Northern Ireland	0–1	
9 Jun 1999	Macedonia	1–0	
1 Sep 1999	Yugoslavia	2–1	1
8 Sep 1999	Malta	3–2	
9 Oct 1999	Macedonia	1–1	
23 Feb 2000	Czech Republic	3–2	
30 May 2000	Scotland	1–2	1
4 Jun 2000	Mexico	2–2	
6 Jun 2000	United States	1–1	
11 Jun 2000	South Africa	2–1	
25 Apr 2001	Andorra	3–1	
15 Aug 2001	Croatia	2–2	
6 Oct 2001	Cyprus	4–0	
13 Feb 2002	Russia	2–0	

352. SHAY GIVEN

Position	Goalkeeper
Born	Lifford, County Donegal, 20 April 1976
Club	Glasgow Celtic; Blackburn Rovers; Swindon Town (loan); Sunderland (loan); Newcastle United
Caps	85

Date	Team	Result	Goals
27 Mar 1996	Russia	0–2	
24 Apr 1996	Czech Republic	0–2	
29 May 1996	Portugal	0–1	
2 Jun 1996	Croatia	2–2	
4 Jun 1996	Holland	1–3	
9 Jun 1996	United States	1–2	
15 Jun 1996	Bolivia	3–0	
31 Aug 1996	Liechtenstein	5–0	
21 May 1997	Liechtenstein	5–0	
20 Aug 1997	Lithuania	0–0	
6 Sep 1997	Iceland	4–2	
10 Sep 1997	Lithuania	2–1	
29 Oct 1997	Belgium	1–1	
16 Nov 1997	Belgium	1–2	
25 Mar 1998	Czech Republic	1–2	
22 Apr 1998	Argentina	0–2	
23 May 1998	Mexico	0–0	
5 Sep 1998	Croatia	2–0	
14 Oct 1998	Malta	5–0	
18 Nov 1998	Yugoslavia	0–1	
10 Feb 1999	Paraguay	2–0	
28 Apr 1999	Sweden	2–0	
29 May 1999	Northern Ireland	0–1	
26 Apr 2000	Greece	0–1	
11 Jun 2000	South Africa	2–1	
15 Nov 2000	Finland	3–0	
24 Mar 2001	Cyprus	4–0	
28 Mar 2001	Andorra	3–0	
25 Apr 2001	Andorra	3–1	
2 Jun 2001	Portugal	1–1	
6 Jun 2001	Estonia	2–0	
15 Aug 2001	Croatia	2–2	
1 Sep 2001	Holland	1–0	
6 Oct 2001	Cyprus	4–0	
10 Nov 2001	Iran	2–0	
15 Nov 2001	Iran	0–1	
13 Feb 2002	Russia	2–0	
17 Apr 2002	United States	2–1	
16 May 2002	Nigeria	1–2	
1 Jun 2002	Cameroon	1–1	
5 Jun 2002	Germany	1–1	
11 Jun 2002	Saudi Arabia	3–0	
16 Jun 2002	Spain	1–1 lost 3–2 on penalties	
21 Aug 2002	Finland	3–0	
7 Sep 2002	Russia	2–4	
16 Oct 2002	Switzerland	1–2	
20 Nov 2002	Greece	0–0	
29 Mar 2003	Georgia	2–1	
2 Apr 2003	Albania	0–0	
30 Apr 2003	Norway	1–0	
7 Jun 2003	Albania	2–1	
11 Jun 2003	Georgia	2–0	
6 Sep 2003	Russia	1–1	
11 Oct 2003	Switzerland	0–2	
18 Nov 2003	Canada	3–0	
18 Feb 2004	Brazil	0–0	
31 Mar 2004	Czech Republic	2–1	
28 Apr 2004	Poland	0–0	
27 May 2004	Romania	1–0	
5 Jun 2004	Holland	1–0	
18 Aug 2004	Bulgaria	1–1	
4 Sep 2004	Cyprus	3–0	
8 Sep 2004	Switzerland	1–1	
9 Oct 2004	France	0–0	
13 Oct 2004	Faroe Islands	2–0	
16 Nov 2004	Croatia	1–0	
9 Feb 2005	Portugal	1–0	
26 Mar 2005	Israel	1–1	
4 Jun 2005	Israel	2–2	
8 Jun 2005	Faroe Islands	2–0	

17 Aug 2005	Italy	1–2
7 Sep 2005	France	0–1
8 Oct 2005	Cyprus	1–0
12 Oct 2005	Switzerland	0–0
1 Mar 2006	Sweden	3–0
24 May 2006	Chile	0–1
2 Sep 2006	Germany	0–1
15 Nov 2006	San Marino	5–0
24 Mar 2007	Wales	1–0
28 Mar 2007	Slovakia	1–0
8 Sep 2007	Slovakia	2–2
12 Sep 2007	Czech Republic	0–1
13 Oct 2007	Germany	0–0
17 Oct 2007	Cyprus	1–1
17 Nov 2007	Wales	2–2

353. KENNY CUNNINGHAM

Position Defender
Born Dublin, 28 June 1971
Club Home Farm; Tolka Rovers; Millwall; Wimbledon; Birmingham City; Sunderland
Caps 72

Date	Team	Result	Goals
24 Apr 1996	Czech Republic	0–2	
29 May 1996	Portugal	0–1	
2 Jun 1996	Croatia	2–2	
4 Jun 1996	Holland	1–3	
9 Jun 1996	United States	1–2	
15 Jun 1996	Bolivia	3–0	
10 Nov 1996	Iceland	0–0	
11 Feb 1997	Wales	0–0	
30 Apr 1997	Romania	0–1	
21 May 1997	Liechtenstein	5–0	
20 Aug 1997	Lithuania	0–0	
6 Sep 1997	Iceland	4–2	
10 Sep 1997	Lithuania	2–1	
29 Oct 1997	Belgium	1–1	
16 Nov 1997	Belgium	1–2	
25 Mar 1998	Czech Republic	1–2	
5 Sep 1998	Croatia	2–0	
14 Oct 1998	Malta	5–0	
18 Nov 1998	Yugoslavia	0–1	
10 Feb 1999	Paraguay	2–0	
28 Apr 1999	Sweden	2–0	
29 May 1999	Northern Ireland	0–1	
9 Jun 1999	Macedonia	1–0	
1 Sep 1999	Yugoslavia	2–1	
4 Sep 1999	Croatia	0–1	
8 Sep 1999	Malta	3–2	
9 Oct 1999	Macedonia	1–1	
13 Nov 1999	Turkey	1–1	
17 Nov 1999	Turkey	0–0	
23 Feb 2000	Czech Republic	3–2	
26 Apr 2000	Greece	0–1	
24 Mar 2001	Cyprus	4–0	
28 Mar 2001	Andorra	3–0	
10 Nov 2001	Iran	2–0	
13 Feb 2002	Russia	2–0	
27 Mar 2002	Denmark	3–0	
17 Apr 2002	United States	2–1	
16 May 2002	Nigeria	1–2	
5 Jun 2002	Germany	1–1	
16 Jun 2002	Spain	1–1 lost 3–2 on penalties	
21 Aug 2002	Finland	3–0	
7 Sep 2002	Russia	2–4	
16 Oct 2002	Switzerland	1–2	
20 Nov 2002	Greece	0–0	
29 Mar 2003	Georgia	2–1	
2 Apr 2003	Albania	0–0	
7 Jun 2003	Albania	2–1	
11 Jun 2003	Georgia	2–0	
19 Aug 2003	Australia	2–1	
6 Sep 2003	Russia	1–1	
18 Nov 2003	Canada	3–0	
18 Feb 2004	Brazil	0–0	
31 Mar 2004	Czech Republic	2–1	
28 Apr 2004	Poland	0–0	

27 May 2004	Romania	1–0
29 May 2004	Nigeria	0–3
5 Jun 2004	Holland	1–0
18 Aug 2004	Bulgaria	1–1
4 Sep 2004	Cyprus	3–0
8 Sep 2004	Switzerland	1–1
9 Oct 2004	France	0–0
13 Oct 2004	Faroe Islands	2–0
16 Nov 2004	Croatia	1–0
9 Feb 2005	Portugal	1–0
26 Mar 2005	Israel	1–1
29 Mar 2005	China	1–0
4 Jun 2005	Israel	2–2
8 Jun 2005	Faroe Islands	2–0
17 Aug 2005	Italy	1–2
7 Sep 2005	France	0–1
8 Oct 2005	Cyprus	1–0
12 Oct 2005	Switzerland	0–0

354. CURTIS FLEMING

Position	Defender
Born	Manchester, 8 October 1968
Club	St Patrick's Athletic; Middlesbrough; Birmingham City (loan); Crystal Palace; Darlington
Caps	**10**

Date	Team	Result	Goals
24 Apr 1996	Czech Republic	0–2	
29 May 1996	Portugal	0–1	
2 Jun 1996	Croatia	2–2	
4 Jun 1996	Holland	1–3	
9 Jun 1996	United States	1–2	
12 Jun 1996	Mexico	2–2	
15 Jun 1996	Bolivia	3–0	
21 May 1997	Liechtenstein	5–0	
11 Oct 1997	Romania	1–1	
23 May 1998	Mexico	0–0	

355. ALAN MOORE

Position	Left-winger
Born	Dublin, 25 November 1974
Club	Middlesbrough; Barnsley (loan); Burnley; Shelbourne
Caps	8

Date	Team	Result	Goals
24 Apr 1996	Czech Republic	0–2	
2 Jun 1996	Croatia	2–2	
4 Jun 1996	Holland	1–3	
12 Jun 1996	Mexico	2–2	
15 Jun 1996	Bolivia	3–0	
31 Aug 1996	Liechtenstein	5–0	
9 Oct 1996	Macedonia	3–0	
10 Nov 1996	Iceland	0–0	

356. GARY BREEN

Position	Central defender
Born	Hendon, 12 December 1973
Club	Maidstone United; Gillingham; Peterborough United; Birmingham City; Coventry City; West Ham United; Sunderland
Caps	63

Date	Team	Result	Goals
29 May 1996	Portugal	0–1	
2 Jun 1996	Croatia	2–2	
4 Jun 1996	Holland	1–3	1
9 Jun 1996	United States	1–2	
12 Jun 1996	Mexico	2–2	
15 Jun 1996	Bolivia	3–0	
31 Aug 1996	Liechtenstein	5–0	
9 Oct 1996	Macedonia	3–0	
10 Nov 1996	Iceland	0–0	
2 Apr 1997	Macedonia	2–3	
10 Sep 1997	Lithuania	2–1	
11 Oct 1997	Romania	1–1	
25 Mar 1998	Czech Republic	1–2	1
22 Apr 1998	Argentina	0–2	
23 May 1998	Mexico	0–0	
14 Oct 1998	Malta	5–0	1

18 Nov 1998	Yugoslavia	0–1	
10 Feb 1999	Paraguay	2–0	
28 Apr 1999	Sweden	2–0	
9 Jun 1999	Macedonia	1–0	
1 Sep 1999	Yugoslavia	2–1	
4 Sep 1999	Croatia	0–1	
8 Sep 1999	Malta	3–2	1
9 Oct 1999	Macedonia	1–1	
13 Nov 1997	Turkey	1–1	
17 Nov 1999	Turkey	0–0	
26 Apr 2000	Greece	0–1	
30 May 2000	Scotland	1–2	
4 Jun 2000	Mexico	2–2	
6 Jun 2000	United States	1–1	
11 Jun 2000	South Africa	2–1	
2 Sep 2000	Holland	2–2	
7 Oct 2000	Portugal	1–1	
11 Oct 2000	Estonia	2–0	
15 Nov 2000	Finland	3–0	
24 Mar 2001	Cyprus	4–0	
28 Mar 2001	Andorra	3–0	
25 Apr 2001	Andorra	3–1	1
6 Oct 2001	Cyprus	4–0	
10 Nov 2001	Iran	2–0	
15 Nov 2001	Iran	0–1	
13 Feb 2002	Russia	2–0	
17 Apr 2002	United States	2–1	
1 Jun 2002	Cameroon	1–1	
5 Jun 2002	Germany	1–1	
11 Jun 2002	Saudi Arabia	3–0	1
16 Jun 2002	Spain	1–1 lost 3–2 on penalties	
21 Aug 2002	Finland	3–0	
7 Sep 2002	Russia	2–4	
16 Oct 2002	Switzerland	1–2	
12 Feb 2003	Scotland	2–0	
29 Mar 2003	Georgia	2–1	
2 Apr 2003	Albania	0–0	
30 Apr 2003	Norway	1–0	

7 Jun 2003	Albania	2–1
11 Jun 2003	Georgia	2–0
19 Aug 2003	Australia	2–1
6 Sep 2003	Russia	1–1
9 Sep 2003	Turkey	2–2
11 Oct 2003	Switzerland	0–2
18 Aug 2004	Bulgaria	1–1
16 Nov 2004	Croatia	1–0
24 May 2006	Chile	0–1

357. DAVID CONNOLLY

Position	Forward
Born	Willesden, 6 June 1977
Club	Watford; Feyenoord (Holland); Wolverhampton Wanderers (loan); Excelsior (Holland); Feyenoord (Holland); Wimbledon; West Ham United; Leicester City; Wigan Athletic; Sunderland
Caps	41

Date	Team	Result	Goals
29 May 1996	Portugal	0–1	
4 Jun 1996	Holland	1–3	
9 Jun 1996	United States	1–2	1
12 Jun 1996	Mexico	2–2	1
30 Apr 1997	Romania	0–1	
21 May 1997	Liechtenstein	5–0	3
20 Aug 1997	Lithuania	0–0	
6 Sep 1997	Iceland	4–2	1
10 Sep 1997	Lithuania	2–1	
29 Oct 1997	Belgium	1–1	
16 Nov 1997	Belgium	1–2	
25 Mar 1998	Czech Republic	1–2	
23 May 1998	Mexico	0–0	
18 Nov 1998	Yugoslavia	0–1	
10 Feb 1999	Paraguay	2–0	1
28 Apr 1999	Sweden	2–0	
29 May 1999	Northern Ireland	0–1	
9 Jun 1999	Macedonia	1–0	
13 Nov 1999	Turkey	1–1	
17 Nov 1999	Turkey	0–0	

Date	Team	Result	Goals
23 Feb 2000	Czech Republic	3–2	
26 Apr 2000	Greece	0–1	
2 Sep 2000	Holland	2–2	
15 Nov 2000	Finland	3–0	
24 Mar 2001	Cyprus	4–0	
28 Mar 2001	Andorra	3–0	
25 Apr 2001	Andorra	3–1	
15 Aug 2001	Croatia	2–2	
6 Oct 2001	Cyprus	4–0	1
15 Nov 2001	Iran	0–1	
27 Mar 2002	Denmark	3–0	
17 Apr 2002	United States	2–1	
16 May 2002	Nigeria	1–2	
16 Jun 2002	Spain	1–1	
		lost 3–2 on penalties	
12 Feb 2003	Scotland	2–0	
30 Apr 2003	Norway	1–0	
7 Jun 2003	Albania	2–1	
19 Aug 2003	Australia	2–1	
9 Sep 2003	Turkey	2–2	1
11 Oct 2003	Switzerland	0–2	
8 Oct 2005	Cyprus	1–0	

358. GARETH FARRELLY

Position Midfield
Born Dublin, 28 August 1975
Club Home Farm; Aston Villa; Rotherham United (loan); Everton; Bolton Wanderers; Rotherham United (loan); Burnley (loan); Bradford City (loan); Wigan Athletic; Bohemians
Caps 6

Date	Team	Result	Goals
29 May 1996	Portugal	0–1	
9 Jun 1996	United States	1–2	
15 Jun 1996	Bolivia	3–0	
25 Mar 1998	Czech Republic	1–2	
23 May 1998	Mexico	0–0	
6 Jun 2000	United States	1–1	

359. KEITH O'NEILL

Position Left-winger
Born Dublin, 16 February 1976
Club Home Farm; Norwich City; Middlesbrough; Coventry City
Caps 13

Date	Team	Result	Goals
29 May 1996	Portugal	0–1	
2 Jun 1996	Croatia	2–2	1
4 Jun 1996	Holland	1–3	
9 Jun 1996	United States	1–2	
12 Jun 1996	Mexico	2–2	
15 Jun 1996	Bolivia	3–0	2
31 Aug 1996	Liechtenstein	5–0	1
9 Oct 1996	Macedonia	3–0	
2 Apr 1997	Macedonia	2–3	
5 Sep 1998	Croatia	2–0	
18 Nov 1998	Yugoslavia	0–1	
29 May 1999	Northern Ireland	0–1	
9 Oct 1999	Macedonia	1–1	

360. DAVE SAVAGE

Position Midfield
Born Dublin, 30 July 1973
Club Kilkenny City; Brighton & Hove Albion; Longford Town; Millwall; Northampton Town; Oxford United; Bristol Rovers
Caps 5

Date	Team	Result	Goals
29 May 1996	Portugal	0–1	
2 Jun 1996	Croatia	2–2	
9 Jun 1996	United States	1–2	
12 Jun 1996	Mexico	2–2	
15 Jun 1996	Bolivia	3–0	

361. IAN HARTE

Position Midfield
Born Drogheda, 31 August 1977
Club Leeds United; Levante (Spain)
Caps 64

Date	Team	Result	Goals
2 Jun 1996	Croatia	2–2	
4 Jun 1996	Holland	1–3	
12 Jun 1996	Mexico	2–2	
15 Jun 1996	Bolivia	3–0	1
31 Aug 1996	Liechtenstein	5–0	1
9 Oct 1996	Macedonia	3–0	
10 Nov 1996	Iceland	0–0	
11 Feb 1997	Wales	0–0	
2 Apr 1997	Macedonia	2–3	
30 Apr 1997	Romania	0–1	
21 May 1997	Liechtenstein	5–0	
20 Aug 1997	Lithuania	0–0	
6 Sep 1997	Iceland	4–2	
10 Sep 1997	Lithuania	2–1	
29 Oct 1997	Belgium	1–1	
16 Nov 1997	Belgium	1–2	
22 Apr 1998	Argentina	0–2	
23 May 1998	Mexico	0–0	
10 Feb 1999	Paraguay	2–0	
4 Sep 1999	Croatia	0–1	
8 Sep 1999	Malta	3–2	
23 Feb 2000	Czech Republic	3–2	1
2 Sep 2000	Holland	2–2	
7 Oct 2000	Portugal	1–1	
11 Oct 2000	Estonia	2–0	
15 Nov 2000	Finland	3–0	
24 Mar 2001	Cyprus	4–0	1
28 Mar 2001	Andorra	3–0	1
25 Apr 2001	Andorra	3–1	
2 Jun 2001	Portugal	1–1	
6 Jun 2001	Estonia	2–0	
15 Aug 2001	Croatia	2–2	
1 Sep 2001	Holland	1–0	
6 Oct 2001	Cyprus	4–0	1
10 Nov 2001	Iran	2–0	1
15 Nov 2001	Iran	0–1	
13 Feb 2002	Russia	2–0	
27 Mar 2002	Denmark	3–0	1
17 Apr 2002	United States	2–1	

Date	Team	Result	Goals
16 May 2002	Nigeria	1–2	
1 Jun 2002	Cameroon	1–1	
5 Jun 2002	Germany	1–1	
11 Jun 2002	Saudi Arabia	3–0	
16 Jun 2002	Spain	1–1 lost 3–2 on penalties	
21 Aug 2002	Finland	3–0	
7 Sep 2002	Russia	2–4	
16 Oct 2002	Switzerland	1–2	
12 Feb 2003	Scotland	2–0	
30 Apr 2003	Norway	1–0	
19 Aug 2003	Australia	2–1	
6 Sep 2003	Russia	1–1	
9 Sep 2003	Turkey	2–2	
11 Oct 2003	Switzerland	0–2	
18 Nov 2003	Canada	3–0	
31 Mar 2004	Czech Republic	2–1	1
28 Apr 2004	Poland	0–0	
4 Jun 2005`	Israel	2–2	1
8 Jun 2005	Faroe Islands	2–0	1
17 Aug 2005	Italy	1–2	
7 Sep 2005	France	0–1	
12 Oct 2005	Switzerland	0–0	
1 Mar 2006	Sweden	3–0	
24 May 2006	Chile	0–1	
7 Feb 2007	San Marino	2–1	

362. KEITH BRANAGAN

Position	Goalkeeper
Born	Fulham, 10 July 1966
Club	Cambridge United; Millwall; Brentford (loan); Gillingham (loan); Bolton Wanderers; Ipswich Town
Caps	1

Date	Team	Result	Goals
11 Feb 1997	Wales	0–0	

363. JON GOODMAN

Position	Forward
Born	Walthamstow, 2 June 1971
Club	Bromley; Millwall; Wimbledon
Caps	4

Date	Team	Result	Goals
11 Feb 1997	Wales	0–0	
2 Apr 1997	Macedonia	2–3	
30 Apr 1997	Romania	0–1	
21 May 1997	Liechtenstein	5–0	

364. KEVIN KILBANE

Position	Left-winger; Midfield
Born	Preston, 1 February 1977
Club	Preston North End; West Bromwich Albion; Sunderland; Everton; Wigan Athletic
Caps	86

Date	Team	Result	Goals
6 Sep 1997	Iceland	4–2	
25 Mar 1998	Czech Republic	1–2	
22 Apr 1998	Argentina	0–2	
28 Apr 1999	Sweden	2–0	
9 Jun 1999	Macedonia	1–0	
1 Sep 1999	Yugoslavia	2–1	
4 Sep 1999	Croatia	0–1	
8 Sep 1999	Malta	3–2	
13 Nov 1999	Turkey	1–1	
17 Nov 1999	Turkey	0–0	
23 Feb 2000	Czech Republic	3–2	
26 Apr 2000	Greece	0–1	
30 May 2000	Scotland	1–2	
4 Jun 2000	Mexico	2–2	
6 Jun 2000	United States	1–1	
11 Jun 2000	South Africa	2–1	
2 Sep 2000	Holland	2–2	
7 Oct 2000	Portugal	1–1	
11 Oct 2000	Estonia	2–0	
15 Nov 2000	Finland	3–0	1
24 Mar 2001	Cyprus	4–0	

Keith Branagan

Date	Team	Result	Goals
28 Mar 2001	Andorra	3–0	1
25 Apr 2001	Andorra	3–1	1
2 Jun 2001	Portugal	1–1	
6 Jun 2001	Estonia	2–0	
15 Aug 2001	Croatia	2–2	
1 Sep 2001	Holland	1–0	
6 Oct 2001	Cyprus	4–0	
10 Nov 2001	Iran	2–0	
15 Nov 2001	Iran	0–1	
13 Feb 2002	Russia	2–0	
17 Apr 2002	United States	2–1	
16 May 2002	Nigeria	1–2	
1 Jun 2002	Cameroon	1–1	
5 Jun 2002	Germany	1–1	
11 Jun 2002	Saudi Arabia	3–0	
16 Jun 2002	Spain	1–1 lost 3–2 on penalties	
21 Aug 2002	Finland	3–0	
7 Sep 2002	Russia	2–4	
16 Oct 2002	Switzerland	1–2	

Date	Team	Result	Goals
12 Feb 2003	Scotland	2–0	1
29 Mar 2003	Georgia	2–1	
2 Apr 2003	Albania	0–0	
30 Apr 2003	Norway	1–0	
7 Jun 2003	Albania	2–1	
11 Jun 2003	Georgia	2–0	
19 Aug 2003	Australia	2–1	
6 Sep 2003	Russia	1–1	
9 Sep 2003	Turkey	2–2	
11 Oct 2003	Switzerland	0–2	
18 Nov 2003	Canada	3–0	
18 Feb 2004	Brazil	0–0	
31 Mar 2004	Czech Republic	2–1	
18 Aug 2004	Bulgaria	1–1	
4 Sep 2004	Cyprus	3–0	
8 Sep 2004	Switzerland	1–1	
9 Oct 2004	France	0–0	
13 Oct 2004	Faroe Islands	2–0	
16 Nov 2004	Croatia	1–0	
9 Feb 2005	Portugal	1–0	
26 Mar 2005	Israel	1–1	
29 Mar 2005	China	1–0	
4 Jun 2005	Israel	2–2	
8 Jun 2005	Faroe Islands	2–0	1
17 Aug 2005	Italy	1–2	
7 Sep 2005	France	0–1	
8 Oct 2005	Cyprus	1–0	
12 Oct 2005	Switzerland	0–0	
1 Mar 2006	Sweden	3–0	
24 May 2006	Chile	0–1	
18 Aug 2006	Holland	0–4	
2 Sep 2006	Germany	0–1	
7 Oct 2006	Cyprus	2–5	
11 Oct 2006	Czech Republic	1–1	1
15 Nov 2006	San Marino	5–0	
7 Feb 2007	San Marino	2–1	1
24 Mar 2007	Wales	1–0	
28 Mar 2007	Slovakia	1–0	
23 May 2007	Ecuador	1–1	
26 May 2007	Bolivia	1–1	

Date	Team	Result	Goals
22 Aug 2007	Denmark	4–0	
8 Sep 2007	Slovakia	2–2	
12 Sep 2007	Czech Republic	0–1	
13 Oct 2007	Germany	0–0	
17 Oct 2007	Cyprus	1–1	
17 Nov 2007	Wales	2–2	

365. LEE CARSLEY

Position	Midfield
Born	Birmingham, 28 February 1974
Club	Derby County; Blackburn Rovers; Coventry City; Everton
Caps	38

Date	Team	Result	Goals
11 Oct 1997	Romania	1–1	
29 Oct 1997	Belgium	1–1	
16 Nov 1997	Belgium	1–2	
25 Mar 1998	Czech Republic	1–2	
22 Apr 1998	Argentina	0–2	
23 May 1998	Mexico	0–0	
5 Sep 1998	Croatia	2–0	
14 Oct 1998	Malta	5–0	
10 Feb 1999	Paraguay	2–0	
29 May 1999	Northern Ireland	0–1	
9 Jun 1999	Macedonia	1–0	
1 Sep 1999	Yugoslavia	2–1	
4 Sep 1999	Croatia	0–1	
8 Sep 1999	Malta	3–2	
13 Nov 1999	Turkey	1–1	
15 Nov 2000	Finland	3–0	
15 Aug 2001	Croatia	2–2	
6 Oct 2001	Cyprus	4–0	
13 Feb 2002	Russia	2–0	
11 Jun 2002	Saudi Arabia	3–0	
21 Aug 2002	Finland	3–0	
20 Nov 2002	Greece	0–0	
12 Feb 2003	Scotland	2–0	
29 Mar 2003	Georgia	2–1	
2 Apr 2003	Albania	0–0	
30 Apr 2003	Norway	1–0	

Date	Team	Result	Goals
7 Jun 2003	Albania	2–1	
11 Jun 2003	Georgia	2–0	
6 Sep 2003	Russia	1–1	
11 Oct 2006	Czech Republic	1–1	
15 Nov 2006	San Marino	5–0	
7 Feb 2007	San Marino	2–1	
24 Mar 2007	Wales	1–0	
28 Mar 2007	Slovakia	1–0	
8 Sep 2007	Slovakia	2–2	
12 Sep 2007	Czech Republic	0–1	
13 Oct 2007	Germany	0–0	
17 Nov 2007	Wales	2–2	

366. MICKY EVANS

Position Forward
Born Plymouth, 1 January 1973
Club Plymouth Argyle; Southampton; West Bromwich Albion; Bristol Rovers; Plymouth Argyle; Torquay United
Caps 1

Date	Team	Result	Goals
11 Oct 1997	Romania	1–1	

367. RORY DELAP

Position Midfield
Born Sutton Coldfield, 6 July 1976
Club Carlisle United; Derby County; Southampton; Sunderland; Stoke City
Caps 11

Date	Team	Result	Goals
25 Mar 1998	Czech Republic	1–2	
22 Apr 1998	Argentina	0–2	
23 May 1998	Mexico	0–0	
13 Nov 1999	Turkey	1–1	
17 Nov 1999	Turkey	0–0	
26 Apr 2000	Greece	0–1	
17 Apr 2002	United States	2–1	
21 Aug 2002	Finland	3–0	
20 Nov 2002	Greece	0–0	
18 Nov 2003	Canada	3–0	
31 Mar 2004	Czech Republic	2–1	

368. DAMIEN DUFF

Position Midfield
Born Dublin, 2 March 1979
Club Lourdes Celtic; Blackburn Rovers; Chelsea; Newcastle United
Caps 66

Date	Team	Result	Goals
25 Mar 1998	Czech Republic	1–2	
23 May 1998	Mexico	0–0	
5 Sep 1998	Croatia	2–0	
14 Oct 1998	Malta	5–0	
18 Nov 1998	Yugoslavia	0–1	
10 Feb 1999	Paraguay	2–0	
28 Apr 1999	Sweden	2–0	
29 May 1999	Northern Ireland	0–1	
9 Jun 1999	Macedonia	1–0	
4 Sep 1999	Croatia	0–1	
8 Sep 1999	Malta	3–2	
13 Nov 1999	Turkey	1–1	
17 Nov 1999	Turkey	0–0	
30 May 2000	Scotland	1–2	
7 Oct 2000	Portugal	1–1	
11 Oct 2000	Estonia	2–0	
24 Mar 2001	Cyprus	4–0	
28 Mar 2001	Andorra	3–0	
2 Jun 2001	Portugal	1–1	
6 Jun 2001	Estonia	2–0	
15 Aug 2001	Croatia	2–2	1
1 Sep 2001	Holland	1–0	
13 Feb 2002	Russia	2–0	
27 Mar 2002	Denmark	3–0	
17 Apr 2002	United States	2–1	
16 May 2002	Nigeria	1–2	
1 Jun 2002	Cameroon	1–1	
5 Jun 2002	Germany	1–1	
11 Jun 2002	Saudi Arabia	3–0	1
16 Jun 2002	Spain	1–1 lost 3–2 on penalties	
21 Aug 2002	Finland	3–0	
7 Sep 2002	Russia	2–4	

Date	Team	Result	Goals
16 Oct 2002	Switzerland	1–2	
29 Mar 2003	Georgia	2–1	
2 Apr 2003	Albania	0–0	
30 Apr 2003	Norway	1–0	1
7 Jun 2003	Albania	2–1	
19 Aug 2003	Australia	2–1	
6 Sep 2003	Russia	1–1	1
9 Sep 2003	Turkey	2–2	
11 Oct 2003	Switzerland	0–2	
18 Nov 2003	Canada	3–0	
31 Mar 2004	Czech Republic	2–1	
18 Aug 2004	Bulgaria	1–1	
4 Sep 2004	Cyprus	3–0	
8 Sep 2004	Switzerland	1–1	
9 Oct 2004	France	0–0	
13 Oct 2004	Faroe Islands	2–0	
16 Nov 2004	Croatia	1–0	
9 Feb 2005	Portugal	1–0	
26 Mar 2005	Israel	1–1	
29 Mar 2005	China	1–0	
4 Jun 2005	Israel	2–2	
8 Jun 2005	Faroe Islands	2–0	
17 Aug 2005	Italy	1–2	
7 Sep 2005	France	0–1	
8 Oct 2005	Cyprus	1–0	
1 Mar 2006	Sweden	3–0	1
24 May 2006	Chile	0–1	
2 Sep 2006	Germany	0–1	
7 Oct 2006	Cyprus	2–5	
11 Oct 2006	Czech Republic	1–1	
15 Nov 2006	San Marino	5–0	
7 Feb 2007	San Marino	2–1	
24 Mar 2007	Wales	1–0	
28 Mar 2007	Slovakia	1–0	

369. GRAHAM KAVANAGH

Position Midfield
Born Dublin, 2 December 1973
Club Home Farm; Middlesbrough; Darlington (loan); Stoke City; Cardiff City; Wigan Athletic; Sunderland
Caps 16

Date	Team	Result	Goals
25 Mar 1998	Czech Republic	1–2	
28 Apr 1999	Sweden	2–0	1
29 May 1999	Northern Ireland	0–1	
18 Nov 2003	Canada	3–0	
18 Feb 2004	Brazil	0–0	
18 Aug 2004	Bulgaria	1–1	
4 Sep 2004	Cyprus	3–0	
8 Sep 2004	Switzerland	1–1	
16 Nov 2004	Croatia	1–0	
9 Feb 2005	Portugal	1–0	
29 Mar 2005	China	1–0	
4 Jun 2005	Israel	2–2	
8 Oct 2005	Cyprus	1–0	
1 Mar 2006	Sweden	3–0	
24 May 2006	Chile	0–1	
18 Aug 2006	Holland	0–4	

370. ROBBIE KEANE

Position Forward
Born Dublin, 8 July 1980
Club Wolverhampton Wanderers; Coventry City; Inter Milan (Italy); Leeds United; Tottenham Hotspur
Caps 78

Date	Team	Result	Goals
25 Mar 1998	Czech Republic	1–2	
22 Apr 12998	Argentina	0–2	
23 May 1998	Mexico	0–0	
5 Sep 1998	Croatia	2–0	
14 Oct 1998	Malta	5–0	2
10 Feb 1999	Paraguay	2–0	
28 Apr 1999	Sweden	2–0	
29 May 1999	Northern Ireland	0–1	
9 Jun 1999	Macedonia	1–0	
1 Sep 1999	Yugoslavia	2–1	1
8 Sep 1999	Malta	3–2	1
9 Oct 1999	Macedonia	1–1	
13 Nov 1999	Turkey	1–1	1
23 Feb 2000	Czech Republic	3–2	1

26 Apr 2000	Greece	0–1	
30 May 2000	Scotland	1–2	
4 Jun 2000	Mexico	2–2	
11 Jun 2000	South Africa	2–1	
2 Sep 2000	Holland	2–2	1
7 Oct 2000	Portugal	1–1	
11 Oct 2000	Estonia	2–0	
15 Nov 2000	Finland	3–0	
24 Mar 2001	Cyprus	4–0	
28 Mar 2001	Andorra	3–0	
2 Jun 2001	Portugal	1–1	
15 Aug 2001	Croatia	2–2	
1 Sep 2001	Holland	1–0	
10 Nov 2001	Iran	2–0	1
15 Nov 2001	Iran	0–1	
13 Feb 2002	Russia	2–0	1
27 Mar 2002	Denmark	3–0	1
17 Apr 2002	United States	2–1	
16 May 2002	Nigeria	1–2	
1 Jun 2002	Cameroon	1–1	
5 Jun 2002	Germany	1–1	1
11 Jun 2002	Saudi Arabia	3–0	1
16 Jun 2002	Spain	1–1 lost 3–2 on penalties	
21 Aug 2002	Finland	3–0	1
7 Sep 2002	Russia	2–4	
16 Oct 2002	Switzerland	1–2	
2 Apr 2003	Albania	0–0	
30 Apr 2003	Norway	1–0	
7 Jun 2003	Albania	2–1	1
11 Jun 2003	Georgia	2–0	1
19 Aug 2003	Australia	2–1	
11 Oct 2003	Switzerland	0–2	
18 Nov 2003	Canada	3–0	2
18 Feb 2004	Brazil	0–0	
31 Mar 2004	Czech Republic	2–1	1
27 May 2004	Romania	1–0	
29 May 2004	Nigeria	0–3	
5 Jun 2004	Holland	1–0	1
4 Sep 2004	Cyprus	3–0	1
8 Sep 2004	Switzerland	1–1	
9 Oct 2004	France	0–0	
13 Oct 2004	Faroe Islands	2–0	2
16 Nov 2004	Croatia	1–0	1
9 Feb 2005	Portugal	1–0	
26 Mar 2005	Israel	1–1	
29 Mar 2005	China	1–0	
4 Jun 2005	Israel	2–2	1
7 Sep 2005	France	0–1	
8 Oct 2005	Cyprus	1–0	
12 Oct 2005	Switzerland	0–0	
1 Mar 2006	Sweden	3–0	1
24 May 2006	Chile	0–1	
2 Sep 2006	Germany	0–1	
7 Oct 2006	Cyprus	2–5	
11 Oct 2006	Czech Republic	1–1	
15 Nov 2006	San Marino	5–0	3
7 Feb 2007	San Marino	2–1	
24 Mar 2007	Wales	1–0	
22 Aug 2007	Denmark	4–0	2
8 Sep 2007	Slovakia	2–2	
12 Sep 2007	Czech Republic	0–1	
13 Oct 2007	Germany	0–0	
17 Oct 2007	Cyprus	1–1	
17 Nov 2007	Wales	2–2	1

371. MARK KINSELLA

Position	Midfield
Born	Dublin, 12 August 1972
Club	Home Farm; Colchester United; Charlton Athletic; Aston Villa; West Bromwich Albion; Walsall
Caps	48

Date	Team	Result	Goals
25 Mar 1998	Czech Republic	1–2	
22 Apr 1998	Argentina	0–2	
5 Sep 1998	Croatia	2–0	
14 Oct 1998	Malta	5–0	
18 Nov 1998	Yugoslavia	0–1	

10 Feb 1999	Paraguay	2–0	
28 Apr 1999	Sweden	2–0	
29 May 1999	Northern Ireland	0–1	
9 Jun 1999	Macedonia	1–0	
1 Sep 1999	Yugoslavia	2–1	
4 Sep 1999	Croatia	0–1	
8 Sep 1999	Malta	3–2	
9 Oct 1999	Macedonia	1–1	
17 Nov 1999	Turkey	0–0	
23 Feb 2000	Czech Republic	3–2	
26 Apr 2000	Greece	0–1	
2 Sep 2000	Holland	2–2	
7 Oct 2000	Portugal	1–1	
11 Oct 2000	Estonia	2–0	1
15 Nov 2000	Finland	3–0	
24 Mar 2001	Cyprus	4–0	
25 Apr 2001	Andorra	3–1	1
2 Jun 2001	Portugal	1–1	
6 Jun 2001	Estonia	2–0	
15 Nov 2001	Iran	0–1	
27 Mar 2002	Denmark	3–0	
17 Apr 2002	United States	2–1	1
16 May 2002	Nigeria	1–2	
1 Jun 2002	Cameroon	1–1	
5 Jun 2002	Germany	1–1	
11 Jun 2002	Saudi Arabia	3–0	
16 Jun 2002	Spain	1–1 lost 3–2 on penalties	
21 Aug 2002	Finland	3–0	
7 Sep 2002	Russia	2–4	
16 Oct 2002	Switzerland	1–2	
12 Feb 2003	Scotland	2–0	
29 Mar 2003	Georgia	2–1	
2 Apr 2003	Albania	0–0	
30 Apr 2003	Norway	1–0	
7 Jun 2003	Albania	2–1	
11 Jun 2003	Georgia	2–0	
19 Aug 2003	Australia	2–1	
9 Sep 2003	Turkey	2–2	

11 Oct 2003	Switzerland	0–2	
31 Mar 2004	Czech Republic	2–1	
28 Apr 2004	Poland	0–0	
29 May 2004	Nigeria	0–3	
2 Jun 2004	Jamaica	1–0	

372. ALAN MAYBURY

Position Full-back
Born Dublin, 8 August 1978
Club St Kevin's BC; Leeds United; Reading (loan); Crewe Alexandra (loan); Heart of Midlothian; Leicester City
Caps 10

Date	Team	Result	Goals
25 Mar 1998	Czech Republic	1–2	
29 May 1999	Northern Ireland	0–1	
31 Mar 2004	Czech Republic	2–1	
28 Apr 2004	Poland	0–0	
27 May 2004	Romania	1–0	
29 May 2004	Nigeria	0–3	
2 Jun 2004	Jamaica	1–0	
5 Jun 2004	Holland	1–0	
4 Sep 2004	Cyprus	3–0	
29 Mar 2005	China	1–0	

373. STEPHEN CARR

Position Full-back
Born Dublin, 29 August 1976
Club Tottenham Hotspur; Newcastle United
Caps 44

Date	Team	Result	Goals
28 Apr 1999	Sweden	2–0	
29 May 1999	Northern Ireland	0–1	
9 Jun 1999	Macedonia	1–0	
1 Sep 1999	Yugoslavia	2–1	
4 Sep 1999	Croatia	0–1	
8 Sep 1999	Malta	3–2	
13 Nov 1999	Turkey	1–1	
17 Nov 1999	Turkey	0–0	

Date	Team	Result	Goals
30 May 2000	Scotland	1–2	
4 Jun 2000	Mexico	2–2	
6 Jun 2000	United States	1–1	
11 Jun 2000	South Africa	2–1	
2 Sep 2000	Holland	2–2	
7 Oct 2000	Portugal	1–1	
11 Oct 2000	Estonia	2–0	
25 Apr 2001	Andorra	3–1	
2 Jun 2001	Portugal	1–1	
6 Jun 2001	Estonia	2–0	
12 Feb 2003	Scotland	2–0	
29 Mar 2003	Georgia	2–1	
2 Apr 2003	Albania	0–0	
30 Apr 2003	Norway	1–0	
7 Jun 2003	Albania	2–0	
11 Jun 2003	Georgia	2–0	
19 Aug 2003	Australia	2–1	
6 Sep 2003	Russia	1–1	
9 Sep 2003	Turkey	2–2	
11 Oct 2003	Switzerland	0–2	
18 Nov 2003	Canada	3–0	
18 Feb 2004	Brazil	0–0	
18 Aug 2004	Bulgaria	1–1	
4 Sep 2004	Cyprus	3–0	
8 Sep 2004	Switzerland	1–1	
9 Oct 2004	France	0–0	
13 Oct 2004	Faroe Islands	2–0	
26 Mar 2005	Israel	1–1	
8 Jun 2005	Faroe Islands	2–0	
17 Aug 2005	Italy	1–2	
7 Sep 2005	France	0–1	
8 Oct 2005	Cyprus	1–0	
12 Oct 2005	Switzerland	0–0	
18 Aug 2006	Holland	0–4	
2 Sep 2006	Germany	0–1	
22 Aug 2007	Denmark	4–0	

374. MATT HOLLAND

Position Midfield
Born Bury, 11 April 1974

Club West Ham United; Bournemouth; Ipswich Town; Charlton Athletic
Caps 49

Date	Team	Result	Goals
9 Oct 1999	Macedonia	1–1	
4 Jun 2000	Mexico	2–2	
6 Jun 2000	United States	1–1	
11 Jun 2000	South Africa	2–1	
7 Oct 2000	Portugal	1–1	1
15 Nov 2000	Finland	3–0	
24 Mar 2001	Cyprus	4–0	
28 Mar 2001	Andorra	3–0	1
25 Apr 2001	Andorra	3–1	
2 Jun 2001	Portugal	1–1	
6 Jun 2001	Estonia	2–0	1
1 Sep 2001	Holland	1–0	
6 Oct 2001	Cyprus	4–0	
10 Nov 2001	Iran	2–0	
15 Nov 2001	Iran	0–1	
13 Feb 2002	Russia	2–0	
27 Mar 2002	Denmark	3–0	
17 Apr 2002	United States	2–1	
16 May 2002	Nigeria	1–2	
1 Jun 2002	Cameroon	1–1	1
5 Jun 2002	Germany	1–1	
11 Jun 2002	Saudi Arabia	3–0	
16 Jun 2002	Spain	1–1	
		lost 3–2 on penalties	
21 Aug 2002	Finland	3–0	
7 Sep 2002	Russia	2–4	
16 Oct 2002	Switzerland	1–2	
20 Nov 2002	Greece	0–0	
12 Feb 2003	Scotland	2–0	
29 Mar 2003	Georgia	2–1	
2 Apr 2003	Albania	0–0	
30 Apr 2003	Norway	1–0	
7 Jun 2003	Albania	2–1	
11 Jun 2003	Georgia	2–0	
19 Aug 2003	Australia	2–1	
6 Sep 2003	Russia	1–1	

Date	Team	Result	Goals
11 Oct 2003	Switzerland	0–2	
18 Nov 2003	Canada	3–0	
18 Feb 2004	Brazil	0–0	
31 Mar 2004	Czech Republic	2–1	
27 May 2004	Romania	1–0	1
29 May 2004	Nigeria	0–3	
2 Jun 2004	Jamaica	1–0	
5 Jun 2004	Holland	1–0	
9 Feb 2005	Portugal	1–0	
26 Mar 2005	Israel	1–1	
4 Jun 2005	Israel	2–2	
17 Aug 2005	Italy	1–2	
8 Oct 2005	Cyprus	1–0	
12 Oct 2005	Switzerland	0–0	

375. DEAN KIELY

Position Goalkeeper
Born Salford, 10 October 1970
Club Coventry City; York City; Bury; Charlton Athletic; Portsmouth; Luton Town (loan); West Bromwich Albion
Caps 8

Date	Team	Result	Goals
13 Nov 1999	Turkey	1–1	
17 Nov 1999	Turkey	0–0	
26 Apr 2000	Greece	0–1	
4 Jun 2000	Mexico	2–2	
13 Feb 2002	Russia	2–0	
27 Mar 2002	Denmark	3–0	
21 Aug 2002	Finland	3–0	
12 Feb 2003	Scotland	2–0	

376. PAUL BUTLER

Position Central defender
Born Manchester, 2 November 1972
Club Rochdale; Bury; Sunderland; Wolverhampton Wanderers; Leeds United; MK Dons
Caps 1

Date	Team	Result	Goals
23 Feb 2000	Czech Republic	3–2	

377. GARY DOHERTY

Position Central defender; Forward
Born Camdonagh, County Donegal, 31 January 1980
Club Luton Town; Tottenham Hotspur; Norwich City
Caps 34

Date	Team	Result	Goals
26 Apr 2000	Greece	0–1	
6 Jun 2000	United States	1–1	
11 Jun 2000	South Africa	2–1	
24 Mar 2001	Cyprus	4–0	
28 Mar 2001	Andorra	3–0	
25 Apr 2003	Andorra	3–1	
2 Jun 2001	Portugal	1–1	
6 Jun 2001	Estonia	2–0	
17 Apr 2002	United States	2–1	1
21 Aug 2002	Finland	3–0	
7 Sep 2002	Russia	2–4	1
16 Oct 2002	Switzerland	1–2	
20 Nov 2002	Greece	0–0	
12 Feb 2003	Scotland	2–0	
29 Mar 2003	Georgia	2–1	1
2 Apr 2003	Albania	0–0	
7 Jun 2003	Albania	2–1	
11 Jun 2003	Georgia	2–0	1
19 Aug 2003	Australia	2–1	
6 Sep 2003	Russia	1–1	
9 Sep 2003	Turkey	2–2	
18 Nov 2003	Canada	3–0	
31 Mar 2004	Czech Republic	2–1	
28 Apr 2004	Poland	0–0	
29 May 2004	Nigeria	0–3	
2 Jun 2004	Jamaica	1–0	
18 Aug 2004	Bulgaria	1–1	
8 Sep 2004	Switzerland	1–1	
13 Oct 2004	Faroe Islands	2–0	
29 Mar 2005	China	1–0	
4 Jun 2005	Israel	2–2	
8 Jun 2005	Faroe Islands	2–0	

Date	Team	Result	Goals
7 Sep 2005	France	0–1	
12 Oct 2005	Switzerland	0–0	

378. RICHARD DUNNE

Position Defender
Born Dublin, 21 September 1979
Club Everton; Manchester City
Caps 39

Date	Team	Result	Goals
26 Apr 2000	Greece	0–1	
30 May 2000	Scotland	1–2	
4 Jun 2000	Mexico	2–2	1
2 Sep 2000	Holland	2–2	
7 Oct 2000	Portugal	1–1	
11 Oct 2000	Estonia	2–0	1
15 Nov 2000	Finland	3–0	
25 Apr 2001	Andorra	3–1	
2 Jun 2001	Portugal	1–1	
6 Jun 2001	Estonia	2–0	1
15 Aug 2001	Croatia	2–2	
1 Sep 2001	Holland	1–0	
13 Feb 2002	Russia	2–0	
27 Mar 2002	Denmark	3–0	
20 Nov 2002	Greece	0–0	
12 Feb 2003	Scotland	2–0	
30 Apr 2003	Norway	1–0	
19 Aug 2003	Australia	2–1	
9 Sep 2003	Turkey	2–2	1
18 Nov 2003	Canada	3–0	
16 Nov 2004	Croatia	1–0	
9 Feb 2005	Portugal	1–0	
29 Mar 2005	China	1–0	
17 Aug 2005	Italy	1–2	
7 Sep 2005	France	0–1	
8 Oct 2005	Cyprus	1–0	
12 Oct 2005	Switzerland	0–0	
1 Mar 2006	Sweden	3–0	
24 May 2006	Chile	0–1	
2 Sep 2006	Germany	0–1	
7 Oct 2006	Cyprus	2–5	1
15 Nov 2006	San Marino	5–0	
7 Feb 2007	San Marino	2–1	
24 Mar 2007	Wales	1–0	
28 Mar 2007	Slovakia	1–0	
22 Aug 2007	Denmark	4–0	
8 Sep 2007	Slovakia	2–2	
12 Sep 2007	Czech Republic	0–1	
13 Oct 2007	Germany	0–0	

379. STEVE FINNAN

Position Right-back
Born Limerick, 20 April 1976
Club Welling United; Birmingham City; Notts County; Fulham; Liverpool
Caps 50

Date	Team	Result	Goals
26 Apr 2000	Greece	0–1	
30 May 2000	Scotland	1–2	
7 Oct 2000	Portugal	1–1	
11 Oct 2000	Estonia	2–0	
15 Nov 2000	Finland	3–0	1
28 Mar 2001	Andorra	3–0	
25 Apr 2001	Andorra	3–1	
15 Aug 2001	Croatia	2–2	
1 Sep 2001	Holland	1–0	
6 Oct 2001	Cyprus	4–0	
10 Nov 2001	Iran	2–0	
15 Nov 2001	Iran	0–1	
13 Feb 2002	Russia	2–0	
17 Apr 2002	United States	2–1	
16 May 2002	Nigeria	1–2	
1 Jun 2002	Cameroon	1–1	
5 Jun 2002	Germany	1–1	
11 Jun 2002	Saudi Arabia	3–0	
16 Jun 2002	Spain	1–1 lost 3–2 on penalties	
7 Sep 2002	Russia	2–4	
20 Nov 2002	Greece	0–0	
30 Apr 2003	Norway	1–0	
19 Aug 2003	Australia	2–1	

Date	Team	Result	Goals
9 Sep 2003	Turkey	2–2	
11 Oct 2003	Switzerland	0–2	
27 May 2004	Romania	1–0	
29 May 2004	Nigeria	0–3	
5 Jun 2004	Holland	1–0	
18 Aug 2004	Bulgaria	1–1	
4 Sep 2004	Cyprus	3–0	
8 Sep 2004	Switzerland	1–1	
9 Oct 2004	France	0–0	
13 Oct 2004	Faroe Islands	2–0	
16 Nov 2004	Croatia	1–0	
9 Feb 2005	Portugal	1–0	
26 Mar 2005	Israel	1–1	
17 Aug 2005	Italy	1–2	
8 Oct 2005	Cyprus	1–0	
18 Aug 2006	Holland	0–4	
2 Sep 2006	Germany	0–1	
7 Oct 2006	Cyprus	2–5	
11 Oct 2006	Czech Republic	1–1	
15 Nov 2006	San Marino	5–0	
7 Feb 2007	San Marino	2–1	
24 Mar 2007	Wales	1–0	
28 Mar 2007	Slovakia	1–0	
22 Aug 2007	Denmark	4–0	
13 Oct 2007	Germany	0–0	
17 Oct 2007	Cyprus	1–1	1
17 Nov 2007	Wales	2–2	

380. ALAN MAHON

Position	Midfield
Born	Dublin, 4 April 1978
Club	Tranmere Rovers; Sporting Lisbon (Portugal); Blackburn Rovers; Cardiff City (loan); Ipswich Town (loan); Wigan Athletic; Burnley
Caps	2

Date	Team	Result	Goals
26 Apr 2000	Greece	0–1	
11 Jun 2000	South Africa	2–1	

381. BARRY QUINN

Position	Midfield
Born	Dublin, 9 May 1979
Club	Coventry City; Rushden and Diamonds (loan); Oxford United
Caps	4

Date	Team	Result	Goals
26 Apr 2000	Greece	0–1	
4 Jun 2000	Mexico	2–2	
6 Jun 2000	United States	1–1	
11 Jun 2000	South Africa	2–1	

382. DOMINIC FOLEY

Position	Forward
Born	Cork, 7 July 1976
Club	St James's Gate; Wolverhampton Wanderers; Watford (loan); Notts County (loan); Ethnikos (Greece) (loan); Watford; Queen's Park Rangers (loan); Swindon Town (loan); Queen's Park Rangers (loan); Southend United (loan); Oxford United (loan); SC Braga (Portugal); Bohemians; KAA Ghent (Belgium)
Caps	6

Date	Team	Result	Goals
30 May 2000	Scotland	1–2	
4 Jun 2000	Mexico	2–2	1
6 Jun 2000	United States	1–1	1
11 Jun 2000	South Africa	2–1	
11 Oct 2000	Estonia	2–0	
15 Nov 2000	Finland	3–0	

383. STEPHEN McPHAIL

Position	Midfield
Born	Westminster, 9 December 1979
Club	Leeds United; Millwall (loan); Nottingham Forest (loan); Barnsley; Cardiff City
Caps	10

Date	Team	Result	Goals
30 May 2000	Scotland	1–2	

6 Jun 2000	United States	1–1	
11 Jun 2000	South Africa	2–1	1
15 Aug 2001	Croatia	2–2	
6 Oct 2001	Cyprus	4–0	
21 Aug 2002	Finland	3–0	
20 Nov 2002	Greece	0–0	
9 Sep 2003	Turkey	2–2	
18 Nov 2003	Canada	3–0	
29 May 2004	Nigeria	0–3	

384. ANDY O'BRIEN

Position	Central defender
Born	Harrogate, 29 June 1979
Club	Bradford City; Newcastle United; Portsmouth; Bolton Wanderers
Caps	27

Date	Team	Result	Goals
11 Oct 2000	Estonia	2–0	
15 Aug 2001	Croatia	2–2	
1 Sep 2001	Holland	1–0	
13 Feb 2002	Russia	2–0	
17 Apr 2002	United States	2–1	
12 Feb 2003	Scotland	2–0	
19 Aug 2003	Australia	2–1	
9 Sep 2003	Turkey	2–2	
18 Feb 2004	Brazil	0–0	
28 Apr 2004	Poland	0–0	
27 May 2004	Romania	1–0	
2 Jun 2004	Jamaica	1–0	
5 Jun 2004	Holland	1–0	
4 Sep 2004	Cyprus	3–0	
8 Sep 2004	Switzerland	1–1	
9 Oct 2004	France	0–0	
13 Oct 2004	Faroe Islands	2–0	
9 Feb 2005	Portugal	1–0	1
26 Mar 2005	Israel	1–1	
29 Mar 2005	China	1–0	
4 Jun 2005	Israel	2–2	
17 Aug 2005	Italy	1–2	
1 Mar 2006	Sweden	3–0	

18 Aug 2006	Holland	0–4	
2 Sep 2006	Germany	0–1	
7 Oct 2006	Cyprus	2–5	
26 May 2007	Bolivia	1–1	

385. CLINTON MORRISON

Position	Forward
Born	Wandsworth, 14 May 1979
Club	Crystal Palace; Birmingham City; Crystal Palace
Caps	36

Date	Team	Result	Goals
15 Aug 2001	Croatia	2–2	1
6 Oct 2001	Cyprus	4–0	
15 Nov 2001	Iran	0–1	
13 Feb 2002	Russia	2–0	
27 Mar 2002	Denmark	3–0	1
17 Apr 2002	United States	2–1	
16 May 2002	Nigeria	1–2	
7 Sep 2002	Russia	2–4	1
16 Oct 2002	Switzerland	1–2	
12 Feb 2003	Scotland	2–0	1
19 Aug 2003	Australia	2–1	1
6 Sep 2003	Russia	1–1	
9 Sep 2003	Turkey	2–2	
11 Oct 2003	Switzerland	0–2	
18 Nov 2003	Canada	3–0	
18 Feb 2004	Brazil	0–0	
31 Mar 2004	Czech Republic	2–1	
28 Apr 2004	Poland	0–0	
27 May 2004	Romania	1–0	
2 Jun 2004	Jamaica	1–0	
5 Jun 2004	Holland	1–0	
18 Aug 2004	Bulgaria	1–1	
4 Sep 2004	Cyprus	3–0	1
8 Sep 2004	Switzerland	1–1	1
9 Oct 2004	France	0–0	
9 Feb 2005	Portugal	1–0	
26 Mar 2005	Israel	1–1	1
29 Mar 2005	China	1–0	1

Date	Team	Result	Goals
4 Jun 2005	Israel	2–2	
8 Jun 2005	Faroe Islands	2–0	
17 Aug 2005	Italy	1–2	
7 Sep 2005	France	0–1	
12 Oct 2005	Switzerland	0–0	
1 Mar 2006	Sweden	3–0	
18 Aug 2006	Holland	0–4	
7 Oct 2006	Cyprus	2–5	

386. JOHN O'SHEA

Position Central defender
Born Waterford, 30 April 1981
Club Waterford; Manchester United; Bournemouth (loan); Royal Antwerp (Belgium) (loan); Manchester United
Caps 43

Date	Team	Result	Goals
15 Aug 2001	Croatia	2–2	
20 Nov 2002	Greece	0–0	
12 Feb 2002	Scotland	2–0	
29 Mar 2003	Georgia	2–1	
2 Apr 2003	Albania	0–0	
7 Jun 2003	Albania	2–1	
11 Jun 2003	Georgia	2–0	
19 Aug 2003	Australia	2–1	1
6 Sep 2003	Russia	1–1	
11 Oct 2003	Switzerland	0–2	
18 Nov 2003	Canada	3–0	
18 Feb 2004	Brazil	0–0	
28 Apr 2004	Poland	0–0	
2 Jun 2004	Jamaica	1–0	
18 Aug 2004	Bulgaria	1–1	
4 Sep 2004	Cyprus	3–0	
9 Oct 2004	France	0–0	
13 Oct 2004	Faroe Islands	2–0	
16 Nov 2004	Croatia	1–0	
9 Feb 2004	Portugal	1–0	
26 Mar 2005	Israel	1–1	
29 Mar 2005	China	1–0	
4 Jun 2005	Israel	2–2	

Date	Team	Result	Goals
8 Jun 2005	Faroe Islands	2–0	
17 Aug 2005	Italy	1–2	
7 Sep 2005	France	0–1	
8 Oct 2005	Cyprus	1–0	
12 Oct 2005	Switzerland	0–0	
1 Mar 2006	Sweden	3–0	
24 May 2006	Chile	0–1	
18 Aug 2006	Holland	0–4	
2 Sep 2006	Germany	0–1	
7 Oct 2006	Cyprus	2–5	
11 Oct 2006	Czech Republic	1–1	
15 Nov 2006	San Marino	5–0	
7 Feb 2007	San Marino	2–1	
24 Mar 2007	Wales	1–0	
28 Mar 2007	Slovakia	1–0	
22 Aug 2007	Denmark	4–0	
8 Sep 2007	Slovakia	2–2	
12 Sep 2007	Czech Republic	0–1	
17 Oct 2007	Cyprus	1–1	
17 Nov 2007	Wales	2–2	

387. STEVEN REID

Position Midfield
Born Kingston, 10 March 1981
Club Millwall; Blackburn Rovers
Caps 20

Date	Team	Result	Goals
15 Aug 2001	Croatia	2–2	
13 Feb 2002	Russia	2–0	1
27 Mar 2002	Denmark	3–0	
17 Apr 2002	United States	2–1	
16 May 2002	Nigeria	1–2	1
1 Jun 2002	Cameroon	1–1	
5 Jun 2002	Germany	1–1	
12 Feb 2003	Scotland	2–0	
7 Jun 2003	Albania	2–1	
6 Sep 2003	Russia	1–1	
9 Sep 2003	Turkey	2–2	
18 Nov 2003	Canada	3–0	
28 Apr 2004	Poland	0–0	

17 Aug 2005	Italy	1–2
8 Oct 2005	Cyprus	1–0
12 Oct 2005	Switzerland	0–0
1 Mar 2006	Sweden	3–0
24 May 2006	Chile	0–1
18 Aug 2006	Holland	0–4
2 Sep 2006	Germany	0–1

388. COLIN HEALY

Position Midfield
Born Cork, 14 March 1980
Club Wilton United; Glasgow Celtic; Coventry City (loan); Sunderland; Livingston; Barnsley; Bradford City (loan)
Caps 13

Date	Team	Result	Goals
13 Feb 2002	Russia	2–0	
27 Mar 2002	Denmark	3–0	
17 Apr 2002	United States	2–1	
21 Aug 2002	Finland	3–0	1
16 Oct 2002	Switzerland	1–2	
20 Nov 2002	Greece	0–0	
12 Feb 2003	Scotland	2–0	
30 Apr 2003	Norway	1–0	
11 Jun 2003	Georgia	2–0	
19 Aug 2003	Australia	2–1	
6 Sep 2003	Russia	1–1	
9 Sep 2003	Turkey	2–2	
11 Oct 2003	Switzerland	0–2	

389. RICHARD SADLIER

Position Forward
Born Dublin, 14 January 1979
Club Belvedere YC; Millwall
Caps 1

Date	Team	Result	Goals
13 Feb 2002	Russia	2–0	

390. NICKY COLGAN

Position Goalkeeper
Born Drogheda, 19 September 1973
Club Chelsea; Brentford (loan); Reading (loan); Bournemouth; Hibernian; Stockport County (loan); Barnsley; Dundee United (loan)
Caps 9

Date	Team	Result	Goals
27 Mar 2002	Denmark	3–0	
12 Feb 2003	Scotland	2–0	
30 Apr 2003	Norway	1–0	
19 Aug 2003	Australia	2–1	
9 Sep 2003	Turkey	2–2	
18 Nov 2003	Canada	3–0	
28 Apr 2004	Poland	0–0	
29 May 2004	Nigeria	0–3	
26 May 2007	Bolivia	1–1	

391. GRAHAM BARRETT

Position Midfield; Forward
Born Dublin, 6 October 1981
Club Arsenal; Bristol Rovers (loan); Crewe Alexandra (loan); Colchester United (loan); Brighton & Hove Albion (loan); Coventry City; Sheffield Wednesday (loan); Livingston
Caps 6

Date	Team	Result	Goals
21 Aug 2002	Finland	3–0	1
28 Apr 2004	Poland	0–0	
29 May 2004	Nigeria	0–3	
2 Jun 2004	Jamaica	1–0	1
5 Jun 2004	Holland	1–0	
16 Nov 2004	Croatia	1–0	

392. TOMMY BUTLER

Position Left-winger
Born Dublin, 25 April 1981
Club Sunderland; Darlington (loan); Dunfermline Athletic; Hartlepool United; Swansea City
Caps 2

Date	Team	Result	Goals
21 Aug 2002	Finland	3–0	
16 Oct 2002	Switzerland	1–2	

393. JIM GOODWIN

Position	Midfield
Born	Waterford, 20 November 1981
Club	Tramore; Glasgow Celtic; Stockport County; Scunthorpe United
Caps	1

Date	Team	Result	Goals
21 Aug 2002	Finland	3–0	

394. GLEN CROWE

Position	Forward
Born	Dublin, 25 December 1977
Club	Wolverhampton Wanderers; Exeter City (loan); Cardiff City (loan); Exeter City (loan); Plymouth Argyle; Bohemians; Shelbourne
Caps	2

Date	Team	Result	Goals
20 Nov 2002	Greece	0–0	
30 Apr 2003	Norway	1–0	

395. ALAN LEE

Position	Forward
Born	Galway, 21 August 1978
Club	Aston Villa, Torquay United (loan); Port Vale (loan); Burnley; Rotherham United; Cardiff City; Ipswich Town
Caps	10

Date	Team	Result	Goals
30 Apr 2003	Norway	1–0	
11 Jun 2003	Georgia	2–0	
31 Mar 2004	Czech Republic	2–1	
28 Apr 2004	Poland	0–0	
29 May 2004	Nigeria	0–3	
2 Jun 2004	Jamaica	1–0	
5 Jun 2004	Holland	1–0	

Date	Team	Result	Goals
4 Sep 2004	Cyprus	3–0	
7 Oct 2006	Cyprus	2–5	
15 Nov 2006	San Marino	5–0	

396. ALAN QUINN

Position	Midfield
Born	Dublin, 13 June 1979
Club	Cherry Orchard; Sheffield Wednesday; Sunderland (loan); Sheffield United
Caps	8

Date	Team	Result	Goals
30 Apr 2003	Norway	1–0	
19 Aug 2003	Australia	2–1	
2 Jun 2004	Jamaica	1–0	
5 Jun 2004	Holland	1–0	
18 Aug 2004	Bulgaria	1–1	
16 Nov 2004	Croatia	1–0	
11 Oct 2006	Czech Republic	1–1	
28 Mar 2007	Slovakia	1–0	

397. JOE MURPHY

Position	Goalkeeper
Born	Dublin, 21 August 1981
Club	Stella Maris; Tranmere Rovers; West Bromwich Albion; Walsall (loan); Sunderland; Walsall (loan); Scunthorpe United
Caps	1

Date	Team	Result	Goals
9 Sep 2003	Turkey	2–2	

398. ANDY REID

Position	Midfield
Born	Dublin, 29 July 1982
Club	Nottingham Forest; Tottenham Hotspur; Charlton Athletic
Caps	26

Date	Team	Result	Goals
18 Nov 2003	Canada	3–0	
18 Feb 2004	Brazil	0–0	

31 Mar 2004	Czech Republic	2–1	
28 Apr 2004	Poland	0–0	
27 May 2004	Romania	1–0	
2 Jun 2004	Jamaica	1–0	
5 Jun 2004	Holland	1–0	
18 Aug 2004	Bulgaria	1–1	1
4 Sep 2004	Cyprus	3–0	1
8 Sep 2004	Switzerland	1–1	
9 Oct 2004	France	0–0	
13 Oct 2004	Faroe Islands	2–0	
9 Feb 2005	Portugal	1–0	
29 Mar 2005	China	1–0	
4 Jun 2005	Israel	2–2	
8 Jun 2005	Faroe Islands	2–0	
17 Aug 2005	Italy	1–2	1
7 Sep 2005	France	0–1	
12 Oct 2005	Switzerland	0–0	
11 Oct 2006	Czech Republic	1–1	
15 Nov 2006	San Marino	5–0	
22 Aug 2007	Denmark	4–0	
12 Sep 2007	Czech Republic	0–1	
13 Oct 2007	Germany	0–0	
17 Oct 2007	Cyprus	1–1	
17 Nov 2007	Wales	2–2	

399. JOHN THOMPSON

Position Midfield; Right-back
Born Dublin, 12 October 1981
Club River Valley Rangers; Home Farm; Nottingham Forest; Tranmere Rovers (loan)
Caps 1

Date	Team	Result	Goals
18 Nov 2003	Canada	3–0	

400. PADDY KENNY

Position Goalkeeper
Born Halifax, 17 May 1978
Club Bradford Park Avenue; Bury; Sheffield United
Caps 7

Date	Team	Result	Goals
31 Mar 2004	Czech Republic	2–1	
2 Jun 2004	Jamaica	1–0	
18 Aug 2004	Bulgaria	1–1	
16 Nov 2004	Croatia	1–0	
29 Mar 2005	China	1–0	
18 Aug 2006	Holland	0–4	
7 Oct 2006	Cyprus	2–5	

401. LIAM MILLER

Position Midfield
Born Cork, 13 February 1981
Club Ballincollig AFC; Glasgow Celtic; Manchester United; Leeds United (loan); Sunderland
Caps 15

Date	Team	Result	Goals
31 Mar 2004	Czech Republic	2–1	
28 Apr 2004	Poland	0–0	
27 May 2004	Romania	1–0	
29 May 2004	Nigeria	0–3	
18 Aug 2004	Bulgaria	1–1	
13 Oct 2004	Faroe Islands	2–0	
16 Nov 2004	Croatia	1–0	
9 Feb 2005	Portugal	1–0	
29 Mar 2005	China	1–0	
17 Aug 2005	Italy	1–2	
1 Mar 2006	Sweden	3–0	1
24 May 2006	Chile	0–1	
18 Aug 2006	Holland	0–4	
17 Oct 2007	Cyprus	1–1	
17 Nov 2007	Wales	2–2	

402. JASON BYRNE

Position Forward
Born Dublin, 23 February 1978
Club Bray Wanderers; Shelbourne
Caps 2

Date	Team	Result	Goals
28 Apr 2004	Poland	0–0	
24 May 2006	Chile	0–1	

403. JONATHAN DOUGLAS

Position	Midfield
Born	Monaghan, 22 November 1981
Club	Blackburn Rovers; Chesterfield (loan); Blackpool (loan); Gillingham (loan); Leeds United
Caps	9

Date	Team	Result	Goals
28 Apr 2004	Poland	0–0	
29 May 2004	Nigeria	0–3	
18 Aug 2006	Holland	0–4	
7 Oct 2006	Cyprus	2–5	
11 Oct 2006	Czech Republic	1–1	
15 Nov 2006	San Marino	5–0	
24 Mar 2007	Wales	1–0	
8 Sep 2007	Slovakia	2–2	
17 Oct 2007	Cyprus	1–1	

404. MARTIN ROWLANDS

Position	Midfield
Born	Hammersmith, 8 February 1979
Club	Farnborough Town; Brentford; Queen's Park Rangers
Caps	3

Date	Team	Result	Goals
27 May 2004	Romania	1–0	
29 May 2004	Nigeria	0–3	
2 Jun 2004	Jamaica	1–0	

405. CLIVE CLARKE

Position	Left-back; Midfield
Born	Dublin, 14 January 1980
Club	Stoke City; West Ham United; Sunderland; Coventry City (loan)
Caps	2

Date	Team	Result	Goals
29 May 2004	Nigeria	0–3	
2 Jun 2004	Jamaica	1–0	

406. AIDEN McGEADY

Position	Midfield
Born	Glasgow, 4 April 1986
Club	Glasgow Celtic
Caps	16

Date	Team	Result	Goals
2 Jun 2004	Jamaica	1–0	
16 Nov 2004	Croatia	1–0	
9 Feb 2005	Portugal	1–0	
24 May 2006	Chile	0–1	
18 Aug 2006	Holland	0–4	
2 Sep 2006	Germany	0–1	
7 Oct 2006	Cyprus	2–5	
15 Nov 2006	San Marino	5–0	
24 Mar 2007	Wales	1–0	
28 Mar 2007	Slovakia	1–0	
22 Aug 2007	Denmark	4–0	
8 Sep 2007	Slovakia	2–2	
12 Sep 2007	Czech Republic	0–1	
13 Oct 2007	Germany	0–0	
17 Oct 2007	Cyprus	1–1	
17 Nov 2007	Wales	2–2	

407. MICHAEL DOYLE

Position	Midfield
Born	Dublin, 8 July 1981
Club	Glasgow Celtic; Coventry City
Caps	1

Date	Team	Result	Goals
5 Jun 2004	Holland	1–0	

408. JON MACKEN

Position	Forward
Born	Manchester, 7 September 1977
Club	Manchester United; Preston North End; Manchester City; Crystal Palace; Ipswich Town (loan); Derby County
Caps	1

Date	Team	Result	Goals
18 Aug 2004	Bulgaria	1–1	

409. STEPHEN ELLIOTT

Position	Forward
Born	Dublin, 6 January 1984
Club	Manchester City; Sunderland
Caps	9

Date	Team	Result	Goals
16 Nov 2004	Croatia	1–0	
29 Mar 2005	China	1–0	
8 Jun 2005	Faroe Islands	2–0	
17 Aug 2005	Italy	1–2	
8 Oct 2005	Cyprus	1–0	1
12 Oct 2005	Switzerland	0–0	
1 Mar 2006	Sweden	3–0	
18 Aug 2006	Holland	0–4	
2 Sep 2006	Germany	0–1	

410. KEVIN DOYLE

Position	Forward
Born	Dublin, 18 September 1983
Club	Adamstown FC; Wexford; St Patrick's Athletic; Cork City; Reading
Caps	15

Date	Team	Result	Goals
1 Mar 2006	Sweden	3–0	
24 May 2006	Chile	0–1	
18 Aug 2006	Holland	0–4	
2 Sep 2006	Germany	0–1	
15 Nov 2006	San Marino	5–0	1
24 Mar 2007	Wales	1–0	
28 Mar 2007	Slovakia	1–0	1
23 May 2007	Ecuador	1–1	1
26 May 2007	Bolivia	1–1	
22 Aug 2007	Denmark	4–0	
8 Sep 2007	Slovakia	2–2	1
12 Sep 2007	Czech Republic	0–1	
13 Oct 2007	Germany	0–0	
17 Oct 2007	Cyprus	1–1	
17 Nov 2007	Wales	2–2	1

411. JOEY O'BRIEN

Position	Right-back
Born	Dublin, 17 February 1986
Club	Bolton Wanderers; Sheffield Wednesday (loan)
Caps	3

Date	Team	Result	Goals
1 Mar 2006	Sweden	3–0	
13 Oct 2007	Germany	0–0	
17 Oct 2007	Cyprus	1–1	

412. WAYNE HENDERSON

Position	Goalkeeper
Born	Dublin, 16 September 1983
Club	Cherry Orchard; Aston Villa; Tamworth (loan); Wycombe Wanderers (loan); Notts County (loan); Brighton & Hove Albion; Preston North End
Caps	6

Date	Team	Result	Goals
1 Mar 2006	Sweden	3–0	
24 May 2006	Chile	0–1	
11 Oct 2006	Czech Republic	1–1	
7 Feb 2007	San Marino	2–1	
26 May 2007	Bolivia	1–1	
22 Aug 2007	Denmark	4–0	

413. STEPHEN IRELAND

Position	Midfield
Born	Cork, 22 August 1986
Club	Manchester City
Caps	6

Date	Team	Result	Goals
1 Mar 2006	Sweden	3–0	
7 Oct 2006	Cyprus	2–5	1
7 Feb 2007	San Marino	2–1	1
24 Mar 2007	Wales	1–0	1
28 Mar 2007	Slovakia	1–0	
8 Sep 2007	Slovakia	2–2	1

414. STEPHEN KELLY

Position	Full-back
Born	Dublin, 6 September 1983
Club	Tottenham Hotspur; Southend United (loan); Queen's Park Rangers (loan); Watford (loan); Birmingham City
Caps	9

Date	Team	Result	Goals
24 May 2006	Chile	0–1	
18 Aug 2006	Holland	0–4	
11 Oct 2006	Czech Republic	1–1	
23 May 2007	Ecuador	1–1	
26 May 2007	Bolivia	1–1	
22 Aug 2007	Denmark	4–0	
8 Sep 2007	Slovakia	2–2	
12 Sep 2007	Czech Republic	0–1	
13 Oct 2007	Germany	0–0	

415. ALAN O'BRIEN

Position	Left-winger
Born	Dublin, 20 February 1985
Club	Newcastle United; Carlisle United (loan)
Caps	5

Date	Team	Result	Goals
18 Aug 2006	Holland	0–4	
2 Sep 2006	Germany	0–1	
7 Oct 2006	Cyprus	2–5	
11 Oct 2006	Czech Republic	1–1	
26 May 2007	Bolivia	1–1	

416. PAUL McSHANE

Position	Central defender
Born	Wicklow, 6 January 1986
Club	Manchester United; Walsall (loan); Brighton & Hove Albion (loan); West Bromwich Albion; Sunderland
Caps	9

Date	Team	Result	Goals
11 Oct 2006	Czech Republic	1–1	

Date	Team	Result	Goals
15 Nov 2006	San Marino	5–0	
7 Feb 2007	San Marino	2–1	
24 Mar 2007	Wales	1–0	
28 Mar 2007	Slovakia	1–0	
8 Sep 2007	Slovakia	2–2	
12 Sep 2007	Czech Republic	0–1	
17 Oct 2007	Cyprus	1–1	
17 Nov 2007	Wales	2–2	

417. STEPHEN HUNT

Position	Midfield
Born	Port Laoise, 1 August 1980
Club	Crystal Palace; Brentford; Reading
Caps	9

Date	Team	Result	Goals
7 Feb 2007	San Marino	2–1	
24 Mar 2007	Wales	1–0	
28 Mar 2007	Slovakia	1–0	
23 May 2007	Ecuador	1–1	
26 May 2007	Bolivia	1–1	
22 Aug 2007	Denmark	4–0	
12 Sep 2007	Czech Republic	0–1	
17 Oct 2007	Cyprus	1–1	
17 Nov 2007	Wales	2–2	

418. SHANE LONG

Position	Forward
Born	Kilkenny, 22 January 1987
Club	Cork City; Reading
Caps	7

Date	Team	Result	Goals
7 Feb 2007	San Marino	2–1	
28 Mar 2007	Slovakia	1–0	
23 May 2007	Ecuador	1–1	
26 May 2007	Bolivia	1–1	1
22 Aug 2007	Denmark	4–0	2
12 Sep 2007	Czech Republic	0–1	
13 Oct 2007	Germany	0–0	

419. ANTHONY STOKES

Position	Forward
Born	Dublin, 25 July 1988
Club	Arsenal; Falkirk (loan); Sunderland
Caps	3

Date	Team	Result	Goals
7 Feb 2007	San Marino	2–1	
23 May 2007	Ecuador	1–1	
26 May 2007	Bolivia	1–1	

420. ALAN BENNETT

Position	Defender
Born	Cork, 4 October 1981
Club	Cork City; Reading; Southampton (loan)
Caps	2

Date	Team	Result	Goals
23 May 2007	Ecuador	1–1	
26 May 2007	Bolivia	1–1	

421. ALEX BRUCE

Position	Midfield; Full-back
Born	Norwich, 28 September 1984
Club	Blackburn Rovers; Oldham Athletic (loan); Birmingham City; Oldham Athletic (loan); Sheffield Wednesday (loan); Tranmere Rovers (loan); Ipswich Town
Caps	1

Date	Team	Result	Goals
23 May 2007	Ecuador	1–1	

422. COLIN DOYLE

Position	Goalkeeper
Born	Cork, 12 August 1985
Club	Birmingham City; Chester City (loan); Nottingham Forest (loan); Millwall (loan)
Caps	1

Date	Team	Result	Goals
23 May 2007	Ecuador	1–1	

423. JOE GAMBLE

Position	Midfield
Born	Cork, 14 January 1982
Club	Cork City; Reading; Cork City
Caps	2

Date	Team	Result	Goals
23 May 2007	Ecuador	1–1	
26 May 2007	Bolivia	1–1	

424. STEPHEN GLEESON

Position	Midfield
Born	Dublin, 3 August 1988
Club	Wolverhampton Wanderers; Stockport County (loan)
Caps	2

Date	Team	Result	Goals
23 May 2007	Ecuador	1–1	
26 May 2007	Bolivia	1–1	

425. ANDY KEOGH

Position	Midfield; Forward
Born	Dublin, 16 May 1986
Club	Leeds United; Scunthorpe United (loan); Bury (loan); Scunthorpe United; Wolverhampton Wanderers
Caps	5

Date	Team	Result	Goals
23 May 2007	Ecuador	1–1	
22 Aug 2007	Denmark	4–0	
12 Sep 2007	Czech Republic	0–1	
13 Oct 2007	Germany	0–0	
17 Oct 2007	Cyprus	1–1	

426. JOSEPH LAPIRA

Position	Forward
Born	Lake Charles, Louisiana, United States, 13 August 1986
Club	Baton Rouge Capitals
Caps	1

Date	Team	Result	Goals
23 May 2007	Ecuador	1–1	

427. DARYL MURPHY

Position	Forward
Born	Waterford, 15 March 1983
Club	Luton Town; Waterford United; Sunderland; Sheffield Wednesday (loan)
Caps	5

Date	Team	Result	Goals
23 May 2007	Ecuador	1–1	
26 May 2007	Bolivia	1–1	
22 Aug 2007	Denmark	4–0	
8 Sep 2007	Slovakia	2–2	
13 Oct 2007	Germany	0–0	

428. JOE O'CEARUILL

Position	Full-back
Born	Edmonton, 9 February 1987
Club	Arsenal; Brighton & Hove Albion (loan)
Caps	2

Date	Team	Result	Goals
23 May 2007	Ecuador	1–1	
26 May 2007	Bolivia	1–1	

429. STEPHEN O'HALLORAN

Position	Defender
Born	Cork, 29 November 1987
Club	Aston Villa; Wycombe Wanderers (loan)
Caps	2

Date	Team	Result	Goals
23 May 2007	Ecuador	1–1	
26 May 2007	Bolivia	1–1	

430. DARREN POTTER

Position	Midfield
Born	Liverpool, 21 December 1984
Club	Liverpool; Southampton (loan); Wolverhampton Wanderers
Caps	4

Date	Team	Result	Goals
23 May 2007	Ecuador	1–1	
26 May 2007	Bolivia	1–1	
22 Aug 2007	Denmark	4–0	
17 Nov 2007	Wales	2–2	

431. PETER MURPHY

Position	Left-back; Midfield
Born	Dublin, 27 October 1980
Club	Blackburn Rovers; Halifax Town (loan); Carlisle United
Caps	1

Date	Team	Result	Goals
26 May 2007	Bolivia	1–1	

432. DARRON GIBSON

Position	Midfield
Born	Derry, 25 October 1987
Club	Manchester United; Royal Antwerp (Belgium) (loan); Wolverhampton Wanderers (loan)
Caps	2

Date	Team	Result	Goals
22 Aug 2007	Denmark	4–0	
8 Sep 2007	Slovakia	2–2	

The Managers

The Managers

Profiles of the Republic of Ireland's twelve managers (including caretakers) along with the teams' playing record and other statistics.

MICK MEAGAN
September 1969–May 1971

MANAGERS

During the 1950s and 1960s, the Republic of Ireland was far down on the European pecking order and its national team was selected by a five-man committee but in September 1969, Mick Meagan became the first Republic of Ireland manager to be given a voice at selection meetings. This was due, in the main, to the campaigning efforts of Eamonn Dunphy and other senior players. Under this new system, Mick Meagan would make his recommendations to the selection committee about whom he would like in the squad before making the decision on the final starting line-up himself.

The devolution of selection power from the Big Five represented a major step forward but this was counterbalanced by the problem that had bedevilled Irish international football for a number of years: most of the players had played League games the day before.

Meagan took the dual role of captain and manager for his first game in charge before handing authority on the field of play to Manchester United full-back Tony Dunne and concentrating on management.

The Meagan era started off reasonably well with a 1–1 draw against Scotland, courtesy of a Don Givens goal, but there then followed the more serious business of World Cup qualifying games for the 1970 tournament. Prior to Meagan's appointment, Ireland had already played three of their Group two games and had yet to register a point – unfortunately, it didn't get much better.

Meagan took to the dug out for his side's next game against Czechoslovakia and gave debuts to four League of Ireland players. However, despite his 'I'm backing Ireland' policy, his team was completely outclassed and lost 3–0 as Adamec netted a hat-trick. Ireland drew 1–1 with Denmark at Dalymount Park in their next World Cup qualifier but there then followed a run of four defeats with friendlies against Poland and West Germany bringing little comfort, except for the debut of Liverpool star Steve Heighway.

There was further disappointment for the Republic and Meagan in the qualifying rounds of the 1972 European Championships. The campaign started brightly enough with a Tommy Carroll penalty securing a 1–1 draw against Sweden but a 1–0 reversal in the return fixture was followed by home and away defeats at the hands of Italy and a 4–1 hammering by Austria at Dalymount Park. It was a disastrous sequence of results and one that brought to an end Mick Meagan's managerial tenure. He had been in office for two years, overseen a dozen internationals and failed to record a victory.

Playing Record

P	W	D	L	F	A
12	0	3	9	7	26

Players Used	30
Debuts Under	10
Most Appearances	Alan Kelly (11); Eamonn Dunphy (11)
Leading Goalscorer	Don Givens (3)
Biggest Win	None
Heaviest Defeat	0–4 v Hungary

LIAM TUOHY
October 1971–May 1973

In October 1971, the position of Republic of Ireland manager was not a particularly attractive one The team had gone almost five years without a win and had very few top class players available. Even so, Liam Tuohy could not resist and in October 1971 he signed a three-year contract with the FAI to become Mick Meagan's successor. He had played most of his football in the League of Ireland and had on occasion taken charge of the League of Ireland representative side.

He was well aware that the greatest difficulty facing the team was the lack of preparation before games, not least because of the difficulty of getting players released by their English clubs in the absence of FIFA regulations. However, unlike his predecessor, he was the team's sole selector.

His first game in charge was the final European Championship qualifier against Austria. The match which had been arranged before his appointment was scheduled for a Sunday and as it was being played in Linz, he was forced to take a scratch team to Austria. The team that lined up had seven new caps and, with the exception of Chelsea's Paddy Mulligan, was entirely comprised of League of Ireland players. Though defeat was predictable, the 6–0 scoreline provided a clear lesson for the FAI and throughout the rest of Tuohy's reign, the manager worked closely with the administrators to ensure that where possible, international matches were played midweek.

Tuohy was determined to create a team spirit among the English and home-based players and as part of this process, his side took part in the Brazilian Independence Cup in the summer of 1972. Coming back from 1–0 down against Iran to win 2–1, Ireland recorded their first victory since Prague in November 1967. A 3–2 victory over Ecuador in the next game was soured when Don Givens was sent off and when Turlough O'Connor received his marching orders in the next game against Chile, Ireland lost 2–1. This was followed by another defeat by the same scoreline against Portugal but even so, morale had been given a much needed fillip.

The first meaningful competitive action of Tuohy's tenure came during the qualifying rounds for the 1974 World Cup. The campaign opened with home games against the USSR and France and although they lost the first of these against a strong USSR team at Lansdowne Road in October 1972, a month later, they recorded an impressive 2–1 victory over the French at Dalymount Park.

However, at the beginning of December 1972, Tuohy dropped a bombshell by announcing his resignation. He had been combining his job as national team manager with that of an area manager for an ice cream firm and he was also in charge of Shamrock Rovers. Something had to give.

Eventually he was persuaded to stay on as Ireland manager until after a run of three World Cup qualifiers that were scheduled for May 1973 but he couldn't be convinced to change his mind on a permanent basis. After defeats away to the USSR and Poland, the boys in green produced a memorable performance to draw 1–1 in France – Liam Tuohy's final match in charge.

Though his time in charge was short, it was undoubtedly significant. In just ten games, the popular Dubliner had done much to lift the national team out of the doldrums. His record of three victories was all the more impressive given the fact that he was quite often without the services of key players. He would later go on to enjoy success with the Republic of Ireland's youth teams during the 1980s.

Playing Record

P	W	D	L	F	A
10	3	1	6	11	20

Players Used	30
Debuts Under	9
Most Appearances	Alan Kelly; Mick Martin; Paddy Mulligan; Ray Treacy (9)
Leading Goalscorer	Terry Conroy; Mick Leech; Mick Martin; Eamonn Rogers (2)
Biggest Win	3–2 v Ecuador
Heaviest Defeat	0–6 v Austria

SEAN THOMAS
June 1973

Following the resignation of Liam Tuohy, the FAI turned to one of the most successful League of Ireland managers: Bohemians' Sean Thomas. He was appointed care-taker-manager for the friendly game against Norway in Oslo.

He had a lot of managerial experience at domestic level. He was in charge at Shamrock Rovers between 1961 and 1964 when the Hoops won the FAI Cup twice and the League Championship once. In 1963–64, Rovers won all the major trophies open to them except the Top 4 trophy.

He then took charge of Bohemians where he was credited with transforming the amateur club into the new glamour club of the League of Ireland. He left the Bohs in the summer of 1973 for business reasons and was out of the game until April 1976 when he replaced Mick Meagan as manager of his former club, Shamrock Rovers. In the late 1970s, he was manager of Athlone Town.

At national level, Thomas was the manager of the League of Ireland XI which beat their English counterparts 2–1 at Dalymount Park in October 1963. He also managed three Republic of Ireland Under-23 games against France, all of which ended in goalless draws.

His one game as national team boss against the amateurs of Norway in Oslo ended in a 1–1 draw.

Playing Record

P	W	D	L	F	A
1	0	1	0	1	1

Players Used   13
Debut Under   1
Goalscorer   Miah Dennehy (1)

JOHNNY GILES
October 1973–March 1980

In October 1973, former Leeds United midfielder Johnny Giles succeeded Liam Tuohy as Republic of Ireland manager. His appointment was a rather surprising show of foresight on the part of the FAI.

The midfielder was still only 32 years old when he took charge of the national team and although he had no managerial experience at club level, he had been one of Ireland's most influential players of the last decade. Giles also possessed an astute footballing brain and was widely tipped for a great future as a coach.

After watching his country finish bottom of the 1970 World Cup and 1972 European Championships, Giles set about reorganising the international set-up. He was able to convince the FAI that they should play their games midweek and on the same dates as England, so that more Irish players would be available for the national side. Under his managership, the Republic was regularly able to field its strongest team.

Giles was an inspirational figure and immediately won the respect of the players and gradually established the Republic as a team to be respected, especially in Dublin.

The Giles era got off to a flying start with a 1–0 defeat of Poland at Dalymount Park, just four days after they had qualified for the World Cup with a 1–1 draw against

England at Wembley. This success was followed by seven months of inactivity before Giles took his side for a three-match tour of South America in May 1974. After defeats by Brazil and Uruguay, Ireland beat Chile and though they may have only won one match, they had been competitive in all three fixtures.

Ticket for the Republic of Ireland v Switzerland game at Lansdowne Road in May 1975, a match the Republic of Ireland won 2–1 with goals from Mick Martin and Ray Treacy.

Expectations of the boys in green were high when the qualifying groups of the 1976 European Championships got underway. They didn't disappoint, for in their opening match against group favourites the USSR, Don Givens netted a hat-trick in a 3–0 win. However, a draw away to Turkey in their next match proved costly. Ireland won both their remaining home games against Switzerland and Turkey (Don Givens scored all four goals in a 4–0 success in the game against Turkey) but a point behind the leaders, the USSR. Normally following failure to qualify for a tournament finals there had been resignation but now there was disappointment.

In 1975 Johnny Giles had taken over from Don Howe as manager of West Bromwich Albion and in his first season at the Hawthorns, led the club to promotion to the First Division. Despite the demands of his new position, he continued with his role as the Republic's player-manager.

The draw for the 1978 World Cup Finals put Ireland in the same group as France and Bulgaria and though they lost the opening game 2–0 in France, the scoreline didn't reflect the Republic's very accomplished display which might well have earned them a draw if an over-eager linesman hadn't ruled out a Frank Stapleton 'goal' when the score was 1–0. Unfortunately there was worse to come. After beating France 1–0 in the return at Lansdowne Road, Ireland were the victims of a number of errors from match officials during the game against Bulgaria in Sofia. A blatant penalty for a push on Givens wasn't given and then a full minute after Giles had put the ball in the net for what looked like the winning goal, the linesman raised his flag! With ten minutes to go, the game erupted into a free-for-all and four players were sent off including Noel Campbell and Mick Martin.

The qualification programme for the 1980 European Championships brought no better fortune for the Irish and, sadly, defeats in Belfast and London did nothing for the manager's popularity. Giles was now back in Dublin full-time, having taken over as player-manager of Shamrock Rovers in the summer of 1977. His return to the capital brought him under intense media scrutiny and he was criticised for selecting himself in the national side. Also, his patient possession football came under attack and by the end of the decade, the situation had deteriorated to the point where a section of the Lansdowne Road crowd booed when Giles' name was read out from the teamsheet.

In March 1980 after a narrow 3–2 defeat of Cyprus in the opening match of the team's 1982 World Cup qualifying campaign, Giles decided that the time was right to resign.

Giles had taken Ireland extremely close to qualifying for a major tournament for the first time in 1976 and though he was ultimately unable to deliver tournament football, he had achieved much during his seven-year management of the national team, being credited with introducing several Irish greats such as Liam Brady, David O'Leary, Frank Stapleton and Mark Lawrenson.

Playing Record

P	W	D	L	F	A
37	14	9	14	49	45

Players Used	53
Debuts Under	33
Most Appearances	Mick Martin; Paddy Mulligan (28)
Leading Goalscorer	Don Givens (13)
Biggest Win	4–0 v Turkey
Heaviest Defeat	1–4 v Czechoslovakia

ALAN KELLY
April 1980

When Johnny Giles left his role as Republic of Ireland manager in the spring of 1980, the position passed to Alan Kelly. He had been Giles' assistant for two games, both of which had ended in victories.

The former Preston North End and Republic of Ireland goalkeeper, however, resigned from the post after just one game as he found it impossible to combine the Ireland job with his role as North End manager.

He had the pleasure of ending his tenure as Ireland boss with a 100 per cent record as goals from Don Givens and Gerry Daly secured a 2–0 victory over Switzerland for the boys in green.

Did you know?

In the Republic of Ireland's 2–0 defeat by England at Wembley in 1980, Arsenal central defender David O'Leary was substituted by his brother Pierce.

Playing Record

P	W	D	L	F	A
1	1	0	0	2	0

Players Used   11
Debuts Under   2
Goalscorers   Gerry Daly; Don Givens (1)

EOIN HAND
April 1980–November 1985

After the brief reign of former goalkeeper Alan Kelly, the responsibility for leading the boys in green fell to Eoin Hand.

The 34–year-old Limerick United manager was on on his appointment, one of the youngest national team bosses in the world. He had won his twenty international caps for the Republic of Ireland whilst at Portsmouth. He was initially given the

Republic of Ireland job on a caretaker basis but after one match – a 1–0 defeat to Argentina in Dublin – he was appointed on a permanent basis.

He had shown great promise at Limerick during his first season at the club, having led them to the 1979–80 League of Ireland Championship. His efforts were recognised when he was voted 'Sports Personality of the Year'. Limerick were runners-up a year later and in his third season with the club, they won the FAI Cup. When Johnny Giles tendered his resignation, Hand was at the forefront of Irish domestic football.

Tactically, Eoin Hand was much more of a pragmatist than his predecessor Giles and his teams tended to move the ball forward with much greater urgency than those of Johnny Giles. The number of English-born players declaring for Ireland certainly increased during Hand's reign. The relaxation in FIFA's qualification criteria prompted many second-generation Irishmen – whose families had emigrated in the 1950s – to declare for the mother country. Hand gave first caps to a host of second-generation Irishmen including Tony Cascarino, Tony Galvin, Mick McCarthy and Jim McDonagh. He also uncovered some superb home-grown talent, Packie Bonner, Paul McGrath and Ronnie Whelan, all of whom went on to serve the Republic for years to come.

The 1982 World Cup qualifying stages were the first test of Hand's mettle as an international manager. The campaign began well with goals from Daly and Lawrenson giving the Irish a 2–1 win over Holland, though they dropped a point in their next home game, being held to a 1–1 draw by Belgium. Following a 1–0 defeat in France, Ireland brushed aside Cyprus 6–0 before facing Belgium in Brussels for the return game. Frank Stapleton's 'perfect' goal for the Republic was ruled out whilst the referee allowed a late Belgian goal despite a clear foul on keeper Jim McDonagh. There followed two great performances in Dublin with Holland being held 2–2 before France were defeated 3–2. At the end of the qualifying campaign, Hand's team found themselves eliminated from the competition on goal difference.

The turning point in the Hand era came in the summer of 1982 when a depleted Republic of Ireland side embarked on an ill-advised tour of South America. Not only did they lose all three matches but the tour took in a record 7–0 defeat against Brazil and a 2–1 reversal against Trinidad and Tobago which was an even greater humiliation.

Hopes of qualifying for the 1984 European Championship were quickly dashed when the Irish lost at home to Holland – their first defeat in a competitive home game for seven years. But even an 8–0 mauling of Malta in the last group game could not deflect the brickbats aimed at the manager. After a 2–0 defeat to Spain, Hand was accused of employing defensive tactics and his ability to manage the side's big name stars was called into question. Though the press and public were baying for his head, Eoin Hand's luck changed and after surviving an attempt to install Bob Paisley as boss, he was still at the helm as the qualifying rounds for the 1986 World Cup got underway.

The campaign started with a 1–0 defeat of the USSR but back-to-back defeats against Norway and Denmark saw the pressure on the manager return. The rest of the campaign was a shambles and after Norway forced a goalless draw at Lansdowne Road, spectators began to call for the manager's head. The announcement of Eoin Hand's resignation came on 16 October 1985 following a 2–0 defeat in Moscow. He was close to tears in the press room of the Lenin Stadium, describing it as the most disappointing night of his life.

Playing Record

P	W	D	L	F	A
40	11	9	20	47	59

Players Used	49
Debuts Under	24
Most Appearances	Frank Stapleton (32)
Leading Goalscorer	Frank Stapleton (11)
Biggest Win	8–0 v Malta
Heaviest Defeat	0–7 v Brazil

Did you know?

Gerry Daly and Don Givens scored their Irish goals under four different managers.

JACK CHARLTON
February 1986–December 1995

A hard uncompromising defender with Leeds United and England, Jack Charlton assembled an impressive trophy collection which included League Championship, FA Cup, League Cup and UEFA Cup winners' medals with the Yorkshire club and a 1966 World Cup winners' medal with Alf Ramsey's side.

Ticket from the famous Republic of Ireland v Romania World Cup match at Genoa in Italia '90 – a match that ended goalless but one that the Republic won 5–4 on penalties.

He began his managerial career with Middlesbrough in 1973 and the following year was voted 'Manager of the Year' after leading Boro to promotion to the top flight as Second Division Champions. He left Ayresome Park in 1977 to take over at Sheffield Wednesday, earning them promotion to the Second Division in 1980. In 1983, he left Hillsborough to devote more time to his hobbies of shooting and fishing, but a year later he took over at Newcastle United, just after Arthur Cox had taken the Magpies into the First Division. Much was expected of him but he didn't deliver and after the club just avoided relegation, he left.

He was appointed Republic of Ireland manager in February 1986 and over the next ten years, became the most revered figure in the history of Irish football.

It was the first time that the FAI had turned to a non-Irishman to lead the national team. Charlton inherited an Ireland team that contained several players of undoubted talent – Frank Stapleton, Liam Brady, Paul McGrath, Mark Lawrenson and David O'Leary being the most conspicuous. Within three months of taking over, Charlton had earned the Republic their first senior trophy by winning two games away from home. It may only have been the triangular tournament in Reykjavik with wins over Iceland and Czechoslovakia but it was a significant start.

The new Irish manager applied much of the simplicity and directness of his own personality into the playing style of the Republic's team. It was the beginning of Ireland's long-ball game. Though it was far from aesthetically pleasing, it was certainly effective. Charlton was often criticised for his tactics but he was a much better tactician than he was given credit for, and when the occasion demanded, the Republic could and did play the passing game. Another measure he took was to increase the number of second-generation Irishmen in the side.

Charlton didn't place undue importance on the strengths and weaknesses of the opposition, as illustrated by his habit of naming his side long before deemed necessary by international football law.

His first major task was qualification for the 1988 European Championships. The Republic produced many fine performances over the eight-game qualifying rounds and finished their campaign top of the group with eleven points. Bulgaria were just a point behind with one match to play against Scotland in Sofia but a dramatic late strike by Gary Mackay made Scotland the victors and put the Republic through to the finals of their first major tournament.

Did you know?

Republic of Ireland manager Jack Charlton received a one-match touchline ban and a £10,000 fine in the 1994 World Cup Finals after arguing with an official during a match against Mexico.

The Irish went to West Germany and took the football world by surprise, defeating England 1–0 with a goal from Ray Houghton. Then they gave one of their best performances in holding the Soviet Union to a 1–1 draw and it was only after Holland, the eventual champions, scored a highly fortuitous winning goal in the final group match that Ireland were eliminated. Jack's boys returned 'home' to Dublin as heroes.

Charlton's no-nonsense approach worked again as Ireland qualified for the 1990 World Cup Finals for the first time. The Irish conceded just two goals en route to Italia '90. Although they did not win a game in normal time in Italy, they made it all the way to the quarter-finals through draws with England, Holland and Egypt and the never-to-be-forgotten penalty shoot-out with Romania, won with a Packie Bonner save from Daniel Timofte and David O'Leary's dramatic spot kick. They faced hosts Italy in Rome, losing 1–0 to a Schillaci goal.

Though Jack Charlton was the man responsible for the Republic of Ireland's new-found sporting glory, he was not without his critics. Charlton appeared to pay short shrift to those who doubted him and though Ireland narrowly missed out on a place at the 1992 European Championships, he led his team to a second consecutive World Cup Finals in 1994.

Ireland again progressed to the second round, where they were beaten by Holland after two uncharacteristically sloppy defensive errors. The highlight of the tournament was, without doubt, Ray Houghton's goal which earned the Irish a much lauded win against eventual finalists Italy in New York.

There were many pundits who predicted that Charlton would stand down after these finals but he was not ready to take his leave. Sadly, his final qualifying campaign was to end in great disappointment when the Republic missed out on a place at Euro '96 after a play-off match against Holland at Anfield.

Jack Charlton, who in May 1994 had been made a freeman of Dublin, pondered his future for eight days but on 21 December 1995, he announced his resignation. The popular manager had exceeded all expectations and had taken the Republic of Ireland to the finals of three major tournaments, not to mention sixth place in the FIFA world rankings, ahead of the likes of Brazil.

Playing Record

P	W	D	L	F	A
94	47	30	17	128	63

Players Used	57
Debuts Under	33
Most Appearances	Packie Bonner (69)
Leading Goalscorer	John Aldridge (19)
Biggest Win	5–0 v Israel; v Turkey
Heaviest Defeat	0–3 v Portugal

MICK McCARTHY
February 1996–November 2002

The job of following Jack Charlton was certainly not an easy one, for though the ex-England centre-half had taken the Republic to new heights, his achievements also had the potential to become a millstone around the neck of any successor.

The FAI deliberated long and hard before whittling the candidates down to just two men – Mick McCarthy and Kevin Moran. Both had enjoyed successful playing careers with Ireland but McCarthy had the added advantage of three years' managerial experience at club level with Millwall and he was appointed Republic manager.

Mick McCarthy has just congratulated Roy Keane as he leaves the field after scoring one of the goals in a 2–0 win over Iran in the first leg of the World Cup play-off in November 2001.

Mick McCarthy proved to be a real motivator and he promised both a new order and a new style. A series of eight tough friendlies were arranged, beginning with the visit of Russia to Dublin in March 1996 and ending with US Cup games in America in the summer. McCarthy had inherited a squad of players that was built around a core coming towards the end of their careers. His problems were further compounded when, in his first game in charge, Roy Keane was sent off. Keane's dismissal was the lowlight of a forgettable debut for the Republic's new manager who watched his team lose 2–0 to Russia before a full house at Lansdowne Road.

The Republic's first victory under McCarthy's reign came in the eighth friendly match against Bolivia in New Jersey, United States. Results at this stage though were not too important – what was of more significance was the progress of the young players blooded by McCarthy, players like Kenny Cunningham, Gary Breen and Ian Harte.

It was the qualifying rounds of the 1998 World Cup that provided McCarthy with his first taste of competitive action as manager of the national team. The Irish started the campaign well but after a goalless home draw against Iceland, disaster struck with a 3–2 defeat in Macedonia. Any lingering hopes of qualification were dashed with a 1–0 loss in Romania. Ireland recovered their form and were unbeaten in their last six games to earn a two-legged play-off game against Group 7 runners-up Belgium. A 3–2 aggregate defeat ended the boys in green hopes of playing in France.

By the start of the 2000 European qualifiers, McCarthy had assembled a new look Republic of Ireland side which bore very little resemblance to that which he had inherited from Jack Charlton. Despite being paired with Yugoslavia and Croatial, both strong teams at that time, Ireland topped the group until injury-time goals in Croatia and then Macedonia condemned them to the play-offs once more. Unfortunately, they lost to an impressive Turkish side over two legs.

The qualifiers for the 2002 World Cup again saw the Irish suffer a certain degree of misfortune as they surrendered a two-goal lead in Holland enabling the Dutch to draw 2–2. Another away draw in Portugal followed before a home victory over Estonia put the side in a strong position to qualify. McCarthy's team then beat Holland 1–0 at Lansdowne Road – a result that effectively secured second place in the group for the Irish, who eventually lost out on the top spot on goal difference to Portugal. That meant the Irish had another chance to qualify for the finals via the play-offs – it was third time lucky for McCarthy's men as they defeated Iran.

The World Cup finals turned out to be the most dramatic period of Mick McCarthy's tenure as Ireland boss. As the team headed out to the Far East with spirits and expectations high, the country looked to the manager and skipper Roy Keane to continue their impressive form. However, after admitting he nearly walked out on the squad in the run-up to the World Cup, Keane publicly criticised the team's training facilities and general attitude. The Manchester United midfielder argued with his manager and, after insulting him in front of the rest of the squad, was subsequently sent home.

Despite this, McCarthy led his team through to the second round of the World Cup where, after drawing with Spain 1–1, they went out after penalties.

As the fall-out from the Keane saga rumbled on, McCarthy focused on the Euro 2004 qualifiers. However, his team made a disastrous start and, amidst growing pressure, he resigned his post in November 2002, having agreed a compensation package with the Irish board. His impact on the Irish side was phenomenal, lifting them from fifty-fourth to thirteenth in FIFA's world rankings in just over five years.

His reputation and international experience meant he was always going to be given a chance to manage in the top flight and in March 2003, he was appointed Sunderland manager. Although he was unable to keep the Black Cats in the Premiership, he did help them return to the top flight two years later when they won the Coca Cola Championship. The Wearsiders then suffered relegation a second time after just one season back in the Premiership and McCarthy parted company with the club to take over the reins at Wolverhampton Wanderers.

Playing Record

P	W	D	L	F	A
70	31	20	19	117	66

Players Used	65
Debuts Under	41
Most Appearances	Gary Breen (52)
Leading Goalscorer	Robbie Keane (14)
Biggest Win	5–0 v Liechtenstein (twice); v Malta
Heaviest Defeat	2–4 v Russia

DON GIVENS
November 2002 and November 2007

Don Givens, who holds the record for scoring Ireland's quickest-ever hat-trick in a 4–0 defeat of Turkey in October 1975, was also sent-off twice while playing for the Republic. A fiery competitor, his commitment to the Irish cause was never in doubt.

After starting out with Manchester United, he later played for Luton Town, Queen's Park

Don Givens

Rangers and Birmingham City before ending his league career with Sheffield United. He then had a spell with Swiss club Xamax Neuchatel before joining the youth set up at Arsenal and overseeing an FA Premier Academy League.

In 2000 he was appointed the Republic of Ireland Under-21 manager. In November 2002 he briefly became caretaker-manager of the senior squad following the departure of Mick McCarthy and managed the team for a goalless draw against Greece. His tenure ended following the appointment of Brian Kerr as manager in January 2003.

Once again appointed caretaker-manager following Steve Staunton's dismissal, Givens was in charge for Ireland's last qualifying game for Euro 2008, a 2–2 draw against Wales at the Millennium Stadium. Givens is currently preparing his Under-21 team for the UEFA Championships.

Playing Record

P	W	D	L	F	A
2	0	2	0	2	2

Players Used	21
Debuts Under	1
Most Appearances	Shay Given; Steve Finnan; John O'Shea; Lee Carsley (2)
Leading Goalscorer	Robbie Keane; Kevin Doyle (1)

BRIAN KERR
January 2003–October 2005

Brain Kerr's appointment as manager of the Republic of Ireland was seen as likely to bring some badly-needed respite to the country's harassed soccer governing body. The appointment was well received by the majority of Irish football supporters who respected him for his achievements with the country's youth sides.

Kerr's playing career was, to say the least, a modest one. He didn't make it to the League of Ireland level and spent most of his playing days with Leinster Senior League club Bluebell United with whom he helped lift the FAI Intermediate Cup. Kerr's day job was that of a laboratory technician at the University College, Dublin where he worked for 25 years before taking a leave of absence after being appointed Irish youth manager in 1996.

His introduction to management came in the late 1970s and early 1980s when he served as assistant manager at Home Farm and later Drogheda. In 1982 his ability was spotted by Ireland youth team manager Liam Tuohy who appointed him to his backroom staff.

Things didn't always run smoothly between Kerr and the FAI and, in 1986, he felt compelled to resign from the position after Tuohy quit his youth managerial role. This came about after new senior team manager Jack Charlton stormed into the Irish

Brian Kerr

dressing-room at half-time during a game against the England Youths and took over the team-talk. For a long time thereafter, Kerr felt somewhat on the outside as regards the Irish football hierarchy.

Brian Kerr's ten-year reign at St Patrick's Athletic saw him turn a club that had been in the doldrums into a force to be reckoned with in the League of Ireland. His knowledge of the League of Ireland game was encyclopaedic.

Less than a year into his reign as Ireland youth team manager, Kerr managed the Irish Under-20s to a remarkable third place in the World Championships in Malaysia. In 1998 his Under-16 and Under-18 squads both claimed European Championship triumphs. Three years later, he managed Ireland to Youth Olympics gold in Spain.

He started his reign as national team manager with a 2–0 defeat of Scotland but in October 2003, needing a win against Switzerland to clinch a play-off place, Ireland bowed out of the European Championships with a 2–0 defeat. Kerr then played a part in convincing Roy Keane to return to the international fold following his bust-up with Mick McCarthy.

Kerr's side made a good start to the 2006 World Cup qualifiers with a 3–0 defeat of Cyprus and draws in Switzerland and France before beating the Faroes. Despite being rocked by a late equaliser by Israel in March 2005 and throwing a two-goal lead away against the same opposition in the summer, Ireland did the double over the Faroes to top the table. A Thierry Henry goal saw Ireland suffer their only defeat but after a narrow win in Cyprus, a goalless home draw with Switzerland ended their interest in the World Cup.

At a meeting in Dublin in October 2005, the FAI chose not to renew Brian Kerr's contract.

Did you know?

A Republic of Ireland international team reached the quarter-finals of the 1924 Olympic Games several years before playing Italy in a full international match.

Playing Record

P	W	D	L	F	A
33	18	11	4	39	20

Players Used	45
Debuts Under	15
Most Appearances	Kenny Cunningham (28)
Leading Goalscorer	Robbie Keane (11)
Biggest Win	3–0 v Canada; v Cyprus
Heaviest Defeat	0–3 v Nigeria

STEVE STAUNTON
January 2006–October 2007

The Republic of Ireland's most capped player, Steve Staunton replaced Brian Kerr as the national team manager in January 2006.

Staunton started his career with his home-town club, Irish National League side, Dundalk but before he had even made an appearance, Liverpool paid £30,000 for his services in September 1986. Playing for the Reds at left-back, Staunton won an FA

Cup winners' medal in 1989 and a League Championship medal a year later before moving to Aston Villa for £1.1 million in August 1991.

At international level, Staunton, who had made his debut against Tunisia in 1988, played in the 1990 World Cup finals in Italy and took part in both 1994 and 2002 World Cups on his way to winning 102 caps for his country.

With Villa, Staunton won League Cup medals in 1994 and 1996 before returning to Liverpool for two seasons. After a brief loan spell with Crystal palace, he spent a second spell at Villa from 2000 to 2003 and a further two seasons at Coventry City. He joined Walsall as assistant manager. The team, managed by former Villa teammate Paul Merson, was also where Staunton had ended his playing days.

On 13 January 2006, Staunton was appointed manager of the Republic of Ireland side with former England coach Bobby Robson acting as his International Football Consultant. Staunton won his first game in charge, a 3–0 friendly victory over Sweden but in their second game of the Euro 2008 qualifying campaign, Ireland suffered a shock 5–2 defeat away to Cyprus. A stoppage-time victory over San Marino and a 1–1 home draw with Cyprus ended Ireland's qualifying hopes with two games to spare.

The FAI terminated Staunton's contract on 24 October 2007.

Playing Record

P	W	D	L	F	A
17	7	5	5	24	18

Players Used	49
Debuts Under	23
Most Appearances	Kevin Kilbane (17)
Leading Goalscorer	Robbie Keane (6)
Biggest Win	5–0 v San Marino
Heaviest Defeat	0–4 v Holland

GIOVANNI TRAPATONI
Feburary 2008–present

Considered the most successful club coach in Italy, Giovanni Trapatoni also had a most successful playing career with AC Milan during the 1960s and 1970s. He began coaching at AC Milan as youth team coach before being appointed first team coach in 1975.

The following year he moved on to Juventus and ten years later in 1986, he went to Inter Milan, being successful with both sides. He returned to Juventus in 1991 before taking his first job in football outside of Italy with Germany's Bayern Munich in 1994.

In 2000 Trapattoni took charge of the Italian national team and led the nation to the 2002 World Cup Finals but after a disappointing tournament and a similar showing in the 2004 European Championships, Trapattoni was replaced by Marcello Lippi. In July 2004 he took over the reins of Benfica, leading them to the Portuguese Championship in his only season with the club. He then returned to Germany to manage VfB Stuttgart but his stay was brief and he moved to FC Red Bull Salzburg. Following a career spanning three decades in which he won ten league titles, a European Cup, a Cup Winners' Cup, three UEFA Cups, the Super Cup and four national cups, Trapattoni agreed to become the Republic of Ireland's new manager.

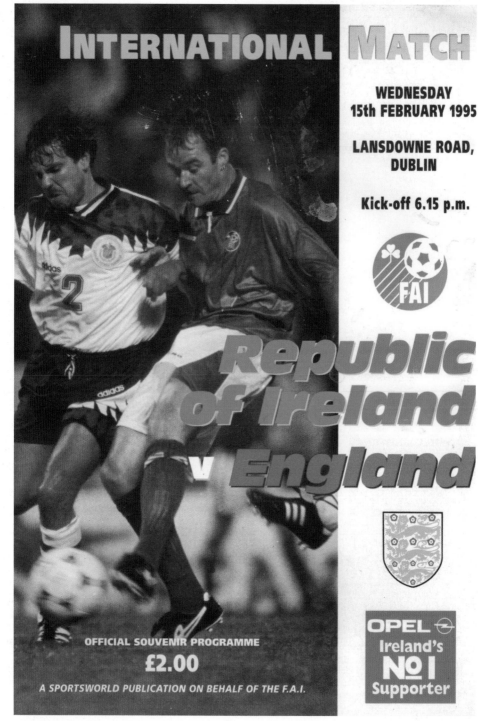

INTERNATIONAL MATCH

WEDNESDAY 15th FEBRUARY 1995

LANSDOWNE ROAD, DUBLIN

Kick-off 6.15 p.m.

FAI

Republic of Ireland v England

OFFICIAL SOUVENIR PROGRAMME
£2.00

A SPORTSWORLD PUBLICATION ON BEHALF OF THE F.A.I.

OPEL
Ireland's
No 1
Supporter

Programme cover for the match against England which was abandoned after twenty-seven minutes because of crowd trouble.

4

The Matches

The Matches

In addition to listing the date, opposition, team line-ups and scorers for every Republic of Ireland match since 1926, this section also contains match reports on 25 featured games.

Match No. 1	
21 March 1926 v ITALY at Turin	
H Cannon	Bohemians
F Brady	Fordson
J McCarthy	Bohemians
M Foley	Shelbourne
D Doyle	Shamrock Rovers
J Connolly	Fordson
JJ Flood	Shamrock Rovers
J Grace	Drumcondra
F Watters	Shelbourne
R Fullam	Shamrock Rovers
J Fagan	Shamrock Rovers

Result	0–3

Match No. 2	
27 April 1927 v ITALY 'B' at Dublin	
F Collins	Jacobs
A Kirkland	Shamrock Rovers
F Brady	Fordson
W Glen	Shamrock Rovers

M O'Brien	Derby County
T Muldoon	Aston Villa
W Lacey	Shelbourne
H Duggan	Leeds United
C Martin	Bowness
R Fullam	Shamrock Rovers
J Kendrick	Everton

Result	1–2
Scorer	R Fullam

Match No. 3	
12 February 1928 v BELGIUM at Liege	
H Cannon	Bohemians
J Robinson	Bohemians
J McCarthy	Bohemians
J Kinsella	Shelbourne
J Byrne	Bray Unknowns
P Barry	Fordson
J Sullivan	Fordson
W Lacey	Shelbourne
JJ White	Bohemians

C Dowdall	Fordson
L Golding	Shamrock Rovers

Result	4–2
Scorers	JJ White (2); W Lacey; J Sullivan (penalty)

Match No. 4
20 April 1929 v BELGIUM at Dublin

T Farquharson	Cardiff City
J Maguire	Shamrock Rovers
J Burke	Shamrock Rovers
W Glen	Shamrock Rovers
M O'Brien	Walsall
P Barry	Fordson
J Bermingham	Bohemians
JJ Flood	Shamrock Rovers
D Byrne	Shelbourne
C Dowdall	Barnsley
R Egan	Dundalk

Result	4–0
Scorers	JJ Flood (3); D Byrne

Match No. 5
11 May 1930 v BELGIUM at Brussels

T Farquharson	Cardiff City
W Lacey	Shelbourne
J McCarthy	Bohemians
W Glen	Shamrock Rovers
M O'Brien	Norwich City
F McLoughlin	Fordson
H Duggan	Leeds United
JJ Flood	Shamrock Rovers
J Dunne	Sheffield United
A Horlacher	Bohemians
L Golding	Shamrock Rovers

Result	3–1
Scorers	J Dunne (2); JJ Flood

Match No. 6
26 April 1931 v SPAIN at Barcelona

T Farquharson	Cardiff City
G Lennox	Dolphin
P Byrne	Dolphin
J Robinson	Dolphin
H Chatton	Shelbourne
S Byrne	Bohemians
JJ Flood	Shamrock Rovers
C Dowdall	Cork
P Moore	Shamrock Rovers
C Reid	Brideville
P Kavanagh	Glasgow Celtic

Result	1–1
Scorer	P Moore

Match No. 7
13 December 1931 v SPAIN at Dublin

T Farquharson	Cardiff City
G Lennox	Shelbourne
L Doyle	Dolphin
W Glen	Shamrock Rovers
H Chatton	Dumbarton
F McLoughlin	Cork
JJ Flood	Shamrock Rovers
P Gallagher	Falkirk
D Byrne	Shamrock Rovers
A Horlacher	Bohemians
P Kavanagh	Glasgow Celtic

Result	0–5

Match No. 8
8 May 1932 v HOLLAND at Amsterdam

M McCarthy	Shamrock Rovers
J Daly	Shamrock Rovers
P Byrne	Shelbourne
J O'Reilly	Brideville
M O'Brien	Watford

O Kinsella	Shamrock Rovers
W Kennedy	St James's Gate
A Stevenson	Dolphin
P Moore	Shamrock Rovers
A Horlacher	Bohemians
J Kelly	Derry City

Result	2–0
Scorers	J O'Reilly; P Moore

Match No. 9

25 February 1934 v BELGIUM at Dublin

J Foley	Cork
J Lynch	Cork Bohemians
T Burke	Cork
P Gaskins	Shamrock Rovers
J O'Reilly	Aberdeen
J Kendrick	Dolphin
W Kennedy	St James's Gate
D Byrne	Coleraine
P Moore	Aberdeen
T O'Keeffe	Cork
J Kelly	Derry City

Result	4–4
Scorer	P Moore

FEATURED MATCH 1

REPUBLIC OF IRELAND 4 BELGIUM 4
At Dalymount Park, Dublin, 25 February 1934

Republic of Ireland
Jim Foley; Miah Lynch; Tom Burke; Paddy Gaskins; Joe O'Reilly; Joe Kendrick; Billy Kennedy; David Byrne; Paddy Moore; Tim O'Keeffe; Jimmy Kelly.

Belgium
A Vande Wijer; J Pappaert; P Smellinckx; J Van Ingelhem; F Welkenhuyzen; D Bourgeois; L Versyp; J Brichaut; J Capelle; A Saeys; S Vanden Eynde; Subs: F Vanden Eynde for S Vanden.

Ireland's first truly competitive international game turned out to be an eight-goal thriller and is remembered most for Paddy Moore's goalscoring exploits. With World Cup points at stake, the football wasn't pretty to watch but there was very little complaint from the 28,000-strong crowd.

Belgium took the lead in the thirteenth minute when CAPELLE, who was unmarked in front of goal, turned in Versyp's cross after the Belgian winger had dispossessed Tom Burke on the by-line. Then Versyp beat a couple of Irish defenders, his cross forcing Foley in the Ireland goal to punch clear. Unfortunately he didn't connect properly and as the ball went up in the air, Stanley VANDEN EYNDE was on hand to lob it into the empty net.

Within a minute, Ireland had pulled a goal back when Paddy MOORE raced on to a through ball from Derry City's Jimmy Kelly. As he shaped to shoot, Welkenhuyzen and Pappaert closed in on him but despite their close attention, he managed to shoot, the ball going under Vande Wijer's despairing dive. Belgium's second goalscorer, Stanley Vanden Eynde broke his leg in an innocuous looking tackle and was replaced by his brother Francois Vanden Eynde. Tim O'Keeffe almost levelled the scores on the stroke of half-time but his effort went into the side netting.

Within two minutes of the restart, the Belgians regained their two-goal lead when Francois VANDEN EYNDE side-footed home Saeys pass following an inch-perfect cross from Van Ingelghem. MOORE replied quickly when he stretched out a leg to convert Billy Kennedy's cross past Vande Wijer. In the fifty-sixth minute, MOORE completed his hat-trick when he latched on to a high cross by Kelly to steer the ball home and in doing so, levelled the scores.

Shortly after the hour mark, a pass by Brichaut allowed Francois VANDEN EYNDE to score his second goal. The substitute cut inside Miah Lynch and fired past the advancing Jim Foley. The Cork keeper then kept out further efforts from Capelle and Saeys before Byrne came close at the other end.

But again Aberdeen's MOORE equalised after 75 minutes when a corner was cleared out to Joe Kendrick and when he lobbed the ball back into the area, Ireland's No. 9 headed home.

With fifteen minutes still to play, both sides went in search of the winning goal. Foley saved well from Bourgeois, whilst Tim O'Keeffe on his debut forced the Belgian keeper into a fine double save in the closing moments.

Match No. 10	
8 April 1934 v HOLLAND at Amsterdam	
J Foley	Cork
P Gaskins	Shamrock Rovers
P Byrne	Drumcondra
J O'Reilly	Aberdeen
H Chatton	Cork
J Kendrick	Dolphin
W Kennedy	St James's Gate
J Squires	Shelbourne
P Moore	Aberdeen
W Jordan*	Bohemians
P Meehan	Drumcondra
A Horlacher *(sub)	Bohemians

Result	2–5
Scorers	P Moore; J Squires

Match No. 11	
16 December 1934 v HUNGARY at Dublin	
J Foley	Glasgow Celtic
P Gaskins	Shamrock Rovers
P Bermingham	St James's Gate
P O'Kane	Bohemians
C Lennon	St James's Gate
A Horlacher	Bohemians
R Griffiths	Walsall
J Donnelly	Dundalk

A Rigby	St James's Gate
P Moore	Aberdeen
WJ Fallon	Notts County

Result	2–4
Scorers	J Donnelly; P Bermingham

Match No. 12	
5 May 1935 v SWITZERLAND at Basel	
J Foley	Glasgow Celtic
P Gaskins	Shamrock Rovers
L Dunne	Manchester City
P O'Kane	Bohemians
C Lennon	St James's Gate
F Hutchinson	Drumcondra
J Daly	Shamrock Rovers
P Ellis	Bohemians
A Rigby	St James's Gate
J Donnelly	Dundalk
P Monahan	Sligo Rovers

Result	0–1

Match No. 13	
8 May 1935 v GERMANY at Dortmund	
J Foley	Glasgow Celtic
P Gaskins	Shamrock Rovers
L Dunne	Manchester City
P O'Kane	Bohemians
C Lennon	St James's Gate
F Hutchinson	Drumcondra
P Ellis	Bohemians
P Moore	Aberdeen

Did you know?

Of the five sets of brothers to appear for the Republic only the O'Flanagans, the O'Learys and the Dunnes have played together on the same team.

A Rigby	St James's Gate
J Donnelly	Dundalk
P Monahan	Sligo Rovers

Result	1–3
Scorer	L Dunne

8 December 1935 v HOLLAND at Dublin

W Harrington	Cork
W O'Neill	Dundalk
W McGuire	Bohemians
W Glen	Shamrock Rovers
P Andrews	Bohemians
J O'Reilly	Brideville
P Ellis	Bohemians
J Donnelly	Dundalk
P Moore	Shamrock Rovers
A Horlacher	Bohemians
J Kendrick	Dolphin

Result	3–5
Scorers	P Ellis; A Horlacher (2)

17 March 1936 v SWITZERLAND at Dublin

W Harrington	Cork
W O'Neill	Dundalk
W Gorman	Bury
W Glen	Shamrock Rovers
C Turner	Southend United
J O'Reilly	Brideville
P Ellis	Bohemians
J Donnelly	Dundalk
J Dunne	Arsenal
A Horlacher	Bohemians
J Kelly	Derry City

Result	1–0
Scorer	J Dunne

3 May 1936 v HUNGARY at Budapest

W Harrington	Cork
W O'Neill	Dundalk
W Gorman	Bury
W Glen	Shamrock Rovers
C Moulson	Lincoln City
J O'Reilly	Brideville
H Duggan	Leeds United
J Donnelly	Dundalk
J Dunne	Arsenal
O Madden	Cork
WJ Fallon	Notts County

Result	3–3
Scorers	J Dunne (2); O Madden

9 May 1936 v LUXEMBOURG at Luxembourg

W Harrington	Cork
W O'Neill	Dundalk
W Gorman	Bury
W Glen	Shamrock Rovers
C Moulson	Lincoln City
J O'Reilly	Brideville
H Duggan	Leeds United
J Donnelly	Dundalk
J Dunne	Arsenal
P Ellis	Bohemians
J Kelly	Derry City

Result	5–1
Scorers	J Dunne (2); J Donnelly; J Kelly (2)

17 October 1936 v GERMANY at Dublin

J Foley	Glasgow Celtic
W O'Neill	Dundalk
W Gorman	Bury

MATCHES

J O'Reilly	St James's Gate
C Turner	Southend United
H Connolly	Cork
P Ellis	Bohemians
J Donnelly	Dundalk
T Davis	Oldham Athletic
P Moore	Shamrock Rovers
M Geoghegan	St James's Gate

| Result | 5–2 |
| Scorers | J Donnelly (2); T Davis (2 – 1 penalty); M Geoghegan |

FEATURED MATCH 2

REPUBLIC OF IRELAND 5 GERMANY 2
At Dalymount Park, Dublin, 17 October 1936

Republic of Ireland
Jim Foley; William O'Neill; Bill Gorman; Joe O'Reilly; Charlie Turner; Hugh Connolly; Plev Ellis; Joey Donnelly; Tom Davis; Paddy Moore; Matty Geoghegan.

Germany
H Jakob; R Muenzenberg; A Munkert; J Rodzinski; L Goldbrunner; A Kitzinger; E Lehner; O Siffling; K Hohmann; F Szepan; S Kobierski;

Ireland's tactics of stopping the Germans' short passing game, coupled with a magnificent display from Paddy Moore paved the way for a famous victory.

Both sides had early chances with Szepan forcing Foley into a good save after just two minutes whilst Oldham Athletic's Tom Davis, making his full international debut, saw his snap shot turned round the post by Jakob in the German goal. The end-to-end game exploded after twenty-five minutes with four goals in under ten minutes. Another debutant Matty Geoghegan sent in a low cross which picked out Joey DONNELLY and he made no mistake from a few yards out. Within a minute the Germans were level when Ireland's defenders failed to pick up KOBIERSKI who easily converted Lehner's cross.

A shot from Paddy Moore rattled the Germans' crossbar before SZEPAN scrambled the ball over the line from close range following excellent work out on the left by Kobierski. The home side equalised after 35 minutes when Davis was brought down from behind by Goldbrunner. The referee Mr Webb of Scotland had no hesitation in awarding Ireland a penalty. DAVIS picked himself up and scored from the spot, sending Jakob the wrong way.

As the half drew to a close, Ireland could easily have been awarded another penalty when Geoghegan was brought down in the box but despite the protests from the home side, the referee waved play on. German went straight down to the other end and almost took the lead when Kobierski's delicate chip forced Foley into making an excellent save.

The Irish had an early scare at the start of the second-half when Joe O'Reilly's back-pass caught Foley unaware but passed just outside the keeper's left-hand post. It was the only scare of a half that saw Ireland completely dominate proceedings. On 59 minutes, an accurate cross by Moore was headed clear by a defender but only to Ellis whose header back into the box found the unmarked GEOGHEGAN who chested the ball over the line. The debutant could have had another goal but headed over from six yards out when it seemed easier to score.

Ten minutes later, Ireland extended their lead when Moore's cross was headed on by Ellis to DONNELLY. His shot was deflected past Jakob by Muenzenberg but the Dundalk forward claimed the goal as the ball was going in anyway. On 76 minutes, Paddy Moore evaded a couple of challenges before sending in a powerfully-struck 25 yard drive. Jakob failed to hold the ball and as it broke loose, DAVIS slid in to ram the ball home.

Match No. 19	
6 December 1936 v HUNGARY at Dublin	
J Foley	Glasgow Celtic
W O'Neill	Dundalk
W Gorman	Bury
J O'Reilly	St James's Gate
C Turner	Southend United
C Moulson	Notts County

P Ellis	Bohemians
J Donnelly	Dundalk
T Davis	Oldham Athletic
P Moore	Shamrock Rovers
WJ Fallon	Notts County

Result	2–3
Scorers	WJ Fallon; T Davis

Match No. 20
17 May 1937 v SWITZERLAND at Berne

T Breen	Manchester United
J Feenan	Sunderland
W O'Neill	Dundalk
C Moulson	Notts County
C Turner	Southend United
J O'Reilly	St James's Gate
J Brown	Coventry City
D Jordan	Wolverhampton Wanderers
J Dunne	Southampton
P Farrell	Hibernian
WJ Fallon	Notts County

Result	1–0
Scorer	J Dunne

Match No. 21
23 May 1937 v FRANCE at Paris

T Breen	Manchester United
W O'Neill	Dundalk
J Feenan	Sunderland
J O'Reilly	St James's Gate
C Turner	Southend United
C Moulson	Notts County
J Brown	Coventry City
D Jordan	Wolverhampton Wanderers
J Dunne	Southampton
P Farrell	Hibernian
WJ Fallon	Notts County

Result	2–2
Scorers	D Jordan; J Brown

Match No. 22
10 October 1937 v NORWAY at Oslo

G McKenzie	Southend United
J Williams	Shamrock Rovers
M Hoy	Dundalk
J O'Reilly	St James's Gate
C Turner	Southend United
O Kinsella	Shamrock Rovers
T Donnelly	Drumcondra
J Donnelly	Dundalk
J Dunne	Shamrock Rovers
W Jordan	Bohemians
M Geoghegan	St James's Gate

Result	2–3
Scorers	M Geoghegan; J Dunne

Match No. 23
7 November 1937 v NORWAY at Dublin

G McKenzie	Southend United
W O'Neill	Dundalk
W Gorman	Bury
J O'Reilly	St James's Gate
C Turner	Southend United
T Arrigan	Waterford
K O'Flanagan	Bohemians
H Duggan	Newport County
J Dunne	Shamrock Rovers
J Carey	Manchester United
T Foy	Shamrock Rovers

Result	3–3
Scorers	J Dunne; K O'Flanagan; H Duggan

Match No. 24

18 May 1938 v CZECHOSLOVAKIA at Prague

G McKenzie	Southend United
P Gaskins	St James's Gate
W Gorman	Bury
J O'Reilly	St James's Gate
M O'Mahoney	Bristol Rovers
C Turner	West Ham United
K O'Flanagan	Bohemians
J Dunne	Shamrock Rovers
T Davis	Tranmere Rovers
J Carey	Manchester United
T O'Keeffe	Waterford

Result	2–2
Scorers	T Davis; J Dunne

Match No. 25

22 May 1938 v POLAND at Warsaw

G McKenzie*	Southend United
P Gaskins	St James's Gate
W Gorman	Bury
J O'Reilly	St James's Gate
M O'Mahoney	Bristol Rovers
C Turner	West Ham United
K O'Flanagan	Bohemians
J Dunne	Shamrock Rovers
T Davis	Tranmere Rovers
J Carey	Manchester United
T O'Keeffe	Waterford
W Harrington* (sub)	Cork

Result	0–6

Match No. 26

18 September 1938 v SWITZERLAND at Dublin

G McKenzie	Southend United
W Gorman	Bury
M Hoy	Dundalk
J O'Reilly	St James's Gate
M O'Mahoney	Bristol Rovers
R Lunn	Dundalk
T Donnelly	Shamrock Rovers
J Dunne	Shamrock Rovers
P Bradshaw	St James's Gate
J Carey	Manchester United
WJ Fallon	Notts County

Result	4–0
Scorers	P Bradshaw (2); J Dunne; T Donnelly

Match No. 27

13 November 1938 v POLAND at Dublin

G McKenzie	Southend United
W Gorman	Bury
M Hoy	Dundalk
J O'Reilly	St James's Gate
M O'Mahoney	Bristol Rovers
R Lunn	Dundalk
K O'Flanagan	Bohemians
J Dunne	Shamrock Rovers
P Bradshaw	St James's Gate
J Carey	Manchester United
WJ Fallon	Notts County

Result	3–2
Scorers	WJ Fallon; J Carey; J Dunne

Match No. 28

19 March 1939 v HUNGARY at Cork

G McKenzie	Southend United
W Gorman	Brentford
M Hoy	Dundalk
J O'Reilly	St James's Gate
C Turner	West Ham United
E Weir	Clyde
K O'Flanagan	Bohemians
J Dunne	Shamrock Rovers

P Bradshaw	St James's Gate
J Carey	Manchester United
T Foy	Shamrock Rovers

| Result | 2–2 |
| Scorers | P Bradshaw; J Carey |

Match No. 29
18 May 1939 v HUNGARY at Budapest

G McKenzie	Southend United
W O'Neill	Dundalk
M Hoy	Dundalk
J O'Reilly	St James's Gate
M O'Mahoney	Bristol Rovers
E Weir	Clyde
K O'Flanagan	Bohemians
J Dunne	Shamrock Rovers
P Bradshaw	St James's Gate
J Carey	Manchester United
WJ Fallon	Sheffield Wednesday

| Result | 2–2 |
| Scorers | K O'Flanagan (2) |

Match No. 30
23 May 1939 v GERMANY at Bremen

G McKenzie	Southend United
W O'Neill	Dundalk
M Hoy	Dundalk
J O'Reilly	St James's Gate
M O'Mahoney	Bristol Rovers
E Weir	Clyde
K O'Flanagan	Bohemians
J Dunne	Shamrock Rovers
P Bradshaw	St James's Gate
J Carey	Manchester United
WJ Fallon	Sheffield Wednesday

| Result | 1–1 |
| Scorer | P Bradshaw |

Match No. 31
16 June 1946 v PORTUGAL at Lisbon

E Courtney*	Cork United
W McMillan	Belfast Celtic
T Aherne	Belfast Celtic
J Carey	Manchester United
J Vernon	Belfast Celtic
PD Farrell	Shamrock Rovers
J O'Reilly	Cork United
W Sloan	Arsenal
D Walsh	West Bromwich Albion
J McAlinden	Portsmouth
T Eglington	Shamrock Rovers
C Martin*(sub)	Glentoran

| Result | 1–3 |
| Scorer | J O'Reilly |

Match No. 32
23 June 1946 v SPAIN at Madrid

C Martin	Glentoran
W McMillan	Belfast Celtic
T Aherne	Belfast Celtic
J Carey	Manchester United
J Vernon	Belfast Celtic
PD Farrell	Shamrock Rovers
J O'Reilly	Cork United
W Sloan	Arsenal
D Walsh	West Bromwich Albion
J McAlinden	Portsmouth
T Eglington	Shamrock Rovers

| Result | 1–0 |
| Scorer | W Sloan |

Match No. 33
30 September 1946 v ENGLAND at Dublin

T Breen	Shamrock Rovers
W Gorman	Brentford
WE Hayes	Huddersfield Town

J Carey	Manchester United
C Martin	Glentoran
W Walsh	Manchester City
K O'Flanagan	Arsenal
P Coad	Shamrock Rovers
M O'Flanagan	Bohemians
A Stevenson	Everton
T Eglington	Everton

Result	0–1

Match No. 34
2 March 1947 v SPAIN at Dublin

T Breen	Shamrock Rovers
J McGowan	Cork United
J Carey	Manchester United
PD Farrell	Everton
C Martin	Leeds United
W Walsh	Manchester City
K O'Flanagan	Arsenal
P Coad	Shamrock Rovers
D Walsh	West Bromwich Albion
A Stevenson	Everton
T Eglington	Everton

Result	3–2
Scorers	D Walsh (2); P Coad

Match No. 35
4 May 1947 v PORTUGAL at Dublin

T Breen	Shamrock Rovers
W Gorman	Brentford
WE Hayes	Huddersfield Town
W Walsh	Manchester City
J Carey	Manchester United
PD Farrell	Everton
K O'Flanagan	Arsenal
P Coad	Shamrock Rovers
D Walsh	West Bromwich Albion

A Stevenson	Everton
T Eglington	Everton

Result	0–2

Match No. 36
23 May 1948 v PORTUGAL at Lisbon

G Moulson	Lincoln City
J Carey	Manchester United
C Martin	Leeds United
W Walsh	Manchester City
K Clarke	Drumcondra
PD Farrell	Everton
B Henderson	Drumcondra
P Coad	Shamrock Rovers
D Walsh	West Bromwich Albion
A Stevenson	Everton
T Eglington	Everton

Result	0–2

Match No. 37
30 May 1948 v SPAIN at Barcelona

G Moulson	Lincoln City
J Carey	Manchester United
C Martin	Leeds United
W Walsh	Manchester City
K Clarke	Drumcondra
PD Farrell	Everton
A Stevenson	Everton
P Coad	Shamrock Rovers
D Walsh	West Bromwich Albion
T Moroney	West Ham United
B Henderson	Drumcondra

Result	1–2
Scorer	T Moroney

Match No. 38

5 December 1948 v SWITZERLAND at Dublin

G Moulson	Lincoln City
J Carey	Manchester United
TR Keane	Swansea Town
E Gannon	Notts County
C Martin	Aston Villa
PD Farrell	Everton
J O'Driscoll	Swansea Town
P Coad	Shamrock Rovers
D Walsh	West Bromwich Albion
A Stevenson	Everton
T Eglington	Everton

Result	0–1

Match No. 39

24 April 1949 v BELGIUM at Dublin

WJ Hayes	Limerick
J Carey	Manchester United
L O'Byrne	Shamrock Rovers
E Gannon	Sheffield Wednesday
C Martin	Aston Villa
W Walsh	Manchester City
J O'Driscoll	Swansea Town
JC Lawlor	Drumcondra
B Carroll	Shelbourne
P Coad	Shamrock Rovers
G Malone	Shelbourne

Result	0–2

Match No. 40

22 May 1949 v PORTUGAL at Dublin

T Godwin	Shamrock Rovers
J Carey	Manchester United
TR Keane	Swansea Town
E Gannon	Sheffield Wednesday
C Martin	Aston Villa
T Moroney	West Ham United

P Corr	Everton
P Coad	Shamrock Rovers
D Walsh*	West Bromwich Albion
D McGowan	West Ham United
T Eglington	Everton
PD Farrell* (sub)	Everton

Result	1–0
Scorer	P Coad (penalty)

Match No. 41

2 June 1949 v SWEDEN at Stockholm

T Godwin	Shamrock Rovers
J Carey	Manchester United
TR Keane	Swansea Town
E Gannon	Sheffield Wednesday
C Martin	Aston Villa
T Moroney	West Ham United
J O'Driscoll	Swansea Town
P Coad	Shamrock Rovers
D Walsh	West Bromwich Albion
D McGowan	West Ham United
T Eglington	Everton

Result	1–3
Scorer	D Walsh

Match No. 42

12 June 1949 v SPAIN at Dublin

T Godwin	Shamrock Rovers
J Carey	Manchester United
TR Keane	Swansea Town
PD Farrell	Everton
C Martin	Aston Villa
T Moroney	West Ham United
P Corr	Everton
E Gannon	Sheffield Wednesday
D Walsh	West Bromwich Albion
D McGowan	West Ham United
J Hartnett	Middlesbrough

MATCHES

Result	1–4
Scorer	C Martin (penalty)

Match No. 43

8 September 1949 v FINLAND at Dublin

T Godwin	Shamrock Rovers
J Carey	Manchester United
T Aherne	Luton Town
E Gannon	Sheffield Wednesday
C Martin	Aston Villa
T Moroney	West Ham United
J Gavin	Norwich City
A Fitzsimons	Middlesbrough
B Carroll*	Shelbourne
P Desmond	Middlesbrough
T O'Connor	Shamrock Rovers
P Daly* (sub)	Shamrock Rovers

Result	3–0
Scorers	J Gavin; C Martin (2–1 penalty)

Match No. 44

21 September 1949 v ENGLAND at Liverpool

T Godwin	Shamrock Rovers
J Carey	Manchester United
T Aherne	Luton Town
W Walsh	Manchester City
C Martin	Aston Villa
T Moroney	West Ham United
P Corr	Everton
PD Farrell	Everton
D Walsh	West Bromwich Albion
P Desmond	Middlesbrough
T O'Connor	Shamrock Rovers

Result	2–0
Scorers	C Martin (penalty); PD Farrell

The Irish team that defeated England 2–0 at Goodison Park in 1949. They were the first foreign team to defeat England on home soil.

9 October 1949 v FINLAND at Helsinki	
T Godwin	Leicester City
J Carey	Manchester United
T Aherne	Luton Town
J Coffey	Drumcondra
C Martin	Aston Villa
T Moroney	West Ham United
J Gavin	Norwich City
PD Farrell	Everton
D Walsh	West Bromwich Albion
P Desmond	Middlesbrough
T O'Connor	Shamrock Rovers

Result	1–1
Scorer	PD Farrell

FEATURED MATCH 3

ENGLAND 0 REPUBLIC OF IRELAND 2
At Goodison Park, Liverpool, 21 September 1949

England
Bert Williams; Bert Mozley; Johnny Aston; Billy Wright; Neil Franklin; Jimmy Dickinson; Peter Harris; Johnny Morris; Jesse Pye; Wilf Mannion; Tom Finney.

Republic of Ireland
Tommy Godwin; Johnny Carey; Tommy Aherne; Willie Walsh; Con Martin; Tommy Moroney; Peter Corr; Peter Farrell; Davy Walsh; Peter Desmond; Tommy O'Connor.

England were undefeated at home against non-British sides prior to this game and opted to blood a number of new players in readiness for the forthcoming British Championships which would double-up as a World Cup qualification group.

They gave debuts to forwards Harris and Pye and it was the Wolves' centre-forward Jesse Pye who had the game's first chance after only three minutes. Preston winger Tom Finney beat Willie Walsh to the ball and set Wilf Mannion free down the left. His pinpoint cross found the head of Pye but he put the ball inches wide of the post. Finney then cut inside Carey to set up Mannion but he too failed to trouble Godwin in the Ireland goal. Pye had another chance to mark his full international debut with a goal but he was well tackled by Bud Aherne and failed.

At the other end, Davy Walsh tested Williams with a snap shot but, in truth, England had dominated the first half-hour. Then on 33 minutes, completely against the run of play, Tommy O'Connor released Peter Desmond who raced into the England box. As he shaped to shoot, his legs were taken from under him by Bert Mozley and the referee, Mr Mowat of Scotland, pointed to the spot. Con MARTIN blasted the spot-kick at goal and although Bert Williams got his hands to the ball, it spun from his grasp and over the line, such was the power of the strike.

Ireland took heart from this goal and in the closing minutes of the half both Davy Walsh and Peter Desmond had chances to extend their side's lead. In fact, Desmond's effort grazed the outside of Williams' left-hand post.

As the second half got underway, England went all out for the equaliser and skipper Billy Wright tested Godwin from 35 yards but the Irish keeper turned the ball round the post. The Shamrock Rovers No. 1 also denied Harris, tipping his goalbound header over the bar. The other England debutant Jesse Pye was having a good game and had the ball taken off his toe by an alert Bud Aherne as he looked likely to level the scores. Then a curling free-kick by Pompey winger Harris came back off the underside of the bar and Con Martin twice cleared off the line as England pressed hard.

The home side continued to dominate but with just five minutes remaining, an England attack broke down and the ball was played to O'Connor. The speedy winger left the England defenders in his wake before passing inside for FARRELL. Playing on his home ground, Farrell chipped the ball over the advancing Williams and into the empty net.

England failed to recover from this late blow and the Republic of Ireland thus inflicted on them their first defeat on home soil by a non-British side.

MATCHES

Match No. 46

13 November 1949 v SWEDEN at Dublin

T Godwin	Leicester City
J Carey	Manchester United
T Aherne	Luton Town
W Walsh	Manchester City
C Martin	Aston Villa
R Ryan	West Bromwich Albion
P Corr	Everton
PD Farrell	Everton
D Walsh	West Bromwich Albion
P Desmond	Middlesbrough
T O'Connor	Shamrock Rovers

Result	1–3
Scorer	C Martin (penalty)

Match No. 47

10 May 1950 v BELGIUM at Brussels

T Godwin	Leicester City
M Clarke	Shamrock Rovers
T Aherne	Luton Town
W Walsh	Manchester City
C Martin	Aston Villa
T Moroney	West Ham United
T Murray	Dundalk
A Fitzsimons	Middlesbrough
B Duffy	Shamrock Rovers
R Ryan	West Bromwich Albion
M Colfer	Shelbourne

Result	1–5
Scorer	B Duffy

Match No. 48

26 November 1950 v NORWAY at Dublin

T Godwin	Leicester City
S Fallon	Glasgow Celtic
T Aherne	Luton Town
E Gannon	Sheffield Wednesday
J Carey	Manchester United
T Moroney	West Ham United
C Giles	Doncaster Rovers
JC Lawlor	Doncaster Rovers
D Walsh	West Bromwich Albion
R Ryan	West Bromwich Albion
T Eglington	Everton

Result	2–2
Scorers	J Carey (penalty); D Walsh

Match No. 49

13 May 1951 v ARGENTINA at Dublin

F Kiernan	Shamrock Rovers
J Carey	Manchester United
T Aherne	Luton Town
R Ryan	West Bromwich Albion
C Martin	Aston Villa
PD Farrell	Everton
A Ringstead	Sheffield United
J Higgins	Birmingham City
D Walsh	Aston Villa
JC Lawlor	Doncaster Rovers
T Eglington	Everton

Result	0–1

Match No. 50	
30 May 1951 v NORWAY at Oslo	
F Kiernan	Shamrock Rovers
TJ Clinton	Everton
T Aherne	Luton Town
R Ryan	West Bromwich Albion
J Carey	Manchester United
T Moroney	West Ham United
A Ringstead	Sheffield United
T Cunneen*	Limerick
D Walsh	Aston Villa
PD Farrell	Everton
M Colfer	Shelbourne
P Coad* (sub)	Shamrock Rovers

Result	3–2
Scorers	A Ringstead; PD Farrell; P Coad

Match No. 51	
17 October 1951 v WEST GERMANY at Dublin	
F Kiernan	Southampton
S Fallon	Glasgow Celtic
T Aherne	Luton Town
T Moroney	West Ham United
F Burke	Cork Athletic
PD Farrell	Everton
A Ringstead	Sheffield United
A Fitzsimons	Middlesbrough
D Glynn	Drumcondra
R Ryan	West Bromwich Albion
T Eglington	Everton

Result	3–2
Scorers	J Posipal (own goal); A Fitzsimons; D Glynn

Republic of Ireland goalkeeper Fred Kiernan is beaten but German centre-forward Morlock fires into the side netting. Ireland won 3–2 with Dessie Glynn netting a late winner.

Match No. 52

4 May 1952 v WEST GERMANY at Cologne

F Kiernan	Southampton
T Aherne	Luton Town
S Fallon	Glasgow Celtic
E Gannon	Sheffield Wednesday
C Martin	Aston Villa
PD Farrell	Everton
A Ringstead	Sheffield United
A Fitzsimons	Middlesbrough
S Gibbons	St Patrick's Athletic
R Ryan	West Bromwich Albion
T Eglington	Everton

Result	0–3

Match No. 53

7 May 1952 v AUSTRIA at Vienna

F Kiernan	Southampton
S Fallon	Glasgow Celtic
T Aherne	Luton Town
E Gannon	Sheffield Wednesday
C Martin	Aston Villa
F O'Farrell	West Ham United
A Ringstead	Sheffield United
A Fitzsimons	Middlesbrough
R Ryan	West Bromwich Albion
PD Farrell	Everton
T Eglington	Everton

Result	0–6

Match No. 54

1 June 1952 v SPAIN at Madrid

J O'Neill	Everton
S Fallon	Glasgow Celtic
T Aherne	Luton Town
PD Farrell	Everton
C Martin	Aston Villa
R Ryan	West Bromwich Albion
A Ringstead	Sheffield United
P Coad	Shamrock Rovers
D Walsh	Aston Villa
A Fitzsimons	Middlesbrough
T Eglington	Everton

Result	0–6

Match No. 55

16 November 1952 v FRANCE at Dublin

J O'Neill	Everton
S Dunne	Luton Town
T Aherne	Luton Town
PD Farrell	Everton
J Carey	Manchester United
S Cusack	Limerick
J Gavin	Norwich City
A Fitzsimons	Middlesbrough
S Fallon	Glasgow Celtic
R Ryan	West Bromwich Albion
T Eglington	Everton

Result	1–1
Scorer	S Fallon

Match No. 56

25 March 1953 v AUSTRIA at Dublin

J O'Neill	Everton
S Dunne	Luton Town
JF Lawler	Fulham
PD Farrell	Everton
J Carey	Manchester United
F O'Farrell	West Ham United
A Ringstead	Sheffield United
A Fitzsimons	Middlesbrough
D Walsh	Aston Villa
R Ryan	West Bromwich Albion
T Eglington	Everton

Result	4–0
Scorers	A Ringstead (2); T Eglington; F O'Farrell

Match No. 57

4 October 1953 v FRANCE at Dublin

J O'Neill	Everton
S Dunne	Luton Town
T Aherne	Luton Town
PD Farrell	Everton
C Martin	Aston Villa
F O'Farrell	West Ham United
A Fitzsimons	Middlesbrough
T Moroney	Evergreen United
D Walsh	Aston Villa
R Ryan	West Bromwich Albion
T Eglington	Everton

Result	3–5
Scorers	R Ryan; D Walsh; F O'Farrell

Match No. 58

28 October 1953 v LUXEMBOURG at Dublin

J O'Neill	Everton
S Dunne	Luton Town
JF Lawler	Fulham
E Gannon	Sheffield Wednesday
N Cantwell	West Ham United
R Ryan	West Bromwich Albion
L Munroe	Shamrock Rovers
GP Cummins	Luton Town
S Gibbons	St Patrick's Athletic
A Fitzsimons	Middlesbrough
T Eglington	Everton

Result	4–0
Scorers	A Fitzsimons (20; R Ryan (penalty); T Eglington

Match No. 59

25 November 1953 v FRANCE at Paris

J O'Neill	Everton
TJ Clinton	Everton
JF Lawler	Fulham
E Gannon	Sheffield Wednesday
C Martin	Aston Villa
PD Farrell	Everton
A Ringstead	Sheffield United
R Ryan	West Bromwich Albion
D Walsh	Aston Villa
A Fitzsimons	Middlesbrough
T Eglington	Everton

Result	0–1

Match No. 60

7 March 1954 v LUXEMBOURG at Luxembourg

T Scannell	Southampton
TJ Clinton	Everton
T Traynor	Southampton
M Gallagher	Hibernian
C Martin	Aston Villa
P Saward	Millwall
J Gavin	Norwich City
N Kelly	Nottingham Forest
FT Kearns	West Ham United
GP Cummins	Luton Town
J Hartnett	Middlesbrough

Result	1–0
Scorer	GP Cummins

Match No. 61

7 November 1954 v NORWAY at Dublin

J O'Neill	Everton
D Donovan	Everton
JF Lawler	Fulham
E Gannon	Shelbourne
C Martin	Aston Villa
PD Farrell	Everton
F Fagan	Manchester City
R Ryan	Derby County
P Ambrose	Shamrock Rovers

GP Cummins	Luton Town
T Eglington	Everton

Result	2–1
Scorers	C Martin; R Ryan (penalty)

Match No. 62

1 May 1955 v HOLLAND at Dublin

J O'Neill	Everton
D Donovan	Everton
JF Lawler	Fulham
PD Farrell	Everton
C Martin	Aston Villa
F O'Farrell	West Ham United
J Gavin	Tottenham Hotspur
P Ambrose	Shamrock Rovers
FJ Fitzgerald	Waterford
A Fitzsimons	Middlesbrough
T Eglington	Everton

Result	1–0
Scorer	FJ Fitzgerald

Match No. 63

25 May 1955 v NORWAY at Oslo

J O'Neill	Everton
D Donovan	Everton
JF Lawler	Fulham
E Gannon	Shelbourne
C Martin	Aston Villa
F O'Farrell	West Ham United
A Ringstead	Sheffield United
GP Cummins	Luton Town
S Fallon	Glasgow Celtic
A Fitzsimons	Middlesbrough
D Glynn	Drumcondra

Result	3–1
Scorers	GP Cummins (2); A Fitzsimons

Match No. 64

28 May 1955 v WEST GERMANY at Hamburg

J O'Neill	Everton
D Donovan	Everton
JF Lawler	Fulham

The Republic of Ireland and Norway teams line up before the international at Dalymount Park in November 1954, a match the Irish won 2–1.

E Gannon	Shelbourne
C Martin	Aston Villa
PD Farrell	Everton
J Gavin	Tottenham Hotspur
GP Cummins	Luton Town
S Fallon	Glasgow Celtic
A Fitzsimons	Middlesbrough
T Eglington	Everton

| Result | 1–2 |
| Scorer | S Fallon |

Match No. 65

19 October 1955 v YUGOSLAVIA at Dublin

J O'Neill	Everton
A Murphy	Clyde
JF Lawler	Fulham
PD Farrell	Everton
C Martin	Aston Villa
F O'Farrell	West Ham United
A Ringstead	Sheffield United
A Fitzsimons	Middlesbrough
S Gibbons	St Patrick's Athletic
GP Cummins	Luton Town
L Tuohy	Shamrock Rovers

| Result | 1–4 |
| Scorer | A Fitzsimons |

Match No. 66

27 November 1955 v SPAIN at Dublin

J O'Neill	Everton
S Dunne	Luton Town
N Cantwell	West Ham United
PD Farrell	Everton
C Martin	Aston Villa
R Ryan	Derby County
A Ringstead	Sheffield United
A Fitzsimons	Middlesbrough
S Gibbons	St Patrick's Athletic

| GP Cummins | Luton Town |
| T Eglington | Everton |

| Result | 2–2 |
| Scorers | A Fitzsimons; A Ringstead |

Match No. 67

10 May 1956 v HOLLAND at Rotterdam

T Godwin	Leicester City
S Dunne	Luton Town
N Cantwell	West Ham United
T Dunne	St Patrick's Athletic
C Martin	Aston Villa
F O'Farrell	West Ham United
A Ringstead	Sheffield United
A Fitzsimons	Middlesbrough
FJ Fitzgerald	Waterford
W Whelan	Manchester United
J Haverty	Arsenal

| Result | 4–1 |
| Scorers | A Fitzsimons (2); J Haverty; A Ringstead |

Match No. 68

3 October 1956 v DENMARK at Dublin

J O'Neill	Everton
S Dunne	Luton Town
N Cantwell	West Ham United
T Dunne	St Patrick's Athletic
G Mackey	Shamrock Rovers
R Nolan	Shamrock Rovers
J Gavin	Norwich City
W Whelan	Manchester United
D Curtis	Shelbourne
A Fitzsimons	Middlesbrough
J Haverty	Arsenal

| Result | 2–1 |
| Scorers | D Curtis; J Gavin (penalty) |

Match No. 69

25 November 1956 v WEST GERMANY at Dublin

A Kelly	Drumcondra
S Dunne	Luton Town
N Cantwell	West Ham United
T Dunne	St Patrick's Athletic
G Mackey	Shamrock Rovers
R Nolan	Shamrock Rovers
J McCann	Shamrock Rovers
N Peyton	Shamrock Rovers
D Curtis	Shelbourne
A Fitzsimons	Middlesbrough
J Haverty	Arsenal

Result	3–0
Scorers	N Cantwell (penalty); J Haverty; J McCann

Match No. 70

8 May 1957 v ENGLAND at Wembley

A Kelly	Drumcondra
D Donovan	Everton
N Cantwell	West Ham United
PD Farrell	Everton
G Mackey	Shamrock Rovers
P Saward	Aston Villa
A Ringstead	Sheffield United
W Whelan	Manchester United
D Curtis	Bristol City
A Fitzsimons	Middlesbrough
J Haverty	Arsenal

Result	1–5
Scorer	D Curtis

Match No. 71

19 May 1957 v ENGLAND at Dublin

T Godwin	Bournemouth
S Dunne	Luton Town
N Cantwell	West Ham United
P Saward	Aston Villa
R Nolan	Shamrock Rovers
C Hurley	Millwall
A Ringstead	Sheffield United
W Whelan	Manchester United
D Curtis	Bristol City
A Fitzsimons	Middlesbrough
J Haverty	Arsenal

Result	1–1
Scorer	A Ringstead

Match No. 72

2 October 1957 v DENMARK at Copenhagen

T Godwin	Bournemouth
S Dunne	Luton Town
N Cantwell	West Ham United
P Saward	Aston Villa
C Hurley	Sunderland
F O'Farrell	Preston North End
A Ringstead	Sheffield United
A Fitzsimons	Middlesbrough
D Curtis	Bristol City
GP Cummins	Luton Town
J Haverty	Arsenal

Result	2–0
Scorers	GP Cummins; D Curtis

Match No. 73

11 May 1958 v POLAND at Katowice

T Godwin	Bournemouth
S Dunne	Luton Town
N Cantwell	West Ham United
R Nolan	Shamrock Rovers
C Hurley	Sunderland
P Saward	Aston Villa
A Ringstead	Sheffield United
GP Cummins	Luton Town

D Curtis	Bristol City
A Fitzsimons	Middlesbrough
J Haverty	Arsenal

Result	2–2
Scorers	D Curtis; GP Cummins

Match No. 74

14 May 1958 v AUSTRIA at Vienna

J O'Neill	Everton
S Dunne	Luton Town
N Cantwell	West Ham United
M McGrath	Blackburn Rovers
C Hurley	Sunderland
P Saward	Aston Villa
A Ringstead	Sheffield United
GP Cummins	Luton Town
D Curtis	Bristol City
A Fitzsimons	Middlesbrough
J Haverty	Arsenal

Result	1–3
Scorer	D Curtis

Match No. 75

5 October 1958 v POLAND at Dublin

J O'Neill*	Everton
S Dunne	Luton Town
N Cantwell	West Ham United
M McGrath	Blackburn Rovers
S Keogh	Shamrock Rovers
P Saward	Aston Villa
A Ringstead	Sheffield United
A Fitzsimons	Middlesbrough
D Curtis	Ipswich Town
GP Cummins	Luton Town
J Haverty	Arsenal
T Taylor* (sub)	Waterford

Result	2–2
Scorer	N Cantwell (2–1 penalty)

Match No. 76

5 April 1959 v CZECHOSLOVAKIA at Dublin

J O'Neill	Everton
B McNally	Luton Town
N Cantwell	West Ham United
M McGrath	Blackburn Rovers
C Hurley	Sunderland
P Saward	Aston Villa
A Ringstead	Sheffield United
T Hamilton	Shamrock Rovers
C Doyle	Shelbourne
GP Cummins	Luton Town
L Tuohy	Shamrock Rovers

Result	2–0
Scorers	L Tuohy; N Cantwell (penalty)

Match No. 77

10 May 1959 v CZECHOSLOVAKIA at Bratislava

J O'Neill	Everton
R Whittaker	Chelsea
N Cantwell	West Ham United
F O'Farrell	Preston North End
C Hurley	Sunderland
M McGrath	Blackburn Rovers
A Ringstead	Sheffield United
T Hamilton	Shamrock Rovers
A Fitzsimons	Lincoln City
GP Cummins	Luton Town
L Tuohy	Shamrock Rovers

Result	0–4

Match No. 78

1 November 1959 v SWEDEN at Dublin

N Dwyer	West Ham United
J Carolan	Manchester United
N Cantwell	West Ham United
M McGrath	Blackburn Rovers

C Hurley	Sunderland
P Saward	Aston Villa
F Fagan	Manchester City
J Giles	Manchester United
D Curtis	Ipswich Town
GP Cummins	Luton Town
J Haverty	Arsenal

Result	3–2
Scorers	J Giles; D Curtis (2)

Match No. 79	
30 March 1960 v CHILE at Dublin	
N Dwyer	West Ham United
J Carolan	Manchester United
N Cantwell	West Ham United
R Nolan	Shamrock Rovers
C Hurley	Sunderland
P Saward	Aston Villa
F Fagan	Derby County
J Giles	Manchester United
D Curtis	Ipswich Town
GP Cummins	Luton Town
J Haverty	Arsenal

Result	2–0
Scorers	N Cantwell (penalty); D Curtis

Match No. 80	
11 May 1960 v WEST GERMANY at Düsseldorf	
N Dwyer	West Ham United
S Dunne	Luton Town
R Nolan	Shamrock Rovers
M McGrath	Blackburn Rovers
C Hurley	Sunderland
P Saward	Aston Villa
A Fogarty	Sunderland
N Peyton	Leeds United
D Curtis	Ipswich Town
GP Cummins	Luton Town
F Fagan	Derby County

Result	1–0
Scorer	F Fagan

Match No. 81	
18 May 1960 v SWEDEN at Malmo	
N Dwyer*	West Ham United
S Dunne	Luton Town
R Nolan	Shamrock Rovers
M McGrath	Blackburn Rovers
C Hurley	Sunderland
P Saward	Aston Villa
D Curtis	Ipswich Town
A Fogarty	Sunderland
N Cantwell**	West ham United
GP Cummins	Luton Town
F Fagan	Derby County

Did you know?

The longest run of scoring in consecutive games is held by Fionan Fagan who scored in four successive games in 1960, whilst Jimmy Dunne holds the longest run of scoring in consecutive appearances with five goals scored during his international career which ran from 1930 to 1937.

M Swan* (sub)	Drumcondra
N Peyton** (sub)	Leeds United

Result	1–4
Scorer	F Fagan (penalty)

Match No. 82

28 September 1960 v WALES at Dublin

N Dwyer	Swansea Town
P Kelly	Wolverhampton Wanderers
J O'Neill	Preston North End
M McGrath	Blackburn Rovers
C Hurley	Sunderland
P Saward	Aston Villa
F Fagan	Derby County
J Giles	Manchester United
P Fitzgerald	Leeds United
N Peyton	Leeds United
J Haverty	Arsenal

Result	2–3
Scorer	F Fagan (2–1 penalty)

Did you know?

The Republic of Ireland and Wales have played each other at five different venues – Croke Park, Lansdowne Road, Tolka Park, Dalymount Park and the Royal Dublin Society Showgrounds.

Match No. 83

6 November 1960 v NORWAY at Dublin

N Dwyer	Swansea Town
P Kelly	Wolverhampton Wanderers
N Cantwell	West Ham United
J Fullam	Preston North End
C Hurley	Sunderland

P Saward	Aston Villa
F Fagan	Derby County
P Fitzgerald	Leeds United
D Curtis	Ipswich Town
J Giles	Manchester United
J Haverty	Arsenal

Result	3–1
Scorers	F Fagan; P Fitzgerald (2)

Match No. 84

3 May 1961 v SCOTLAND at Glasgow

N Dwyer	Swansea Town
B McNally	Luton Town
N Cantwell	Manchester United
A McEvoy	Blackburn Rovers
C Hurley	Sunderland
P Saward	Huddersfield Town
J Giles	Manchester United
A Fogarty	Sunderland
D Curtis	Ipswich Town
GP Cummins	Luton Town
J Haverty	Arsenal

Result	1–4
Scorer J Haverty	

Match No. 85

7 May 1961 v SCOTLAND at Dublin

N Dwyer	Swansea Town
P Kelly	Wolverhampton Wanderers
N Cantwell	Manchester United
A McEvoy	Blackburn Rovers
C Hurley	Sunderland
M Meagan	Everton
F Fagan	Derby County
J Giles	Manchester United
P Fitzgerald	Leeds United
GP Cummins	Luton Town
J Haverty	Arsenal

Result	0–3

Match No. 86

8 October 1961 v CZECHOSLOVAKIA at Dublin

N Dwyer	Swansea Town
P Kelly	Wolverhampton Wanderers
N Cantwell	Manchester United
M McGrath	Blackburn Rovers
C Hurley	Sunderland
R Nolan	Shamrock Rovers
A Fogarty	Sunderland
J Giles	Manchester United
P Fitzgerald	Chester
F O'Neill	Shamrock Rovers
J Haverty	Blackburn Rovers

Result	1–3
Scorer	J Giles

Match No. 87

29 October 1961 v CZECHOSLOVAKIA at Prague

N Dwyer	Swansea Town
P Kelly	Wolverhampton Wanderers
N Cantwell	Manchester United
R Nolan	Shamrock Rovers
C Hurley	Sunderland
M McGrath	Blackburn Rovers
F O'Neill	Shamrock Rovers
A Fogarty	Sunderland
P Fitzgerald	Chester
J Giles	Manchester United
J Haverty	Blackburn Rovers

Result	1–7
Scorer	A Fogarty

Match No. 88

8 April 1962 v AUSTRIA at Dublin

A Kelly*	Preston North End
A Dunne	Manchester United
T Traynor	Southampton
P Saward	Huddersfield Town
C Hurley	Sunderland
M Meagan	Everton
A Hale	Aston Villa
J Giles	Manchester United
N Cantwell	Manchester United
D Curtis	Ipswich Town
L Tuohy	Newcastle United
D Lowry* (sub)	St Patrick's Athletic

Result	2–3
Scorers	N Cantwell; L Tuohy

Match No. 89

12 August 1962 v ICELAND at Dublin

A Kelly	Preston North End
A Dunne	Manchester United
T Traynor	Southampton
P Saward	Huddersfield Town
C Hurley	Sunderland
M Meagan	Everton
A Hale	Doncaster Rovers
J Giles	Manchester United
N Cantwell	Manchester United
A Fogarty	Sunderland
L Tuohy	Newcastle United

Result	4–2
Scorers	L Tuohy; A Fogarty; N Cantwell (2)

Match No. 90

2 September 1962 v ICELAND at Reykjavik

A Kelly	Preston North End
B McNally	Luton Town
T Traynor	Southampton
R Nolan	Shamrock Rovers
C Hurley	Sunderland
P Saward	Huddersfield Town
D Curtis	Ipswich Town
A Fogarty	Sunderland

N Cantwell	Manchester United
N Peyton	Leeds United
L Tuohy	Newcastle United

Result	1–1

Scorer L Tuohy

FEATURED MATCH 4

REPUBLIC OF IRELAND 4 ICELAND 2
At Dalymount Park, Dublin, 12 August 1962

Republic of Ireland
Alan Kelly; Tony Dunne; Tommy Traynor; Pat Saward; Charlie Hurley; Mick Meagan; Alfie Hale; Johnny Giles; Noel Cantwell; Ambrose Fogarty; Liam Tuohy.

Iceland
H Danielsson; A Njalsson; B Felixson; G Arnason; H Felixson; S Jonsson; S Agustsson; T Beck; R Jonsson; EB Schram; T Jonsson.

During the early stages of this European Championship match, both sides had opportunities with the best falling to Noel Cantwell but Icelandic keeper Danielsson was quickly off his line to smother the effort. At the other end, Tony Dunne cleared a Beck shot off the goal-line, but it was the visitors' only chance as the Irish dominated the opening exchanges.

Ireland went ahead after eleven minutes when TUOHY stooped low to head home Johnny Giles' cross. The home side could have gone 2–0 up minutes later but Fogarty miscued his shot when through on goal. Gradually, Iceland began to claw their way back into the game and Kelly had to be alert to save from both Beck and Rikharour Jonsson in the space of five minutes. On the half-hour mark, Tuohy was denied a certain second goal when Njalsson handled on the goal-line and a penalty was awarded. Cantwell smashed the ball against the bar and though Fogarty scored from the rebound, it was disallowed because Cantwell was in an offside position.

Cantwell then had a shot well saved by Danielsson and Tuohy headed inches wide but on 37 minutes, Iceland drew level when the usually reliable Hurley was caught in two minds and robbed by Rikharour JONSSON. The Icelandic forward had no trouble in beating Kelly from the edge of the box. Just before half-time, a cross from Traynor was headed goalwards by Cantwell and though Danielsson got his hands to the ball, he couldn't hold it and FOGARTY was the first to react to turn the ball over the line.

Early in the second half, Thorour Jonsson forced a good save from Alan Kelly, whilst Doncaster's Alfie Hale, playing in only his second international, was foiled by the skill of the Icelandic keeper. Danielsson made outstanding stops from both Giles and Cantwell but on 65 minutes he was powerless to stop Noel CANTWELL from extending Ireland's lead with a 20-yard shot that took a slight deflection. Ten minutes later CANTWELL outjumped Danielsson and Felixson to head home another accurate cross from Hale.

Ireland continued to press forward in search of further goals and both Hurley and Tuohy had shots turned round the post before Noel Cantwell, who would have had a hat-trick if he'd converted his penalty, had a chance to make amends but he miskicked in front of goal with only Danielsson to beat.

With just four minutes to play, Iceland were awarded a free-kick, a yard outside Ireland's penalty area. As the kick was taken, the Irish defence moved out en masse, leaving three Icelandic forwards offside. The linesman kept his flag down though and Rikharour JONSSON scored his and his side's second goal.

Match No. 91	
9 June 1963 v SCOTLAND at Dublin	
A Kelly	Preston North End
A Dunne	Manchester United
T Traynor	Southampton
A McEvoy	Blackburn Rovers
C Hurley	Sunderland
M McGrath	Blackburn Rovers
J Giles	Manchester United
P Turner	Glasgow Celtic
N Cantwell	Manchester United
N Peyton*	Leeds United

| J Haverty | Blackburn Rovers |
| A Fogarty* (sub) | Sunderland |

Result	1–0
Scorer	N Cantwell

Match No. 92

23 September 1963 v AUSTRIA at Vienna

A Kelly	Preston North End
W Browne	Bohemians
T Traynor	Southampton
R Brady	Queen's Park Rangers
C Hurley	Sunderland
M McGrath	Blackburn Rovers
J Giles	Leeds United
R Whelan	St Patrick's Athletic
D Curtis	Exeter City
A Fogarty	Sunderland
L Tuohy	Shamrock Rovers

Result	0–0

Match No. 93

13 October 1963 v AUSTRIA at Dublin

A Kelly	Preston North End
A Dunne	Manchester United
T Traynor	Southampton
R Brady	Queen's Park Rangers
C Hurley	Sunderland
M McGrath	Blackburn Rovers
J Giles	Leeds United
A McEvoy	Blackburn Rovers
N Cantwell	Manchester United
A Fogarty	Sunderland
J Haverty	Millwall

Result	3–2
Scorers	N Cantwell (2–1 penalty); A Fogarty

FEATURED MATCH 5

REPUBLIC OF IRELAND 3 AUSTRIA 2
At Dalymount Park, Dublin, 13 October 1963

Republic of Ireland
Alan Kelly; Tony Dunne; Tommy Traynor; Ray Brady; Charlie Hurley; Mick McGrath; Johnny Giles; Andy McEvoy; Noel Cantwell; Ambrose Fogarty; Joe Haverty.

Austria
G Fraydl; P Vargo; W Glechner; E Hasenkopf; J Frank; K Koller; W Koleznik; H Jank; J Buzek; H Nemee; R Flogel.

After a goalless first leg, the second leg of the European Championship tie against Austria was a hard fought game, one filled with both incident and atmosphere. Though the official attendance was 40,000, there were many more who got into the ground without paying and this overcrowding caused problems. Over the course of the 90 minutes, there were four pitch invasions that not only forced play to be stopped but could have led to the match being abandoned.

Ambrose Fogarty had an early chance to put Ireland ahead but shot wide when well placed, while at the other end, Koleznik blazed over the bar with only Kelly to beat. Noel Cantwell headed into the side netting but after just fifteen minutes, the home side was reduced to ten men when Blackburn's Mick McGrath was forced to retire with a nasty-looking head injury. His Blackburn teammate Andy McEvoy moved into the left-half position and was immediately called into action to tackle Koller when the Austrian was through on goal.

Playing against ten men, the Austrians gradually began to get on top and after Buzek had a header saved by Kelly, they went ahead on 39 minutes when KOLEZNIK accepted a pass from Frank, cut inside Dunne and fired past Kelly. Ireland equalised with just a minute to go until the interval when Cantwell latched on to a fine through ball by Fogarty. His shot was touched on to the underside of the bar by Fraydl but as the ball bounced back into play CANTWELL beat his teammate Haverty to the ball to head it over the line.

One of four pitch invasions occurred during the half-time interval and both teams were kept in the dressing-rooms for twenty minutes before the game could get under way. When Ireland emerged for the second half, Mick McGrath was with them. He went out on to the wing but proved to be little more than a passenger. Ireland took the lead after 65 minutes when Haverty's corner was met by Fogarty, whose powerful header entered the net off the chest of KOLLER for an own goal. This, of course, led to another pitch invasion.

When it had been cleared, Ireland went in search of another goal and Giles, Cantwell and Haverty all went close before McEvoy tested Fraydl from a distance. Then with just eight minutes remaining, a stunning cross field pass from Koleznik found FLOGEL whose first time shot rocketed into the net past a flat-footed Kelly. With just a minute left on the clock, Haverty's cross deep into the Austrian penalty area was handled by Frank and the referee had no hesitation in pointing to the spot. This resulted in another pitch invasion but when the playing area was cleared, up stepped Noel CANTWELL to send Fraydl the wrong way with a well-struck penalty.

Amid chaotic scenes, Dalymount Park was invaded again. Following this delay, injury time was played but Ireland hung on to record a famous victory and with it, qualify for the quarter-finals of the European Nations Championship.

Match No. 94
11 March 1964 v SPAIN at Seville

A Kelly	Preston North End
T Foley	Northampton Town
T Traynor	Southampton
R Brady	Queen's Park Rangers
C Hurley	Sunderland
M Meagan	Everton
J Giles	Leeds United
A McEvoy	Blackburn Rovers
A Hale	Doncaster Rovers
A Fogarty	Hartlepool United
J Haverty	Millwall

Result	1–5
Scorer	A McEvoy

Match No. 95
8 April 1964 v SPAIN at Dublin

A Kelly	Preston North End
A Dunne	Manchester United
W Browne	Bohemians
R Brady	Queen's Park Rangers
C Hurley	Sunderland
J Fullam	Shamrock Rovers
J Giles	Leeds United
A McEvoy	Blackburn Rovers
N Cantwell	Manchester United
P Turner	Glasgow Celtic
A Hale	Doncaster Rovers

Result	0–2

Match No. 96
10 May 1964 v POLAND at Krakow

A Kelly*	Preston North End
T Foley	Northampton Town
A Dunne	Manchester United
R Brady	Queen's Park Rangers
C Hurley	Sunderland
F Strahan	Shelbourne
J Giles	Leeds United
A McEvoy	Blackburn Rovers
P Ambrose	Shamrock Rovers
J Fullam	Shamrock Rovers
J Haverty	Millwall
N Dwyer* (sub)	Swansea Town

Result	1–3
Scorer	P Ambrose

Match No. 97
13 May 1964 v NORWAY at Oslo

N Dwyer	Swansea Town
T Foley	Northampton Town
A Dunne	Manchester United
R Brady	Queen's Park Rangers

F Strahan	Shelbourne
J Fullam	Shamrock Rovers
J Giles	Leeds United
A McEvoy	Blackburn Rovers
C Hurley	Sunderland
P Ambrose	Shamrock Rovers
J Haverty	Millwall

Result	4–1
Scorers	C Hurley (2); J Giles; A McEvoy

Match No. 98
24 May 1964 v ENGLAND at Dublin

N Dwyer	Swansea Town
A Dunne	Manchester United
N Cantwell	Manchester United
F Strahan	Shelbourne
W Browne	Bohemians
M McGrath	Blackburn Rovers
J Giles	Leeds United
A McEvoy	Blackburn Rovers
E Bailham	Shamrock Rovers
J Haverty*	Millwall
R Whelan * (sub)	St Patrick's Athletic

Result	1–3
Scorer	F Strahan

Match No. 99
25 October 1964 v POLAND at Dublin

N Dwyer	Swansea Town
T Foley	Northampton Town
A Dunne	Manchester United
F Strahan	Shelbourne
N Cantwell	Manchester United
M McGrath	Blackburn Rovers
F O'Neill	Shamrock Rovers
A McEvoy	Blackburn Rovers
J Mooney	Shamrock Rovers

J Hennessey	Shelbourne
J Haverty	Glasgow Celtic

Result	3–2
Scorers	A McEvoy (2); J Mooney

Match No. 100
24 March 1965 v BELGIUM at Dublin

A Kelly	Preston North End
T Foley	Northampton Town
M Meagan	Huddersfield Town
M McGrath	Blackburn Rovers
F Brennan	Drumcondra
J Hennessey	Shelbourne
F O'Neill	Shamrock Rovers
O Conmy	Peterborough United
J Mooney	Shamrock Rovers
A McEvoy	Blackburn Rovers
L Tuohy	Shamrock Rovers

Result	0–2

Match No. 101
5 May 1965 v SPAIN at Dublin

P Dunne	Manchester United
S Brennan	Manchester United
A Dunne	Manchester United
M McGrath	Blackburn Rovers
C Hurley	Sunderland
J Hennessey	Shelbourne
F O'Neill	Shamrock Rovers
J Giles	Leeds United
N Cantwell	Manchester United
A McEvoy	Blackburn Rovers
J Haverty	Bristol Rovers

Result	1–0
Scorer	Iribar (own goal)

Match No. 102

27 October 1965 v SPAIN at Seville

P Dunne	Manchester United
T Foley	Northampton Town
A Dunne	Manchester United
M McGrath	Blackburn Rovers
N Cantwell	Manchester United
M Meagan	Huddersfield Town
F O'Neill	Shamrock Rovers
A McEvoy	Blackburn Rovers
E Barber	Shelbourne
J Giles	Leeds United
J Haverty	Shelbourne

Result	1–4
Scorer	A McEvoy

Match No. 103

10 November 1965 v SPAIN at Paris

P Dunne	Manchester United
S Brennan	Manchester United
A Dunne	Manchester United
T Foley	Northampton Town
N Cantwell	Manchester United
M Meagan	Huddersfield Town
F O'Neill	Shamrock Rovers
E Dunphy	York City
A McEvoy	Blackburn Rovers
J Giles	Leeds United
J Haverty	Shelbourne

Result 0–1

Match No. 104

4 May 1966 v WEST GERMANY at Dublin

P Dunne	Manchester United
T Foley*	Northampton Town
F Strahan	Shelbourne
M McGrath	Bradford City
C Hurley	Sunderland
J Hennessey	Shelbourne

F O'Neill	Shamrock Rovers
R Treacy	West Bromwich Albion
R Gilbert	Shamrock Rovers
E Dunphy	Millwall
J Haverty	Shelbourne
J Keogh* (sub)	Shamrock Rovers

Result	0–4

Match No. 105

22 May 1966 v AUSTRIA at Vienna

A Kelly	Preston North End
S Brennan	Manchester United
A Dunne	Manchester United
M McGrath	Bradford City
C Hurley	Sunderland
M Meagan	Huddersfield Town
F O'Neill	Shamrock Rovers
J Fullam	Shamrock Rovers
N Cantwell	Manchester United
J Giles	Leeds United
J Haverty	Shelbourne

Result	0–1

Match No. 106

25 May 1966 v BELGIUM at Liege

A Kelly	Preston North End
S Brennan	Manchester United
A Dunne	Manchester United
M McGrath	Bradford City
C Hurley	Sunderland
M Meagan	Huddersfield Town
E Barber	Shelbourne
J Fullam	Shamrock Rovers
N Cantwell	Manchester United
J Giles	Leeds United
J Haverty	Shelbourne

Result	3–2
Scorers	N Cantwell (2); J Fullam

Match No. 107

23 October 1966 v SPAIN at Dublin

A Kelly	Preston North End
S Brennan	Manchester United
A Dunne	Manchester United
J Conway	Fulham
N Cantwell	Manchester United
M Meagan	Huddersfield Town
F O'Neill	Shamrock Rovers
A McEvoy	Blackburn Rovers
R Treacy	West Bromwich Albion
J Giles	Leeds United
A O'Connell	Dundalk

Result	0–0

Match No. 108

16 November 1966 v TURKEY at Dublin

P Dunne	Manchester United
S Brennan	Manchester United
A Dunne	Manchester United
J Conway	Fulham
C Hurley	Sunderland
M Meagan	Huddersfield Town
F O'Neill	Shamrock Rovers
E Dunphy	Millwall
A McEvoy	Blackburn Rovers
J Giles	Leeds United
J Haverty	Shelbourne

Result	2–1
Scorers	F O'Neill; A McEvoy

Match No. 109

7 December 1966 v SPAIN at Valencia

A Kelly	Preston North End
S Brennan	Manchester United
A Dunne	Manchester United
J Dempsey	Fulham
C Hurley	Sunderland
M Meagan	Huddersfield Town
F O'Neill	Shamrock Rovers
J Conway	Fulham
A Hale	Waterford
E Dunphy	Millwall
J Haverty	Shelbourne

Result	0–2

Match No. 110

22 February 1967 v TURKEY at Ankara

A Kelly	Preston North End
J Kinnear	Tottenham Hotspur
M Meagan	Huddersfield Town
A Finucane	Limerick
C Hurley	Sunderland
M McGrath	Bradford City
F O'Neill	Shamrock Rovers
C Gallagher	Glasgow Celtic
N Cantwell	Manchester United
J Giles	Leeds United
E Dunphy	Millwall

Result	1–2
Scorer	N Cantwell

Match No. 111

21 May 1967 v CZECHOSLOVAKIA at Dublin

A Kelly	Preston North End
T Foley	Northampton Town
J Dempsey	Fulham
A Finucane	Limerick
C Hurley	Sunderland
M Meagan	Huddersfield Town
C Gallagher	Glasgow Celtic
A McEvoy	Blackburn Rovers
R Treacy	West Bromwich Albion
E Dunphy	Millwall
O Conmy	Peterborough United

Result	0–2

Match No. 112

22 November 1967 v CZECHOSLOVAKIA at Prague

A Kelly	Preston North End
J Kinnear	Tottenham Hotspur
M Meagan	Huddersfield Town
J Dempsey	Fulham
C Hurley	Sunderland
J Conway	Fulham
E Rogers	Blackburn Rovers
E Dunphy	Millwall
O Conmy	Peterborough United
R Treacy	Charlton Athletic
T O'Connor	Fulham

Result	2–1
Scorers	R Treacy; T O'Connor

Match No. 113

15 May 1968 v POLAND at Dublin

A Kelly	Preston North End
J Kinnear	Tottenham Hotspur
T Carroll	Ipswich Town
J Fullam	Shamrock Rovers
C Hurley	Sunderland
M Meagan	Huddersfield Town
O Conmy	Peterborough United
R Treacy	Charlton Athletic
J Dempsey	Fulham
E Dunphy	Millwall
E Rogers*	Blackburn Rovers
A Hale * (sub)	Waterford

Result	2–2
Scorers	J Dempsey; A Hale

Match No. 114

30 October 1968 v POLAND at Katowice

A Kelly*	Preston North End
T Carroll	Ipswich Town

A Dunne	Manchester United
J Fullam	Shamrock Rovers
C Hurley	Sunderland
J Dempsey	Fulham
F O'Neill	Shamrock Rovers
R Treacy	Charlton Athletic
A Hale	Waterford
E Dunphy	Millwall
E Rogers	Blackburn Rovers
M Smythe* (sub)	Shamrock Rovers

Result	0–1

FEATURED MATCH 6

CZECHOSLOVAKIA 1 REPUBLIC OF IRELAND 2
At Slavia Stadium, Prague, 22 November 1967

Czechoslovakia
A Kramerius; J Lala; J Popluhar; V Taborsky; A Horvath; J Geleta; J Levicky; J Szikora; L Kuna; J Jurkanin; V Vrana.

Republic of Ireland
Alan Kelly; Joe Kinnear; Mick Meagan; John Dempsey; Charlie Hurley; Jimmy Conway; Eamonn Rogers; Eamonn Dunphy; Oliver Conmy; Ray Treacy; Turlough O'Connor.

Having already beaten the Republic of Ireland in Dublin, Czechoslovakia went into the last game in Group One of the European Championship qualifiers needing only a draw to be sure of a place in the quarter-finals. Remembering their last visit to Prague six years ago, when they were beaten 7–1, the Irish came to defend.

In the opening five minutes, the Czechs had three corners in the space of as many minutes but Alan Kelly and his defence were able to deal comfortably with them. On eleven minutes, Czech inside-forward Jurkanin was put clean through on goal when Charlie Hurley miscued his clearance, but he pulled his shot wide of Kelly's goal. The same player then had two further opportunities to give the home side the lead but on each occasion

MATCHES

he was denied by the agility of keeper Alan Kelly. Ireland's only shot of a rather one-sided first half was by Conmy but it didn't cause the Czech keeper too much trouble. On the stroke of half time, a Kuna header hit Kelly's crossbar with the Irish keeper well beaten and as it bounced back into play, Hurley was on hand to clear the danger.

Early in the second half, Joe Kinnear cleared a Popluhar shot off the line, then on 58 minutes, after Czech winger Levicky had got in a cross, Mick Meagan deflected the ball into the path of DEMPSEY who was unable to steady himself and sliced his clearance past Kelly for an own goal. Ireland came under a lot of pressure and in a hard-fought rearguard action, both Dunphy and Rogers were booked.

Seven minutes later, Ireland were level when Peterborough's Conmy broke from defence and gave the ball to Eamonn Rogers. Conmy continued his run, expecting a return pass but the Blackburn midfielder switched the ball out to the other wing where Conway put in Dunphy. He beat Lala and crossed to the far post where TREACY rose above a static Czech defence to make the score 1–1.

With a little over fifteen minutes to go, Szikora was badly injured in a 50–50 challenge with big Charlie Hurley and he had to be stretchered-off with a broken leg. The ten men of Czechoslovakia then opted to play defensively, knowing that if the result stayed as it was, they would be through to the quarter-finals. But this proved to be their undoing. There were just four minutes left on the clock when Ray Treacy robbed Popluhar on the edge of his own penalty area and crossed for O'CONNOR to score with a diving header.

Match No. 115

10 November 1968 v AUSTRIA at Dublin

A Kelly	Preston North End
J Kinnear	Tottenham Hotspur
T Carroll	Ipswich Tow
J Fullam	Shamrock Rovers
J Dempsey	Fulham
J Hennessey*	St Patrick's Athletic
F O'Neill	Shamrock Rovers
E Dunphy	Millwall
A Hale	Waterford
J Giles	Leeds United

E Rogers	Blackburn Rovers
J Conway* (sub)	Fulham
Result	2–2
Scorers	E Rogers; A Hale

Match No. 116

4 December 1968 v DENMARK at Dublin

A Kelly	Preston North End
T Carroll	Ipswich Town
A Dunne	Manchester United
J Dempsey	Fulham
C Hurley	Sunderland
J Fullam	Shamrock Rovers
F O'Neill	Shamrock Rovers
E Dunphy	Millwall
A Hale	Waterford
J Giles	Leeds United
E Rogers	Blackburn Rovers
Result	1–1 The match was abandoned after 51 minutes due to fog.
Scorers	J Giles (penalty)

Match No. 117

4 May 1969 v CZECHOSLOVAKIA at Dublin

A Kelly	Preston North End
S Brennan	Manchester United
P Mulligan	Shamrock Rovers
A Finucane	Limerick
C Hurley	Sunderland
J Dempsey	Chelsea
F O'Neill	Shamrock Rovers
M Leech*	Shamrock Rovers
R Treacy	Charlton Athletic
J Giles	Leeds United
E Rogers	Blackburn Rovers
E Hand* (sub)	Portsmouth
Result	1–2
Scorer	E Rogers

Match No. 118

27 May 1969 v DENMARK at Copenhagen

A Kelly	Preston North End
S Brennan	Manchester United
P Mulligan	Shamrock Rovers
A Finucane	Limerick
J Dempsey	Chelsea
W Newman*	Shelbourne
E Rogers	Blackburn Rovers
M Leech	Shamrock Rovers
D Givens	Manchester United
E Dunphy	Millwall
R Treacy	Charlton Athletic
F O'Neill* (sub)	Shamrock Rovers

Result	0–2

Match No. 119

8 June 1969 v HUNGARY at Dublin

A Kelly	Preston North End
S Brennan	Manchester United
A Dunne	Manchester United
J Conway	Fulham
A Finucane	Limerick
P Mulligan	Shamrock Rovers
E Dunphy	Millwall
M Leech	Shamrock Rovers
C Hurley*	Bolton Wanderers
E Rogers	Blackburn Rovers
D Givens	Manchester United
F O'Neill* (sub)	Shamrock Rovers

Result	1–2
Scorer	D Givens

Match No. 120

21 September 1969 v SCOTLAND at Dublin

A Kelly	Preston North End
S Brennan	Manchester United
M Meagan	Drogheda
A Finucane	Limerick
P Mulligan	Shamrock Rovers
J Conway	Fulham
E Rogers	Blackburn Rovers
J Giles	Leeds United
D Givens	Manchester United
A Hale	Waterford
R Treacy	Charlton Athletic

Result	1–1
Scorer	D Givens

Match No. 121

7 October 1969 v CZECHOSLOVAKIA at Prague

K Fitzpatrick	Limerick
S Brennan	Manchester United
T Carroll	Ipswich Town
A Finucane	Limerick
P Mulligan	Shamrock Rovers
J Kinnear	Tottenham Hotspur
J Conway	Fulham
G Conroy	Stoke City
D Givens*	Manchester United
A Hale	Waterford
O Conmy	Peterborough United
J Fullham* (sub)	Shamrock Rovers

Result	0–3

Did you know?

In 1963, Stoke City had both Irish goalkeepers on their books: the Republic's Jimmy O'Neill and Northern Ireland's Bobby Irvine.

Match No. 122
15 October 1969 v DENMARK at Dublin

A Kelly	Preston North End
J Kinnear	Tottenham Hotspur
S Brennan	Manchester United
P Mulligan	Shamrock Rovers
A Byrne	Southampton
J Conway	Fulham
E Dunphy	Millwall
E Rogers	Blackburn Rovers
G Conroy	Stoke City
D Givens	Manchester United
R Treacy	Charlton Athletic

Result	1–1
Scorer	D Givens

Match No. 123
5 November 1969 v HUNGARY at Budapest

A Kelly	Preston North End
S Brennan	Manchester United
A Dunne	Manchester United
P Mulligan	Chelsea
J Dempsey	Chelsea
J Kinnear	Tottenham Hotspur
G Conroy*	Stoke City
J Conway	Fulham
D Givens	Manchester United
E Dunphy	Millwall
E Rogers	Blackburn Rovers
R Treacy* (sub)	Charlton Athletic

Result	0–4

Match No. 124
6 May 1970 v POLAND at Poznan

A Kelly	Preston North End
J Kinnear	Tottenham Hotspur
T Carroll*	Ipswich Town
E Hand	Portsmouth
P Mulligan	Chelsea
A Byrne	Southampton
E Dunphy	Millwall
J Giles	Leeds United
J Conway**	Fulham
G Conroy	Stoke City
D Givens	Manchester United
S Brennan* (sub)	Manchester United
R Treacy** (sub)	Charlton Athletic

Result	1–2
Scorer	D Givens

Match No. 125
9 May 1970 v WEST GERMANY at West Berlin

A Kelly	Preston North End
S Brennan	Manchester United
T Carroll	Ipswich Town
E Hand	Portsmouth
J Dempsey	Chelsea
P Mulligan	Chelsea
J Conway*	Fulham
J Giles	Leeds United
D Givens**	Luton Town
A Byrne	Southampton
G Conroy	Stoke City
E Dunphy* (sub)	Millwall
R Treacy** (sub)	Charlton Athletic

Result	1–2
Scorer	P Mulligan

Match No. 126
23 September 1970 v POLAND at Dublin

A Kelly*	Preston North End
S Brennan	Waterford
A Byrne	Southampton
E Hand	Portsmouth
J Dempsey	Chelsea
P Mulligan	Chelsea

G Conroy	Stoke City
E Dunphy	Millwall
R Treacy	Charlton Athletic
M Lawlor**	Shamrock Rovers
S Heighway***	Liverpool
M Kearns* (sub)	Oxford United
T O'Connell** (sub)	Bohemians
A Hale*** (sub)	Waterford

Result	0–2

Match No. 127

14 October 1970 v SWEDEN at Dublin

A Kelly	Preston North End
T Carroll*	Ipswich Town
A Dunne	Manchester United
P Mulligan	Chelsea
J Dempsey	Chelsea
A Byrne	Southampton
G Conroy	Stoke City
E Dunphy	Millwall
D Givens**	Luton Town
M Lawlor	Shamrock Rovers
S Heighway	Liverpool
J Kinnear* (sub)	Tottenham Hotspur
R Treacy** (sub)	Charlton Athletic

Result	1–1
Scorer	T Carroll (penalty)

Match No. 128

28 October 1970 v SWEDEN at Stockholm

A Kelly	Preston North End
S Brennan	Manchester United
J Dempsey	Chelsea
P Dunning	Shelbourne
A Byrne	Southampton
E Dunphy	Millwall
A Finucane	Limerick
M Lawlor	Shamrock Rovers

G Conroy	Stoke City
R Treacy	Charlton Athletic
S Heighway	Liverpool

Result	0–1

Match No. 129

8 December 1970 v ITALY at Florence

A Kelly	Preston North End
S Brennan	Waterford
A Byrne	Southampton
J Dempsey	Chelsea
P Dunning	Shelbourne
G Conroy	Stoke City
E Dunphy*	Millwall
A Finucane	Limerick
E Rogers	Blackburn Rovers
D Givens	Luton Town
R Treacy	Charlton Athletic
M Lawlor* (sub)	Shamrock Rovers

Result	0–3

Match No. 130

10 May 1971 v ITALY at Dublin

A Kelly	Preston North End
A Byrne	Southampton
A Dunne	Manchester United
J Kinnear	Tottenham Hotspur
P Mulligan	Chelsea
E Dunphy	Millwall
E Rogers*	Blackburn Rovers
J Conway	Fulham
D Givens	Luton Town
J Giles	Leeds United
S Heighway	Liverpool
A Finucane* (sub)	Limerick

Result	1–2
Scorer	J Conway

Match No. 131

30 May 1971 v AUSTRIA at Dublin

A Kelly	Preston North End
A Byrne	Southampton
A Dunne	Manchester United
E Hand	Portsmouth
JC Dunne	Fulham
E Dunphy*	Millwall
E Rogers	Blackburn Rovers
J Conway	Fulham
D Givens**	Luton Town
R Treacy	Charlton Athletic
S Heighway	Liverpool
N Campbell* (sub)	St Patrick's Athletic
J Holmes** (sub)	Coventry City

Result	1–4
Scorer	E Rogers (penalty)

Match No. 132

10 October 1971 v AUSTRIA at Linz

P Roche	Shelbourne
M Gannon	Shelbourne
J Herrick	Cork Hibernians
T McConville	Dundalk
A Finucane	Limerick
P Mulligan	Chelsea
M Kearin*	Shamrock Rovers
F O'Neill	Shamrock Rovers
M Leech	Shamrock Rovers
M Martin**	Bohemians
T O'Connor	Dundalk
D Richardson* (sub)	Shamrock Rovers
A Hale** (sub)	Waterford

Result	0–6

Match No. 133

11 June 1972 v IRAN at Recife

A Kelly	Preston North End
J Kinnear	Tottenham Hotspur
J Dempsey	Chelsea
P Mulligan	Chelsea
T Carroll	Birmingham City
N Campbell	Fortuna Cologne
M Martin	Bohemians
E Rogers	Charlton Athletic
R Treacy	Swindon Town
M Leech*	Shamrock Rovers
D Givens	Luton Town
T O'Connor* (sub)	Dundalk

Result	2–1
Scorers	M Leech; D Givens

Match No. 134

18 June 1972 v ECUADOR at Recife

A Kelly	Preston North End
J Kinnear	Tottenham Hotspur
P Mulligan	Chelsea
J Dempsey	Chelsea
T Carroll	Birmingham City
N Campbell	Fortuna Cologne
M Martin	Bohemians
E Rogers	Charlton Athletic
R Treacy*	Swindon Town
D Givens	Luton Town
M Leech**	Shamrock Rovers
T O'Connor* (sub)	Dundalk
J Dennehey** (sub)	Cork Hibernians

Result	3–2
Scorers	E Rogers; M Martin; T O'Connor

Match No. 135

21 June 1972 v CHILE at Recife

A Kelly	Preston North End
J Kinnear	Tottenham Hotspur
P Mulligan	Chelsea

J Dempsey	Chelsea
T Carroll*	Birmingham City
N Campbell	Fortuna Cologne
M Martin	Bohemians
E Rogers	Charlton Athletic
R Treacy	Swindon Town
T O'Connor	Dundalk
J Dennehey	Cork Hibernians
J Herrick* (sub)	Cork Hibernians

| Result | 1–2 |
| Scorer | E Rogers |

Match No. 136

25 June 1972 v PORTUGAL at Recife

A Kelly	Preston North End
J Kinnear	Tottenham Hotspur
P Mulligan	Chelsea
J Dempsey	Chelsea
T Carroll	Birmingham City
N Campbell	Fortuna Cologne
M Martin	Bohemians
E Rogers	Charlton Athletic
R Treacy*	Swindon Town
D Givens	Luton Town
M Leech	Shamrock Rovers
T O'Connor* (sub)	Dundalk

| Result | 1–2 |
| Scorer | M Leech |

Match No. 137

18 October 1972 v USSR at Dublin

A Kelly	Preston North End
J Kinnear	Tottenham Hotspur
T Carroll	Birmingham City
T McConville	Waterford
E Hand	Portsmouth
N Campbell	Fortuna Cologne
E Rogers*	Charlton Athletic

M Martin	Bohemians
S Heighway	Liverpool
R Treacy	Swindon Town
G Conroy	Stoke City
M Leech* (sub)	Shamrock Rovers

| Result | 1–2 |
| Scorer | G Conroy |

Match No. 138

15 November 1972 v FRANCE at Dublin

A Kelly	Preston North End
J Kinnear	Tottenham Hotspur
J Holmes	Coventry City
P Mulligan	Crystal Palace
T McConville	Waterford
E Hand	Portsmouth
A Byrne*	Southampton
J Giles	Leeds United
G Conroy**	Stoke City
R Treacy	Swindon Town
D Givens	Queen's Park Rangers
N Campbell* (sub)	Fortuna Cologne
T O'Connor** (sub)	Bohemians

| Result | 2–1 |
| Scorers | G Conroy; R Treacy |

FEATURED MATCH 7

REPUBLIC OF IRELAND 2 FRANCE 1
At Dalymount Park, Dublin, 15 November 1972

Republic of Ireland
Alan Kelly; Joe Kinnear; Jimmy Holmes; Paddy Mulligan; Tommy McConville; Eoin Hand; Tony Byrne (Noel Campbell); Johnny Giles; Terry Conroy (Turlough O'Connor); Ray Treacy; Don Givens.

MATCHES

France

G Carnus; J Broissart; C Quittet; M Tresor;
J-P Rostagni; J-N Huck; J-P Adams; C Loubet;
(J Molitor) H Revelli; J-M Larque; G Bereta.

This match proved to be a watershed for Republic of Ireland football. With the side not having won a home game for six years, it was imperative that this World Cup qualifier against France resulted in victory. In fact, team boss Liam Tuohy told his players that victory was not only vital for the Republic's World Cup hopes but for the game in the country as a whole. Despite the ups and downs that were to follow in the coming years, this result was the beginning of a recovery.

Ireland almost fell behind after four minutes and it was all their own doing. Joe Kinnear attempted a back pass to keeper Alan Kelly but overhit the ball past the custodian, thankfully inches to the wrong side of the post. This encouraged the French and Revelli headed just over the bar before a powerful strike from Larque flew wide. After fifteen minutes, Revelli fired against the post and minutes later Bereta shot straight into the grateful arms of Alan Kelly.

Ireland's first real attack of the game resulted in a goal. A free-kick taken by Johnny Giles was knocked into the air by Tresor. The midfielder was quickly on to it and headed it back into the area. French defender Quittet headed it down but Terry CONROY was on it like a flash and smashed a great shot off the underside of the bar and into the back of the net. The Republic continued to press and some good work by Giles and Byrne set up Don Givens whose shot was well saved by Carnus. The French were beginning to look a little shaky and Tresor's back-pass was hit so hard that Carnus only managed to save at the second attempt. In the last minute of the half, Conroy headed against the crossbar while the French keeper was forced to turn a Tresor deflected header out for a corner.

Though the Irish dominated the early exchanges of the second half, it was France who scored the game's next goal. In the sixty-sixth minute, substitute Molitor, who had only been on the pitch for about two minutes, sent over a perfect cross for LARQUE to volley past Kelly.

However, the home side continued to force the pace and a free-kick from Giles was met by

Conroy who forced Carnus into making yet another great save. The French keeper couldn't hold the ball and Mulligan, up from the back, hacked the ball over the bar. On 75 minutes, a long ball out of defence by Kinnear was chased by Eoin Hand and Rostagni. The Irishman got to the ball first and crossed into the middle where TREACY flicked the ball over Carnus and into the net with the back of his head.

Giles and Conroy had late chances to extend the lead as the referee played about five minutes of injury time but dropped back to help the defence as the Irish contained the visitors until the final whistle was blown.

Match No. 139	
13 May 1973 v USSR at Moscow	
A Kelly	Preston North End
T Carroll	Birmingham City
P Mulligan	Crystal Palace
T McConville	Waterford
J Holmes	Coventry City
E Hand	Portsmouth
J Giles*	Leeds United
M Martin	Manchester United
R Treacy	Swindon Town
D Givens	Queen's Park Rangers
G Conroy**	Stoke City
A Byrne* (sub)	Southampton
J Dennehey** (sub)	Nottingham Forest

Result	0–1

Match No. 140	
16 May 1973 v POLAND at Wroclaw	
A Kelly	Preston North End
T Carroll	Birmingham City
P Mulligan	Crystal Palace
T McConville	Waterford
J Holmes	Coventry City
E Hand	Portsmouth
M Martin	Manchester United
M Lawlor*	Shamrock Rovers

R Treacy	Swindon Town
D Givens	Queen's Park Rangers
J Dennehey**	Nottingham Forest
G Daly* (sub)	Manchester United
T O'Connor** (sub)	Bohemians

Result	0–2

Match No. 141

19 May 1973 v FRANCE at Paris

A Kelly	Preston North End
T Carroll*	Birmingham City
J Holmes	Coventry City
P Mulligan	Crystal Palace
T McConville	Waterford
E Hand	Portsmouth
M Martin	Manchester United
A Byrne	Southampton
J Dennehey	Nottingham Forest
R Treacy	Swindon Town
D Givens	Queen's Park Rangers
J Herrick* (sub)	Shamrock Rovers

Result	1–1
Scorer	M Martin

Match No. 142

6 June 1973 v NORWAY at Oslo

A Kelly	Preston North End
T Carroll	Birmingham City
M Martin	Manchester United
P Mulligan	Crystal Palace
J Holmes	Coventry City
A Byrne*	Southampton
J Dennehey	Nottingham Forest
G Daly	Manchester United
D Givens	Queen's Park Rangers
R Treacy**	Swindon Town
G Conroy	Stoke City
D Richardson* (sub)	Gillingham
E Fagan** (sub)	Shamrock Rovers

Result	1–1
Scorer	J Dennehey

Match No. 143

21 October 1973 v POLAND at Dublin

P Thomas*	Waterford
J Kinnear	Tottenham Hotspur
J Holmes	Coventry City
P Mulligan	Crystal Palace
T Mancini	Queen's Park Rangers
M Martin	Manchester United
E Hand	Portsmouth
A Byrne	Southampton
G Conroy**	Stoke City
R Treacy	Swindon Town
D Givens***	Queen's Park Rangers
M Kearns* (sub)	Walsall
J Dennehey** (sub)	Nottingham Forest
A Hale*** (sub)	Waterford

Result	1–0
Scorer	J Dennehey

Match No. 144

5 May 1974 v BRAZIL at Rio de Janeiro

P Thomas	Waterford
J Kinnear	Tottenham Hotspur
J Holmes*	Coventry City
P Mulligan	Crystal Palace
T Mancini	Queen's Park Rangers
M Martin	Manchester United
E Hand	Portsmouth
G Conroy	Stoke City
R Treacy**	Preston North End
J Giles	Leeds United
D Givens	Queen's Park Rangers
A Dunne* (sub)	Bolton Wanderers
G Daly** (sub)	Manchester United

Result	1–2
Scorer	T Mancini

Match No. 145

8 May 1974 v URUGUAY at Montevideo

M Kearns	Walsall
J Kinnear	Tottenham Hotspur
A Dunne	Bolton Wanderers
P Mulligan	Crystal Palace
T Mancini	Queen's Park Rangers
M Martin	Manchester United
E Hand	Portsmouth
G Conroy	Stoke City
J Conway	Fulham
J Giles	Leeds United
D Givens*	Queen's Park Rangers
G Daly* (sub)	Manchester United

Result	0–2

Match No. 146

12 May 1974 v CHILE at Santiago

M Kearns	Walsall
J Kinnear	Tottenham Hotspur
P Mulligan	Crystal Palace
T Mancini	Queen's Park Rangers
A Dunne	Bolton Wanderers
E Hand	Portsmouth
M Martin	Manchester United
J Giles	Leeds United
G Conroy	Stoke City
J Conway	Fulham
D Givens	Queen's Park Rangers

Result	2–1
Scorers	E Hand; J Conway

Match No. 147

30 October 1974 v USSR at Dublin

P Roche	Manchester United
J Kinnear	Tottenham Hotspur
P Mulligan	Crystal Palace
T Mancini	Arsenal
J Holmes	Coventry City
M Martin	Manchester United
J Giles	Leeds United
L Brady	Arsenal
S Heighway	Liverpool
D Givens	Queen's Park Rangers
R Treacy	Preston North End

Result	3–0
Scorer	D Givens 3

FEATURED MATCH 8

REPUBLIC OF IRELAND 3 USSR 0
At Dalymount Park, Dublin, 30 October 1974

Republic of Ireland
Paddy Roche; Joe Kinnear; Paddy Mulligan; Terry Mancini; Jimmy Holmes; Mick Martin; Johnny Giles; Liam Brady; Steve Heighway; Ray Treacy; Don Givens.

USSR
V Pilgui; S Nikulin; V Kaplichny; S Olshansky; E Lovchev; V Matvienko; V Kolotov; V Veremeev (V Fedorov); V Onischenko; V Fedotov; O Blokhin.

In the opening fifteen minutes of this European Championship qualifier, Ireland created three good chances. A Johnny Giles free-kick gave Mancini a free header on goal but he failed to trouble Pilgui. Treacy then headed a Mick Martin cross into the path of Givens but he shot wide. The Queen's Park Rangers man was pulled down in the box but Swedish referee Axelryd deemed the challenge not worthy of a penalty.

Ireland took the lead after 23 minutes when Giles swept a long ball out to full-back Joe Kinnear racing down the right-wing. He had time to pick out GIVENS who got between two defenders and placed the ball past the Soviet keeper. The visitors then came into the game a little more and both Blokhin and Fedotov forced good saves from Paddy Roche in the Irish goal. In the Republic of Ireland's next attack, they went 2–0. A long throw by Steve Heighway was flicked on by Ray Treacy for Givens. But the ball was intercepted and headed back to the Preston forward who, in turn, knocked it to the near post where GIVENS hooked it past the keeper for his and Ireland's second goal.

Ireland continued to press and shortly afterwards, as Giles shaped to take a free-kick, Terry Mancini and Soviet defender Kaplichny were involved in a scuffle. Mancini knocked Kaplichny to the floor and was immediately ordered off as was Kaplichny once he had received treatment.

Mick Martin dropped back into the back four for the remainder of the first half but the home side began to lose much of their composure and were lucky not to concede late in the opening period when Kinnear cleared a Blokhin shot off the line. Even so, the last chance of the first 45 minutes fell to Steve Heighway whose shot was well saved by Pilgui.

At the start of the second half, the Soviets went all out to reduce the arrears but, in fact, the first real effort of the half came from debutant Liam Brady whose 30-yard shot was turned over the bar by Pilgui. At the other end, Roche was finally called into action, saving well from Blokhin and Onischenko. The Manchester United keeper then parried a shot from Fedotov but Kolotov following up, fired the rebound wide.

On 70 minutes, a free-kick by Johnny Giles was headed into the roof of the Soviet net by Don GIVENS, completing a memorable hat-trick for the Irish forward. The home side finished victorious in this entertaining international could have seen even more goals as first, Treacy poked a shot inches wide and then an excellent volley from Giles forced Pilgui into a fingertip save.

Match No. 148	
20 November 1974 v TURKEY at Izmir	
P Roche	Manchester United
J Kinnear	Tottenham Hotspur
P Mulligan	Crystal Palace
E Hand	Portsmouth
A Dunne	Bolton Wanderers
L Brady	Arsenal
M Martin	Manchester United

J Giles	Leeds United
S Heighway	Liverpool
G Conroy*	Stoke City
D Givens	Queen's Park Rangers
J Dennehey* (sub)	Nottingham Forest

Result	1–1
Scorer	D Givens

Match No. 149	
11 March 1975 v WEST GERMANY 'B' at Dublin	
P Roche	Manchester United
J Kinnear	Tottenham Hotspur
M Martin	Manchester United
E Hand	Portsmouth
A Dunne	Bolton Wanderers
N Campbell*	Fortuna Cologne
G Daly**	Manchester United
L Brady	Arsenal
R Treacy***	Preston North End
S Heighway	Liverpool
D Givens	Queen's Park Rangers
J Conway* (sub)	Fulham
J Dennehey** (sub)	Nottingham Forest
G Conroy*** (sub)	Stoke City

Result	1–0
Scorer	J Conway

Match No. 150	
10 May 1975 v SWITZERLAND at Dublin	
P Roche	Manchester United
J Kinnear	Tottenham Hotspur
P Mulligan	Crystal Palace
E Hand	Portsmouth
A Dunne	Bolton Wanderers
M Martin	Manchester United
J Giles	Leeds United
L Brady	Arsenal
R Treacy	Preston North End

D Givens	Queen's Park Rangers
G Conroy	Stoke City

Result	2–1
Scorers	M Martin; R Treacy

Match No. 151
18 May 1975 v USSR at Kiev

P Roche	Manchester United
J Kinnear	Tottenham Hotspur
P Mulligan	Crystal Palace
E Hand	Portsmouth
A Dunne	Bolton Wanderers
M Martin	Manchester United
J Giles	Leeds United
L Brady	Arsenal
G Conroy	Stoke City
D Givens	Queen's Park Rangers
S Heighway	Liverpool

Result	1–2
Scorer	E Hand

Match No. 152
21 May 1975 v SWITZERLAND at Berne

P Roche	Manchester United
A Dunne	Bolton Wanderers
P Mulligan	Crystal Palace
E Hand	Portsmouth
J Holmes	Coventry City
M Martin	Manchester United
J Giles*	Leeds United
L Brady	Arsenal
G Conroy	Stoke City
R Treacy	Preston North End
D Givens	Queen's Park Rangers
G Daly* (sub)	Manchester United

Result	0–1

Match No. 153
29 October 1975 v TURKEY at Dublin

P Roche	Manchester United
A Dunne*	Bolton Wanderers
J Holmes	Coventry City
P Mulligan	West Bromwich Albion
E Hand	Portsmouth
M Martin	West Bromwich Albion
L Brady	Arsenal
J Giles	West Bromwich Albion
R Treacy	Preston North End
D Givens	Queen's Park Rangers
S Heighway**	Liverpool
J Kinnear* (sub)	Brighton and Hove Albion
G Conroy** (sub)	Stoke City

Result	4–0
Scorer	D Givens

Match No. 154
24 March 1976 v NORWAY at Dublin

M Kearns	Walsall
A Grealish	Orient
M Martin	West Bromwich Albion
J Holmes	Coventry City
R O'Brien	Notts County
N Campbell	Fortuna Cologne
J Conway	Fulham
L Brady	Arsenal
S Heighway	Liverpool
D Givens*	Queen's Park Rangers
M Walsh	Blackpool
R Treacy* (sub)	Preston North End

Result	3–0
Scorers	L Brady; J Holmes (penalty); M Walsh

REPUBLIC OF IRELAND 4 TURKEY 0
At Dalymount Park, Dublin, 29 October 1975

Republic of Ireland
Paddy Roche; Tony Dunne (Joe Kinnear); Paddy Mulligan; Eoin Hand; Jimmy Holmes; Mick Martin; Johnny Giles; Liam Brady; Steve Heighway (Terry Conroy); Ray Treacy; Don Givens.

Turkey
Yasin (Rasim); Sabahattin; Ismail (Zafor); Fatih; Kadir; Alpaslan; Engin; Necati; Ali Kemal; Gokmen; T Cemil.

The Republic of Ireland finished off the European Championship qualifying group with their biggest win for 22 years and Don Givens' four goals equalled a 41-year-old national record for the most goals in a match. This result brought a successful end to a qualifying campaign which began brightly but faltered in the final run-in despite this victory.

Jimmy Holmes set up Mick Martin for the first chance of the match in the opening minutes but the West Bromwich Albion midfielder finished rather weakly. Ireland continued to dominate the opening exchanges and both Heighway and Treacy missed chances before Turkey missed the easiest chance so far. Eoin Hand left a cross from Ali Kemal to his goalkeeper but Roche didn't come and Gokmen nipped in to head wide.

Ireland went ahead after 27 minutes when Paddy Mulligan's cross was headed down by Treacy for GIVENS. He evaded the desperate challenge of Turkish defender Fatih and powered a shot past Yasin in the Turkey goal. Five minutes later a, deep cross from Tony Dunne saw Yasin under pressure from a rather hefty challenge by Treacy. He could only punch the ball on to the head of Don GIVENS who scored his and Ireland's second goal. The Queen's Park Rangers forward completed a nine-minute hat-trick when Heighway sent Treacy away to send in an inch-perfect cross for GIVENS to head home. Another robust challenge by Treacy on the Turkish goalkeeper and captain, saw the visitors' keeper carried off as a result of his injuries and he was replaced by Rasim.

Three minutes after the restart, the substitute keeper was involved in an incident that almost saw the game abandoned. He was suddenly pelted with missiles from the crowd behind his goal. Whilst the Guardaí dived into the crowd to find the culprits, the referee stopped the game and had to do so again some five minutes later when he said he would abandon the game should there be another occurrence of the misbehaviour. Thankfully there wasn't but these delays plus another of four minutes in getting the floodlights lit, meant that almost fifteen minutes of lost time had to be played. The interruptions certainly put the home side off their game and Turkey came back into it. On the hour mark, Turkey were awarded a free-kick and Alpaslan curled the ball over the Irish wall and into the net. The referee immediately disallowed the goal as the kick was indirect but neither team was aware of that.

Five minutes later Treacy was brought down as he attempted to round the keeper but from the resulting spot-kick, Holmes saw his penalty turned on to the post by Rasim, who also saved the full-back's follow up. With a little over ten minutes remaining, Martin and Alpaslan were involved in a punch-up and both received their marching orders. Two minutes before the long-awaited final whistle GIVENS side-footed home Paddy Mulligan's cross to end one of the most action-packed international matches.

Match No. 155	
26 May 1976 v POLAND at Poznan	
M Kearns	Walsall
A Grealish	Orient
R O'Brien	Notts County
P Mulligan	West Bromwich Albion
J Holmes	Coventry City
M Martin	West Bromwich Albion
J Conway*	Fulham
L Brady	Arsenal
G Conroy	Stoke City
M Walsh**	Blackpool
D Givens	Queen's Park Rangers
J Dennehey* (sub)	Walsall
R Treacy** (sub)	Preston North End
Result	2–0
Scorer	D Givens

Match No. 156

8 September 1976 v ENGLAND at Wembley

M Kearns	Walsall
P Mulligan	West Bromwich Albion
J Holmes	Coventry City
M Martin	West Bromwich Albion
D O'Leary	Arsenal
L Brady	Arsenal
G Daly	Derby County
G Conroy	Stoke City
S Heighway	Liverpool
J Giles	West Bromwich Albion
D Givens	Queen's Park Rangers

Result	1–1
Scorer	G Daly (penalty)

Match No. 157

13 October 1976 v TURKEY at Ankara

M Kearns	Walsall
J Waters	Grimsby Town
P Mulligan	West Bromwich Albion
M Martin	West Bromwich Albion
J Holmes	Coventry City
G Daly	Derby County
J Giles	West Bromwich Albion
L Brady	Arsenal
G Conroy	Stoke City
F Stapleton	Arsenal
D Givens	Queen's Park Rangers

Result	3–3
Scorers	F Stapleton; G Daly; J Waters

Match No. 158

17 November 1976 v FRANCE at Paris

M Kearns	Walsall
P Mulligan	West Bromwich Albion
J Holmes	Coventry City
G Daly	Derby County
D O'Leary	Arsenal
M Martin	West Bromwich Albion
L Brady	Arsenal
F Stapleton*	Arsenal
S Heighway	Liverpool
J Giles	West Bromwich Albion
D Givens	Queen's Park Rangers
M Walsh* (sub)	Blackpool

Result	0–2

Match No. 159

9 February 1977 v SPAIN at Dublin

M Kearns*	Walsall
M Martin	West Bromwich Albion
D O'Leary	Arsenal
J Holmes	Tottenham Hotspur
R O'Brien	Notts County
A Macken	Derby County
N Campbell	Fortuna Cologne
L Brady	Arsenal
D Givens	Queen's Park Rangers
F Stapleton	Arsenal
S Heighway	Liverpool
G Peyton* (sub)	Fulham

Result	0–1

30 March 1977 v France at Dublin

M Kearns	Walsall
P Mulligan	West Bromwich Albion
D O'Leary	Arsenal
M Martin	West Bromwich Albion
J Holmes	Tottenham Hotspur
G Daly	Derby County
J Giles	West Bromwich Albion
D Givens	Queen's Park Rangers
S Heighway	Liverpool

| L Brady | Arsenal |
| R Treacy | West Bromwich Albion |

| Result | 1–0 |
| Scorer | L Brady |

FEATURED MATCH 10

REPUBLIC OF IRELAND 1 FRANCE 0
At Lansdowne Road, Dublin, 30 March 1977

Republic of Ireland
Mick Kearns; Paddy Mulligan; David O'Leary; Mick Martin; Jimmy Holmes; Gerry Daly; Johnny Giles; Don Givens; Steve Heighway; Liam Brady; Ray Treacy.

France
A Rey; G Janvion; P Rio; C Lopez; T Tusseau; D Bathenay; M Platini; C Synaeghal; D Rocheteau; B Lacombe; O Rouyer.

Though officially there was an all-ticket crowd of 36,000 for this World Cup qualifier against France, in fact, almost 48,000 packed into Lansdowne Road to see if Ireland could win and put themselves into a great position to qualify for the finals.

All the early pressure was from Ireland and it came as no surprise when they took the lead with only ten minutes played. A free-kick by Johnny Giles was headed clear by Lopez but only to Liam Brady who was 30 yards from goal, As the French back four moved out to catch Treacy and Givens offside, BRADY broke through the back-line avoiding the challenges of Lopez and Bathenay to slide the ball under French keeper Rey.

France were almost level within a minute but Bathenay's powerful shot from the edge of the area was inches too high. At the other end, Don Givens was played on-side and appeared to have a great chance until he was scythed down by Janvion–remarkably the Austrian referee waved play on. On 26 minutes, a Johnny Giles shot cannoned back off Rey's right upright but though Givens was the first to react, his header sailed over the bar.

As the first half drew to a close, the French side came close to scoring on three occasions. Synaeghal's shot was turned into the side netting by Mick Kearns. The resultant corner was only partially cleared and Bathenay, Synaeghal and Rocheteau combined in a move which ended with the latter's 20-yard shot scraping the outside of the post. In the final minute of the half, a Bathenay shot looked like it was heading for the top left-hand corner of the goal but Kearns rose magnificently to tip the ball away to safety. However, there was still time for Giles to get the ball in the net only to see the linesman's flag raised for an offside decision against Gerry Daly.

The second half began at the same hectic pace with Rey tipping over a dipping 20-yard shot from Liam Brady. France counter-attacked and Michel Platini came close when, after intercepting a misplaced Mulligan pass, he raced clear of the Irish defence only to be thwarted by a superb last-ditch tackle by David O'Leary.

The French continued to press and Rocheteau kicked wide before heading Platini's cross into the arms of Mick Kearns. Tusseau found Lacombe with a superb defence-splitting pass but he delayed his shot, allowing Paddy Mulligan to clear the danger. The home side came under heavy pressure but stood firm despite being reduced to clearing the ball upfield and into touch.

Match No. 161	
24 April 1977 v POLAND at Dublin	
R Healey	Cardiff City
P Mulligan	West Bromwich Albion
R O'Brien	Notts County
M Lawrenson*	Preston North End
J Holmes	Tottenham Hotspur
J Conway	Manchester City
M Martin	West Bromwich Albion
R Treacy	West Bromwich Albion
M Walsh	Blackpool
J Giles	West Bromwich Albion
G Conroy	Stoke City
J Dennehey* (sub)	Walsall

| Result | 0–0 |

Match No. 162

1 June 1977 v BULGARIA at Sofia

M Kearns	Walsall
P Mulligan	West Bromwich Albion
M Martin	West Bromwich Albion
D O'Leary	Arsenal
J Holmes	Tottenham Hotspur
L Brady	Arsenal
G Daly*	Derby County
F Stapleton	Arsenal
J Giles	West Bromwich Albion
S Heighway	Liverpool
D Givens	Queen's Park Rangers
N Campbell* (sub)	Fortuna Cologne

Result	1–2
Scorer	D Givens

Match No. 163

12 October 1977 v BULGARIA at Dublin

G Peyton	Fulham
P Mulligan	West Bromwich Albion
D O'Leary	Arsenal
M Lawrenson	Brighton & Hove Albion
J Holmes	Tottenham Hotspur
G Daly	Derby County
J Giles	Shamrock Rovers
L Brady	Arsenal
D Givens	Queen's Park Rangers
F Stapleton	Arsenal
S Heighway	Liverpool

Result	0–0

Match No. 164

5 April 1978 v TURKEY at Dublin

G Peyton	Fulham
D Langan	Derby County
N Synnott	Shamrock Rovers
J Holmes	Tottenham Hotspur
M Daly	Wolverhampton Wanderers
G Daly*	Derby County
J Giles	Shamrock Rovers
A Grimes	Manchester United
P McGee	Queen's Park Rangers
R Treacy	Shamrock Rovers
G Ryan	Derby County
S Braddish* (sub)	Dundalk

Result	4–2
Scorers	J Giles; P McGee; R Treacy (2)

Match No. 165

12 April 1978 v POLAND at Lodz

G Peyton	Fulham
E Gregg	Bohemians
M Lawrenson	Brighton & Hove Albion
N Synnott	Shamrock Rovers
J Holmes	Tottenham Hotspur
S Braddish	Dundalk
J Giles*	Shamrock Rovers
A Grimes	Manchester United
C Muckian	Drogheda United
R Treacy	Shamrock Rovers
M Daly	Wolverhampton Wanderers
J Clarke* (sub)	Drogheda United

Result	0–3

Did you know?

Don Givens scored five goals in three games against Turkey – the most number of goals scored by an Irish striker against one nation.

Match No. 166

21 May 1978 v NORWAY at Oslo

M Kearns	Walsall
D Langan*	Derby County
D O'Leary	Arsenal
P Mulligan	West Bromwich Albion
J Holmes	Tottenham Hotspur
A Grealish	Orient
J Giles	Shamrock Rovers
L Brady**	Arsenal
S Heighway	Liverpool
F Stapleton	Arsenal
D Givens***	Queen's Park Rangers
M Lawrenson* (sub)	Brighton & Hove Albion
A Grimes** (sub)	Manchester United
P McGee*** (sub)	Queen's Park Rangers

Result 0–0	

Match No. 167

24 May 1978 v DENMARK at Copenhagen

M Kearns	Walsall
P Mulligan	West Bromwich Albion
D O'Leary	Arsenal
G Daly	Derby County
J Holmes*	Tottenham Hotspur
M Lawrenson	Brighton & Hove Albion
J Giles	Shamrock Rovers
A Grealish	Orient
F Stapleton	Arsenal
S Heighway	Liverpool
D Givens**	Queen's Park Rangers
E Gregg* (sub)	Bohemians
P McGee** (sub)	Queen's Park Rangers

Result	3–3
Scorers	F Stapleton; A Grealish; G Daly

Match No. 168

20 September 1978 v NORTHERN IRELAND at Dublin

M Kearns	Walsall
A Grealish	Orient
M Lawrenson	Brighton & Hove Albion
N Synnott	Shamrock Rovers
J Holmes	Tottenham Hotspur
L Brady	Arsenal
G Daly	Derby County
J Giles	Shamrock Rovers
P McGee	Queen's Park Rangers
F Stapleton*	Arsenal
S Heighway**	Liverpool
M Walsh* (sub)	Everton
D Givens** (sub)	Birmingham City

Result	0–0

Match No. 169

25 October 1978 v ENGLAND at Dublin

M Kearns	Walsall
P Mulligan	West Bromwich Albion
M Lawrenson	Brighton & Hove Albion
D O'Leary*	Arsenal
J Holmes	Tottenham Hotspur
G Daly	Derby County
L Brady	Arsenal
A Grealish	Orient
P McGee**	Queen's Park Rangers
G Ryan	Brighton & Hove Albion
D Givens	Birmingham City
E Gregg * (sub)	Bohemians
F Stapleton ** (sub)	Arsenal

Result	1–1
Scorer	G Daly

Match No. 170

2 May 1979 v DENMARK at Dublin

G Peyton	Fulham
E Gregg	Bohemians
M Martin	Newcastle United
P Mulligan	West Bromwich Albion
J Holmes	Tottenham Hotspur
G Daly	Derby County
J Giles	Shamrock Rovers
L Brady	Arsenal
A Hayes*	Southampton
F Stapleton	Arsenal
D Givens**	Birmingham City
M Walsh* (sub)	Queen's Park Rangers
P McGee** (sub)	Queen's Park Rangers

Result	2–0
Scorers	G Daly; D Givens

Match No. 171

19 May 1979 v BULGARIA at Sofia

G Peyton	Fulham
E Gregg	Bohemians
D O'Leary	Arsenal
M Martin	Newcastle United
J Holmes*	Tottenham Hotspur
G Daly	Derby County
J Giles	Shamrock Rovers
L Brady	Arsenal
M Walsh**	Queen's Park Rangers
D Givens	Birmingham City
S Heighway	Liverpool
P Mulligan* (sub)	West Bromwich Albion
P McGee ** (sub)	Queen's Park Rangers

Result	0–1

Match No. 172

22 May 1979 v WEST GERMANY at Dublin

G Peyton	Fulham
E Gregg	Bohemians
M Martin	Newcastle United
D O'Leary	Arsenal
P Mulligan	West Bromwich Albion
A Grealish	Orient
J Giles	Shamrock Rovers
L Brady	Arsenal
F Stapleton*	Arsenal
D Givens**	Birmingham City
G Ryan	Brighton & Hove Albion
M Walsh* (sub)	Queen's Park Rangers
B O'Callaghan** (sub)	Stoke City

Result	1–3
Scorer	G Ryan

Match No. 173

11 September 1979 v WALES at Swansea

G Peyton	Fulham
E Gregg	Bohemians
D O'Leary	Arsenal
M Martin	Newcastle United
P Mulligan	Shamrock Rovers
A Grealish	Luton Town
L Brady	Arsenal
J Murphy	Crystal Palace
F Stapleton	Arsenal
B O'Callaghan	Stoke City
G Ryan	Brighton & Hove Albion

Result	1–2
Scorer	J Jones (own goal)

Match No. 174

26 September 1979 v CZECHOSLOVAKIA at Prague

G Peyton	Fulham
P Mulligan	Shamrock Rovers

E Gregg	Bohemians
P O'Leary	Shamrock Rovers
J Devine*	Arsenal
M Martin	Newcastle United
A Grealish	Luton Town
F O'Brien	Philadelphia Furies
D Richardson**	Gillingham
P McGee	Queen's Park Rangers
T Donovan***	Aston Villa
J Anderson* (sub)	Preston North End
J Chandler** (sub)	Leeds United
R Treacy*** (sub)	Shamrock Rovers

Result	1–4
Scorer	P McGee

Match No. 175

17 October 1979 v BULGARIA at Dublin

G Peyton	Fulham
P Mulligan	Shamrock Rovers
D O'Leary	Arsenal
P O'Leary	Shamrock Rovers
A Grimes	Manchester United
A Grealish	Luton Town
M Martin	Newcastle United
L Brady	Arsenal
F Stapleton	Arsenal
P McGee	Queen's Park Rangers
S Heighway	Liverpool

Result	3–0
Scorers	M Martin; A Grealish; F Stapleton

Match No. 176

29 October 1979 v UNITED STATES at Dublin

M Kearns	Wolverhampton Wanderers
C Hughton	Tottenham Hotspur
M Martin	Newcastle United
P O'Leary*	Shamrock Rovers

A Grimes	Manchester United
J Chandler**	Leeds United
A Grealish	Luton Town
J Murphy	Crystal Palace
P McGee***	Preston North End
B O'Callaghan	Stoke City
S Heighway	Liverpool
J Anderson* (sub)	Preston North End
P Mulligan** (sub)	Shamrock Rovers
D Givens*** (sub)	Birmingham City

Result	3–2
Scorers	A Grealish; D Givens; J Anderson

Match No. 177

21 November 1979 v NORTHERN IRELAND at Belfast

M Kearns	Wolverhampton Wanderers
J Devine	Arsenal
D O'Leary	Arsenal
M Martin	Newcastle United
A Grimes	Manchester United
G Daly*	Derby County
P O'Leary	Shamrock Rovers
A Grealish	Luton Town
S Heighway	Liverpool
F Stapleton	Arsenal
P McGee**	Preston North End
J Waters* (sub)	Grimsby Town
D Givens** (sub)	Birmingham City

Result	0–1

Match No. 178

6 February 1980 v ENGLAND at Wembley

G Peyton*	Fulham
C Hughton	Tottenham Hotspur
D O'Leary**	Arsenal
M Lawrenson	Brighton & Hove Albion

A Grimes	Manchester United
A Grealish	Luton Town
G Daly	Derby County
L Brady	Arsenal
F O'Brien	Philadelphia Furies
F Stapleton	Arsenal
S Heighway	Liverpool
R Healey* (sub)	Cardiff City
P O'Leary** (sub)	Shamrock Rovers

Result	0–2

Match No. 179

26 March 1980 v CYPRUS at Nicosia

G Peyton	Fulham
A Grealish	Luton Town
A Grimes	Manchester United
M Lawrenson	Brighton & Hove Albion
D O'Leary	Arsenal
L Brady	Arsenal
G Daly	Derby County
J Murphy*	Crystal Palace
S Heighway**	Liverpool
F Stapleton	Arsenal
P McGee	Preston North End
F O'Brien* (sub)	Philadelphia Furies
G Ryan** (sub)	Brighton & Hove Albion

Result	3–2
Scorers	P McGee (2); M Lawrenson

Match No. 180

30 April 1980 v SWITZERLAND at Dublin

G Peyton	Fulham
M Lawrenson	Brighton & Hove Albion
D Langan	Derby County
K Moran	Manchester United
C Hughton	Tottenham Hotspur
G Daly	Derby County
A Grealish	Luton Town
G Waddock	Queen's Park Rangers

P McGee	Preston North End
D Givens	Birmingham City
G Ryan	Brighton & Hove Albion

Result	2–0
Scorers	D Givens; G Daly

Match No. 181

16 May 1980 v ARGENTINA at Dublin

G Peyton	Fulham
D Langan	Derby County
C Hughton	Tottenham Hotspur
P O'Leary	Shamrock Rovers
K Moran	Manchester United
A Grealish*	Luton Town
G Daly	Derby County
G Waddock**	Queen's Park Rangers
S Heighway	Liverpool
P McGee	Preston North End
D Givens	Birmingham City
R O'Brien* (sub)	Notts County
G Ryan** (sub)	Brighton & Hove Albion

Result	0–1

Match No. 182

10 September 1980 v HOLLAND at Dublin

G Peyton	Fulham
D Langan	Birmingham City
D O'Leary	Arsenal
P O'Leary	Shamrock Rovers
C Hughton	Tottenham Hotspur
M Lawrenson	Brighton & Hove Albion
G Daly	Coventry City
A Grealish	Luton Town
L Brady	Juventus
F Stapleton	Arsenal
D Givens	Birmingham City

Result	2–1
Scorers	G Daly; M Lawrenson

Match No. 183

15 October 1980 v BELGIUM at Dublin

G Peyton	Fulham
D Langan	Birmingham City
K Moran	Manchester United
M Lawrenson	Brighton & Hove Albion
C Hughton	Tottenham Hotspur
L Brady	Juventus
G Daly	Coventry City
A Grealish	Luton Town
F Stapleton	Arsenal
S Heighway	Liverpool
D Givens*	Birmingham City
P McGee* (sub)	Preston North End

Result	1–1
Scorer	A Grealish

Match No. 184

28 October 1980 v FRANCE at Paris

G Peyton	Fulham
D Langan	Birmingham City
M Lawrenson	Brighton& Hove Albion
K Moran	Manchester United
C Hughton	Tottenham Hotspur
M Martin*	Newcastle United
L Brady	Juventus
A Grealish	Luton Town
S Heighway	Liverpool
F Stapleton	Arsenal
M Robinson	Brighton & Hove Albion
G Ryan* (sub)	Brighton & Hove Albion

Result	0–2

Match No. 185

19 November 1980 v CYPRUS at Dublin

G Peyton	Fulham
D Langan	Birmingham City
C Hughton	Tottenham Hotspur

M Lawrenson	Brighton & Hove Albion
K Moran	Manchester United
G Daly	Coventry City
A Grealish	Luton Town
L Brady	Juventus
F Stapleton	Arsenal
S Heighway	Liverpool
M Robinson*	Brighton & Hover Albion
D Givens* (sub)	Birmingham City

Result	6–0
Scorers	G Daly (2–1 penalty); A Grealish; M Robinson; F Stapleton; C Hughton

Match No. 186

24 February 1981 v WALES at Dublin

J McDonough	Everton
D Langan	Birmingham City
B O'Callaghan	Stoke City
J Holmes	Vancouver Whitecaps
C Hughton	Tottenham Hotspur
A Grealish	Luton Town
G Daly	Coventry City
G Waddock	Queen's Park Rangers
D Givens*	Birmingham City
E O'Keefe	Everton
S Heighway	Liverpool
K Moran* (sub)	Manchester United

Result	1–3
Scorer	A Grealish

Match No. 187

25 March 1981 v BELGIUM at Brussels

J McDonough	Everton
D Langan	Birmingham City
M Martin	Newcastle United
K Moran	Manchester United
C Hughton	Tottenham Hotspur

G Daly	Coventry City
A Grealish	Luton Town
L Brady	Juventus
M Robinson	Brighton & Hove Albion
F Stapleton*	Arsenal
S Heighway	Liverpool
M Walsh* (sub)	FC Porto

Result	0–1

Match No. 188

29 April 1981 v CZECHOSLOVAKIA at Dublin

J McDonough	Everton
D Langan	Birmingham City
D O'Leary	Arsenal
K Moran	Manchester United
J Devine	Arsenal
G Daly*	Coventry City
M Martin	Newcastle United
A Grimes	Manchester United
F Stapleton	Arsenal
M Walsh	FC Porto
K O'Callaghan	Ipswich Town
R Whelan* (sub)	Liverpool

Result	3–1
Scorers	K Moran (2); F Stapleton

Match No. 189

21 May 1981 v WEST GERMANY 'B' at Bremen

J McDonough	Everton
D Langan	Birmingham City
D O'Leary	Arsenal
K Moran	Manchester United
J Devine	Arsenal
M Martin*	Newcastle United
A Grealish	Luton Town
F Stapleton	Arsenal
G Daly	Coventry City
M Robinson**	Brighton & Hove Albion

K O'Callaghan***	Ipswich Town
A Grimes* (sub)	Manchester United
T Donovan** (sub)	Aston Villa
G Ryan*** (sub)	Brighton & Hove Albion

Result	0–3

Match No. 190

24 May 1981 v POLAND at Bydgoszcz

P Bonner	Glasgow Celtic
D Langan	Birmingham City
M Lawrenson	Brighton & Hove Albion
D O'Leary	Arsenal
C Hughton	Tottenham Hotspur
A Grimes*	Manchester United
K Moran**	Manchester United
A Grealish	Luton Town
M Robinson	Brighton & Hove Albion
F Stapleton	Arsenal
K O'Callaghan***	Ipswich Town
G Daly* (sub)	Coventry City
G Waddock** (sub)	Queen's Park Rangers
G Ryan*** (sub)	Brighton & Hove Albion

Result	0–3

Match No. 191

9 September 1981 v HOLLAND at Rotterdam

J McDonough	Bolton Wanderers
D Langan	Birmingham City
J Devine	Arsenal
M Lawrenson	Liverpool
D O'Leary	Arsenal
L Brady	Juventus
M Martin*	Newcastle United
A Grealish	Brighton & Hove Albion
S Heighway**	Liverpool
F Stapleton	Manchester United
M Robinson	Brighton & Hove Albion
R Whelan* (sub)	Liverpool

G Ryan** (sub)	Brighton & Hove Albion

Result	2–2
Scorers	M Robinson; F Stapleton

FEATURED MATCH 11

HOLLAND 2 REPUBLIC OF IRELAND 2
At Feynoord Stadium, Rotterdam, 9 September 1981

Holland
P Schrijvers; B Wijnstekers; E Brandts; M Vander Korput; R Krol; A Muhren; F Thijssen; T La Ling (R Vander Kerkhof); K Van Kooten; R Geeles (J Peters); J Rep.

Republic of Ireland
Seamus McDonagh; David Langan; John Devine; Mark Lawrenson; David O'Leary; Liam Brady; Mick Martin (Ronnie Whelan); Tony Grealish; Steve Heighway (Gerry Ryan); Frank Stapleton; Michael Robinson.

Just seconds into this World Cup qualifier, Liam Brady and Frank Stapleton combined to put Devine away on the left. His low cross found its way through a crowded penalty area for Michael Robinson to slide in and put the ball inches wide of the target. A little over ten minutes had been played when the Dutch went ahead courtesy of a mistake by Steve Heighway. The Liverpool player gifted the ball to THIJSSEN who played a one-two with Van Kooten before rifling his shot past McDonagh in the Ireland goal.

The home side continued to dominate and Wijnstekers fired in a shot from 30 yards which McDonagh did well to turn round the post. Mark Lawrenson then cleared Arnold Muhren's shot off the line with McDonagh beaten and Johnny Rep fired wide when he had two colleagues unmarked at the back post.

Tony Grealish tried his luck from 35 yards but failed to trouble Schrijvers. Five minutes before half time, Ireland drew level when Steve Heighway's pinpoint cross was volleyed into the net by Michael ROBINSON.

The Dutch dominated the early exchanges of the second half and McDonagh was forced to save a Van Kooten header with his legs before turning over an Arnold Muhren lob that had him back-pedalling. Johnny Rep created a great opening for La Ling but he slipped as he looked to put the ball into the empty net. Dutch winger Rep outpaced Langan and was brought down from behind as he raced into the box. McDonagh got a hand to MUHREN's penalty but he couldn't keep the ball out.

On 71 minutes, Lawrenson cut past Muhren and Brandts to get to the by-line before crossing to the back post where Frank STAPLETON headed home. Moments later, Robinson had a chance to put Ireland into the lead but his header from Dave Langan's cross landed on the roof of the net. There was little time left when Johnny Rep beat two Irish defenders before being brought down by Lawrenson a yard outside the Irish penalty area. As the Irish formed a wall, the Dutch took their time in deciding who should take the kick with the result that the referee blew for full-time before it could be taken.

Match No. 192	
14 October 1981 v FRANCE at Dublin	
J McDonagh	Bolton Wanderers
D Langan	Birmingham City
D O'Leary	Arsenal
K Moran	Manchester United
C Hughton	Tottenham Hotspur
R Whelan	Liverpool
M Martin	Newcastle United
M Lawrenson	Liverpool
L Brady	Juventus
F Stapleton*	Manchester United
M Robinson	Brighton & Hove Albion
D Givens* (sub)	Neuchatel Xamax

Result	3–2
Scorers	Mahut (own goal); F Stapleton; M Robinson

Republic of Ireland's Arsenal contingent. From left to right: John Murphy, David O'Leary, Frank Stapleton and Liam Brady, pictured in 1973.

FEATURED MATCH 12

REPUBLIC OF IRELAND 3 FRANCE 2
At Lansdowne Road, Dublin, 14 October 1981

Republic of Ireland
Seamus McDonagh; David Langan; David O'Leary; Kevin Moran; Chris Hughton; Ronnie Whelan; Mick Martin; Mark Lawrenson; Liam Brady; Frank Stapleton (Don Givens); Michael Robinson.

France
J Castaneda; M Bossis; P Mahut (F Bracci); C Lopez; G Janvion; R Girand; J-F Larios; D Christophe; M Platini; A Couriol; B Bellone (D Six).

The Republic of Ireland's hopes for a place in the 1982 World Cup Finals lay not only with victory in this match against France but also with their opponents' two remaining home games.

Only five minutes had been played when Liverpool's Ronnie Whelan dispossessed Janvion and put Robinson in the clear. The Irish forward knocked the ball past Lopez and got into the box before his low cross was diverted into his own net by MAHUT under pressure from Frank Stapleton. However, within three minutes the French were level when Curiol's cross found BELLONE who turned and put a 20-yard shot out of McDonagh's reach. France almost went ahead a minute later when Bossis put in a speculative long-range shot which McDonagh held at the second attempt.

In Ireland's next real attack of the game, Kevin Moran had an overhead kick well saved by Castaneda whilst at the other end, Platini played a beautiful one-two with Larios before sending his shot inches wide of McDonagh's left-hand post. Just over midway through the first-half, Ireland took the lead when Martin's high ball into the French box found O'Leary. The Arsenal defender could have shot but with two defenders racing back to cover he squared to his former Highbury teammate Frank STAPLETON who smashed the ball into the roof of the net. Ireland began to dominate and Ronnie Whelan smacked a shot against the crossbar. On 39 minutes, a header from Robinson to Stapleton was intercepted by Larios but his attempted back-pass to Mahut fell wide of the mark and ROBINSON raced on to the loose ball to fire home.

Ireland began the second half in a similar fashion with Stapleton curling a shot just wide of the goal but then France got back into the game with Platini the architect of many of their moves. The French captain was denied by some outstanding goalkeeping by Bolton's McDonagh but even when he was beaten, David O'Leary popped up on the goal-line to clear. There were just eight minutes remaining when a mistake by Chris Hughton allowed the visitors to reduce the arrears. A French corner was only half cleared by the Spurs defender and as the ball fell to PLATINI, he crashed home his shot from around 20 yards.

Ireland had a couple of chances to extend their lead but both Stapleton and Whelan shot wide, although the latter's effort looked to have got a deflection. Didier Six, the French substitute, found himself completely unmarked in the box from Curiol's pass but McDonagh reacted superbly to turn his shot out for a corner.

Ireland had achieved the first of the prerequisites but a second became clear when the boys in green could only match France's goal difference and this was, unfortunately, cost Ireland its finals place.

Match No. 193	
28 April 1982 v ALGERIA at Algiers	
P Bonner	Glasgow Celtic
J Devine	Arsenal
K Moran*	Manchester United
M Martin	Newcastle United
A Grimes	Manchester United
A Grealish	Brighton & Hove Albion
G Waddock**	Queen's Park Rangers
G Daly	Coventry City
K O'Callaghan	Ipswich Town
F Stapleton	Manchester United
M Robinson***	Brighton & Hove Albion
E Deacy* (sub)	Aston Villa
G Ryan** (sub)	Brighton & Hove Albion

M Walsh*** (sub)	FC Porto
Result	0–2

Match No. 194	
21 May 1982 v CHILE at Santiago	
J McDonagh	Bolton Wanderers
E Deacy	Aston Villa
M Martin	Newcastle United
J Anderson	Preston North End
M Walsh	Everton
L Brady	Juventus
S O'Driscoll*	Fulham
A Grealish	Brighton & Hove Albion
G Daly	Coventry City
M Robinson**	Brighton & Hove Albion
K O'Callaghan	Ipswich Town
M Fairclough* (sub)	Dundalk
G Ryan** (sub)	Brighton& Hove Albion
Result	0–1

Match No. 195	
27 May 1982 v BRAZIL at Uberlandia	
J McDonagh	Bolton Wanderers
E Deacy	Aston Villa
M Martin	Newcastle United
J Anderson	Preston North End
M Walsh	Everton
S O'Driscoll	Fulham
L Brady	Juventus
A Grealish	Brighton & Hove Albion
G Daly	Coventry City
B O'Callaghan*	Stoke City
K O'Callaghan	Ipswich Town
G Ryan* (sub)	Brighton & Hove Albion
Result	0–7

Match No. 196

30 May 1982 v TRINIDAD & TOBAGO at Port of Spain

G Peyton	Fulham
E Deacy*	Aston Villa
M Walsh	Everton
J Anderson	Preston North End
M Martin	Newcastle United
A Grealish	Brighton & Hove Albion
J Walsh	Limerick United
B O'Callaghan**	Stoke City
G Daly	Coventry City
L Brady	Juventus
G Ryan***	Brighton & Hove Albion
S O'Driscoll* (sub)	Fulham
M Fairclough** (sub)	Dundalk
K O'Callaghan*** (sub)	Ipswich Town

Result	1–2
Scorer	L Brady

Tony Galvin

Match No. 197

22 September 1982 v HOLLAND at Rotterdam

J McDonagh	Bolton Wanderers
M Martin	Newcastle United
M Lawrenson	Liverpool
D O'Leary	Arsenal
C Hughton	Tottenham Hotspur
A Grealish	Brighton & Hove Albion
F Stapleton	Manchester United
G Daly*	Coventry City
A Galvin**	Tottenham Hotspur
L Brady	Sampdoria
M Robinson	Brighton & Hove Albion
M Walsh* (sub)	FC Porto
G Waddock** (sub)	Queen's Park Rangers

Result	1–2
Scorer	G Daly

Match No. 198

13 October 1982 v ICELAND at Dublin

J McDonagh	Bolton Wanderers
K Moran	Manchester United
M Lawrenson	Liverpool
D O'Leary	Arsenal
M Walsh	Everton
R Whelan	Liverpool
A Grealish	Brighton & Hove Albion
G Waddock	Queen's Park Rangers
L Brady*	Sampdoria
M Robinson	Brighton & Hive Albion
F Stapleton	Manchester United
K O'Callaghan* (sub)	Ipswich Town

Result	2–0
Scorers	F Stapleton; A Grealish

Match No. 199	
17 November 1982 v SPAIN at Dublin	
J McDonagh	Bolton Wanderers
J Devine	Arsenal
M Lawrenson	Liverpool
M Martin	Newcastle United
C Hughton	Tottenham Hotspur
A Grealish*	Brighton & Hove Albion
L Brady	Sampdoria
A Grimes	Manchester United
M Robinson	Brighton & Hove Albion
F Stapleton	Manchester United
K O'Callaghan	Ipswich Town
M Walsh* (sub)	FC Porto

Result	3–3
Scorers	A Grimes; F Stapleton (2)

FEATURED MATCH 13

REPUBLIC OF IRELAND 3 SPAIN 3
At Lansdowne Road, Dublin, 17 November 1982

Republic of Ireland
Seamus McDonagh; John Devine; Mark Lawrenson; Mick Martin; Chris Hughton; Tony Grealish (Mickey Walsh); Liam Brady; Ashley Grimes; Michael Robinson; Frank Stapleton; Kevin O'Callaghan.

Spain
L Arconada; Juan Jose; A Meceda; F Bonet; JA Camacho; Senor; Victor; R Gordillo; JC Pedraza (E Martin); Santillana (F Roberto); Marcos.

Ireland made a great start to this European Championship qualifier when they opened the scoring after only two minutes. Tony Grealish slid in to beat Gordillo to the ball but when it ran loose, Grimes laid it in the path of Robinson, whose shot was blocked. The Brighton forward regained possession and rolled the ball back for GRIMES to drive the ball high into Arconada's goal. Five minutes later, Frank Stapleton should have had a second goal but he dwelled too long on the ball, allowing Maceda to take it from him. Grimes had a powerfully struck free-kick well saved by Arconada, after which the rest of the half belonged to Spain.

A free-kick by Gordillo wide on the right found MACEDA completely unmarked ten yards from goal and his volley gave McDonagh no chance whatsoever. Santillana and Pedraza combined well to create an opening but the latter's curling shot was well held by McDonagh.

A minute into the second half, a ball from Victor saw Senor racing into the Irish penalty area. His low cross eluded McDonagh but Mick MARTIN, trying to cut it out, succeeded only in putting the ball into his own net. On the hour mark, Marcos rounded the unfortunate Martin and sent a through ball into the box for VICTOR. Victor rounded the advancing McDonagh and waited for Lawrenson to commit himself before tapping the ball into the empty net. Tony Grealish, who had been limping badly for a few minutes, was replaced by FC Porto's Mickey Walsh, as the Irish went in search of retrieving the two-goal deficit.

Ashley Grimes

Within three minutes, they had reduced the arrears when, following Liam Brady's free-kick, STAPLETON completely outwitted his marker to send a free header past Arconada. Moments later, the Spanish keeper parried a close-range header from Ashley Grimes to the far post where Walsh got in a shot only to see Arconada save with his legs. There was a little under a quarter of an hour left when Ireland equalised with an absolutely brilliant goal. Kevin O'Callaghan beat Gordillo with a drag-back, then as Victor came across to provide cover, he knocked the ball past him and with the outside of his boot, sent a pinpoint cross to the far post where STAPLETON met it with a firm header that gave Arconada no chance.

Six players were booked in this game which could still have had a winning goal with O'Callaghan having a powerful shot saved by the Spanish keeper and Roberto, who had come on for Santillana, seeing his effort pass just outside McDonagh's left upright.

Match No. 200	
30 March 1983 v MALTA at Valletta	
J McDonough	Bolton Wanderers
J Devine	Arsenal
C Hughton	Tottenham Hotspur
M Lawrenson	Liverpool
M Martin	Newcastle United
L Brady	Sampdoria
R Whelan	Liverpool
F Stapleton	Manchester United
A Galvin*	Tottenham Hotspur
G Waddock	Queen's Park Rangers
M Robinson	Brighton & Hove Albion
K O'Callaghan* (sub)	Ipswich Town

Result	1–0
Scorer	F Stapleton

Match No. 201	
27 April 1983 v SPAIN at Zaragoza	
J McDonough	Bolton Wanderers
M Lawrenson	Liverpool

M Martin	Newcastle United
D O'Leary	Arsenal
C Hughton	Tottenham Hotspur
R Whelan*	Liverpool
A Grealish	Brighton & Hove Albion
A Grimes**	Manchester United
G Waddock	Queen's Park Rangers
M Walsh	FC Porto
F Stapleton	Manchester United
G Daly* (sub)	Coventry City
K O'Callaghan** (sub)	Ipswich Town

Result	0–2

Match No. 202	
21 September 1983 v ICELAND at Reykjavik	
J McDonough	Notts County
J Devine	Norwich City
M Lawrenson	Liverpool
K Moran	Manchester United
C Hughton	Tottenham Hotspur
L Brady	Sampdoria
G Waddock	Queen's Park Rangers
A Grealish	Brighton & Hove Albion
K O'Callaghan	Ipswich Town
F Stapleton	Manchester United
M Robinson*	Liverpool
M Walsh* (sub)	FC Porto

Result	3–0
Scorers	G Waddock; M Robinson; M Walsh

Match No. 203	
12 October 1983 v HOLLAND at Dublin	
J McDonough	Notts County
J Devine	Norwich City
C Hughton	Tottenham Hotspur
M Lawrenson	Liverpool
K Moran	Manchester United

L Brady	Sampdoria
G Waddock	Queen's Park Rangers
A Grealish*	Brighton & Hove Albion
F Stapleton	Manchester United
M Robinson	Liverpool
K O'Callaghan**	Ipswich Town
K Sheedy* (sub)	Everton
A Galvin** (sub)	Tottenham Hotspur

Result	2–3
Scorers	G Waddock; L Brady (penalty)

Match No. 204

16 November 1983 v MALTA at Dublin

P Bonner	Glasgow Celtic
K O'Regan	Brighton & Hove Albion
K Moran*	Manchester United
M Lawrenson**	Liverpool
C Hughton	Tottenham Hotspur
G Daly	Coventry City
K Sheedy	Everton
L Brady	Sampdoria
M Walsh	FC Porto
F Stapleton	Manchester United
K O'Callaghan	Ipswich Town
J McDonagh* (sub)	Shamrock Rovers
G Waddock** (sub)	Queen's Park Rangers

Result	8–0
Scorers	M Lawrenson (2); F Stapleton (penalty); K O'Callaghan; K Sheedy; L Brady (2); G Daly

Match No. 205

4 April 1984 v ISRAEL at Tel Aviv

P Bonner	Glasgow Celtic
J Devine	Norwich City
D O'Leary	Arsenal
K Moran	Manchester United

A Grimes	Coventry City
G Waddock	Queen's Park Rangers
M Lawrenson	Liverpool
R Whelan*	Liverpool
L Brady	Sampdoria
F Stapleton	Manchester United
M Robinson**	Liverpool
A Galvin* (sub)	Tottenham Hotspur
G Daly** (sub)	Coventry City

Result	0–3

FEATURED MATCH 14

REPUBLIC OF IRELAND 8 MALTA 0
At Dalymount Park, Dublin, 16 November 1983

Republic of Ireland
Packie Bonner; Kieran O'Regan; Kevin Moran (Jacko McDonagh); Mark Lawrenson (Gary Waddock); Chris Hughton; Gary Daly; Kevin Sheedy; Liam Brady; Mickey Walsh; Frank Stapleton; Kevin O'Callaghan.

Malta
J Bonello; C Consiglio; J Holland; Edwin Farrugia; A Azzopardi; Emanuel Farrugia; S Demanuelle; Mario Farrugia (E Fabri); N Attard (G Xuereb); C Busuttil; E Spiteri-Gonzi.

The Republic of Ireland ended their European Championship campaign with this record score in what was the seventy-fifth international match to be played at Dalymount Park.

The home side pressed from the start and Bonello was called into action in the opening minute to deny Kevin O'Callaghan. The Maltese keeper saved well from Mickey Walsh and Kevin Moran as Ireland went in search of an opening goal. O'Callaghan must have thought he had put Ireland ahead in the eleventh minute when he beat Bonello but Consiglio appeared from nowhere to clear off the line. Kevin SHEEDY then produced a piece of magic, cutting inside two defenders and curling the ball onto the roof of the net.

Ireland eventually took the lead in the twenty-fourth minute when the overlapping Hughton found Walsh in the box. He beat two defenders but his goalbound effort was headed clear by Edwin Farruigia. The ball fell to LAWRENSON at the edge of the box, he chested the ball down and drove it home off the inside of the post. Two minutes later, Ireland had gone 2–0 up when STAPLE-TON was brought down from behind in the area by Azzopardi as both players chased a long ball. He picked himself up to send Bonello the wrong way. It was all one-way traffic and on 34 minutes, Liam Brady wriggled his way past three defenders before laying the ball into the path of O'CALLAGHAN who gave Bonello little chance.

Ireland continued to mount a series of attacks in the second half and though the forwards were given a number of opportunities to add to their lead, a mixture of bad finishing and brave goal-keeping prevented any further scoring until the sixty-fourth minute when Brady put LAWRENSON in to score his second goal. Ten minutes later Kevin SHEEDY, who was making his first start for Ireland, made it 5–0 after Brady and Lawrenson had combined to set up his chance.

On 76 minutes, BRADY, who'd been at the centre of most of the goals, got on the scoresheet himself when firing past Bonello after Stapleton had provided him with the opportunity. Within the space of four minutes, BRADY scored his second goal following another long ball, this time from Sheedy, enabled him to round Bonello and roll the ball into the unguarded net. With just two minutes remaining on the clock, the scoring was completed when Gerry DALY hooked up Mickey Walsh's downward header.

As far as goalscoring goes, these eight goals represent a pinnacle in manager Eoin Hand's term of office because over the next couple of years, Ireland scored just eight goals in a total of sixteen matches.

P Byrne	Shamrock Rovers
L Brady	Sampdoria
A Grealish	West Bromwich Albion
M Walsh	FC Porto
A Grimes	Coventry City
F Stapleton**	Manchester United
G Ryan	Brighton & Hove Albion
J McDonagh* (sub)	Shamrock Rovers
L Buckley** (sub)	Shamrock Rovers

| Result | 0–0 |

Match No. 207

3 June 1984 v CHINA at Sapporo

P Bonner	Glasgow Celtic
J Anderson	Newcastle United
D O'Leary	Arsenal
M McCarthy	Manchester City
J Beglin	Liverpool
G Ryan	Brighton & Hove Albion
A Grealish	West Bromwich Albion
P Byrne*	Shamrock Rovers
E O'Keefe	Port Vale
F Stapleton	Manchester United
M Walsh	FC Porto
G Howlett* (sub)	Brighton & Hove Albion

| Result | 1–0 |
| Scorer | E O'Keefe |

Did you know?

Eamonn O'Keefe scored four goals in an Under-21 tournament for the Republic of Ireland in a 5–1 win over China in Toulon, France in June 1982 – he was 29 years old at the time.

Match No. 206

23 May 1984 v POLAND at Dublin

J McDonough	Notts County
K O'Regan	Brighton & Hove Albion
M McCarthy	Manchester City
D O'Leary*	Arsenal

Match No. 208

8 August 1984 v MEXICO at Dublin

J McDonough*	Notts County
K O'Regan**	Brighton & Hove Albion
K Moran	Manchester United
M McCarthy	Manchester City
J Beglin	Liverpool
P Byrne****	Shamrock Rovers
A Grealish	West Bromwich Albion
G Ryan	Brighton & Hove Albion
E O'Keefe	Port Vale
L Buckley	Waregem
A Galvin*****	Tottenham Hotspur
G Peyton* (sub)	Fulham
C Hughton** (sub)	Tottenham Hotspur
J McDonagh*** (sub)	Shamrock Rovers
G Daly**** (sub)	Birmingham City
K O'Callaghan*****(sub)	Ipswich Town

Result	0–0

Match No. 209

12 September 1984 v USSR at Dublin

J McDonough	Notts County
J Devine	Norwich City
D O'Leary	Arsenal
M Lawrenson	Liverpool
C Hughton	Tottenham Hotspur
R Whelan	Liverpool
A Grealish	West Bromwich Albion
L Brady	Inter Milan
M Robinson	Liverpool
M Walsh*	FC Porto
A Galvin	Tottenham Hotspur
E O'Keefe* (sub)	Port Vale

Result	1–0
Scorer	M Walsh

Match No. 210

17 October 1984 v NORWAY at Oslo

J McDonough	Notts County
J Devine	Norwich City
D O'Leary	Arsenal
M Lawrenson	Liverpool
C Hughton	Tottenham Hotspur
A Grealish	West Bromwich Albion
R Whelan*	Liverpool
L Brady	Inter Milan
M Robinson**	Liverpool
F Stapleton	Manchester United
A Galvin	Tottenham Hotspur
K O'Callaghan* (sub)	Ipswich Town
M Walsh** (sub)	FC Porto

Result	0–1

Match No. 211

14 November 1984 v DENMARK at Copenhagen

J McDonough	Notts County
M Lawrenson	Liverpool
M McCarthy	Manchester City
D O'Leary	Arsenal
J Beglin	Liverpool
K Sheedy	Everton
L Brady	Inter Milan
A Grealish	West Bromwich Albion
A Galvin*	Tottenham Hotspur
F Stapleton	Manchester United
M Walsh	FC Porto
K O'Callaghan* (sub)	Ipswich Town

Result	0–3

Match No. 212

5 February 1985 v ITALY at Dublin

P Bonner	Glasgow Celtic
C Hughton	Tottenham Hotspur
J Beglin	Liverpool

M Lawrenson*	Liverpool
M McCarthy	Manchester City
L Brady	Inter Milan
K Sheedy	Everton
G Waddock	Queen's Park Rangers
A Galvin**	Tottenham Hotspur
F Stapleton	Manchester United
J Byrne***	Queen's Park Rangers
P McGrath* (sub)	Manchester United
R Whelan** (sub)	Liverpool
A Campbell*** (sub)	RC Santander

Result	1–2
Scorer	G Waddock

Match No. 213

27 February 1985 v ISRAEL at Tel Aviv

P Bonner	Glasgow Celtic
C Hughton	Tottenham Hotspur
M McCarthy	Manchester City
D O'Leary	Arsenal
J Beglin	Liverpool
R Whelan	Liverpool
G Waddock	Queen's Park Rangers
P McGrath	Manchester United
K Sheedy	Everton
A Campbell	RC Santander
F Stapleton*	Manchester United
J Byrne* (sub)	Queen's Park Rangers

Result	0–0

Match No. 214

26 Match 1985 v ENGLAND at Wembley

P Bonner	Glasgow Celtic
C Hughton	Tottenham Hotspur
M Lawrenson	Liverpool
M McCarthy	Manchester City
J Beglin	Liverpool
R Whelan*	Liverpool

G Waddock	Queen's Park Rangers
L Brady	Inter Milan
P McGrath**	Manchester United
E O'Keefe***	Port Vale
F Stapleton	Manchester United
K O'Callaghan* (sub)	Portsmouth
D O'Leary** (sub)	Arsenal
J Byrne*** (sub)	Queen's Park Rangers

Result	1–2
Scorer	L Brady

Match No. 215

1 May 1985 v NORWAY at Dublin

P Bonner	Glasgow Celtic
D Langan*	Oxford United
M Lawrenson	Liverpool
D O'Leary	Arsenal
J Beglin	Liverpool
G Waddock	Queen's Park Rangers
G Daly	Birmingham City
L Brady**	Inter Milan
A Galvin	Tottenham Hotspur
F Stapleton	Manchester United
M Robinson	Queen's Park Rangers
P McGrath* (sub)	Manchester United
R Whelan** (sub)	Liverpool

Result	0–0

Match No. 216

26 May 1985 v SPAIN at Cork

J McDonough	Notts County
D Langan*	Oxford United
D O'Leary	Arsenal
M McCarthy	Manchester City
C Hughton**	Tottenham Hotspur
G Daly	Birmingham City
L Brady	Inter Milan
G Waddock	Queen's Park Rangers

A Galvin***	Tottenham Hotspur
A Campbell	RC Santander
M Robinson	Queen's Park Rangers
P Byrne* (sub)	Shamrock Rovers
K O'Regan** (sub)	Brighton & Hove Albion
A Grealish*** (sub)	West Bromwich Albion

Result	0–0

Match No. 217

2 June 1985 v SWITZERLAND at Dublin

J McDonough	Gillingham
D Langan	Oxford United
D O'Leary	Arsenal
M McCarthy	Manchester City
J Beglin	Liverpool
G Daly*	Birmingham City
A Grealish**	West Bromwich Albion
L Brady	Inter Milan
K Sheedy	Everton
M Robinson	Queen's Park Rangers
F Stapleton	Manchester United
R Whelan* (sub)	Liverpool
P McGrath** (sub)	Manchester United

Result	3–0
Scorers	F Stapleton; A Grealish; K Sheedy

Match No. 218

11 September 1985 v SWITZERLAND at Berne

J McDonagh	Sunderland
C Hughton	Tottenham Hotspur
J Beglin	Liverpool
M McCarthy	Manchester City
D O'Leary	Arsenal
L Brady	Inter Milan
G Daly*	Birmingham City
M Lawrenson	Liverpool
A Cascarino	Gillingham
K Sheedy**	Everton
P McGrath* (sub)	Manchester United
K O'Callaghan** (sub)	Portsmouth

Result	0–0

Match No. 219

16 October 1985 v USSR at Moscow

J McDonagh	Notts County
C Hughton	Tottenham Hotspur
J Beglin*	Liverpool
M McCarthy	Manchester City
D O'Leary	Arsenal
L Brady	Inter Milan
G Waddock	Queen's Park Rangers
M Lawrenson	Liverpool
A Cascarino	Gillingham
F Stapleton	Manchester United
A Grealish**	West Bromwich Albion
K O'Callaghan* (sub)	Portsmouth
R Whelan** (sub)	Liverpool

Result	0–2

Did you know?

Kevin O'Callaghan is the only Irish player (so far!) to star in a film. He was one of a number of soccer players picked by director John Huston to star in the 1981 movie Escape to Victory. In the film he played a goalkeeper who got his arm broken by Michael Caine so that Sylvester Stallone could play in goal for the Allies team.

Match No. 220

13 November 1985 v DENMARK at Dublin

J McDonagh	Wichita Wings
M Lawrenson	Liverpool
J Beglin	Liverpool
K Moran	Manchester United
D O'Leary	Arsenal
L Brady	Inter Milan
P McGrath	Manchester United
A Grealish*	West Bromwich Albion
A Cascarino	Gillingham
F Stapleton	Manchester United
K Sheedy**	Everton
P Byrne* (sub)	Shamrock Rovers
M Robinson** (sub)	Queen's Park Rangers

Result	1–4
Scorer	F Stapleton

Match No. 221

26 March 1986 v WALES at Dublin

G Peyton	Fulham
D Langan	Oxford United
J Beglin	Liverpool
J Anderson*	Newcastle United
D O'Leary	Arsenal
L Brady	Inter Milan
P McGrath	Manchester United
R Houghton	Oxford United
J Aldridge	Oxford United
M Robinson**	Queen's Park Rangers
R Whelan	Liverpool
M McCarthy* (sub)	Manchester City
P Byrne** (sub)	Shamrock Rovers

Result	0–1

Match No. 222

23 April 1986 v URUGUAY at Dublin

P Bonner	Glasgow Celtic
D Langan	Oxford United
B Murphy	Bohemians
M McCarthy	Manchester City
C Hughton*	Tottenham Hotspur
G Daly	Shrewsbury Town
L O'Brien	Shamrock Rovers
R Houghton	Oxford United
A Galvin	Tottenham Hotspur
J Aldridge	Oxford United
F Stapleton**	Manchester United
P Eccles* (sub)	Shamrock Rovers
J Byrne** (sub)	Queen's Park Rangers

Result	1–1
Scorer	G Daly (penalty)

Match No. 223

25 May 1986 v ICELAND at Reykjavik

P Bonner	Glasgow Celtic
J Anderson	Preston North End
C Hughton*	Tottenham Hotspur
K Moran	Manchester United
M McCarthy	Manchester City
M Kennedy	Portsmouth
P McGrath**	Manchester United
R Houghton	Oxford United
J Aldridge***	Oxford United
F Stapleton	Manchester United
A Galvin	Tottenham Hotspur
P Byrne* (sub)	Shamrock Rovers
G Daly** (sub)	Shrewsbury Town
N Quinn*** (sub)	Arsenal

Result	2–1
Scorers	P McGrath; G Daly

Match No. 224

27 May 1986 v CZECHOSLOVAKIA at Reykjavik

G Peyton	Fulham
K Moran	Manchester United
P Byrne	Shamrock Rovers
J Anderson*	Newcastle United
M McCarthy	Manchester City
M Robinson**	Queen's Park Rangers
P McGrath	Manchester United
R Houghton	Oxford United
J Aldridge	Oxford United
N Quinn***	Arsenal
A Galvin	Tottenham Hotspur
M Kennedy* (sub)	Portsmouth
G Daly** (sub)	Shrewsbury Town
F Stapleton*** (sub)	Manchester United

Result	1–0
Scorer	F Stapleton

Match No. 225

10 September 1986 v BELGIUM at Brussels

P Bonner	Glasgow Celtic
D Langan	Oxford United
C Hughton*	Tottenham Hotspur
M Lawrenson	Liverpool
K Moran	Manchester United
L Brady	Ascoli
R Houghton	Oxford United
P McGrath	Manchester United
F Stapleton	Manchester United
J Aldridge	Oxford United
A Galvin**	Tottenham Hotspur
J Beglin* (sub)	Liverpool
R Whelan** (sub)	Liverpool

Result	2–2
Scorers	F Stapleton; L Brady (penalty)

Match No. 226

15 October 1986 v SCOTLAND at Dublin

P Bonner	Glasgow Celtic
D Langan	Oxford United
J Beglin	Liverpool
M McCarthy	Manchester City
K Moran*	Manchester United
L Brady	Ascoli
P McGrath	Manchester United
R Houghton	Oxford United
F Stapleton	Manchester United
J Aldridge	Oxford United
K Sheedy	Everton
G Daly* (sub)	Shrewsbury Town

Result	0–0

Match No. 227

12 November 1986 v POLAND at Warsaw

P Bonner	Glasgow Celtic
D Langan	Oxford United
M McCarthy	Manchester City
K Moran	Manchester United
J Beglin	Liverpool
R Houghton	Oxford United
P McGrath	Manchester United
L Brady	Ascoli
K Sheedy	Everton
F Stapleton	Manchester United
J Aldridge	Oxford United

Result	0–1

Match No. 228

18 February 1987 v SCOTLAND at Glasgow

P Bonner	Glasgow Celtic
P McGrath	Manchester United
R Whelan	Liverpool
M McCarthy	Manchester City
K Moran	Manchester United

L Brady*	Ascoli
M Lawrenson	Liverpool
R Houghton	Oxford United
F Stapleton	Manchester United
J Aldridge	Oxford United
A Galvin	Tottenham Hotspur
J Byrne* (sub)	Queen's Park Rangers

Result	1–0
Scorer	M Lawrenson

Match No. 229
1 April 1987 v BULGARIA at Sofia

P Bonner	Glasgow Celtic
J Anderson	Newcastle United
C Hughton	Tottenham Hotspur
K Moran	Manchester United
M McCarthy	Manchester City
R Whelan	Liverpool
P McGrath	Manchester United
L Brady	West Ham United
A Galvin	Tottenham Hotspur
J Aldridge	Liverpool
F Stapleton*	Manchester United
N Quinn* (sub)	Arsenal

Result	1–2
Scorer	F Stapleton

Match No. 230
29 April 1987 v BELGIUM at Dublin

P Bonner	Glasgow Celtic
J Anderson	Newcastle United
M McCarthy	Manchester City
K Moran	Manchester United
P McGrath	Manchester United
R Whelan	Liverpool
R Houghton	Oxford United
L Brady*	West Ham United
A Galvin	Tottenham Hotspur

F Stapleton	Manchester United
J Aldridge	Liverpool
J Byrne* (sub)	Queen's Park Rangers

Result	0–0

Match No. 231
23 May 1987 v BRAZIL at Dublin

P Bonner	Glasgow Celtic
J Anderson	Newcastle United
M McCarthy*	Glasgow Celtic
K Moran	Manchester United
R Whelan**	Liverpool
L O'Brien***	Manchester United
P McGrath	Manchester United
L Brady	West Ham United
K O'Callaghan	Portsmouth
J Aldridge	Liverpool
J Byrne	Queen's Park Rangers
K de Mange* (sub)	Liverpool
D Langan** (sub)	Oxford United
N Quinn*** (sub)	Arsenal

Result	1–0
Scorer	L Brady

Match No. 232
28 May 1987 v LUXEMBOURG at Luxembourg

P Bonner	Glasgow Celtic
J Anderson*	Newcastle United
R Whelan	Liverpool
M McCarthy	Glasgow Celtic
K Moran**	Manchester United
L Brady	West Ham United
P McGrath	Manchester United
R Houghton	Oxford United
F Stapleton	Manchester United
J Aldridge	Liverpool
A Galvin	Tottenham Hotspur
D Langan* (sub)	Oxford United

J Byrne** (sub)	Queen's Park Rangers

Result	2–0
Scorers	A Galvin; R Whelan

FEATURED MATCH 15

REPUBLIC OF IRELAND 1 BRAZIL 0
At Lansdowne Road, Dublin, 23 May 1987

Republic of Ireland
Packie Bonner; John Anderson; Mick McCarthy (Ken de Mange); Kevin Moran; Ronnie Whelan (Dave Langan); Liam O'Brien (Niall Quinn); Paul McGrath; Liam Brady; Kevin O'Callaghan; John Aldridge; John Byrne.

Brazil
Carlos; Josimar; Ricardo II; Geraldao; Nelsinho; Silas; Valdo; Douglas; Edu I (Rai); Muller (Joao Paulo); Mirandinha (Romario).

A crowd of only 17,000 turned up at Lansdowne Road to see Ireland record their first victory over the mighty Brazil in three attempts and to watch Liam Brady score the game's only goal. It was sweet revenge for, along with John Anderson and Kevin O'Callaghan, Brady had been the only survivors of the side that was demolished 7–0 by Brazil five years earlier.

Muller had an early snap shot well saved by Bonner, and Nelsinho, up for a corner, sent a header inches over the bar. Ireland's best chance in the opening exchanges fell to Paul McGrath but his shot from just outside the area went the wrong side of the post. Muller and Mirandinha combined well to put Douglas through but Bonner was quickly off his line to smother the ball.

Then Ireland began to dominate the game and Aldridge and Byrne both came close with headers before Mick McCarthy tried his luck from long range; the ball trickled harmlessly through to Carlos in the Brazilian goal. Ireland took the lead after 33 minutes when Brady turned inside two players and passed the ball to Aldridge, who, in turn, flicked it onto John Byrne. The Queen's Park Rangers man was tackled as he shaped to shoot

by Geraldao but the ball bounced loose to BRADY who, after shaping to cross to the far post, changed feet and sent a low shot inside Carlos' near post after the keeper had advanced off his line in anticipation of a cross.

Soon after this, Brazil's Muller beat three players in a mazy run down the left but his shot-cum-cross was well held by Bonner. Geraldao then sent a long-range free-kick inches wide of Bonner's right-hand upright but as the half drew to a close, it was Ireland who came nearest to scoring when Liam O'Brien was only inches away from connecting with O'Callaghan's cross from just six yards out.

Early in the second half, Valdo's shot was blocked by Moran and Mirandinha fired the rebound over the bar. Then Valdo and Josimar played a neat one-two before the latter crossed to the far post where Muller headed over. It was all Brazil now and a tremendous shot from Silva was blocked by Moran but as the ball ran free to Aldridge, the Liverpool forward attempted a back-pass which was intercepted by Mirandinha. He took too long on the ball, allowing the Irish defence time to get back and clear the danger. Then Rai, who had come on for Edu, wriggled his way past a couple of Irish defenders but his shot was turned round the post by Bonner.

It seemed only a matter of time before Brazil drew level but with five minutes remaining, Kevin O'Callaghan broke clear with only Carlos to beat. The Brazilian keeper advanced off his line to narrow the angle and bravely dived at his feet to prevent the Republic from going 2–0 up. In the dying moments, Romario came close to an equaliser but after Bonner had saved his first effort, he scuffed the rebound wide.

Match No. 233	
9 September 1987 v LUXEMBOURG at Dublin	
G Peyton	Bournemouth
D Langan	Oxford United
P McGrath	Manchester United
K Moran	Manchester United
A Grimes	Luton Town
R Houghton	Oxford United
R Whelan	Liverpool
L Brady	West Ham United
A Galvin*	Sheffield Wednesday
F Stapleton	Ajax

J Byrne	Queen's Park Rangers
N Quinn* (sub)	Arsenal

Result	2–1
Scorers	F Stapleton; P McGrath

Match No. 234

14 October 1987 v BULGARIA at Dublin

P Bonner	Glasgow Celtic
P McGrath	Manchester United
R Whelan	Liverpool
K Moran	Manchester United
M McCarthy	Glasgow Celtic
L Brady	West Ham United
M Lawrenson	Liverpool
R Houghton	Oxford United
F Stapleton	Ajax
J Aldridge*	Liverpool
A Galvin**	Sheffield Wednesday
N Quinn* (sub)	Arsenal
J Byrne** (sub)	Queen's Park Rangers

Result	2–0
Scorers	P McGrath; K Moran

Match No. 235

10 November 1987 v ISRAEL at Dublin

K O'Hanlon	Rotherham United
C Morris	Glasgow Celtic
C Hughton	Tottenham Hotspur
K Moran	Manchester United
M McCarthy	Glasgow Celtic
J Byrne	Queen's Park Rangers
M Lawrenson	Liverpool
R Houghton*	Liverpool
N Quinn	Arsenal
D Kelly	Walsall
K Sheedy	Everton
L O'Brien* (sub)	Manchester United

Result	5–0
Scorers	J Byrne; D Kelly (3–1 penalty); N Quinn

David Kelly

Match No. 236

23 March 1988 v ROMANIA at Dublin

P Bonner	Glasgow Celtic
C Morris	Glasgow Celtic
A Grimes	Luton Town
M McCarthy*	Glasgow Celtic
K Moran	Manchester United
J Sheridan	Leeds United
A Galvin**	Sheffield Wednesday
J Byrne	Queen's Park Rangers
F Stapleton***	Derby County
D Kelly	Walsall

K Sheedy	Everton
J Anderson* (sub)	Newcastle United
L O'Brien** (sub)	Manchester United
N Quinn*** (sub)	Arsenal

| Result | 2–0 |
| Scorers | K Moran; D Kelly |

Match No. 237

27 April 1988 v YUGOSLAVIA at Dublin

P Bonner	Glasgow Celtic
C Morris	Glasgow Celtic
C Hughton*	Tottenham Hotspur
M McCarthy	Glasgow Celtic
K Moran	Manchester United
J Sheridan	Leeds United
P McGrath	Manchester United
R Houghton	Liverpool
F Stapleton	Derby County
M Kelly**	Portsmouth
D Kelly***	Walsall
J Anderson* (sub)	Newcastle United
L O'Brien** (sub)	Manchester United
J Byrne*** (sub)	Queen's Park Rangers

| Result | 2–0 |
| Scorers | M McCarthy; K Moran |

Match No. 238

22 May 1988 v POLAND at Dublin

G Peyton	Bournemouth
C Morris	Glasgow Celtic
C Hughton	Tottenham Hotspur
P McGrath*	Manchester United
K Moran	Manchester United
J Sheridan**	Leeds United
R Whelan***	Liverpool
J Aldridge	Liverpool
A Galvin****	Sheffield Wednesday
A Cascarino	Millwall

K Sheedy	Everton
N Quinn* (sub)	Arsenal
M Kelly** (sub)	Portsmouth
J Byrne*** (sub)	Queen's Park Rangers
L O'Brien**** (sub)	Manchester United

| Result | 3–1 |
| Scorers | K Sheedy; A Cascarino; J Sheridan |

Match No. 239

1 June 1988 v NORWAY at Oslo

P Bonner`	Glasgow Celtic
C Morris	Glasgow Celtic
C Hughton	Tottenham Hotspur
M McCarthy	Glasgow Celtic
K Moran	Manchester United
P McGrath	Manchester United
R Whelan	Liverpool
R Houghton	Liverpool
J Aldridge	Liverpool
F Stapleton*	Derby County
A Galvin**	Sheffield Wednesday
A Cascarino* (sub)	Millwall
J Sheridan** (sub)	Leeds United

| Result | 0–0 |

Match No. 240

12 June 1988 v ENGLAND at Stuttgart

P Bonner	Glasgow Celtic
C Morris	Glasgow Celtic
M McCarthy	Glasgow Celtic
K Moran	Manchester United
C Hughton	Tottenham Hotspur
R Houghton	Liverpool
P McGrath	Manchester United
R Whelan	Liverpool
A Galvin*	Sheffield Wednesday
J Aldridge	Liverpool

F Stapleton**	Derby County
K Sheedy* (sub)	Everton
N Quinn** (sub)	Arsenal

Result	1–0
Scorer	R Houghton

FEATURED MATCH 16

ENGLAND 0 REPUBLIC OF IRELAND 1
At Neckarstadion, Stuttgart, 12 June 1988

England
Peter Shilton; Gary Stevens; Mark Wright; Tony Adams; Kenny Sansom; Neil Webb (Glenn Hoddle); Bryan Robson; Chris Waddle; Peter Beardsley (Mark Hateley); Gary Lineker; John Barnes.

Republic of Ireland
Packie Bonner; Chris Morris; Mick McCarthy; Kevin Moran; Chris Hughton; Ray Houghton; Paul McGrath; Ronnie Whelan; Tony Galvin (Kevin Sheedy); John Aldridge; Frank Stapleton (Niall Quinn).

Jack Charlton

Ireland achieved one of their greatest ever victories in this European Championship Finals match at Stuttgart after making a dream start.

In the opening minute, McGrath scuffed his shot which was easily saved by Peter Shilton but five minutes later after their next attack, the Irish took the lead. A long free-kick taken by Moran was challenged for by Stapleton, Stevens and Wright, with the ball landing at the feet of Galvin. The winger's cross was miskicked into the air by Sansom, and Aldridge headed the ball across to the diminutive HOUGHTON who looped his header into the corner of the net.

Minutes later, Packie Bonner was in action, diving at the feet of the on-rushing Lineker but that was one of only a couple of chances England had in the opening half. Ireland dominated proceedings and Chris Morris' shot through a crowd of players almost caught Shilton unawares but he produced a brilliant save to turn the ball round the post for a corner. In the twenty-sixth minute, England had strong claims for a penalty when Barnes was pulled down by Moran but the East German referee waved play on. England's other gilt-edged chance towards the end of the half fell to Chris Waddle but he fired into the side netting. Even so, the last chance of the half fell to Ireland's goalscorer Ray Houghton who, having broken through England's offside trap, saw Shilton save by bravely diving at his feet.

England were in charge in the second half they should have drawn level three minutes after the interval when Lineker found himself with only Bonner to beat but his shot was beaten out by Bonner and Beardsley put the rebound over the bar. Beardsley and Barnes both curled shots inches wide before Neil Webb forced Bonner into making a good stop. On the hour mark, Robson sent Lineker away again as Bonner advanced, he chipped the ball over his head but it just clipped the bar as it went over.

A minute later, Ronnie Whelan, in a rare Irish attack, also clipped the bar, after a Mick McCarthy free-kick was only partially cleared. At the other end, Hoddle had a free-kick well saved by Bonner and then Lineker screwed a shot across the face of Bonner's goals. The Irish keeper then denied Beardsley and Barnes with good saves but made an even better one to prevent Robson levelling the scores. England pressed hard and Hoddle sent a flashing volley inches wide, whilst Moran hacked the ball clear after Bonner had spilt a Robson shot with Lineker waiting to pounce. Aldridge and

Whelan wasted good opportunities to put the game beyond doubt but in injury time, Lineker got his head to a Hoddle cross. Even though Bonner was completely out of position, he managed to twist in mid-air and turn the ball against the post and out for a rather inconsequential corner.

Match No. 241

15 June 1988 v USSR at Hanover

P Bonner	Glasgow Celtic
C Morris	Glasgow Celtic
M McCarthy	Glasgow Celtic
K Moran	Manchester United
C Hughton	Tottenham Hotspur
R Houghton	Liverpool
R Whelan	Liverpool
K Sheedy	Everton
A Galvin	Sheffield Wednesday
F Stapleton*	Derby County
J Aldridge	Liverpool
A Cascarino* (sub)	Millwall

Result	1–1
Scorer	R Whelan

Match No. 242

18 June 1988 v HOLLAND at Gelsenkirchen

P Bonner	Glasgow Celtic
C Morris*	Glasgow Celtic
M McCarthy	Glasgow Celtic
K Moran	Manchester United
C Hughton	Tottenham Hotspur
R Houghton	Liverpool
P McGrath	Manchester United
R Whelan	Liverpool
A Galvin	Sheffield Wednesday
J Aldridge	Liverpool
F Stapleton**	Derby County
K Sheedy* (sub)	Everton
A Cascarino** (sub)	Millwall

Result	0–1

Match No. 243

14 September 1988 v NORTHERN IRELAND at Belfast

G Peyton	Bournemouth
C Morris	Glasgow Celtic
M McCarthy	Glasgow Celtic
K Moran	Sporting Gijon
C Hughton	Tottenham Hotspur
R Houghton	Liverpool
P McGrath	Manchester United
R Whelan	Liverpool
K Sheedy	Everton
A Cascarino	Millwall
J Aldridge	Liverpool

Result	0–0

Match No. 244

19 October 1988 v TUNISIA at Dublin

G Peyton	Bournemouth
C Morris*	Glasgow Celtic
M McCarthy	Glasgow Celtic
J Anderson	Newcastle United
S Staunton	Liverpool
R Houghton**	Liverpool
L O'Brien	Manchester United
K Sheedy	Everton
M Kelly	Portsmouth
A Cascarino***	Millwall
J Aldridge****	Liverpool
P Scully* (sub)	Arsenal
D Kelly** (sub)	West Ham United
K de Mange*** (sub)	Hull City
N Quinn**** (sub)	Arsenal

Result	4–0
Scorers	A Cascarino (2); J Aldridge; K Sheedy

MATCHES

Match No. 245

16 November 1988 v SPAIN at Seville

P Bonner	Glasgow Celtic
C Morris	Glasgow Celtic
M McCarthy	Glasgow Celtic
D O'Leary	Arsenal
S Staunton	Liverpool
J Sheridan*	Leeds United
K Moran	Sporting Gijon
R Houghton	Liverpool
A Galvin	Sheffield Wednesday
J Aldridge**	Liverpool
A Cascarino	Millwall
L O'Brien* (sub)	Newcastle United
N Quinn** (sub)	Arsenal

Result	0–2

Match No. 246

7 February 1989 v FRANCE at Dublin

P Bonner	Glasgow Celtic
C Morris	Glasgow Celtic
C Hughton	Tottenham Hotspur
M McCarthy	Glasgow Celtic
L Brady	West Ham United
P McGrath	Manchester United
R Whelan	Liverpool
R Houghton	Liverpool
F Stapleton*	Le Havre
A Cascarino	Millwall
A Townsend	Norwich City
J Aldridge* (sub)	Liverpool

Result	0–0

Match No. 247

8 March 1989 v HUNGARY at Budapest

P Bonner	Glasgow Celtic
C Morris	Glasgow Celtic
M McCarthy	Glasgow Celtic
K Moran	Sporting Gijon
C Hughton	Tottenham Hotspur
R Houghton	Liverpool
P McGrath	Manchester United
R Whelan	Liverpool
K Sheedy	Everton
J Aldridge*	Liverpool
A Cascarino**	Millwall
L Brady* (sub)	West Ham United
N Quinn** (sub)	Arsenal

Result	0–0

Match No. 248

26 April 1989 v SPAIN at Dublin

P Bonner	Glasgow Celtic
C Hughton	Tottenham Hotspur
S Staunton	Liverpool
M McCarthy	Glasgow Celtic
K Moran	Sporting Gijon
R Whelan	Liverpool
P McGrath	Manchester United
R Houghton	Liverpool
F Stapleton*	Le Havre
A Cascarino	Millwall
K Sheedy	Everton
A Townsend* (sub)	Norwich City

Result	1–0
Scorer	Michel (own goal)

Match No. 249

28 May 1989 v MALTA at Dublin

P Bonner	Glasgow Celtic
C Hughton	Tottenham Hotspur
S Staunton	Liverpool
D O'Leary	Arsenal
K Moran	Sporting Gijon
R Whelan	Liverpool
P McGrath	Manchester United

R Houghton*	Liverpool
F Stapleton**	Le Havre
A Cascarino	Millwall
K Sheedy	Everton
A Townsend* (sub)	Norwich City
J Aldridge** (sub)	Liverpool

Result	2–0
Scorers	R Houghton; K Moran

Match No. 250

4 July 1989 v HUNGARY at Dublin

P Bonner	Glasgow Celtic
C Hughton	Tottenham Hotspur
S Staunton	Liverpool
D O'Leary	Arsenal
K Moran	Sporting Gijon
A Townsend	Norwich City
P McGrath*	Manchester United
R Houghton	Liverpool
J Aldridge**	Liverpool
A Cascarino	Millwall
K Sheedy	Everton
C Morris* (sub)	Glasgow Celtic
L Brady** (sub)	West Ham United

Result	2–0
Scorers	P McGrath; A Cascarino

Match No. 251

6 September 1989 v WEST GERMANY at Dublin

P Bonner	Glasgow Celtic
C Morris	Glasgow Celtic
S Staunton	Liverpool
M McCarthy	Olympique Lyon
D O'Leary	Arsenal
L Brady*	West Ham United
P McGrath	Aston Villa
J Aldridge**	Liverpool
F Stapleton***	Blackburn Rovers

R Whelan	Liverpool
A Galvin	Swindon Town
A Townsend* (sub)	Norwich City
A Cascarino** (sub)	Millwall
J Byrne*** (sub)	Le Havre

Result	1–1
Scorer	F Stapleton

Match No. 252

11 October 1989 v NORTHERN IRELAND at Dublin

P Bonner	Glasgow Celtic
C Morris	Glasgow Celtic
S Staunton*	Liverpool
M McCarthy	Olympique Lyon
K Moran	Sporting Gijon
R Whelan	Liverpool
A Townsend	Norwich City
R Houghton	Liverpool
J Aldridge	Real Sociedad
A Cascarino	Millwall
K Sheedy	Everton
D O'Leary* (sub)	Arsenal

Result	3–0
Scorers	R Whelan; A Cascarino; R Houghton

Match No. 253

15 November 1989 v MALTA at Valletta

P Bonner	Glasgow Celtic
P McGrath	Aston Villa
K Moran*	Sporting Gijon
S Staunton	Liverpool
D O'Leary	Arsenal
R Houghton	Liverpool
K Sheedy	Everton
A Townsend	Norwich City
R Whelan	Liverpool

MATCHES

J Aldridge	Real Sociedad
A Cascarino	Millwall
C Morris* (sub)	Glasgow Celtic

Result	2–0
Scorer	J Aldridge (2–1 penalty)

Match No. 254

28 March 1990 v WALES at Dublin

P Bonner	Glasgow Celtic
C Morris	Glasgow Celtic
S Staunton*	Liverpool
M McCarthy	Millwall
K Moran**	Blackburn Rovers
R Whelan***	Liverpool
A Townsend	Norwich City
J Byrne	Le Havre
B Slaven	Middlesbrough
A Cascarino	Aston Villa
J Sheridan	Sheffield Wednesday
C Hughton* (sub)	Tottenham Hotspur
D O'Leary** (sub)	Arsenal
K Sheedy*** (sub)	Everton

Result	1–0
Scorer	B Slaven

Match No. 255

25 April 1990 v USSR at Dublin

G Peyton	Bournemouth
C Morris*	Glasgow Celtic
S Staunton	Liverpool
M McCarthy	Millwall

D O'Leary**	Arsenal
G Waddock	Millwall
P McGrath	Aston Villa
A Townsend	Norwich City
N Quinn	Manchester City
D Kelly	Leicester City
K Sheedy	Everton
C Hughton* (sub)	Tottenham Hotspur
K Moran** (sub)	Blackburn Rovers

Result	1–0
Scorer	S Staunton

Match No. 256

16 May 1990 v FINLAND at Dublin

P Bonner	Glasgow Celtic
C Hughton	Tottenham Hotspur
S Staunton*	Liverpool
M McCarthy	Millwall
D O'Leary	Arsenal
L Brady**	West Ham United
P McGrath	Aston Villa
R Houghton	Liverpool
B Slaven***	Middlesbrough
A Cascarino	Aston Villa
J Byrne****	Le Havre
C Morris* (sub)	Glasgow Celtic
A Townsend** (sub)	Norwich City
J Aldridge*** (sub)	Real Sociedad
K Sheedy**** (sub)	Everton

Result	1–1
Scorer	K Sheedy

Did you know?

John Aldridge's second-half penalty against Malta in November 1989 was the first penalty the Republic had been awarded in World Cup football in 55 years.

Match No. 257

27 May 1990 v TURKEY at Izmir

P Bonner	Glasgow Celtic
C Morris	Glasgow Celtic
M McCarthy	Millwall
D O'Leary*	Arsenal
S Staunton**	Liverpool
G Waddock***	Millwall
P McGrath	Aston Villa
A Townsend****	Norwich City
K Sheedy	Everton
A Cascarino	Aston Villa
J Aldridge	Real Sociedad
B Slaven* (sub)	Middlesbrough
C Hughton** (sub)	Tottenham Hotspur
J Byrne*** (sub)	Le Havre
J Sheridan**** (sub)	Sheffield Wednesday

Result	0–0

Match No. 258

2 June 1990 v MALTA at Valletta

G Peyton	Bournemouth
C Hughton	Tottenham Hotspur
S Staunton	Liverpool
D O'Leary	Arsenal
K Moran	Blackburn Rovers
A McLoughlin	Swindon Town
J Sheridan	Sheffield Wednesday
J Byrne	Le Havre
N Quinn	Manchester City
D Kelly*	Leicester City
B Slaven**	Middlesbrough
F Stapleton* (sub)	Blackburn Rovers
A Townsend** (sub)	Norwich City

Result	3–0
Scorers	N Quinn; A Townsend; F Stapleton

Match No. 259

11 June 1990 v ENGLAND at Cagliari

P Bonner	Glasgow Celtic
C Morris	Glasgow Celtic
S Staunton	Liverpool
M McCarthy	Millwall
K Moran	Blackburn Rovers
R Houghton	Liverpool
P McGrath	Aston Villa
A Townsend	Norwich City
K Sheedy	Everton
A Cascarino	Aston Villa
J Aldridge*	Real Sociedad
A McLoughlin* (sub)	Swindon Town

Result	1–1
Scorer	K Sheedy

Match No. 260

17 June 1990 v EGYPT at Palermo

P Bonner	Glasgow Celtic
C Morris	Glasgow Celtic
M McCarthy	Millwall
K Moran	Blackburn Rovers
S Staunton	Liverpool
R Houghton	Liverpool
P McGrath	Aston Villa
A Townsend	Norwich City
K Sheedy	Everton
A Cascarino*	Aston Villa
J Aldridge**	Real Sociedad
N Quinn* (sub)	Manchester City
A McLoughlin** (sub)	Swindon Town

Result	0–0

FEATURED MATCH 17

ENGLAND 1 REPUBLIC OF IRELAND 1
At Sant 'Elia Stadium, Cagliari, 11 June 1990

England
Peter Shilton; Gary Stevens; Des Walker; Terry Butcher; Stuart Pearce; Chris Waddle; Paul Gascoigne; Bryan Robson; John Barnes; Peter Beardsley (Steve McMahon); Gary Lineker (Steve Bull).

Republic of Ireland
Packie Bonner; Chris Morris; Steve Staunton; Mick McCarthy; Kevin Moran; Ray Houghton; Paul McGrath; Andy Townsend; Kevin Sheedy; Tony Cascarino; John Aldridge (Alan McLoughlin).

Ireland had the first goalscoring opportunity in this World Cup encounter in Italia '90 but Sheedy's low effort was saved easily by Peter Shilton in the England goal. Bryan Robson got his head to a Paul Gascoigne free-kick but the ball flew past Bonner's right-hand post. However, a minute later, England took the lead, a result of poor marking by the Irish defence. A throw-in by Steve Staunton was headed towards touch by Stevens and although the Irish players expected the ball to go out of play, Chris Waddle somehow kept the ball in. Therefore the defence was at sixes and sevens as Waddle's cross was chested past Bonner by LINEKER who followed the ball up and scrambled it over the line.

Ireland responded immediately and Sheedy shot narrowly wide before Paul McGrath's header was saved by Shilton. Peter Beardsley came close after good work by Barnes but as the half drew towards a close, a John Aldridge header shaved the bar before McGrath wasted a good chance from a Sheedy free-kick.

As the teams came out for the second half, they were met by a thunder storm and torrential rain. Ireland continued where they had left off in the first half and a powerful drive by Cascarino was well held by Shilton. On 56 minutes, McGrath sent a shot inches over the bar before Andy Townsend tried his luck from 30 yards but failed to trouble the England keeper.

One of the game's most exciting moments came when Chris Waddle's run down the left took him past Steve Staunton and Andy Townsend. He then cut into the box only to have his legs taken from under him by a desperate lunge by Kevin Moran. Surprisingly the West Germany referee did not award a penalty. England continued to press and Pearce had a long range shot turned round the post by Bonner.

Even so, the next goal was scored by Ireland and it came courtesy of their substitute Steve McMahon who had replaced Beardsley. Bonner's long punt downfield was headed down by Terry Butcher under pressure from Cascarino for Sheedy. His first time ball was then intercepted by McMahon who, under pressure from Townsend, lost control on the edge of the box and as the ball ran free, Kevin SHEEDY thumped a low shot into the corner of Shilton's net.

In the seventy-fourth minute, England should have regained their lead but Butcher's header from Paul Gascoigne's free-kick flew well wide. As well as being responsible for the Irish goal, McMahon, who came off the bench in the sixty-ninth minute, was also booked for retaliation. In the end, a draw was a fair result.

Match No. 261	
21 June 1990 v HOLLAND at Palermo	
P Bonner	Glasgow Celtic
C Morris	Glasgow Celtic
M McCarthy	Millwall
K Moran	Blackburn Rovers
S Staunton	Liverpool
R Houghton	Liverpool
P McGrath	Aston Villa
A Townsend	Norwich City
K Sheedy*	Everton
N Quinn	Manchester City
J Aldridge**	Real Sociedad
R Whelan* (sub)	Liverpool
A Cascarino** (sub)	Aston Villa

Result	1–1
Scorer	N Quinn

Match No. 262	
25 June 1990 v ROMANIA at Genoa	
P Bonner	Glasgow Celtic
C Morris	Glasgow Celtic
M McCarthy	Millwall
K Moran	Blackburn Rovers
S Staunton*	Liverpool
R Houghton	Liverpool
P McGrath	Aston Villa
A Townsend	Norwich City
K Sheedy	Everton
N Quinn	Manchester City
J Aldridge**	Real Sociedad
D O'Leary* (sub)	Arsenal
A Cascarino** (sub)	Aston Villa

Result	0–0
Republic of Ireland won 5–4 on penalties after extra time	

FEATURED MATCH 18

ROMANIA 0 REPUBLIC OF IRELAND 0
(4–5 on penalties after extra time)

At Luigi Ferraris Stadium, Genoa, 25 June 1990

Romania
S Lung; M Rednic; I Andone; G Popesca; I Lupescu; M Klein; G Hagi; I Sabau (D Timofte); J Rotariu; G Balint; F Radociou (D Lupu).

Republic of Ireland
Packie Bonner; Chris Morris; Mick McCarthy; Kevin Moran; Steve Staunton (David O'Leary); Ray Houghton; Paul McGrath; Andy Townsend; Kevin Sheedy; Niall Quinn; John Aldridge (Tony Cascarino).

In their first World Cup Finals the Republic of Ireland had qualified for Round Two where they faced tricky opponents, Romania who were hoping to reach the quarter-finals for the first time in their fifth World Cup finals tournament.

Romania was the stronger of the teams in the first fifteen minutes, almost taking the lead after three minutes when Hagi and Sabau played a neat one-two before the latter shot wide with Bonner beaten. Sabau continued to impress and moments later he set up Balint whose shot was well saved by Bonner. The Irish keeper was called into action again, saving from Rotariu before Aldridge was injured in a tackle on Hagi for which he was booked. Only 22 minutes had been played when the Real Sociedad forward limped off to be replaced by Cascarino. A minute later, Hagi ran clear of the Irish defence and his shot went across the face of the Irish goal before going out of play.

After both Sheedy and Hagi had tested the respective keepers from range, Ireland had a couple of chances to open the scoring in the last few minutes of the first half. Sheedy's shot was turned round the post by Lung and Quinn headed Ray Houghton's cross just wide.

Early in the second half, Cascarino had a shot saved by Lung and then the Irish substitute headed over from six yards out after good work by Quinn. Romania had a couple of shots off target before Bonner brought off a magnificent save from Raducioiu. With fifteen minutes remaining, Hagi cut inside Staunton and unleashed a powerful shot which Bonner did well to keep out. As the full-time whistle loomed, Quinn headed narrowly wide from a Morris cross and McGrath lost the advantage of being temporarily unmarked when he headed Sheedy's corner-kick over the bar.

In extra time, Steve Staunton almost broke the deadlock in the opening minute but his free-kick flew just inches wide. Soon after, he was replaced by David O'Leary who set up Sheedy to cross to the far post where Houghton headed over. Play flowed from end to end and Hagi and Townsend both had shots off target, but neither side could find a way through and the game went to a penalty shoot-out.

The scores were level at 4–4 with Sheedy, Houghton, Townsend and Cascarino scoring Ireland's goals and then it was down to the two substitutes. Timofte sent his penalty low to Bonner's right but the Irish keeper, who had guessed right on all of the previous kicks but had not been able to keep them out, turned the ball away for a brilliant save. The pressure was now on O'Leary but despite never having taken a spot-kick before, he sent Lung the wrong way and put

Ireland into the quarter-finals. This achievement was in spite of the fact that Ireland had not won a game and had set a new World Cup Finals record of four successive draws.

Match No. 263

30 June 1990 v ITALY at Rome

P Bonner	Glasgow Celtic
C Morris	Glasgow Celtic
M McCarthy	Millwall
K Moran	Blackburn Rovers
S Staunton	Liverpool
R Houghton	Liverpool
P McGrath	Aston Villa
A Townsend	Norwich City
K Sheedy	Everton
N Quinn*	Manchester City
J Aldridge**	Real Sociedad
A Cascarino* (sub)	Aston Villa
J Sheridan** (sub)	Sheffield Wednesday

Result	0–1

Match No. 264

12 September 1990 v MOROCCO at Dublin

P Bonner	Glasgow Celtic
D Irwin	Manchester United
S Staunton	Liverpool
M McCarthy	Millwall
D O'Leary	Arsenal
R Whelan	Liverpool
A Townsend*	Chelsea
R Houghton	Liverpool
D Kelly	Leicester City
N Quinn**	Manchester City
M Kelly***	Portsmouth
J Sheridan* (sub)	Sheffield Wednesday
A Cascarino** (sub)	Aston Villa
A McLoughlin*** (sub)	Swindon Town

Result	1–0
Scorer	D Kelly

Match No. 265

17 October 1990 v TURKEY at Dublin

P Bonner	Glasgow Celtic
D Irwin	Manchester United
S Staunton	Liverpool
M McCarthy	Millwall
D O'Leary	Arsenal
C Hughton	Tottenham Hotspur
A Townsend*	Chelsea
R Houghton	Liverpool
N Quinn**	Manchester City
J Aldridge	Real Sociedad
J Sheridan	Sheffield Wednesday
K Moran* (sub)	Blackburn Rovers
A Cascarino** (sub)	Aston Villa

Result	5–0
Scorers	J Aldridge (3–1 pen); D O'Leary; N Quinn

Match No. 266

14 November 1990 v ENGLAND at Dublin

P Bonner	Glasgow Celtic
C Morris	Glasgow Celtic
S Staunton	Liverpool
M McCarthy	Millwall
D O'Leary	Arsenal
R Whelan*	Liverpool
P McGrath	Aston Villa
R Houghton	Liverpool
N Quinn**	Manchester City
J Aldridge	Real Sociedad
A Townsend	Chelsea
A McLoughlin* (sub)	Swindon Town
A Cascarino** (sub)	Aston Villa

Result	1–1
Scorer	A Cascarino

REPUBLIC OF IRELAND 5 TURKEY 0

At Lansdowne Road, Dublin, 17 October 1990

Republic of Ireland

Packie Bonner; Denis Irwin; Steve Staunton; Mick McCarthy; David O'Leary; Chris Hughton; Andy Townsend (Kevin Moran); Ray Houghton; Niall Quinn (Tony Cascarino); John Aldridge; John Sheridan.

Turkey

Engin; Riza; Kemal; K Gokhan; Ercan (Metin); Tugay; Oguz; Mehmet; Bulent; Hami; Sercan (Tanju).

The visitors made a lively start to this European Championship qualifier with Packie Bonner saving a deflected shot from Hami and then racing out of his area to kick clear from the on-rushing Sercan. Hami and Sercan played some attractive football but the former shot wide even when he was well placed. Ireland's first real attack of the game saw Aldridge put in a header from a Ray Houghton cross but it was well saved by Engin.

Ireland took the lead after fifteen minutes when Chris Hughton's shot was only partially saved by Engin. As the ball spun away from the keeper, ALDRIDGE was the first to react and smashed the ball home from close range. The home side continued to press forward and Aldridge almost had a second goal but Engin turned his shot behind, before bravely diving at the feet of Quinn to deny the Manchester City striker.

Turkey should have been awarded a penalty after 35 minutes when Bonner brought down Sercan when he was clean through on goal. Mr Fredriksen, the Swedish referee, was the only man on the ground who didn't think this way. Ireland profited and four minutes later, a free-kick from Sheridan was headed goalwards by McCarthy. Engin appeared to have it covered but it was deflected by Ercan to O'LEARY who shot home. In the final minute of the half, a long punt downfield by Bonner was headed on by Quinn to Townsend but his first time shot was well held by Engin.

Ireland extended their lead after 57 minutes when a pass from John Sheridan found O'Leary

completely unmarked in the Turkish box. The Arsenal defender unselfishly squared the ball for ALDRIDGE to fire past Engin. Sheridan then had a header turned over the bar by Engin before the unlucky Turkish keeper was beaten for a fourth time. Aldridge headed down a Denis Irwin cross and Niall QUINN was on hand to blast the ball home.

On 70 minutes, a goalbound shot by Aldridge was handled by Gokhan and a penalty awarded. There followed a couple of minutes' protest by the Turkish players before ALDRIDGE scored from the spot to complete his hat-trick.

Turkey's Tanju volleyed over from close range but the last chance of an entertaining game, fell to John Aldridge, whose shot was deflected onto the crossbar by Kemal.

Match No. 267	
6 February 1991 v WALES at Wrexham	
P Bonner	Glasgow Celtic
D Irwin	Manchester United
S Staunton	Liverpool
P McGrath	Aston Villa
K Moran	Blackburn Rovers
A McLoughlin	Southampton
A Townsend	Chelsea
J Byrne	Brighton & Hove Albion
N Quinn	Manchester City
B Slaven*	Middlesbrough
K Sheedy	Everton
D Kelly* (sub)	Leicester City

Result	3–0
Scorers	N Quinn 2; J Byrne

Match No. 268	
27 March 1991 v ENGLAND at Wembley	
P Bonner	Glasgow Celtic
D Irwin	Manchester United
S Staunton	Liverpool
D O'Leary	Arsenal
K Moran	Blackburn Rovers
A Townsend	Chelsea

P McGrath	Aston Villa
R Houghton	Liverpool
N Quinn	Manchester City
J Aldridge*	Real Sociedad
K Sheedy	Everton
A Cascarino* (sub)	Aston Villa

Result	1–1
Scorer	N Quinn

Match No. 269
1 May 1991 v POLAND at Dublin

P Bonner	Glasgow Celtic
D Irwin	Manchester United
S Staunton	Liverpool
D O'Leary	Arsenal
K Moran	Blackburn Rovers
A Townsend	Chelsea
P McGrath	Aston Villa
R Houghton	Liverpool
N Quinn*	Manchester City
J Aldridge**	Real Sociedad
K Sheedy	Everton
A Cascarino* (sub)	Aston Villa
B Slaven** (sub)	Middlesbrough

Result	0–0

Match No. 270
22 May 1991 v CHILE at Dublin

G Peyton	Bournemouth
C Hughton	West Ham United
S Staunton	Liverpool
D O'Leary*	Arsenal
K Moran	Blackburn Rovers
A Townsend	Chelsea
R Keane	Nottingham Forest
R Houghton**	Liverpool
J Sheridan	Sheffield Wednesday
D Kelly	Leicester City

K Sheedy***	Everton
P McGrath* (sub)	Aston Villa
A McLoughlin** (sub)	Southampton
A Cascarino*** (sub)	Aston Villa

Result	1–1
Scorer	D Kelly

Match No. 271
1 June 1991 v UNITED STATES at Boston

P Bonner	Glasgow Celtic
D Irwin*	Manchester United
S Staunton	Liverpool
M McCarthy	Millwall
K Moran	Blackburn Rovers
A Townsend	Chelsea
P McGrath	Aston Villa
R Houghton	Liverpool
A Cascarino	Aston Villa
D Kelly	Leicester City
K Sheedy	Everton
J Sheridan* (sub)	Sheffield Wednesday

Result	1–1
Scorer	A Cascarino

Match No. 272
11 September 1991 v HUNGARY at Gyor

P Bonner	Glasgow Celtic
D Irwin	Manchester United
T Phelan*	Wimbledon
D O'Leary	Arsenal
M McCarthy	Millwall
J Sheridan**	Sheffield Wednesday
R Keane	Nottingham Forest
R Houghton	Liverpool
N Quinn	Manchester City
D Kelly***	Leicester City
K Sheedy	Everton
C Morris* (sub)	Glasgow Celtic

A McLoughlin** (sub) Southampton

J Aldridge*** (sub)   Tranmere Rovers

Result	2–1
Scorers	D Kelly; K Sheedy

Match No. 273

16 October 1991 v POLAND at Poznan

P Bonner	Glasgow Celtic
D Irwin	Manchester United
S Staunton*	Aston Villa
D O'Leary	Arsenal
K Moran	Blackburn Rovers
A Townsend	Chelsea
P McGrath	Aston Villa
C Morris	Glasgow Celtic
R Keane	Nottingham Forest
A Cascarino	Glasgow Celtic
K Sheedy	Everton
T Phelan* (sub)	Wimbledon

Result	3–3
Scorers	P McGrath; A Townsend; A Cascarino

Match No. 274

13 November 1991 v TURKEY at Istanbul

P Bonner	Glasgow Celtic
C Hughton	West Ham United
T Phelan	Wimbledon
D O'Leary	Arsenal
M McCarthy	Millwall
S Staunton	Aston Villa
P McGrath	Aston Villa
J Byrne	Sunderland
A Cascarino	Glasgow Celtic
J Aldridge	Tranmere Rovers
K Sheedy	Everton

Result	3–1
Scorers	J Byrne 2; A Cascarino

Match No. 275

19 February 1992 v WALES at Dublin

P Bonner	Glasgow Celtic
C Morris	Glasgow Celtic
D Irwin	Manchester United
D O'Leary	Arsenal
L Daish	Cambridge United
A Townsend*	Chelsea
T Phelan**	Wimbledon
J Byrne	Sunderland
R Keane	Nottingham Forest
A Cascarino***	Chelsea
K Sheedy	Everton
A McLoughlin* (sub)	Southampton
J Aldridge** (sub)	Tranmere Rovers
N Quinn*** (sub)	Manchester City

Result	0–1

Match No. 276

25 March 1992 v SWITZERLAND at Dublin

P Bonner	Glasgow Celtic
C Morris	Glasgow Celtic
T Phelan	Wimbledon
D O'Leary*	Arsenal
P McGrath	Aston Villa
R Keane	Nottingham Forest
R Whelan	Liverpool
E McGoldrick**	Crystal Palace
T Coyne***	Glasgow Celtic
A Cascarino	Chelsea
S Staunton****	Aston Villa
L Daish* (sub)	Cambridge United
L O'Brien** (sub)	Newcastle United
J Aldridge*** (sub)	Tranmere Rovers
K Sheedy**** (sub)	Newcastle United

Result	2–1
Scorers	T Coyne; J Aldridge (penalty)

MATCHES

Match No. 277

29 April 1992 v UNITED STATES at Dublin

G Peyton	Everton
C Morris	Glasgow Celtic
D Irwin*	Manchester United
D O'Leary**	Arsenal
P McGrath	Aston Villa
A Townsend	Chelsea
E McGoldrick	Crystal Palace
A McLoughlin	Portsmouth
N Quinn***	Manchester City
T Coyne****	Glasgow Celtic
S Staunton	Aston Villa
M Milligan* (sub)	Oldham Athletic
B Carey** (sub)	Manchester United
A Cascarino*** (sub)	Chelsea
J Aldridge**** (sub)	Tranmere Rovers

Result	4–1
Scorers	A Townsend; D Irwin; N Quinn; A Cascarino

Match No. 278

26 May 1992 v ALBANIA at Dublin

P Bonner	Glasgow Celtic
D Irwin	Manchester United
S Staunton	Aston Villa
D O'Leary	Arsenal
P McGrath	Aston Villa
A Townsend	Chelsea
R Keane	Nottingham Forest
R Houghton	Liverpool
N Quinn	Manchester City
J Aldridge*	Tranmere Rovers
K Sheedy**	Newcastle United
T Coyne* (sub)	Glasgow Celtic
M McCarthy** (sub)	Millwall

Result	2–0
Scorers	J Aldridge; P McGrath

Match No. 279

30 May 1992 v UNITED STATES at Washington

G Peyton	Everton
C Morris*	Glasgow Celtic
M McCarthy	Millwall
K Moran	Blackburn Rovers
T Phelan	Wimbledon
R Houghton	Liverpool
R Keane**	Nottingham Forest
P McGrath	Aston Villa
A Townsend	Chelsea
S Staunton***	Aston Villa
N Quinn	Manchester City
D Irwin* (sub)	Manchester United
A McLoughlin** (sub)	Portsmouth
T Coyne*** (sub)	Glasgow Celtic

Result	1–3
Scorer	M McCarthy

Match No. 280

4 June 1992 v ITALY at Boston

P Bonner	Glasgow Celtic
D Irwin*	Manchester United
M McCarthy**	Millwall
D O'Leary	Arsenal
S Staunton	Aston Villa
E McGoldrick***	Crystal Palace
A Townsend	Chelsea
P McGrath	Aston Villa
R Houghton	Liverpool
N Quinn****	Manchester City
J Aldridge*****	Tranmere Rovers
G Peyton* (sub)	Everton
A McLoughlin** (sub)	Portsmouth
T Phelan*** (sub)	Wimbledon
T Coyne**** (sub)	Glasgow Celtic
D Kelly***** (sub)	Newcastle United

Result	0–2

Did you know?

Packie Bonner is the only Irish goalkeeper to have been sent off: he fouled an opponent in the penalty area during a match against Italy on 4 June 1992.

Match No. 281

7 June 1992 v PORTUGAL at Boston

G Peyton	Everton
S Staunton	Aston Villa
M McCarthy	Millwall
D O'Leary	Arsenal
C Morris	Glasgow Celtic
R Houghton	Liverpool
A McLoughlin	Portsmouth
P McGrath	Aston Villa
T Phelan*	Wimbledon
D Kelly**	Newcastle United
N Quinn***	Manchester City
E McGoldrick* (sub)	Crystal Palace
T Coyne** (sub)	Glasgow Celtic
J Aldridge*** (sub)	Tranmere Rovers

Result	2–0
Scorers	S Staunton; T Coyne

Match No. 282

9 September 1992 v LATVIA at Dublin

P Bonner	Glasgow Celtic
D Irwin	Manchester United
S Staunton	Aston Villa
A Kernaghan	Middlesbrough
P McGrath	Aston Villa
A Townsend	Chelsea
R Keane	Nottingham Forest
R Whelan	Liverpool
N Quinn*	Manchester City
J Aldridge	Tranmere Rovers
K Sheedy**	Newcastle United
T Coyne* (sub)	Glasgow Celtic
T Phelan** (sub)	Manchester City

Result	4–0
Scorers	K Sheedy; J Aldridge (3–1 penalty)

Match No. 283

14 October 1992 v DENMARK at Copenhagen

P Bonner	Glasgow Celtic
D Irwin	Manchester United
T Phelan	Manchester City
K Moran	Blackburn Rovers
A Kernaghan	Middlesbrough
R Keane	Nottingham Forest
A Townsend	Chelsea
R Houghton	Aston Villa
N Quinn	Manchester City
J Aldridge*	Tranmere Rovers
E McGoldrick	Crystal Palace
D Kelly* (sub)	Newcastle United

Result	0–0

Match No. 284

18 November 1992 v SPAIN at Seville

P Bonner	Glasgow Celtic
D Irwin	Manchester United
T Phelan	Manchester City
P McGrath	Aston Villa
K Moran	Blackburn Rovers
R Keane	Nottingham Forest
A Townsend	Chelsea

R Houghton	Aston Villa
N Quinn	Manchester City
J Aldridge	Tranmere Rovers
S Staunton	Aston Villa

| Result | 0–0 |

17 February 1993 v WALES at Dublin

P Bonner*	Glasgow Celtic
C Morris	Middlesbrough
E McGoldrick	Crystal Palace
B Carey	Manchester United
D O'Leary**	Arsenal
R Keane	Nottingham Forest
L O'Brien	Newcastle United
J Byrne	Millwall
A Cascarino***	Chelsea
D Kelly****	Newcastle United
A McLoughlin	Portsmouth
A Kelly* (sub)	Sheffield United
R Whelan** (sub)*****Liverpool
B Slaven*** (sub)	Middlesbrough
T Coyne**** (sub)	Glasgow Celtic
K Sheedy*****(sub)	Newcastle United

| Result | 2–1 |
| Scorers | K Sheedy; T Coyne |

Match No. 286

31 March 1993 v NORTHERN IRELAND at Dublin

P Bonner	Glasgow Celtic
D Irwin	Manchester United
T Phelan	Manchester City
K Moran	Blackburn Rovers
P McGrath	Aston Villa
R Keane	Nottingham Forest
A Townsend	Chelsea
R Houghton	Aston Villa

N Quinn*	Manchester City
T Coyne**	Tranmere Rovers
S Staunton	Aston Villa
E McGoldrick* (sub)	Crystal Palace
A Cascarino** (sub)	Chelsea

| Result | 3–0 |
| Scorers | A Townsend; N Quinn; S Staunton |

Match No. 287

28 April 1993 v DENMARK at Dublin

P Bonner	Glasgow Celtic
D Irwin	Manchester United
E McGoldrick	Crystal Palace
P McGrath	Aston Villa
A Kernaghan	Middlesbrough
R Houghton	Aston Villa
A Townsend	Chelsea
R Keane	Nottingham Forest
S Staunton	Aston Villa
J Aldridge*	Tranmere Rovers
N Quinn	Manchester City
A Cascarino* (sub)	Chelsea

| Result | 1–1 |
| Scorer | N Quinn |

Match No. 288

26 May 1993 v ALBANIA at Tirana

P Bonner	Glasgow Celtic
D Irwin	Manchester United
T Phelan	Manchester City
K Moran	Blackburn Rovers
A Kernaghan	Middlesbrough
R Houghton	Aston Villa
R Keane	Nottingham Forest
A Townsend	Chelsea
S Staunton	Aston Villa
J Aldridge*	Tranmere Rovers

| N Quinn | Manchester City |
| A Cascarino* (sub) | Chelsea |

Result	2–1
Scorer	S Staunton; A Cascarino

Match No. 289

9 June 1993 v LATVIA at Riga

P Bonner	Glasgow Celtic
D Irwin	Manchester United
T Phelan	Manchester City
P McGrath	Aston Villa
A Kernaghan	Middlesbrough
R Houghton	Aston Villa
R Keane	Nottingham Forest
A Townsend	Chelsea
S Staunton	Aston Villa
J Aldridge*	Tranmere Rovers
N Quinn**	Manchester City
J Sheridan* (sub)	Sheffield Wednesday
A Cascarino** (sub)	Chelsea

Result	2–0
Scorers	J Aldridge; P McGrath

Match No. 290

16 June 1993 v LITHUANIA at Vilnius

P Bonner	Glasgow Celtic
D Irwin	Manchester United
T Phelan	Manchester City
P McGrath	Aston Villa
A Kernaghan	Middlesbrough
R Houghton	Aston Villa
R Keane	Nottingham Forest
A Townsend	Chelsea
S Staunton	Aston Villa
J Aldridge*	Tranmere Rovers
N Quinn	Manchester City
R Whelan* (sub)	Liverpool

Result	1–0
Scorer	S Staunton

Match No. 291

8 September 1993 v LITHUANIA at Dublin

P Bonner	Glasgow Celtic
D Irwin	Manchester United
T Phelan	Manchester City
A Kernaghan	Manchester City
P McGrath	Aston Villa
R Houghton	Aston Villa
R Keane	Manchester United
A Townsend*	Aston Villa
S Staunton	Aston Villa
N Quinn**	Manchester City
J Aldridge	Tranmere Rovers
R Whelan* (sub)	Liverpool
A Cascarino** (sub)	Chelsea

Result	2–0
Scorer	J Aldridge; A Kernaghan

Match No. 292

13 October 1993 v SPAIN at Dublin

P Bonner	Glasgow Celtic
D Irwin	Manchester United
T Phelan	Manchester City
A Kernaghan	Manchester City
K Moran*	Blackburn Rovers
R Whelan	Liverpool
R Keane	Manchester United
A Townsend	Aston Villa
R Houghton	Aston Villa
N Quinn	Manchester City
S Staunton**	Aston Villa
J Sheridan* (sub)	Sheffield Wednesday
A Cascarino** (sub)	Chelsea

Result	1–3
Scorer	J Sheridan

Match No. 293

17 November 1993 v NORTHERN IRELAND at Belfast

P Bonner	Glasgow Celtic
D Irwin	Manchester United
T Phelan	Manchester City
A Kernaghan	Manchester City
P McGrath	Aston Villa
R Houghton*	Aston Villa
R Keane	Manchester United
A Townsend	Aston Villa
E McGoldrick	Arsenal
N Quinn	Manchester City
J Aldridge**	Tranmere Rovers
A McLoughlin* (sub)	Portsmouth
A Cascarino** (sub)	Chelsea

Result	1–1
Scorer	A McLoughlin

Match No. 294

23 March 1994 v RUSSIA at Dublin

P Bonner*	Glasgow Celtic
G Kelly	Leeds United
E McGoldrick	Arsenal
B Carey	Leicester City
P Babb	Coventry City
J McAteer	Bolton Wanderers
L O'Brien	Tranmere Rovers
R Whelan	Liverpool
A McLoughlin	Portsmouth
D Kelly**	Wolverhampton Wanderers
A Cascarino	Chelsea
A Kelly* (sub)	Sheffield United
T Coyne** (sub)	Motherwell

Result	0–0

Match No. 295

20 April 1994 v HOLLAND at Tilburg

P Bonner	Glasgow Celtic
G Kelly	Leeds United
T Phelan*	Manchester City
K Moran	Blackburn Rovers
P Babb	Coventry City
R Whelan	Liverpool
A Townsend	Aston Villa
E McGoldrick**	Arsenal
T Coyne***	Motherwell
J Sheridan	Sheffield Wednesday
S Staunton	Aston Villa
A McLoughlin* (sub)	Portsmouth
J McAteer** (sub)	Bolton Wanderers
O Coyle*** (sub)	Bolton Wanderers

Result	1–0
Scorer	T Coyne

Match No. 296

24 May 1994 v BOLIVIA at Dublin

P Bonner	Glasgow Celtic
D Irwin*	Manchester United
T Phelan	Manchester City
K Moran**	Blackburn Rovers
P Babb	Coventry City
R Houghton***	Aston Villa
R Keane	Manchester United
A Townsend	Aston Villa
J Sheridan	Sheffield Wednesday
S Staunton	Aston Villa
T Coyne****	Motherwell
G Kelly* (sub)	Leeds United
A Kernaghan** (sub)	Manchester City
J McAteer*** (sub)	Bolton Wanderers
A Cascarino**** (sub)	Chelsea

Result	1–0
Scorer	J Sheridan

Match No. 297

29 May 1994 v GERMANY at Hanover

A Kelly	Sheffield United
T Phelan	Manchester City
D Irwin*	Manchester United
P McGrath	Aston Villa
P Babb	Coventry City
J McAteer**	Bolton Wanderers
R Keane	Manchester United
A Townsend	Aston Villa
J Sheridan***	Sheffield Wednesday
A Cascarino****	Chelsea
S Staunton	Aston Villa
G Kelly* (sub)	Leeds United
R Houghton** (sub)	Aston Villa
R Whelan*** (sub)	Liverpool
T Coyne**** (sub)	Motherwell

Result	2–0
Scorers	A Cascarino; G Kelly

Match No. 298

5 June 1994 v CZECH REPUBLIC at Dublin

P Bonner	Glasgow Celtic
G Kelly	Leeds United
T Phelan	Manchester City
P McGrath*	Aston Villa
A Kernaghan	Manchester City
E McGoldrick**	Arsenal
A Townsend	Aston Villa
J Sheridan	Sheffield Wednesday
J Aldridge***	Tranmere Rovers
S Staunton	Aston Villa
A Cascarino****	Chelsea
P Babb* (sub)	Coventry City
R Keane** (sub)	Manchester United
J McAteer*** (sub)	Bolton Wanderers
T Coyne**** (sub)	Motherwell

Result	1–3
Scorers	A Townsend

Match No. 299

18 June 1994 v ITALY at New Jersey

P Bonner	Glasgow Celtic
D Irwin	Manchester United
T Phelan	Manchester City
P McGrath	Aston Villa
P Babb	Coventry City
R Houghton*	Aston Villa
R Keane	Manchester United
A Townsend	Aston Villa
J Sheridan	Sheffield Wednesday
S Staunton	Aston Villa
T Coyne**	Motherwell
J McAteer* (sub)	Bolton Wanderers
J Aldridge** (sub)	Tranmere Rovers

Result	1–0
Scorer	R Houghton

Match No. 300

24 June 1994 v MEXICO at Orlando

P Bonner	Glasgow Celtic
D Irwin	Manchester United
T Phelan	Manchester City
P McGrath	Aston Villa
P Babb	Coventry City
R Houghton	Aston Villa
R Keane	Manchester United
A Townsend	Aston Villa
J Sheridan	Sheffield Wednesday
S Staunton*	Aston Villa
T Coyne**	Motherwell
J McAteer* (sub)	Bolton Wanderers
J Aldridge** (sub)	Tranmere Rovers

Result	1–2
Scorer	J Aldridge

FEATURED MATCH 20

ITALY 0 REPUBLIC OF IRELAND 1
At Giants Stadium, East Rutherford, New York,
18 June 1994

Italy
G Pagliuca; A Costacurta; P Maldini; F Baresi; M
Tassotti; D Albertini; D Baggio; R Donadoni; A
Evani (D Massaro); R Baggio; G Signori (N Berti).

Republic of Ireland
Packie Bonner; Denis Irwin; Terry Phelan; Paul
McGrath; Phil Babb; Ray Houghton (Jason
McAteer); Roy Keane; Andy Townsend; John
Sheridan; Steve Staunton; Tommy Coyne (John
Aldridge).

Back-to-back games with the same opponents in
consecutive World Cups was something of an
oddity and it was certainly a tough task for the Irish
who had lost all previous seven internationals
against Italy, who were highly fancied for this tournament.

The opening exchanges were quite tense as
might be expected in a match of this magnitude but
the Italians seemed to be settling when Ireland took
the lead completely against the run of play.
Costacurta headed Sheridan's long ball forward up
in the air and Franco Baresi, attempting a headed
pass out, directed it straight at the onrushing Ray
HOUGHTON. The Aston Villa midfielder was side
on to the ball and couldn't connect with the ball
fully. The outcome was half lob, half shot, the ball
coming down over Pagliuca's head without the
Italian keeper making the faintest attempt to save it.

Italy failed to respond to this early setback and
moments later, Staunton found Townsend
unmarked in front of goal but his first touch let him
down and the chance went begging. As the first
half wore on, Italy came back into the game but
each of their attacks was met by firm resistance
from Ireland's back four, Babb and McGrath in
particular though Terry Phelan was cautioned for a
reckless challenge on Donadoni.

At the start of the secondhalf, Italy brought on
ace goalscorer Daniele Massaro and switched to a
4–3–3 formation. Yet it was Dino Baggio who
almost levelled the scores in the fifty-eighth
minute when he cut inside Phelan only to be

Republic of Ireland and Italy line up before their 1994 World Cup meeting.

tackled by Babb as he shaped to shoot. Though the Coventry defender won the ball cleanly, he went through Baggio's legs from behind but despite the Italians' claim for a penalty, Dutch referee Mario van der Ende waved play on. Ireland now came under a lot of pressure and Bonner beat out a powerful shot from Signori before Massaro tested the keeper with an unsuccessful low drive.

Goalscorer Ray Houghton was waiting to be substituted by Jason McAteer, who was celebrating his twenty-third birthday, when the ball fell at his feet. He just had time to test Pagliuca at the foot of his post before being replaced. Roy Keane got to the by-line and pulled the ball back. Tommy Coyne dummied, leaving Sheridan to drive the ball against the crossbar – the Sheffield Wednesday man should have done better.

Thankfully it didn't prove a costly miss as Ireland survived four minutes' injury time to record their first victory over Italy and their first in a World Cup Finals.

Match No. 301
28 June 1994 v NORWAY at New Jersey

P Bonner	Glasgow Celtic
G Kelly	Leeds United
S Staunton	Aston Villa
P McGrath	Aston Villa
P Babb	Coventry City
J McAteer	Bolton Wanderers
R Keane	Manchester United
A Townsend*	Aston Villa
J Sheridan	Sheffield Wednesday
R Houghton	Aston Villa
J Aldridge**	Tranmere Rovers
R Whelan* (sub)	Liverpool
D Kelly** (sub)	Wolverhampton Wanderers

Result	0–0

Match No. 302
4 July 1994 v HOLLAND at Orlando

P Bonner	Glasgow Celtic
G Kelly	Leeds United
T Phelan	Manchester City
P McGrath	Aston Villa
P Babb	Coventry City
R Houghton	Aston Villa
R Keane	Manchester United
A Townsend	Aston Villa
J Sheridan	Sheffield Wednesday
S Staunton*	Aston Villa
T Coyne**	Motherwell
J McAteer* (sub)	Bolton Wanderers
A Cascarino** (sub)	Chelsea

Result	0–2

Match No. 303
7 September 1994 v LATVIA at Riga

A Kelly	Sheffield United
G Kelly	Leeds United
D Irwin	Manchester United
P Babb	Liverpool
P McGrath	Aston Villa
J McAteer*	Bolton Wanderers
J Sheridan	Sheffield Wednesday
A Townsend	Aston Villa
S Staunton	Aston Villa
N Quinn**	Manchester City
J Aldridge	Tranmere Rovers
E McGoldrick* (sub)	Arsenal
A Cascarino** (sub)	Marseille

Result	3–0
Scorers	J Aldridge (2); J Sheridan

Match No. 304
12 October 1994 v LIECHTENSTEIN at Dublin

P Bonner	Glasgow Celtic
G Kelly	Leeds United
D Irwin*	Manchester United
A Kernaghan	Manchester City
P Babb	Liverpool

J McAteer	Bolton Wanderers
E McGoldrick	Arsenal
J Sheridan	Sheffield Wednesday
S Staunton	Aston Villa
N Quinn	Manchester City
T Coyne	Motherwell
A McLoughlin* (sub)	Portsmouth

Result	4–0
Scorers	T Coyne (2); N Quinn (2)

Match No. 305

16 November 1994 v NORTHERN IRELAND at Belfast

A Kelly	Sheffield United
G Kelly	Leeds United
D Irwin	Manchester United
P Babb	Liverpool
P McGrath	Aston Villa
R Keane*	Manchester United
A Townsend	Aston Villa
J Sheridan	Sheffield Wednesday
S Staunton	Aston Villa
N Quinn	Manchester City
J Aldridge**	Tranmere Rovers
J McAteer* (sub)	Bolton Wanderers
T Coyne** (sub)	Motherwell

Result	4–0
Scorers	J Aldridge; R Keane; J Sheridan; A Townsend

Match No. 306

15 February 1995 v ENGLAND at Dublin

A Kelly	Sheffield United
D Irwin	Manchester United
T Phelan	Manchester City
A Kernaghan	Manchester City
P McGrath	Aston Villa
S Staunton	Aston Villa

D Kelly	Wolverhampton Wanderers
N Quinn	Manchester City
A Townsend	Aston Villa
E McGoldrick	Arsenal

Result	1–0
The match was abandoned after 27 minutes due to crowd trouble.	
Scorer	D Kelly

FEATURED MATCH 21

NORTHERN IRELAND 0 REPUBLIC OF IRELAND 4

At Windsor Park, Belfast, 16 November 1994

Northern Ireland

Vic Kee; Gary Fleming; Nigel Worthington; Gerry Taggart; Sam Morrow; Michael O'Neill (Darren Patterson); Keith Gillespie (Kevin Wilson); Jim Magilton; Ian Dowie; Phil Gray; Michael Hughes.

Republic of Ireland

Alan Kelly; Gary Kelly; Denis Irwin; Phil Babb; Paul McGrath; Roy Keane (Jason McAteer); Andy Townsend; John Sheridan; Steve Staunton; Niall Quinn; John Aldridge (Tommy Coyne).

After winning their opening two matches of the Euro '96 Championship qualifiers, the Republic went in search of another three points in their match against Northern Ireland.

Early pressure from the home side was comfortably dealt with by the Republic's Phil Babb and Paul McGrath, and Niall Quinn came close to giving his side the lead when his glancing header went the wrong side of Kee's near post. However, only six minutes had been played when the Republic took the lead through John ALDRIDGE who latched on to a fine through ball from Keane to fire his side ahead. The Republic were dominating the game and five minutes later Roy KEANE extended their lead with a shot from the edge of the area that gave Kee no chance whatsoever.

A rare Northern Ireland attack midway through the first half saw Dowie head the ball down for

Hughes but he mis-hit his shot. The Republic had further chances to score but some good goal-keeping and a couple of last-ditch tackles saved the day. A fine ball from Steve Staunton put Townsend clear but he delayed his shot allowing Taggart to get back and block. In the thirty-eighth minute, the Republic went 3–0 up when John SHERIDAN fired the ball home from 20 yards with the Northern Ireland defence backing off and allowing him room to shoot. It could have been worse but Worthington cleared a Niall Quinn header off the line moments before the referee blew to end the first 45 minutes.

The Republic continued their tremendous form at the start of the second half and Sheridan nearly scored again before Andy TOWNSEND fired his side's fourth goal. Other chances went astray with Quinn and substitutes McAteer and Coyne the major culprits, but the side was playing such incredible football that these misses didn't matter.

Northern Ireland tried desperately to get back in the game but their only worthy efforts on goal came from long-range efforts by Jim Magilton and Michael Hughes – neither of which troubled Alan Kelly in the Republic goal. The Republic's back four can seldom have had such an easy ride as a long-range Sheridan shot finished off one of the side's greatest victories away from home.

Match No. 307

29 March 1995 v NORTHERN IRELAND at Dublin

A Kelly	Sheffield United
G Kelly	Leeds United
D Irwin	Manchester United
P McGrath	Aston Villa
P Babb	Liverpool
J Sheridan	Sheffield Wednesday
A Townsend	Aston Villa
R Keane	Manchester United
S Staunton	Aston Villa
N Quinn*	Manchester City
D Kelly**	Wolverhampton Wanderers
A Cascarino* (sub)	Marseille
J McAteer** (sub)	Bolton Wanderers

Result	1–1
Scorer	N Quinn

Match No. 308

26 April 1995 v PORTUGAL at Dublin

A Kelly	Sheffield United
G Kelly	Leeds United
D Irwin	Manchester United
P Babb	Liverpool
P McGrath	Aston Villa
R Houghton*	Crystal Palace
A Townsend	Aston Villa
J Sheridan	Sheffield Wednesday
S Staunton	Aston Villa
N Quinn	Manchester City
J Aldridge**	Tranmere Rovers
J Kenna* (sub)	Blackburn Rovers
A Cascarino** (sub)	Marseille

Result	1–0
Scorer	S Staunton

Match No. 309

3 June 1995 v LIECHTENSTEIN at Vaduz

A Kelly	Sheffield United
G Kelly	Leeds United
D Irwin	Manchester United
P Babb	Liverpool
P McGrath	Aston Villa
R Whelan	Southend United
J McAteer*	Bolton Wanderers
J Sheridan	Sheffield Wednesday
S Staunton	Aston Villa
N Quinn**	Manchester City
J Aldridge	Tranmere Rovers
J Kenna* (sub)	Blackburn Rovers
A Cascarino** (sub)	Marseille

Result	0–0

Match No. 310

11 June 1995 v AUSTRIA at Dublin

A Kelly	Sheffield United
G Kelly	Leeds United
D Irwin	Manchester United
P Babb	Liverpool
P McGrath	Aston Villa
R Whelan	Southend United
R Houghton	Crystal Palace
J Sheridan	Sheffield Wednesday
S Staunton*	Aston Villa
T Coyne	Motherwell
N Quinn**	Manchester City
J Kenna* (sub)	Blackburn Rovers
A Cascarino** (sub)	Marseille

Result	1–3
Scorer	R Houghton

Match No. 311

6 September 1995 v AUSTRIA at Vienna

A Kelly	Sheffield United
G Kelly	Leeds United
D Irwin	Manchester United
A Kernaghan	Manchester City
P McGrath	Aston Villa
R Houghton*	Crystal Palace
A Townsend	Aston Villa
R Keane	Manchester United
J Sheridan	Sheffield Wednesday
M Kennedy	Liverpool
N Quinn	Manchester City
A Cascarino* (sub)	Marseille

Result	1–3
Scorer	P McGrath

Match No. 312

11 October 1995 v LATVIA at Dublin

A Kelly	Sheffield United

G Kelly	Leeds United
T Phelan	Manchester City
P Babb	Liverpool
P McGrath	Aston Villa
J McAteer	Liverpool
A Townsend	Aston Villa
J Kenna	Blackburn Rovers
S Staunton	Aston Villa
N Quinn	Manchester City
J Aldridge*	Tranmere Rovers
D Kelly* (sub)	Sunderland

Result	2–1
Scorer	J Aldridge (2–1 penalty)

Match No. 313

15 November 1995 v PORTUGAL at Lisbon

A Kelly	Sheffield United
G Kelly	Leeds United
D Irwin	Manchester United
P Babb	Liverpool
P McGrath	Aston Villa
J McAteer	Liverpool
M Kennedy*	Liverpool
J Kenna	Blackburn Rovers
S Staunton**	Aston Villa
N Quinn	Manchester City
J Aldridge	Tranmere Rovers
A Cascarino* (sub)	Marseille
A Kernaghan** (sub)	Manchester City

Result	0–3

Match No. 314

13 December 1995 v HOLLAND at Liverpool

A Kelly	Sheffield United
G Kelly	Leeds United
D Irwin	Manchester United
P Babb	Liverpool
P McGrath	Aston Villa

J Kenna	Blackburn Rovers	A Cascarino	Marseille
A Townsend*	Aston Villa	J McAteer* (sub)	Liverpool
J Sheridan	Sheffield Wednesday	A Kernaghan** (sub)	Manchester City
T Phelan	Chelsea		
J Aldridge**	Tranmere Rovers	Result	0–2

Programme cover from the European Championship play-off match at Anfield. The Dutch won 2–0.

Match No. 315	
27 March 1996 v RUSSIA at Dublin	
S Given	Blackburn Rovers
T Phelan	Chelsea
S Staunton	Aston Villa
A Kernaghan	Manchester City
P McGrath	Aston Villa
R Keane	Manchester United
A Townsend*	Aston Villa
J McAteer	Liverpool
N Quinn**	Manchester City
J Aldridge***	Tranmere Rovers
M Kennedy	Liverpool
J Kenna* (sub)	Blackburn Rovers
T Coyne** (sub)	Motherwell
A Cascarino*** (sub)	Marseille
Result	0–2

Match No. 316	
24 April 1996 v CZECH REPUBLIC at Prague	
S Given	Blackburn Rovers
J Kenna	Blackburn Rovers
D Irwin*	Manchester United
K Cunningham	Wimbledon
P Babb**	Liverpool
P McGrath	Aston Villa
R Houghton	Crystal Palace
M Kennedy	Liverpool
A Townsend	Aston Villa
A Moore	Middlesbrough
N Quinn	Manchester City

C Fleming* (sub)	Middlesbrough
L Daish** (sub)	Coventry City
Result	0–2

Match No. 317	
29 May 1996 v PORTUGAL at Dublin	
S Given	Blackburn Rovers
C Fleming	Middlesbrough
T Phelan	Chelsea
A Kernaghan*	Manchester City
K Cunningham	Wimbledon
J Kenna	Blackburn Rovers
A Townsend	Aston Villa
A McLoughlin	Portsmouth
D Connolly**	Watford
A Cascarino***	Marseille
G Farrelly****	Aston Villa
G Breen* (sub)	Birmingham City
K O'Neill** (sub)	Norwich City
N Quinn*** (sub)	Manchester City
D Savage**** (sub)	Millwall
Result	0–1

Match No. 318	
2 June 1996 v CROATIA at Dublin	
S Given	Blackburn Rovers
G Breen*	Birmingham City
L Daish	Coventry City
J Kenna**	Blackburn Rovers
K Cunningham***	Wimbledon

Did you know?

Roy Keane was sent off against Russia in March 1996 in Mick McCarthy's first game as national team boss. McCarthy, Niall Quinn and Liam Daish were all shown the red card in a match against Mexico in June 1996.

A McLoughlin****	Portsmouth
M Kennedy	Liverpool
L O'Brien	Tranmere Rovers
T Phelan*****	Chelsea
N Quinn	Manchester City
K O'Neill******	Norwich City
A Cascarino* (sub)	Marseille
A Kernaghan** (sub)	Manchester City
C Fleming*** (sub)	Middlesbrough
D Savage**** (sub)	Millwall
I Harte***** (sub)	Leeds United
A Moore****** (sub)	Middlesbrough

| Result | 2–2 |
| Scorers | K O'Neill; N Quinn |

Match No. 319

4 June 1996 v HOLLAND at Rotterdam

S Given	Blackburn Rovers
G Breen	Birmingham City
A Kernaghan	Manchester City
J Kenna*	Blackburn Rovers
I Harte	Leeds United
L O'Brien**	Tranmere Rovers
A McLoughlin	Portsmouth
T Phelan	Chelsea
A Moore***	Middlesbrough
D Connolly****	Watford
A Cascarino*****	Marseille
C Fleming* (sub)	Middlesbrough
K Cunningham** (sub)	Wimbledon
M Kennedy*** (sub)	Liverpool
N Quinn**** (sub)	Manchester City
K O'Neill***** (sub)	Norwich City

| Result | 1–3 |
| Scorer | G Breen |

Match No. 320

9 June 1996 v UNITED STATES at Foxboro

S Given	Blackburn Rovers
G Breen	Birmingham City
A Kernaghan	Manchester City
K Cunningham	Wimbledon
J Kenna*	Blackburn Rovers
L O'Brien**	Tranmere Rovers
G Farrelly***	Aston Villa
A McLoughlin	Portsmouth
T Phelan	Chelsea
N Quinn****	Manchester City
D Connolly	Watford
C Fleming* (sub)	Middlesbrough
D Savage** (sub)	Millwall
M Kennedy*** (sub)	Liverpool
K O'Neill**** (sub)	Norwich City

| Result | 1–2 |
| Scorer D Connolly | |

Match No. 321

12 June 1996 v MEXICO at New Jersey

P Bonner	Glasgow Celtic
C Fleming	Middlesbrough
G Breen	Birmingham City
L Daish	Coventry City
I Harte	Leeds United
M Kennedy*	Liverpool
D Savage	Millwall
A McLoughlin	Portsmouth
A Moore	Middlesbrough
K O'Neill	Norwich City
D Connolly	Watford
T Phelan* (sub)	Chelsea

| Result | 2–2 |
| Scorers | D Connolly; Davino (own goal) |

Match No. 322

15 June 1996 v BOLIVIA at New Jersey

S Given*	Blackburn Rovers
K Cunningham	Wimbledon
A Kernaghan**	Manchester City
I Harte	Leeds United
C Fleming	Middlesbrough
D Savage	Millwall
L O'Brien***	Tranmere Rovers
G Farrelly****	Aston Villa
T Phelan	Chelsea
K O'Neill	Norwich City
A Moore	Middlesbrough
P Bonner* (sub)	Glasgow Celtic
G Breen** (sub)	Birmingham City
A McLoughlin*** (sub)	Portsmouth
M Kennedy**** (sub)	Liverpool

Result	3–0
Scorers	K O'Neill (2); I Harte

Match No. 323

31 August 1996 v LIECHTENSTEIN at Liechtenstein

S Given	Blackburn Rovers
D Irwin	Manchester United
I Harte	Leeds United
J Kenna	Blackburn Rovers
G Breen	Birmingham City
S Staunton	Aston Villa
A Townsend*	Aston Villa
R Houghton	Crystal Palace
N Quinn	Sunderland
A McLoughlin	Portsmouth
K O'Neill**	Norwich City
A Cascarino* (sub)	Marseille
A Moore** (sub)	Middlesbrough

Result	5–0
Scorers	A Townsend; K O'Neill; N Quinn (2); I Harte

Match No. 324

9 October 1996 v MACEDONIA at Dublin

A Kelly	Sheffield United
J Kenna	Blackburn Rovers
D Irwin	Manchester United
J McAteer	Liverpool
G Breen	Birmingham City
S Staunton	Aston Villa
A Townsend	Aston Villa
A McLoughlin*	Portsmouth
A Cascarino	Marseille
I Harte**	Leeds United
K O'Neill***	Norwich City
L O'Brien* (sub)	Tranmere Rovers
A Moore** (sub)	Middlesbrough
J Aldridge*** (sub)	Tranmere Rovers

Result	3–0
Scorers	J McAteer; A Cascarino (2)

Match No. 325

10 November 1996 v ICELAND at Dublin

A Kelly	Sheffield United
J Kenna*	Blackburn Rovers
D Irwin**	Manchester United
R Keane	Manchester United
G Breen	Birmingham City
P Babb	Liverpool
A McLoughlin	Portsmouth
J McAteer	Liverpool
D Kelly***	Sunderland
A Cascarino	Marseille
A Townsend	Aston Villa
K Cunningham* (sub)	Wimbledon
I Harte** (sub)	Leeds United
A Moore*** (sub)	Middlesbrough

Result	0–0

Match No. 326

11 February 1997 v WALES at Cardiff

K Branagan	Bolton Wanderers
J McAteer	Liverpool
T Phelan	Everton
K Cunningham	Wimbledon
P McGrath	Aston Villa
I Harte	Leeds United
A McLoughlin*	Portsmouth
R Keane**	Manchester United
J Goodman	Wimbledon
A Cascarino	Nancy
S Staunton	Aston Villa
G Kelly* (sub)	Leeds United
D Kelly** (sub)	Sunderland

Result	0–0

Match No. 327

2 April 1997 v MACEDONIA at Skopje

A Kelly	Sheffield United
J McAteer	Liverpool
D Irwin	Manchester United
A McLoughlin	Portsmouth
G Breen	Coventry City
S Staunton	Aston Villa
A Townsend	Aston Villa
R Keane	Manchester United
A Cascarino*	Nancy
J Goodman	Wimbledon
T Phelan***	Everton
K O'Neill* (sub) **	Norwich City
D Kelly** (sub)	Sunderland
I Harte*** (sub)	Leeds United

Result	2–3
Scorers	A McLoughlin; D Kelly

Match No. 328

30 April 1997 v ROMANIA at Bucharest

A Kelly	Sheffield United
G Kelly	Leeds United
D Irwin*	Manchester United
K Cunningham	Wimbledon
S Staunton	Aston Villa
I Harte**	Leeds United
A Townsend	Aston Villa
R Keane	Manchester United
D Connolly***	Watford
R Houghton	Crystal Palace
M Kennedy	Liverpool
J Kenna* (sub)	Blackburn Rovers
A Cascarino** (sub)	Nancy
J Goodman*** (sub)	Wimbledon

Result	0–1

Match No. 329

21 May 1997 v LIECHTENSTEIN at Dublin

S Given	Blackburn Rovers
J Kenna	Blackburn Rovers
K Cunningham	Wimbledon
R Keane	Manchester United
I Harte	Leeds United
S Staunton	Aston Villa
R Houghton*	Crystal Palace
G Kelly	Leeds United
D Connolly**	Watford
A Townsend	Aston Villa
M Kennedy***	Liverpool
A Cascarino* (sub)	Nancy
J Goodman** (sub)	Wimbledon
C Fleming*** (sub)	Middlesbrough

Result	5–0
Scorers	D Connolly (3); A Cascarino (2)

MATCHES

Match No. 330

20 August 1997 v LITHUANIA at Dublin

S Given	Newcastle United
J Kenna	Blackburn Rovers
S Staunton	Aston Villa
K Cunningham	Wimbledon
I Harte	Leeds United
R Keane	Manchester United
A Townsend*	Middlesbrough
R Houghton	Reading
N Quinn**	Sunderland
D Connolly	Feyenoord
M Kennedy***	Liverpool
D Kelly* (sub)	Tranmere Rovers
A Cascarino** (sub)	Nancy
A McLoughlin*** (sub)	Portsmouth

Result	0–0

Match No. 331

6 September 1997 v ICELAND at Reykjavik

S Given	Newcastle United
J Kenna*	Blackburn Rovers
S Staunton	Aston Villa
K Cunningham	Wimbledon
I Harte	Leeds United
G Kelly	Leeds United
A McLoughlin	Portsmouth
R Keane	Manchester United
D Connolly	Feyenoord
A Townsend**	Middlesbrough
K Kilbane***	West Bromwich Albion
J McAteer* (sub)	Liverpool
A Cascarino** (sub)	Nancy
M Kennedy*** (sub)	Liverpool

Result	4–2
Scorers	D Connolly; R Keane (2); Finnbogason (own goal)

Match No. 332

10 September 1997 v LITHUANIA at Vilnius

S Given	Newcastle United
G Kelly	Leeds United
D Irwin	Manchester United
J McAteer*	Liverpool
K Cunningham	Wimbledon
I Harte	Leeds United
A McLoughlin	Portsmouth
R Keane	Manchester United
D Connolly**	Feyenoord
A Cascarino	Nancy
S Staunton	Aston Villa
P Babb* (sub)	Liverpool
G Breen** (sub)	Coventry City

Result	2–1
Scorer	A Cascarino

Match No. 333

11 October 1997 v ROMANIA at Dublin

A Kelly	Sheffield United
J Kenna	Blackburn Rovers
T Phelan*	Everton
J McAteer	Liverpool
G Breen	Coventry City
P Babb	Liverpool
A McLoughlin**	Portsmouth
R Houghton	Reading
A Cascarino***	Nancy
L Carsley	Derby County
M Kennedy	Liverpool
C Fleming* (sub)	Middlesbrough
D Kelly** (sub)	Feyenoord
M Evans*** (sub)	Southampton

Result	1–1
Scorer	A Cascarino

Match No. 334

29 October 1997 v BELGIUM at Dublin

S Given	Newcastle United
G Kelly	Leeds United
D Irwin	Manchester United
I Harte	Leeds United
K Cunningham	Wimbledon
S Staunton	Aston Villa
M Kennedy*	Liverpool
R Houghton	Reading
D Connolly**	Feyenoord
A Cascarino	Nancy
A Townsend***	Middlesbrough
J Kenna* (sub)	Blackburn Rovers
T Coyne** (sub)	Motherwell
L Carsley*** (sub)	Derby County

Result	1–1
Scorer	D Irwin

Match No. 335

16 November 1997 v BELGIUM at Brussels

S Given	Newcastle United
J Kenna	Blackburn Rovers
S Staunton	Aston Villa
G Kelly	Leeds United
K Cunningham	Wimbledon
I Harte	Leeds United
L Carsley	Derby County
A McLoughlin*	Portsmouth
A Cascarino	Nancy
A Townsend**	Middlesbrough
M Kennedy***	Liverpool
R Houghton* (sub)	Reading
D Kelly** (sub)	Tranmere Rovers
D Connolly*** (sub)	Feyenoord

Result	1–2
Scorer	R Houghton

Match No. 336

25 March 1998 v CZECH REPUBLIC at Olomouc

S Given	Newcastle United
A Maybury*	Leeds United
J Kenna	Blackburn Rovers
L Carsley**	Derby County
K Cunningham	Wimbledon
G Breen	Coventry City
M Kinsella	Charlton Athletic
G Farrelly***	Everton
D Connolly****	Feyenoord
G Kelly	Leeds United
D Duff*****	Blackburn Rovers
RD Keane* (sub)	Wolverhampton Wanderers
G Kavanagh** (sub)	Stoke City
A McLoughlin*** (sub)	Portsmouth
K Kilbane**** (sub)	West Bromwich Albion
R Delap***** (sub)	Derby County

Result	1–2
Scorer	G Breen

Match No. 337

22 April 1998 v ARGENTINA at Dublin

S Given*	Newcastle United
J Kenna**	Blackburn Rovers
S Staunton	Aston Villa
G Kelly	Liverpool
G Breen	Coventry City
I Harte***	Leeds United
L Carsley	Derby County
M Kinsella	Charlton Athletic
N Quinn	Sunderland
RD Keane	Wolverhampton Wanderers
K Kilbane****	West Bromwich Albion
A Kelly* (sub)	Sheffield United
R Delap** (sub)	Derby County
P Babb*** (sub)	Liverpool
D Irwin**** (sub)	Manchester United

Result	0–2

MATCHES

Match No. 338

23 May 1998 v MEXICO at Dublin

S Given	Newcastle United
C Fleming	Middlesbrough
I Harte	Leeds United
P Babb	Liverpool
G Breen	Coventry City
G Kelly	Leeds United
L Carsley	Derby County
G Farrelly	Everton
D Connolly*	Feyenoord
RD Keane	Wolverhampton Wanderers
D Duff**	Blackburn Rovers
R Delap* (sub)	Derby County
M Kennedy** (sub)	Wimbledon

Result	0–0

Match No. 339

5 September 1998 v CROATIA at Dublin

S Given	Newcastle United
D Irwin	Manchester United
S Staunton	Liverpool
J McAteer	Liverpool
K Cunningham	Wimbledon
P Babb	Liverpool
M Kinsella	Charlton Athletic
RM Keane	Manchester United
K O'Neill*	Norwich City
RD Keane**	Wolverhampton Wanderers
D Duff***	Blackburn Rovers
A Cascarino* (sub)	Nancy
L Carsley** (sub)	Derby County
J Kenna*** (sub)	Blackburn Rovers

Result	2–0
Scorers	D Irwin (penalty); RM Keane

Match No. 340

14 October v MALTA at Dublin

S Given	Newcastle United
J Kenna	Blackburn Rovers
S Staunton	Liverpool
J McAteer*	Liverpool
K Cunningham	Wimbledon
G Breen	Coventry City
M Kinsella	Charlton Athletic
RM Keane	Manchester United
N Quinn**	Sunderland
RD Keane***	Wolverhampton Wanderers
D Duff	Blackburn Rovers
L Carsley* (sub)	Derby County
A Cascarino** (sub)	Nancy
M Kennedy*** (sub)	Wimbledon

Result	5–0
Scorers	RD Keane (2); RM Keane; N Quinn; G Breen

Match No. 341

18 November 1998 v YUGOSLAVIA at Belgrade

S Given	Newcastle United
K Cunningham	Wimbledon
D Irwin	Manchester United
A McLoughlin*	Portsmouth
G Breen	Coventry City
S Staunton	Liverpool
M Kinsella	Charlton Athletic
RM Keane	Manchester United
N Quinn**	Sunderland
J McAteer***	Liverpool
D Duff	Blackburn Rovers
D Connolly* (sub)	Wolverhampton Wanderers
A Cascarino** (sub)	Nancy
K O'Neill*** (sub)	Norwich City

Result	0–1

Match No. 342

10 February 1999 v PARAGUAY at Dublin

S Given*	Newcastle United
D Irwin	Manchester United
I Harte**	Leeds United
J McAteer***	Blackburn Rovers
K Cunningham	Wimbledon
G Breen	Coventry City
M Kinsella****	Charlton Athletic
RM Keane	Nottingham Forest
N Quinn*****	Sunderland
RD Keane******	Wolverhampton Wanderers
D Duff	Blackburn Rovers
A Kelly* (sub)	Sheffield United
P Babb** (sub)	Liverpool
A McLoughlin*** (sub)	Portsmouth
L Carsley**** (sub)	Derby County
A Cascarino*****(sub)	Nancy
D Connolly******(sub)	Wolverhampton Wanderers

Result	2–0
Scorers	D Irwin (penalty); D Connolly

Match No. 343

28 April 1999 v SWEDEN at Dublin

S Given	Newcastle United
S Carr	Tottenham Hotspur
S Staunton	Liverpool
J McAteer*	Blackburn Rovers
K Cunningham	Wimbledon
G Breen**	Coventry City
M Kinsella***	Charlton Athletic
A McLoughlin	Portsmouth
N Quinn****	Sunderland
D Connolly*****	Wolverhampton Wanderers
M Kennedy******	Wimbledon
K Kilbane* (sub)	West Bromwich Albion
P Babb** (sub)	Liverpool
G Kavanagh*** (sub)	Stoke City

RD Keane**** (sub)	Wolverhampton Wanderers
A Cascarino*****(sub)	Nancy
D Duff****** (sub)	Blackburn Rovers

Result	2–0
Scorers	G Kavanagh; M Kennedy

Match No. 344

29 May 1999 v NORTHERN IRELAND at Dublin

S Given	Newcastle United
S Carr	Tottenham Hotspur
A Maybury	Leeds United
L Carsley*	Blackburn Rovers
K Cunningham	Wimbledon
P Babb	Liverpool
M Kinsella**	Charlton Athletic
RD Keane***	Wolverhampton Wanderers
N Quinn****	Sunderland
D Duff*****	Blackburn Rovers
M Kennedy	Wimbledon
A McLoughlin* (sub)	Portsmouth
G Kavanagh** (sub)	Stoke City
D Connolly*** (sub)	Wolverhampton Wanderers
A Cascarino**** (sub)	Nancy
K O'Neill ***** (sub)	Middlesbrough

Result	0–1

Match No. 345

9 June 1999 v MACEDONIA at Dublin

A Kelly	Sheffield United
S Carr	Tottenham Hotspur
D Irwin	Manchester United
D Duff*	Blackburn Rovers
K Cunningham	Wimbledon
G Breen	Coventry City
M Kennedy	Wimbledon
M Kinsella	Charlton Athletic
N Quinn**	Sunderland
RD Keane***	Wolverhampton Wanderers

L Carsley	Blackburn Rovers
K Kilbane* (sub)	West Bromwich Albion
D Connolly** (sub)	Wolverhampton Wanderers
A Cascarino*** (sub)	Nancy

Result	1–0
Scorer	N Quinn

Match No. 346

1 September 1999 v YUGOSLAVIA at Dublin

A Kelly	Blackburn Rovers
D Irwin*	Manchester United
S Staunton	Liverpool
G Breen	Coventry City
K Cunningham	Wimbledon
RM Keane**	Manchester United
M Kinsella	Charlton Athletic
RD Keane	Coventry City
N Quinn***	Sunderland
K Kilbane	West Bromwich Albion
M Kennedy	Manchester City
S Carr* (sub)	Tottenham Hotspur
L Carsley** (sub)	Blackburn Rovers
A Cascarino*** (sub)	Nancy

Result	2–1
Scorers	RD Keane; M Kennedy

Match No. 347

4 September 1999 v CROATIA at Zagreb

A Kelly	Blackburn Rovers
S Carr	Tottenham Hotspur
G Kelly*	Leeds United
G Breen	Coventry City
K Cunningham	Wimbledon
S Staunton	Liverpool
L Carsley	Blackburn Rovers
M Kinsella	Charlton Athletic
A Cascarino**	Nancy
A McLoughlin	Portsmouth

D Duff***	Blackburn Rovers
I Harte* (sub)	Leeds United
N Quinn** (sub)	Sunderland
K Kilbane*** (sub)	West Bromwich Albion

Result	0–1

Match No. 348

8 September 1999 v MALTA at Valletta

A Kelly	Blackburn Rovers
S Carr	Tottenham Hotspur
S Staunton	Liverpool
L Carsley	Blackburn Rovers
K Cunningham	Wimbledon
G Breen*	Coventry City
M Kennedy**	Manchester City
RD Keane	Coventry City
N Quinn	Sunderland
K Kilbane***	West Bromwich Albion
M Kinsella	Charlton Athletic
I Harte* (sub)	Leeds United
A McLoughlin** (sub)	Portsmouth
D Duff*** (sub)	Blackburn Rovers

Result	3–2
Scorers	RD Keane; G Breen; S Staunton

Match No. 349

9 October 1999 v MACEDONIA at Skopje

A Kelly	Blackburn Rovers
D Irwin	Manchester United
S Staunton	Liverpool
A McLoughlin	Portsmouth
K Cunningham	Wimbledon
G Breen	Coventry City
G Kelly	Leeds United
M Kinsella	Charlton Athletic
RD Keane*	Coventry City
N Quinn**	Sunderland

M Kennedy***	Manchester City
K O'Neill* (sub)	Middlesbrough
A Cascarino** (sub)	Nancy
M Holland*** (sub)	Ipswich Town

| Result | 1–1 |
| Scorer | N Quinn |

Match No. 350
13 November 1999 v TURKEY at Dublin

A Kelly*	Blackburn Rovers
S Carr	Tottenham Hotspur
D Irwin	Manchester United
G Breen	Coventry City
K Cunningham	Wimbledon
L Carsley	Blackburn Rovers
R Delap**	Derby County
RM Keane	Manchester United
RD Keane	Coventry City
A Cascarino***	Nancy
K Kilbane	West Bromwich Albion
D Kiely* (sub)	Charlton Athletic
D Duff** (sub)	Blackburn Rovers
D Connolly*** (sub)	Excelsior

| Result | 1–1 |
| Scorer | RD Keane |

Match No. 351
17 November 1999 v TURKEY at Bursa

D Kiely	Charlton Athletic
S Carr*	Tottenham Hotspur
D Irwin	Manchester United
R Delap	Derby County
K Cunningham	Wimbledon
G Breen	Coventry City
M Kinsella	Charlton Athletic
RM Keane	Manchester United
N Quinn	Sunderland
D Connolly***	Excelsior

K Kilbane	West Bromwich Albion
J Kenna* (sub)**	Blackburn Rovers
A Cascarino** (sub)	Nancy
D Duff*** (sub)	Blackburn Rovers

| Result | 0–0 |

Match No. 352
23 February 2000 v CZECH REPUBLIC at Dublin

A Kelly	Blackburn Rovers
G Kelly	Leeds United
I Harte	Leeds United
K Kilbane*	Sunderland
K Cunningham	Wimbledon
P Butler**	Sunderland
M Kennedy***	Manchester City
M Kinsella	Charlton Athletic
N Quinn	Sunderland
RD Keane****	Coventry City
RM Keane	Manchester United
S Staunton* (sub)	Liverpool
P Babb** (sub)	Liverpool
J McAteer*** (sub)	Blackburn Rovers
D Connolly**** (sub)	Excelsior

| Result | 3–2 |
| Scorers | Rada (own goal); I Harte; RD Keane |

Match No. 353
26 April 2000 v GREECE at Dublin

S Given*	Newcastle United
K Cunningham	Wimbledon
G Breen	Coventry City
R Dunne	Everton
S Staunton	Liverpool
B Quinn**	Coventry City
S Finnan***	Fulham
M KInsella	Charlton Athletic
RD Keane	Coventry City

MATCHES

K Kilbane	Sunderland	
D Connolly****	Excelsior	
D Kiely	* (sub)	Charlton Athletic
R Delap** (sub)	Derby County	
G Doherty*** (sub)	Luton Town	
A Mahon**** (sub)	Tranmere Rovers	

Result	0–1

Match No. 354
30 May 2000 v SCOTLAND at Dublin

A Kelly	Blackburn Rovers
S Carr	Tottenham Hotspur
G Breen*	Coventry City
P Babb	Liverpool
K Kilbane	Sunderland
J McAteer	Blackburn Rovers
S Finnan	Fulham
S McPhail**	Leeds United
M Kennedy***	Manchester City
N Quinn****	Sunderland
RD Keane	Coventry City
D Foley* (sub)	Watford
T Phelan** (sub)	Fulham
D Duff*** (sub)	Blackburn Rovers
R Dunne**** (sub)	Everton

Result	1–2
Scorer	M Kennedy

Match No. 355
4 June 2000 v MEXICO at Chicago

D Kiely	Charlton Athletic
S Carr	Tottenham Hotspur
G Breen	Coventry City
R Dunne*	Everton
T Phelan	Fulham
J McAteer	Blackburn Rovers
B Quinn**	Coventry City
M Holland	Ipswich Town

M Kennedy	Manchester City
N Quinn	Sunderland
RD Keane***	Coventry City
P Babb* (sub)	Liverpool
K Kilbane** (sub)	Sunderland
D Foley*** (sub)	Watford

Result	2–2
Scorers	R Dunne; D Foley

Match No. 356
6 June 2000 v UNITED STATES at Foxboro

A Kelly	Blackburn Rovers
S Carr	Tottenham Hotspur
G Breen	Coventry City
P Babb	Liverpool
T Phelan	Fulham
G Farrelly*	Bolton Wanderers
M Holland	Ipswich Town
S McPhail**	Leeds United
K Kilbane	Sunderland
G Doherty***	Tottenham Hotspur
D Foley****	Watford
M Kennedy* (sub)	Manchester City
J McAteer** (sub)	Blackburn Rovers
N Quinn*** (sub)	Sunderland
B Quinn**** (sub)	Coventry City

Result	1–1
Scorer	D Foley

Match No. 357
11 June 2000 v SOUTH AFRICA at East Rutherford

S Given	Newcastle United
S Carr	Tottenham Hotspur
P Babb	Liverpool
G Breen	Coventry City
T Phelan	Fulham
J McAteer*	Blackburn Rovers

M Holland	Ipswich Town
A Mahon**	Tranmere Rovers
S McPhail***	Leeds United
D Foley****	Watford
N Quinn*****	Sunderland
M Kennedy* (sub)	Manchester City
K Kilbane** (sub)	Sunderland
B Quinn*** (sub)	Coventry City
RD Keane**** (sub)	Coventry City
G Doherty***** (sub)	Tottenham Hotspur

Result	2–1
Scorers	S McPhail; N Quinn

Match No. 358

2 September 2000 v HOLLAND at Amsterdam

A Kelly	Blackburn Rovers
S Carr	Tottenham Hotspur
I Harte	Leeds United
R Dunne	Everton
G Breen	Coventry City
RM Keane	Manchester United
J McAteer*	Blackburn Rovers
M Kinsella	Charlton Athletic
N Quinn**	Sunderland
RD Keane	Inter Milan
K Kilbane***	Sunderland
G Kelly* (sub)	Leeds United
D Connolly** (sub)	Excelsior
S Staunton*** (sub)	Liverpool

Result	2–2
Scorers	RD Keane; J McAteer

Match No. 359

7 October 2000 v PORTUGAL at Lisbon

A Kelly	Blackburn Rovers
S Carr	Tottenham Hotspur
I Harte	Leeds United
R Dunne	Everton

G Breen	Coventry City
RM Keane	Manchester United
J McAteer*	Blackburn Rovers
M Kinsella	Charlton Athletic
N Quinn**	Sunderland
RD Keane***	Inter Milan
K Kilbane	Sunderland
D Duff* (sub)	Blackburn Rovers
M Holland** (sub)	Ipswich Town
S Finnan*** (sub)	Fulham

Result	1–1
Scorer	M Holland

Match No. 360

11 October 2000 v ESTONIA at Dublin

A Kelly	Blackburn Rovers
S Carr	Tottenham Hotspur
I Harte	Leeds United
R Dunne	Everton
G Breen	Coventry City
RM Keane	Manchester United
J McAteer*	Blackburn Rovers
M Kinsella	Charlton Athletic
N Quinn	Sunderland
RD Keane**	Inter Milan
K Kilbane***	Sunderland
D Duff* (sub)	Blackburn Rovers
D Foley** (sub)	Watford
S Finnan*** (sub)	Fulham

Result	2–0
Scorers	M Kinsella; R Dunne

Match No. 361

15 November 2000 v FINLAND at Dublin

S Given	Newcastle United
G Kelly*	Leeds United
I Harte**	Leeds United
S Finnan	Fulham

G Breen	Coventry City
R Dunne	Manchester City
M Kinsella	Charlton Athletic
M Holland	Ipswich Town
RD Keane***	Inter Milan
D Foley****	Watford
K Kilbane	Sunderland
J McAteer* (sub)	Blackburn Rovers
S Staunton** (sub)	Liverpool
D Connolly*** (sub)	Excelsior
L Carsley**** (sub)	Blackburn Rovers

Result	3–0
Scorers	S Finnan; K Kilbane; S Staunton

24 March 2001 v CYPRUS at Nicosia

S Given	Newcastle United
G Kelly	Leeds United
I Harte	Leeds United
RM Keane	Manchester United
G Breen	Coventry City
K Cunningham	Wimbledon
J McAteer*	Blackburn Rovers
M Kinsella	Charlton Athletic
D Connolly	Excelsior
RD Keane**	Inter Milan
K Kilbane***	Sunderland
M Holland* (sub)	Ipswich Town
G Doherty** (sub)	Tottenham Hotspur
D Duff*** (sub)	Blackburn Rovers

Result	4–0
Scorers	RM Keane (2); I Harte (penalty) G Kelly

Match No. 363

28 March 2001 v ANDORRA at Barcelona

S Given	Newcastle United
G Kelly	Leeds United
I Harte	Leeds United
RM Keane	Manchester United
G Breen	Coventry City
K Cunningham	Wimbledon
M Holland	Ipswich Town
K Kilbane*	Sunderland
D Connolly**	Excelsior
RD Keane	Inter Milan
D Duff	Blackburn Rovers
S Finnan* (sub)	Fulham
G Doherty** (sub)	Tottenham Hotspur

Result	3–0
Scorers	I Harte (penalty); K Kilbane; M Holland

Match No. 364

25 April 2001 v ANDORRA at Dublin

S Given	Newcastle United
G Kelly	Leeds United
I Harte	Leeds United
G Breen*	Coventry City
R Dunne	Manchester City
M Holland	Ipswich Town
M Kennedy**	Manchester City
M Kinsella***	Charlton Athletic
D Connolly	Feyenoord
G Doherty	Tottenham Hotspur
K Kilbane	Sunderland
S Staunton* (sub)	Aston Villa
S Carr** (sub)	Tottenham Hotspur
S Finnan*** (sub)	Fulham

Result	3–1
Scorers	K Kilbane; M Kinsella; G Breen

Match No. 365

2 June 2001 v PORTUGAL at Dublin

S Given	Newcastle United
S Carr	Tottenham Hotspur
I Harte	Leeds United
G Kelly	Leeds United
R Dunne	Manchester City
S Staunton	Aston Villa
M Kinsella*	Charlton Athletic
RM Keane	Manchester United
N Quinn**	Sunderland
RD Keane***	Inter Milan
K Kilbane	Sunderland
G Doherty* (sub)	Tottenham Hotspur
M Holland** (sub)	Ipswich Town
D Duff*** (sub)	Blackburn Rovers

Result	1–1
Scorers	RM Keane

Match No. 366

6 June 2001 v ESTONIA at Tallinn

S Given	Newcastle United
S Carr	Tottenham Hotspur
I Harte	Leeds United
G Kelly	Leeds United
R Dunne	Manchester City
S Staunton	Aston Villa
M Kinsella	Charlton Athletic
M Holland	Ipswich Town
N Quinn*	Sunderland
K Kilbane	Sunderland
D Duff**	Blackburn Rovers
G Doherty* (sub)	Tottenham Hotspur
A O'Brien** (sub)	Newcastle United

Result 2–0	
Scorers	R Dunne; M Holland

Match No. 367

15 August 2001 v CROATIA at Dublin

S Given*	Newcastle United
G Kelly**	Leeds United
I Harte***	Leeds United
L Carsley	Coventry City
R Dunne****	Manchester City
S Staunton	Aston Villa
S Reid*****	Millwall
RM Keane******	Manchester United
RD Keane*******	Leeds United
D Duff********	Blackburn Rovers
M Kennedy*********	Wolverhampton Wanderers
A Kelly* (sub)	Blackburn Rovers
J O'Shea** (sub)	Manchester United
S McPhail*** (sub)	Leeds United
A O'Brien**** (sub)	Newcastle United
S Finnan*****(sub)	Fulham
J McAteer******(sub)	Blackburn Rovers
C Morrison*******(sub)	Crystal Palace
D Connolly********(sub)	Wimbledon
K Kilbane*********(sub)	Sunderland

Result	2–2
Scorers	D Duff; C Morrison

Match No. 368

1 September 2001 v HOLLAND at Dublin

S Given	Newcastle United
G Kelly	Leeds United
I Harte	Leeds United
R Dunne	Manchester City
S Staunton	Aston Villa
M Holland	Ipswich Town
J McAteer*	Blackburn Rovers
RM Keane	Manchester United
RD Keane**	Leeds United
K Kilbane	Sunderland
D Duff***	Blackburn Rovers
A O'Brien* (sub)	Newcastle United

| S Finnan** (sub) | Fulham |
| N Quinn*** (sub) | Sunderland |

| Result | 1–0 |
| Scorer | J McAteer |

Match No. 369
6 October 2001 v CYPRUS at Dublin

S Given	Newcastle United
S Finnan	Fulham
I Harte	Leeds United
G Breen	Coventry City
S Staunton	Aston Villa
M Holland	Ipswich Town
M Kennedy*	Wolverhampton Wanderers
RM Keane	Manchester United
N Quinn**	Sunderland
D Connolly	Wimbledon
K Kilbane***	Sunderland
L Carsley* (sub)	Coventry City
C Morrison** (sub)	Crystal Palace
S McPhail*** (sub)	Leeds United

| Result | 4–0 |
| Scorers | I Harte; N Quinn; D Connolly; RM Keane |

FEATURED MATCH 22

REPUBLIC OF IRELAND 1 HOLLAND 0
At Lansdowne Road, Dublin, 1 September 2001

Republic of Ireland
Shay Given; Gary Kelly; Ian Harte; Richard Dunne; Steve Staunton; Matt Holland; Jason McAteer (Andy O'Brien); Roy Keane; Robbie Keane (Steve Finnan); Kevin Kilbane; Damien Duff (Niall Quinn).

Holland
Van der Sar; Melchiot; Numan (Van Hooijdonk); Cocu; Stam; Hofland; Zenden (Hasselbaink); Van Bommel; Kluivert; Van Nistelrooy; Overmars (Van Bronckhorst).

There was a stormy opening to this vital World Cup qualifier against Holland when, after just thirty seconds, Roy Keane was warned for a hefty challenge on Cocu. Just two minutes had been played when Patrick Kluivert shot wide from a great position after dispossessing Gary Kelly. The Dutch continued to have the better of the early play and after five minutes, Shay Given got down well to his right to save from Van Bommel.

Robbie Keane had Ireland's first shot on goal after thirteen minutes but it was straight at Van der Sar who had no trouble in saving. At the other end, Zenden wasted a good chance by firing his shot inches wide and minutes later, was booked for a foul on Kevin Kilbane. Rangers defender Arthur Numan was stretchered off after sustaining a facial cut following a collision with Jason McAteer but he was soon back in the thick of the action. Gary Kelly was also shown a yellow card and from the resulting free-kick, Van Nistelrooy just failed to connect with Overmars' cross at the far post.

Following the goalless first half, Ian Harte tried his luck from a distance but he failed to catch Van der Sar unawares. Shay Given then turned a Van Nistelrooy effort round the post and clung on to a powerful Marc Overmars shot after Richard Dunne had given the ball away. The Dutch winger then cut inside Kelly and forced Given into making yet another save. Moments later, the Leeds United full-back was sent off after picking up his second yellow card for a needless foul on Overmars near the halfway line. The Republic make an immediate substitution with Finnan replacing Robbie Keane.

Just after the hour mark, a dreadful mix-up between Given and Steve Staunton nearly gifted Holland the opening goal. Van Nistelrooy collided with the Irish keeper but the German referee turned down the Dutch penalty appeals. Holland then replaced Numan with another striker in Pierre van Hooijdonk but two minutes after the substitution, Ireland took the lead. An unmarked Jason McATEER shot the ten–man Republic into the lead after Steve Finnan's right-wing cross eluded the Dutch defence.

The Dutch brought on Giovanni van Bronckhorst and piled on the pressure in search of the equaliser with Kluivert shooting into the side-netting from close range during a goalmouth scramble. The Dutch striker then shot narrowly over with his left foot, whilst in the final minute of added time, Van Nistelrooy headed the ball inches wide with Given rooted to the spot.

Action from the featured match against Holland. Roy Keane is under pressure from Mark Van Bommel and Mario Melchiot in a game Ireland won 1–0.

Match No. 370	
10 November 2001 v IRAN at Dublin	
S Given	Newcastle United
S Finnan	Fulham
I Harte	Leeds United
G Breen	Coventry City
S Staunton*	Aston Villa
M Holland	Ipswich Town
J McAteer**	Sunderland
RM Keane	Manchester United
RD Keane	Leeds United
N Quinn	Sunderland
K Kilbane	Sunderland
K Cunningham* (sub) Wimbledon	
G Kelly** (sub)	Leeds United
Result	2–0
Scorers	I Harte (penalty); RD Keane

Match No. 371	
15 November 2001 v IRAN at Tehran	
S Given	Newcastle United
S Finnan	Fulham
I Harte	Leeds United
M Holland	Ipswich Town
S Staunton	Aston Villa
G Breen	Coventry City
J McAteer	Sunderland
M Kinsella	Charlton Athletic
RD Keane*	Leeds United
D Connolly	Wimbledon
K Kilbane**	Sunderland
C Morrison (sub)	Crystal Palace
G Kelly** (sub)	Leeds United
Result	0–1

MATCHES

Match No. 372

13 February 2002 v RUSSIA at Dublin

S Given*	Newcastle United
S Finnan**	Fulham
I Harte****	Leeds United
RM Keane*****	Manchester United
A O'Brien******	Newcastle United
K Cunningham*******	Wimbledon
S Reid********	Millwall
C Healy*********	Glasgow Celtic
RD Keane**********	Leeds United
D Duff***********	Blackburn Rovers
K Kilbane************	Sunderland
D Kiely* (sub)	Charlton Athletic
J McAteer** (sub)***	Sunderland
N Quinn*** (sub)	Sunderland
S Staunton**** (sub)	Aston Villa
M Holland***** (sub)	Ipswich Town
R Dunne******(sub)	Manchester City
G Breen*******(sub)	Coventry City
G Kelly********(sub)	Leeds United
L Carsley*********(sub)	Coventry City
R Sadlier**********(sub)	Millwall
C Morrison***********(sub)	Crystal Palace
M Kennedy************(sub)	Wolverhampton Wanderers

Result	2–0
Scorers	S Reid; RD Keane

Match No. 373

27 March 2002 v DENMARK at Dublin

D Kiely*	Charlton Athletic
G Kelly	Leeds United
I Harte	Leeds United
M Holland	Ipswich Town
K Cunningham	Wimbledon
S Staunton	Aston Villa
J McAteer**	Sunderland
M Kinsella***	Charlton Athletic

RD Keane****	Leeds United
C Morrison	Crystal Palace
D Duff*****	Blackburn Rovers
N Colgan* (sub)	Hibernian
S Reid** (sub)	Millwall
C Healy*** (sub)	Glasgow Celtic
D Connolly**** (sub)	Wimbledon
R Dunne***** (sub)	Manchester City

Result	3–0
Scorers	I Harte; RD Keane; C Morrison

Match No. 374

17 April 2002 v UNITED STATES at Dublin

S Given	Newcastle United
S Finnan*	Fulham
I Harte**	Leeds United
M Kinsella***	Charlton Athletic
A O'Brien****	Newcastle United
G Breen*****	Coventry City
R Delap	Southampton
C Healy	Glasgow Celtic
RD Keane******	Leeds United
D Duff*******	Blackburn Rovers
K Kilbane********	Sunderland
G Kelly* (sub)	Leeds United
S Staunton** (sub)	Aston Villa
M Holland*** (sub)	Ipswich Town
K Cunningham****(sub)	Wimbledon
G Doherty***** (sub)	Tottenham Hotspur
C Morrison******(sub)	Crystal Palace
D Connolly*******(sub)	Wimbledon
S Reid********(sub)	Millwall

Result 2–1	
Scorers	M Kinsella; G Doherty

Match No. 375

16 May 2002 v NIGERIA at Dublin

S Given	Newcastle United
S Finnan	Fulham
I Harte	Leeds United
M Holland	Ipswich Town
K Cunningham	Wimbledon
S Staunton	Aston Villa
J McAteer*	Sunderland
RM Keane**	Manchester United
RD Keane***	Leeds United
D Duff****	Blackburn Rovers
K Kilbane*****	Sunderland
S Reid* (sub)	Millwall
M Kinsella** (sub)	Charlton Athletic
C Morrison*** (sub)	Crystal Palace
D Connolly**** (sub)	Wimbledon
G Kelly***** (sub)	Leeds United

Result	1–2
Scorer	S Reid

Match No. 376

1 June 2002 v CAMEROON at Niigata

S Given	Newcastle United
G Kelly	Leeds United
I Harte*	Leeds United
G Breen	Coventry City
S Staunton	Aston Villa
M Kinsella	Charlton Athletic
J McAteer**	Sunderland
M Holland	Ipswich Town
RD Keane	Leeds United
D Duff	Blackburn Rovers
K Kilbane	Sunderland
S Reid* (sub)	Millwall
S Finnan** (sub)	Fulham

Result	1–1
Scorer	M Holland

Match No. 377

5 June 2002 v GERMANY at Ibaraki

S Given	Newcastle United
G Kelly*	Leeds United
I Harte**	Leeds United
G Breen	Coventry City
S Staunton***	Aston Villa
M Kinsella	Charlton Athletic
S Finnan	Fulham
M Holland	Ipswich Town
RD Keane	Leeds United
K Kilbane	Sunderland
D Duff	Blackburn Rovers
N Quinn* (sub)	Sunderland
S Reid** (sub)	Millwall
K Cunningham*** (sub)	Wimbledon

Result	1–1
Scorer	RD Keane

Match No. 378

11 June 2002 v SAUDI ARABIA at Yokohama

S Given	Newcastle United
S Finnan	Fulham
I Harte*	Leeds United
M Kinsella**	Charlton Athletic
G Breen	Coventry City
S Staunton	Aston Villa
G Kelly***	Leeds United
M Holland	Ipswich Town
RD Keane	Leeds United
K Kilbane	Sunderland
D Duff	Blackburn Rovers
N Quinn* (sub)	Sunderland
L Carsley** (sub)	Everton
J McAteer*** (sub)	Sunderland

Result	3–0
Scorers	RD Keane; G Breen; D Duff

MATCHES

Match No. 379	
16 June 2002 v SPAIN at Suwon	
S Given	Newcastle United
S Finnan	Fulham
I Harte*	Leeds United
M Kinsella	Charlton Athletic
G Breen	Coventry City
S Staunton**	Aston Villa
G Kelly***	Leeds United
M Holland	Ipswich Town
RD Keane	Leeds United
D Duff	Blackburn Rovers
K Kilbane	Sunderland
D Connolly* (sub)	Wimbledon
K Cunningham** (sub)	Wimbledon
N Quinn*** (sub)	Sunderland

Result	1–1
Scorer	RD Keane (penalty)

Spain won 3–2 on penalties

FEATURED MATCH 23

SAUDI ARABIA 0 REPUBLIC OF IRELAND 3

At Yokohama, Japan, 11 June 2002

Saudi Arabia
Al-Deayea; Al-Jahani (Ahmed Al-Dossari); Sulimnai; Tukar; Zubromawi (Abdullah Al-Dossari); Al Shehri; Ibrahim; Al-Shahrani; Al-Temyat; Al-Yami; Khamis Al-Dossari; Al-Khathran (Al-Shalhoub).

Republic of Ireland
Shay Given; Steve Finnan; Ian Harte (Niall Quinn); Mark Kinsella (Lee Carsley); Gary Breen; Steve Staunton; Gary Kelly (Jason McAteer); Matt Holland; Robbie Keane; Kevin Kilbane; Damien Duff.

Ireland needed to beat Saudi Arabia by two goals to qualify for the second round – a task made all the harder by the fact that the Irish had never won by more than one goal in the World Cup Finals.

World Cup ticket for the 2002 World Cup match against Saudi Arabia.

The players were welcomed by swirling rain and strong warm winds with the Irish contingent being swelled by even more Japanese fans in green! Ireland made a great start to the game, taking the lead after just seven minutes when Robbie KEANE volleyed home Gary Kelly's cross, the ball slipping through Mohammed Al-Deayea's hands. Although Saudi Arabia made a few penetrating moves towards the danger zone, they didn't look like scoring until the final minute of the half when Khamis Al-Dossari's shot caused Given a problem.

Niall Quinn replaced Ian Harte for the start of the second half as Ireland went in search of further goals. One or two chances went begging during the early stages of the second half but Ireland extended their lead after 62 minutes when Gary BREEN guided the ball home with his head after Steve Staunton's free-kick was not dealt with by Saudi Arabia. Ireland were then in the driving seat, having scored more than one goal in the Finals for the first time and hearing that ten–man Germany were leading Cameroon.

Al-Temyat, who had been booked minutes earlier, was lucky not to receive his marching orders for a crunching tackle on Robbie Keane as Ireland did the bulk of the attacking. Damien Duff caused untold problems for the Saudi defence and came close to netting Ireland's third goal from an acute angle.

Matt Holland and Kevin Kilbane got close with long range efforts but with just three minutes remaining, Ireland put the game beyond doubt when Damien DUFF was rewarded for his endless runs and credited with the goal, although the Saudi goalkeeper played his part. In fact, it was reminiscent of the goal that Packie Bonner let in against the Dutch in the United States in 1994.

FEATURED MATCH 24

SPAIN 1 REPUBLIC OF IRELAND 1
Spain won 3–2 on penalties

At Suwon, South Korea, 16 June 2002

Spain
Casillas; Puyol; Helguera; Hierro; Juanfran; Baraja; Valeron; De Pedro (Mendieta); Luis Enrique; Raul (Luque); Morientes (Albelda).

Republic of Ireland
Shay Given; Steve Finnan; Ian Harte (David Connolly); Mark Kinsella; Gary Breen; Steve Staunton (Kenny Cunningham); Gary Kelly (Niall Quinn); Matt Holland; Robbie Keane; Damien Duff; Kevin Kilbane.

The Republic of Ireland went out of the 2002 World Cup on penalties after staging a superb comeback against Spain in Suwon.

Spain, so comfortable in possession and threatening on the break, completely dominated the first half and took the lead after eight minutes through Morientes. The goal was magnificently taken but Spain were undoubtedly aided by some awful Irish defending. Carlos Puyol picked up the ball from a throw-in and was able to get his cross in far too easily. MORIENTES got in front of Breen at the near post and glanced his header past Shay Given. Spain, with Raul and Morientes showing excellent movement in attack, and Valeron showing some excellent touches in midfield, almost added to their lead on numerous occasions. Luis Enrique did get the ball into the net but his effort was disallowed for offside.

The Republic had to make a change and it was no surprise when Mick McCarthy brought on veteran striker Niall Quinn for Gary Kelly after ten minutes of the second half. Duff moved out to the wing and immediately began to pose more of a threat to the Spanish defence. The Blackburn winger cut in from the right and was in the box when he was tripped by Juanfran. The referee awarded Ireland a penalty but the normally reliable Harte struck his penalty too close to Casillas and it was pushed out. Kevin Kilbane followed up but his shot from the rebound went rather embarrassingly wide of the post.

Ireland piled forward in the closing stages and Duff shot narrowly wide of the far post after a thrilling run before Keane forced Casillas into producing a magnificent save. The game was in its final minute when Fernando Hierro was deemed to have pulled Niall Quinn's shirt at a free-kick, and Ireland were awarded another spot-kick. This time Robbie KEANE stepped up and sent his penalty to the right of Casillas.

In extra time Ireland had the better of their opponents who had been reduced to ten men due to a groin injury to substitute David Abelda. Breen

Spanish 'keeper Casillas celebrates after saving Ian Harte's second–half penalty. Harte, Kilbane and Holland hold their heads in a World Cup second round game Ireland drew 1–1 but then lost 3–2 on penalties.

and Robbie Keane went close but the game went to penalties.

Sadly, Matt Holland, David Connolly and Kevin Kilbane missed in the shoot-out and allowed Gaizka Mendieta to score the penalty that sent Spain into the last eight teams of the tournament.

Match No. 380	
21 August 2002 v FINLAND at Helsinki	
D Kiely*	Charlton Athletic
G Kelly	Leeds United
I Harte**	Leeds United
G Breen	West Ham United
K Cunningham**	Birmingham City
L Carsley***	Everton
T Butler****	Sunderland
M Kinsella*****	Charlton Athletic
J McAteer******	Sunderland
RD Keane*******	Leeds United
D Duff********	Blackburn Rovers
S Given*(sub)	Newcastle United

G Barrett** (sub)	Arsenal
G Doherty*** (sub)	Tottenham Hotspur
M Holland**** (sub)	Ipswich Town
K Kilbane***** (sub)	Sunderland
S McPhail****** (sub)	Leeds United
C Healy******* (sub)	Glasgow Celtic
J Goodwin********(sub)	Stockport County
R Delap*********(sub)	Southampton

Result	3–0
Scorers	RD Keane; C Healy; G Barrett

Match No. 381	
7 September 2002 v RUSSIA at Moscow	
S Given	Newcastle United
S Finnan	Fulham
I Harte	Leeds United
K Cunningham	Birmingham City

G Breen	West Ham United
M Kinsella	Aston Villa
J McAteer*	Sunderland
M Holland	Ipswich Town
RD Keane	Tottenham Hotspur
D Duff**	Blackburn Rovers
K Kilbane***	Sunderland
G Doherty* (sub)	Tottenham Hotspur
C Morrison** (sub)	Birmingham City
P Babb*** (sub)	Sunderland

| Result | 2–4 |
| Scorers | G Doherty; C Morrison |

Match No. 382

16 October 2002 v SWITZERLAND at Dublin

S Given	Newcastle United
G Kelly	Leeds United
I Harte*	Leeds United
M Holland	Ipswich Town
G Breen	West Ham United
K Cunningham	Birmingham City
C Healy	Glasgow Celtic
M Kinsella	Aston Villa
RD Keane	Tottenham Hotspur
D Duff**	Blackburn Rovers
K Kilbane***	Sunderland
G Doherty* (sub)	Tottenham Hotspur
T Butler** (sub)	Sunderland
C Morrison*** (sub)	Birmingham City

| Result | 1–2 |
| Scorer | Magnin (own goal) |

Match No. 383

20 November 2002 v GREECE at Athens

S Given	Newcastle United
S Finnan	Fulham
R Dunne	Manchester City
J O'Shea	Manchester United

K Cunningham	Birmingham City
M Holland	Ipswich Town
C Healy	Glasgow Celtic
L Carsley	Everton
S McPhail	Leeds United
G Crowe*	Bohemians
G Doherty	Tottenham Hotspur
R Delap* (sub)	Southampton

| Result | 0–0 |

Match No. 384

12 February 2003 v SCOTLAND at Glasgow

D Kiely*	Charlton Athletic
S Carr	Tottenham Hotspur
I Harte	Leeds United
G Breen**	West Ham United
J O'Shea***	Manchester United
M Holland	Ipswich Town
M Kinsella****	Aston Villa
S Reid*****	Millwall
C Morrison	Birmingham City
G Doherty******	Tottenham Hotspur
K Kilbane	Sunderland
N Colgan* (sub)	Hibernian
A O'Brien** (sub)	Newcastle United
R Dunne*** (sub)	Manchester City
C Healy**** (sub)	Glasgow Celtic
L Carsley***** (sub)	Everton
D Connolly******(sub)	Wimbledon

| Result | 2–0 |
| Scorers | K Kilbane; C Morrison |

Match No. 385

29 March 2003 v GEORGIA at Tbilisi

S Given	Newcastle United
S Carr	Tottenham Hotspur
J O'Shea	Manchester United
M Kinsella	Aston Villa

MATCHES

G Breen	West Ham United
K Cunningham	Birmingham City
L Carsley	Everton
M Holland	Ipswich Town
G Doherty	Tottenham Hotspur
K Kilbane	Sunderland
D Duff	Blackburn Rovers

Result	2–1
Scorers	D Duff; G Doherty

Match No. 386

2 April 2003 v ALBANIA at Tirana

S Given	Newcastle United
S Carr	Tottenham Hotspur
J O'Shea	Manchester United
M Holland	Ipswich Town
G Breen	West Ham United
K Cunningham	Birmingham City
L Carsley	Everton
M Kinsella	Aston Villa
RD Keane*	Tottenham Hotspur
D Duff	Blackburn Rovers
K Kilbane	Sunderland
G Doherty* (sub)	Tottenham Hotspur

Result	0–0

Match No. 387

30 April 2003 v NORWAY at Dublin

S Given*	Newcastle United
S Carr	Tottenham Hotspur
I Harte**	Leeds United
G Breen	West Ham United
R Dunne	Manchester City
M Holland	Ipswich Town
M Kinsella***	Aston Villa
K Kilbane****	Sunderland
RD Keane*****	Tottenham Hotspur
D Connolly******	Wimbledon

D Duff*******	Blackburn Rovers
N Colgan* (sub)	Hibernian
S Finnan** (sub)	Fulham
L Carsley*** (sub)	Everton
A Quinn**** (sub)	Sheffield Wednesday
G Crowe***** (sub)	Bohemians
C Healy****** (sub)	Glasgow Celtic
A Lee******* (sub)	Rotherham United

Result	1–0
Scorer	D Duff

Match No. 388

7 June 2003 v ALBANIA at Dublin

S Given	Newcastle United
S Carr	Tottenham Hotspur
J O'Shea	Manchester United
M Kinsella*	Aston Villa
K Cunningham	Birmingham City
G Breen	West Ham United
K Kilbane**	Sunderland
M Holland	Ipswich Town
RD Keane	Tottenham Hotspur
D Connolly***	Wimbledon
D Duff	Blackburn Rovers
L Carsley* (sub)	Everton
S Reid** (sub)	Millwall
G Doherty*** (sub)	Tottenham Hotspur

Result	2–1
Scorers	RD Keane; Aliaj (own goal)

Match No. 389

11 June 2003 v GEORGIA at Dublin

S Given	Newcastle United
S Carr	Tottenham Hotspur
J O'Shea	Manchester United
L Carsley	Everton
K Cunningham	Birmingham City
G Breen	West Ham United

C Healy*	Glasgow Celtic
M Holland	Ipswich Town
RD Keane	Tottenham Hotspur
G Doherty**	Tottenham Hotspur
K Kilbane	Sunderland
M Kinsella* (sub)	Aston Villa
A Lee** (sub)	Rotherham United

Result	2–0
Scorers	G Doherty; RD Keane

Match No. 390

19 August 2003 v AUSTRALIA at Dublin

N Colgan	Stockport County
S Carr*	Tottenham Hotspur
G Breen**	Sunderland
K Cunningham***	Birmingham City
J O'Shea	Manchester United
S Finnan****	Fulham
M Kinsella	Aston Villa
M Holland*****	Ipswich Town
D Duff******	Chelsea
G Doherty*******	Tottenham Hotspur
RD Keane********	Tottenham Hotspur
I Harte* (sub)	Leeds United
A O'Brien** (sub)	Newcastle United
R Dunne*** (sub)	Manchester City
K Kilbane**** (sub)	Sunderland
C Healy***** (sub)	Sunderland
A Quinn****** (sub)	Sheffield Wednesday
C Morrison*******(sub)	Birmingham City
D Connolly********(sub)	West Ham United

Result	2–1
Scorers	J O'Shea; C Morrison

Match No. 391

6 September 2003 v RUSSIA at Dublin

S Given	Newcastle United
S Carr	Tottenham Hotspur

G Breen	Sunderland
K Cunningham	Birmingham City
J O'Shea*	Manchester United
L Carsley**	Everton
M Holland	Charlton Athletic
C Healy	Sunderland
K Kilbane	Everton
D Duff	Chelsea
C Morrison***	Birmingham City
I Harte* (sub)	Leeds United
S Reid** (sub)	Blackburn Rovers
G Doherty*** (sub)	Tottenham Hotspur

Result	1–1
Scorer	D Duff

Match No. 392

9 September 2003 v TURKEY at Dublin

N Colgan*	Stockport County
S Finnan	Liverpool
G Breen**	Sunderland
A O'Brien***	Newcastle United
I Harte****	Leeds United
M Kinsella	Aston Villa
C Healy*****	Sunderland
K Kilbane	Everton
D Duff******	Chelsea
D Connolly	West Ham United
G Doherty	Tottenham Hotspur
J Murphy* (sub)	West Bromwich Albion
C Morrison** (sub)	Birmingham City
R Dunne*** (sub)	Manchester City
S Carr**** (sub)	Tottenham Hotspur
S McPhail***** (sub)	Leeds United
S Reid****** (sub)	Blackburn Rovers

Result	2–2
Scorers	D Connolly; R Dunne

Match No. 393

11 October 2003 v SWITZERLAND at Basel

S Given	Newcastle United
S Carr	Tottenham Hotspur
G Breen	Sunderland
J O'Shea	Manchester United
I Harte	Leeds United
D Duff	Chelsea
M Holland*	Charlton Athletic
C Healy	Sunderland
K Kilbane**	Everton
RD Keane	Tottenham Hotspur
D Connolly***	West Ham United
M Kinsella* (sub)	Aston Villa
S Finnan** (sub)	Liverpool
C Morrison*** (sub)	Birmingham City

Result	0–2

Match No. 394

18 November 2003 v CANADA at Dublin

S Given*	Newcastle United
S Carr**	Tottenham Hotspur
K Cunningham	Birmingham City
R Dunne	Manchester City
J O'Shea***	Manchester United
S Reid****	Blackburn Rovers
G Kavanagh*****	Cardiff City
A Reid******	Nottingham Forest
D Duff*******	Chelsea
G Doherty********	Tottenham Hotspur
RD Keane	Tottenham Hotspur
N Colgan* (sub)	Stockport County
I Harte** (sub)	Leeds United
J Thompson *** (sub)	Nottingham Forest
R Delap**** (sub)	Southampton
M Holland***** (sub)	Charlton Athletic
S McPhail****** (sub)	Leeds United
K Kilbane******* (sub)	Everton
C Morrison******** (sub)	Birmingham City

Result	3–0
Scorers	D Duff; RD Keane (2)

Match No. 395

18 February 2004 v BRAZIL at Dublin

S Given	Newcastle United
S Carr	Tottenham Hotspur
A O'Brien	Newcastle United
K Cunningham	Birmingham City
J O'Shea	Manchester United
M Holland	Charlton Athletic
G Kavanagh	Cardiff City
K Kilbane	Everton
A Reid*	Nottingham Forest
C Morrison	Birmingham City
RD Keane	Tottenham Hotspur
J McAteer* (sub)	Sunderland

Result	0–0

Match No. 396

31 March 2004 v CZECH REPUBLIC at Dublin

S Given*	Newcastle United
A Maybury	Heart of Midlothian
G Doherty*	Tottenham Hotspur
K Cunningham	Birmingham City
I Harte	Leeds United
A Reid**	Nottingham Forest
M Holland	Charlton Athletic
K Kilbane	Everton
D Duff***	Chelsea
RD Keane	Tottenham Hotspur
C Morrison****	Birmingham City
P Kenny* (sub)	Sheffield United
L Miller** (sub)	Glasgow Celtic
M Kinsella*** (sub)	West Bromwich Albion
A Lee**** (sub)	Cardiff City

Result	2–1
Scorers	I Harte; RD Keane

Match No. 397

28 April 2004 v POLAND at Bydgoszcz

S Given*	Newcastle United
J O'Shea	Manchester United
G Doherty**	Tottenham Hotspur
K Cunningham	Birmingham City
I Harte***	Leeds United
S Reid	Blackburn Rovers
L Miller	Glasgow Celtic
M Kinsella	West Bromwich Albion
A Reid****	Nottingham Forest
A Lee*****	Cardiff City
C Morrison******	Birmingham City
N Colgan* (sub)	Hibernian
A O'Brien** (sub)	Newcastle United
A Maybury*** (sub)	Heart of Midlothian
J Douglas**** (sub)	Blackburn Rovers
G Barrett***** (sub)	Coventry City
J Byrne****** (sub)	Shelbourne

Result	0–0

Match No. 398

27 May 2004 v ROMANIA at Dublin

S Given	Newcastle United
S Finnan	Liverpool
K Cunningham	Birmingham City
A O'Brien	Newcastle United
A Maybury	Heart of Midlothian
L Miller	Glasgow Celtic
RD Keane	Manchester United
M Holland	Charlton Athletic
A Reid*	Nottingham Forest
RD Keane	Tottenham Hotspur
C Morrison	Birmingham City
M Rowlands* (sub)	Queen's Park Rangers

Result	1–0
Scorer	M Holland

Roy Keane bursts past Romania's Ganea Ioan Virol in a 1–0 win for the Irish at Lansdowne Road.

N Colgan	Hibernian
S Finnan	Liverpool
G Doherty	Tottenham Hotspur
K Cunningham	Birmingham City
A Maybury*	Heart of Midlothian
L Miller**	Glasgow Celtic
M Kinsella	West Bromwich Albion
M Holland***	Charlton Athletic
S McPhail	Leeds United
RD Keane****	Tottenham Hotspur
A Lee	Cardiff City
C Clarke* (sub)	Stoke City
M Rowlands** (sub)	Queen's Park Rangers
J Douglas*** (sub)	Blackburn Rovers
G Barrett**** (sub)	Coventry City
Result	0–3

P Kenny	Sheffield United
A Maybury	Heart of Midlothian
G Doherty	Tottenham Hotspur
A O'Brien	Newcastle United
J O'Shea*	Manchester United
G Barrett	Coventry City
M Kinsella	West Bromwich Albion
A Quinn**	Sheffield Wednesday
A Reid***	Nottingham Forest
C Morrison	Birmingham City
A Lee****	Cardiff City
C Clarke* (sub)	Stoke City
M Holland** (sub)	Charlton Athletic
M Rowlands*** (sub)	Queen's Park Rangers
A McGeady**** (sub)	Glasgow Celtic
Result	1–0
Scorer	G Barrett

S Given	Newcastle United
S Finnan	Liverpool
A O'Brien	Newcastle United
K Cunningham	Birmingham City
A Maybury*	Heart of Midlothian
G Barrett	Coventry City
M Holland	Charlton Athletic
A Quinn	Sheffield Wednesday
A Reid	Nottingham Forest
C Morrison**	Birmingham City
RD Keane	Tottenham Hotspur
M Doyle* (sub)	Coventry City
A Lee** (sub)	Cardiff City
Result	1–0
Scorer	RD Keane

S Given*	Newcastle United
S Finnan**	Liverpool
K Cunningham	Birmingham City
G Doherty***	Tottenham Hotspur
J O'Shea	Manchester United
L Miller****	Manchester United
RM Keane*****	Manchester United
K Kilbane	Everton
A Reid	Nottingham Forest
D Duff	Chelsea
C Morrison******	Birmingham City
P Kenny* (sub)	Sheffield United
A Quinn** (sub)	Sheffield United
G Breen*** (sub)	Sunderland
S Carr**** (sub)	Newcastle United
G Kavanagh***** (sub)	Cardiff City
J Macken****** (sub)	Manchester City
Result	1–1
Scorer	A Reid

4 September 2004 v CYPRUS at Dublin

S Given	Newcastle United
S Carr*	Newcastle United
A O'Brien	Newcastle United
K Cunningham	Birmingham City
J O'Shea**	Manchester United
A Reid	Nottingham Forest
G Kavanagh	Cardiff City
K Kilbane	Everton
D Duff	Chelsea
RD Keane	Tottenham Hotspur
C Morrison***	Birmingham City
S FInnan* (sub)	Liverpool
A Maybury** (sub)	Heart of Midlothian
A Lee*** (sub)	Cardiff City
Result	3–0
Scorers	C Morrison; A Reid; RD Keane (penalty)

8 September 2004 v SWITZERLAND at Basel

S Given	Newcastle United
S Carr	Newcastle United
A O'Brien	Newcastle United
K Cunningham	Birmingham City
S Finnan	Liverpool
A Reid*	Nottingham Forest
RM Keane	Manchester United
K Kilbane	Everton
D Duff	Chelsea
RD Keane	Tottenham Hotspur
C Morrison**	Birmingham City
G Kavanagh* (sub)	Cardiff City
G Doherty** (sub)	Norwich City
Result	1–1
Scorer	C Morrison

9 October 2004 v FRANCE at Paris

S Given	Newcastle United
S Carr	Newcastle United
A O'Brien	Newcastle United
K Cunningham	Birmingham City
J O'Shea	Manchester United
S Finnan	Liverpool
RM Keane	Manchester United
K Kilbane	Everton
D Duff	Chelsea
C Morrison*	Birmingham City
RD Keane	Tottenham Hotspur
A Reid* (sub)	Nottingham Forest
Result	0–0

13 October 2004 v FAROE ISLANDS at Dublin

S Given	Newcastle United
S Carr	Newcastle United
A O'Brien	Newcastle United
K Cunningham	Birmingham City
J O'Shea*	Manchester United
S Finnan	Liverpool
RM Keane	Manchester United
K Kilbane	Everton
A Reid	Nottingham Forest
D Duff	Chelsea
RD Keane	Tottenham Hotspur
L Miller* (sub)	Manchester United
Result	2–0
Scorers	RD Keane (2–1 penalty)

16 November 2004 v CROATIA at Dublin

P Kenny*	Sheffield United
S Finnan	Liverpool
G Breen**	Sunderland
R Dunne	Manchester City

J O'Shea	Manchester United
L Miller	Manchester United
G Kavanagh	Cardiff City
K Kilbane***	Everton
D Duff	Chelsea
S Elliott****	Sunderland
RD Keane*****	Tottenham Hotspur
S Given* (sub)	Newcastle United
K Cunningham** (sub)	Birmingham City
A Quinn*** (sub)	Sheffield United
G Barrett **** (sub)	Coventry City
A McGeady***** (sub)	Glasgow Celtic

Result	1–0
Scorer	RD Keane

9 February 2005 v PORTUGAL at Dublin	
S Given	Newcastle United
S Finnan	Liverpool
A O'Brien	Newcastle United
K Cunningham*	Birmingham City
J O'Shea	Manchester United
A Reid	Tottenham Hotspur
M Holland	Charlton Athletic
K Kilbane**	Everton
D Duff***	Chelsea
C Morrison	Birmingham City
RD Keane****	Tottenham Hotspur
R Dunne* (sub)	Manchester City
G Kavanagh** (sub)	Cardiff City
L Miller*** (sub)	Manchester United
A McGeady**** (sub)	Glasgow Celtic

Result	1–0
Scorer	A O'Brien

Match No. 409
26 March 2005 v ISRAEL at Tel Aviv

S Given	Newcastle United
S Carr	Newcastle United
A O'Brien	Newcastle United
K Cunningham	Birmingham City
J O'Shea	Manchester United
S Finnan	Liverpool
RM Keane	Manchester United
K Kilbane	Everton
D Duff	Chelsea
C Morrison*	Birmingham City
RD Keane	Tottenham Hotspur
M Holland* (sub)	Charlton Athletic

Result	1–1
Scorer	C Morrison

Match No. 410
29 March 2005 v CHINA at Dublin

P Kenny	Sheffield United
A Maybury	Leicester City
R Dunne	Manchester City
K Cunningham*	Birmingham City
J O'Shea	Manchester United
A Reid	Tottenham Hotspur
G Kavanagh	Wigan Athletic
K Kilbane**	Everton
D Duff***	Chelsea
RD Keane****	Tottenham Hotspur
S Elliott*****	Sunderland
A O'Brien* (sub)	Newcastle United
RM Keane**	Manchester United
L Miller*** (sub)	Manchester United
C Morrison**** (sub)	Birmingham City
G Doherty***** (sub)	Norwich City

Result	1–0
Scorer	C Morrison

Republic of Ireland and Manchester United defender John O'Shea holds off Portugal's Petit in a 1–0 win for the boys in green.

Match No. 411	
4 June 2005 v ISRAEL at Dublin	
S Given	Newcastle United
J O'Shea	Manchester United
K Cunningham	Birmingham City
A O'Brien	Newcastle United
I Harte	Levante
A Reid*	Tottenham Hotspur
M Holland	Charlton Athletic
K Kilbane	Everton
D Duff	Chelsea
RD Keane**	Tottenham Hotspur
C Morrison	Birmingham City
G Doherty* (sub)	Norwich City
G Kavanagh** (sub)	Wigan Athletic

Result	2–2
Scorers	I Harte; RD Keane

Match No. 412	
8 June 2005 v FAROE ISLANDS at Torshavn	
S Given	Newcastle United
S Carr	Newcastle United
J O'Shea	Manchester United
K Cunningham	Birmingham City
I Harte	Levante
A Reid	Tottenham Hotspur
RM Keane	Manchester United
K Kilbane	Everton
D Duff	Chelsea
C Morrison*	Birmingham City
S Elliott	Sunderland
G Doherty* (sub)	Norwich City

Result	2–0
Scorers	I Harte (penalty); K Kilbane

Match No. 413

17 August 2005 v ITALY at Dublin

S Given	Newcastle United
S Finnan*	Liverpool
J O'Shea**	Manchester United
M Holland***	Charlton Athletic
K Cunningham	Birmingham City
R Dunne****	Manchester City
A Reid*****	Tottenham Hotspur
S Reid	Blackburn Rovers
C Morrison	Birmingham City
K Kilbane	Everton
D Duff	Chelsea
S Carr* (sub)	Newcastle United
L Miller** (sub)	Manchester United
I Harte*** (sub)	Levante
A O'Brien**** (sub)	Portsmouth
S Elliott***** (sub)	Sunderland

Result	1–2
Scorer	A Reid

Match No. 414

7 September 2005 v FRANCE at Dublin

S Given	Newcastle United
S Carr	Newcastle United
J O'Shea	Manchester United
RM Keane	Manchester United
K Cunningham	Birmingham City
R Dunne	Manchester City
A Reid	Tottenham Hotspur
K Kilbane*	Everton
RD Keane	Tottenham Hotspur
C Morrison**	Crystal Palace
D Duff	Chelsea
G Doherty* (sub)	Norwich City
I Harte** (sub)	Levante

Result	0–1

Match No. 415

8 October 2005 v CYPRUS at Nicosia

S Given	Newcastle United
S Carr	Newcastle United
J O'Shea	Manchester United
G Kavanagh	Wigan Athletic
R Dunne	Manchester City
K Cunningham	Birmingham City
S Finnan*	Liverpool
K Kilbane	Everton
RD Keane**	Tottenham Hotspur
S Elliott	Sunderland
D Duff***	Chelsea
M Holland* (sub)	Charlton Athletic
D Connolly** (sub)	Wigan Athletic
A Reid*** (sub)	Tottenham Hotspur

Result	1–0
Scorer	S Elliott

Match No. 416

12 October 2005 v SWITZERLAND at Dublin

S Given	Newcastle United
S Carr	Newcastle United
I Harte	Levante
J O'Shea	Manchester United
R Dunne	Manchester City
K Cunningham	Birmingham City
M Holland	Charlton Athletic
A Reid*	Tottenham Hotspur
C Morrison**	Crystal Palace
RD Keane***	Tottenham Hotspur
K Kilbane	Everton
S Reid* (sub)	Blackburn Rovers
G Doherty** (sub)	Norwich City
S Elliott*** (sub)	Sunderland

Result	0–0

Match No. 417

1 March 2006 v SWEDEN at Dublin

S Given*	Newcastle United
J O'Brien**	Bolton Wanderers
I Harte***	Levante
J O'Shea****	Manchester United
A O'Brien	Portsmouth
R Dunne	Manchester City
S Elliott*****	Sunderland
S Reid	Blackburn Rovers
RD Keane	Tottenham Hotspur
K Doyle******	Reading
D Duff	Chelsea
W Henderson* (sub)	Brighton & Hove Albion
L Miller** (sub)	Manchester United
K Kilbane*** (sub)	Everton
S Ireland**** (sub)	Manchester City
G Kavanagh*****(sub)	Wigan Athletic
C Morrison******(sub)	Crystal Palace

Result	3–0
Scorers	D Duff; RD Keane; L Miller

Match No. 418

24 May 2006 v CHILE at Dublin

S Given*	Newcastle United
S Kelly**	Tottenham Hotspur
R Dunne	Manchester City
G Breen***	Sunderland
K Kilbane	Everton
L Miller****	Manchester United
S Reid	Blackburn Rovers
J O'Shea*****	Manchester United
K Doyle******	Reading
RD Keane	Tottenham Hotspur
D Duff	Chelsea
W Henderson* (sub)	Brighton & Hove Albion
A Reid** (sub)	Tottenham Hotspur
I Harte*** (sub)	Levante
G Kavanagh**** (sub)	Wigan Athletic
A McGeady***** (sub)	Glasgow Celtic

J Byrne****** (sub)	Shelbourne

Result	0–1

Match No. 419

18 August 2006 v HOLLAND at Dublin

P Kenny	Sheffield United
S Carr*	Newcastle United
S Finnan**	Liverpool
AJ O'Brien	Portsmouth
G Kavanagh***	Wigan Athletic
J O'Shea	Manchester United
A McGeady	Glasgow Celtic
S Reid****	Blackburn Rovers
C Morrison*****	Crystal Palace
S Elliott	Sunderland
K Kilbane	Everton
A O'Brien* (sub)	Newcastle United
S Kelly** (sub)	Tottenham Hotspur
J Douglas*** (sub)	Blackburn Rovers
L Miller****(sub)	Manchester United
K Doyle***** (sub)	Reading

Result	0–4

Match No. 420

2 September 2006 v GERMANY at Stuttgart

S Given	Newcastle United
S Carr	Newcastle United
S Finnan	Liverpool
AJ O'Brien	Portsmouth
R Dunne	Manchester City
J O'Shea	Manchester United
D Duff*	Newcastle United
S Reid	Blackburn Rovers
RD Keane	Tottenham Hotspur
K Doyle**	Reading
K Kilbane***	Wigan Athletic
A McGeady* (sub)	Glasgow Celtic
S Elliott** (sub)	Sunderland

A O'Brien*** (sub)   Newcastle United

Result	0–1

Match No. 421

7 October 2006 v CYPRUS at Nicosia

P Kenny	Sheffield United
S Finnan	Liverpool
J O'Shea	Manchester United
AJ O'Brien*	Portsmouth
R Dunne	Manchester City
K Kilbane	Wigan Athletic
A McGeady**	Glasgow Celtic
S Ireland***	Manchester City
C Morrison	Crystal Palace
RD Keane	Tottenham Hotspur
D Duff	Newcastle United
A Lee* (sub)	Ipswich Town
A O'Brien** (sub)	Newcastle United
J Douglas*** (sub)	Leeds United

Result	2–5
Scorers	S Ireland; R Dunne

Match No. 422

11 October 2006 v CZECH REPUBLIC at Dublin

W Henderson	Brighton & Hove Albion
S Kelly	Birmingham City
S Finnan	Liverpool
J O'Shea	Manchester United
P McShane	West Bromwich Albion
L Carsley	Everton
A Reid*	Charlton Athletic
J Douglas	Leeds United
RD Keane	Tottenham Hotspur
K Kilbane**	Wigan Athletic
D Duff	Newcastle United
A Quinn* (sub)	Sheffield United
A O'Brien** (sub)	Newcastle United

Result	1–0
Scorer	K Kilbane

Match No. 423

15 November 2006 v SAN MARINO at Dublin

S Given	Newcastle United
S Finnan	Liverpool
J O'Shea	Manchester United
R Dunne	Manchester City
P McShane	West Bromwich Albion
L Carsley*	Everton
A Reid	Charlton Athletic
K Doyle**	Reading
RD Keane	Tottenham Hotspur
D Duff	Newcastle United
K Kilbane***	Wigan Athletic
J Douglas* (sub)	Leeds United
A McGeady** (sub)	Glasgow Celtic
A Lee*** (sub)	Ipswich Town

Result	5–0
Scorers	Simoncini (own goal); K Doyle; RD Keane (3–1 penalty)

Match No. 424

7 February 2007 v SAN MARINO at Serravalle

W Henderson	Preston North End
S Finnan	Liverpool
I Harte*	Levante
R Dunne	Manchester City
J O'Shea**	Manchester United
L Carsley	Everton
D Duff	Newcastle United
S Ireland	Manchester City
RD Keane	Tottenham Hotspur
S Long***	Reading
K Kilbane	Wigan Athletic
S Hunt* (sub)	Reading
P McShane** (sub)	West Bromwich Albion
A Stokes*** (sub)	Sunderland

Result	2–1
Scorers	K Kilbane; S Ireland

24 March 2007 v WALES at Dublin	
S Given	Newcastle United
S Finnan	Liverpool
J O'Shea	Manchester United
R Dunne	Manchester City
P McShane	West Bromwich Albion
L Carsley	Everton
J Douglas*	Leeds United
S Ireland**	Manchester City
RD Keane***	Tottenham Hotspur
K Kilbane	Wigan Athletic
D Duff	Newcastle United
S Hunt* (sub)	Reading
K Doyle** (sub)	Reading
A McGeady*** (sub)	Glasgow Celtic

Result	1–0
Scorer	S Ireland

FEATURED MATCH 25

REPUBLIC OF IRELAND 1 WALES 0
At Croke Park, Dublin, 24 March 2007

Republic of Ireland
Shay Given; Steve Finnan; John O'Shea; Richard Dunne; Paul McShane; Lee Carsley; John Douglas (Stephen Hunt); Stephen Ireland (Kevin Doyle); Robbie Keane (Aiden McGeady); Kevin Kilbane; Damien Duff.

Wales
Danny Coyne; Sam Ricketts; Gareth Bale (Danny Collins); James Collins; Steve Evans; Lewin Nyatanga; Joe Ledley (Carl Fletcher); Carl Robinson (Jermaine Easter); Simon Davies; Craig Bellamy; Ryan Giggs.

Stephen Ireland's goal in the thirty-ninth minute gave the boys in green a vital Euro 2008 win in the historic first football match at Dublin's Croke Park.

After a quiet start, Steve Staunton's side created the first opening in the fourteenth minute when Robbie Keane flashed a shot narrowly wide after Simon Davies lost possession in a dangerous position. Eight minutes later, the Spurs striker had an even better chance following Stephen Ireland's ball over the top of the Welsh defence. Despite a neat chest down to control, Keane's finish was poorly executed as he dragged his shot wide. Wales' best chance of breaking the deadlock came on the half-hour mark when Craig Bellamy burst clear and looked certain to score until Shay Given raced off his line to narrow the angle and smother his shot.

Ireland began to play with a greater degree of purpose, pressing Wales further into their shell. Kevin Kilbane headed a Duff corner wide and the legs of Danny Coyne denied the Wigan winger a goal moments later. Running on to a fine through ball by Keane, Duff's attempted flick over Coyne was blocked at point-blank range. Then on 39 minutes, the Republic took the lead when Stephen IRELAND took a lay-off from Keane in his stride, rounded Coyne and, from the tightest of angles, lifted the ball into the empty net. It was his third goal in only four appearances for his country.

The second half was a scrappy affair as Wales struggled to get back into the game. Indeed, the Republic went closest to adding to their lead after the interval. Lee Carsley's deflected fifty-second-minute effort from the edge of the area was saved easily by Coyne and with fifteen minutes left, Kevin Kilbane headed into the side-netting from a tight angle. In the eighty-first minute, substitute Kevin Doyle, who had replaced the Republic's goalscorer on the hour, curled in an effort that beat Coyne but came back off the crossbar. Keane was then unable to get a shot on goal despite being brilliantly set up by Duff.

Ryan Giggs curled a late shot straight into Given's midriff but the Welsh star, along with Craig Bellamy, was off colour and did not score.

28 March 2007 v SLOVAKIA at Dublin	
S Given	Newcastle United
J O'Shea	Manchester United
S Finnan	Liverpool
P McShane	West Bromwich Albion
R Dunne	Manchester City

L Carsley	Everton
S Ireland*	Manchester City
A McGeady**	Glasgow Celtic
K Kilbane	Wigan Athletic
D Duff	Newcastle United
K Doyle***	Reading
S Hunt* (sub)	Reading
A Quinn** (sub)	Sheffield United
S Long*** (sub)	Reading

Result	1–0
Scorer	K Doyle

Match No. 427

23 May 2007 v ECUADOR at New Jersey

C Doyle	Birmingham City
S Kelly	Birmingham City
S O'Halloran*	Aston Villa
D Potter	Wolverhampton Wanderers
A Bennett	Reading
A Bruce	Ipswich Town
D Murphy**	Sunderland
S Hunt***	Reading
A Keogh****	Wolverhampton Wanderers
K Doyle*****	Reading
K Kilbane******	Wigan Athletic
J O'Cearuill* (sub)	Arsenal
J Lapira** (sub)	Notre Dame
A Stokes*** (sub)	Sunderland
J Gamble**** (sub)	Cork City
S Long***** (sub)	Reading
S Gleeson****** (sub)	Wolverhampton Wanderers

Result	1–1
Scorer	K Doyle

Match No. 428

26 May 2007 v BOLIVIA at Boston

N Colgan*	Barnsley
J O'Cearuill	Arsenal

S Kelly	Birmingham City
J Gamble**	Cork City
A Bennett	Reading
P Murphy***	Carlisle United
AJ O'Brien****	Portsmouth
D Potter	Wolverhampton Wanderers
A Stokes	Sunderland
S Long*****	Reading
K Kilbane******	Wigan Athletic
W Henderson* (sub)	Preston North End
D Murphy** (sub)	Sunderland
S O'Halloran*** (sub)	Aston Villa
S Gleeson**** (sub)	Wolverhampton Wanderers
K Doyle***** (sub)	Reading
S Hunt****** (sub)	Reading

Result	1–1
Scorer	S Long

Match No. 429

22 August 2007 v DENMARK at Aarhus

W Henderson	Preston North End
S Carr	Newcastle United
J O'Shea	Manchester United
R Dunne	Manchester City
S Finnan*	Liverpool
A McGeady	Glasgow Celtic
D Potter**	Wolverhampton Wanderers
A Reid***	Charlton Athletic
S Hunt****	Reading
K Doyle*****	Reading
RD Keane******	Tottenham Hotspur
K Kilbane* (sub)	Wigan Athletic
S Kelly** (sub)	Birmingham City
D Gibson*** (sub)	Wolverhampton Wanderers
A Keogh**** (sub)	Wolverhampton Wanderers
S Long***** (sub)	Reading
D Murphy****** (sub)	Sunderland

Result	4–0
Scorers	RD Keane (2); S Long (2)

Kevin Kilbane fires in a shot on the Slovakia goal in the 2008 Euro qualifier that the Republic of Ireland won 1–0.

Match No. 430	
8 September 2007 v SLOVAKIA at Bratislava	
S Given	Newcastle United
J O'Shea	Manchester United
R Dunne	Manchester City
S Kelly	Birmingham City
P McShane	Sunderland
L Carsley	Everton
S Ireland*	Manchester City
K Kilbane	Wigan Athletic
RD Keane	Tottenham Hotspur
A McGeady**	Glasgow Celtic
K Doyle***	Reading
J Douglas* (sub)	Leeds United
D Gibson** (sub)	Wolverhampton Wanderers
D Murphy*** (sub)	Sunderland

Result	2–2
Scorers	S Ireland; K Doyle

Match No. 431	
12 September 2007 v CZECH REPUBLIC at Prague	
S Given	Newcastle United
R Dunne	Manchester City
S Kelly	Birmingham City
P McShane	Sunderland
J O'Shea*	Manchester United
L Carsley**	Everton
K Kilbane	Wigan Athletic
A McGeady***	Glasgow Celtic
A Reid	Charlton Athletic
K Doyle	Reading
RD Keane	Tottenham Hotspur
S Hunt* (sub)	Reading
A Keogh** (sub)	Wolverhampton Wanderers
S Long*** (sub)	Reading

Result	0–1

Match No. 432

13 October 2007 v GERMANY at Dublin

S Given	Newcastle United
S Finnan	Liverpool
R Dunne	Manchester City
J O'Brien	Bolton Wanderers
S Kelly	Birmingham City
A Keogh*	Wolverhampton Wanderers
A Reid	Charlton Athletic
L Carsley	Everton
K Kilbane**	Wigan Athletic
K Doyle***	Reading
RD Keane	Tottenham Hotspur
A McGeady* (sub)	Glasgow Celtic
D Murphy** (sub)	Sunderland
S Long*** (sub)	Reading

Result	0–0

Match No. 433

17 October 2007 v CYPRUS at Dublin

S Given	Newcastle United
S Finnan	Liverpool
P McShane	Sunderland
J O'Brien*	Bolton Wanderers
K Kilbane	Wigan Athletic
A Keogh**	Wolverhampton Wanderers
J O'Shea	Manchester United
A Reid	Charlton Athletic
S Hunt***	Reading
K Doyle	Reading
RD Keane	Tottenham Hotspur
L Miller* (sub)	Sunderland
A McGeady** (sub)	Glasgow Celtic
J Douglas*** (sub)	Leeds United

Result	1–1
Scorer	S Finnan

Match No. 434

17 November 2007 v WALES at Cardiff

S Given	Newcastle United
S Finnan	Liverpool
P McShane	Sunderland
J O'Shea	Manchester United
L Carsley	Everton
K Kilbane	Wigan Athletic
L Miller*	Sunderland
A Reid**	Charlton Athletic
RD Keane	Tottenham Hotspur
K Doyle	Reading
A McGeady	Glasgow Celtic
S Hunt* (sub)	Reading
D Potter** (sub)	Wolverhampton Wanderers

Result	2–2
Scorers	RD Keane; K Doyle

5

The Republic of Ireland's Top 50 Players

The Republic of Ireland's Top 50 Players

JOHN ALDRIDGE

A Liverpool fan since childhood, John Aldridge harboured an ambition to play for the Anfield club. When he was fourteen years old, he had a trial for the Reds and was told they'd be in touch, but it took another fourteen years for the phone to ring.

He played his early football on Merseyside for South Liverpool before getting his break in the professional game with Welsh side Newport County. At Somerton Park,

John Aldridge (wearing Number 8 and heading the ball).

TOP 50 PLAYERS

he partnered Tommy Tynan for four years, helping the club to move from the Fourth Division and into the European Cup Winners' Cup quarter-finals. In March 1984 he took his goalscoring touch – 78 goals in 198 games for Newport – to Oxford United, who paid £78,000 for his services.

He was used sparingly in the club's run-in to the Third Division title but the following season he forged a great partnership with Billy Hamilton and became the first Second Division player for nineteen years to score 30 goals in a campaign. He actually broke the club's record of goals in a season in 1984–85 with 34 goals, 30 of them in the League. He netted six goals in the U's League Cup winning run in 1986 when they beat Queen's Park Rangers 3–0 in the final. Aldo went on to score 90 goals in 141 games for Oxford including four against Gillingham in a 1986–87 League Cup tie and three hat-tricks, the first in a 5–2 defeat of Leeds United in November 1984.

International honours eluded Aldridge until he was 27 when, under the grandparent rule, he made his Republic of Ireland debut against Wales in Jack Charlton's first match in charge. However, to everyone's surprise, Aldridge failed to score in his first twenty internationals, finally breaking his duck against Tunisia. Despite his lack of goals, John Aldridge was a crucial factor in the Ireland side. He played in seven of the eight qualifiers for the 1988 European Championships and appeared in all three matches at the tournament finals in Germany.

Liverpool lost their chief striker Ian Rush at the end of the 1986–87 season and needed a proven and experienced replacement. Aldridge, who even bore a physical resemblance to Rush, joined Kenny Dalglish's Liverpool for £750,000 in January 1987. Aldo flourished at Anfield, where he had three highly successful seasons, scoring 61 goals in 103 League and Cup games. It was in 1987–88 that he hit the headlines, for after scoring in the opening nine League games, his clinical finishing brought him 29 League and Cup goals. However, though he was usually a ferocious and accurate penalty-taker, he was devastated to miss in that season's FA Cup Final against Wimbledon, as it robbed the Reds of a much-deserved double. When Rush returned from Italy it was obvious that Anfield was not big enough for both of them and Aldridge joined Spanish club Real Sociedad for £1.1 million.

It was as a Sociedad player that Aldridge travelled to Italy for the 1990 World Cup Finals. He didn't score in the tournament where the Republic lost to the host nation in the last eight but though he played in all five games, he was substituted in each.

His exploits in Spain earned him the nickname 'El Zorro' but after two seasons in which he scored 40 goals in 76 games he returned to the Football League and Merseyside with Tranmere Rovers. In his first season at Prenton Park, he equalled Bunny Bell's record from 1933–34 by scoring 40 goals. The move to the Wirral-based club also preceded his best run of scoring for the national side.

Aldridge hit six goals in ten games during qualification for the 1994 World Cup Finals and made three appearances in the finals in the United States. In the game against Mexico, he was on the bench and about to replace Tommy Coyne when the officials intervened to prevent him from doing so until an administrative hitch had been resolved. After a six-minute delay during which time Ireland were down to ten men, Aldridge entered the fray and scored with a well-taken header. The goal proved decisive to the team's progress to the second round. He went on to score five goals in his last nine appearances, finishing with a highly respectable total of nineteen goals.

At Tranmere, he was the club's top scorer for six successive seasons before becoming player-manager in April 1996 following the departure of John King. Having scored 174 goals in 294 games for Rovers, he decided to concentrate fully on management. Though the club was involved in some memorable runs and giant-killing acts including reaching the 2000 League Cup Final, it was eventually relegated to English football's third tier in 2001. Aldridge parted company with the club just before it went down.

He is now a pundit with various media organisations, having recently gained media celebrity status in Ireland by appearing in RTÉ's *Charity You're a Star* competition. He won and in the process raised money for his nominated charity, Temple Street Children's Hospital.

Did you know?

Irish internationals Paddy Mulligan and Gary Waddock were both born on St Patrick's Day: Paddy in 1945 and Gary in 1962.

PACKIE BONNER

Jock Stein's eye for spotting real talent was legendary and Packie Bonner became the Big Man's last signing for Celtic when he joined the Hoops in May 1978. Along with Willie Miller and Ronnie Simpson, he is considered the greatest of Celtic's post-war goalkeepers.

Bonner, who was also a highly-rated Gaelic footballer, was spotted playing for Leicester City's youth team and very little persuasion was required to entice him over from his home in County Donegal. He made his Celtic debut on St Patrick's Day 1979 in a 2–1 victory over Motherwell and a year later had displaced Peter Latchford as the club's regular keeper. Not always blessed with the cream of the defensive world in front of him, Packie – a master shot-stopper with few peers in a one-on-one situation – went on to win four League Championship medals, three Scottish Cup medals and a League Cup medal in a career which saw him turn out for the club on well over 600 occasions.

However, Bonner will be best remembered for his heroics at international level. Having won caps for the Republic of Ireland at youth and Under-21 level, he was called into the senior squad for a tour of Germany and Poland in the summer of 1981. He made his full international debut on his twenty-first birthday in the game against Poland.

The arrival of Jack Charlton as Republic of Ireland team manager in 1986 proved the watershed in the international career of Packie Bonner. He missed just one of the Republic's qualifying matches ahead of the 1988 European Championships and despite missing Celtic's 1988 Scottish Cup Final victory over Dundee United due to injury, he played in each of the country's three matches during the tournament finals. His performance in the defeat of England in Stuttgart – especially the save late on to deny Gary Lineker – was memorable.

In the 1990 World Cup Finals in Italy, Packie Bonner conceded just two goals in the group matches but it was his display in the second round tie against Romania that made him a legend. After two hours of football, the game remained goalless and went to a penalty shoot-out. After each team had successfully converted four spot-kicks, the weary Bonner produced a superb save to deny Romania's Daniel Timofte. Although the Irish lost out to hosts Italy in the quarter-finals, Bonner was brilliant and unlucky to concede the game's only goal after making an excellent save from Donadini.

Back at club level, Bonner was dropped by Liam Brady and then given a free transfer by his successor Lou Macari. He was, however, persuaded to stay, although a little pressure was needed, when new boss Tommy Burns took over the reins months later. He then crowned a glorious career at Parkhead with a clean sheet in the 1995 Scottish Cup Final triumph over Airdrie.

Packie was subsequently a coach at Parkhead and, later, Reading, before being named as technical director and goalkeeping coach for the Football Association of Ireland under Brian Kerr in February 2003. He did not keep this position when Kerr was sacked and replaced with Steve Staunton. In addition, he has worked as a football presenter with TV3, Ireland.

LIAM BRADY

Arguably the most talented footballer ever produced by the Republic of Ireland, Liam Brady left Dublin at the age of fifteen for North London and Arsenal. His influence in his seven years at Highbury has only been matched by a handful of players – Alex James, Joe Mercer, Frank McLintock, Tony Adams and, of course, Thierry Henry.

The seventh son of a Dublin docker, Brady made his Arsenal debut against Birmingham City in October 1973, becoming a regular in the side in 1974–75, a season in which he won the first of his 72 caps for the Republic of Ireland. Brady was called into the national side for the European Championship qualifier against the USSR. On a memorable afternoon at Dalymount Park, Brady performed with great skill in a 3–0 win, the goals courtesy of a Don Givens hat-trick.

Liam Brady

Ever-present for Arsenal in seasons 1975–76 and 1976–77, the latter of which saw him create most of the goals scored by Malcolm Macdonald and Frank Stapleton. In 1977–78 he was a regular in the Gunners side which reached the League Cup semi-final and FA Cup Final.

His golden display in the 1979 FA Cup Final earned Brady the only winners' medal of his Arsenal career. He was the general who plotted Manchester United's downfall in that final, dancing a merry Irish jig on the famous sward in the most exciting climax to a Cup Final. Arsenal somehow managed to lose a two-goal cushion in the dying minutes of the game, only to snatch victory with a Brady-inspired winner in the last seconds to run out 3–2 winners. He also played in the 1980 FA Cup Final which Arsenal lost 1–0 to West Ham United.

The newly-crowned PFA 'Footballer of the Year' was also a member of Arsenal's European Cup Winners' Cup side which lost on penalties to Valencia.

During the close season he turned down Manchester United's bid of £1.5 million – which would have smashed the British transfer record – and opted for a £600,000 move to Italian giants, Juventus. Few foreign players can have settled so quickly into Italian football. He won the Italian League Championship in each of his two seasons with the club before being surprisingly replaced by Michel Platini. He moved to newly promoted Sampdoria before, two seasons later, signing for Inter Milan. Lastly, he played for Ascoli before returning to the Football League with West Ham United.

In 1985 Brady became the youngest player to record 50 appearances for the national team when he played against England at Wembley. The following year his status within Irish football met a new challenge when the FAI appointed Jack Charlton as manager. Though he tried hard, Brady could never disguise his creative instincts enough for Big Jack. There was one brief period of harmony in the qualifying rounds for the 1988 European Championships. Brady played in all of the games but in the dying minutes of the final group match against Bulgaria, he was sent-off for fouling his marker. The red card combined with a serious knee injury forced him to miss the finals. His international career was almost at an end when, in the friendly match against West Germany in September 1989, Charlton substituted him after only 35 minutes. Furious at the humiliation, Brady announced his retirement from international football.

After more than 100 games for the Hammers, Brady decided to call it a day during the summer of 1990.

A year later he became the first manager of Celtic not to have played for the Glasgow giants. He resigned in October 1993 after a string of poor results, later managing Brighton & Hove Albion. In 1996 he rejoined Arsenal as Head of Youth Development and Academy Director. Overseeing the club's two FA Youth Cup wins in 2000 and 2001, Liam Brady remains at the club where he proved he was the most outstanding player of his generation.

GARY BREEN

After his first club Maidstone United dropped out of the Football League at the end of the 1992–93 season, defender Gary Breen joined Gillingham where his impressive displays at the heart of the Kent club's defence led to Peterborough United paying the Gills £70,000 for his services. However, his career only really took off when in February 1996 he joined Birmingham City as a replacement for Liam Daish who had left St Andrew's to play for Coventry City.

Only three months after joining Birmingham, Breen won the first of his 63 full international caps for the Republic of Ireland when he came off the bench in the eighty-ninth minute of the 1–0 defeat to Portugal to replace Alan Kernaghan. It was Breen who was given the unenviable task of filling the boots of Paul McGrath and he emerged with great credit after a handful of appearances later that summer. Breen also proved him-self as an attacking threat, especially at set pieces, with a goal in the game against Holland. By the time the 1998 World Cup qualifiers came around, Breen was the Republic of Ireland's first-choice centre-half.

Rather surprisingly, Gary Breen's stay at St Andrews lasted just a year before Coventry City paid £2.4 million to take him to Highfield Road. A defender who likes to carry the ball out of defence, Breen is also very good in the air and in 1998–99 he played an important part in the Sky Blues' unbeaten FA Cup run. Playing for Coventry at both right-back and in central defence, he continued to appear on a regular basis for the Republic of

Gary Breen

Ireland. In 2000–01 he was voted Coventry City's Player of the Year and equalled the club's record for the most international appearances. Having become something of a cult figure at Highfield Road, his refusal to discuss new terms somewhat soured his relationship with the City fans.

After a number of outstanding performances for the Republic in the 2002 World Cup Finals, Breen was a target for a number of Premiership clubs, but it was West Ham United who won the race for his signature. Yet after just one season at Upton Park, he was on the move again, this time to Sunderland.

His first season at the Stadium of Light was disrupted when a medial ligament injury kept him out of first team action for over three months. However, on his return to full fitness he capped an excellent 2004–05 campaign by leading the Black Cats back to the Premiership and being selected in the PFA Championship team of the season. However, Sunderland's stay in the top flight lasted just one season and the club found themselves back in the Championship for the 2006–07 campaign.

Not every Sunderland supporter was convinced that the decision to release Gary Breen was the correct one as the majority of them thought he was the man to lead them back to the Premiership at the first attempt.

Breen joined Wolverhampton Wanderers on a free transfer in July 2006. A model professional, the central defender was calm and assured and was probably the Molineux club's best player in the early months of the 2006–07 campaign. He didn't miss a League game until January but after his second red card of the season, he was suspended for three games. He later returned to the club's starting line-up and he was made club captain by Wolves' boss Mick McCarthy.

NOEL CANTWELL

Having played his early football with Cork Athletic, Noel Cantwell joined West Ham United in the summer of 1952 and together with John Bond, formed one of the best full-back pairings ever seen at Upton Park.

West Ham and, in particular, Noel Cantwell began the 1953–54 season in good form but sadly the same couldn't be said for the Republic of Ireland. A disastrous World Cup qualifier defeat at the hands of France in the autumn of 1953 led the Irish selection committee to make a number of changes for the next game against Luxembourg. Cantwell, in his first match for the national side, played at centre-half and performed commendably in a 4–0 win. However, it turned out to be the West Ham player's only contribution to the 1954 qualifying campaign and it was another two years before he won his second cap. That came in a friendly against Spain at Dalymount Park in November 1955 and this time he appeared in his more customary left-back position.

He soon became a fixture in the Republic of Ireland side and was later chosen to replace Peter Farrell as the team's captain. He led the Irish out for the first time against England in a World Cup qualifying game at Dalymount Park in May 1957. Alf Ringstead had given the boys in green the lead but Cantwell, stretching to clear, accidentally presented a simple chance to John Atyeo and the 1–1 draw ended the Republic's hopes of reaching the 1958 World Cup Finals.

Cantwell led the Hammers to the 1957–58 Second Division title and the following season was a customary presence in the club's first season back in the top flight. His achievements at Upton Park were recognised in Ireland when he was voted 'Footballer of the Year' for 1958–59.

When he joined Manchester United for £29,500 in November 1960, it was a record fee for a full-back, though he had played at centre-half and occasional games as a centre-forward. He was signed by Matt Busby as part of his team re-building in the aftermath of the Munich disaster. Busby needed Cantwell to provide stability, character and knowledge, to inspire and cajole the younger players along what the manager realised could be a long and arduous road back to the top. Cantwell followed in a long line of fine captains and led United to victory in the 1963 FA Cup Final against Leicester City.

On the international scene, the Irish selection committee decided that they needed to add a strong presence to the national side's lacklustre forward line. Asked to lead the attack, Cantwell responded in typical fashion – cracking home a 40-yard drive against Austria in April 1962. Having picked up his bronze statuette for reaching 25 international caps, Cantwell celebrated with a goal against Scotland.

Without doubt though, the highlight of Noel Cantwell's international career came on 13 October 1963 during a European nations game against Austria. With the scores level at 2–2, the Irish were awarded a last-minute penalty. The Dalymount crowd erupted as Cantwell slotted home his second goal to earn the Republic of Ireland a quarter-final tie against Spain.

Towards the end of his playing days, Cantwell concentrated on the coaching side of the game and there were many who expected him to succeed Matt Busby at Old Trafford. Indeed, to this day, there are those who believe he would have been the best choice. Instead, Cantwell surprised everyone by replacing Jimmy Hill at Coventry City, later leading them into Europe.

Noel Cantwell

In 1972 he took over the reins at Peterborough United but in 1977 he quit the English game to enjoy brief spells in the NASL. He later returned to Peterborough but parted company with the club in 1989. A former PFA Chairman, Noel Cantwell was a double international, having also played cricket for his country.

JOHNNY CAREY

Johnny Carey had an illustrious playing career at club and international level which was followed by a successful but largely underrated series of managerial appointments. Above all else, Carey had a reputation for sportsmanship which won him the respect of teammates and opponents alike and made him a natural choice as captain.

Johnny Carey arrived at Old Trafford as a youngster and had the distinction of representing the Republic of Ireland before he had fully established himself in Manchester United's first team. He was spotted by United's talent scout Louis Rocca who, rumour has it, had gone to watch another player. It was allegedly only Carey's third game of football but Rocca was so keen that the seventeen–year-old was signed before he even had time to take off his boots!

In 1937–38 he helped United win promotion to the First Division and though he went on to appear in 53 games before the war intervened, he faced stiff competition from Stan Pearson. They were so equally matched that the state of the pitch often decided whether Carey or the more heavily-built Pearson played.

Army service in the Middle East, Italy and elsewhere interrupted his career. He returned to a bomb-devastated Old Trafford in 1945 and began a seven-year run with the first of Busby's great sides. Before the first League season had ended, Carey had switched from inside-forward to half-back and finally to full-back., the position in which he is best remembered.

He captained United's 1948 FA Cup winning team and the one that finally lifted the League Championship in 1951–52 after several near misses. A versatile player, he figured in nine different positions for the Reds, ten if you include the occasion he pulled on the goalkeeper's jersey when Jack Crompton was taken ill at an away match. He was also adaptable on the international stage, appearing in seven different positions for the Republic of Ireland.

During the 1952–53 season, Carey was awarded a statuette by the Football Association of Ireland to mark his record twenty-fifth appearance for the national side. Carey was capped 29 times by the Republic of Ireland – including leading his country to a famous 2–0 win over England at Everton's Goodison Park in 1949 – and played seven times for Northern Ireland. Carey also captained the Rest of Europe against Great Britain in 1947 and was voted 'Footballer of the Year' in 1949 and 'Sportsman of the Year' in 1950.

A thoroughly polished performer, Carey ended his playing career whilst still at the top, making 32 First Division appearances in 1952–53 and by the time he hung up his boots, he had made 344 appearances and scored 18 goals for United. He could have remained at Old Trafford as coach but he chose to move into management with Blackburn Rovers.

He led Rovers to promotion to the First Division and this success led to him being appointed manager of Everton in 1958. This was the one club in which he failed to make a big impact – he was famously fired by Everton chairman John Moores in a London taxi. From Everton he went to Brisbane Road and guided Leyton Orient into the top flight for the first and only time in the O's history. Carey then had five seasons in charge of Nottingham Forest, taking them to an FA Cup semi-final and runners-up spot in the First Division in 1966–67. Carey's last job in football was a second spell in charge of Blackburn which ended in 1971.

He left football to work for a textile machine company and ended his working days in 1984 in the Treasurer's Office of Trafford Borough Council. His retirement was spent in Bramall, Cheshire where he indulged in his passion for golf and made regular visits to his beloved Old Trafford.

> ## Did you know?
> The last time the Republic fielded a team comprised wholly of players born in Ireland was in the 4–0 European Championship victory over Turkey in October 1975.

TONY CASCARINO

Though he had more than his fair share of criticism throughout his playing career, be it at club or international level, Tony Cascarino always bounced back to let his football do the talking.

Cascarino started out with Gillingham but his displays soon led to him making his international debut for the Republic of Ireland in a World Cup qualifier against Switzerland in Berne. Though the game ended goalless, Cascarino had impressed enough to keep his place for the next couple of games. He became eligible to pull on the green shirt of Ireland when FIFA altered their rules to allow a mother's origins to be taken into account: his maternal grandfather came from Westport in County Mayo.

Cascarino stayed at the Priestfield Stadium for six seasons, four of which saw him as the club's leading scorer, netting 78 goals in 219 League appearances. In June 1987 he was transferred to Millwall for a fee of £250,000. For a player who had supported the Lions from the terraces as a youngster, it was a dream come true.

At the Den, Cascarino linked up with Teddy Sheringham to form the most feared and prolific strike force in the Second Division. The partnership paid dividends immediately: in his first season, Cascarino netted 20 goals in 39 games compared to Sheringham's 22 in 43 games; and the Lions were Second Division champions, moving into the top flight for the first time in their history. Cascarino spent a further two seasons at Millwall, scoring 22 more goals in a further 66 games.

His goalscoring feats saw Cascarino return to the Republic of Ireland side in a friendly against Poland which the Irish won 3–1. It proved enough to earn him a place in the squad for Euro '88 and he was ever-present in the Republic's qualifying campaign for the 1990 World Cup Finals.

Towards the end of 1990–91, Aston Villa were in a Championship dogfight with Liverpool and Villa boss Graham Taylor smashed the club's transfer record by paying Millwall £1.5 million for the Irish international. Cascarino didn't have time to acclimatise and only found the net in the last two games of the season as Villa were pipped at the post.

There was more disappointment for Cascarino in the 1990 World Cup Finals in Italy. After two games without a goal he was relegated to the bench for the Republic's next match against Holland. During the next decade, Cascarino became a specialist No. 12 for the Irish. In fact, no player has made more appearances off the bench for the boys in green than Tony Cascarino.

After another season with Villa, Cascarino joined Celtic at a cut price fee of £1.1 million. He also failed to hit form with the Glasgow giants and spent most of 1991–92 on the bench. In January 1992 he joined Chelsea in a straight swap deal that saw Tommy Boyd move to Parkhead. Initially his fortunes took a turn for the better after he scored on his debut but it turned out to be a false dawn as he scored just once more in ten further outings that season. The following season was a disaster for the big man as he was laid low by two cartilage operations. He recovered in time to be a playing substitute when Chelsea lost the 1994 FA Cup Final to Manchester United.

In the summer of 1994 he was freed by Chelsea and subsequently joined French Second Division club Marseille. His career took an upward swing in France and as he began scoring regularly, he became something of a cult figure at the club. He ended his first season at Marseille as top scorer with 38 League goals. He later enjoyed further success in France when he joined AS Nancy-Lorraine.

A regular with the Irish side, Cascarino scored 19 goals in 88 international appearances.

KENNY CUNNINGHAM

Having played his early football with Tolka Rovers and Home Farm, Kenny Cunningham had a trial for Millwall and after a series of impressive displays, signed professional forms for the Lions. He made his League debut in a 1–1 draw with Norwich City in March 1990 and in the remaining matches lined up alongside his future international manager Mick McCarthy. But at the end of the season, Millwall lost their top flight status, and were relegated to the old Second Division.

After securing a regular spot at right-back, the stylish and versatile Glasnevin defender's displays led to him winning four caps for the Republic of Ireland at Under-21 level. After 136 League appearances for Millwall, Cunningham's reputation was growing and in November 1994, manager McCarthy cashed in by accepting Wimbledon's offer of £1.3 million in a joint deal which also took Jon Goodman to Selhurst Park.

Kenny Cunningham

Progress in the Premiership was followed by a full international debut for the Republic of Ireland against the Czech Republic in Prague in April 1996. Two years later, Cunningham's increasing importance to the national side was twice rewarded: when he was handed the captaincy for the friendly against the Czech Republic; and when he was named the FAI/Opel International Player of the Year towards the end of 1998.

One of the game's most versatile defenders, Cunningham captained the Dons. In 1999–2000 he played in every game except the 'Black Sunday' match against Southampton at The Dell, in which the Dons were relegated from the Premiership. The hugely popular player missed most of the following campaign with a groin injury but returned to action in 2001–02 when he was voted Wimbledon's 'Player of the Year'.

Cunningham was transferred to Birmingham City for a fee of £600,000 in the summer of 2002 and was outstanding at the heart of the Blues' defence and instrumental in the club avoiding relegation. Deservedly named the club's 'Player of the

Year' in his first season at St Andrew's, he was appointed club captain. Though he initially suffered a spate of injuries, when fit he produced quiet but highly-efficient performances. He continued to provide a steadying influence at the back during some fraught games for City but after a public bust-up with then Birmingham boss Steve Bruce, he left the Midlands club to sign for Sunderland.

Prior to his arrival at the Stadium of Light, Sunderland charirman Niall Quinn praised his leadership qualities and his exceptional reading of the game. He played regularly during the early part of the 2006–7 season but after October didn't get a look in as the Black Cats went on to win the Championship and promotion to the Premiership. Released in the close season, Kenny Cunningham, who won 72 caps for the Republic of Ireland, was unable to find a new club and decided to retire.

He has recently worked for RTÉ as a pundit.

GERRY DALY

Gerry Daly

Midfielder Gerry Daly was one of the bright young stars in Tommy Docherty's Manchester United side after his arrival from Dublin club Bohemians for a fee of £12,500 in April 1973.

His time at Old Trafford was a mixture of joy and despair: he was on the fringes of the 1973–74 relegation side; an integral part of the team which won the Second Division Championship the following season; and a losing finalist at Wembley in 1976 when United lost 1–0 to Southampton in the FA Cup Final. He was also United's penalty-taker and had netted 23 goals in 111 games for the club when a disagreement with the manager brought his United career to an abrupt end. In March 1977 Derby County boss Colin Murphy stepped in and secured his services for £190,000, making him Ireland's most expensive player at the time.

Daly had an immediate impact on a struggling Derby side. His hard work and battling qualities helped the club to a position of safety in the First Division. He was enjoying his football at the Baseball ground but when Tommy Docherty arrived from Old Trafford in 1977 to take over from Colin Murphy, Daly asked for a transfer. The request was later withdrawn but the two men had an uneasy relationship. In August 1980, after 112 League games and 31 goals, Daly was sold by Colin Addison, who had replaced Docherty in the Derby hot seat. Daly went to Derby's First Division rivals Coventry City for £300,000

In four years at Highfield Road, Daly scored 19 goals in 84 League games. He also scored once in seventeen games for Leicester City with whom he had a loan spell, contributing to the Foxes' promotion to the top flight. In August 1984 he was transferred to Birmingham City for a meagre £10,000 – a fee set by a tribunal. Exactly a decade after helping Manchester United win the Second Division title, Daly helped the Blues to second place in the Second Division. He had 32 League outings for Birmingham before joining Second Division Shrewsbury Town in October 1985. He later made 22 First Division appearances for Stoke City before signing for his final League club, Fourth Division Doncaster Rovers.

Around the time of Daly's move to Coventry City, Eoin Hand was appointed coach of the Republic of Ireland – this coincided with Gerry Daly's best run of form in the green shirt. Daly scored three times in Hand's first four games in charge and proved a highly-valued source of both goals and inspiration in an Irish side which narrowly missed out on qualification for the 1982 World Cup Finals.

Daly, who had made his international debut for the Republic Ireland as a substitute against Poland shortly after joining Manchester United, appeared in three other games from the bench before he was given his first start by Johnny Giles in the match against West Germany 'B'. From September 1976, following his superb performance against England – when he scored from the penalty-spot in a 1–1 draw – he became a regular in the national side for the rest of the decade.

Not content with donning the colours of eight Football League clubs, Daly also spent May 1973 and May 1979 with New England Tea Men in the North American Soccer League (NASL).

At the beginning of the 1990–91 season, he became player-manager of Vauxhall Conference club Telford United, a post from which he was dismissed in October 1993. Sadly, Gerry Daly, who scored 13 goals in 48 games for the Republic of Ireland, is now unable to work because of a back problem.

Damien Duff

DAMIEN DUFF

Damien Duff joined Blackburn Rovers after playing for Leicester Celtic, St Kevin's Boys and Lourdes Celtic as a schoolboy in Dublin. Impressive displays in the club's reserve side saw him make his debut for Rovers as an eighteen–year-old on the final day of the 1996–97 season against Leicester City.

Although he was used sparingly the following season, he showed himself to be fast with great control – a player who could comprehensively beat opponents. By the end of the season he was billed as a big star of the future and, despite not having played for the Republic of Ireland at Under-21 level, was handed a full international debut by Mick McCarthy in the game against the Czech Republic in March 1998. After impressing in Ireland's next game against Mexico, he was chosen in the side to begin the Euro 2000 qualifiers as the national team's first-choice left-winger.

Despite Blackburn's relegation the following season, Duff stayed loyal to the club and did not ask for a transfer, despite the obvious attention he was receiving from top flight clubs. He helped Rovers achieve promotion back to the Premiership in 2000–01 when he was honoured by his fellow professionals with a place in the PFA's First Division team. Having helped Blackburn win the League Cup in 2002, he went on to have an outstanding World Cup including a goal in the 3–0 defeat of Saudi Arabia and was voted the Republic's Player of the Tournament.

Identified as a world-class player, rumours were rife that Duff would move to a bigger club. However, he signed a new four-year contract with Rovers. He then suffered a frustrating time by recurring hamstring problems but was still the club's top-scorer in that injury-ravaged season of 2002–03 with eleven goals. Buoyed by new owner Roman Abramovich's money, Chelsea made a series of bids for Duff, with a £17 million offer eventually triggering a release clause in the player's contract.

His first season at Stamford Bridge was somewhat plagued by injury and crucially he missed the latter stages of the season including the Champions League semi-final against Liverpool. However, he was instrumental in securing for Chelsea the highest League finish for 49 years as well as the Champions League run but the season ultimately ended trophy-less and with the sacking of Claudio Ranieri. New manager Jose Mourinho did not play Duff in the early part of the 2004–05 season but his versatility eventually saw him win a place and he went on to become an important member of the side that won both the Premiership and the Carling Cup. The 2005–06 season was a disappointing one for Duff and at the end of the campaign he completed a £5 million move to Newcastle United.

His displays for the Magpies during the early stages of his first season at St James's Park failed to live up to those with both Blackburn and Chelsea, although he did score for the Republic of Ireland in a 3–0 defeat of Sweden in what was Steve Staunton's first match in charge. A knee injury in November 2006 kept him out of action for four months. Shortly after his return to the side, he suffered a career-threatening injury against Portsmouth and this winner of 66 caps for the Republic of Ireland only made his return to first-team action in December 2007 when he came off the bench against bottom of the league Derby County. Since then, he has featured prominently in Kevin Keegan's plans.

JIMMY DUNNE

Jimmy Dunne was the first Irishman to figure prominently in the English Football League's scoring records and as a result, was idolised by football fans in Ireland.

His football career was put on hold during the Irish Civil War when he was interned by the Irish Free State authorities for alleged Republican sympathies – his brother Christy was an active Republican. He subsequently joined Shamrock Rovers where he did enough to impress a scout who recommended him to New Brighton of the Third Division (North). Joining them in November 1925, he made an immediate impact, scoring six goals in eight League games.

He soon attracted the attention of the leading clubs and in February 1926, he was signed by Sheffield United. He had to wait until the start of the 1926–27 season before making his debut in a 4–0 defeat of Arsenal but struggled to hold down a regular place, making just eleven appearances in his first three seasons at Bramall Lane and at one stage, he even found himself on the transfer list.

It wasn't until the 1929–30 season that Dunne became a goalscoring sensation. His first hat-trick against Leicester City in a 3–3 draw in September was followed by successive four-goal hauls against West Ham United (4–2) on New Year's Day and Leicester City (7–1) three days later. He scored another hat-trick against Blackburn Rovers in March and finished the season as the club's top goalscorer with 36 goals in 39 games. His goals helped the Blades avoid relegation to the Second Division on goal average.

Dunne was subsequently top goalscorer at United for four consecutive seasons between 1929 and 1933. This included scoring over 30 First Division goals in three consecutive seasons between 1930 and 1933. His best season was 1930–31 when he scored 41 League goals plus a further nine in other competitions, including nine hat-tricks! Outstanding with his head, his total included a hat-trick of headers against Portsmouth. The following season he scored in twelve successive games with a haul of eighteen goals. A legend in Sheffield United's history, where only three players have bettered his total of 143 League goals, Dunne's prolific scorer attracted the interest of Arsenal who, after having a bid of £10,000 turned down, got their man for a reduced fee of £8,250 after United hit financial trouble.

When Dunne began his international career, there were, in effect, two Ireland teams, chosen by two rival associations. Both associations, the Northern Ireland-based IFA and the Irish Free State-based FAI, claimed jurisdiction over the whole of Ireland and selected players from the whole island. As a result several players including Dunne played for both teams. His debut for the Republic saw him score twice in a 3–1 win in Belgium and over the course of nine years in which he scored thirteen goals in fifteen games, he also netted 'doubles' against Hungary and Luxembourg.

In his first season at Highbury, Dunne scored nine goals in 23 outings to help Arsenal win the First Division title. However, the arrival of Ted Drake in the summer of 1934 saw Dunne lose his first team place and over the next two seasons he made just eight appearances. He later played for Southampton and was their leading scorer during the 1936–37 season when his goals helped the club avoid relegation to the Third Division. Opting not to renew his contract, he returned to Shamrock Rovers as player-manager and was the inspiration behind the Hoops winning League of Ireland titles in 1938 and 1939. He also helped Rovers win the FAI Cup in 1940. Dunne went on to coach Bohemians from 1942 to 1947 before returning to Rovers once again.

Jimmy Dunne died suddenly from a heart attack at the age of just 44 in November 1949.

TONY DUNNE

Capped by the Republic of Ireland as both an amateur and a professional, Tony Dunne cost Manchester United a bargain £5,000 when he joined them from Shelbourne in April 1960. In the week before his transfer he won an FAI Cup winners' medal when Shelbourne beat Cork Hibernians 2–0 at Dalymount Park.

He was a centre-forward during his junior days in Dublin with St Finbarr's and Tara United and matured in United's reserve side before claiming a regular first team place midway through the 1961–62 season, replacing his international colleague Noel Cantwell in the left-back position. The wiry Dunne did so well that for some time after Cantwell's recovery from injury, he was unable to displace his young countryman.

Dunne won the first of his 33 international caps against Austria in Dublin in April 1962. In his early days with the Republic, he was played at right-back but his best performances at national level came when he was paired at left-back with his United teammate Shay Brennan playing at right-back. Dunne was an important player in the Irish team that narrowly missed out on qualification for the 1966 World Cup Finals.

The pinnacle of Tony Dunne's international career came three years later when he was appointed captain of the Republic of Ireland side for the first time. The honour came shortly after he had been named Ireland's 'Player of the Year'. Playing alongside

Tony Dunne

his brother Pat, he skippered his country on four more occasions over the next six years but in the summer of 1972 he fell out with manager Liam Tuohy and was only recalled to the side after Johnny Giles had taken over as team boss.

One of the top full-backs in Manchester United's history, the loyal and consistent Dunne was an FA Cup winner with United in 1963, won League Championships in 1964–65 and 1966–67, and won a European Cup winners' medal in 1968 when he turned in an outstanding display in the final against Benfica. He frustrated the Benfica attackers with resolute defending, moved forward at will and curved long accurate passes into the paths of the front men. He had thirteen seasons at Old Trafford in which he appeared in 530 League and Cup games but in April 1973, Dunne – with six other players including Denis Law – was freed by United boss Tommy Docherty.

In August 1973, Tony Dunne was transferred to Third Division Bolton Wanderers. During a five- year spell at Burnden Park, his high standards never faltered and he was a key member of the 1977–78 side which won the championship of the Second Division. At the end of the following season and following 192 League and Cup appearances for Bolton, Dunne retired from League football.

He then jetted off to the United States to play for Detroit Express in the NASL.

Tony Dunne, who still follows the fortunes of both United and the Wanderers, later managed the golf-driving range he built in Altrincham shortly after hanging up his boots.

TOMMY EGLINGTON

One of the early giants of Irish football, Tommy Eglington also excelled at Hurling and Gaelic football during his schooldays but in the late 1940s and early 1950s, just the mention of his name sent shivers down the spines of First Division defenders.

He joined Everton from Shamrock Rovers in the summer of 1946 in a double transfer deal involving the Blues' other immediate post-war great, Peter Farrell. Eglington had had just one season with Shamrock Rovers before his move to Merseyside and ended that 1945–46 campaign as the Hoops' leading scorer with eleven goals from his left-wing berth. The double deal which cost Everton £10,000 has often been described as the best piece of business in the club's history.

Elegant and unruffled, with an explosive burst of pace and a thundering shot, Tommy Eglington was the Republic of Ireland's regular outside-left for a decade in the immediate post-war years. During that time he won 24 caps, scored two goals – both in 4–0 wins against Austria and Luxembourg respectively and was national team captain on two occasions.

Eglington made his Everton debut in a 3–2 home win over Arsenal in September 1946, going on to claim a regular place for the next eleven seasons – all but three of which were spent in the top flight. Following Everton's relegation at the end of the 1950–51 season, they were promoted back to the First Division in 1953–54 having finished runners-up to Leicester City on goal difference.

During the club's spell in the Second Division, Eglington guaranteed himself a place in the pages of the club's history. On 27 September 1952 he almost single-handedly demolished Doncaster Rovers at Goodison Park, scoring five times in a 7–1 win. He ended that season as the club's leading scorer in the Football League with 14 goals in 39 games.

Eglington was one of only a handful of players to have appeared for both Northern Ireland and the Republic. He was a member of the Irish side which recorded an historic 2–0 victory over an England side – appropriately enough at Goodison Park – in 1949. They became the first overseas side to defeat England on English soil.

He was a poised and graceful player, head down; fast; haring straight for the corner flag before firing off pinpoint crosses. Tommy Eglington was a winger of the old school but after scoring 76 times in 394 League games, he left Everton for Tranmere Rovers in the summer of 1957.

Tommy Eglington

TOP 50 PLAYERS

For a little over three seasons, he gave the Wirral-based club the same wholehearted service that he had given the Blues, before finally hanging up his boots and returning to his native Dublin, where, for many years, he ran a butcher's shop.

PETER FARRELL

Peter Farrell, whose career coincided with that of Tommy Eglington, played for Shamrock Rovers' first team as a schoolboy. In August 1946 he and Tommy joined Everton in a combined deal of £10,000 spread over two years. Considering that the transaction was regarded by many as one of Everton's most successful transfer deals, it is ironic that the Merseyside club scouts had actually gone to Dublin to see another player in an Inter City Cup Final!

Peter Farrell

Peter Farrell was an archetypal wing-half, a tireless worker who thrived on one-to-one situations and never shirked a tackle. Like his close friend Eglington, he had eleven seasons at Goodison Park, during which he became something of a living legend. In fact, he is one of the few footballers to have a street named after him – Farrell Close, near Goodison Park.

His Everton debut was postponed until late November 1946 because of an injury he sustained playing tennis. After that, he was a popular choice in the Everton side – never dropped, he went on to make 453 League and Cup appearances.

On the international front, Peter Farrell appeared at left-half for Northern Ireland in seven internationals between September 1946 and March 1949, while he was a regular in the Republic of Ireland side from 1946 to 1957, making a total of 28 appearances – the last following a 5–1 World Cup qualifying defeat at the hands of England in 1957. He scored one of the goals in the Republic's epic 2–0 defeat of England at Goodison Park in September 1949. Farrell also achieved the unusual distinction of captaining his country in his first international, an honour bestowed on him in a further eleven internationals.

Peter Farrell, who was Everton captain when the Blues dropped down to the Second Division at the end of the 1950–51 season – only the second time this had happened in the club's history – led the side back to the First Division three seasons later. An inspiration to all around him and very popular on the field, Farrell was also something of a hero off it, mixing freely with the club's supporters in a down-to-earth manner.

In October 1957, less than six months after Tommy Eglington left Everton for Tranmere Rovers, Peter Farrell embarked on the same short journey across the River Mersey to link up yet again with his close friend and colleague. Not surprisingly, Farrell was immediately appointed captain at Prenton Park. Although his three seasons on the Wirral were not the happiest of his long career, he continued to play as enthusiastically as ever, more than justifying Tranmere's £2,500 investment in a player heading towards the end of his career.

After a brief spell as caretaker-boss of Tranmere, he left Tranmere at the end of 1960 to join Welsh non-League side Hydhist Town as player-manager, later returning to Ireland to continue in management before working in broadcasting with RTÉ in Dublin.

STEVE FINNAN

Though he was born in Limerick, Steve Finnan moved to England at a young age. He began his career with non-League Welling United, before being spotted by scouts for Birmingham City. He had appeared in only a handful of matches for the Blues, including scoring on his debut at Watford, when he found himself on his way to Notts County, initially on loan. On his return to St Andrew's he was selected for the Republic of Ireland's Under-21 side against Norway in May 1996, scoring the equaliser in a 1–1 draw. Having impressed in his loan spell at Meadow Lane, he joined Notts County on a permanent basis in October 1996. The following season he was selected for the Republic of Ireland 'B' side and helped County run away with the Third Division Championship.

His performances that season prompted Fulham boss Kevin Keegan to pay £600,000 for the defender in November 1998. He became a instant regular at Craven

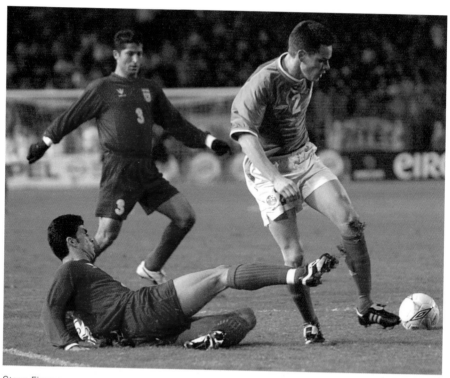

Steve Finnan

Cottage and a fans' favourite, playing in a variety of positions including right-wing back and central midfield. A Second Division Championship medal was the prize as the Cottagers revival continued. It is not often that a player wins Championship medals in successive seasons with different clubs, but Finnan did. He was also selected for the PFA award-winning divisional side.

In April 2000, Finnan won his first cap for the Republic of Ireland when he appeared against Greece, following this with the end-of-season friendly against Scotland. He cemented his place in the Irish starting line-up towards the end of qualification for the 2002 World Cup, supplying the cross for Jason McAteer to score the only goal in the crucial 1–0 home win against Holland in September 2001.

In 2000–01, Finnan was Fulham's most outstanding player, helping the Cottagers win the First Division Championship and winning selection for the PFA First Division side. He was selected for every match in Fulham's first season in the Premiership, he was named as the club's 'Player of the Season' and selected for the PFA Premiership team ahead of the likes of Gary Neville.

Not surprisingly, Finnan was named in the Irish squad for the 2002 World Cup Finals, going on to play in all of the nation's four matches in South Korea and Japan.

On his return to Craven Cottage he continued to show the form that had made him a target for a number of top Premiership clubs and after continuing as a regular selection for the Republic under new boss Brian Kerr, he joined Liverpool in June 2003 for a fee of £3.5 million.

Finnan's first season at Anfield was disrupted by a succession of injuries and, not surprisingly, he struggled to settle into his new surroundings. The appointment of a new manager at Anfield in the summer of 2004 prompted some to cast doubt on his future at the club, but his ultra-professionalism and composed defending won the day. He won a European Champions' League medal in 2005 despite being substituted at half-time and playing no part in Liverpool's stunning recovery.

He had a highly successful 2005–06 season, adding another medal to his collection as Liverpool won the FA Cup. In May 2007 he featured in his second Champions' League final, playing 88 minutes before Benitez introduced Alvaro Arbeloa. The popular defender signed a new two-year deal in August 2007 with the option of a further year but, sadly, has suffered more than his fair share of injuries throughout 2007–08.

JOHNNY GILES

Another product of the famous Dublin nursery, Home Farm, Johnny Giles left Ireland at the age of fifteen to join Manchester United. After working his way up through the ranks at Old Trafford, Giles made his first team debut but it wasn't the best of starts as United crashed 5–1 at home to Spurs.

A couple of months later, Giles played for the Republic of Ireland and scored just sixteen minutes into the 3–2 defeat of Sweden – at 19 years 304 days old, Giles was the youngest player to score for the boys in green.

With United he won an FA Cup winners' medal after they beat Leicester City 3–1 in 1963 – it was his last appearance for the Old Trafford outfit. Surprisingly, he was sold to United's

John Giles

TOP 50 PLAYERS

Yorkshire rivals Leeds United for a fee of £32,000. It has been said on many occasions since that the worst decision ever made by the Red Devils.

Giles was a brilliant tactician, a player with one of the game's shrewdest brains. He was transformed by Leeds manager Don Revie from a winger into one of the greatest midfield dynamos of the 1960s and even 1970s. In his first season at Elland Road, Giles helped Leeds win the Second Division Championship, which marked the beginning of the most successful era in the Yorkshire club's history. In the next ten seasons with Leeds, Giles won a number of honours including League Championship medals in 1968–69 and 1973–74; an FA Cup winners' medal in 1972; a League Cup winners' medal in 1968 and UEFA Cup winners' medals in 1968 and 1971.

Success with Leeds United had an adverse effect upon Johnny Giles' international career. Cup runs both domestically and in Europe resulted in a hectic fixture schedule. This meant it was not always possible for the Republic of Ireland to gain Johnny Giles' release for inter-national matches. The tension between the midfield maestro and the national selection committee was growing. The situation came to a head in 1969 when Giles was inexplicably dropped for the World Cup qualifier against Denmark in Copenhagen. He was not even considered good enough to sit on the bench. The Leeds player then reacted by making himself unavailable for the next game and though he soon returned to national action, the Republic's selection committee had made an enemy.

Over the next couple of seasons, Giles played a major role in the successful campaign to reform the Republic of Ireland's antiquated selection process.

In the summer of 1975 after appearing in 527 League and Cup games for Leeds United, Giles joined West Bromwich Albion. As player-manager of the Baggies, he took the club into the First Division at the end of his first season. After two more seasons at the Hawthorns, he returned to Ireland to play for and manage Shamrock Rovers, guiding the Hoops to victory in the 1978 FAI Cup Final.

Giles, who had been appointed player-manager of the Republic of Ireland in October 1973, continued playing until May 1979, making 59 appearances and captaining his country a record 30 times. He quit as manager in March 1980.

He later had brief spells in management with Vancouver Whitecaps and again at West Brom before eventually moving into work with the media.

SHAY GIVEN

Destined to be vice captain of both his club and country, goalkeeper Shay Given was invited to join Glasgow Celtic on a pre-season tour of Ireland when he was just fourteen years old and signed terms when he was sixteen under the stewardship of Republic of Ireland legend, Liam Brady. He spent two years playing for the Parkhead club's youth and Under-18 sides with one of his highlights being when he made the bench for the Old Firm clash against Rangers.

In 1994 he was transferred to Blackburn Rovers by new Hoops boss Kenny Dalglish. Despite some outstanding displays when he was given first team opportunities, he was unable to dislodge Tim Flowers on a permanent basis. He then went on loan to Swindon Town and then Sunderland, keeping twelve clean sheets in seventeen starts for the Black Cats. He picked up a First Division Championship medal and won his first full cap for Ireland, having earlier played at Under-21 level.

He went on to play in Mick McCarthy's first six games in charge before losing his place because he wasn't playing regular first team football at Blackburn. Desperate for first team football and out of contract at Ewood Park, Given joined Newcastle United for a tribunal-set fee of £1.5 million.

Given immediately established himself in the Magpies first team, beating fellow keeper Pavel Srnicek, Shaka Hislop and Steve Harper to the No. 1 jersey. He played in the 1998 FA Cup Final but missed out on the following season's FA Cup Final when Harper was preferred. The move to St James Park certainly enhanced his international prospects as he became a regular between the posts for the Republic of Ireland.

While training with the national team in the 1999 close season, he nicked a cartilage in his right knee and had to undergo surgery. In his second game back, he broke a bone in his wrist but following further treatment and rest, re-established himself as Newcastle's first-choice keeper. Over the next couple of seasons, Given proved himself to be one of the top goalkeepers in the Premiership.

In 2001–02 he played in every Premiership match and was named in the PFA Premiership team of the season. He was also voted 'Player of the Year' by the north-east football writers. He had an outstanding World Cup for the Republic in Japan and Korea but was powerless to stop his side exiting the tournament on penalties to Spain.

In April 2003, he became Newcastle's most capped player when he won his forty-first cap (fiftieth in total) and in doing so, overtook Alf McMichael's record. He set a new record for consecutive appearances in the competition (which was later surrendered to Chelsea's Frank Lampard) during the third season in succession but his run of 140 appearances came to an end when he was absent to attend the birth of his first child. Given also became the first Newcastle player to reach 50 European appearances and in 2005–06 again won selection to the PFA Premiership team of the year.

Having signed a new contract with Newcastle, he suffered a serious injury at West Ham United in September 2006 which necessitated emergency surgery to repair a tear in his abdomen. He joined United's '400' club in January 2007 and is currently sixth on the Magpies all-time appearance list. Having equalled Packie Bonner's total of 80 caps in the game against Slovakia in March 2007, when he was made captain for the day, Shay Given has now taken his total of appearances for the Republic of Ireland to 85.

DON GIVENS

Don Givens made his full international debut for the Republic of Ireland in a World Cup qualifier against Denmark in May 1969. It marked the beginning of a colourful and certainly action-packed international career which spanned 12 years and brought him 19 goals in 56 appearances.

He holds the record for scoring Ireland's quickest-ever hat-trick. It came in the 4–0 defeat of Turkey in October 1975 and took him just nine minutes. This was the first treble scored by a Republic of Ireland player since Paddy Moore 40 years before. For good measure, he also scored the Republic's fourth goal in that game.

He could be a volatile player and was sent off twice while playing for Ireland – against Ecuador in June 1972 and against Chile in May 1974. His final appearance for the boys in green came in October 1981 in the epic 3–2 victory over France. At that time, he headed the Republic of Ireland's scoring charts until he was overtaken by Frank Stapleton.

Don Givens

He started out with Manchester United, captaining the club's youth team and hadn't even appeared in their League side when he won his first full cap. Despite scoring four goals in his first seven internationals, he was unable to hold down a regular place at Old Trafford, and was transferred to Second Division Luton Town for £15,000 in April 1970.

After a couple of seasons at Kenilworth Road in which he scored 19 goals in 83 League outings, Givens joined Queen's Park Rangers for a fee of £40,000. Don Givens enjoyed the most settled and productive spell of his career at Loftus Road. The dangerous hitman spent six seasons with Rangers, netting 76 times in 242 League games and helping them win promotion to the First Division in 1972–73 as runners-up to Burnley.

Towards the end of his international career, Givens joined Birmingham City and his transfer fee soared to £165,000. He helped the Midlands club win promotion to the First Division in his first season at St Andrew's but following their immediate relegation, he had a loan spell with Bournemouth prior to ending his League career with Sheffield United. Whilst on loan with the Cherries, Givens scored four goals in five games.

His last kick for the Blades in the Football League was a missed penalty in the relegation dogfight with Walsall in May 1981. Walsall had a one-point lead before the game but Sheffield United had a vastly superior goal difference which meant that a point would be sufficient to keep them up. United lost the game 1–0 and Givens' missed spot-kick condemned the Yorkshire club to Fourth Division football the following season.

Givens then joined Swiss club Xamax prior to coaching at Arsenal's FA Academy. Later he was appointed the Republic of Ireland Under-21 manager, a position he still holds, though he has on two occasions taken temporary charge of the full national side.

TONY GREALISH

Though he was born in London, Tony Grealish enjoyed an Irish upbringing as his parents were both involved in the city's Gaelic Athletic Association. As a youngster he showed great promise as a Gaelic footballer and represented London in the All-Ireland Minor Football Championships.

The tigerish midfielder was a schoolboy footballer with Leyton Orient before joining the club as an apprentice in the summer of 1972. Two years later he signed professional forms and in 1976 was voted the O's 'Player of the Year'. Just prior to winning this award, the nineteen–year-old won the first of 45 caps for the Republic of Ireland in a friendly against Norway. Tony Dunne and Joe Kinnear had just ended their international careers, so it was in the unusual position of full-back that Grealish played his first international in a 3–0 win. He kept his place in the side for the next game against Poland but then found himself out of the side as Johnny Giles' team made an unsuccessful attempt to qualify for the 1978 World Cup Finals in Argentina.

Grealish had five seasons with Leyton Orient, scoring 10 goals in 171 Second Division appearances before in the summer of 1979 transferring to the O's rivals, Luton Town, for a fee of £150,000. Orient had wanted £350,000 but manager David Pleat

Tony Grealish

had refused to agree to their asking price and the fee was eventually decided by an independent tribunal.

It was whilst with the Hatters that Grealish enjoyed his best football with the Republic of Ireland. Together with Liam Brady and Gerry Daly, he formed a top midfield trio – the driving force behind Ireland's impressive but sadly unsuccessful bid to qualify for the 1982 World Cup Finals. Grealish skippered the side in Alan Kelly's sole match in charge but took over the captain's armband on a regular basis following the appointment of Eoin Hand.

In two seasons at Kenilworth Road, Tony Grealish made 78 League appearances before joining Brighton and Hove Albion for £100,000 in July 1981. He was captain of the Seagulls side which drew 2–2 with Manchester United in the 1983 FA Cup Final and then lost the replay 4–0. That season, 1982–83, the south coast club were relegated to the Second Division.

When former Republic of Ireland international Johnny Giles was appointed manager of West Bromwich Albion, he targeted Tony Grealish as the man to be his midfield general. In March 1984, Grealish became Giles' first major signing in a £75,000 transfer deal. In one and a half seasons at the Hawthorns, Grealish made 65 First Division appearances before Manchester City boss Jimmy Frizzell took him to Maine Road. He made his City debut in the derby against Manchester United, having an outstanding game in a 1–1 draw. However, at the end of the season, City were relegated and Grealish moved on to Third Division Rotherham United.

His three seasons at Millmoor included a loan spell in Portugal with Salgueros but his 110 appearances for the Yorkshire club also saw him win a Fourth Division Championship medal in 1988–89 after the Millers had been relegated the previous season.

He later wound down his League career with Walsall before prior to the start of the 1992–93 season joining non-League Bromsgrove Rovers.. He later had spells with Atherstone United and Halesowen Harriers where he was player-coach.

IAN HARTE

When Ian Harte came off the bench for Leeds United in the Coca Cola Cup game against Reading, it completed an amazing family double – his uncle, Gary Kelly, who at 21 was just three years older than Harte, was already on the pitch. Uncle and nephew helped Leeds to a 2–1 win to take the Yorkshire club further down the road to Wembley.

Having joined Leeds from Home Farm in 1995, Harte developed into a key player for United, especially under the management of David O'Leary. He had made just four appearances for the Elland Road club when Ireland boss Mick McCarthy handed him his full international debut against Croatia in June 1996. McCarthy was impressed by the youngster and included him in his next eight games in charge.

Harte was an integral part of the Leeds United team for nine seasons, although on occasions his passing let him down and at one point, when United bought Dominic Matteo, it looked as though Harte might become second choice. Thanks to injury, Matteo ended up playing at centre-half and Harte kept his place on the left. A proficient left-footed free-kick and penalty-taker, his performances for both club and country prompted Spurs to offer £2 million for his services but this was turned down by new Leeds manager George Graham.

Ian Harte

TOP 50 PLAYERS

In 1997–98 he had the unusual distinction of making more international appearances for the Republic of Ireland than for Leeds United's first team. Despite the signing of Danny Granville from Chelsea, Harte was Leeds' first-choice left-back in 1998–99. Though he continued to play on a regular basis for Leeds – scoring a hat-trick of free-kicks at Blackburn prior to the start of the 2000–01 season, he found himself out of the reckoning at international level until he returned to play in the 2002 World Cup qualifiers.

Harte played every minute as the Republic of Ireland reached the World Cup Finals, notching up four goals including a penalty against Iran in the play-off, though he struggled at the World Cup because of a toe injury. Though the emergence of John O'Shea restricted his appearances under new manager Brian Kerr, Harte later resumed his international career, taking his total of appearances for the boys in green to 64.

Towards the end of the 2002–03 season, Harte contributed three valuable goals as United narrowly avoided relegation. But then injuries began to hamper his progress at Elland Road and even when deemed fit, he failed to win a regular place in the Leeds side.

Though earlier in his career there had been rumours that clubs including Barcelona and AC Milan were willing to offer £11 million for his services, in the end, it was Spanish club Levante that signed him in 2004, following the financial crisis at the Yorkshire club.

Harte, who had played in 288 games for Leeds, had a couple of seasons in Spain before being released at the end of the 2006–07 La Liga season. In August 2007, it was announced that he had joined his former national teammate Roy Keane at Sunderland on a one-year contract. He made his Sunderland debut as a late substitute in the Black Cats' 3–2 defeat away at Arsenal but later, he was placed on the transfer list.

STEVE HEIGHWAY

Dublin-born Steve Heighway did not see a game of football until he moved to England with his parents at the age of ten. He was with Manchester City when he was seventeen and though they gave him every opportunity to enjoy a footballer's life, his education always came first. A graduate from Warwick University, he wasn't contemplating turning professional and was playing as an amateur for Skelmersdale United who were earning a growing reputation in the old Amateur Cup.

Heighway later signed for Liverpool and made his international debut for the Republic of Ireland against Poland in Dublin before he had even played in the Liverpool League side.

Heighway brought pace and width to the Reds attack, having a two-footed talent which enabled him to cut inside opponents or to pass them on the outside. In the months following his first team debut, he turned the tide in the Merseyside derby with Liverpool 2–0 down. He scored the first goal from an acute angle and then provided the pinpoint cross for John Toshack to equalise before Chris Lawler hit the third from a Heighway cross. He ended his first campaign with the club with a near post shot that deceived Arsenal goalkeeper Bob Wilson to give Liverpool the lead in the 1971 FA Cup Final, although the Gunners came back to win 2–1.

Steve Heighway

Despite wearing the No. 9 shirt, Steve Heighway was a winger with the audacity to take on defenders and confound then, running at them and getting past them time and time again.

The mercurial wing wizard helped Liverpool to European Cup success in 1977 and 1978 after victories over Borussia Moenchengladbach and FC Bruges respectively. The same teams provided the opposition in 1973 and 1976 when Liverpool won the UEFA Cup. Four First Division medals were added to his collection in 1972–73, 1975–76, 1976–77 and 1978–79; he won an FA Cup winners' medal in 1974 when he scored in the 3–0 win over Newcastle United.

Renowned for his athleticism, electrifying speed and intelligent football, Heighway, who became known as 'Big Bamber' at Anfield, played a major role in Liverpool's emergence under Bill Shankly as the dominant force in both British and European football.

In 1981 after 329 League appearances for the Reds, he jetted off to America to join Minnesota Kicks where he shimmied, darted and dashed in his own inimitable style for three seasons before becoming a coach and guiding the American Under-19 team to the last sixteen of the Junior World Cup.

At full international level, Heighway made 34 appearances for the Republic of Ireland. It is a total that would have been much higher had it not been for Liverpool's success both at home and abroad, which meant he wasn't always available for international fixtures.

When the position of youth development officer at Anfield became available in 1988, Steve Heighway jumped at the chance to return to what was his spiritual home. His experience with the youngsters in the States and his inside knowledge of the 'Liverpool way' made him the obvious choice for the job. He later became youth team manager and led his young charges to success in the FA Youth Cup in 1996.

According to Liverpool manager Bill Shankly, Steve Heighway was 'an individualist who could win a match with one flash of genius'.

MATT HOLLAND

Initially rejected by Arsenal for being 'too small', Matt Holland went to West Ham United where he moved up the ranks of the academy but never played for the

Matt Holland

Hammers' first team. In order to play first team football, Holland joined south coast club Bournemouth in January 1995.

In his first full season at Dean Court, Holland swept the board in the 'Player of the Year' awards. Playing mainly in a central midfield position, with a number of games as sweeper, he was appointed the Cherries' captain, and went on to score 18 goals in 116 games before joining Ipswich Town for a fee of £800,000 in the summer of 1997.

He soon became a firm favourite with the Portman Road crowd and was again appointed captain. Influential in Town's second-half surge up the table, he played in a variety of positions, displaying his wholehearted endeavour in every game he played. His most eventful experience came in the game against Oxford United, when he took over from the injured Richard Wright in goal while the keeper received stitches for a facial injury. Though he was powerless to prevent Kevin Francis from scoring, he scored the fourth goal himself in a 5–2 win, before, unfortunately, conceding a penalty.

Not surprisingly, Holland was voted the supporters' 'Player of the Year'. Instrumental in the club reaching the Premiership via the play-offs, Holland was rewarded with club captaincy.

Holland made his full international debut for the Republic of Ireland against Macedonia in October 1999 and also appeared in the end-of-season Nike Cup games in America. The following season he netted his first international goals against Andorra and Portugal, whilst at club level, he continued to epitomise all that is good about the Suffolk club – playing in the right spirit, hard but fair.

Holland captained Ipswich to fifth place in the Premiership and qualification for the UEFA Cup and in doing so, established himself as one of the best midfielders in the country. Though Ipswich were relegated at the end of the 2001–02 season, Holland stayed with the club after he turned down a £4.5 million move to Aston Villa. He went to the 2002 World Cup Finals with the boys in green and scored the equaliser against Cameroon in their opening game.

Again voted Ipswich Town's 'Player of the Year' for 2002–03, Holland left Portman Road in the close season following the club's failure to regain their top flight status. Having scored 46 goals in 314 games, including a spell of 223 consecutive games and only missing one League game (because of international duty), he signed for Charlton Athletic for an initial £750,000 fee which later rose to £900,000.

Holland, who was made club captain on his Addicks debut, soon became a huge crowd favourite. Forming a good understanding with Danny Murphy, he chipped in with some valuable goals and remains one of the longest-serving players at The Valley.

Following the Republic of Ireland's failure to qualify for the 2006 World Cup Finals, Matt Holland – one short of 50 caps – announced his retirement from international football.

RAY HOUGHTON

One of the most consistent performers of the Jack Charlton era, industrious midfielder Ray Houghton was brought up in Scotland but began his football career south of the border in London at West Ham United where he came through the ranks before signing professional forms. He failed to make much of an impression at Upton Park, making just a single substitute appearance in three years with the club and in July 1982 he moved to Fulham on a free transfer.

It was at Craven Cottage that his reputation as a hard-working, ball-playing midfielder flourished. In 1982–83, having won promotion to the Second Division the previous season, Houghton was part of the side that, for much of the campaign, looked as if they would win back-to-back promotions. It wasn't to be but over the next two seasons, his form was such that higher division sides began to sit up and take notice.

Jim Smith had taken Oxford United to the top flight and looked to Houghton to solidify their place in the First Division after he had paid the Cottagers £125,000 for his services in September 1985. Making his debut in a 2–2 draw with Liverpool, Houghton helped steer United clear of the relegation places but most notable he scored the second goal in the club's 3–0 League Cup Final victory over Queen's Park Rangers at Wembley.

Ray Houghton

His form for Oxford led to him winning the first of 73 caps for the Republic of Ireland in what was also Jack Charlton's first match in charge – a 1–0 defeat by Wales at Lansdowne Road in March 1986.

In October 1987 Houghton joined Liverpool, his value having soared to £825,000 and finished his first season at Anfield with a League Championship winners' medal. During the course of the campaign he contributed some fantastic displays as a marauding creator from the flank. He scored his fair share of goals too including the first in an era-defining 5–0 defeat of Nottingham Forest. Houghton did his best in the club's run to that season's FA Cup Final too, scoring the winning goal in the fifth round clash with rivals Everton and another in the quarter-final defeat of Manchester City.

Houghton joined teammates John Aldridge and Ronnie Whelan in the Republic of Ireland side for the 1988 European Championships. He played in all three of Ireland's group games and scored his first international goal with a much-celebrated header after five minutes of the opening game against England. The goal gave the Republic victory over a much-fancied England team and made Houghton a hero in his adopted country. However, after that great performance, they still failed to get through the group stage after a draw with USSR and a defeat against eventual champions, Holland.

He was in outstanding form in 1988–89 and was a strong presence on the Liverpool side. They narrowly failed to take the League title but won the FA Cup after beating Everton 3–2 in the final. Sadly, injuries caused the midfielder to miss much of the 1989–90 season but he bounced back towards the end of the campaign to help the Liverpool cause.

Having appeared in all eight qualifying matches for the 1990 World Cup, Houghton was again selected in the Irish squad for the finals. Ireland drew all three group games and then beat Romania on penalties in the knockout stages before losing 1–0 to hosts Italy in the quarter-finals.

Houghton helped Liverpool win another League title in 1990–91 and he picked an FA Cup winners' medal in 1992 but in the close season, new boss Graeme Souness allowed him to join Aston Villa. He helped his new club win the League Cup before returning to London and Crystal Palace.

In the summer of 1994 he was again in the Irish squad and once again he was the goalscoring hero in a shock win as Ireland beat Italy 1–0 at the Giants Stadium. Houghton's final appearance on the international stage came in a World Cup play-off match against Belgium in 1997.

He helped Palace to regain their top flight status via the play-offs and then joined Reading as player-coach.. After a couple of years with the Royals, he left to wind down his playing career with Stevenage Borough of the Nationwide Conference. One of the game's true gentlemen, Ray Houghton now works in the media for RTÉ, talkSPORT and Sky Sports.

CHRIS HUGHTON

A credit to both club and country, full-back Chris Hughton is widely respected as one of football's most articulate and finest ambassadors.

Chris Hughton joined Spurs as a thirteen–year-old in 1972. It was the beginning of a relationship between player and club which spanned almost three decades. He became a part-time defender at White Hart Lane in the summer of 1977 after completing a four-year apprenticeship as a lift engineer and made his League debut two years later in September 1979 against Manchester United.

A month later, Hughton, who qualified to play for the Republic of Ireland through his Limerick-born mother, made history by becoming the first black player to repre-

Chris Hughton

sent Ireland when he played against the United States. His pace, competitiveness and resolute defensive qualities endeared him to the Irish fans and he became an integral part of the Irish set-up for over ten years, making 53 appearances – his one goal coming in a 6–0 drubbing of Cyprus in November 1980.

Formerly a winger, Hughton was converted into a fast, overlapping full-back, ever keen to attack and get a shot in on goal. He was also capable of playing in either full-back berth.

Hughton was a cup winner with Spurs on three occasions in the early 1980s. He picked up FA Cup winners' medals in 1981 and 1982 after victories in replayed finals over Manchester City and Queen's Park Rangers respectively. He added another winners' medal to his collection when Spurs beat Anderlecht of Belgium on penalties in the 1984 UEFA Cup Final. The only runners-up medal of his career came in 1982 when Spurs lost that year's League Cup Final 3–1 to Liverpool.

For both Spurs and the Republic of Ireland, Hughton formed an effective and industrious partnership with Tony Galvin. The pair of them were important figures in Ireland's qualification for the 1988 European Championships. Both Spurs players appeared in all three matches for the boys in green in West Germany. Hughton travelled to the 1990 World Cup Finals in Italy but by then he had lost his place in the Spurs team and was struggling somewhat for form.

His great service to Spurs was rewarded with a free transfer in the summer of 1990 and although several clubs were interested in acquiring his services, no permanent moves were immediately forthcoming. In November 1990 he was loaned to West Ham United to cover for long-term injury victim Julian Dicks and the following month, the move was made permanent. He made 33 League appearances for the Hammers and played a key role in the club's 1990–91 promotion-winning season before joining Brentford on a free transfer in February 1992.

His vast experience helped the Bees lift the Third Division title but shortly after the season ended he decided that the time was right to hang up his boots.

Chris Hughton later returned to White Hart Lane to join the club's coaching staff prior to being appointed assistant-manager under both Gerry Francis and George Graham. He later became the North London club's first team coach but like manager Martin Jol, he lost his job following Spurs' poor start to the 2007–08 season.

CHARLIE HURLEY

Charlie Hurley is best remembered from his time at Sunderland, where he was named the Black cats' 'Player of the Century' by their fans on the occasion of the club's centenary in 1979. Nicknamed 'The King' Hurley, who was rightly admitted to the FAI Hall of Fame, was a classy defender, a commanding figure, combining power in the air with an assured touch and the confidence to carry the ball out of defence.

Though he was born in Cork, he moved to live in Hornchurch, East London, when he was seven. He was spotted by Millwall scout Bill Voisey whilst playing with Rainham Youth Centre and signed amateur forms with the club in 1953. In October 1953 he turned professional and made his League debut, aged seventeen, ousting fellow Irishman Gerry Bowler from the side. Hurley wasted little time in winning over the notoriously critical Millwall crowd and became a firm favourite at the Den. Reports of his outstanding displays at the heart of the Lions' defence made their way to the FAI selection committee and in November 1955 he was called into the Republic

Charlie Hurley

of Ireland squad for the match against Spain.

Unfortunately, a knee injury sustained in a match whilst playing for the Army Catering Corps whom he was representing whilst on National Service forced him to withdraw from the national squad. However, eighteen months later he made his international debut against an England side who, eleven days earlier, had beaten Ireland 5–1. Marking Manchester United's Tommy Taylor, Hurley was outstanding in a 1–1 draw.

Shortly afterwards, Hurley, who had made 105 League appearances for Millwall, left to join Sunderland for a fee of £20,000. His first game for the north-east club could not have been worse as they were beaten 7–0 by Blackpool and Hurley put through his own goal. His next appearance in Sunderland colours wasn't much better as Burnley beat the Wearsiders 6–0. Many Sunderland supporters must have wondered what sort of centre-half manager Alan Brown had signed but they need not have worried. Charlie Hurley proved himself over the next twelve seasons to be one of the best central defenders in the country.

However, at the end of Hurley's first season at Roker Park, Sunderland were relegated to the Second Division for the first time in their history. Matters did improve and in 1963–64 they regained their place in the top flight, by which time Hurley had established himself as the team's skipper and defensive lynchpin.

His international career had also blossomed during those six years. When the Republic of Ireland began their European Nations Cup games in 1962, Hurley was appointed team captain. Thereafter, he shared the honour of leading the national side with fellow defender Noel Cantwell. During his twelve–year career with the national side, he scored two goals, both of which came during a rare appearance at centre-forward in a 4–1 win over Norway in Oslo in May 1964.

'King Charlie' went on to play in 402 games for Sunderland before he was given a free transfer in the summer of 1969 as a thank you for the loyal service he had shown the club.

He was allowed to negotiate his own contract and joined Bolton Wanderers. After a couple of seasons with the Trotters, he entered the world of management with Reading and took them to promotion from the Fourth Division in 1975–76. The Royals were relegated the following year and Hurley resigned, saying that the players were not responding to his methods of management.

DENIS IRWIN

It is hard to believe that full-back Denis Irwin once suffered the ignominy of being released on a free transfer from his first club Leeds United. He was quickly snapped up by Oldham Athletic and in his first season at Boundary Park, he helped the Latics reach the play-offs. Irwin stayed with Oldham for four years – the highlight of his stay was in 1989–90, his last season at Boundary Park, when Oldham reached the League Cup Final only to lose 1–0 to Nottingham Forest. Oldham were also involved in two exciting FA Cup semi-finals against Manchester United before losing out to a Mark Robins goal in extra-time.

Denis Irwin

When Manchester United manager Alex Ferguson paid Oldham £625,000 for Denis Irwin in 1990, it was surely one of the best transfer bargains in modern football history. United got eleven years of solid professional reliability from the quiet man from Cork.

His first season with the Reds was certainly one to remember, for not only did he win his first full international cap for the Republic of Ireland against Morocco but he helped United win the European Cup Winners' Cup by beating Barcelona in the final. In 1991–92 with the purchase of Paul Parker, he switched to left-back and helped United win the League Cup whilst the following season he missed just a couple of games as the Reds won the first-ever Premiership title – the trophy returning to Old Trafford after a 26–year gap.

Ireland's qualifiers for the 1994 World Cup coincided with Irwin's best form for United and he travelled to the United States in possession of the No. 2 shirt. Irwin had an outstanding game against Italy in the Giants Stadium in New York but after suspension against Norway, he lost his place in the starting line-up.

One of United's least high-profile players, Irwin's overall contribution to the side was beyond reproach. In 1995–96 he helped the Reds win the Premier League and FA Cup double, once again proving to be the club's 'Mr Dependable'. A specialist goalscorer from set pieces, Irwin won another Championship medal the following season. On the international front, the Republic of Ireland failed to qualify for France '98 but Irwin scored a well-taken goal in the play-offs against Belgium.

During the course of the 1998–99 season, a red card issued in the game against Liverpool, ruled him out of that season's FA Cup Final but in one of United's best-ever campaigns, he was delighted to add a European Cup and a fifth Premiership League winners' medal to his growing collection of honours. One of five Manchester United players selected by their fellow professionals for the PFA award-winning team, Irwin celebrated a few milestones including becoming United's top man in Europe when he surpassed Peter Schmeichel's seventeen–match record in the Champions' League.

At international level, he appeared in the European Championship play-off matches against Turkey before announcing his retirement from the international game after 56 appearances for his country.

After winning his sixth Premiership title in 2000–01, Irwin went on to celebrate five hundred senior game at Old Trafford on St Patrick's Day and establish a new club record with his seventieth appearance in a European competition.

He was allowed to leave Old Trafford in the summer of 2002 but he wasn't ready to give up playing just yet and joined Wolverhampton Wanderers. His first season at Molineux ended with selection for the PFA's First Division team of the season. He thought long and hard about retiring but gave it one more season. On 15 May 2004 he was given a tremendous ovation as he retired after a long and successful career spanning more than 900 club appearances.

ROBBIE KEANE (RD KEANE)

The Republic of Ireland's top goalscorer, Robbie Keane started his career with South Dublin schoolboy side, Crumlin United, where his talent was recognised at an early age. He was soon being watched by scouts from a number of Premiership League clubs including Liverpool. However, Keane turned down the Merseyside club to join Wolverhampton Wanderers, reasoning that he had a greater chance of breaking into the first team at the First Division side.

He was just seventeen when he made his League debut for Wolves against Norwich City on the opening day of the 1997–98 season. The first player to score two goals on his debut since Ted Farmer, he went on to score 11 goals in 37 games that season, playing in the 'hole' behind the front two and showing remarkable composure throughout his first campaign in the senior side.

On the international scene, Keane was part of the 'Golden Generation' of Republic of Ireland youth football of the late 1990s. Under the guidance of Brian Kerr, the unfancied Ireland won the UEFA Under-16 and Under-18 European Championships in 1998 and Robbie Keane was part of the victorious Under-18 team. In 1999 he played at the World Youth Cup in Nigeria where the Republic reached the quarter-finals before going out on penalties to the hosts. Having progressed to the 'B' team, he became the Republic of Ireland's second-youngest full international, coming on for most of the second-half in Czechoslovakia in March 1998. Clearly the find of the season, he was selected in the PFA divisional XI, having scored eight goals in Wolves' first twelve games of the 1998–99 season along with two for the Republic of Ireland in a 5–0 win over Malta. In August 1999, Keane left Wolves to join Coventry City for a fee of £6 million, then a British record for a teenager. After a successful season at Highfield Road, where he scored 12 goals in 34 games, he became one of the hottest properties in English football and was being courted by many of the biggest clubs in football. Runner-up in the PFA's 'Young Player of the Year' award, he was sorely missed in the second leg of the European Championship play-off against Turkey when suspension kept him out.

Keane was signed by Marcello Lippi of Inter Milan in July 2000 for £13 million yet within a matter of months following Lippi's sacking, Keane was back in the Football League with Leeds United; the Yorkshire club paid £12 million for his services.

His Leeds career got off to an impressive start as he scored five times in his first seven games, including a spectacular overhead kick to beat his former club Coventry.

Robbie Keane

He netted a hat-trick during the early part of the 2001–02 season as Leeds beat Leicester City 6–0 in a Worthington Cup tie at the Walker's Stadium.

He continued to be a crucial figure for the Republic of Ireland and had a superb 2002 World Cup, netting goals in the games against Germany – the only one against them in the competition until the final – Saudi Arabia and Spain, when his last-minute equaliser took the game to extra-time and then penalties.

Meanwhile, Leeds United were experiencing financial troubles, forcing the club to sell many of its players and Keane joined the exodus when he was sold to Tottenham Hotspur in August 2002 for a fee of £7 million. He didn't take long to settle at White Hart Lane and netted a hat-trick against Everton to end the season as the club's leading scorer. He was the club's 'Player of the Year' in his first two seasons at the club. Having scored thirteen and sixteen goals respectively in those campaigns, Keane, despite netting seventeen times in 2004–05, found himself playing second-fiddle to Jermain Defoe for much of the season. Keane was much more of a regular after he started playing some of the best football of his career and his partnership with Dimitar Berbatov is now one of the most-feared in the Premiership.

Following Steve Staunton's appointment as Republic of Ireland manager, Robbie Keane was appointed captain for the game against Sweden which the Republic won 3–0 with Keane netting one of the goals. On 15 November 2006, he celebrated the final match at Lansdowne Road (before the stadium closed for refurbishment) against San Marino with a hat-trick in a 5–0 win. Consistently rising to the occasion for both club and country, Robbie Keane is the Republic of Ireland's highest-ever scorer with 32 goals in his 78 appearances. The 2007–08 season saw Keane reach two milestones – he scored his hundredth competitive goal for Spurs and picked up his first senior honours when the North London club beat Chelsea 2–1 to win the League Cup.

ROY KEANE (RM KEANE)

A footballer and now manager who provokes extreme reactions, Roy Keane played his early football for Cobh Ramblers before being signed by Nottingham Forest manager Brian Clough in the summer of 1990. The Forest manager plunged him straight into first team action and after making his debut against Liverpool at Anfield in August 1990, Roy finished the season playing for Forest in the FA Cup Final against Tottenham Hotspur, a match they lost 2–1.

This disappointment was tempered somewhat four days later when he won the first of 67 full caps for the Republic of Ireland against Chile.

Keane confirmed the progress he had made in his first season with another excellent campaign in 1991–92 when Forest reached the finals of two Cup competitions. They beat Southampton 3–2 in the ZDS Final but lost to Manchester United in the League Cup Final. Once it became clear that Forest's days in the top flight were numbered, Keane made it clear that he wanted to stay in the Premiership – an announcement that immediately alerted the leading clubs. It looked as if he would join Blackburn Rovers but once Manchester United joined the chase, there was only one club in it. United originally offered £3.5 million and refused to increase their bid even though Forest wanted £4 million. The period of intransigence was broken when Alex Ferguson increased his offer by a further £250,000 – it was a British record transfer fee and in his first season at Old Trafford, the midfielder proved his worth when he helped United to the League and Cup double.

Keane, who had become an established figure in the Republic of Ireland's midfield, played in all four of their matches at the 1994 World Cup finals, giving a memorable performance against Italy in New York. Even in the heat of Orlando, against Mexico and Holland, Keane maintained his all-action style. His efforts were recognised by RTÉ viewers, who voted him the Republic's player of USA '94. Over the next two years, his appearances for the national side became all too rare – he played in just three of Ireland's ten Euro '96 qualifiers – a series of niggling injuries being the cause of his absence.

The 1995–96 season saw Keane again producing brilliant competitive displays in midfield. However, his greatest performance was reserved for the FA Cup Final against Liverpool when he won the 'Man-of-the-Match' award – he also won a Premiership Championship medal as United won their second-ever double. Despite missing a number of games through injury the following season, he still ended the campaign as the proud possessor of a third Championship medal as United surged to their fourth title in five years.

The appointment of Mick McCarthy as manager of the Republic of Ireland saw the United midfielder sent off in his first match in charge. The situation deteriorated even further when, despite being named skipper for the 1996 US Cup, he withdrew from the trip. After an absence of over a year, he returned to the green shirt for a World Cup qualifier against Iceland. He found that a section of the Dublin crowd had grown hostile to him but Keane, a most determined character, soon won back both the fans and the captaincy.

He was appointed Manchester United's skipper prior to the start of the 1997–98 season and was named the Republic of Ireland's 'Player of the Year'. Around this time, Keane suffered cruciate knee ligament damage following a challenge with Leeds United's Alf-Inge Haaland. He returned to full fitness in 1998–99, leading United to success in the League and FA Cup. A yellow card in the European Cup semi-final against Juventus ruled him out of the final and a question mark hung over Keane's future at Old Trafford. But he eventually signed a new contract and led the Reds to another Premiership title. Fittingly he won both the PFA and Football Writers' 'Player of the Year' awards. He won his sixth Premiership medal in 2000–01 and remained a cornerstone of the national team as they made a very promising start to qualifying for the 2004 World Cup Finals.

Controversy then followed as the well-publicised spat with manager Mick McCarthy saw him ruled out of the World Cup Finals and he announced his retirement from the international scene. In April 2004, Keane ended his enforced absence from the Republic of Ireland side, hoping for one last chance of glory on the international stage.

He quickly put the furore over his autobiography behind him and led United to another Premiership title in 2003. The winner of 67 caps, he criticised a number of his Manchester United colleagues and parted company with the club. He signed for Glasgow Celtic in 2005 but hung up his boots at the end of the season.

In August 2006 he became the manager of Sunderland, replacing Mick McCarthy, his former national team boss, in an ironic twist. In his first season at the Stadium of Light, he led the Black Cats to promotion from the Championship. Following some fighting displays from the north-east club, Keane has successfully kept the club in the top flight.

ALAN KELLY SNR

Alan Kelly senior is the Republic of Ireland's third most capped goalkeeper after Shay Given and Packie Bonner and only a serious injury sustained in September 1973 whilst playing for Preston North End against Bristol City, prevented him from winning more caps.

His early promise was noted by the scouts attending schoolboy matches and after being snapped up by League of Ireland side Drumcondra, he won an FAI Cup winners' medal when they defeated Shamrock Rovers 2–0 in the 1957 Final. A year later in April 1958, Alan Kelly moved to Preston North End.

Kelly had already made his full international debut for the Republic of Ireland by the time he arrived at Deepdale, playing first against West Germany and then suffering the traumatic experience of losing 5–1 to England in a World Cup qualifier at Wembley in May 1957. The goals he conceded were not Kelly's fault but more that of the outfield players who seemed to freeze on the big occasion. He then had to wait almost five years for his next cap but from then on, his inspired displays made him a regular in the Ireland side.

He made his Preston debut in the FA Cup fourth round tie at Swansea – it was a late decision to play him after Fred Else fell ill. It was touch and go whether he would arrive on time but North End fan Jack Whalley used his own car to take Kelly to the Vetch Field. His first two League games for North End saw him concede five goals against both Sheffield Wednesday and Spurs.

During thirteen seasons as a player with the Lancashire club, Alan Kelly experienced all the highs and lows associated with a top flight club. He saw Preston slide from a peak of second place in the First Division in 1957–58 to Division Three for the first time in their history at the end of the 1969–70 season. On the other hand, the Lilywhites won the Division Three Championship the following season and were narrowly beaten 3–2 by West Ham United in the FA Cup Final of 1964.

TOP 50 PLAYERS

Alan Kelly Snr

Alan Kelly was one of the most consistent keepers in the Football League and in five seasons from 1966, he missed just five out of a possible 214 League games and was never ever dropped.

At the time of his injury, Kelly had made 47 appearances for the Republic of Ireland and until recently was the only goalkeeper to have captained the national side – a role he performed against the USSR in October 1972. He also took over the managerial reins for one game against Switzerland in April 1980. There is no doubt that further appearances for the Republic would have come his way but the shoulder injury he sustained led to serious complications – he lost the power in his right hand and had to learn to write with his left.

On his retirement, Alan Kelly remained loyal to Preston. He became assistant-manager and in 1983 was elevated to the manager's post. He resigned his position in February 1985 and was later attached to the coaching staff at Everton. Today, he runs goalkeeping clinics in Washington DC but in 2001 he returned to Deepdale as guest of honour when the Alan Kelly Town End Stand was opened.

GARY KELLY

The youngest of a family of thirteen, Gary Kelly signed for Leeds United from Dublin club Home Farm in 1992, after which his progress was quite remarkable. He was a striker in the Yorkshire club's reserve side when he was pitched into first team action as a seventeen–year-old winger in a League Cup tie against Scunthorpe United in October 1991. Apart from a few appearances off the bench it wasn't until 1993–94 when he broke into Leeds' Premiership side, making the right-back berth his own.

Gary Kelly

Kelly matured so quickly that Republic of Ireland manager Jack Charlton awarded his first full international cap for the game against Russia in March 1994. Though he hadn't scored for Leeds, he netted in the international friendly against World Cup holders Germany in Hanover.

Jack Charlton had seen enough and the nineteen–year-old full-back headed west for the 1998 World Cup Final in the United States. When Denis Irwin collected a second booking in the heated match against Mexico, Kelly got his chance in the next game against Norway. In doing so, he became the youngest player to appear for the Republic of Ireland in a World Cup Finals. Even with Irwin and Phelan available for the final group match, Kelly retained his place for the game against Holland, but the Irish lost 2–0.

It wasn't long before Gary Kelly was regarded as one of the best right-backs in the Premiership. Although he had spells playing under new managers at both club level (George Graham) and international level (Mick McCarthy), he continued to produce performances of the highest quality.

Occasionally playing on the right of midfield, where his searing pace was used to good effect, Kelly also captained the Leeds side and demonstrated his versatility when used at the heart of the United defence. A serious shin injury kept him out of action for the whole of the 1998–99 season. Despite Leeds signing England full-back Danny Mills for £4 million from Charlton Athletic, Kelly won back his place and was selected by his fellow professionals in the PFA award-winning Premiership side.

By the turn of the century, Gary Kelly was Leeds United's longest-serving player, though a spate of niggling injuries reduced his first team opportunities. Following Mills' departure to Middlesbrough, Kelly regained his first team place, this in spite of the club's relegation from the Premiership and its financial upheaval.

He opened a cancer-care centre in his home town of Drogheda in May 2002, having donated a substantial sum from his testimonial game against Celtic in memory of his sister Mandy who had died of the illness.

Gary Kelly was capped 52 times by the Republic of Ireland and appeared in 531 League and Cup games for Leeds United before bringing the curtain down on a sixteen–year-long distinguished career with Leeds United. After starting the majority of games in the opening third of the season, a back injury forced him out of action and he was deemed not fit enough to play his part in the club's battle against relegation. He was presented with a silver salver at the end of the final ill-fated home game against Ipswich Town on 28 April 2007. It spoke volumes for the affection in which he was held by Leeds fans, that the majority of the 31,000 crowd, though disappointed, stayed on to watch the presentation once the game was ended.

KEVIN KILBANE

Though of Irish parentage, Kevin Kilbane came up through the ranks of his home-town club Preston North End and in his very first season with the club, demonstrated his ability to beat men at pace and whip in dangerous crosses. This form led to him being called up to the Republic of Ireland Under-21 squad and it wasn't long before his performances began to attract attention from other clubs. North End received a bid of £900,000 from West Bromwich Albion but this was rejected. However, the Baggies came back with an increased offer and in the 1997 close season, he signed for Albion for a fee of £1 million

This heralded a bright new era for Kilbane, as he quickly became a fan favourite at the Hawthorns and at the same time broke into the Republic of Ireland set up, making his debut in a 4–2 World Cup qualifier against Iceland in September 1997. Back at the Hawthorns, Kilbane lacked consistency although in 1998–99, he scored the 'Goal of the Season' against Bolton Wanderers and netted the clincher in the tension-packed local derby win over Wolverhampton Wanderers. His performances improved during the early part of the following campaign and this prompted Sunderland boss Peter Reid to pay £2.5 million for the left-winger's services.

Signed to fill the void left by Scottish international flier Allan Johnston, it took Kilbane some time to settle and adapt to his new surroundings and the step up into the Premiership.

Throughout his time at all his clubs, he was a regular for the Republic of Ireland and was chosen as part of Mick McCarthy's Ireland squad for the 2002 World Cup Finals in South Korea and Japan. The team did relatively well at the tournament, progressing to the last sixteen where they were unlucky to lose out to Spain in a shoot-out – Kilbane missed one of the Irish penalties. He was known affectionately in some quarters as 'Zinedine Kilbane', and there were, at one point, t-shirts printed with this nickname for sale outside Lansdowne Road after international matches.

In spite of his best efforts on the pitch for Sunderland, he eventually became a target for the Black Cats to vent their frustrations, as the team's drop in form under Peter Reid continued and the team was relegated from the Premiership. The constant booing proved too much for Kilbane and on the last day of the transfer window at the start of the 2003–04 season, Kilbane moved to Everton for £750,000.

Having scored the first goal for Ireland under the reign of new manager Brain Kerr and reunited with his old boss David Moyes at Goodison Park, Kilbane began to demonstrate great versatility and was deployed right across the midfield, at left-back or even as a support striker as well as his preferred left-wing position. In 2004–05 he became the first Everton outfield player to appear in every game for thirteen years. His consistent displays for his country in a more central role also saw him voted as the Republic of Ireland's 'Player of the Year' for the 2004–05 season.

Sent off on what was his last game for Everton, Kilbane, who has appeared in 86 full internationals for the Republic of Ireland, later joined Wigan Athletic and made his Latics debut against his former club on 16 September 2006. He has since been a regular in the Wigan side and one of their most consistent performers as they fight to avoid relegation from the Premiership.

MARK KINSELLA

Having played his early football with Home Farm, midfielder Mark Kinsella joined Colchester United in August 1989. He spent seven seasons at Layer Road, helping the club win the GM Vauxhall Conference title and FA Trophy in 1991–92. After scoring 36 goals, the majority from distance in 212 League and Cup appearances for Colchester, he joined Charlton Athletic for a fee of £150,000 in September 1996.

An intelligent player with a good work ethic and an eye for goal, Kinsella was made the Addicks' captain and in 1997–98 he lead the side to the Premiership following a dramatic victory over Sunderland in the First Division play-off final. Not surprisingly, he was voted the club's 'Player of the Year'.

During the course of that 1997–98 season, having played for the Republic of Ireland 'B' side, Kinsella was called up to the full international side for the games against Czech Republic and Argentina. He retained his place in the national side when the Euro 2000 qualifiers got underway the following autumn – a campaign in which he was named the Addicks' 'Player of the Year' for the second successive season.

Following Charlton's relegation, Kinsella led the club back to the top flight as First Division champions in 1999–2000. This earned him a place in the PFA award-winning First Division side. Continuing to read the game well, Kinsella also proved his ability as an excellent passer of the ball who was not afraid to hit a 40–yard pass to change the direction of play. Midway through the 2001–02 season, Kinsella suffered injuries – first an operation to cure a double hernia and then a knee problem. His absence allowed Scott Parker to take his place in the team and even when fully fit, Kinsella could not reclaim his place in the Charlton starting line-up. He had scored 22 goals in 226 games for Charlton when he was sold to Aston Villa in the summer of 2002 for a fee of £750,000.

Mark Kinsella

Solid, reliable and consistent for both Villa and the Republic of Ireland, he then began to struggle with injuries. Unable to win back his first team place, Kinsella moved to Villa's neighbours West Bromwich Albion in January 2004 on a short-term contract. Despite helping the Baggies win promotion to the Premiership, he was released.

Kinsella, who captained the Republic of Ireland in a friendly against Finland in November 2000 and went on to make 48 appearances for the national side, was outstanding in the qualifying stages of the 2002 World Cup, forming a good understanding with Roy Keane. After Keane's much-publicised dismissal from the squad before the 2002 World Cup, Kinsella formed a solid midfield partnership with Matt Holland.

In the summer of 2004, Kinsella was transferred to another Midlands club, Walsall, and after two injury-ravaged seasons, took charge of the Saddlers on a caretaker-basis following Kevin Broadhurst's sacking in April 2006. He continued to combine playing and coaching at Walsall until December of that year when he was lured back to Charlton Athletic. Since the appointment of new manager Alan Pardew, Kinsella now finds himself reserve team manager at The Valley.

MARK LAWRENSON

Mark Lawrenson was one of the most stylish and polished defenders of the modern game, winning almost every honour in the book with Liverpool in the 1980s.

Born just a stone's throw away from Preston North End's Deepdale ground, he followed in his father Tommy's footsteps by joining the Lilywhites, having rejected the opportunity to pursue a first-class cricketing career with Lancashire. It was whilst he was at Deepdale that a chance conversation with former North End favourite Alan Kelly (who was then coach to both Preston and the Republic of Ireland) led to Lawrenson, whose mother was born in Waterford, playing for the Irish.

Lawrenson won the first of his 38 international caps against Poland in April 1977 but three months later he was on his way from Preston to Brighton and Hove Albion for £100,000. He didn't particularly want to leave Deepdale but North End were in urgent need of the money and so cashed in their most valuable asset. At the time the deal went through, Lawrenson was on holiday and agreed transfer terms in a café on the sea front at Benidorm!

He spent four years on the south coast, helping the Seagulls win promotion to the First Division in 1978–79. In the summer of 1981 Liverpool paid a record-breaking £900,000 for his services.

It was around this time that Mark Lawrenson started to play in midfield for the Republic of Ireland. In Eoin Hand's first game in charge, a World Cup qualifier against Holland in Dublin, Lawrenson grabbed the winning goal in a 2–1 victory.

With the likes of Phil Neal, Alan Hansen and Steve Nicol alongside him at Anfield, Lawrenson reached the pinnacle of his career with the Reds. He remained a regular in the Liverpool side in various positions throughout the decade. In doing so, he picked up League Championship and League Cup winners' medals in 1981–82, 1982–83

Mark Lawrenson

and 1983–84. He won a European Cup winners' medal in 1984 and in 1985–86 was a double winner when Liverpool won both the League title and the FA Cup. Another League Championship medal was added to the collection in his last season on Merseyside in 1987–88.

At international level, Mark Lawrenson scored five goals, including a couple in the record 8–0 home victory over Malta in November 1983. His most memorable contribution to Ireland's cause was the goal that beat Scotland at Hampden Park in February 1987 and sent the boys in green on their way to the 1988 European Championships in Germany. He also captained the national side on his final international appearance, leading them to a 5–0 victory over Israel.

In April 1988 he took up the offer of a managerial post with Oxford United. After some success, he was sacked after a disagreement with the club's directors over the sale of Dean Saunders to Derby County.

After a spell as player-coach at Tampa Bay Rowdies, Lawrenson became manager of Peterborough United but is now a prominent television and radio personality.

JASON McATEER

A direct hard-running midfielder, Jason McAteer was spotted by Bolton Wanderers manager Phil Neal whilst playing Lancashire League football for Marine. He was invited to Burnden Park for a trial and after being offered terms, it was not long before he made his League debut, coming off the bench in a 4–0 win over Burnley in November 1992. He kept his place in the Wanderers side for the next game, a

Jason McAteer

second round FA Cup tie against Rochdale and scored one of the goals in Bolton's 4–0 win.

McAteer made rapid progress at Bolton and by the following February he was a regular in the centre of the club's midfield. He took part in every League game in 1993–94 and also began to find the net – scoring in both memorable FA Cup fourth round ties against Arsenal.

He made his debut for the Republic of Ireland in March 1994 in the goalless draw with Russia and further impressive displays secured his place in Ireland's 1994 World Cup squad for the tournament in the United States. Becoming the first Bolton player to appear in a World Cup Finals since England's Tommy Banks in 1958, he returned to Burnden Park and enjoyed a spectacular season with the Lancashire club. It was a campaign that ended in promotion via the play-offs and an appearance in the League Cup final at Wembley where the Wanderers lost 2–1 to Liverpool. He had made just four Premiership appearances the following season when Liverpool paid £4.5 million for his signature.

He was quickly installed into the Liverpool side, playing as an attacking wing-back on the right-hand side. In his first season at Anfield he helped the Reds reach the FA Cup Final which ended in defeat against Manchester United.

> **Did you know?**
>
> Jason McAteer is nicknamed 'Trigger' after the character from *Only Fools and Horses.*

For the Republic of Ireland though, he continued to play in midfield and was a regular in the national side during the qualifying rounds for Euro '96. He scored his first international goal in the 3–0 defeat of Macedonia in October 1996 but in the return match the following April, he was red-carded for an uncharacteristically rash challenge.

The following season whilst playing for Liverpool, he suffered a broken left fibula and missed almost six months of action. On his return he scored twice in a 5–0 defeat of West Ham United but though he continued to play for Ireland, it appeared his days at Anfield were numbered.

In January 1999 he joined Blackburn Rovers for a fee of £4 million but his early days at Ewood Park were hampered by both injuries and disciplinary problems. Used sparingly by Rovers boss Graeme Souness, McAteer opted for a move to the north-east and Sunderland; the Black Cats paid £1 million for his services.

He made an immediate impact at the Stadium of Light before injuries again took their toll, including surgery on an abdominal hernia. Starting the 2003–04 season as club captain, he led the Wearsiders to the FA Cup semi-finals and earned a recall to the Ireland side before surprisingly being released by Sunderland in the close season. He then made the decision to head back to Birkenhead, signing a two-year deal with Tranmere Rovers, hoping to play out his career with his local club.

Appointed captain, he led Rovers to the First Division play-off finals where they eventually lost on penalties to Hartlepool United. Capped 52 times by the Republic of Ireland, he was released in the summer of 2007 and announced his retirement from the game immediately afterwards.

Did you know?

Seven sets of fathers and sons have played for Ireland. They are the Fagans (Jack and Fionan), the Dunnes (Jimmy and Tommy), the Lawlors ('Kit' and Mick), the Martins (Con and Mick), the Whelans (Ronnie Snr and Ronnie Jnr), the Donovans (Don and Terry) and the Kellys (Alan Snr and Alan Jnr).

MICK McCARTHY

Mick McCarthy began his career with his home-town club Barnsley, making his debut in August 1977 in a 4–0 win over Rochdale. He was a firm favourite during his time at Oakwell, helping the Yorkshire club climb from the Fourth Division to the Second Division with promotions in 1978–79 and 1980–81. His rugged and uncompromising displays at the heart of the Barnsley defence brought him to the attention of a number of higher division clubs and in December 1983, he crossed the Pennines to join newly relegated Manchester City for a fee of £20,000.

The switch of clubs brought McCarthy to the attention of Ireland boss Eoin Hand and McCarthy, who qualified for the Republic by virtue of his Waterford-born father, made his full international debut in a friendly against Poland in May 1984. He gave a most-assured display alongside David O'Leary as the teams played out a goalless draw.

The then Maine Road club won promotion to the First Division in 1984–85, in what was Mick McCarthy's first full season. His first season in the top flight was steady enough as the club hovered around mid-table but relegation struck the following year and McCarthy opted for a move north of the border to Glasgow Celtic. His first season at Parkhead ended in glory when the Hoops claimed the 'double' of the Premier League title and Scottish Cup. The following campaign brought further success in the Cup but in the League, the Bhoys finished a rather disappointing third.

Following the appointment of Jack Charlton as Republic of Ireland team manager, McCarthy found himself paired at the heart of the defence with Kevin Moran. He played in six of the side's eight 1988 European Championship qualifiers and kept his place in the side for all three of the Republic's matches in the finals in Germany. McCarthy was later appointed skipper of the national side leading to the nickname 'Captain Fantastic'.

In the summer of 1989, McCarthy was on the move again, this time to French club Olympique Lyon but in less than a year he was back in the Football League with Millwall. Though much of his time at the Den was spent on the treatment table – including needing surgery on a knee for a third time – he was able to help the boys in green qualify for Italia '90.

McCarthy was Ireland's captain and he saw his side reach the last eight of the

Mick McCarthy

competition following a penalty shoot-out win over Romania. Despite the 1–0 defeat by hosts Italy, both McCarthy and manager Charlton returned from the tournament as heroes. McCarthy, who went on to win 57 caps for the Republic, had the unenviable record of having committed the most fouls in the finals.

In March 1992, McCarthy became player-manager of Millwall succeeding Bruce Rioch. He took the club to the play-offs in 1993–94 but they lost out to Derby County. Following Jack Charlton's resignation as Republic of Ireland manager, McCarthy became the prime candidate for the vacancy and in February 1996 he was officially appointed national team boss.

After two narrow failures to qualify for the 1998 World Cup and Euro 2000, McCarthy took the nation to the 2002 World Cup Finals. Though their tournament was overshadowed by his public and very bitter row with Roy Keane, McCarthy's team had a relatively successful campaign, reaching the second round where they were eliminated on penalties. After a disappointing start to Ireland's Euro 2004 campaign, McCarthy resigned.

In March 2003 he was appointed manager of Sunderland but he couldn't prevent the Black Cats losing their Premiership status. The following season he took Sunderland to the First Division promotion play-offs but they lost to Crystal Palace in a penalty shoot-out. In 2004–05 he took Sunderland back into the top flight as First Division champions but in March 2006 with the club looking certain to be relegated, he was sacked.

Appointed manager of Wolverhampton Wanderers, he took the Midlands club to the promotion play-offs but they lost out to rivals West Bromwich Albion. Despite the club going through a number of rough patches and McCarthy being linked to a number of managerial vacancies, he has persistently confirmed his desire to remain at Molineux.

PAUL McGRATH

One of the greatest players ever to pull on the green shirt of the Republic of Ireland, Paul McGrath was born in Ealing, west London but when he was two months old, his mother took him to live in Monkstown, County Dublin. McGrath played his early football for Pearse Rovers before moving on to Leinster Senior League side, Dalkey United. It was whilst playing for the latter that he first came to the attention of Manchester United scout Billy Behan but in the autumn of 1981, it was League of Ireland club St Patrick's Athletic that he joined.

McGrath, who had worked briefly as an apprentice sheet metal worker and as a security guard, proved a revelation at St Pat's too and in 1981–82 he was voted PFAI 'Player of the Year'. Nicknamed 'The Black Pearl of Inchicore', McGrath joined

Manchester United in April 1982 for a bargain £30,000 plus extra payments for international and first team appearances.

It was midway through the 1984–85 season before McGrath established himself in the United side, a campaign in which international recognition also came his way. He made his Ireland debut as a substitute in the 2–1 defeat by Italy at Dalymount Park. Despite the reversal, McGrath had given a polished display against the World Cup holders. At the end of that season, McGrath claimed an FA Cup winners' medal after United had beaten Everton 1–0 – a match in which Kevin Moran was sent off and Norman Whiteside scored the winning goal.

Paul McGrath

Following the appointment of Jack Charlton as Ireland manager, Paul McGrath played in all but one of the new manager's first fourteen games in charge. It was during this spell that McGrath played in a new pivotal role – a midfield sweeper playing just in front of the back four. The switch proved a huge success and the boys in green qualified for the 1988 European Championships in Germany, with McGrath scoring in each of the last two qualifying games against Luxembourg and Bulgaria.

Sadly, a number of injuries prevented McGrath from becoming a regular at Old Trafford under United's new manager Alex Ferguson. The two had a somewhat turbulent relationship and McGrath's alcohol addiction and troublesome knees led to United offering him a retirement package of £100,000 with testimonial. McGrath turned the offer down and after Ferguson informed clubs of his availability, McGrath joined Aston Villa for £400,000.

His new surroundings at Villa Park seemed to agree with him and he began to play some of the best football of his career, this in spite of his problems with his knees. He was the fulcrum around which an impressive Villa side finished runners-up to Liverpool but then struggled in 1991–92 following the departure of manager Graham Taylor to take charge of England. However, when new manager Ron Atkinson was appointed, Villa came close again in 1992–93, finishing as runners-up to McGrath's former club Manchester United. At the end of the season, McGrath was voted the PFA 'Player of the Year'.

At international level, McGrath helped the Republic of Ireland to the final stages of both the 1990 and 1994 World Cups. In his latter years in the national side he reverted to his preferred position of centre-half and had spells captaining the side. It was from this position that he gave one of his best performances in a green shirt – the 1–0 victory over Italy in New York at USA '94. He continued to command a place in the national starting line-up until the end of the qualifying campaign for Euro '96, taking his tally of international caps to 83. McGrath later had brief spells with Derby County and Sheffield United before hanging up his boots in 1998.

ALAN McLOUGHLIN

Alan McLoughlin began his career as a trainee at Manchester United but when he was unable to break into the Old Trafford club's League side, he joined Swindon Town in the summer of 1986. After making his debut for the Robins, McLoughlin had a brief spell on loan with Torquay United before returning to the County Ground. His Swindon career looked to be over when he returned to Plainmoor at the start of the following season for another loan spell but following suspensions to other players, McLoughlin was given another chance in the first team and soon established himself as a regular for Swindon.

It was under the watchful eye of Ossie Ardiles that McLoughlin really blossomed. He was played every match in Ardiles' first season in charge, scoring sixteen goals and capping off a fine season by scoring the winning goal in the play-off final at Wembley against Sunderland. The celebrations were short-lived, however: Swindon were denied their place in the top flight due to financial irregularities.

McLoughlin's performances for the Wiltshire club, displaying his excellent vision, driving energy and passing ability earned him an international call-up for the Republic of Ireland's game against Malta in June 1990. Named in the Ireland squad for Italia '90, he made two appearances in the tournament, coming off the bench in the games with England and Egypt.

With Swindon in financial trouble, they were forced to sell their star midfielder – now recognised as one of the most talented footballers in British football – to Southampton for a fee of £1 million. The move wasn't a success and in February 1992 he moved along the south coast to Portsmouth for £400,000.

During his time at Fratton Park, McLoughlin, who became club captain, played in two FA Cup semi-finals as well as a couple of play-off semi-finals.

In November 1993, the Pompey midfielder earned his place in the annals of Irish football. Within six minutes of coming on as a substitute in the World Cup qualifier against Northern Ireland, he scored a second-half equaliser – the goal that would take the Republic of Ireland to USA '94. It was whilst with Portsmouth that McLoughlin's international fortunes were revived following the appointment of Mick McCarthy as successor to Jack Charlton. McLoughlin played in seven of the ten qualifying matches for the 1998 World Cup Finals, going on to win a total of 42 caps for the Republic of Ireland.

In December 1999, McLoughlin was transferred to Wigan Athletic for £260,000, having appeared in 361 games for Portsmouth. Though he helped the Latics reach the play-offs, he was troubled by a slipped disc and eventually left the north-west club to join Rochdale. He more than played his part in helping Rochdale reach the play-offs in 2001–02 and scored a twice-taken penalty for them on his last appearance in the Football League.

With his career winding down, McLoughlin joined Forest Green as player-coach for the 2002–03 season and later retired from playing to concentrate on coaching with the club. He is currently co-commentator on Portsmouth-based radio station The Quay.

CON MARTIN

Nicknamed 'Mr Versatility', Con Martin played in nearly every position during his football career including goalkeeping appearances for both the Republic of Ireland and Aston Villa.

He played Gaelic football in his youth and was called into the Dublin senior panel at the age of eighteen, going on to help them win the Leinster title. However, at the same time as playing for Dublin, he was playing soccer for Drumcondra. When this was discovered, the Gaelic Athletic Association, which maintained a ban on 'foreign sports', expelled Martin and withheld his winners' medal. He eventually received the medal in 1971 after the ban was lifted.

He had been introduced to soccer while serving in the Irish Air Corps and after helping Drumcondra win the FAI Cup and representing a League of Ireland XI against an Irish League XI, he was signed by Glentoran who then bought him out of the Air Corps. He was with the Glens when he became the Republic's first-ever substitute. Sitting on the bench for the friendly against Portugal in June 1946, the Irish were already 3–0 down when Ned Courtney was injured. The selectors put Martin in goal and he kept a clean sheet in a 3–1 reversal.

He kept his place between the posts for Ireland's next game and kept another clean sheet in a 1–0 win over Spain. His third appearance, against England, found him playing as a defender before he later moved into the forward line. He scored four goals in three successive internationals including two in a 3–0 World Cup qualifying match against Finland. Martin also found the net from the penalty spot when the Republic became the first non-UK team to beat England on their home soil.

Martin, who went on to play in 30 internationals for the Republic of Ireland, also appeared six times for Northern Ireland. Without doubt the best utility player of his time, scoring six goals, he also captained the national side.

Midway through the 1946–47 season, Con Martin left Glentoran to join Leeds United for a fee of £8,000. He arrived at Elland Road too late to prevent the Yorkshire club's relegation to the Second Division and with Leeds hard up for cash, he was sold to Aston Villa for £10,000 in October 1948.

He enjoyed his best playing days at Villa Park, becoming a permanent fixture in the club's defence before injury curtailed his appearances. He started the 1951–52 season at left-back but a goalkeeping crisis saw Martin take over duties between the posts. He made 27 appearances as a keeper for Villa before reverting back to the centre-half position. Between 1948 and 1956 Martin made 213 appearances for Villa, 193 of them in the First Division.

After leaving Villa, Martin played briefly for Watford before becoming player-manager at Waterford and manager at Shelbourne. He later assisted Cork Hibernians while working as an insurance agent in Dublin. His sons Mick and Con were both footballers and his grandson, Owen Garvan currently plays for Ipswich Town.

MICK MARTIN

Mick Martin, the son of Con, he began his career in Ireland with Home Farm before joining Sean Thomas's Bohemians in 1968. He spent a year learning his trade in the youth and reserve teams before progressing to the first team and his debut against Dundalk. He gave a good account of himself and soon became a regular in the side which challenged for title honours. After an outstanding display in a league match against Shelbourne in January 1973, the watching Tommy Docherty, manager of Manchester United, liked what he saw and within 48 hours, Martin was on his way to Old Trafford.

The cost of his transfer, £20,000, was at the time, a record receipt for a League of Ireland club. At Old Trafford, Mick Martin was in the Reds side for the remainder of that season but in 1973–74 he only appeared occasionally as the club lost its top flight status.

Despite being unable to hold down a regular place in the United side, he continued to command a spot in the Republic of Ireland line-up and during the managerial reigns of both Liam Tuohy and Johnny Giles, he made more international appearances than any other player. Operating in front of the back four, he was a hardworking individual, the perfect foil for the likes of Giles and Liam Brady.

In September 1975, Martin left Manchester United to join Johnny Giles' West Bromwich Albion and in his first season at the Hawthorns, he helped the Baggies win promotion to the First Division. However, when Giles was replaced as manager by Ron Atkinson, Martin found himself out of the side and in December 1978 he was sold to Newcastle United for £100,000.

A big favourite on Tyneside, Martin was appointed captain and spent six seasons with the club. His consistent displays soon won over the Magpies' supporters but just as Arthur Cox's side embarked on an entertaining season which ended in the club winning promotion, Martin was left to wander around the country and even trying North America to continue his football career.

Mick Martin, who captained the Irish national side in five of his 52 international appearances, was also dismissed twice while playing for his country. The second occasion against Bulgaria in June 1977 when he and Noel Campbell were involved in a four-man brawl, signalled the start of a near two-year exile from international football and though he was later reinstated, he played the last of his international games against Spain in April 1983.

Martin later had brief spells with Cardiff City, Preston North End, Peterborough United and Rotherham United. After hanging up his boots, Martin was a member of the coaching staff at his beloved Newcastle as well as serving under former Ireland teammate Liam Brady during his time as manager of Glasgow Celtic.

After ending his involvement with the game, Mick Martin went into business on Tyneside, running a sports shop.

PADDY MOORE

In February 1934, Paddy Moore scored four goals for the Republic of Ireland in a World Cup qualifier against Belgium, the first player ever to score four goals in a World Cup game. However, injury and alcoholism combined to blight both his career and his life and he was only 41 years old when he died.

As a youth, Moore played for several teams including Richmond Rovers before joining Shamrock Rovers for the first of three spells. In 1929, he joined Cardiff City but made just a single appearance for the Bluebirds. After brief periods with Merthyr Town and Tranmere Rovers, he rejoined Shamrock Rovers. In 1931–32 he helped the Hoops win both the League of Ireland Championship and the League of Ireland

Shield. He also helped Rovers win the FAI Cup in 1931 and 1932, scoring in both finals.

Moore made his international debut for the Republic of Ireland in April 1931, playing well in a respectable 1–1 draw against Spain in Barcelona. He marked his debut by scoring his side's goal. Moore coolly lobbed the ball over the advancing Zamora and into the back of the goal. The keeper subsequently tore off his shirt in disgust and threw it into the back of the net, suffering the derision of his own fans.

Moore missed the return game with the Spanish through injury but won his second cap against Holland just over a year later, scoring again in a 2–0 win. However, the highlight of Paddy Moore's international career came on 25 February 1934 at Dalymount Park when Ireland made their World Cup debut in the qualifier against Belgium. He scored all four goals as they came from behind on three occasions to draw 4–4. Two months later in another qualifier, Moore scored his seventh and last goal in a 5–2 defeat against Holland.

Another high point of Moore's international career was in October 1936 when he masterminded Ireland's 5–2 win against Germany, again at Dalymount Park. Despite not scoring himself, he helped set up four of the goals.

His impressive display against Holland in May 1932 resulted in Moore, together with Joe O'Reilly and Jimmy Daly, signing for Aberdeen. The trio were signed for a combined fee of less than £1,000. Moore made an impressive start for the Dons, scoring 27 goals in 29 Scottish League matches during the 1932–33 season. However, in subsequent campaigns, his problems with alcoholism began to emerge.

Aberdeen manager Paddy Travers was aware that Moore had developed a drink problem that would end his career prematurely. He accompanied Moore when the forward was on international duty in order to help him keep away from alcohol. In May 1935 Moore had been selected to play for Ireland against Switzerland but he was declared unfit to play after drinking too heavily while travelling to the game. Other similar incidents resulted in Moore being released by Aberdeen. He returned to Shamrock Rovers and in 1936 he helped them win a third FAI Cup by scoring in his third final.

During the 1940s, Moore coached Stella Maris where he nurtured the talents of a number of future internationals including Ronnie Whelan Snr whose skills, according to legend, were spotted by Moore's wife who then brought him to the attention of her husband.

KEVIN MORAN

Kevin Moran's name will forever be in the record books as the first man to be sent off in an FA Cup Final. Durham referee Peter Willis was the man who ensured the Irishman's infamy when he controversially dismissed him in the 1985 FA Cup Final between Manchester United and Everton.

Moran was a noted Gaelic footballer, winning two All-Ireland Championship medals with Dublin in 1976 and 1977. He was also part of the side that, in 1976–77, won the National Football League for Dublin with a win over Derry in the final. But it was his ability as a soccer player – he played with Dublin side Pegasus – that led to Manchester United scout Billy Behan recommending Moran to Reds' boss Dave Sexton.

The tough-tackling defender made his United debut against Southampton in April 1979 but it was the 1980–81 season before he became a first team regular at Old Trafford. He had by then made his full international debut for the Republic of Ireland, being called into the side for the friendly against Switzerland in April 1980 in what

Kevin Moran

was Alan Kelly's only match in charge. The appointment of Eoin Hand as Ireland boss shortly afterwards did nothing to hinder the Manchester United defender's progress, as he played in five of the eight qualifiers for the 1982 World Cup.

Moran's bravery became legendary at Old Trafford as he literally gave blood in the Reds' cause – collecting well over 100 stitches in what were mostly facial injuries. As a United player he won two FA Cup winners' medals in 1983 and 1985, although he was denied his medal in the latter final until a few weeks later when officials decided that he deserved a medal despite being sent off during the game.

The appointment of Jack Charlton as national team manager in 1986 brought about Kevin Moran's best form for the Republic of Ireland. Two years later after a run of three goals in four games, he was made captain for the first time. Moran played a major role in Ireland's qualification for the 1988 European Championships and was included in the squad for the tournament in Germany, appearing in all three of his side's games.

By then Moran had left United and joined Spanish club Sporting Gijon on a free transfer. He spent two seasons there before returning to England to join Second Division Blackburn Rovers. He helped the Ewood Park club win their place in the Premiership by beating Leicester City in the Second Division play-off final in May 1992. Moran helped Blackburn finish fourth in the Premiership in 1992–93 and runners-up in 1993–94, retiring just before the club won the Premiership title the following season.

Kevin Moran remained a key figure throughout the reign of Jack Charlton and was a key player at Italia '90. Four years later at the age of 38, he was included in the Republic of Ireland squad that travelled to the World Cup in the United States. Unfortunately, injury prevented him from adding to his most impressive collection of 71 caps.

Kevin Moran currently works as a pundit on Irish television channel TV3.

PADDY MULLIGAN

After playing his early football for Home Farm, full-back Paddy Mulligan had a couple of games for Bohemians before signing for Shamrock Rovers in February 1964. Whilst with the Hoops, Mulligan combined playing with work as an office furniture salesman.

With Rovers, Mulligan won FAI Cup winners' medals in 1965, 1966, 1967 and 1969 and won the first of his 50 full international caps for the Republic of Ireland in the ill-tempered World Cup qualifier against Czechoslovakia on 4 May 1969.

In the autumn of 1969, Mulligan left Shamrock Rovers, signing for Chelsea for a fee of £17,500 but it took him some time to adapt to the level of fitness expected at Stamford Bridge. The fee was a record for a League of Ireland player but it was still a surprise move for Mulligan who, at the age of 24, was older than most of the footballers who were making their way across the Irish Sea.

It was a long-term injury to Chelsea's Scottish international defender Eddie McCreadie that eventually allowed Mulligan to establish himself in the Chelsea side. He featured in Chelsea's UEFA Cup Winners' Cup success in 1971, making a late substitute appearance in the first final against Real Madrid in Athens. Despite suffering a spate of niggling injuries, he collected a League Cup runners-up medal the following season after the Blues had lost 2–1 to Stoke City. In fact, an injury in the game compelled Mulligan to leave the fray at the interval and his absence is said to have contributed to Chelsea's downfall.

Although he was a regular in the Republic of Ireland side, Mulligan struggled to hold down a first team place at the Bridge and in September 1972 he opted for a move to Crystal Palace who willingly paid £80,000 for his services.

His three seasons at Selhurst Park witnessed a steady decline in the fortunes of Palace as they dropped from the First to the Third Division in successive seasons. In September 1975 Mulligan was on the move again, this time to West Bromwich Albion who had just appointed Ireland legend Johnny Giles as their manager. In his first season at the Hawthorns, Mulligan helped Albion win promotion to the top flight.

He returned to Ireland with Shamrock Rovers in 1977 and later had a spell as assistant-manager at Panathinaikos before becoming player-manager of Galway United and later taking over the reins at Shelbourne.

Mulligan, who captained his country on thirteen occasions, made the last of his 50 international appearances against the United States at Dalymount Park in October 1979.

DAVID O'LEARY

David O'Leary was born in Stoke Newington but at a very young age, his family moved to Dublin where he played his early football as a junior for Shelbourne. By the time he was fifteen, O'Leary, who was captain of the Republic of Ireland schoolboys team, was on his way back to London to join Arsenal as an apprentice.

He soon settled in at Highbury and manager Bertie Mee gave him his League debut as a seventeen–year-old in August 1975 in the game against Burnley. Despite his tender years, O'Leary played in 30 games that season. He was only a year older when he made his full international debut for the Republic of Ireland in a friendly against England at Wembley, playing a key role in a 1–1 draw.

A calm and collected central defender, O'Leary helped Arsenal to the 1978 FA Cup Final against Ipswich Town before winning an FA Cup winners' medal against Manchester United the following year. He appeared again at Wembley in the 1980 FA Cup Final against West Ham United. It was around this time that David O'Leary was considered not only the best centre-back in the First Division but also in Europe. Throughout his long career, it was his ability to read the game so well that made his job look easy. He used the ball as well as any in his position and possessed great speed of thought as well as a great positional sense – it was very rare that he was dragged out of position.

David O'Leary

Following Jack Charlton's appointment as manager of the national team, O'Leary surprisingly found himself left out of the squad for the summer tour of Iceland in 1986. The relationship between the Gunners' defender and Irish manager deterior-ated further when, just before the tour, the squad was decimated by with-drawals. Charlton went back to O'Leary to ask if he would join them as a late replace-ment but he declined the offer. It was the beginning of a two-and-a-half year absence from the Ireland side, when the defender was at his peak.

He missed Euro '88 but returned to the international arena for Italia '90. It was here that O'Leary enjoyed the greatest highlight of his 68–cap international career. O'Leary, on as a substitute in the second round tie against Romania – his first appearance at a World Cup Finals – was asked to take a spot-kick in the ensuing penalty shoot-out. The scores stood at 4–4 and he needed to beat the Romanian keeper to earn his team a place in the quarter-finals. He coolly sent Lung the wrong way before dispatching the ball into the top right-hand corner of the net. O'Leary remained in the Republic of Ireland squad until 1993, contributing to his fifth World Cup qualifying programme.

O'Leary went on to make a record 558 League appearances, breaking the previous record held by George Arm-strong. Towards the end of his playing days at Highbury, O'Leary became something of a utility player. Injuries and suspensions meant that he could bring the curtain down on his Arsenal career with two Wembley appearances as the Gunners beat Sheffield Wednesday in the League Cup and FA Cup Finals of 1993.

He then joined Leeds United on a free transfer after nineteen years at Highbury. A regular at Elland Road until he suffered an Achilles-tendon injury, he later announced his retirement from the playing side of the game at the age of 37. He remained with Leeds, first as assistant-manager to George Graham and later as the man in charge. He took Leeds to fourth in the Premiership and qualification for the UEFA Cup in 1998–99. The following season, United finished third and qualified for the Champions League. Though their Premiership form dipped, they reached the semi-finals of the Champions League. A finish of sixth and another UEFA Cup spot was achieved in 2001–02 but at the end of the season, he lost his job.

Following a year out of work, he was appointed manager of Aston Villa. He spent three years with the Midlands club but results were mixed and in the summer of 2006, his contract was terminated by mutual consent. Despite many managerial positions becoming available, O'Leary, who was linked with the vacant Republic of Ireland manager's job, is still looking for a return to football management.

NIALL QUINN

Niall Quinn played his early football for Manortown United and after being spotted by Arsenal, signed professional forms for the North London club in 1983. He made his Arsenal debut in December 1985, scoring a goal in a 2–0 win over Liverpool. Prior to joining the Gunners, he had played in the 1983 All-Ireland Minor Hurling Championship final with Dublin.

The young Arsenal forward won his first full cap for the Republic of Ireland against Iceland in May 1986 and became a regular on the national side's bench thereafter. Having earned a League Cup winners' medal with Arsenal in 1987, he made three appearances off the bench for the Republic in the qualifying rounds of the 1988 European Championships and gained a place in the squad for

Niall Quinn

the finals. However, his only action at Euro '88 was as a second-half substitute for Frank Stapleton in the game against England.

Following the signing of Leicester City's Alan Smith, Quinn's first team opportunities at Highbury were limited and he found himself languishing in the club's reserves. Having missed out on a League Championship winners' medal in 1989 after failing to appear in enough games, he was eventually rescued by signing for Manchester City for a fee of £800,000 in March 1990.

He marked his debut for the then Maine Road club with a goal in a 1–1 draw with Chelsea and his form in the remaining weeks of the campaign secured his place in Ireland's World Cup squad for Italia '90. He was on the bench for the opening game against England. Another substitute appearance followed in the second match against Egypt before Quinn at last made the starting line-up for the Republic's match against Holland. In that game, he scored the equaliser which sent the boys in green into the second round of the World Cup. Quinn kept his place for the remainder of the tournament, playing a full role in the run to the quarter-finals.

In his first full season with Manchester City, Quinn scored 22 goals as the club climbed to fifth place in the First Division. Included in that total was his first hat-trick for the club in a 3–1 win at Crystal Palace. One of Quinn's most memorable games for City came in April 1991 when, in the game against Derby County, he scored early on and then, after going in goal following an injury to Tony Coton, he saved a Dean Saunders' penalty in a 2–1 win. This result saw the Rams relegated from the top flight.

Very few forwards caused as much havoc in the air as Niall Quinn. Coupled with his fantastic work-rate, neat distribution and the superb way he held the ball up, it made him one of the best forwards in Europe.

Playing in all twelve qualifying matches ahead of the 1994 World Cup Finals, Quinn ruptured a cruciate ligament and was forced to sit out not only USA '94 but also a year of his career. The 1995–96 season was to provide the amiable Quinn with a double disappointment. Not only did the Republic miss out on a place in Euro '96 after a play-off defeat by Holland but following Manchester City's relegation, he was sold to Sunderland for £1.3 million, the Black Cats' record fee.

After a number of impressive displays in the early part of the 1996–97 season, he damaged an ankle which kept him out of action for over six months. Following a third operation, it looked as if he would miss most of the 1997–98 campaign but he surprisingly returned to action and scored the first goal in the new Stadium of Light. Quinn also scored twice in the First Division play-of final against Charlton Athletic, which Sunderland lost 7–6 on penalties after drawing 4–4. He was outstanding the following season as Sunderland won the First Division Championship.

Continuing to appear on a regular basis for the Republic of Ireland, Quinn scored with headers in the Premiership games against his former clubs Arsenal and Manchester City in 2000–01. For the Republic of Ireland, Quinn eventually scored the goal that gave him his country's out-right goalscoring record in the game against Cyprus in October 2001. Six months later he received a PFA Merit Award and was granted a benefit by the north-east club. Following Sunderland's relegation in 2001–02, Quinn, a true Black Cats' legend, decided to retire.

Typical of the man, he donated all the proceeds from his May 2002 testimonial to children's charities and, not surprisingly, received the prestigious Beacon Fellowship Prize for his contribution to medical and children's charities.

In June 2006, Quinn successfully brokered a deal to buy a controlling stake in his beloved Sunderland and he became the club's chairman and manager. He soon retired as manager, paving the way for Roy Keane to take charge. This was highly unexpected considering the huge rift between the two, arising from Keane's famous ejection from the 2002 World Cup.

KEVIN SHEEDY

Though he was Welsh by birth, his father was born in County Clare and Kevin Sheedy opted to play inter-national football for the Republic of Ireland, believing that they offered him better prospects at this level.

Sheedy began his Football League career with Hereford United before an £80,000 move took him to Liverpool in the summer of 1978. Things didn't work out for him at Anfield and the young midfielder spent most of his four years with the club in the reserves, winning the Central League Championship in each of those four seasons.

In the summer of 1982, Sheedy was rescued from obscurity when Everton manager Howard Kendall paid £100,000 to secure his services.

Kevin Sheedy

In his first season at Goodison, Sheedy scored 11 goals in 40 games and this form earned him a call-up to Eoin Hand's Republic of Ireland squad.

For the match against Holland at Dalymount Park in October 1983, Sheedy came off the bench with eight minutes to play to replace Tony Grealish. Although the Irish lost 3–2, he kept his place in the side for the next game against Malta and scored in an 8–0 win.

He continued to impress for Everton though injury forced him to miss the club's 1984 FA Cup Final victory over Watford. He was back in action the following season, playing a vital role as the Blues lifted the League Championship. He also scored Everton's third goal in the European Cup Winners' Cup Final triumph over Rapid Vienna. In 1986–87 he helped the Merseyside club to another League Championship title. The following year, he played his part in Ireland's 1988 European Championship campaign, appearing in the vital qualifier against Scotland and making two appearances in the tournament finals in Germany.

Arguably one of the best midfielders of the 1980s, Kevin Sheedy was famed for his cultured left foot, from which he combined accurate passing – usually superb-timed through balls over square defences – with deadly shooting. He scored some goals of excellent quality – against Ipswich Town in the sixth round of the 1984–85 FA Cup, he scored twice from a re-taken free-kick. He bent the first attempt over the wall and into the net on Paul Cooper's right but the referee hadn't blown for it to be taken. When the kick was re-taken, he bent it over the wall again, this time to Cooper's left!

He played in all five of Ireland's games in Italia '90 but it was against England in Ireland's first game that he made his greatest contribution. With England leading 1–0 and little over fifteen minutes remaining, he crashed a low drive beyond Peter Shilton to register a deserved equaliser and the Republic's first goal at a World Cup Finals. Later in the tournament in the penalty shoot-out with Romania, Sheedy took the first spot-kick and scored to help his side on their way to the quarter-finals.

Towards the end of his career at Goodison Park, Sheedy found it difficult to hold down a place and giving up a testimonial, joined Newcastle United. He helped the Magpies win the First Division Championship before later ending his career with Blackpool. After a spell as youth team manager at Blackburn Rovers, Sheedy was appointed assistant-manager to his former international colleague John Aldridge at Tranmere Rovers. He spent some time in a similar capacity at Hartlepool United before he returned to Goodison Park as a member of Everton's coaching staff in November 2002.

JOHN SHERIDAN

Having been unable to make much headway with his first club Manchester City, midfielder John Sheridan moved to Leeds United in March 1982 and in November of that year, made his League debut in a goalless draw at Middlesbrough. By then he had already won Irish youth international honours – his parents were from Dublin – and soon went on to represent the Republic at Under-21, Under-23 and 'B' international level.

Sheridan was in the Leeds Second Division side of 1984–85 and two seasons later was a member of the side that reached the FA Cup semi-finals. That season, United reached the Second Division play-offs, only to go down to Charlton Athletic in the final – Sheridan finding the net in the Elland Road leg of the tie. The

John Sheridan

following season, Sheridan was Leeds United's leading scorer and it was this form that led to him winning the first of his 34 caps for the Republic of Ireland against Romania at Lansdowne Road.

The midfielder made an impressive start to his international career, winning caps in four consecutive matches and scoring one of his side's goals in a 3–1 defeat of Poland. Finally establishing himself in Jack Charlton's squad, he remained only a fringe player due to the rapid rise of fellow midfielders Roy Keane and Andy Townsend. As a result, John Sheridan made just one appearance at Italia '90, coming off the bench in the seventy-eighth minute of the quarter-final clash with hosts Italy.

After falling out with Leeds new manager Howard Wilkinson, Sheridan was sold to Brian Clough's Nottingham Forest but after just one appearance he was transferred to Sheffield Wednesday for £500,000. There was a double celebration for the Owls in 1990–91. Sheridan played in every game as the Hillsborough club won promotion to the top flight and then scored the winning goal in the League Cup Final that defeated Manchester United. In 1991–92, he helped Wednesday to third spot in the First

Division and the following season to a Cup Final double that saw them go down to Arsenal in both the FA and League Cup.

After an absence of over eighteen months, Sheridan was recalled to the national side and scored Ireland's goal in a 3–1 defeat by Spain. The Republic, however, qualified for the 1994 World Cup Finals. After impressive displays in the pre-tournament friendlies, Sheridan lined up for the opening match against Italy in New York. He went on to play in all four matches and returned with a much-enhanced reputation. His international career came to an end following the Euro '96 play-off defeat against Holland at Anfield.

After a brief loan spell with Birmingham City, Sheridan joined Bolton Wanderers and was a regular in the club's 1996–97 First Division Championship-winning side. Injuries hampered his progress the following season when non-League Doncaster Rovers offered him a chance to play for them. In 1998 he was offered another shot at League football by Oldham Athletic and he went on to play in a further 150 games before hanging up his boots and joining the club's coaching staff. He was later replaced by Brian Talbot who was, in turn, succeeded by Ronnie Moore. Moore was shown the door and in the summer of 2006, Sheridan stepped in to fill in the manager's position on a permanent basis.

He guided the Latics to the League One play-offs where their promotion challenge was ended in the semi-finals by eventual winners Blackpool.

FRANK STAPLETON

Frank Stapleton, who finished his international career as the Republic of Ireland's leading goalscorer with 20 goals in 71 appearances, showed great promise at Gaelic football as a youngster. But after impressing with Dublin-based junior side Bolton Athletic, he began his career as an apprentice with Arsenal in 1972.

He made his first team debut for the Gunners against Stoke City in March 1975 and established himself in the Arsenal side the following season. In 1976–77, Stapleton became an automatic choice and formed a great goalscoring partnership with England international Malcolm Macdonald. His form led to him winning his first full cap in the friendly with Turkey – a match that ended all-square at 3–3 with Stapleton heading home a Giles' free-kick at the near post after just three minutes! It marked the start of a magnificent international career for the quiet and reserved Stapleton.

Stapleton helped Arsenal to three consecutive FA Cup Finals from 1978 to 1980, scoring one of the goals in the 1979 FA Cup Final against Manchester United. By this time he had found a new goalscoring partner in Alan Sunderland and many of the goals this duo scored were set up by another Irish international, Liam Brady. Like

Brady, Stapleton wanted to leave Highbury after the expiry of his contract and in the summer of 1981, he joined Manchester United for a tribunal-set fee of £900,000.

Stapleton played a significant role in Ireland's attempt to qualify for the World Cup in Spain in 1982. Goals against Cyprus, Holland and France for Stapleton in the qualifying matches were not enough as Ireland were denied a place in the finals by a superior French goal difference. Stapleton was made captain of the national team for the qualifying campaign for the 1986 Wold Cup though Ireland failed to emulate their fine performance of the previous qualifiers.

Back at Old Trafford, Stapleton was United's leading scorer in his first three seasons with the club. He was also in the United side that lost the 1983 League Cup Final 2–1 to Liverpool and faced Brighton and Hove Albion in that year's FA Cup Final and replay, which the Reds won 4–0. The first game ended 2–2 and when Stapleton scored United's first goal in that match, he wrote himself into the history books by becoming the first player to score in two different FA Cup winning teams.

In the summer of 1987, Stapleton was given a free transfer by Manchester United as a reward for his long and loyal service. He joined Ajax but after an unhappy eight months in Amsterdam when he also needed a back operation for the removal of a disc, he had a loan spell with Derby County before signing for French club Le Havre. He failed to settle in France and returned to the north-west of England with Blackburn Rovers. He later played for Aldershot and had a brief stint with Huddersfield Town before being appointed player-manager of Bradford City.

Sacked after failing to steer the Bantams into the Second Division play-offs, he had a brief spell playing with Brighton before working for a number of clubs in a coaching capacity. He was also manager of New England Revolution in the new American Soccer League.

Stapleton, who had remained Ireland captain under Jack Charlton, this despite a sometimes uneasy relationship between the two men, skippered the national side at the 1988 European Championships including the victory over England. Widely regarded as one of the Republic of Ireland's greatest and most committed strikers, he netted the only goal of the friendly with West Germany before following it with one more against Malta to make him his country's leading scorer in June 1990.

STEVE STAUNTON

Former manager of the Republic of Ireland and his country's most-capped player with 102 appearances for the national side, Steve Staunton played his early football for League of Ireland side Dundalk before joining Liverpool in September 1986, bought

Steve Staunton

by Reds boss Kenny Dalglish for a bargain £20,000. He spent over a year at Anfield without first team football before he was loaned out to Bradford City where he made his League debut in the Yorkshire derby against Sheffield United in November 1987.

He eventually broke into the Liverpool side in September 1988 playing in the 1–1 draw against Spurs at Anfield. His performance was so impressive that he remained in the side for the rest of the season. Also during that campaign, he broke into the full Republic of Ireland side, making his international debut against Tunisia at Lansdowne Road, a match the Irish won 4–0. He kept his place in the side for the World Cup qualifier against Spain in Seville a few weeks later and was included in Jack Charlton's 22–man squad for the World Cup Finals in Italy in 1990. At just 21, he was the youngest player at the finals.

Substituted in the 1989 FA Cup final win over Everton, he suffered huge disappointment in the League title decider with Arsenal when Michael Thomas scored late on to prevent Liverpool from gaining a second League and FA Cup double. Though by now an automatic choice for Ireland, he was finding it more difficult to hold down a regular place at Anfield and in the summer of 1991, he was sold to Aston Villa for £1.1 million.

In a dream debut for his new club, Staunton scored the winner in a 3–2 defeat of Sheffield Wednesday on the opening day of the 1991–92 season. He settled into life at Villa Park and after helping the club finish runners-up in the first-ever Premiership season in 1992–93, he won a Coca Cola League Cup winners' medal in 1994 as Villa surprisingly beat Manchester United 3–1. Over the next four years with the Midlands club, he won another Coca Cola League Cup winners' medal as a non-playing substitute against Leeds United.

As the Republic of Ireland kicked off their qualifying programme for the 1994 World Cup, Staunton began in his familiar left-back position but with Sheedy injured he moved into midfield for the game against Spain. He continued in midfield throughout all the qualifiers, scoring in the games against Northern Ireland, Albania and Lithuania. Named FAI 'Player of the Year' for 1993, he unfortunately suffered more than most in the heat of Orlando and was substituted in both games played there.

Staunton was outstanding in the Euro '96 qualifying campaign, missing just one game ahead of the play-off defeat against Holland at Liverpool's Anfield. Following the appointment of Mick McCarthy as Ireland boss, Steve Staunton was asked to revert to defence. Over the next few seasons his vast experience was vital, especially as Paul McGrath and Kevin Moran had decided to retire from international football.

In the summer of 1998, Staunton left Villa to rejoin Liverpool under the Bosman ruling which allows a player to move anywhere he wants without a fee once his contract expires. In his second spell on Merseyside, Staunton found it difficult to hold down a regular first team place, although he continued to turn out for Ireland regularly. After a loan spell with Crystal Palace, he decided to return to Villa Park. Having appeared in 148 games for Liverpool, he took his total of appearances for Aston Villa to 350 before moving on to Coventry City. He spent two seasons with the Sky Blues, clocking up a further 75 appearances before playing for his final League club, Walsall.

After playing his final game on New Year's Eve 2005, Staunton was plucked from the obscurity of being Walsall's assistant-coach to be appointed manager of the Republic of Ireland national side. His international management career enjoyed a dream start as Sweden were beaten 3–0, however, Ireland's 4–0 thrashing by Holland, the country's worst home reverse in 40 years along with failure to qualify for the 2008 European Championships, cost him his job.

ANDY TOWNSEND

Midfielder Andy Townsend began his playing career in non-League football with Welling United of the Southern League whilst working as a computer operator for Greenwich Borough Council in south-east London. In 1984 he joined Weymouth and it was there that his performances brought him to the attention of a number of leading clubs.

In January 1985, Lawrie McMenemy signed him for Southampton for a fee of £35,000 and he made his debut for the Saints against Aston Villa three months later. Southampton qualified for Europe at the end of that 1984–85 season but were later banned (along with all other English teams) in the aftermath of the Heysel Stadium disaster. In a pre-season friendly against his former club Weymouth in August 1986, Townsend broke his leg but fought his way back to fitness and won back his place in the 1999–2000 side. He was a big part of the team in 1987–88 and it came as a shock when he was allowed to join First Division rivals Norwich City for £300,000.

He helped to establish the Canaries' reputation as a classy passing team. They achieved their highest-ever Football League placing of fourth and reached the FA Cup semi-final. At the end of his first season at Carrow Road, Townsend was short listed for the PFA Players' 'Player of the Year' award which was won by Mark Hughes. His contribution to Norwich's successful season saw him selected for the Republic of Ireland and he made his international debut against France in February 1989.

Though the game ended goalless, Townsend did not look out of place in a Republic of Ireland midfield that boasted the likes of Brady, Houghton and Whelan. By the time the 1990 World Cup Finals came around, he had become an important member of the Irish side and his performances against England and Holland were very impressive.

Townsend became the subject of intense transfer speculation after Ireland's exit from Italia '90. Within a week of the Republic's elimination, Norwich sold him to Chelsea for 31.2 million. The job of leading the Stamford Bridge club was to prove good experience for a player who would go on to become the Republic's longest-serving captain.

Andy Townsend

He first wore the captain's armband at international level in the 1–0 defeat by Wales in February 1992 before being given the job on a permanent basis at the start of the qualifying campaign for the 1994 World Cup Finals.

His form at both club and international level saw him linked with a move away from the Bridge and in the summer of 1993 he joined Aston Villa for £2 million. Villa Park had become something of an Irish enclave during the early 1990s: Townsend joined fellow Ireland internationals Ray Houghton, Paul McGrath and Steve Staunton at the Midlands club.

Despite missing only one game in the qualifiers, he saved his best form for the finals and his energetic display was instrumental in his side's famous 1–0 victory against Italy. He skippered Villa to success in the 1996 League Cup Final – which was some consolation for the Republic missing out on qualification for the 1996 European Championships. Though he retained the captaincy of the national side following the appointment of Mick McCarthy, things were changing at Villa Park and in August 1998 he was sold to Middlesbrough for £500,000.

He proved a big hit in his first season on Teesside, helping Boro win promotion to the Premiership – it was as a Middlesbrough player that Ireland's longest-serving skipper won his last cap in the second leg of the World Cup play-off against Belgium. Appointed Middlesbrough's captain for the 1998–99 Premiership season, he continued to belie his advancing years and was a perfect role model for the other players.

Early in the following season he left to play for West Bromwich Albion but a recurring knee injury forced his retirement in July 2000. He can currently be seen as part of ITV's Sport's live coverage and reviewing the Football League Championship highlights show as well as hosting TalkSPORT's Weekend Sports Breakfast programme alongside Mike Parry.

RONNIE WHELAN JNR

Ronnie Whelan Jnr was a skilful and industrious midfielder signed from Home Farm by Liverpool manager Bob Paisley in September 1979. His father was a former international who had won two caps for the Republic of Ireland and had been a key member of the successful St Patrick's Athletic side of the late 1950s and early 1960s.

Ronnie made a goalscoring debut for Liverpool in a 3–0 win over Stoke City in April 1981 and later that month, he came off the bench in the friendly against Czechoslovakia to make his international debut at Lansdowne Road. It was 1981–82 before Whelan won a regular place in the Liverpool side, scoring ten League goals as the club won the Championship title and two in the 1982 League Cup Final as the Reds beat Spurs 3–1 after extra-time. In 1983 he popped up again to score the winner in extra-time as Liverpool retained the trophy by defeating Manchester United 2–1. Whelan then played a major role in Liverpool's treble of League title, League Cup and European Cup of 1984, although he was injured for part of this season.

Liverpool's 1984–85 season (which culminated in the Heysel disaster) was followed by a much more successful season for Whelan and Liverpool under the new

Ronnie Whelan Jnr

management of Kenny Dalglish. The Reds clinched another League title with Whelan netting a hat-trick in a 5–0 defeat of Coventry City and added the FA Cup with Whelan setting up two of the goals in a 3–1 victory over Merseyside rivals Everton.

Under Jack Charlton, Ronnie Whelan became a more industrious and resolute footballer. He was selected for both the 1988 European Championship Finals in Germany and the 1990 World Cup Finals in Italy. In the European Championship game against the USSR, Whelan scored a breathtaking goal: a long throw from Mick McCarthy eluded all the Soviet defenders and fell to Whelan, who leapt into the air to strike a perfect left-footed scissor-kick into the corner of the net. Sadly, he was troubled by injury and he played little part in the Republic's remarkable progress to the World Cup quarter-finals.

On his return from Italia '90, Whelan had two injury-plagued seasons before returning to first team action on a more regular basis in 1992–93. He stayed at Liverpool until 1994 and remained a regular in Jack Charlton's squad. In 1994 at the age of 32, he was included in his second World Cup Finals squad.

Whelan later left Anfield to join Southend United, having won six League Championship medals, two FA Cup winners' medals and a European Cup winners' medal. He began his managerial career at Roots Hall but things started to go wrong for him and in February 1997 the club suspended him from team manager duties after an incident with match officials.

He then worked with clubs in Greece (Panionios) and Cyprus (Apollon Limassol and most notably, Olympiakos Nicosia). His greatest success as a manager was with Panionios in 1999 when his team reached the quarter-finals of the European Cup Winners' Cup. Ronnie Whelan, still a firm favourite with Liverpool supporters everywhere, now works on the after-dinner circuit and does a spot of punditry.

Statistics

Statistics

World Cup and European Championship Results
Republic of Ireland's record against all other nations.
Top 50 Appearances and Goalscorers

THE REPUBLIC OF IRELAND'S WORLD CUP GROUPS

1930 World Cup

Did not enter

1934 World Cup

Group 11

25 Feb 1934	Dublin	Republic of Ireland 4 Belgium 4
8 Apr 1934	Amsterdam	Holland 5 Republic of Ireland 2
29 Apr 1934	Antwerp	Belgium 2 Holland 4

	P	W	D	L	F	A	Pts
Holland	2	2	0	0	9	4	4
Belgium	2	0	1	1	6	8	1
REPUBLIC OF IRELAND	2	0	1	1	6	9	1

Appearances

T Burke 1; D Byrne 1; P Byrne 1; H Chatton 1; J Foley 2; P Gaskins 2; F Horlacher 1; B Jordan 1 J Kelly 1; J Kendrick 2; B Kennedy 2; M Lynch 1; P Meehan 1; P Moore 2; T O'Keeffe 1; J O'Reilly 1; J Squires 1.

Goals

P Moore 5; J Squires 1.

1938 World Cup

Group 2

10 Oct 1937	Oslo	Norway 3 Republic of Ireland 2
7 Nov 1937	Dublin	Republic of Ireland 3 Norway 3

Norway qualified 6–5 on aggregate.

Appearances

T Arrigan 1; J Carey 1; J Donnelly 1; T Donnelly 1; H Duggan 1; J Dunne 2; T Foy 1; M Geoghegan 1; B Gorman 1; M Hoy 1; B Jordan 1; O Kinsella 1; G McKenzie 2; K O'Flanagan 1; W O'Neill 1; J O'Reilly 2; C Turner 2; J Williams 1.

Goals

J Dunne 2; H Duggan 1; M Geoghegan 1; K O'Flanagan 1.

1950 World Cup

Group 5

2 Jun 1949	Stockholm	Sweden 3 Republic of Ireland 1
8 Sep 1949	Dublin	Republic of Ireland 3 Finland 0
9 Oct 1949	Helsinki	Finland 1 Republic of Ireland 1
13 Nov 1949	Dublin	Republic of Ireland 1 Sweden 3

The games between Sweden and Finland were not played when Finland withdrew from the competition.

	P	W	D	L	F	A	Pts
Sweden	2	2	0	0	6	2	4
REPUBLIC OF IRELAND	4	1	1	2	6	7	3
Finland	2	0	1	1	1	4	1

Appearances

T Aherne 3; J Carey 4; B Carroll 1; P Coad 1; J Coffey 1; P Corr 1; P Daly 1; P Desmond 3; T Eglington 1; P Farrell 2; A Fitzsimons 1; E Gannon 2; J Gavin 2; T Godwin 4; T Keane 1; D McGowan 1; C Martin 4; T Moroney 3; T O'Connor 3; J O'Driscoll 1; R Ryan 1; D Walsh 3; W Walsh 1.

Goals

C Martin 3; P Farrell 1; J Galvin 1; D Walsh 1.

Group 4

20 Sep 1953	Luxembourg	Luxembourg 1 France 6
4 Oct 1953	Dublin	Republic of Ireland 3 France 5
28 Oct 1953	Dublin	Republic of Ireland 4 Luxembourg 0
25 Nov 1953	Paris	France 1 Republic of Ireland 0
17 Dec 1953	Paris	France 8 Luxembourg 0
7 Mar 1954	Luxembourg	Luxembourg 0 Republic of Ireland 1

	P	W	D	L	F	A	Pts
France	4	4	0	0	20	4	8
REPUBLIC OF IRELAND	4	2	0	2	8	6	4
Luxembourg	4	0	0	4	1	19	0

Appearances

T Aherne 1; N Cantwell 1; T Clinton 2; G Cummins 2; S Dunne 2; T Eglington 3; P Farrell 2; A Fitzsimons 3; M Gallagher 1; E Gannon 2; J Gavin 1; S Gibbons 1; J Hartnett 1; F Kearns 1; N Kelly 1; J Lawler 2; C Martin 3; T Moroney 1; L Munroe 1; F O'Farrell 1; J O'Neill 3; A Ringstead 1; R Ryan 3; P Saward 1; T Scannell 1; T Traynor 1; D Walsh 2 .

Goals

A Fitzsimons 2; R Ryan 2; G Cummins 1; T Eglington 1; F O'Farrell 1; D Walsh 1.

Group 1

3 Oct 1956	Dublin	Republic of Ireland 2 Denmark 1
5 Dec 1956	Wolverhampton	England 5 Denmark 2
8 May 1957	London	England 5 Republic of Ireland 1
15 May 1957	Copenhagen	Denmark 1 England 4
19 May 1957	Dublin	Republic of Ireland 1 England 1
2 Oct 1957	Copenhagen	Denmark 0 Republic of Ireland 2

	P	W	D	L	F	A	Pts
England	4	3	1	0	15	5	7
REPUBLIC OF IRELAND	4	2	1	1	6	7	5
Denmark	4	0	0	4	4	13	0

Appearances

N Cantwell 4; G Cummins 1; D Curtis 4; D Donovan 1; S Dunne 3; T Dunne 1; P Farrell 1; A Fitzsimons 4; J Gavin 1; T Godwin 2; J Haverty 4; C Hurley 2; A Kelly 1; G Mackey 2; R Nolan 2; F O'Farrell 1; J O'Neill 1; A Ringstead 3; P Saward 3; L Whelan 3.

Goals

D Curtis 3; G Cummins 1; J Gavin 1; A Ringstead 1.

1962 World Cup

Group 8

3 May 1961	Glasgow	Scotland 4 Republic of Ireland 1
7 May 1961	Dublin	Republic of Ireland 0 Scotland 3
14 May 1961	Bratislava	Czechoslovakia 4 Scotland 0
26 Sep 1961	Glasgow	Scotland 3 Czechoslovakia 2
8 Oct 1961	Dublin	Republic of Ireland 1 Czechoslovakia 3
29 Oct 1961	Prague	Czechoslovakia 7 Republic of Ireland 1

	P	W	D	L	F	A	Pts
Czechoslovakia	4	3	0	1	16	5	6
Scotland	4	3	0	1	10	7	6
REPUBLIC OF IRELAND	4	0	0	4	3	17	0

Appearances

N Cantwell 4; G Cummins 2; D Curtis 1; N Dwyer 4; F Fagan 1; P Fitzgerald 3; A Fogarty 3; J Giles 4; J Haverty 4; C Hurley 4; P Kelly 3; A McEvoy 2; M McGrath 2; B McNally 1; M Meagan 1; R Nolan 2; F O'Neill 2; P Saward 1.

Goals

A Fogarty 1; J Giles 1; J Haverty 1.

1966 World Cup

Group 9

| 5 May 1965 | Dublin | Republic of Ireland 1 Spain 0 |
| 27 Oct 1965 | Seville | Spain 4 Republic of Ireland 1 |

	P	W	D	L	F	A	Pts
Spain	2	1	0	1	4	2	2
REPUBLIC OF IRELAND	2	1	0	1	2	4	2

Syria withdrew in support of the African teams who declined to play in protest against the allocation of places.

Play-Off

| 10 Nov 1965 | Paris | Spain 1 Republic of Ireland 0 |

Appearances

E Barber 1; S Brennan 2; N Cantwell 3; P Dunne 3; T Dunne 3; E Dunphy 1; T Foley 2; J Giles 3; J Haverty 3; J Hennessey 1; C Hurley 1; A McEvoy 3; M McGrath 2; M Meagan 2; F O'Neill 3.

Goals

A McEvoy 1; Iribar own goal.

Group 2

25 Sep 1968	Copenhagen	Denmark 0 Czechoslovakia 3
20 Oct 1968	Bratislava	Czechoslovakia 1 Denmark 0
4 Dec 1968	Dublin	Republic of Ireland 1 Denmark 1*
4 May 1969	Dublin	Republic of Ireland 1 Czechoslovakia 2
25 May 1969	Budapest	Hungary 2 Czechoslovakia 0
27 May 1969	Copenhagen	Denmark 2 Republic of Ireland 0
8 Jun 1969	Dublin	Republic of Ireland 1 Hungary 2
15 Jun 1969	Copenhagen	Denmark 3 Hungary 2
14 Sep 1969	Prague	Czechoslovakia 3 Hungary 3
7 Oct 1969	Prague	Czechoslovakia 3 Republic of Ireland 0
15 Oct 1969	Dublin	Republic of Ireland 1 Denmark 1
22 Oct 1969	Budapest	Hungary 3 Denmark 0
5 Nov 1969	Budapest	Hungary 4 Republic of Ireland 0

*Abandoned; the game is not counted in statistics but in Irish appearances and goals.

	P	W	D	L	F	A	Pts
Hungary	6	4	1	1	16	7	9
Czechoslovakia	6	4	1	1	12	6	9
Denmark	6	2	1	3	6	10	5
REPUBLIC OF IRELAND	6	0	1	5	3	14	1

Play-Off

| 3 Dec 1969 | Marseille | Czechoslovakia 4 Hungary 1 |

Appearances

S Brennan 6; T Byrne 1; T Carroll 2; O Conmy 1; T Conroy 3; J Conway 4; J Dempsey 4; T Dunne 3; E Dunphy 5; A Finucane 4; K Fitzpatrick 1; J Fullam 2; J Giles 2; D Givens 5; A hale 2; E Hand 1; C Hurley 3; A Kelly 6; J Kinnear 3; M Leech 3; P Mulligan 6; B Newman 1; F O'Neill 4; E Rogers 6; R Treacy 4.

Goals

D Givens 2; J Giles 1; E Rogers 1.

Group 9

13 Oct 1972	Paris	France 1 USSR 0
18 Oct 1972	Dublin	Republic of Ireland 1 USSR 2
15 Nov 1972	Dublin	Republic of Ireland 2 France 1
13 May 1973	Moscow	USSR 1 Republic of Ireland 0
19 May 1973	Paris	France 1 Republic of Ireland 1
26 May 1973	Moscow	USSR 2 France 0

	P	W	D	L	F	A	Pts
USSR	4	3	0	1	5	2	6
REPUBLIC OF IRELAND	4	1	1	2	4	5	3
France	4	1	1	2	3	5	3

Appearances

T Byrne 3; N Cantwell 2; T Carroll 3; T Conroy 3; M Dennehy 2; J Giles 2; D Givens 3; E Hand 4; S Heighway 1; J Herrick 1; J Holmes 3; A Kelly 4; J Kinnear 2; M Leech 1; T McConville 4; M Martin 3; P Mulligan 3; T O'Connor 1; E Rogers 1; R Treacy 4.

Goals

T Conroy 2; M Martin 1; R Treacy 1.

1978 World Cup

Group 5

9 Oct 1976	Sofia	Bulgaria 2 France 2
17 Nov 1976	Paris	France 2 Republic of Ireland 0
30 Mar 1977	Dublin	Republic of Ireland 1 France 0
1 Jun 1977	Sofia	Bulgaria 2 Republic of Ireland 1
12 Oct 1977	Dublin	Republic of Ireland 0 Bulgaria 0
16 Nov 1977	Paris	France 3 Bulgaria 1

	P	W	D	L	F	A	Pts
France	4	2	1	1	7	4	5
Bulgaria	4	1	2	1	5	6	4
REPUBLIC OF IRELAND	4	1	1	2	2	4	3

Appearances

L Brady 4; N Campbell 1; G Daly 4; J Giles 4; D Givens 4; S Heighway 4; J Holmes 4; M Kearns 3; M Lawrenson 1; M Martin 3; P Mulligan 4; D O'Leary 4; G Peyton 1; F Stapleton 3; R Treacy 1; M Walsh 1.

Goals

L Brady 1; D Givens 1.

1982 World Cup

Group 2

26 Mar 1980	Nicosia	Cyprus 2 Republic of Ireland 3
10 Sep 1980	Dublin	Republic of Ireland 2 Holland 1
11 Oct 1980	Limassol	Cyprus 0 France 7
15 Oct 1980	Dublin	Republic of Ireland 1 Belgium 1
28 Oct 1980	Paris	France 2 Republic of Ireland 0

Date	Venue	Result
19 Nov 1980	Dublin	Republic of Ireland 6 Cyprus 0
19 Nov 1980	Brussels	Belgium 1 Holland 0
21 Dec 1980	Nicosia	Cyprus 0 Belgium 2
18 Feb 1981	Brussels	Belgium 3 Cyprus 2
22 Feb 1981	Groningen	Holland 3 Cyprus 0
25 Mar 1981	Brussels	Belgium 1 Republic of Ireland 0
25 Mar 1981	Rotterdam	Holland 1 France 0
29 Apr 1981	Paris	France 3 Belgium 2
29 Apr 1981	Nicosia	Cyprus 0 Holland 1
9 Sep 1981	Rotterdam	Holland 2 Republic of Ireland 2
9 Sep 1981	Brussels	Belgium 2 France 0
14 Oct 1981	Dublin	Republic of Ireland 3 France 2
14 Oct 1981	Rotterdam	Holland 3 Belgium 0
18 Nov 1981	Paris	France 2 Holland 0
5 Dec 1981	Paris	France 4 Cyprus 0

	P	W	D	L	F	A	Pts
Belgium	8	5	1	2	12	9	11
France	8	5	0	3	20	8	10
REPUBLIC OF IRELAND	8	4	2	2	17	11	10
Holland	8	4	1	3	11	7	9
Cyprus	8	0	0	8	4	29	0

Appearances

L Brady 8; G Daly 5; J Devine 1; T Grealish 7; A Grimes 1; D Givens 4; S Heighway 6; C Hughton 6; D Langan 7; M Lawrenson 7; S McDonough 3; P McGee 2; M Martin 4; K Moran 5; J Murphy 1; F O'Brien 1; D O'Leary 4; P O'Leary 1; G Peyton 5; M Robinson 5; G Ryan 3; F Stapleton 8; M Walsh 1; R Whelan 2.

Goals

G Daly 3; M Robinson 3; F Stapleton 3; T Grealish 2; M Lawrenson 2; P McGee 2; C Hughton 1; Mahut own goal.

1986 World Cup

Group 6

Date	Venue	Result
12 Sep 1984	Dublin	Republic of Ireland 1 USSR 0
12 Sep 1984	Oslo	Norway 0 Switzerland 1
26 Sep 1984	Copenhagen	Denmark 1 Norway 0
10 Oct 1984	Oslo	Norway 1 USSR 1
17 Oct 1984	Oslo	Norway 1 Republic of Ireland 0
17 Oct 1984	Berne	Switzerland 1 Denmark 0
14 Nov 1984	Copenhagen	Denmark 3 Republic of Ireland 0
17 Apr 1985	Berne	Switzerland 2 USSR 2
1 May 1985	Dublin	Republic of Ireland 0 Norway 0

Date	Venue	Result
2 May 1985	Moscow	USSR 4 Switzerland 0
2 Jun 1985	Dublin	Republic of Ireland 3 Switzerland 0
5 Jun 1985	Copenhagen	Denmark 4 USSR 2
11 Sep 1985	Berne	Switzerland 0 Republic of Ireland 0
25 Sep 1985	Moscow	USSR 1 Denmark 0
9 Oct 1985	Copenhagen	Denmark 0 Switzerland 0
16 Oct 1985	Oslo	Norway 1 Denmark 5
19 Oct 1985	Moscow	USSR 2 Republic of Ireland 0
30 Oct 1985	Moscow	USSR 1 Norway 0
13 Nov 1985	Dublin	Republic of Ireland 1 Denmark 4
13 Nov 1985	Lucerne	Switzerland 1 Norway 1

	P	W	D	L	F	A	Pts
Denmark	8	5	1	2	17	6	11
USSR	8	4	2	2	13	8	10
Switzerland	8	2	4	2	5	10	8
REPUBLIC OF IRELAND	8	2	2	4	5	10	6
Norway	8	1	3	4	4	10	5

Appearances

J Beglin 6; P Bonner 1; L Brady 8; P Byrne 1; T Cascarino 3; G Daly 3; J Devine 2; T Galvin 4; T Grealish 6; C Hughton 4; D Langan 2; M Lawrenson 7; M McCarthy 4; S McDonough 7; P McGrath 4; K Moran 1; K O'Callaghan 4; E O'Keefe 1; D O'Leary 8; M Robinson 5; K Sheedy 4; F Stapleton 7; G Waddock 2; M Walsh 3; R Whelan 5.

Goals

F Stapleton 2; T Grealish 1; K Sheedy 1; M Walsh 1.

1990 World Cup

Group 6

Date	Venue	Result
21 May 1988	Belfast	Northern Ireland 3 Malta 0
14 Sep 1988	Belfast	Northern Ireland 0 Republic of Ireland 0
19 Oct 1988	Budapest	Hungary 1 Northern Ireland 0
16 Nov 1988	Seville	Spain 2 Republic of Ireland 0
11 Dec 1988	Valetta	Malta 2 Hungary 2
21 Dec 1988	Seville	Spain 4 Northern Ireland 0
22 Jan 1989	Valetta	Malta 0 Spain 2
8 Feb 1989	Belfast	Northern Ireland 0 Spain 2
8 Mar 1989	Budapest	Hungary 0 Republic of Ireland 0
23 Mar 1989	Seville	Spain 4 Malta 0
12 Apr 1989	Budapest	Hungary 1 Malta 1
26 Apr 1989	Dublin	Republic of Ireland 1 Spain 0
26 Apr 1989	Valetta	Malta 0 Northern Ireland 2

Date	Venue	Result
28 May 1989	Dublin	Republic of Ireland 2 Malta 0
4 Jun 1989	Dublin	Republic of Ireland 2 Hungary 0
6 Sep 1989	Belfast	Northern Ireland 1 Hungary 2
11 Oct 1989	Dublin	Republic of Ireland 3 Northern Ireland 0
11 Oct 1989	Budapest	Hungary 2 Spain 2
15 Nov 1989	Valetta	Malta 0 Republic of Ireland 2
15 Nov 1989	Seville	Spain 4 Hungary 0

	P	W	D	L	F	A	Pts
Spain	8	6	1	1	20	3	13
REPUBLIC OF IRELAND	8	5	2	1	10	2	12
Hungary	8	2	4	2	8	12	8
Northern Ireland	8	2	1	5	6	12	5
Malta	8	0	2	6	3	18	2

Republic of Ireland qualified for the finals in Italy.

Appearances

J Aldridge 7; P Bonner 7; L Brady 2; T Cascarino 8; T Galvin 1; R Houghton 8; C Hughton 5; M McCarthy 5; P McGrath 6; K Moran 8; C Morris 6; L O'Brien 1; D O'Leary 5; G Peyton 1; N Quinn 2; K Sheedy 7; J Sheridan 1; F Stapleton 2; S Staunton 6; A Townsend 5; R Whelan 6.

Goals

J Aldridge 2; T Cascarino 2; R Houghton 2; P McGrath 1; K Moran 1; R Whelan 1; Michel own goal.

REPUBLIC OF IRELAND SQUAD FOR THE FINALS

No	Name	Position	Club	Age	Caps	Goals
1	Packie Bonner	Goalkeeper	Glasgow Celtic	30	38	-
2	Chris Morris	Full-back	Glasgow Celtic	26	21	-
3	Steve Staunton	Full-back	Liverpool	21	13	1
4	Mick McCarthy (Capt)	Central defence	Millwall	31	42	1
5	Kevin Moran	Central defence	Blackburn Rovers	34	50	6
6	Ronnie Whelan	Midfield	Liverpool	28	38	3
7	Paul McGrath	Central defence	Aston Villa	30	36	4
8	Ray Houghton	Midfield	Liverpool	28	29	3
9	John Aldridge	Forward	Real Sociedad	31	30	3
10	Tony Cascarino	Forward	Aston Villa	27	21	5
11	Kevin Sheedy	Midfield	Everton	30	28	5
12	David O'Leary	Central defence	Arsenal	32	51	-
13	Andy Townsend	Midfield	Norwich City	26	12	1
14	Chris Hughton	Full-back	Tottenham Hotspur	31	50	1
15	Bernie Slaven	Midfield	Middlesbrough	29	4	1
16	John Sheridan	Midfield	Sheffield Wednesday	25	8	1

17	Niall Quinn	Forward	Manchester City	23	15	2
18	Frank Stapleton	Forward	Blackburn Rovers	33	71	20
19	David Kelly	Forward	Leicester City	24	6	4
20	John Byrne	Forward	Le Havre	29	19	1
21	Alan McLoughlin	Midfield	Swindon Town	23	1	-
22	Gerry Peyton	Goalkeeper	Bournemouth	34	28	-
			Averages	28.4	27.2	

1990 Final Group F

11 Jun 1990	Cagliari	England 1 Republic of Ireland 1
12 Jun 1990	Palermo	Holland 1 Egypt 1
16 Jun 1990	Cagliari	England 0 Holland 0
17 Jun 1990	Palermo	Egypt 0 Republic of Ireland 0
21 Jun 1990	Palermo	Holland 1 Republic of Ireland 1
21 Jun 1990	Cagliari	England 1 Egypt 0

	P	W	D	L	F	A	Pts
England	3	1	2	0	2	1	4
REPUBLIC OF IRELAND	3	0	3	0	2	2	3
Holland	3	0	3	0	2	2	3
Egypt	3	0	2	1	1	2	2

Round Two

				Extra time	Penalties
23 Jun 1990	Naples	Cameroon 0 Colombia 0		2–1	
23 Jun 1990	Bari	Czechoslovakia 4 Costa Rica 1			
24 Jun 1990	Turin	Argentina 1 Brazil 0			
24 Jun 1990	Milan	West Germany 2 Holland 1			
25 Jun 1990	Genoa	Romania 0 Republic of Ireland 0		0–0	4–5
25 Jun 1990	Rome	Italy 2 Uruguay 0			
26 Jun 1990	Verona	Yugoslavia 1 Spain 1		2–1	
26 Jun 1990	Bologna	England 0 Belgium 0		1–0	

Quarter-Finals

				Extra time	Penalties
30 Jun 1990	Florence	Argentina 0 Yugoslavia 0		0–0	3–2
30 Jun 1990	Rome	Italy 1 Republic of Ireland 0			
1 Jul 1990	Milan	West Germany 1 CSSR 0			
1 Jul 1990	Naples	England 2 Cameroon 2		3–2	

Semi-Finals

				Extra time	Penalties
3 Jul 1990	Naples	Italy 1 Argentina 1		1–1	3–4
4 Jul 1990	Turin	West Germany 1 England 1		1–1	4–3

Third & Fourth Place Play-Off

| 7 Jul 1990 | Bari | Italy 2 England 1 |

Final

| 8 Jul 1990 | Rome | West Germany 1 Argentina 0 |

Appearances

J Aldridge 5; P Bonner 5; T Cascarino 5; R Houghton 5; M McCarthy 5; P McGrath 5; A McLoughlin 2; K Moran 5; C Morris 5; D O'Leary 1; N Quinn 4; K Sheedy 5; J Sheridan 1; S Staunton 5; A Townsend 5; R Whelan 1.

Goals

N Quinn 1; K Sheedy 1.

1994 World Cup

Group 3

22 Apr 1992	Seville	Spain 3 Albania 0
28 Apr 1992	Belfast	Northern Ireland 2 Lithuania 2
26 May 1992	Dublin	Republic of Ireland 2 Albania 0
3 Jun 1992	Tirana	Albania 1 Lithuania 0
12 Aug 1992	Riga	Latvia 1 Lithuania 2]
26 Aug 1992	Riga	Latvia 0 Denmark 0
9 Sep 1992	Dublin	Republic of Ireland 4 Latvia 0
9 Sep 1992	Belfast	Northern Ireland 3 Albania 0
23 Sep 1992	Riga	Latvia 0 Spain 0
23 Sep 1992	Vilnius	Lithuania 0 Denmark 0
14 Oct 1992	Belfast	Northern Ireland 0 Spain 0
14 Oct 1992	Copenhagen	Denmark 0 Republic of Ireland 0
28 Oct 1992	Vilnius	Lithuania 1 Latvia 1
11 Nov 1992	Tirana	Albania 1 Latvia 1
18 Nov 1992	Seville	Spain 0 Republic of Ireland 0
18 Nov 1992	Belfast	Northern Ireland 0 Denmark 1
16 Dec 1992	Seville	Spain 5 Latvia 0
17 Feb 1993	Tirana	Albania 1 Northern Ireland 2
24 Feb 1993	Seville	Spain 5 Lithuania 0
31 Mar 1993	Dublin	Republic of Ireland 3 Northern Ireland 0
31 Mar 1993	Copenhagen	Denmark 1 Spain 0
14 Apr 1993	Copenhagen	Denmark 2 Latvia 0
14 Apr 1993	Vilnius	Lithuania 3 Albania 1
28 Apr 1993	Seville	Spain 3 Northern Ireland 1
28 Apr 1993	Dublin	Republic of Ireland 1 Denmark 1
15 May 1993	Riga	Latvia 0 Albania 0
25 May 1993	Vilnius	Lithuania 0 Northern Ireland 1
26 May 1993	Tirana	Albania 1 Republic of Ireland 2

2 Jun 1993	Riga	Latvia 1 Northern Ireland 2
2 Jun 1993	Copenhagen	Denmark 4 Albania 0
2 Jun 1993	Vilnius	Lithuania 0 Spain 2
9 Jun 1993	Riga	Latvia 0 Republic of Ireland 2
16 Jun 1993	Vilnius	Lithuania 0 Republic of Ireland 1
25 Aug 1993	Copenhagen	Denmark 4 Lithuania 0
8 Sep 1993	Belfast	Northern Ireland 2 Latvia 0
8 Sep 1993	Dublin	Republic of Ireland 2 Lithuania 0
8 Sep 1993	Tirana	Albania 0 Denmark 1
22 Sep 1993	Tirana	Albania 1 Spain 5
13 Oct 1993	Copenhagen	Denmark 1 Northern Ireland 0
13 Oct 1993	Dublin	Republic of Ireland 1 Spain 3
17 Nov 1993	Belfast	Northern Ireland 1 Republic of Ireland 1
17 Nov 1993	Seville	Spain 1 Denmark 0

	P	W	D	L	F	A	Pts
Spain	12	8	3	1	27	4	19
REPUBLIC OF IRELAND	12	7	4	1	19	6	18
Denmark	12	7	4	1	15	2	18
Northern Ireland	12	5	3	4	14	13	13
Lithuania	12	2	3	7	8	21	7
Latvia	12	0	5	7	4	21	5
Albania	12	1	2	9	6	26	4

Republic of Ireland qualified for the finals in the United States.

Appearances

J Aldridge 10; P Bonner 12; T Cascarino 7; T Coyne 3; R Houghton 11; D Irwin 12; R Keane 12; D Kelly 1; A Kernaghan 9; M McCarthy 1; E McGoldrick 4; P McGrath 9; K Moran 6; D O'Leary 1; T Phelan 10; N Quinn 12; K Sheedy 2; J Sheridan 2; S Staunton 10; A Townsend 11; R Whelan 4.

Goals

J Aldridge 6; S Staunton 3; P McGrath 2; N Quinn 2; T Cascarino 1; A Kernaghan 1; A McLoughlin 1; K Sheedy 1; J Sheridan 1; A Townsend 1.

REPUBLIC OF IRELAND SQUAD FOR THE FINALS

No	Name	Position	Club	Age	Caps	Goals
1	Packie Bonner	Goalkeeper	Glasgow Celtic	34	73	-
2	Denis Irwin	Full-back	Manchester United	28	26	1
3	Terry Phelan	Full-back	Manchester City	27	22	-
4	Kevin Moran	Central defence	Blackburn Rovers	38	71	6
5	Paul McGrath	Defence	Aston Villa	34	65	7
6	Roy Keane	Midfield	Manchester United	22	22	-
7	Andy Townsend (Capt)	Midfield	Aston Villa	30	45	4

8	Ray Houghton	Midfield	Aston Villa	32	58	3
9	John Aldridge	Forward	Tranmere Rovers	35	58	13
10	John Sheridan	Midfield	Sheffield Wednesday	29	20	3
11	Steve Staunton	Midfield	Aston Villa	25	47	5
12	Gary Kelly	Full-back	Leeds United	19	4	1
13	Alan Kernaghan	Central defence	Manchester City	27	11	1
14	Phil Babb	Central defence	Coventry City	23	4	-
15	Tommy Coyne	Forward	Motherwell	31	14	4
16	Tony Cascarino	Forward	Chelsea	31	50	12
17	Eddie McGoldrick	Utility	Arsenal	29	11	-
18	Ronnie Whelan	Midfield	Liverpool	32	50	3
19	Alan McLoughlin	Midfield	Portsmouth	27	17	1
20	David Kelly	Forward	Wolverhampton Wands	27	16	7
21	Jason McAteer	Midfield	Bolton Wanderers	23	5	-
22	Alan Kelly	Goalkeeper	Sheffield United	25	3	-
			Averages	28.5	31.5	

1994 Final Group E

18 Jun 1994	New York	Italy 0 Republic of Ireland 1
19 Jun 1994	Washington	Norway 1 Mexico 0
23 Jun 1994	New York	Italy 1 Norway 0
24 Jun 1994	Florida	Mexico 2 Republic of Ireland 1
28 Jun 1994	New York	Republic of Ireland 0 Norway 0
28 Jun 1994	Washington	Italy 1 Mexico 1

	P	W	D	L	F	A	Pts
Mexico	3	1	1	1	3	3	4
REPUBLIC OF IRELAND	3	1	1	1	2	2	4
Italy	3	1	1	1	2	2	4
Norway	3	1	1	1	1	1	4

Round Two

			Extra time	Penalties
2 Jul 1994	Chicago	Germany 3 Belgium 2		
2 Jul 1994	Washington	Spain 3 Switzerland 0		
3 Jul 1994	Dallas	Saudi Arabia 1 Sweden 3		
3 Jul 1994	Los Angeles	Romania 3 Argentina 2		
4 Jul 1994	Orlando	Holland 2 Republic of Ireland 0		
4 Jul 1994	San Francisco	Brazil 1 United States 0		
5 Jul 1994	Boston	Nigeria 1 Italy 1	1–2	
5 Jul 1994	New York	Mexico 1 Bulgaria 1	1–1	3–1

Quarter-Finals

			Extra time	Penalties
9 Jul 1994	Boston	Italy 2 Spain 1		
9 Jul 1994	Dallas	Holland 2 Brazil 3		
10 Jul 1994	New York	Bulgaria 2 Germany 1		
10 Jul 1994	San Francisco	Sweden 1 Romania 1	2–2	5–4

Semi-Finals

13 Jul 1994	New York	Italy 2 Bulgaria 1	
13 Jul 1994	Los Angeles	Brazil 1 Sweden 0	

Third & Fourth Place Play-Off

16 Jul 1994	Los Angeles	Sweden 4 Bulgaria 0

Final

			Extra time	Penalties
17 Jul 1994	Los Angeles	Brazil 0 Italy 0	0–0	3–2

Appearances

J Aldridge 3; P Babb 4; P Bonner 4; T Cascarino 1; T Coyne 3; R Houghton 4; D Irwin 2; R Keane 4; D Kelly 1; G Kelly 2; J McAteer 4; P McGrath 4; T Phelan 3; J Sheridan 4; S Staunton 4; A Townsend 4; R Whelan 1.

Goals

J Aldridge 1; R Houghton 1.

1998 World Cup

Group 8

24 Apr 1996	Skopje	Macedonia 3 Liechtenstein 0
1 Jun 1996	Reykjavik	Iceland 1 Macedonia 1
31 Aug 1996	Eschen	Liechtenstein 0 Republic of Ireland 5
31 Aug 1996	Bucharest	Romania 3 Lithuania 0
5 Oct 1996	Vilnius	Lithuania 2 Iceland 0
9 Oct 1996	Reykjavik	Iceland 0 Romania 4
9 Oct 1996	Vilnius	Lithuania 2 Liechtenstein 1
9 Oct 1996	Dublin	Republic of Ireland 3 Macedonia 0
9 Nov 1996	Eschen	Liechtenstein 1 Macedonia 11
10 Nov 1996	Dublin	Republic of Ireland 0 Iceland 0
14 Dec 1996	Skopje	Macedonia 0 Romania 3
29 Mar 1997	Bucharest	Romania 8 Liechtenstein 0
2 Apr 1997	Vilnius	Lithuania 0 Romania 1
2 Apr 1997	Skopje	Macedonia 3 Republic of Ireland 2
30 Apr 1997	Vaduz	Liechtenstein 0 Lithuania 2
30 Apr 1997	Bucharest	Romania 1 Republic of Ireland 0
21 May 1997	Dublin	Republic of Ireland 5 Liechtenstein 0

7 Jun 1997	Skopje	Macedonia 1 Iceland 0					
11 Jun 1997	Reykjavik	Iceland 0 Lithuania 0					
20 Aug 1997	Eschen	Liechtenstein 0 Iceland 4					
20 Aug 1997	Dublin	Republic of Ireland 0 Lithuania 0					
20 Aug 1997	Bucharest	Romania 4 Macedonia 2					
6 Sep 1997	Reykjavik	Iceland 2 Republic of Ireland 4					
6 Sep 1997	Eschen	Liechtenstein 1 Romania 8					
6 Sep 1997	Vilnius	Lithuania 2 Macedonia 0					
10 Sep 1997	Vilnius	Lithuania 1 Republic of Ireland 2					
10 Sep 1997	Bucharest	Romania 4 Iceland 0					
11 Oct 1997	Reykjavik	Iceland 4 Liechtenstein 0					
11 Oct 1997	Skopje	Macedonia 1 Lithuania 2					
11 Oct 1997	Dublin	Republic of Ireland 1 Romania 1					

	P	W	D	L	F	A	Pts
Romania	10	9	1	0	37	4	28
REPUBLIC OF IRELAND	10	5	3	2	22	8	18
Lithuania	10	5	2	3	11	8	17
Macedonia	10	4	1	5	22	18	13
Iceland	10	2	3	5	11	16	9
Liechtenstein	10	0	0	10	3	52	0

Appearances

J Aldridge 1; P Babb 3; G Breen 6; L Carsley 1; T Cascarino 10; D Connolly 5; K Cunningham 6; S Evans 1; C Fleming 2; S Given 5; J Goodman 3; I Harte 9; R Houghton 5; D Irwin 6; RM Keane 7; A Kelly 5; D Kelly 4; G Kelly 4; J Kenna 8; M Kennedy 5; K Kilbane 1; J McAteer 6; A McLoughlin 8; A Moore 3; L O'Brien 1; K O'Neill 3; T Phelan 2; N Quinn 2; S Staunton 8; A Townsend 8.

Goals

T Cascarino 7; D Connolly 4; RM Keane 2; N Quinn 2; I Harte 1; D Kelly 1; J McAteer 1; A McLoughlin 1; K O'Neill 1; A Townsend 1; Finnbogason (own goal).

2002 World Cup

Group 2

16 Aug 2000	Tallinn	Estonia 1 Andorra 0
2 Sep 2000	La Vella	Andorra 2 Cyprus 3
2 Sep 2000	Amsterdam	Holland 2 Republic of Ireland 2
3 Sep 2000	Tallinn	Estonia 1 Portugal 3
7 Oct 2000	La Vella	Andorra 1 Estonia 2
7 Oct 2000	Nicosia	Cyprus 0 Holland 4
7 Oct 2000	Lisbon	Portugal 1 Republic of Ireland 1
11 Oct 2000	Rotterdam	Holland 0 Portugal 2
11 Oct 2000	Dublin	Republic of Ireland 2 Estonia 0

15 Nov 2000	Nicosia	Cyprus 5 Andorra 0
28 Feb 2001	Madeira	Portugal 3 Andorra 0
24 Mar 2001	Barcelona	Andorra 0 Holland 5
24 Mar 2001	Nicosia	Cyprus 0 Republic of Ireland 4
28 Mar 2001	Barcelona	Andorra 0 Republic of Ireland 3
28 Mar 2001	Limassol	Cyprus 2 Estonia 2
28 Mar 2001	Oporto	Portugal 2 Holland 2
25 Apr 2001	Eindhoven	Holland 4 Cyprus 0
25 Apr 2001	Dublin	Republic of Ireland 3 Andorra 1
2 Jun 2001	Tallinn	Estonia 2 Holland 4
2 Jun 2001	Dublin	Republic of Ireland 1 Portugal 1
6 Jun 2001	Tallinn	Estonia 0 Republic of Ireland 2
6 Jun 2001	Lisbon	Portugal 6 Cyprus 0
15 Aug 2001	Tallinn	Estonia 2 Cyprus 2
1 Sep 2001	Lleida	Andorra 1 Portugal 7
1 Sep 2001	Dublin	Republic of Ireland 1 Holland 0
5 Sep 2001	Larnaca	Cyprus 1 Portugal 3
5 Sep 2001	Eindhoven	Holland 5 Estonia 0
6 Oct 2001	Arnhem	Holland 4 Andorra 0
6 Oct 2001	Lisbon	Portugal 5 Estonia 0
6 Oct 2001	Dublin	Republic of Ireland 4 Cyprus 0

Did you know?

Gary Kelly is the uncle of Ian Harte. Both players featured in the same squad for the Republic of Ireland's 2002 World Cup campaign.

	P	W	D	L	F	A	Pts
Portugal	10	7	3	0	33	7	24
REPUBLIC OF IRELAND	10	7	3	0	23	5	24
Holland	10	6	2	2	30	9	20
Estonia	10	2	2	6	10	26	8
Cyprus	10	2	2	6	13	31	8
Andorra	10	0	0	10	5	36	0

Republic of Ireland qualified for play-offs.

Play-offs

| 10 Nov 2001 | Dublin | Republic of Ireland 2 Iran 0 |
| 15 Nov 2001 | Teheran | Iran 1 Republic of Ireland 0 |

Republic of Ireland qualified for finals in South Korea and Japan.

Appearances

G Breen 9; S Carr 6; L Carsley 1; D Connolly 6; K Cunningham 3; G Doherty 5; R Dunne 7; D Duff 7; S Finnan 8; D Foley 1; S Given 9; I Harte 12; M Holland 10; RD Keane 10; RM Keane 10; A Kelly 3; G Kelly 9; M Kennedy 2; K KIlbane 12; M Kinsella 8; J McAteer 7; S McPhail 1; C Morrison 2; A O'Brien 2; N Quinn 8; S Staunton 8.

Goals

I Harte 4; RM Keane 4; M Holland 3; R Dunne 2; RD Keane 2; K Kilbane 2; M Kinsella 2; J McAteer 2; G Breen 1; D Connolly 1; G Kelly 1; N Quinn 1.

REPUBLIC OF IRELAND SQUAD FOR THE FINALS

No	Name	Position	Club	Age	Caps	Goals
1	Shay Given	Goalkeeper	Newcastle United	26	39	-
2	Steve Finnan	Full-back	Fulham	26	15	1
3	Ian Harte	Full-back	Leeds United	24	40	8
4	Kenny Cunningham	Defender	Wimbledon	31	38	-
5	Steve Staunton	Midfield	Aston Villa	33	98	7
6	Roy Keane	Midfield	Manchester United	30	58	9
7	Jason McAteer	Midfield	Sunderland	31	47	3
8	Matt Holland	Midfield	Ipswich Town	28	19	3
9	Damien Duff	Forward	Blackburn Rovers	23	26	1
10	Robbie Keane	Forward	Leeds United	22	33	10
11	Kevin Kilbane	Midfield	Sunderland	25	33	3
12	Mark Kinsella	Midfield	Charlton Athletic	31	28	3
13	David Connolly	Forward	Wimbledon	25	33	8
14	Gary Breen	Defender	Coventry City	28	43	5
15	Richard Dunne	Defender	Manchester City	22	14	3
16	Dean Kiely	Goalkeeper	Charlton Athletic	31	6	-
17	Niall Quinn	Forward	Sunderland	35	88	21
18	Gary Kelly	Full-back	Leeds United	28	46	2
19	Clinton Morrison	Forward	Crystal Palace	23	7	2
20	Andy O'Brien	Defender	Newcastle United	23	5	-
21	Steven Reid	Midfield	Millwall	21	5	2
22	Lee Carsley	Midfield	Everton	28	19	-
23	Alan Kelly	Goalkeeper	Sheffield United	33	34	-
			Average	27.2	33.6	

2002 Final group E

1 Jun 2002	Sapporo	Germany 8 Saudi Arabia 0
1 Jun 2002	Niigata	Republic of Ireland 1 Cameroon 1
5 Jun 2002	Ibaraki	Germany 1 Republic of Ireland 1
6 Jun 2002	Saitama	Cameroon 1 Saudi Arabia 0

	P	W	D	L	F	A	Pts
11 Jun 2002	Shizuoka		Cameroon 0 Germany 2				
11 Jun 2002	Yokohama		Saudi Arabia 0 Republic of Ireland 3				

	P	W	D	L	F	A	Pts
Germany	3	2	1	0	11	1	7
REPUBLIC OF IRELAND	3	1	2	0	5	2	5
Cameroon	3	1	1	1	2	3	4
Saudi Arabia	3	0	0	3	0	12	0

Ticket for 2002 World Cup finals match against Germany. The result was a 1–1 draw.

Round Two

			Extra time	Penalties
15 Jun 2002	Niigata	Denmark 0 England 3		
15 Jun 2002	Seogwipo	Germany 1 Paraguay 0		
16 Jun 2002	Suwon	Spain 1 Republic of Ireland 1	1–1	3–2
16 Jun 2002	Oita	Sweden 1 Senegal 1	1–2	
17 Jun 2002	Kobe	Brazil 2 Belgium 0		
17 Jun 2002	Jeonju	Mexico 0 United States 2		
18 Jun 2002	Miyagi	Japan 0 Turkey 1		
18 Jun 2002	Daejeon	South Korea 1 Italy 1	1–1	2–1 on sudden death

Quarter-Finals

			Extra time	Penalties
21 Jun 2002	Shizuoka	England 1 Brazil 2		
21 Jun 2002	Ulsan	Germany 1 United States 0		
22 Jun 2002	Osaka	Senegal 0 Turkey 0		0–1 on sudden death
22 Jun 2002	Gwangju	Spain 0 South Korea 0	0–0	3–5

Semi-Finals

25 Jun 2002	Seoul	Germany 1 South Korea 0
26 Jun 2002	Saitama	Brazil 1 Turkey 0

Third & Fourth Place Play-Off

29 Jun 2002	Daegu	South Korea 2 Turkey 3

Final

30 Jun 2002	Yokohama	Germany 0 Brazil 2

Appearances

G Breen 4; L Carsley 1; D Connolly 1; K Cunningham 2; D Duff 4; S Finnan 4; S Given 4; I Harte 4; M Holland 4; RD Keane 4; G Kelly 4; K Kilbane 4; M Kinsella 4; J McAteer 2; N Quinn 3; S Reid 2; S Staunton 4.

Goals

RD Keane 3; G Breen 1; D Duff 1; M Holland 1.

Ticket for 2002 World Cup finals second–round match against Spain. The game went to penalties after a 1–1 draw and Spain won 3–2.

Group 4

4 Sep 2004	Saint-Denis	France 0 Israel 0
4 Sep 2004	Dublin	Republic of Ireland 3 Cyprus 0
4 Sep 2004	Basel	Switzerland 6 Faroes 0
8 Sep 2004	Torshavn	Faroes 0 France 2
8 Sep 2004	Tel Aviv	Israel 2 Cyprus 1
8 Sep 2004	Basel	Switzerland 1 Republic of Ireland 1
9 Oct 2004	Nicosia	Cyprus 2 Faroes 2
9 Oct 2004	Saint-Denis	France 0 Republic of Ireland 0
9 Oct 2004	Tel Aviv	Israel 2 Switzerland 2
13 Oct 2004	Nicosia	Cyprus 0 France 2
13 Oct 2004	Dublin	Republic of Ireland 2 Faroes 0
17 Nov 2004	Nicosia	Cyprus 1 Israel 2
26 Mar 2005	Paris	France 0 Switzerland 0
26 Mar 2005	Tel Aviv	Israel 1 Republic of Ireland 1
30 Mar 2005	Tel Aviv	Israel 1 France 1
30 Mar 2005	Zurich	Switzerland 1 Cyprus 0
4 Jun 2005	Toftir	Faroes 1 Switzerland 3
4 Jun 2005	Dublin	Republic of Ireland 2 Israel 2
8 Jun 2005	Torshavn	Faroes 0 Republic of Ireland 2
17 Aug 2005	Toftir	Faroes 0 Cyprus 3
3 Sep 2005	Lens	France 3 Faroes 0
3 Sep 2005	Basel	Switzerland 1 Israel 1
7 Sep 2005	Nicosia	Cyprus 1 Switzerland 3
7 Sep 2005	Torshavn	Faroes 0 Israel 2
7 Sep 2005	Dublin	Republic of Ireland 0 France 1
8 Oct 2005	Nicosia	Cyprus 0 Republic of Ireland 1
8 Oct 2005	Tel Aviv	Israel 2 Faroes 1
8 Oct 2005	Berne	Switzerland 1 France 1
12 Oct 2005	Saint-Denis	France 4 Cyprus 0
12 Oct 2005	Dublin	Republic of Ireland 0 Switzerland 0

	P	W	D	L	F	A	Pts
France	10	5	5	0	14	2	20
Switzerland	10	4	6	0	18	7	18
Israel	10	4	6	0	15	10	18
REPUBLIC OF IRELAND	10	4	5	1	12	5	17
Cyprus	10	1	1	8	8	20	4
Faroes	10	0	1	9	4	27	1

Appearances

S Carr 9; D Connolly 1; K Cunningham 10; G Doherty 5; D Duff 9; R Dunne 3; S Elliott 3; S Finnan 6; S Given 10; I Harte 4; M Holland 4; G Kavanagh 4; RD Keane 9; RM Keane 6; K Kilbane 10; A Lee 1; A Maybury 1; L Miller 1; C Morrison 8; A O'Brien 6; J O'Shea 9; A Reid 8; S Reid 2.

Goals

RD Keane 4; C Morrison 3; I Harte 2; S Elliott 1; K Kilbane 1; A Reid 1.

THE REPUBLIC OF IRELAND'S EUROPEAN CHAMPIONSHIP GROUPS

1960 European Championship

Preliminary Round

5 Apr 1959	Dublin	Republic of Ireland 2 Czechoslovakia 0
10 May 1959	Bratislava	Czechoslovakia 4 Republic of Ireland 0

Czechoslovakia won 4–2 on aggregate.

Appearances

N Cantwell 2; G Cummins 2; C Doyle 1; A Fitzsimons 1; T Hamilton 2; C Hurley 2; B McNally 1; M McGrath 2; F O'Farrell 1; J O'Neill 2; A Ringstead 2; P Saward 1; L Tuohy 2; R Whittaker 1.

Goals

N Cantwell 1; L Tuohy 1.

1964 European Championship

First Round

12 Aug 1962	Dublin	Republic of Ireland 4 Iceland 2
2 Sep 1962	Reykjavik	Iceland 1 Republic of Ireland 1

Republic of Ireland won 5–3 on aggregate.

Second Round

23 Sep 1963	Vienna	Austria 0 Republic of Ireland 0
13 Oct 1963	Dublin	Republic of Ireland 3 Austria 2

Republic of Ireland won 3–2 on aggregate.

Quarter-Finals

11 Mar 1964	Seville	Spain 5 Republic of Ireland 1
8 Apr 1964	Dublin	Republic of Ireland 0 Spain 2

Spain won 7–1 on aggregate.

Appearances

R Brady 4; W Browne 2; N Cantwell 4; D Curtis 2; T Dunne 3; A Fogarty 5; T Foley 1; J Fullam 1; J Giles 5; A Hale 3; J Haverty 2; C Hurley 6; A Kelly 6; A McEvoy 3; M McGrath 2; B McNally 1; M Meagan 2; R Nolan 1; N Peyton 1; P Saward 2; T Traynor 5; L Tuohy 3; P Turner 1; R Whelan 1.

Goals

N Cantwell 4; L Tuohy 2; A Fogarty 1; A McEvoy 1; Koller (own goal).

1968 European Championship

Group 1

23 Oct 1966	Dublin	Republic of Ireland 0 Spain 0
19 Nov 1966	Dublin	Republic of Ireland 2 Turkey 1
7 Dec 1966	Valencia	Spain 2 Republic of Ireland 0
1 Feb 1967	Istanbul	Turkey 0 Spain 0
22 Feb 1967	Ankara	Turkey 2 Republic of Ireland 1
21 May 1967	Dublin	Republic of Ireland 0 Czechoslovakia 2
31 May 1967	Bilbao	Spain 2 Turkey 0
18 Jun 1967	Bratislava	Czechoslovakia 3 Turkey 0
1 Oct 1967	Prague	Czechoslovakia 1 Spain 0
22 Oct 1967	Madrid	Spain 2 Czechoslovakia 1
15 Nov 1967	Ankara	Turkey 0 Czechoslovakia 0
22 Nov 1967	Prague	Czechoslovakia 1 Republic of Ireland 2

	P	W	D	L	F	A	Pts
Spain	6	3	2	1	6	2	8
Czechoslovakia	6	3	1	2	8	4	7
REPUBLIC OF IRELAND	6	2	1	3	5	5	5
Turkey	6	1	2	3	3	8	4

Appearances

S Brennan 3; N Cantwell 2; O Conmy 2; J Conway 4; J Dempsey 3; P Dunne 1; T Dunne 3; E Dunphy 5; A Finucane 2; T Foley 1; C Gallagher 2; J Giles 3; A Hale 1; J Haverty 2; C Hurley 5; A Kelly 5; J Kinnear 2; A McEvoy 3; M McGrath 1; M Meagan 6; T O'Connell 1; T O'Connor 1; F O'Neill 4; E Rogers 1; R Treacy 3.

Goals

N Cantwell 1; A McEvoy 1; T O'Connor 1; F O'Neill 1; R Treacy 1.

1972 European Championship

Group 6

14 Oct 1970	Dublin	Republic of Ireland 1 Sweden 1
28 Oct 1970	Stockholm	Sweden 1 Republic of Ireland 0
30 Oct 1970	Vienna	Austria 1 Italy 2
8 Dec 1970	Florence	Italy 3 Republic of Ireland 0
10 May 1971	Dublin	Republic of Ireland 1 Italy 2
26 May 1971	Stockholm	Sweden 1 Austria 0

	30 May 1971	Dublin	Republic of Ireland 1 Austria 4
9 Jun 1971	Stockholm	Sweden 0 Italy 0
4 Sep 1971	Vienna	Austria 1 Sweden 0
9 Oct 1971	Milan	Italy 3 Sweden 0
10 Oct 1971	Linz	Austria 6 Republic of Ireland 0
20 Nov 1971	Rome	Italy 2 Austria 2

	P	W	D	L	F	A	Pts
Italy	6	4	2	0	12	4	10
Austria	6	3	1	2	14	6	7
Sweden	6	2	2	2	3	5	6
REPUBLIC OF IRELAND	6	0	1	5	3	17	1

Appearances

S Brennan 2; T Byrne 5; N Campbell 1; T Carroll 1; T Conroy 3; J Conway 2; J Dempsey 3; J Dunne 1; T Dunne 3; P Dunning 2; E Dunphy 5; A Finucane 4; M Gannon 1; J Giles 1; D Givens 4; A Hale 1; E Hand 1; S Heighway 4; J Herrick 1; J Holmes 1; M Kearin 1; A Kelly 5; J Kinnear 2; M Lawlor 3; M Leech 1; T McConville 1; M Martin 1; P Mulligan 3; T O'Connor 1; F O'Neill 1; D Richardson 1; P Roche 1; E Rogers 3; R Treacy 4.

Goals

T Carroll 1; J Conway 1; E Rogers.

1976 European Championship

Group 8

30 Oct 1974	Dublin	Republic of Ireland 3 USSR 0
20 Nov 1974	Izmir	Turkey 1 Republic of Ireland 1
1 Dec 1974	Izmir	Turkey 2 Switzerland 1
2 Apr 1975	Kiev	USSR 3 Turkey 0
30 Apr 1975	Zurich	Switzerland 1 Turkey 1
10 May 1975	Dublin	Republic of Ireland 2 Switzerland 1
18 May 1975	Kiev	USSR 2 Republic of Ireland 1
21 May 1975	Berne	Switzerland 1 Republic of Ireland 0
12 Oct 1975	Zurich	Switzerland 0 USSR 1
29 Oct 1975	Dublin	Republic of Ireland 4 Turkey 0
12 Nov 1975	Kiev	USSR 4 Switzerland 1
23 Nov 1975	Izmir	Turkey 1 USSR 0

	P	W	D	L	F	A	Pts
USSR	6	4	0	2	10	6	8
REPUBLIC OF IRELAND	6	3	1	2	11	5	7
Turkey	6	2	2	2	5	10	6
Switzerland	6	1	1	4	5	10	3

Appearances

L Brady 6; T Conroy 5; G Daly 1; M Dennehy 1; T Dunne 5; J Giles 6; D Givens 6; E Hand 5; S Heighway 4; J Holmes 3; J Kinnear 5; T Mancini 1; M Martin 6; P Mulligan 6; P Roche 6; R Treacy 4.

Goals

D Givens 8; E Hand 1; M Martin 1; R Treacy 1.

1980 European Championship

Group 1

24 May 1978	Copenhagen	Denmark 3 Republic of Ireland 3
20 Sep 1978	Dublin	Republic of Ireland 0 Northern Ireland 0
20 Sep 1978	Copenhagen	Denmark 3 England 4
11 Oct 1978	Copenhagen	Denmark 2 Bulgaria 2
25 Oct 1978	Dublin	Republic of Ireland 1 England 1
25 Oct 1978	Belfast	Northern Ireland 2 Denmark 1
29 Nov 1978	Sofia	Bulgaria 0 Northern Ireland 2
7 Feb 1979	London	England 4 Northern Ireland 0
2 May 1979	Dublin	Republic of Ireland 2 Denmark 0
2 May 1979	Belfast	Northern Ireland 2 Bulgaria 0
19 May 1979	Sofia	Bulgaria 1 Republic of Ireland 0
6 Jun 1979	Sofia	Bulgaria 0 England 3
6 Jun 1979	Copenhagen	Denmark 4 Northern Ireland 0
12 Sep 1979	London	England 1 Denmark 0
17 Oct 1979	Dublin	Republic of Ireland 3 Bulgaria 0
17 Oct 1979	Belfast	Northern Ireland 1 England 5
31 Oct 1979	Sofia	Bulgaria 3 Denmark 0
21 Nov 1979	Belfast	Northern Ireland 1 Republic of Ireland 0
22 Nov 1979	London	England 2 Bulgaria 0
6 Feb 1980	London	England 2 Republic of Ireland 0

	P	W	D	L	F	A	Pts
England	8	7	1	0	22	5	15
Northern Ireland	8	4	1	3	8	14	9
REPUBLIC OF IRELAND	8	2	3	3	9	8	7
Bulgaria	8	2	1	5	6	14	5
Denmark	8	1	2	5	13	17	4

Appearances

L Brady 6; G Daly 7; J Devine 1; J Giles 4; D Givens 6; T Grealish 6; E Gregg 4; A Grimes 3; A Hayes 1; R Healey 1; S Heighway 6; J Holmes 5; C Hughton 1; M Kearns 4; M Lawrenson 4; P McGee 7; M Martin 4; P Mulligan 5; F O'Brien 1; D O'Leary 6; P O'Leary 3; G Peyton 4; G Ryan 1; F Stapleton 7; N Synnott 1; M Walsh 3; J Walters 1.

Goals

G Daly 3; T Grealish 2; F Stapleton 2; D Givens 1; M Martin 1.

Group 7

5 Jun 1982	Messina, Italy	Malta 2 Iceland 1
1 Sep 1982	Reykjavik	Iceland 1 Holland 1
22 Sep 1982	Rotterdam	Holland 2 Republic of Ireland 1
13 Oct 1982	Dublin	Republic of Ireland 2 Iceland 0
27 Oct 1982	Malaga	Spain 1 Iceland 0
17 Nov 1982	Dublin	Republic of Ireland 3 Spain 3
19 Dec 1982	Aachen	Malta 0 Holland 6
16 Feb 1983	Seville	Spain 1 Holland 0
30 Mar 1983	Valetta	Malta 0 Republic of Ireland 1
27 Apr 1983	Zaragoza	Spain 2 Republic of Ireland 0
15 May 1983	Valetta	Malta 2 Spain 3
29 May 1983	Reykjavik	Iceland 0 Spain 1
5 Jun 1983	Reykjavik	Iceland 1 Malta 0
7 Sep 1983	Groningen	Holland 3 Iceland 0
21 Sep 1983	Reykjavik	Iceland 0 Republic of Ireland 3
12 Oct 1983	Dublin	Republic of Ireland 2 Holland 3
16 Nov 1983	Rotterdam	Holland 2 Spain 1
16 Nov 1983	Dublin	Republic of Ireland 8 Malta 0
17 Dec 1983	Rotterdam	Holland 5 Malta 0
21 Dec 1983	Seville	Spain 12 Malta 1

	P	W	D	L	F	A	Pts
Spain	8	6	1	1	24	8	13
Holland	8	6	1	1	22	6	13
REPUBLIC OF IRELAND	8	4	1	3	20	10	9
Iceland	8	1	1	6	3	13	3
Malta	8	1	0	7	5	37	2

Appearances

P Bonner 1; L Brady 7; G Daly 3; J Devine 4; T Galvin 3; T Grealish 6; A Grimes 2; C Hughton 7; M Lawrenson 8; J McDonough 1; S McDonough 7; M Martin 4; K Moran 4; K O'Callaghan 7; D O'Leary 3; K O'Regan 1; M Robinson 6; K Sheedy 2; F Stapleton 8; G Waddock 7; Mickey Walsh 5; Mike Walsh 1; R Whelan 3.

Goals

F Stapleton 5; L Brady 3; G Daly 2; M Lawrenson 2; G Waddock 2; T Grealish 1; A Grimes 1; K O'Callaghan 1; M Robinson 1; K Sheedy 1; Mickey Walsh 1.

Group 7

10 Sep 1986	Brussels	Belgium 2 Republic of Ireland 2
10 Sep 1986	Glasgow	Scotland 0 Bulgaria 0
14 Oct 1986	Luxembourg	Luxembourg 0 Belgium 6
15 Oct 1986	Dublin	Republic of Ireland 0 Scotland 0
12 Nov 1986	Glasgow	Scotland 3 Luxembourg 0
19 Nov 1986	Brussels	Belgium 1 Bulgaria 1
18 Feb 1987	Glasgow	Scotland 0 Republic of Ireland 1
1 Apr 1987	Sofia	Bulgaria 2 Republic of Ireland 1
1 Apr 1987	Brussels	Belgium 4 Scotland 1
29 Apr 1987	Dublin	Republic of Ireland 0 Belgium 0
30 Apr 1987	Luxembourg	Luxembourg 1 Bulgaria 4
20 May 1987	Sofia	Bulgaria 3 Luxembourg 0
28 May 1987	Luxembourg	Luxembourg 0 Republic of Ireland 2
9 Sep 1987	Dublin	Republic of Ireland 2 Luxembourg 1
23 Sep 1987	Sofia	Bulgaria 2 Belgium 0
14 Oct 1987	Dublin	Republic of Ireland 2 Bulgaria 0
14 Oct 1987	Glasgow	Scotland 2 Belgium 0
11 Nov 1987	Brussels	Belgium 3 Luxembourg 0
11 Nov 1987	Sofia	Bulgaria 0 Scotland 1
12 Nov 1987	Esch	Luxembourg 0 Scotland 0

	P	W	D	L	F	A	Pts
REPUBLIC OF IRELAND	8	4	3	1	10	5	11
Bulgaria	8	4	2	2	12	6	10
Belgium	8	3	3	2	16	8	9
Scotland	8	3	3	2	7	5	9
Luxembourg	8	0	1	7	2	23	1

Republic of Ireland qualified for finals in Germany.

Appearances

J Aldridge 7; J Anderson 3; J Beglin 2; P Bonner 7; L Brady 8; J Byrne 5; G Daly 1; T Galvin 7; A Grimes 1; R Houghton 7; C Hughton 2; D Langan 4; M Lawrenson 3; M McCarthy 6; P McGrath 8; K Moran 8; G Peyton 1; N Quinn 3; K Sheedy 1; F Stapleton 8; R Whelan 7.

Did you know?

A number of Irish players have scored on their international debuts but David Kelly is the only player to have netted a hat-trick on his first appearance for the national side – it came in a 5–0 defeat of Israel in November 1987.

Goals

F Stapleton 3; P McGrath 2; L: Brady 1; T Galvin 1; M Lawrenson 1; K Moran 1; R Whelan 1.

REPUBLIC OF IRELAND SQUAD FOR THE FINALS

No	Name	Position	Club	Age	Caps	Goals
1	Packie Bonner	Goalkeeper	Glasgow Celtic	28	23	-
2	Chris Moi.	Full-back	Glasgow Celtic	24	5	-
3	Chris Hughton	Full-back	Tottenham Hotspur	29	36	1
4	Mick McCarthy	Central defence	Glasgow Celtic	29	27	1
5	Kevin Moran	Central defence	Manchester United	32	36	5
6	Ronnie Whelan	Midfield	Liverpool	26	26	1
7	Paul McGrath	Defender	Manchester United	28	23	3
8	Ray Houghton	Midfield	Liverpool	26	15	-
9	John Aldridge	Forward	Liverpool	29	15	-
10	Frank Stapleton	Forward	Derby County	32	63	18
11	Tony Galvin	Winger	Sheffield Wednesday	31	24	1
12	Tony Cascarino	Forward	Millwall	25	5	1
13	Liam O'Brien	Midfield	Manchester United	23	6	-
14	David Kelly	Forward	Walsall	22	3	4
15	Kevin Sheedy	Midfield	Everton	28	13	3
16	Gerry Peyton	Goalkeeper	Bournemouth	32	24	-
17	John Byrne	Forward	Le Havre	27	14	1
18	John Sheridan	Midfield	Leeds United	23	4	1
19	John Anderson	Full-back	Newcastle United	28	15	1
20	Niall Quinn	Forward	Arsenal	21	9	1

1988 Final Group B

12 Jun 1988	Stuttgart	England 0 Republic of Ireland 1
12 Jun 1988	Cologne	USSR 1 Holland 0
15 Jun 1988	Dusseldorf	Holland 3 England 1
15 Jun 1988	Hanover	USSR 1 Republic of Ireland 1
18 Jun 1988	Gelsenkirchen	Holland 1 Republic of Ireland 0
18 Jun 1988	Frankfurt	USSR 3 England 1

	P	W	D	L	F	A	Pts
USSR	3	2	1	0	5	2	5
Holland	3	2	0	1	4	2	4
REPUBLIC OF IRELAND	3	1	1	1	2	2	3
England	3	0	0	3	2	7	0

Semi-Finals

| 21 Jun 1988 | Hamburg | Holland 2 West Germany 1 |
| 22 Jun 1988 | Stuttgart | USSR 2 Italy 0 |

Final

| 25 Jun 1988 | Munich | Holland 2 USSR 0 |

Appearances

J Aldridge 3; P Bonner 3; T Cascarino 3; T Galvin 23; R Houghton 3; C Hughton 3; M McCarthy 3; P McGrath 2; K Moran 3; C Morris 3; N Quinn 1; K Sheedy 3; F Stapleton 3; R Whelan 3.

Goals

R Houghton 1; R Whelan 1.

1992 European Championships

Group 7

17 Oct 1990	Dublin	Republic of Ireland 5 Turkey 0
17 Oct 1990	London	England 2 Poland 0
14 Nov 1990	Dublin	Republic of Ireland 1 England 1
14 Nov 1990	Istanbul	Turkey 0 Poland 1
27 Mar 1991	London	England 1 Republic of Ireland 1
17 Apr 1991	Warsaw	Poland 3 Turkey 0
1 May 1991	Dublin	Republic of Ireland 0 Poland 0
1 May 1991	Izmir	Turkey 0 England 1
16 Oct 1991	Poznan	Poland 3 Republic of Ireland 3
16 Oct 1991	London	England 1 Turkey 0
13 Nov 1991	Istanbul	Turkey 1 Republic of Ireland 3
13 Nov 1991	Poznan	Poland 1 England 1

	P	W	D	L	F	A	Pts
England	6	3	3	0	7	3	9
REPUBLIC OF IRELAND	6	2	4	0	13	6	8
Poland	6	2	3	1	8	6	7
Turkey	6	0	0	6	1	14	0

Appearances

J Aldridge 5; P Bonner 6; J Byrne 1; T Cascarino 6; R Houghton 4; C Hughton 2; D Irwin 4; RM Keane 1; M McCarthy 3; P McGrath 5; A McLoughlin 1; K Moran 4; C Morris 2; D O'Leary 6; T Phelan 2; N Quinn 4; K Sheedy 4; J Sheridan 1; B Slaven 1; S Staunton 6; A Townsend 5; R Whelan 1.

Goals

J Aldridge 3; T Cascarino 3; J Byrne 2; N Quinn 2; P McGrath 1; D O'Leary 1; A Townsend 1.

Group 6

20 Apr 1994	Belfast	Northern Ireland 4 Liechtenstein 1
7 Sep 1994	Riga	Latvia 0 Republic of Ireland 3
7 Sep 1994	Eschen	Liechtenstein 0 Austria 4
7 Sep 1994	Belfast	Northern Ireland 1 Portugal 2
9 Oct 1994	Riga	Latvia 1 Portugal 3
12 Oct 1994	Vienna	Austria 1 Northern Ireland 2
12 Oct 1994	Dublin	Republic of Ireland 4 Liechtenstein 0
13 Nov 1994	Lisbon	Portugal 1 Austria 0
15 Nov 1994	Eschen	Liechtenstein 1 Latvia 0
16 Nov 1994	Belfast	Northern Ireland 0 Republic of Ireland 4
18 Dec 1994	Lisbon	Portugal 8 Liechtenstein 0
29 Mar 1995	Vienna	Austria 5 Latvia 0
29 Mar 1995	Dublin	Republic of Ireland 1 Northern Ireland 1
26 Apr 1995	Vienna	Austria 7 Liechtenstein 0
26 Apr 1995	Dublin	Republic of Ireland 1 Portugal 0
26 Apr 1995	Riga	Latvia 0 Northern Ireland 1
3 Jun 1995	Vaduz	Liechtenstein 0 Republic of Ireland 0
3 Jun 1995	Lisbon	Portugal 3 Latvia 2
7 Jun 1995	Belfast	Northern Ireland 1 Latvia 2
11 Jun 1995	Dublin	Republic of Ireland 1 Austria 3
15 Aug 1995	Eschen	Liechtenstein 0 Portugal 7
16 Aug 1995	Riga	Latvia 3 Austria 2
3 Sep 1995	Lisbon	Portugal 1 Northern Ireland 1
6 Sep 1995	Vienna	Austria 3 Republic of Ireland 1
6 Sep 1995	Riga	Latvia 1 Liechtenstein 0
11 Oct 1995	Vienna	Austria 1 Portugal 1
11 Oct 1995	Dublin	Republic of Ireland 2 Latvia 1
11 Oct 1995	Eschen	Liechtenstein 0 Northern Ireland 4
15 Nov 1995	Belfast	Northern Ireland 5 Austria 3
15 Nov 1995	Lisbon	Portugal 3 Republic of Ireland 0

	P	W	D	L	F	A	Pts
Portugal	10	7	2	1	29	7	23
REPUBLIC OF IRELAND	10	5	2	3	17	11	17
Northern Ireland	10	5	2	3	20	15	17
Austria	10	5	1	4	29	14	16
Latvia	10	4	0	6	11	20	12
Liechtenstein	10	0	1	9	1	40	1

Republic qualified for play-offs.

Play-Offs

| 13 Dec 1995 | Liverpool | Holland 2 Republic of Ireland 0 |

Appearances

J Aldridge 7; P Babb 10; P Bonner 1; T Cascarino 8; T Coyne 3; R Houghton 3; D Irwin 10; RM Keane 3; A Kelly 10; D Kelly 1; G Kelly 11; J Kenna 6; M Kennedy 2; A Kernaghan 4; J McAteer 8; E McGoldrick 2; P McGrath 10; A McLoughlin 1; T Phelan 2; N Quinn 10; J Sheridan 9; S Staunton 9; A Townsend 7; R Whelan 2.

Goals

J Aldridge 5; N Quinn 3; T Coyne 2; S Staunton 2; R Houghton 1; RM Keane 1; P McGrath 1; J Sheridan 1; A Townsend 1.

2000 European Championships

Group 8

5 Sep 1998	Dublin	Republic of Ireland 2 Croatia 0
6 Sep 1998	Skopje	Macedonia 4 Malta 0
10 Oct 1998	Ta'Qali	Malta 1 Croatia 4
14 Oct 1998	Zagreb	Croatia 3 Macedonia 2
14 Oct 1998	Dublin	Republic of Ireland 5 Malta 0
18 Nov 1998	Valetta	Malta 1 Macedonia 2
18 Nov 1998	Belgrade	Yugoslavia 1 Republic of Ireland 0
10 Feb 1999	Valetta	Malta 0 Yugoslavia 3
5 Jun 1999	Skopje	Macedonia 1 Croatia 1
8 Jun 1999	Salonika	Yugoslavia 4 Malta 1
9 Jun 1999	Dublin	Republic of Ireland 1 Macedonia 0
18 Aug 1999	Belgrade	Yugoslavia 0 Croatia 0
21 Aug 1999	Zagreb	Croatia 2 Malta 1
1 Sep 1999	Dublin	Republic of Ireland 2 Yugoslavia 1
4 Sep 1999	Zagreb	Croatia 1 Republic of Ireland 0
5 Sep 1999	Belgrade	Yugoslavia 3 Macedonia 1
8 Sep 1999	Skopje	Macedonia 2 Yugoslavia 4
8 Sep 1999	Valetta	Malta 2 Republic of Ireland 3
9 Oct 1999	Zagreb	Croatia 2 Yugoslavia 2
9 Oct 1999	Skopje	Macedonia 1 Republic of Ireland 1

	P	W	D	L	F	A	Pts
Yugoslavia	8	5	2	1	18	8	17
REPUBLIC OF IRELAND	8	5	1	2	14	6	16
Croatia	8	4	3	1	13	9	15
Macedonia	8	2	2	4	13	14	8
Malta	8	0	0	8	6	27	0

Appearances

P Babb 1; G Breen 7; S Carr 4; L Carsley 6; T Cascarino 7; D Connolly 2; K Cunningham 8; D Duff 6; S Given 3; I Harte 2; M Holland 1; D Irwin 5; RD Keane 6; RM Keane 4; A Kelly 5; G Kelly 2; J Kenna 2; M Kennedy 5; K Kilbane 4; M Kinsella 8; J McAteer 3; A McLoughlin 4; K O'Neill 3; N Quinn 7; S Staunton 7.

Goals

RD Keane 4; N Quinn 3; G Breen 2; RM Keane 2; D Irwin 1; M Kennedy 1; S Staunton 1.

2004 European Championships

Group 10

7 Sep 2002	Moscow	Russia 4 Republic of Ireland 2
7 Sep 2002	Basel	Switzerland 4 Georgia 1
12 Oct 2002	Tirana	Albania 1 Switzerland 1
16 Oct 2002	Dublin	Republic of Ireland 1 Switzerland 2
16 Oct 2002	Moscow	Russia 4 Albania 1
29 Mar 2003	Tirana	Albania 3 Russia 1
29 Mar 2003	Tbilisi	Georgia 1 Republic of Ireland 2
2 Apr 2003	Tirana	Albania 0 Republic of Ireland 0
2 Apr 2003	Tbilisi	Georgia 0 Switzerland 0
30 Apr 2003	Tbilisi	Georgia 1 Russia 0
7 Jun 2003	Dublin	Republic of Ireland 2 Albania 1
7 Jun 2003	Basel	Switzerland 2 Russia 2
11 Jun 2003	Dublin	Republic of Ireland 2 Georgia 0
11 Jun 2003	Geneva	Switzerland 3 Albania 2
6 Sep 2003	Tbilisi	Georgia 3 Albania 0
6 Sep 2003	Dublin	Republic of Ireland 1 Russia 1
10 Sep 2003	Tirana	Albania 3 Georgia 1
10 Sep 2003	Moscow	Russia 4 Switzerland 1
11 Oct 2003	Moscow	Russia 3 Georgia 1
11 Oct 2003	Basel	Switzerland 2 Republic of Ireland 0

	P	W	D	L	F	A	Pts
Switzerland	8	4	3	1	15	11	15
Russia	8	4	2	2	19	12	14
REPUBLIC OF IRELAND	8	3	2	3	10	11	11
Albania	8	2	2	4	11	15	8
Georgia	8	2	1	5	8	14	7

Appearances

P Babb 1; G Breen 8; T Butler 1; S Carr 6; L Carsley 5; K Cunningham 7; D Connolly 2; G Doherty 7; D Duff 7; S Finnan 2; S Given 8; I Harte 4; C Healy 4; M Holland 8; RD Keane 6; G Kelly 1; K Kilbane 8; M Kinsella 7; A Lee 1; J McAteer 1; C Morrison 4; J O'Shea 6; S Reid 2.

Goals

G Doherty 3; D Duff 2; RD Keane 2; C Morrison 1; Aliaj (own goal) Magnin (own goal).

2008 European Championships		
2 Sep 2006	Teplice	Czech Republic 2 Wales 1
2 Sep 2006	Bratislava	Slovakia 6 Cyprus 1
2 Sep 2006	Stuttgart	Germany 1 Republic of Ireland 0
6 Sep 2006	Bratislava	Slovakia 0 Czech Republic 3
6 Sep 2006	Serravalle	San Marino 0 Germany 13
7 Oct 2006	Cardiff	Wales 1 Slovakia 5
7 Oct 2006	Liberec	Czech Republic 7 San Marino 0
7 Oct 2006	Nicosia	Cyprus 5 Republic of Ireland 2
11 Oct 2006	Dublin	Republic of Ireland 1 Czech Republic 1
11 Oct 2006	Bratislava	Slovakia 1 Germany 4
11 Oct 2006	Cardiff	Wales 3 Cyprus 1
15 Nov 2006	Nicosia	Cyprus 1 Germany 1
15 Nov 2006	Dublin	Republic of Ireland 5 San Marino 0
7 Feb 2007	Serravalle	San Marino 1 Republic of Ireland 2
24 Mar 2007	Dublin	Republic of Ireland 1 Wales 0
24 Mar 2007	Nicosia	Cyprus 1 Slovakia 3
24 Mar 2007	Prague	Czech Republic 1 Germany 2
28 Mar 2007	Liberec	Czech Republic 1 Cyprus 0
28 Mar 2007	Dublin	Republic of Ireland 1 Slovakia 0
28 Mar 2007	Cardiff	Wales 3 San Marino 0
2 Jun 2007	Cardiff	Wales 0 Czech Republic 0
2 Jun 2007	Nuremberg	Germany 6 San Marino 0
6 Jun 2007	Hamburg	Germany 1 Slovakia 0
22 Aug 2007	Serravalle	San Marino 0 Cyprus 1
8 Sep 2007	Serravalle	San Marino 0 Czech Republic 3
8 Sep 2007	Bratislava	Slovakia 2 Republic of Ireland 2
8 Sep 2007	Cardiff	Wales 0 Germany 2
12 Sep 2007	Bratislava	Slovakia 2 Wales 5
12 Sep 2007	Nicosia	Cyprus 3 San Marino 0
12 Sep 2007	Prague	Czech Republic 1 Republic of Ireland 0
13 Oct 2007	Bratislava	Slovakia 7 San Marino 0
13 Oct 2007	Nicosia	Cyprus 3 Wales 1
13 Oct 2007	Dublin	Republic of Ireland 0 Germany 0
17 Oct 2007	Serravalle	San Marino 1 Wales 2
17 Oct 2007	Dublin	Republic of Ireland 1 Cyprus 1
17 Oct 2007	Munich	Germany 0 Czech Republic 3
17 Nov 2007	Cardiff	Wales 2 Republic of Ireland 2

17 Nov 2007	Hanover	Germany 4 Cyprus 0
17 Nov 2007	Prague	Czech Republic 3 Slovakia 1
21 Nov 2007	Serravalle	San Marino 0 Slovakia 5
21 Nov 2007	Nicosia	Cyprus 0 Czech Republic 2
21 Nov 2007	Frankfurt	Germany 0 Wales 0

	P	W	D	L	F	A	Pts
Czech Republic	12	9	2	1	27	5	29
Germany	12	8	3	1	35	7	27
REPUBLIC OF IRELAND	12	4	5	3	17	14	17
Slovakia	12	5	1	6	33	23	16
Wales	12	4	3	5	18	19	15
Cyprus	12	4	2	6	17	24	14
San Marino	12	0	0	12	2	57	0

Appearances

S Carr 1; L Carsley 9; J Douglas 6; K Doyle 9; D Duff 7; R Dunne 9; S Elliott 1; S Finnan 10; D Gibson 1; S Givens 9; I Harte 1; W Henderson 2; S Hunt 6; S Ireland 5; RD Keane 11; S Kelly 4; P Kenny 1; A Keogh 3; K Kilbane 12; A Lee 2; S Long 4; A McGeady 10; P McShane 8; L Miller 2; C Morrison 1; D Murphy 2; A O'Brien 3; AJ O'Brien 2; J O'Brien 2; J O'Shea 10; D Potter 1; A Quinn 2; A Reid 6; S Reid 1; A Stokes 1.

Goals

K Doyle 4; S Ireland 4; RD Keane 4; K Kilbane 2; R Dunne 1; S Finnan 1; Simoncini (own goal).

REPUBLIC OF IRELAND RECORD AGAINST ALL NATIONS

	P	W	D	L	F	A
Albania	4	3	1	0	6	2
Algeria	1	0	0	1	0	2
Andorra	2	2	0	0	6	1
Argentina	3	0	0	3	0	4
Australia	1	1	0	0	2	1
Austria	12	2	2	8	15	33
Belgium	14	4	5	5	24	25
Bolivia	3	2	1	0	5	1
Brazil	4	1	1	2	2	9
Bulgaria	7	2	2	3	8	6
Cameroon	1	0	1	0	1	1
Canada	1	1	0	0	3	0
Chile	6	2	1	3	6	6

China	2	2	0	0	2	0
Croatia	5	2	2	1	7	5
Cyprus	8	6	1	1	24	8
Czechoslovakia	12	4	1	7	14	29
Czech Republic	7	2	1	4	8	12
Denmark	13	5	5	3	20	16
Ecuador	2	1	1	0	4	3
Egypt	1	0	1	0	0	0
England	14	3	6	5	13	19
Estonia	2	2	0	0	4	0
Faroes	2	2	0	0	4	0
Finland	5	3	2	0	11	2
France	13	4	4	5	13	16
Georgia	2	2	0	0	4	1
Germany	7	2	3	2	10	8
West Germany	11	4	1	6	12	20
Greece	2	0	1	1	0	1
Holland	19	7	3	9	26	34
Hungary	10	2	4	4	16	21
Iceland	7	5	2	0	16	6
Iran	3	2	0	1	4	2
Israel	5	1	3	1	8	6
Italy	9	1	0	8	5	17
Jamaica	1	1	0	0	1	0
Latvia	4	4	0	0	11	2
Liechtenstein	4	3	1	0	14	0
Lithuania	4	3	1	0	5	1
Luxembourg	5	5	0	0	14	2
Macedonia	4	2	1	1	7	4
Malta	7	7	0	0	24	2
Mexico	5	0	4	1	5	6
Morocco	1	1	0	0	1	0
Nigeria	2	0	0	2	1	5
Northern Ireland	9	3	4	2	12	4
Norway	16	8	6	2	27	16
Paraguay	1	1	0	0	2	0
Poland	22	5	8	9	23	37
Portugal	12	4	2	6	9	15
Romania	5	2	2	1	4	2
Russia	5	1	2	2	5	7

San Marino	2	2	0	0	7	1
Saudi Arabia	1	1	0	0	3	0
Scotland	8	3	2	3	7	10
Slovakia	2	1	1	0	3	2
South Africa	1	1	0	0	2	1
Spain	24	4	7	13	18	48
Sweden	8	3	1	4	12	14
Switzerland	15	7	3	5	17	10
Trinidad & Tobago	1	0	0	1	1	2
Tunisia	1	1	0	0	4	0
Turkey	12	5	6	1	26	13
United States of America	7	3	3	1	13	11
Uruguay	2	0	1	1	1	3
USSR	8	3	1	4	8	8
Wales	11	4	2	5	13	13
Yugoslavia	4	2	0	2	5	6

Played	434
Won	171
Drawn	114
Lost	149
Goals Scored	628
Goals Against	572

TOP 50 APPEARANCES

Former manager Steve Staunton leads the way with 102 caps, winning his first in a 4–0 home win over Tunisia on 19 October 1988 and his last in the World Cup match against Spain on 16 June 2002.

	Player	Career Dates	Total Appearances
1	Steve Staunton	1989–2002	102
2	Niall Quinn	1986–2002	91
3	Tony Cascarino	1986–2000	88
4	Kevin Kilbane	1998–present	86
5	Shay Given	1996–present	85
6	Paul McGrath	1985–1997	83
7	Packie Bonner	1981–1996	80
8	Robbie Keane	1998–present	78
9	Ray Houghton	1986–1998	73
10=	Liam Brady	1975–1990	72
	Kenny Cunningham	1996–present	72

12=	Kevin Moran	1980–1994	71
	Frank Stapleton	1977–1990	71
14	Andy Townsend	1989–1998	70
15	John Aldridge	1986–1997	69
16	David O'Leary	1977–1993	68
17	Roy Keane	1991–2006	67
18	Damien Duff	1998–present	66
19	Ian Harte	1996–present	64
20	Gary Breen	1996–present	63
21	Johnny Giles	1960–1979	59
22	Mick McCarthy	1984–1992	57
23=	Don Givens	1969–1982	56
	Denis Irwin	1991–2000	56
25=	Chris Hughton	1980–1992	53
	Ronnie Whelan	1981–1995	53
27=	Gary Kelly	1994–2003	52
	Jason McAteer	1994–2004	52
	Mick Martin	1972–1983	52
30=	Steve Finnan	2000–present	50
	Paddy Mulligan	1969–1980	50
32	Matt Holland	2000–2006	49
33=	Gerry Daly	1973–1987	48
	Mark Kinsella	1998–2004	48
35	Alan Kelly Snr	1957–1973	47
36	Kevin Sheedy	1984–1993	46
37	Tony Grealish	1976–1986	45
38	Stephen Carr	1999–present	44
39	John O'Shea	2002–present	43
40=	Alan McLoughlin	1990–2000	42
	Terry Phelan	1992–2000	42
	Ray Treacy	1966–1980	42
43	David Connolly	1996–2006	41
44	Charlie Hurley	1957–1969	40
45=	Richard Dunne	2000–present	39
	Mark Lawrenson	1977–1988	39
47	Lee Carsley	1998–present	38
48=	Noel Cantwell	1954–1967	36
	Clinton Morrison	2002–present	36
50=	Phil Babb	1994–2003	35
	Chris Morris	1988–1993	35

TOP 50 GOALSCORERS

In terms of strike-rate (dividing goals scored by the number of matches played) the leader of the pack is Tom Davis who scored four goals in as many games. However, Jimmy Dunne, who netted thirteen goals in fifteen appearances also has a healthy strike-rate of 0.86 goals per game. It should be remembered, though, that substitute appearances are included as full games in these totals.

	Player	Career Dates	Total	Games Played	Strike-Rate
1	Robbie Keane	1998–present	32	78	0.41
2	Niall Quinn	1986–2002	21	91	0.23
3	Frank Stapleton	1977–1990	20	71	0.28
4=	John Aldridge	1986–1997	19	69	0.27
	Tony Cascarino	1986–2000	19	88	0.21
	Don Givens	1969–1982	19	56	0.33
7	Noel Cantwell	1954–1967	14	36	0.38
8=	Gerry Daly	1973–1987	13	48	0.27
	Jimmy Dunne	1930–1939	13	15	0.86
10	Ian Harte	1996–present	11	64	0.17
11=	Liam Brady	1975–1990	9	72	0.12
	David Connolly	1996–2006	9	41	0.21
	Roy Keane	1991–2006	9	67	0.13
	David Kelly	1988–1998	9	26	0.34
	Clinton Morrison	2002–present	9	36	0.25
	Kevin Sheedy	1984–1993	9	46	0.19
17=	Dermot Curtis	1957–1964	8	17	0.47
	Tony Grealish	1976–1986	8	45	0.17
	Paul McGrath	1985–1997	8	83	0.09
20=	Gary Breen	1996–present	7	63	0.11
	Damien Duff	1998–present	7	66	0.11
	Arthur Fitzsimons	1950–1959	7	26	0.26
	Kevin Kilbane	1998–present	7	86	0.08
	Paddy Moore	1931–1937	7	9	0.77

Alf Ringstead	1951–1959	7	20	0.35
Steve Staunton	1989–2002	7	102	0.06
Andy Townsend	1989–1998	7	70	0.10
28= Tommy Coyne	1992–1998	6	22	0.27
Ray Houghton	1986–1998	6	73	0.08
Andy McEvoy	1961–1967	6	17	0.35
Con Martin	1946–1956	6	30	0.20
Kevin Moran	1980–1994	6	71	0.08
33= George Cummins	1954–1961	5	19	0.26
Kevin Doyle	2006–present	5	15	0.33
Richard Dunne	2000–present	5	39	0.12
Patsy Fagan	1955–1961	5	8	0.62
Johnny Giles	1960–1979	5	59	0.08
Matt Holland	2000–2006	5	49	0.10
Mark Lawrenson	1977–1988	5	39	0.12
Eamonn Rogers	1968–1973	5	19	0.26
John Sheridan	1988–1996	5	34	0.14
Ray Treacy	1966–1980	5	42	0.11
Davy Walsh	1946–1954	5	20	0.25
44= Paddy Bradshaw	1938–1939	4	5	0.80
Johnny Byrne	1985–1993	4	23	0.17
Tommy Davis	1937–1938	4	4	1.00
Gary Doherty	2000–present	4	34	0.11
Joey Donnelly	1935–1938	4	10	0.40
John Joe Flood	1926–1932	4	5	0.80
Stephen Ireland	2006–present	4	6	0.66
Denis Irwin	1991–2000	4	56	0.07
Mick Kennedy	1996–2002	4	34	0.11
Paul McGee	1978–1981	4	15	0.26
Mick Martin	1972–1983	4	52	0.07
Keith O'Neill	1996–2000	4	13	0.30
Andy Reid	2004–present	4	22	0.18
Mick Robinson	1981–1986	4	24	0.16
Liam Tuohy	1956–1965	4	8	0.50